AUTOMOBILE ENGINEERING

For the Students of B.E./B.Tech. of all Technical Universities of India

Er. A.K. Babu
B.E. (Mech), M.E. (Auto)
Assistant Professor (SG)
School of Mechanical & Building Sciences,
VIT University, Chennai Campus
Chennai - 600 127

Er. Ajit Pal Singh
B.E., M.E. (IIT Delhi)
Assistant Professor
Department of Production Engineering
Defence University, Ethiopia

S. CHAND
PUBLISHING

S Chand And Company Limited
(ISO 9001 Certified Company)

S Chand And Company Limited
(ISO 9001 Certified Company)
Head Office: Block B-1, House No. D-1, Ground Floor, Mohan Co-operative Industrial Estate, New Delhi – 110 044 | Phone: 011-66672000
Registered Office: A-27, 2nd Floor, Mohan Co-operative Industrial Estate, New Delhi – 110 044
Phone: 011-49731800
www.**schandpublishing.com**; e-mail: **info@schandpublishing.com**

Branches

Ahmedabad	:	Ph: 27542369, 27541965; ahmedabad@schandpublishing.com
Bengaluru	:	Ph: 22354008, 22268048; bangalore@schandpublishing.com
Bhopal	:	Ph: 4274723, 4209587; bhopal@schandpublishing.com
Bhubaneshwar	:	Ph: 2951580; bhubaneshwar@schandpublishing.com
Chennai	:	Ph: 23632120; chennai@schandpublishing.com
Guwahati	:	Ph: 2738811, 2735640; guwahati@schandpublishing.com
Hyderabad	:	Ph: 40186018; hyderabad@schandpublishing.com
Jaipur	:	Ph: 2291317, 2291318; jaipur@schandpublishing.com
Jalandhar	:	Ph: 4645630; jalandhar@schandpublishing.com
Kochi	:	Ph: 2576207, 2576208; cochin@schandpublishing.com
Kolkata	:	Ph: 23357458, 23353914; kolkata@schandpublishing.com
Lucknow	:	Ph: 4003633; lucknow@schandpublishing.com
Mumbai	:	Ph: 25000297; mumbai@schandpublishing.com
Nagpur	:	Ph: 2250230; nagpur@schandpublishing.com
Patna	:	Ph: 2260011; patna@schandpublishing.com
Ranchi	:	Ph: 2361178; ranchi@schandpublishing.com
Sahibabad	:	Ph: 2771238; info@schandpublishing.com

First Edition 2013
Revised Edition 2014; Reprint 2018
Reprint 2020

ISBN: 978-81-219-9770-6 **Product Code:** H3AUE62AUTO10ENZX14O

PRINTED IN INDIA

By Vikas Publishing House Private Limited, Plot 20/4, Site-IV, Industrial Area Sahibabad, Ghaziabad – 201 010 and Published by S Chand And Company Limited, A-27, 2nd Floor, Mohan Co-operative Industrial Estate, New Delhi – 110 044

FOREWORD

There is a long-felt need for a comprehensive text-book cover the major portions of the syllabi of Automobile Engineering subject of all Technical Universities of India. This void is filled by this book authored by Er. A.K.Babu and Er. Ajit Pal Singh.

Er. A.K.Babu has a rich experience in teaching this subject for a long time and this has been very well utilised to rightly reflect the treatment of various topics in this book. Besides, he has used his thorough knowledge that he has gained in bringing out his handouts, which have been well appreciated in Technical Colleges and Universities in India and abroad as well.

The authors have been serving in academic sphere for more than a decade and have undertaken a stupendous task which I hope will be of immense help and use to the students community as well as people engaged in teaching. The effort of the authors in bringing out this concise yet elaborate text is appreciated and deserves encouragement.

Dr. S.Parthasarathy
Former Professor and Head
Department of Automobile Engineering
M.I.T., Anna University
Chennai

This Page has been intentionally left blank

PREFACE

This book is an introductory text for students undertaking a subject '*Automobile Engineering*' in the branches of Mechanical Engineering at Engineering Colleges and Technical Universities in India. This book has been updated to reflect the latest syllabus of most of the universities in India and features state-of-the-art coverage of alternate fuels, electric and hybrid vehicles, electronic ignition systems, fuel injection systems, and more.

This well-written, comprehensive book contains an incredible amount of information about the working of automobiles. The text is very readable, and it presumes no previous knowledge about automobiles. Chapters on introduction and vehicle structures will appeal to beginners, while their subsequent chapters build on this knowledge and get quite in-depth.

The strengths of the book are unique illustrations and content for all the topics than the same level of books available in the Indian market.

The book begins with an introduction that describes the vehicle structures. The chapters that follow describe the main systems of vehicles and pollutants produced by the automobiles and their control. The book concludes with a discussion of the future and alternative energy resources for automobiles.

We hope that students and teachers enjoy reading this book and that they find its contents informative and useful.

Suggestions to improve the utility of the book will be gratefully acknowledged and incorporated in the subsequent editions.

Finally, our healthy thanks to the Management Team and Editorial Staff of S. Chand & Company Pvt. Ltd., New Delhi for bringing out the book in such a good layout and within a short duration of time.

AUTHORS

BRIEF CONTENTS

CONTENTS

1 CHAPTER

INTRODUCTION

AUTOMOBILE

The automobile is defined as a self-propelling vehicle. In the past, the automobile was only required to serve as the legs for the people, but today many more things are demanded such as comfort and convenience, high mobility and maneuverability, running safety, economy and personnel safety.

The automobile has five basic components or parts:

1. The power plant or engine, which is the source of power.
2. The chassis, which supports the engine and body and includes the brake, steering and suspension systems.
3. The power train or drive train, which is the power-transmission system that carries power from the engine to the drive wheels. This unit includes clutch, gearbox, drive axle assembly, final drive, differential and the wheel axles.
4. The car body.
5. The car-body accessories, which include the heater and air conditioner, lights, radio and music player, windshield wiper and washer, power windows and seat adjusters.

VEHICLE LAYOUT

The following Fig.1.1 shows a basic structure and simplified layout of various transmission components used on a vehicle.

Transmission system

The transmission system covers the complete driveline between the engine and the road wheels. However, in many countries the term "transmission" refers to the gearbox unit.

Power unit

The normal source of power is provided by an internal combustion engine. The gasoline (petrol) engine is the most popular for its superior performance, but if the vehicle is used extensively, the excellent fuel economy given by a diesel engine makes this type attractive. The economy feature of the diesel engine offsets the higher initial cost and slightly reduced output.

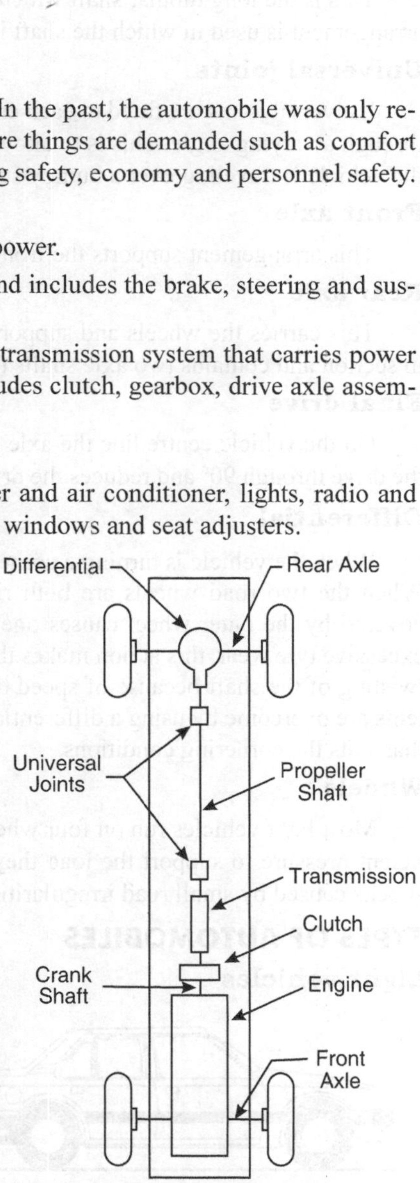

Fig. 1.1: Transmission layout

Clutch

The gears in a manual gearbox have to be changed. This action should only be performed when the gears are not under load, so a clutch is fitted to meet this need. This enables the driver to disconnect the engine from the gearbox.

Gearbox

Gearbox consists of sets of gears that amplify the engine torque to enable the driving force at the road wheels to be increased sufficiently to overcome the resistance to movement of the vehicle. Also the gearbox enables the engine speed to be kept within its working limits irrespective of the speed of the vehicle. In addition it provides neutral, where the engine can run without moving the vehicle and a reverse to drive the vehicle backwards.

Propeller shaft

This is the long tubular shaft which links the gearbox to the final drive. Normally an open type arrangement is used in which the shaft is exposed.

Universal joints

Universal joints are fitted to each end of the propeller shaft to enable the drive to be transmitted through a varying angle. This is to allow for the flexing of the chassis components that occurs when the vehicle is traveling over a bumpy surface.

Front axle

This arrangement supports the front of the vehicle and is also used for steering.

Rear axle

This carries the wheels and supports the weight of the rear of the vehicle. The axle is tubular in section and contains two axle shafts (half shafts) to drive the road wheels in rear wheel drives.

Final drive

On the vehicle centre line the axle is enlarged to house the final drive. This pair of gears turns the drive through 90° and reduces the driving speed which is suitable for the size of the road wheels.

Differential

When the vehicle is turning a corner, the inner and outer road wheels travel at different speeds. When the two road wheels are both rigidly connected to single axle shaft, the greater distance covered by the outer wheel causes one or both wheels to slip on the road. In addition to causing excessive tyre wear, this action makes the vehicle difficult to steer. Also axle shaft may break due to twisting of the shaft because of speed difference between the outer and inner wheels. These problems are overcome by using a differential. This unit ensures each wheel can rotate at different speed that suits the cornering conditions.

Wheels

Most light vehicles run on four wheels fitted with hollow rubber tyres filled with air under sufficient pressure to support the load they have to carry. These provide grip to the road and absorb shocks caused by small road irregularities.

TYPES OF AUTOMOBILES

Light vehicles

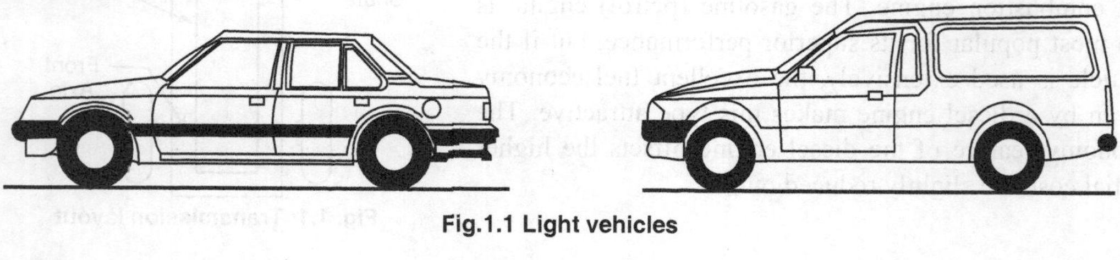

Fig.1.1 Light vehicles

Vehicles classified in this category have a laden mass of less than three tonnes. A wide range of different body shapes and sizes come into this light vehicle category. These range from two-seater cars to personnel carriers (mini-buses) and small trucks.

Commercial vehicles

Commercial vehicles are used to transport goods and people safely and efficiently. Commercial vehicles can be divided up not only according to the position of their engine but also according to their use, their body or their trailer type.

Light commercial vehicles

These small commercial vehicles are used for the conveyance of relatively light goods usually over short distances, e.g. the type of vehicles used by tradesmen to carry their equipment or by shopkeepers to make local deliveries to their customers. Common types are vans, pick-up and light trucks and mini-buses.

a. Vans

Vans are light commercial vehicles with a maximum weight of 7.5 t. They are generally used for short-range distribution of goods and passengers. Most vans have a load-carrying capacity of about 0.5 tonnes.

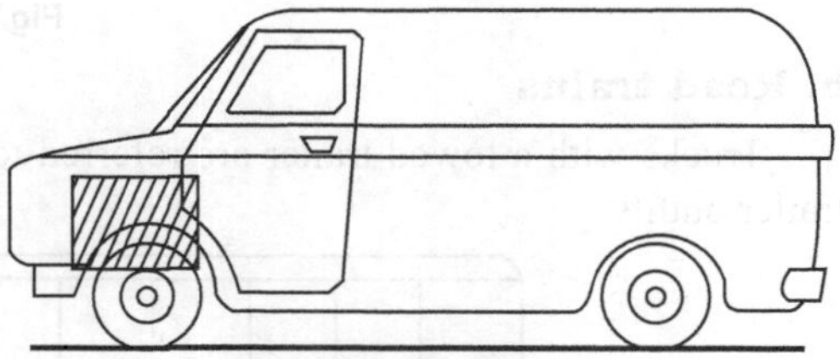

Fig .1.2 Van

b. Pick-up

When a vehicle is required for the transportation of bulky equipment, e.g. materials carried by builders and decorators, an open body is often preferred. A light vehicle having this partly enclosed body is called a pick-up.

Fig. 1.3 Pick-up

c. Light trucks and mini-buses

Larger vehicles such as light trucks and minibuses need to carry heavier loads, so they require a stronger construction and have to be specially designed to suit the application. Since low-cost operation is an essential factor, most of these vehicles are fitted with a diesel engine.

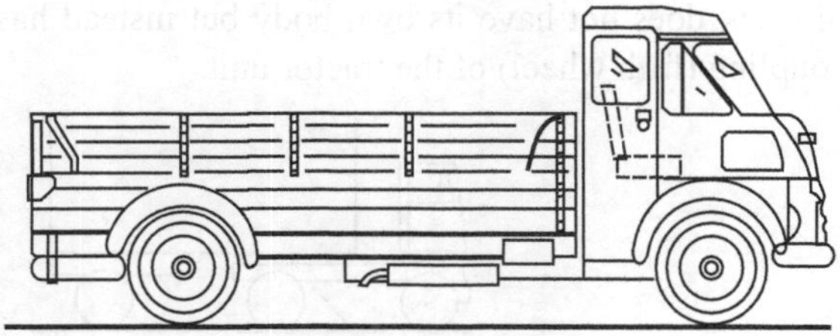

Fig. 1.4 Light truck

Heavy commercial vehicles

Although this book concentrates mainly on light vehicles, a review of some heavier vehicles is included for comparison purposes. Common types are:

- Trucks
- Road trains (truck and trailer outfits)
- Semi-trailer trucks
- Buses
- Special-purpose vehicles

a. Trucks

A heavy vehicle has a load-carrying capacity in excess of about 3 tonnes. For long-distance transportation of goods a truck is used and these come in various shapes and sizes. Depending on their size and weight, trucks have different numbers of axles and these can be steered or driven.

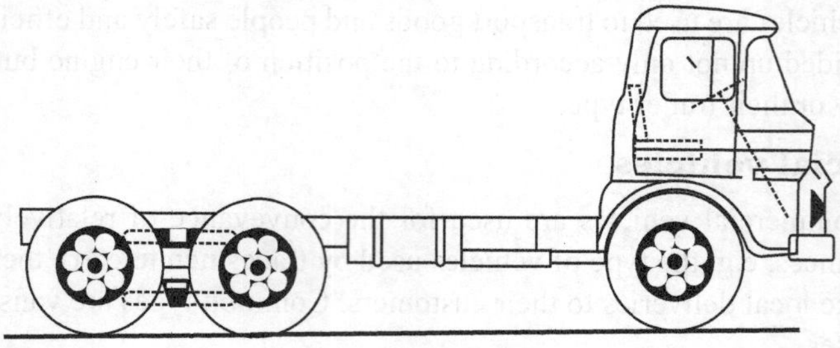

Fig. 1.5 Truck

b. Road trains

Trucks with a towed trailer are referred to as road trains, articulated road trains or truck-and-trailer outfits.

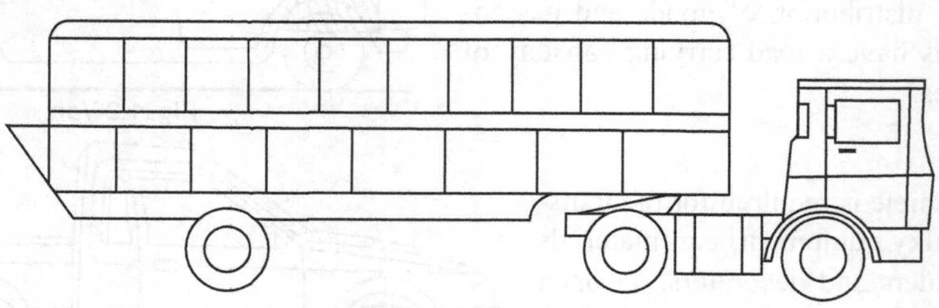

Fig. 1.6 Road train

c. Semi-trailer trucks

The term semi-trailer truck refers to a combination of a tractor vehicle and a trailer. This type of truck does not have its own body but instead has a semi-trailer which rests on the semi-trailer coupling (fifth wheel) of the tractor unit.

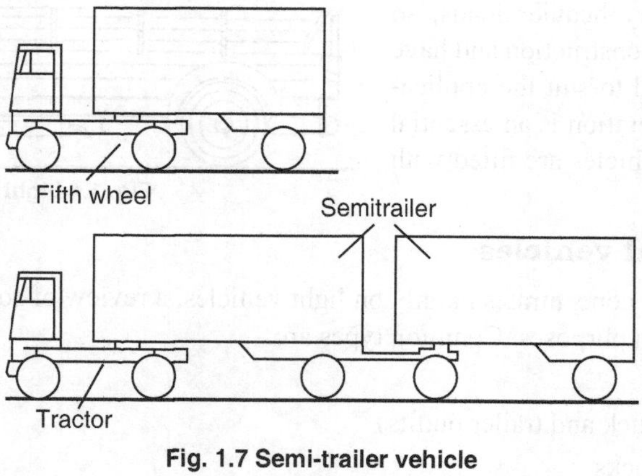

Fig. 1.7 Semi-trailer vehicle

d. Buses

These are used for short-and-long distance passenger transport and are referred to as scheduled-service buses and coaches respectively.

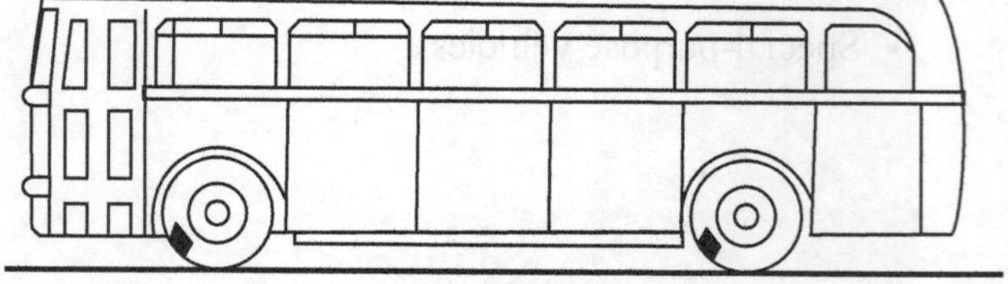

Fig. 1.8 Buse

e. Special-purpose vehicles

These are large vehicles for the transportation of very heavy loads. They also include fire engines and trucks with crane or concrete-pump bodies. Because of their high permissible gross weight and their unusual dimensions, special-purpose vehicles often require a special operating license.

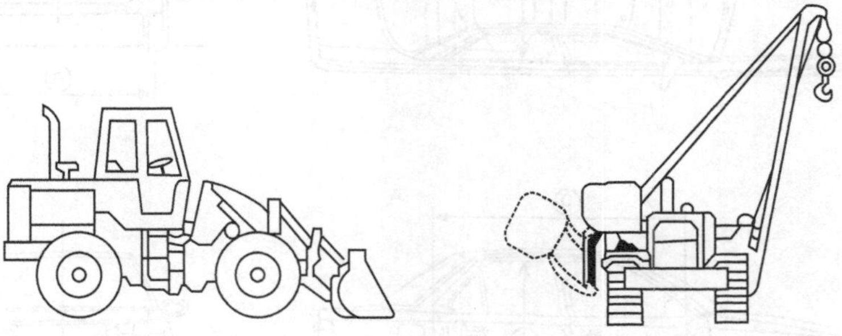

Fig. 1.9 Special-purpose vehicles

VEHICLE WEIGHTS & DIMENSIONS

Major weights and dimensions of a vehicle are explained below:

Weights

Payload

The total weight of passengers and cargo that a vehicle carries or can carry.

Gross Vehicle Weight (GVW)

GVW is the weight of the vehicle, plus the weight of all passengers the vehicle is designed to carry, plus the maximum allowable payload (passengers and cargo) or luggage load. It is also known as laden weight.

Curb Weight (CW) or Kerb Weight (KW)

CW is the weight of a vehicle wet, meaning with a full tank of fuel and all fluids filled, but without passengers or cargo (luggage).

Dimensions

(*a*) **Overall length:** The distance between the front and rear of the vehicle measured along the longitudinal centre line, including bumper guards, if the vehicle has them.

(*b*) **Overall width:** The maximum lateral distance measured between the sides of the vehicle. It includes bumpers, moldings, sheet metal protrusions, etc., measured to the outside of the metal.

(*c*) **Overall height:** The maximum vertical distance from the top of the roof to the road surface, measured with the vehicle in a curb weight condition.

(*d*) **Wheelbase:** The distance between the center lines of the front and rear axles.

(*e*) **Wheel tread (or) wheel track:** The distance between the longitudinal axes of the impressions (on the road surface) of the right and left wheels of a single axle of a vehicle.

(*f*) **Minimum running ground clearance:** The minimum clearance measured from ground with the vehicle in a gross vehicle weight condition.

(*g*) **Room length:** The horizontal distance along the vehicle's longitudinal (lengthwise) center line from the top of the instrument safety pad to the point directly above the top of the rear seatback.

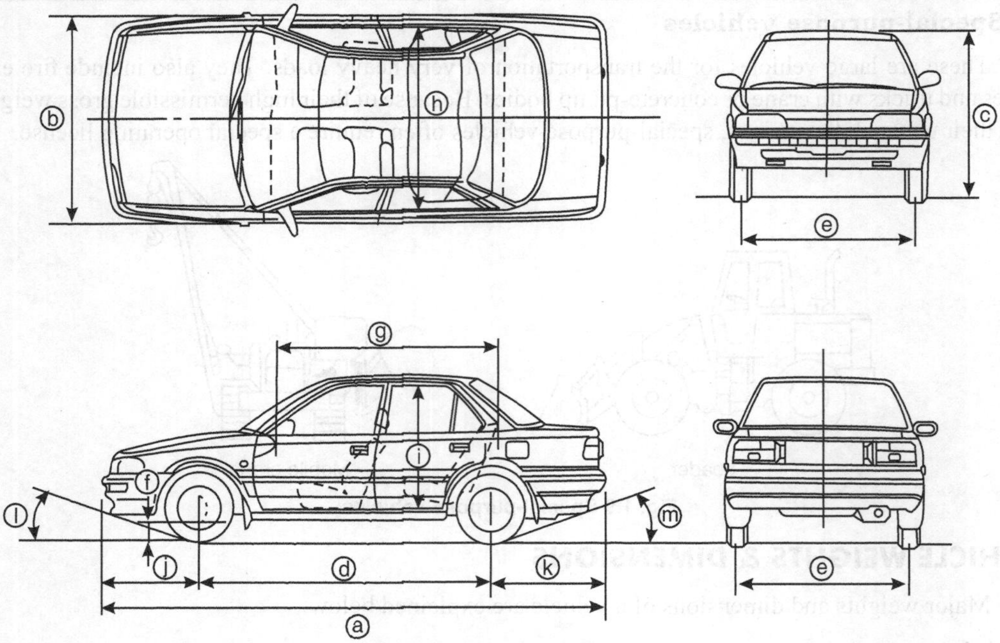

Fig. 1.10 Vehicle dimensions

(*h*) **Room width:** The maximum lateral distance between the trimmed interior body surfaces.

(*i*) **Room height:** The maximum vertical distance from the top of the floor covering to the headlining.

(*j*) **Overhang-front:** The distance from the center line of the front wheels to the front of the vehicle, including bumper guards if they are standard equipment.

(*k*) **Overhang-rear:** The distance from the center line of the rear wheels to the rear of the vehicle, including bumper guards if they are standard equipment.

(*l*) **Angle of approach:** The angle formed by the ground and the line tangent to the front tyre static loaded radius are and the first point of interference (i.e. bumper, guard, gravel deflector, fender or other components excluding license plate).

(*m*) **Angle of departure:** The angle formed by the ground and the line tangent to the rear tyre static loaded radius arc and the first point of interference (i.e. bumper, guard, gravel deflector, tail pipe, fender or other components excluding license plate).

HISTORICAL DEVELOPMENT OF AUTOMOBILES

Development of the motor vehicle, that is to say a land based vehicle not limited to travelling on rails and driven by an engine or motor, received a decisive stimulus when the internal combustion engine was invented.

The pioneer years

1860 The Frenchman Lenoir constructs the first internal combustion engine capable of driving itself, with coal gas as a fuel. Efficiency was ~3%.

1867 Otto and Langen exhibit an improved internal combustion engine at the world exhibition in Paris. Efficiency was ~9%.

1878 Otto constructs the first gas engine using mixture compression and the four-stroke operating principle. Efficiency approx.15%. Almost simultaneously, the Englishman Clerk builds the first two-stroke gas engine.

1883 Daimler and maybach develop the first high-speed four stroke gasoline engine with hot-tube ignition.

1885 Carl Benz builds the first practical, petrol-burning car.

1886 Gottlieb Daimler installs a 1.5 hp engine in a carriage.

1887 Bosch invents the magneto-ignition with make-and-break for the internal combustion engine.

1889 Daimler introduces the first sliding pinion 4-speed gear system. The Englishman Dunlop begins to produce pneumatic tyres.

1891 Panhard and Levassor pioneer the front-engined car.

1892 Maybach develops a float-type jet carburetor.

1893 The American Ford builds his first car and Diesel patents his heavy oil engine operating principle.

1894 The 2.75 hp Benz "Velo" is the first car to be produced in quantity. The Vacheron car has the first steering wheel.

1895 Panhard builds the first closed car. The Michelin brothers, Andre and Edouard, introduce the first pneumatic car tyres. The Lanchester brothers, of Britain, patent propellershaft transmission.

1897 Mors, of France, produces the first V4 engine. Graf and Stift, of Austria, build the first front-wheel drive petrol car. The M.A.N. company manufacturers the first operational diesel engine.

1898 Percy Riley, of Coventry, pioneers use of the mechanically operated inlet valve. Daimler builds the first in-line 4-cylinder engine. Opel starts to build motor vehicles.

1899 Daimler introduces the honeycomb type radiator with integral water tank, gate gear change and foot accelerator. Renault, of France, pioneers use of shaft drive with sprung rear axle, using universal joints. Dietrich-Bollee offers windscreens as optional extras. The Fiat company is established in Turin.

1900 Establishment of the Horch company in Cologne.

Age of the Model T

1901 Daimler, of Germany, introduces the Mercedes, first true forerunner of the modern car.

1902 Spyker, of Holland, builds 4-wheel drive car with 6 cylinder, in-line engine. Amedee Bollee patents a system of direct fuel injection. Dr Frederick Lanchester designs disc brake.

1903 Adler, of Germany, patents first swing rear axles, designed by Dr.E.Rumpler. Mors sells a car with shock absorbers. Maudslay, of Britain, produces first overhead camshaft car engine. Ader, of France, builds first V8 engine.

1904 Sturtevant, of USA, sells first car with automatic transmission. Cadillac, of USA, offers anti-theft ignition lock as optional extra.

1905 Antifreeze sold in USA. Heaters, working off engine exhaust, are introduced in America.

1906 Rolls-Royce launches the Silver Ghost. France introduces detachable wheel rims; UA bumper bars.

1907 Chadwick, of USA, produces first supercharged car.

1908 Ford announces the Model T. Delco, of USA, produces the first coil and distributor ignition system. Herbert Frood, in England, uses asbestos for brake and clutch linings.

1909 Christie, of USA, mounts 4-cylinder engine and gearbox transversely to drive front wheels. Triplex, in France, sells the first 'shatterproof' safety glass.

The quest for comfort

1911 Cadillac introduces electric starter and electric lighting with dynamo. First car telephone used in Los Angeles, USA. Isotta-Fraschini, of Italy, develops the first effective four-wheel brakes.

1912 Peugeot introduces the twin overhead camshaft engine. Delahaye, of France, sells V6-engined car. Oakland and Hupmobile, of USA, pioneer the all-steel body.

1913 Two types of direction indicator are introduced in USA, both cable operated. Forced feed, dry-sump lubrication is introduced by Peugeot. The British SU constant-vacuum carburetor with sliding piston is introduced.

1915 Windscreen wipers worked by vacuum from the engine introduced in USA. Cadillac pioneers thermostatic control of the cooling system.

1916 Packard sells the first production car with a V12 engine, the Twin Six. Brake stop-lights used in the USA. The Bavarian Motor Works (BMW) are set up, initially as an aircraft engine manufacturer under the name "Bayerische Flugzeugwerke AG".

1917 The first push button electric gear selector is fitted to the American Premier car.

1919 Hispano-Suiza od Spain and France introduces servo-assisted brakes.

1920 Duesenberg, of USA, fits hydraulic, internally expanding four-wheel brakes. Torsion bars are used in the suspension of the Leyland Eight. Columbia, of USA, introduces automatic radiator shutters.

The jazz age

1921 Automatic reversing light devised in America.

1922 Unitary construction and independent front suspension pioneered on Lancia Lambda. Austin announces the Seven, a baby car with 747 cc, engine and four seats. In the USA, Trico introduces electric windscreen wipers and Cadillac an automatic choke. Marconi and the British Daimler Company experiment with car radio.

1923 Ethyl lead is added to petrol to reduce pinking (knocking). Dodge, of USA, produces the first all-steel saloon body. Fiat, of Italy, fits an adjustable steering column. The first diesel-engined trucks appear from Benz and M.A.N.

1925 Front and rear bumpers are fitted as standard in USA.

1926 Hot-water car heaters introduced in USA. Riley announces 9 hp Monaco saloon with a built-in boot. The Belgian-invented Silentbloc non-lubricated bearing is launched.

1927 Studebaker and Oldsmobile, of USA, use chromium plating.

1928 Cadillac and la Salle, USA, introduce the synchromesh gearbox.

1929 The British Luvax hydraulic shock absorber is announced. Body rustproofing and dual tail lights are among the year's innovations. Car radios are available as extras.

1930 The Vauxhall Cadet is the first European car with synchromesh.

Coping with the slump

1931 Automatic clutches, worked by engine vacuum, adopted by Standard and Rover. Wolseley and Triumph build small 6-cylinder cars; Hillman launches Minx. Swallow Coach building Co. announces the SS1, ancestor of the Jaguar.

1932 Trend to independent front suspension on popular cars led by Peugeot and Adler. Wolseley Hornet has engine mounted over front axle to gain extra body space. Illuminated semaphore-type direction indicators come into general use. The Auto-Union is set up by the fusion of the Wanderer, Audi, Horch and DKW companies.

1933 General Motors, of USA, introduces the 'No-Draft' ventilation system.

1934 Citroen, of France, launches the 7CV. It has front drive, unitary construction and all-independent suspension. Chrysler, of USA, launches streamlined airflow car.

1935 Fiat 1500 has 6-cylinder engine, backbone chassis, hydraulic brakes, independent front suspension and streamlined body.

1936 Daimler-Benz begins to build diesel-engined car. Fiat 500 has engine ahead of front wheels, four synchromesh gears, hydraulic bikes and independent front suspension. Wilson, of Leicester, builds electric car-a 32 mph 2 seater.

1937 Studebaker offers windscreen washers.

1938 The Volkswagenwerk is set up.

1939 Fully automatic Hydra-Matic transmission is offered on Oldmobiles.

1940 Chrysler offers 2-speed wipers.

Post-war expansion

1945 Renault becomes the first car company in the west to be state-owned. Philips, of Holland, produces the double filament bulb for dipping lights.

1946 Power-operated windows fitted in USA.

1947 The first Ferrari announced the 1.5 litres V12type 125 with 5 speeds.

1948 Morris introduces the new Minor with torsion bar independent front suspension. Jaguar launches the 120 mph XK120 sports car with 3.5 litres, twin overhead camshaft, 6-cylinder engine. In USA the Tucker Torpedo has rear engine, advanced safety features, disc brakes and turning headlamps. Michelin introduces the X radial-ply tyre. Triplex makes the curved windscreen. Goodrich, of USA, produces the first tubeless tyre. Warning lights are generally adopted in place of some instruments.

1949 Combined coil spring/damper unit and strut-type telescopic damper introduced on Triumph Mayflower. Cadillac inaugurates the tail-fin era of styling.

1950 Ford, of Britain, adopts Macpherson strut independent front suspension on Mk 1 Consul, Zephyr and Zodiac models. Dunlop, of Britain, announces patent disc brake with pads applied by caliper. Rover builds the first jet car with front-mounted 200 hp gas turbine engine. Buick, of USA, introduces tinted glass.

From jet to mini

1951 Chrysler and Buick introduce power steering.

1952 General Motors introduces air conditioning. Austin and Morris combine to form the British Motor Corporation. The Mercedes-Benz 300 SL sports car has vertically opening doors and the engine canted at 45 degrees to lower body. Rover's JET 1 establishes a gas turbine car record of 152 mph.

1954 Cadillac uses twin headlamps. Buick uses wrap-round windscreen. Bosch, of Germany, produces petrol injection for 4-stroke car, the Mercedes-Benz 300SL.

1955 Citroen's DS19 has replaceable body panels, glass-fibre roof, hydro-pneumatic suspension, front disc brakes, hydraulic gear change, steering and automatic clutch.

1956 Jensen 541 is the first British road car with disc brakes on all four wheels.

1957 Chrysler makes the Auto-pilot, a push-button device to hold constant throttle positions for motorway driving. Felix Wankel, of Germany, runs his first rotary petrol engine.

1958 DAF, of Holland, produces Variomatic automatic transmission which drives through belts on expanding pulleys.

1959 BMC introduces the Mini with front drive, transverse engine and independent rubber suspension. The Triump Herald abandons grease points.

Years of innovation

1961 The Renault R4 has a cooling system sealed for life.

1962 BMC announces the 1100, a descendant of the Mini, with Hydrolastic suspension.

1963 Rootes launches the Hillman Imp with the first mass-produced engine using die-cast aluminium parts. Dunlop demonstrates aqua planning.

1964 The rear-engined NSU Spider is the first Wankel-engined car. Ford introduces Aeroflow ventilation for family cars. Cibie, of France, and Philips jointly develop the iodine vapour bulb.

1965 The Renault 16 combines features of both estate car and saloon.

1966 The USA adopts legislation to establish car safety standards. Californian air pollution laws set the pace in the USA for producing engines with less noxious exhaust fumes.

1967 Cibie develops the self-levelling headlamp for Citroen.

1968 Cibie produces headlamps which turn with steering on the Citroen DS21. Citroen introduces the Mehari estate car with moulded plastic body.

1969 Mercedes-Benz builds the C111 prototype with first triple-rotor Wankel engine. The USA experiments with safety airbags designed to inflate and cushion a car's occupants in a crash.

1970 Maserati-engined Citroen SM has power-assisted rack and pinion steering with power-centring device.

Exemplary modern cars

1966 Present Toyota Corolla, a simple small Japanese saloon/sedan that has come to be the best-selling car of all time.

1970 Present Range Rover, the first take on the combination of luxury and four-wheel drive utility, the original 'SUV'. Such was the popularity of the original Range Rover Classic that a new model was not brought out until 1994.

1973 Present Mercedes-Benz S-Class, electronic Anti-lock Braking System, supplemental restraint airbags, seat belt pre-tensioners, and electronic traction control systems all made their debut on the S-Class. These features would later become standard throughout the car industry.

1975 Present BMW 3 Series, the 3 Series has been on Car and Driver magazine's annual Ten Best list 17 times, making it the longest running entry in the list.

1977 Present Honda Accord saloon/sedan, this Japanese sedan became the most popular car in the United States in the 1990s, pushing the Ford Taurus aside, and setting the stage for today's upscale Asian sedans.

1981 Dodge Aries and Plymouth Reliant, the "K-cars" that saved Chrysler as a major to manufacturer. These models were some of the first successful American front-wheel

1989 drive, fuel-efficient compact cars.

1983 Present Chrysler minivans, the two-box minivan design nearly pushed the station wagon out of the market, and presaged today's crossover SUVs.

1984 Present Renault Espace, first mass one-volume car of non-commercial MPV class.

1986 Present Ford Taurus, this mid-sized front-wheel drive sedan with modern computer-assisted design dominated the American market in the late 1980s, and created a design revolution in North America.

1989

to

1999 Pontiac Trans Sport was one of the first of the one box cars.

1997 Present Toyota Prius was launched in the Japanese market, in September 2010 reached worldwide cumulative sales of 2.0 million units, becoming the most iconic hybrid electric vehicle in the world.

1998 Present Ford Focus is one of the most popular hatchbacks across the globe, that is also one of Ford's best selling world cars.

2008 Present Tata Nano is an inexpensive, rear-engined, four-passenger city car built by the Indian company Tata Motors and is aimed primarily at the Indian domestic market.

2010 Present, Nissan Leaf and Chevrolet Volt, an all-electric car and a plug-in hybrid correspondingly, were launched in the U.S. and Japanese markets in December 2010, becoming the first mass production vehicles of their kind.

THE MOTOR VEHICLES ACT, 1988

This volume examines laws regarding motor vehicles and their operation, including traffic violations and infractions, with significant focus on two major areas of public interest: speeding, and drinking and driving. It covers laws related to victims of accidents, young drivers, licensing requirements, vehicle safety issues, helmet use laws, seat belts, child restraints, and air bags, and the Transportation Equity Act.

The first enactment relating to motor vehicles in India was the Indian Motor Vehicles Act, 1914, which was subsequently replaced by the Motor Vehicles Act, 1939. The Act of 1939 had been amended several times. Inspite of several amendments it was felt necessary to bring out a comprehensive legislation keeping in view the changes in the transport technology, pattern of passenger and freight movements, development of the road network in the country and particularly the improved techniques in the motor vehicles management. Various committees as well as the Law Commission had gone into different aspects of road transport. Several members of parliament have also urged for comprehensive review of the Motor Vehicles act, 1939. A working group was, therefore, constituted in January, 1984 to review all the provisions of the act of 1939. This working group took into account the suggestions and recommendations earlier made by various bodies and institutions and made certain recommendations. On the recommendations of the working group state governments were asked to submit their comments. The recommendations made by the working group and comments received from the state governments were discussed at a special meeting of transport ministers of all states and union territories. Based on the conclusions reached in the meeting of transport ministers and suggestions made by the Supreme Court in a case the motor vehicles bill was introduced in the parliament.

Review Questions

1. What is meant by Automobile?
2. List the components of an automobile.
3. Who invented automobile?
4. Who first commercially manufactured motor vehicles?
5. What are the different types of motor vehicles on the basis of their construction?
6. What are the main units of a motorcar?
7. Which car set the pattern for many of those in use today?
8. Define body of a car.
9. What are the nominal requirements of a body?
10. What is meant by a saloon body?
11. What is meant by a coupe in an automobile?

2
CHAPTER

VEHICLE STRUCTURE

CHASSIS (OR) RUNNING GEAR

A VEHICLE WITHOUT BODY IS CALLED CHASSIS

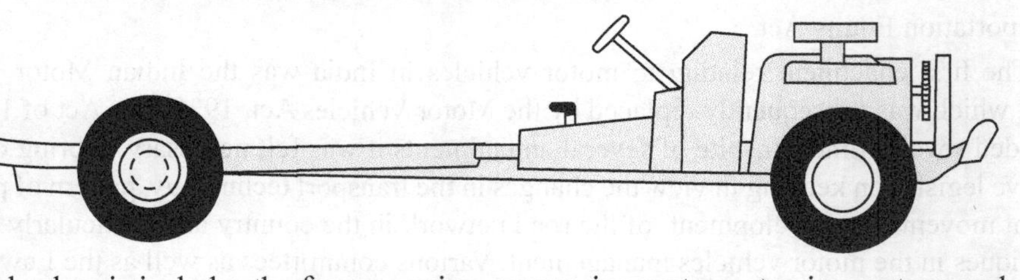

The vehicle chassis includes the frame, engine, suspension system, steering system, and other mechanical parts with the body removed. These systems have direct impacts on riding comfort, the vehicle stability, steering feeling, etc, and vary widely in mechanisms and devices.

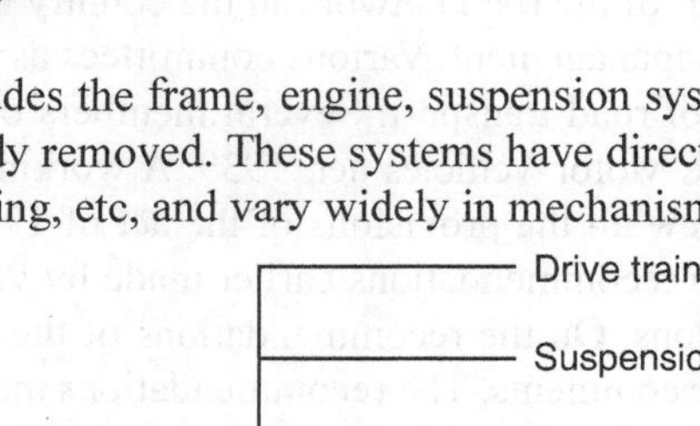

CHASSIS LAYOUT

Chassis layout refers to location of an engine and driveline components and also how power is transmitted from the engine to the drive wheels.

Chassis layout with reference to drive

Rear wheel drive

This layout has the engine in the front, mounted longitudinally, and the drive axle in the rear. The transmission is usually right behind the engine, and a drive shaft transfers power back to the rear axle. In this arrangement the rear wheels act as the driving wheels and the front wheels swivel to allow the vehicle to be steered. Spacing out the main components in this layout makes each unit accessible but a drawback is the intrusion of the transmission components into the passenger compartment. These create a large bulge in the region of the gearbox and a raised long bulge, called a tunnel, down the centre of the car floor for the accommodation of the propeller shaft. Using the rear wheels to propel the car utilizes the load transfer that takes place from the front to rear of the vehicle when the car is climbing a hill or accelerating and therefore good traction is obtained.

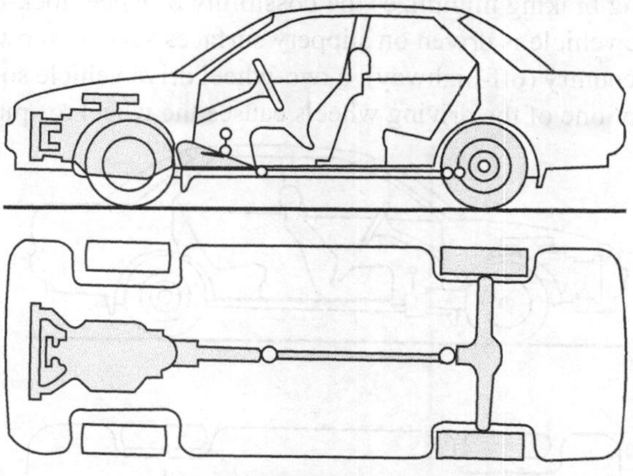

Fig. 2.1 Front engine rear-wheel drive

Front wheel drive

The compactness of the layout has made it very popular for use on cars. The vehicle has both the engine and transaxle in the front. Accommodating all the main components under the bonnet (hood) in one compartment give maximum space within the car for the occupants, also the absence of floor bulges and tunnel provides more room for the rear passengers. Transverse mounting of the engine simplifies the transmission, because the output shafts from the engine and gearbox move in a similar direction to the wheels. This avoids the need for a bevel-type final drive. Instead a simple reduction gear, incorporating a differential, transmits the power by short drive shafts to the road wheels. The heavy drive train adds weight to the front drive wheels for good traction on slippery pavement. Mounting the main units in one assembly sometimes makes it difficult to gain access to some parts.

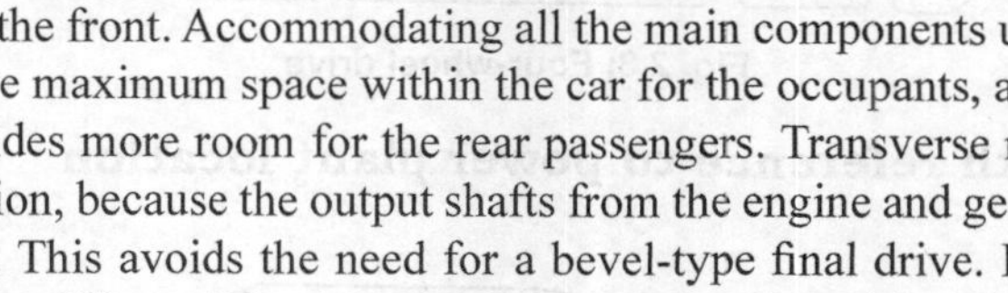

Fig. 2.2 Front engine front-wheel drive

The major criticism of front-wheel drive is that the driving wheels have less grip on the road when the vehicle is accelerating and hill-climbing. Although this characteristic can be partly corrected by placing the engine well forward to increase the load on the driving wheels, the car is then liable to become "nose-heavy". The effect of this is to make the steering of the car more difficult. For this case the car is to be fitted with power steering. Using the front wheels for steering allows the driving force to act in the same direction as the wheel is pointing. This feature improves vehicle handling especially in slippery conditions.

Four wheel drive

This arrangement is safer because it distributes the drive to all four wheels. The sharing of the load between the four wheels during acceleration reduces the risks of wheel spin. Also the positive drive to each wheel during braking minimizes the possibility of wheel lock-up. A further advantage of this layout is when the vehicle is driven on slippery surfaces such as snow and mud. When on an icy road or driven cross-country (off-highway), a two-wheel drive vehicle soon becomes undrivable because the loss of grip of one of the driving wheels causes the wheel to spin.

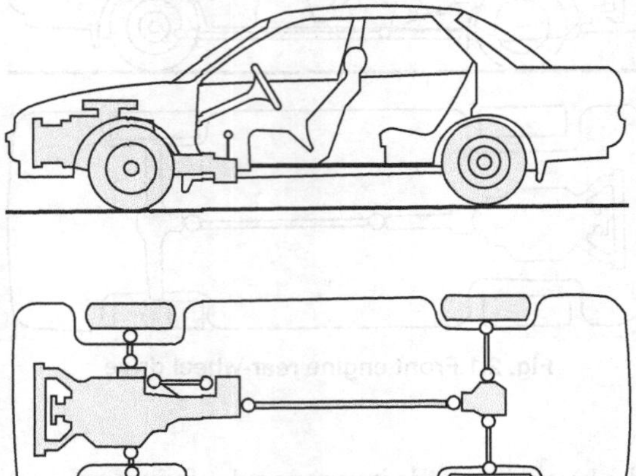

Fig. 2.3: Four-wheel drive

Chassis layout with reference to power plant location

Front engine

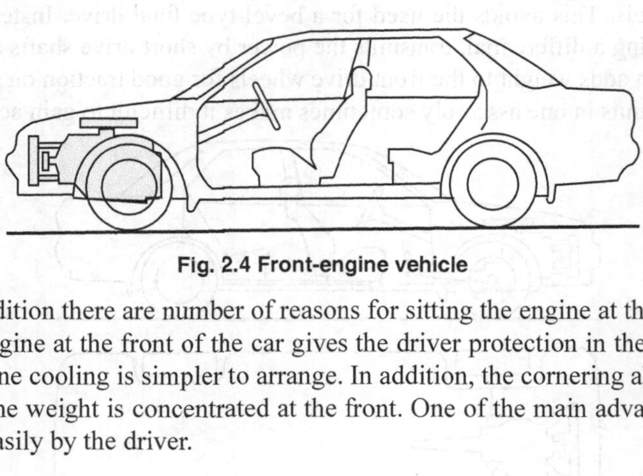

Fig. 2.4 Front-engine vehicle

Apart from tradition there are number of reasons for sitting the engine at the front of a car. The large mass of an engine at the front of the car gives the driver protection in the event of a head-on collision. Also engine cooling is simpler to arrange. In addition, the cornering ability of a vehicle is normally better if the weight is concentrated at the front. One of the main advantage is that engine can be controlled easily by the driver.

Rear engine

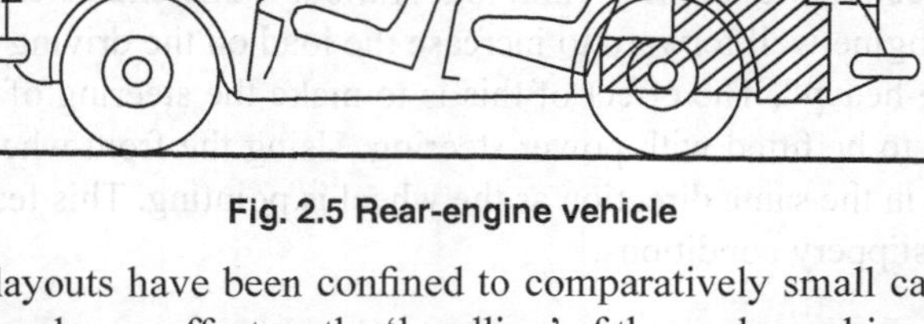

Fig. 2.5 Rear-engine vehicle

Most rear-engine layouts have been confined to comparatively small cars, because the heavy engine at the rear has an adverse effect on the 'handling' of the car by making it 'tail heavy'. Also it takes up a good deal of space that would be used on a front-engined car for carrying luggage. Most of the space vacated by the engine at the front end can be used for luggage, but this space is usually less than that available at the rear.

One advantage attributed to a rear-engined layout is that it increases the load on the rear driving wheels, giving them better grip of the road.

One of the most famous rear-engined cars is the Volkswagen Beetle.

Central (or) mid engine

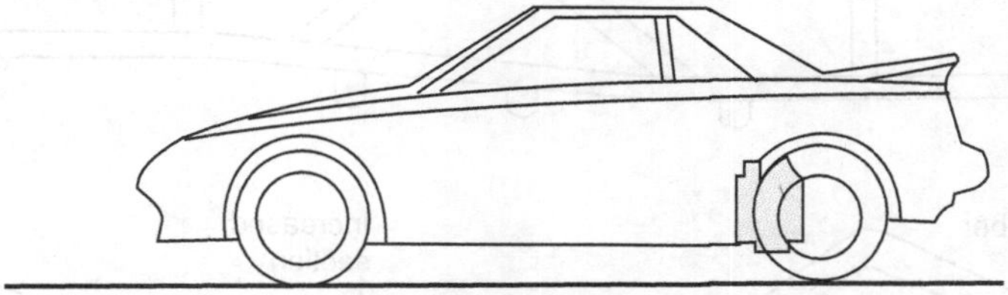

Fig. 2.6 Mid-engine vehicle

The term mid-engine is used because the engine is mounted in front of the rear axle line. This situations generally apply to sports cars because the engine sitting gives a load distribution that achieves both good handling and maximum traction from the driving wheels.

CHASSIS FRAME

The vehicle frame is a high-strength structure used to support all other parts of the vehicle. Besides bolt-on body panels, the frame holds the engine, transmission, suspension, and other parts in position. The frame can be separate from the body or integrated into the body shell as in the case of unitized body design.

Purpose of a frame

The vehicle frame is used:

- to support engine, body, road wheels and transmission assemblies.
- to withstand the accelerating and braking torque.
- to accommodate suspension system.
- to resist centrifugal force while taking a turn.
- to withstand bending and twisting stresses due to the fluctuation of rear and front axle.

Constructional details

The chassis frame is usually constructed from steel pressings which may be welded, riveted or bolted together and reinforced where necessary. There are two major types: conventional construction and unitized body construction.

Conventional construction

In this type of chassis construction the frame is the basic unit to which various components are attached and body is bolted on the frame later on. It is also known as framed construction.

Conventional construction for passenger cars

The actual chassis frame consists of two longitudinal members which are referred to as side members. These members are braced by cross members (horizontal members) at the front and rear of the frame. To improve the torsional stiffness of the frame a diagonal cross-brace arrangement is added to the centre of the frame. The side members must taper in (narrow) at the front to provide shorter turning radius of front wheel and give improved support to the engine assembly. It is widening out at the rear end to provide a bigger space for body.

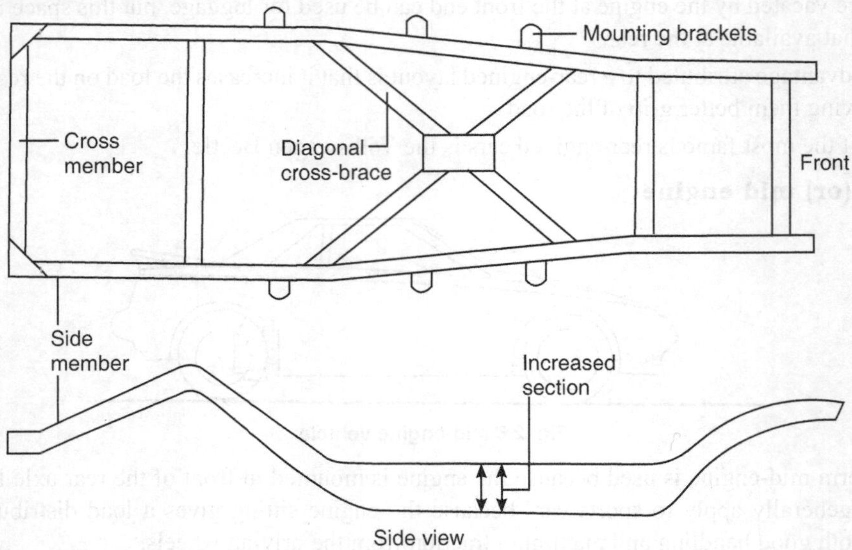

Fig. 2.7 SUV/Passenger car chassis frame

The front and rear ends of the side members are swept upwards (curved upwards) to accommodate the movement of the axle due to springing and also kept the chassis height low (lower ground clearance). This also avoids impact due to the rear axle bouncing. It is also common practice to provide the side members with an increased depth of section towards the centre, where there is a tendency for the greatest bending loads to occur. A number of brackets are attached to the main chassis members to provide a means of mounting and securing the vehicle body and components.

Although the use of a separate chassis frame is now restricted to low volume production cars it is still the main method of construction of commercial vehicle chassis.

Conventional construction for commercial vehicles

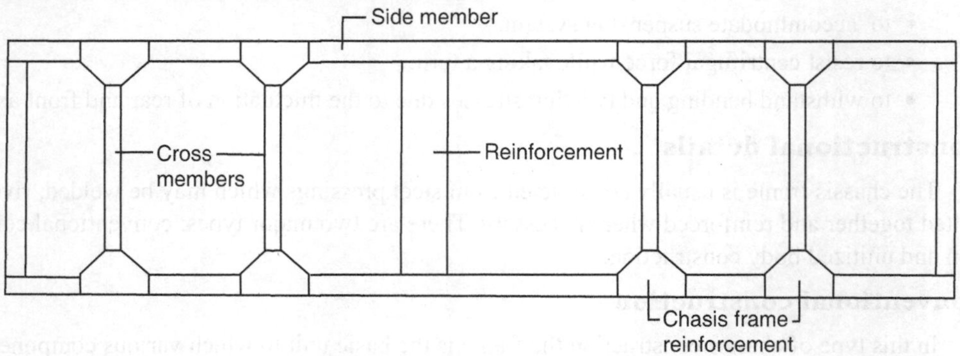

Fig. 2.8 Commercial vehicle chassis frame

The arrangement of the commercial vehicle chassis frame is similar to that of the SUVs/passenger cars frame but it must be capable of carrying heavier and more varied loads. The various parts of the chassis frame are usually manufactured from relatively heavy gauge steel plate and are of much deeper section than those in the SUVs/passenger cars chassis frame. Diagonal cross-bracing is rarely used. Instead a series of channel or tubular section cross members are welded or riveted to the side members, as illustrated in Fig.2.8. In most designs the side members are not swept up at the front and rear to allow for the vertical movement of the axles. The front end of the chassis is not swept in to allow for the movement of the steered wheels. This is because the engine is usually mounted higher in the chassis frame than a SUV/passenger car engine and therefore there is more space available for the front road wheels to turn on the larger vehicle and the ground clearance is greater.

Unitized body design (Frameless construction)

Today, almost all passenger cars, most vanes and even some buses are of integral construction, also known as integral or monocoque construction.

In this type of construction heavy side members used in conventional construction are eliminated and the floor is strengthened by cross members and the body, all welded.

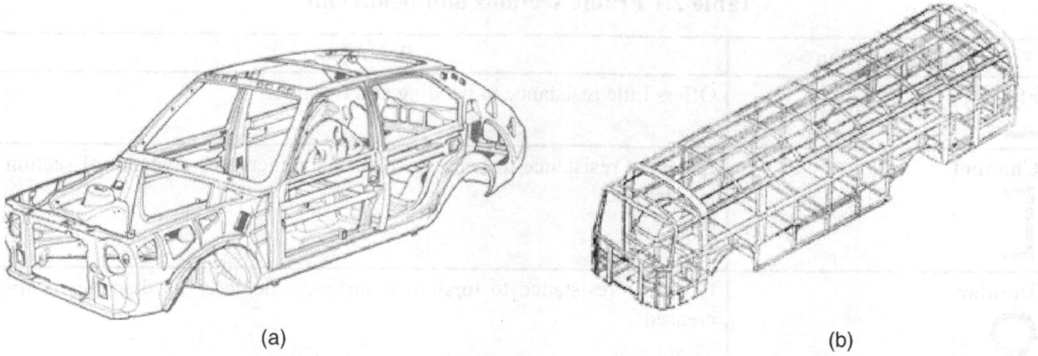

Fig. 2.9 Unitized body designs: (a) passenger car and (b) bus

Most of the modern cars have this integral construction. In this body design, the frame and body are combined as one unit. All the members of a unitized body are load carrying members. Panels or members that share the load are called stressed panels. Very often their creases and bends are there to increase strength rather than change the vehicle's appearance. Unstressed panels are those that do not contribute significantly to the strength of the structure. The floor pan, roof, inner aprons, quarter panels, pillars and rocker panels are integrally joined to form an unitized body. The unitized body has a complex design that spreads collision forces throughout the body to help protect the vehicle occupants.

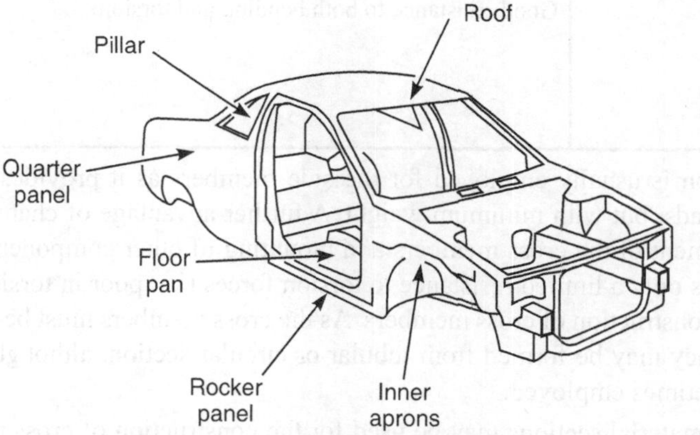

Fig. 2.10 Parts of an unitized body of a car

The strength and rigidity of the unitized body is achieved by body design rather than by having a heavy steel frame to support the body. In this body design, body sheet metal is fabricated into a box design which provides good resistance to bending and torsion.

The advantages of this construction are low weight and the ability to style the outer body panels as desired.

Design and production costs are very high, which means that integral construction is used only for mass-produced vehicles. A further disadvantage of this type of construction is that the resulting box-like shape tends to amplify road and engine noise for the occupants. Special sound-deadening materials are used to minimize the transmission of noise.

FRAME SECTIONS

In order to provide a good resistance to bending and torsional effect, the frame sections are made of proper forms.

Table 2.1 Frame sections and behaviours

Frame Section	Behaviour
Flat 	Offers little resistance to bending and twisting.
Channel 	Excellent resistance to bending. Resistance increases as depth of section is increased.
Tubular 	Excellent resistance to torsion. Resistance increases as diameter is increased.
Box 	Good resistance to both bending and torsion.
Top-hat 	Not commonly used due to weakness and a propensity to rust.
I 	Good resistance to both bending and torsion.

Channel section is usually employed for the side members as it provides good resistance to vertical bending loads, but with minimum weight. A further advantage of channel section is that it allows easy attachment of the cross members and mounting of other components. However, channel section provides only a limited resistance to torsion forces (i.e. poor in torsion) and is therefore unsuitable for the construction of cross members. As the cross members must be capable of resisting torsional effects, they may be formed from tubular or circular section, although for convenience a box section is sometimes employed.

Various other material sections may be used for the construction of cross members. These include the top-hat section and the I-section which is manufactured from two channel sections placed back-to-back. Provided the correct material section is used, the chassis frame can be made rigid enough to withstand the loads placed upon it.

FRAME MATERIALS

Frames are usually made of steel or aluminium and sometimes composite materials. Most frames used on light vehicles are made of low-carbon steel having a carbon content of 0.15-0.25

percent. Alloy steels (nickel chrome) which are responsive to heat treatment are used for truck frames of the better grade.

Some of the components in a unitized body are made from high-strength steel (HSS) to provide additional protection in a collision.

CRUMPLE ZONE

The purpose of a crumple zone or deformation element is to ensure that in the event of a severe front or rear impact the vehicle's structure absorbs as much energy as possible. This reduces the rate of deceleration felt by the occupants and reduces the risk of injury.

Fig. 2.11 Crumble Zore

Fig. 2.12 (b) shows the internal structure of an integral body. The front arrows show how the shock of a frontal collision is transferred along the front body members, which are designed to collapse progressively, absorbing energy as they do so and protecting the passenger compartment. The intention is to create a passenger safety cell in which the occupants are protected from physical impact and excessive body stresses.

The rear of the vehicle acts in exactly the same way. Note that if the spare wheel lies flat in the boot floor, it may be part of the rear crumple zone and if so it must be kept inflated.

IMPACT BEAMS

To prevent intrusion into the passenger area as a result of side impact, an increasing number of vehicles are now designed with side impact protection features.

One of the most common types comprises strengthening beams fitted into the frame of each door. Side impact beams are metal bars or corrugated panels that bolt or weld inside the door assemblies as shown in Fig. 2.12 (a), to protect the passengers. They prevent the door from opening upon impact and help protect the passenger area. The side arrows in Fig. 2.12 (b) show how these beams help to spread the load of a side impact.

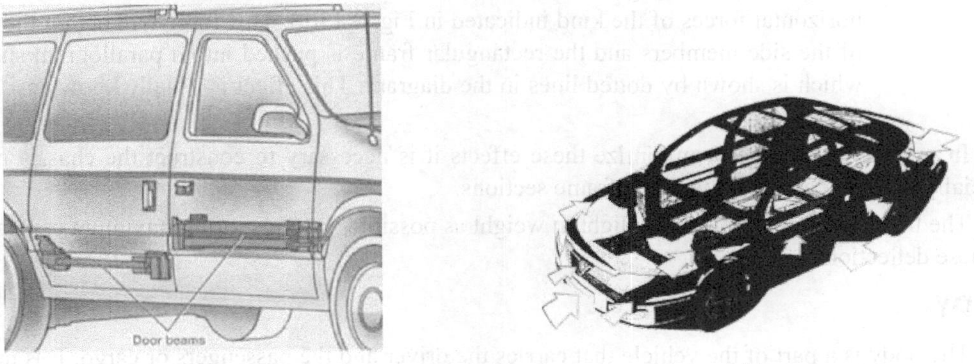

(a) (b)

Fig. 2.12 (a) Impact beams and (b) Impact beams spreading side impact load

LOADS ON FRAMES

Whether it is a car or a truck, the vehicle structure has to withstand various static and dynamic loads. The deflections of a simple rectangular frame, consisting of two side members connected together with two cross members, are shown in Fig. 2.13. These deflections are caused by the following forces:

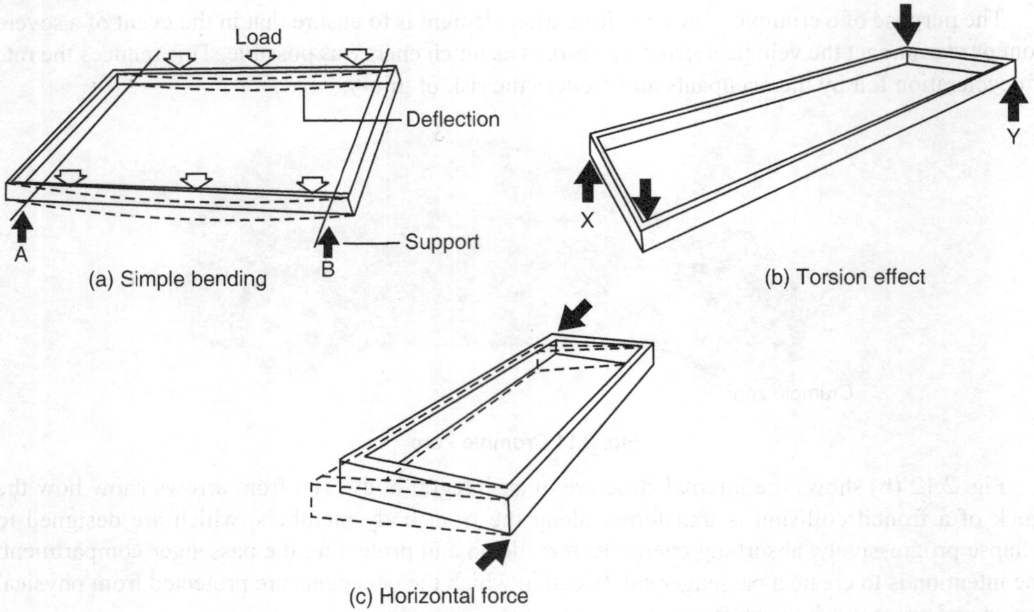

Fig. 2.13 Distortion of a simple frame

1. Weight of the components and passengers gives a bending action. This causes the frame to sag, which is shown in Fig. 2.13(a).
2. Road shocks, caused by vehicle motion or impact with an obstacle, produces two deflections of the frame:
   (*a*) Twisting due to a deflection at one corner of the frame. As road surfaces tend to be uneven the chassis frame is subjected to a twisting or torsion effect. This is illustrated diagrammatically in Fig. 2.13(b) where the opposite corners of the frame X and Y receive a loading in the upward direction. As the wheels run over an uneven surface the vehicle will experience this form of twisting action.
   (*b*) In addition to bending and torsion, the frame of the chassis must be able to withstand horizontal forces of the kind indicated in Fig. 2.13(c). This force will act on the end of the side members and the rectangular frame is pushed into a parallogram shape, which is shown by dotted lines in the diagram. This effect is usually known as 'lozenging'.

In order to overcome or minimize these effects it is necessary to construct the chassis from specially designed and manufactured frame sections.

The body and frame must be as light in weight as possible, yet must offer maximum resistance to these deflections.

BODY

The body is a part of the vehicle that carries the driver and the passengers or cargo. It is made of steel sheets 0.6 mm to 3 mm thick, welded into a box shape. It is a beam supported at each end by the wheels. So it has to be strong enough not to sag in the middle. A car must also have torsional stiffness i.e. the ability to resist the twisting stresses imposed by any irregular road surface. Structural strength is also necessary to cope with particular loads, such as the weight of the engine, thrust of the springs and minor impacts.

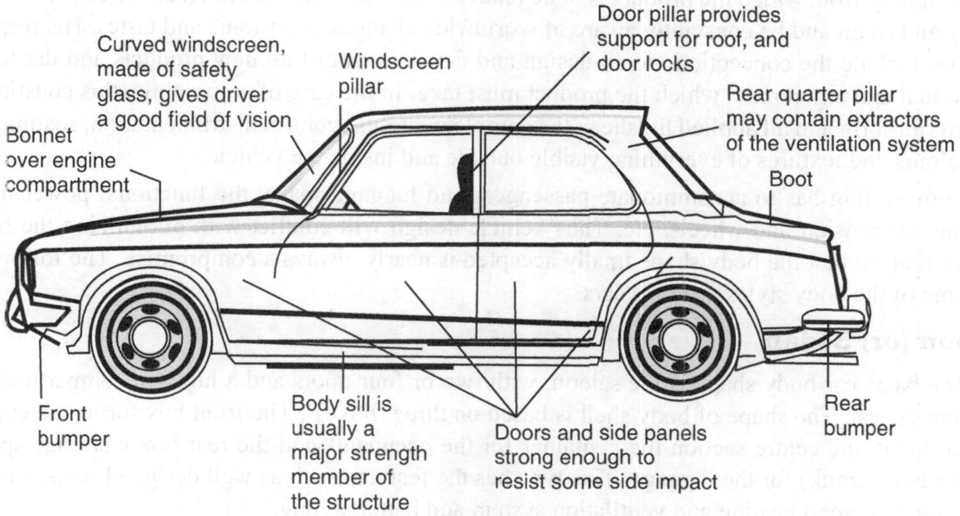

Fig. 2.14 Parts of a car body

The main parts of the car body are:

- **Bonnet** (or hood) over the engine compartment.
- Curved **windscreen**, made of safety glass, gives driver a good field of vision.
- **Windscreen pillar** provides support for windscreen glass.
- **Body sill** is usually a major strength member of the structure.
- **Door pillar** provides support for roof, and carries hinges and door locks.
- **Rear quarter pillar** may contain extractors of the ventilation system.
- **Boot** over the luggage compartment.
- **Doors and side panels** strong enough to resist some side impact.
- **Bumpers**, a horizontal bar fixed across the front or back of a motor vehicle to reduce serious damage in a collision or as a trim
- **Floor panels** ribbed for stiffness.

Bodywork materials

Steel (mild steel) is still the cheapest and the most efficient material for mass-produced separate bodies. It is strong and easily formed. The parts are stamped out by machine presses from varying thicknesses of sheet steel. Apart from steel, cast iron, aluminum, magnesium, copper, zinc, glass, and polymers are also the most commonly used materials.

Styling forms and role of stylist

Designing a form based on artistic vision is known as 'styling'. Styling enables high-volume production articles to be both attractive and functional. In fact in an age where mechanical reliability is almost automatic it is aesthetic value that provides the truly commercial success of a specific product.

Thus the stylists responsibilities in modern industry cover a very wide range. That is today's automotive stylist is required to be a combination of artist, inventor, craftsman, engineer and to some extent psychologist. He must have the ability to conceive new ideas with inventive flair and imagination and bring them to an economical reality using modern techniques and facilities, correctly selecting for the specific project in hand. To do this, he must thoroughly understand the product, its function and its appeal, have a thorough knowledge of the materials available, costs, capacities of the machinery from which the product is to be made, in an economical manner, as well as sources of supply and so on and be constantly aware of worldwide changes in customs and tastes. His responsibilities include the conception, detail design and development of all new products and the form, both visual and ergonomic, which the product must take. In the case of automobile, this constitutes the exterior form and all applied finishers, the complete interior, control instrumentation, seating, etc and colours and textures of everything visible outside and inside the vehicle.

Body styling has to accommodate passengers and luggage space, the functional power train, steering, suspension and wheels, etc. Thus vehicle design will conflict with minimizing the body surface drag so that the body shape finally accepted is nearly always a compromise. The following are some of the body styles used for cars.

Saloon (or) Sedan

The basic car body shape is the saloon, with two or four doors and a luggage compartment at the front or rear. The shape of body shell is based on three 'boxes'. The front box forms the engine compartment, the centre section the container for the occupants and the rear box a storage space, called a boot (trunk) for the luggage. This type has the features such as well designed seats, ease of entry and exit, good heating and ventilation system and better styling.

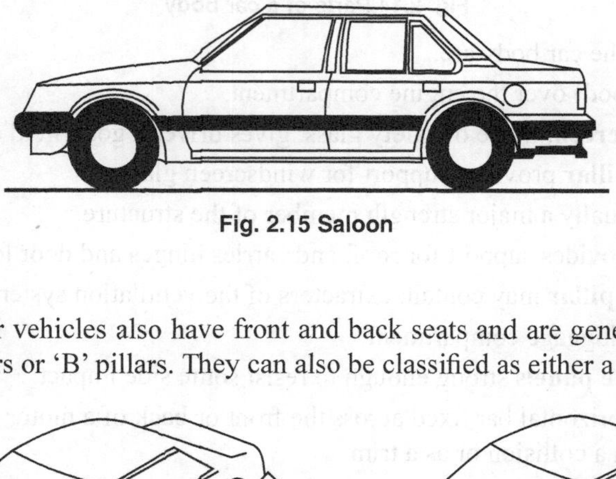

Fig. 2.15 Saloon

Hardtop

Hardtop passenger vehicles also have front and back seats and are generally characterized by their lack of door pillars or 'B' pillars. They can also be classified as either a 2 or 4-door hardtop.

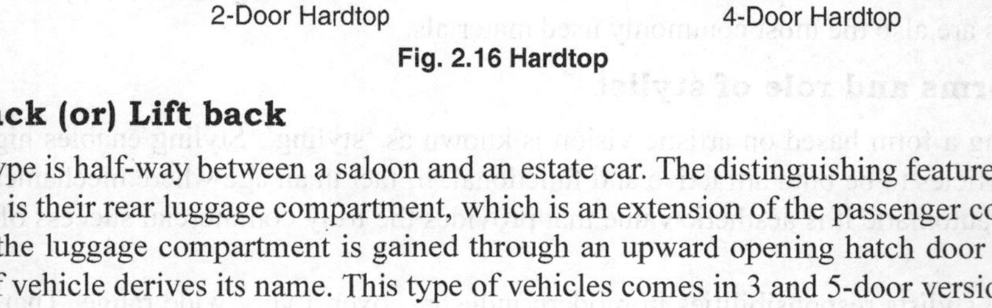

2-Door Hardtop 4-Door Hardtop

Fig. 2.16 Hardtop

Hatchback (or) Lift back

This type is half-way between a saloon and an estate car. The distinguishing feature of this type of vehicles is their rear luggage compartment, which is an extension of the passenger compartment. Access to the luggage compartment is gained through an upward opening hatch door from which this type of vehicle derives its name. This type of vehicles comes in 3 and 5-door versions.

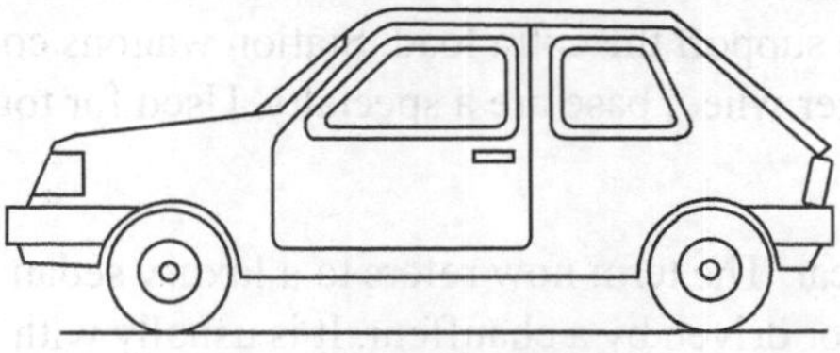

Fig. 2.17 Hatchback

Convertible (or) Drop-head coupe

This type has a folding roof, but when closed is often draughtier, noisier and less roomy than the equivalent saloon. Prior to the introduction of air-conditioning this type was widely used in hot countries.

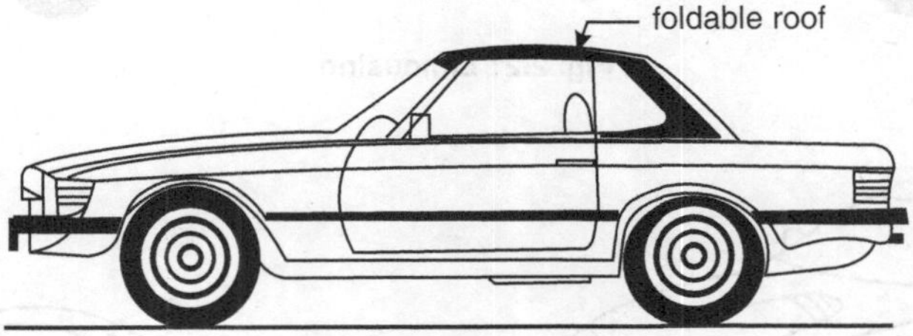

Fig. 2.18 Convertible

Sports coupe

It is a small car with two seats, for a driver and a passenger. It has better aerodynamic shape and better acceleration. Styling is not much important. Lightness combined with rigidity is the special feature.

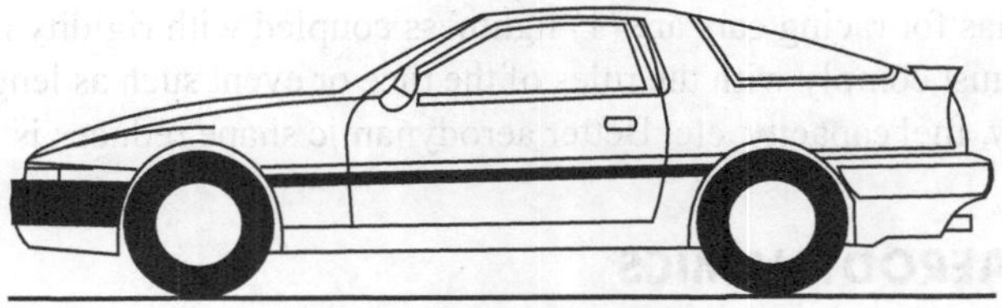

Fig. 2.19 Sports Coupe

Today some coupe models are called '2 + 2'. This generally suggests that the rear seat accommodation is rather cramped for adults but is suitable for children or for occasional adult use.

Estate car (or) Station wagon

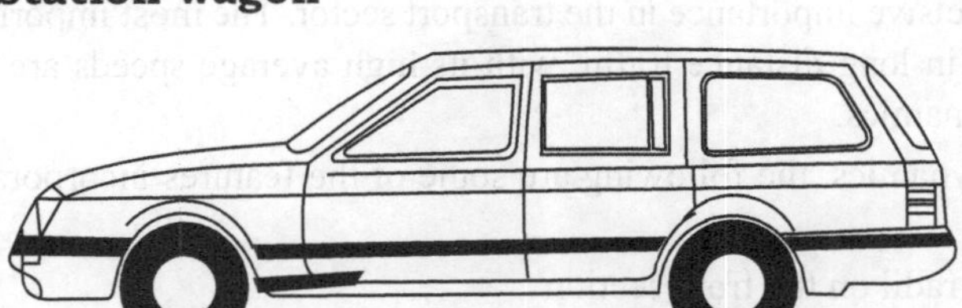

Fig. 2.20 Estate car

Station wagons are characterized by their roof, which extends straight back the length of the vehicle, allowing a spacious interior luggage compartment in the rear. The rear door, which can be opened in various ways depending on the model, provides access to the luggage compartment. Some manufacturers have successfully combined the best features of saloon and estate car in the versatile 'five-door' body. Folding the rear seats down gives a larger floor area for the carriage of luggage or goods. A door at the rear enables bulky or long objects to be loaded easily. Stronger suspension springs are fitted at the rear to support the extra load. Station wagons come in 2 and 4-door versions. More luggage space and longer wheel base are a specialty. Used for touring, picnics, etc.

Limousine

Limousine is the luxury car. The term now refers to a luxury sedan or saloon car, especially one with a lengthened wheelbase or driven by a chauffeur. It is usually with high quality equipments and best finish. Cushioned seats, air conditioning system, cooling glasses, etc., are other features.

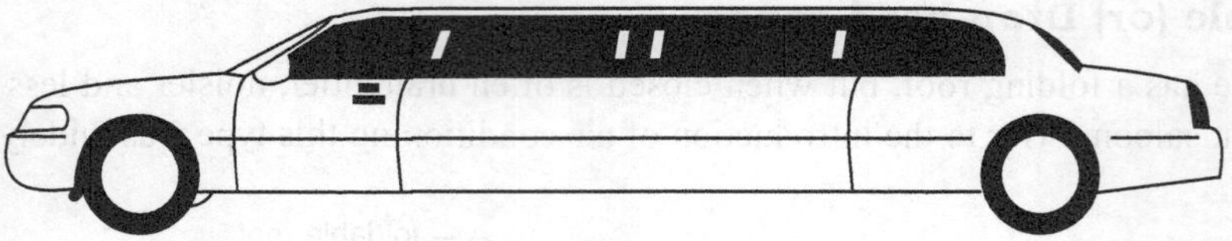

Fig. 2.21 Limousine

Racing car

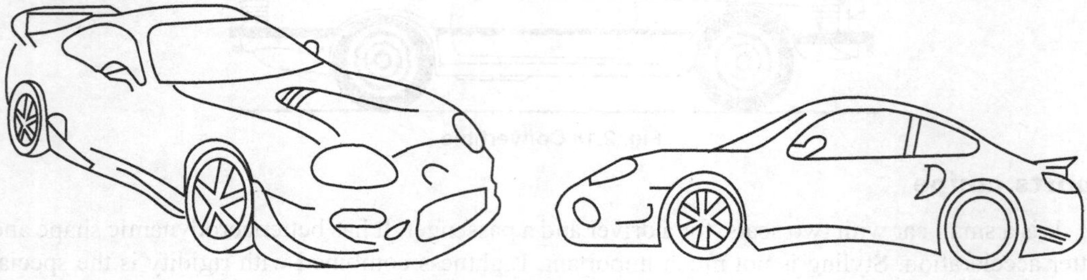

Fig. 2.22 Racing cars

Two prime criterias for racing cars are (1) lightness coupled with rigidity regardless of comfort and (2) body design must comply with the rules of the race or event such as length, width and height of car, engine capacity, fuel capacity, etc. Better aerodynamic shape reduces is the unique feature of this design.

VEHICLE BODY AERODYNAMICS

Aerodynamics is a branch of physics and is concerned with all the processes which can be observed when air flows around a body. This study deals with a solid body moving through the atmosphere and the interaction which takes place between the body surfaces and the surrounding air with varying relative speeds and wind direction.

Economy is of decisive importance in the transport sector. The most important factors in reducing fuel consumption in long distance traffic with its high average speeds are the economy of the drive train and aerodynamics.

As regards aerodynamics, the following are some of the features incorporated into the vehicle design.

- Large corner radii on the front section
- Low-level front skirts
- Fairings above and behind the driver's cab
- Aerodynamically shaped mirrors
- Enclosed steps

In addition to optimizing the shape of the driver's cab in terms of air flow to improve fuel consumption, there are a number of other aims to be considered in aerodynamic design, namely:

- Intensive air flow around cooling units
- Optimized air flow through the interior of cab

- Minimizing dirt deposition on visible areas
- Reducing impairment of the vision of other drivers in the wet

Importance of aerodynamic study

With proper aerodynamic design, the following advantages could be achieved :

1. Drag force is reduced. So maximum speed and acceleration are obtained for the same power output.
2. Fuel consumption of the vehicle can be reduced to the maximum (about 35% of fuel cost).
3. Gives better appearance and styling.
4. By reducing the various forces and moments, good stability and safety can be achieved.
5. Helps to provide proper ventilation system.
6. Helps to understand the dirt flow and exhaust gas flow patterns.
7. Aerodynamic noise could be reduced which results in quite running of the vehicle.

AERODYNAMIC DRAG

This study concerns about the airflow around the vehicle body. Drag is caused by the movement of a vehicle in the atmosphere. This term is used to describe the resistance presented by the air to the moving object as it progresses. Aerodynamic drag is usually insignificant at low vehicle speed but the magnitude of air resistance becomes considerable with rising speed. This can be seen in Fig. 2.23 which compares the aerodynamic drag forces of a poorly streamlined and a very highly streamlined medium sized car against its constant rolling resistance over a typical speed range. A vehicle with a high drag resistance tends only marginally to hinder its acceleration but it does inhibit its maximum speed and increases the fuel consumption with increasing speed.

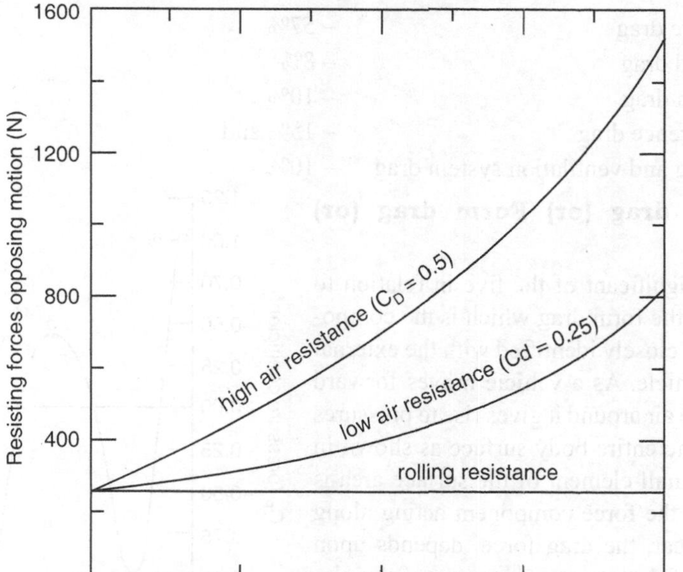

Fig. 2.23 Comparison of low and high aerodynamic drag forces with rolling resistance

Drag force depends on the following factors:

- The size and shape of the vehicle (area of nose end, vehicle super structures, shape of the loads being carried).

- Travel speed.
- Air density (air density decreases at higher temperatures and increases at higher atmospheric pressure).
- Wind direction and strength.

The aerodynamic resistance of a vehicle in air is referred to as drag force F_L. It is calculated according to the following formula:

$$F_L = \frac{1}{2} Cd\, A\rho v^2$$

Cd : Vehicle's drag co-efficient

A : Area of vehicle's nose end

ρ : Density of air

v : Velocity of the vehicle

To overcome drag, a vehicle must develop a specific amount of power. The drag power P_L is the result of drag force multiplied by travel speed *v*:

$$P_L = F_L v = \frac{1}{2} Cd\, A\rho\, v^3$$

At increasing travel speed, drag force increases by a power of two and drag power by a power of three. The increase in drag is as the square of the speed, i.e. if the speed doubles, the drag quadruples.

TYPES OF DRAG

The drag force is most easily understood if it is broken down into five constituent elements. This includes:

(*a*) Pressure drag – 57%

(*b*) Induced drag – 8%

(*c*) Friction drag – 10%

(*d*) Interference drag – 15% and

(*e*) Cooling and ventilation system drag – 10%

(a) Pressure drag (or) Form drag (or) Profile drag

The most significant of the five in relation to road vehicles is the form drag which is the component that is most closely identified with the external shape of the vehicle. As a vehicle moves forward the motion of the air around it gives rise to pressures that vary over the entire body surface as shown in Fig. 2.24. If a small element of the surface area is considered then the force component acting along the axis of the car, the drag force, depends upon the magnitude of the pressure, the area of the element upon which it acts and the inclination of that surface element (Fig.2.25). Thus it is possible for two different designs, each having a similar frontal area, to have very different values of form drag.

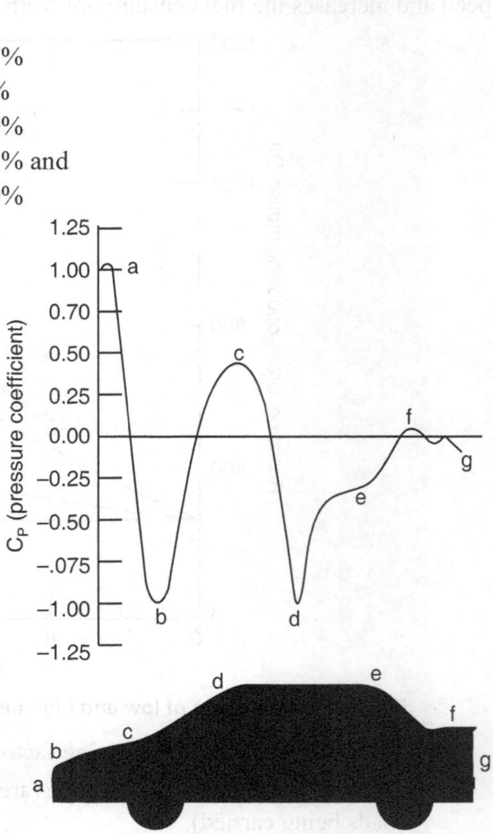

Fig. 2.24 Typical static pressure coefficient distribution

Form drag depends upon the longitudinal section of the vehicle body. For low drag coefficient a careful choice of body profile is essential, i.e.

streamlines should be continuous and separation of boundary layer with its vortices should be avoided.

Body shapes that minimize positive aerodynamic forces on the front of the vehicle and minimize negative aerodynamic forces or suction on the rear of the vehicle will exhibit low form drag. The trend to lower vehicles has reduced the frontal area significantly which has reduced form drag appreciably. Constantly retarding fast back bodies may lead to passenger car shape of relatively low form drag.

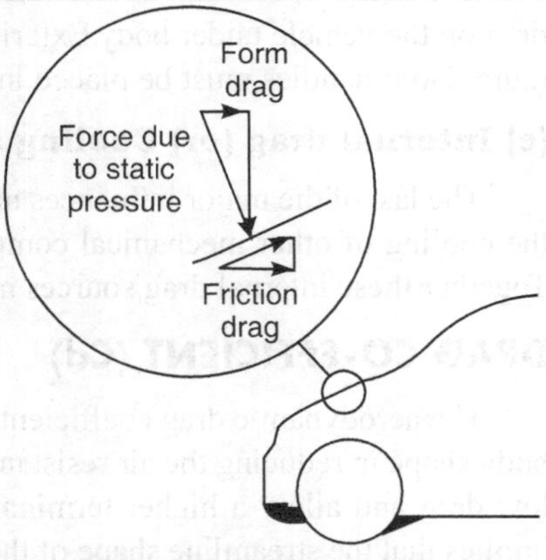

Fig. 2.25 The force acting on a surface element

(b) Friction drag (or) Surface drag

As air flows across the surface of the car frictional forces are generated giving rise to the second drag component which is usually referred to as surface drag or skin friction drag. If the viscosity of air is considered to be almost constant, the frictional forces at any point on the body surface depend upon the shear stresses generated in the boundary layer. The boundary layer is that layer of fluid close to the surface in which the air velocity changes from zero at the surface (relative to the vehicle) to its local maximum some distance from the surface.

This is caused by friction force between the boundary layer and the body surface. If this surface is kept smooth, a laminar boundary layer will be maintained. Thus a well-polished surface is not only attractive but also makes the vehicle more economical.

Body paint surface roughness has considerable effect on friction drag. Body smoothness is of the order of 0.5 to 1.0 microns.

(c) Induced drag (or) Lift drag

A consequence of the constraints imposed by realistic passenger space and mechanical design requirements is the creation of a profile which in most situations is found to generate a force with a vertical component. That lift, whether positive (upwards) or negative, induces changes in the character of the flow which the selves create an induced drag force. This is caused by vortices formed at the side of the vehicle. These vortices are in turn caused by the aerodynamic lift of the vehicle.

A car body produces accelerated air flow and the corresponding low pressure on its upper surface, especially in such areas of the lending edge of the hood, wind shield corners and the leading edge of the roof. Because of the low pressure developed on the upper surface than on the under body, aerodynamic lift results. This lift force depends on the contour of the body, underbody and ground clearance.

Lift is not a serious problem at normal speeds but it possesses a serious problem at very high speeds such as in racing cars. It also affects stability and braking performance of the vehicle. In general modification to the body so as to reduce accelerated flow and corresponding low pressure on the upper side and to reduce deceleration flow and corresponding high pressure on the underside of the body will reduce the aerodynamic lift.

(d) Interference drag

The flow over many exterior components interact with the flow over basic body shape and this lead to interference drag. Exterior components include projecting door handles, mirrors, aerials and badges which project out of the normal surface of the body. Also projectors below the vehicle such as axles, etc contribute towards the interference drag.

The various mechanical components project from under the vehicle such as an engine parts, suspension arms, exhaust system, frame rail and rear suspension also contribute to the interference drag on the vehicle under body.Exterior body ornaments must be placed where the velocity is minimum. Door handles must be placed in a close proximity and longitudinally in line with each other.

(e) Internal drag (or) Cooling and ventilation system drag

The last of the major influences upon vehicle drag is that arising from the cooling of the engine, the cooling of other mechanical components such as the brakes and from cabin ventilation flows. Together these internal drag sources may typically contribute in excess of 10% of the overall drag.

DRAG CO-EFFICIENT (Cd)

The aerodynamic drag coefficient is a measure of the effectiveness of a streamline aerodynamic body shape in reducing the air resistance to the forward motion of a vehicle. Low Cd values indicate low drag and allow a higher terminal speed and lower fuel consumption. A low drag coefficient implies that the streamline shape of the vehicle's body is such as to enable it to move easily through the surrounding viscous air with the minimum of resistance. Conversely a high drag coefficient is caused by poor streamlining of the body profile so that there is a high air resistance when the vehicle is in motion. The drag coefficient is calculated in tests carried out in aerodynamic or wind tunnels. It indicates the magnitude of a vehicle's drag as a result of its shape.

Typical drag coefficients for various classes of vehicles can be seen as follows:

Vehicle type	Drag coefficient (Cd)
Saloon car	0.22 – 0.4
Sports car	0.28 – 0.4
Light van	0.35 – 0.5
Buses and coaches	0.4 – 0.8
Articulated trucks	0.55 – 0.8
Ridged truck and draw bar trailer	0.7 – 0.9

The drag coefficient of a vehicle can be significantly reduced by rounding the front section and using a front apron, a roof spoiler and side skirts. Only a slight improvement in the drag coefficient is possible by altering the external shape of a commercial vehicle body since rounding the corners and edges reduces the load space and hence the payload. In combination with air deflectors, an aerodynamically optimized cab provides significant reductions in the drag of the vehicle as a whole.

Another measure for reducing resistance is to enclose the exposed running gear of the vehicle with fairings. This reduces the air resistance of the vehicle especially in a cross-wind.

AERODYNAMIC FORCES

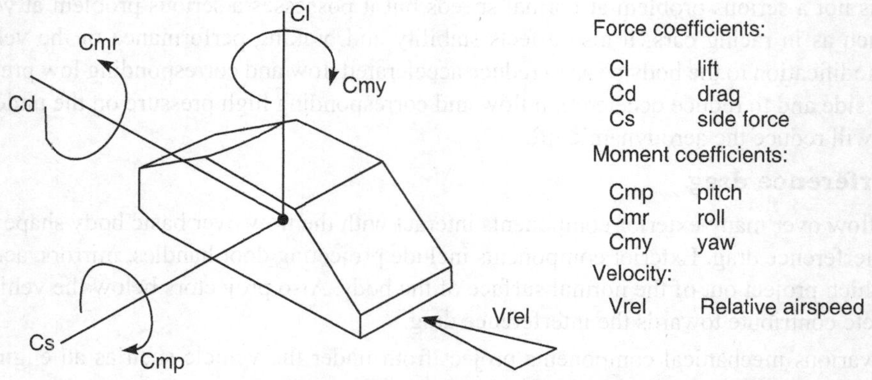

Fig. 2.26 Lift, drag, side force and moment axes

Aerodynamic research initially focused upon drag reduction, but it soon became apparent that the lift and side forces were also of great significance in terms of vehicle stability.

The aerodynamic forces and moments that act upon a vehicle are shown in coefficient form in Fig. 2.26. The forces may be considered to act along three, mutually perpendicular axes. Those forces are the drag, which is a measure of the aerodynamic force that resists the forward motion of the car, the lift which may act upwards or downwards and the side force which only occurs in the event of a cross-wind or when the vehicle is in close proximity to another. The lift, drag and pitching moments are a measure of the tendency of those three forces to cause the car to rotate about some datum, usually the centre of gravity. The moment effect is most easily observed in cross-wind conditions when the effective aerodynamic side force acts forward of the centre of gravity, resulting in the vehicle tending to steer away from the wind. In extreme, gusting conditions the steering correction made by the driver can lead to a loss of control.

In order to analyze the various aerodynamic forces and moments acting on the vehicle body, consider the vehicle as a mass having six degrees of freedom.

Now the various aerodynamic forces acting on the vehicle body can be summarized as follows:

Px – Force of air drag in the direction of motion with wind angle along the longitudinal axis

Py – Cross wind force

Pz – Aerodynamic lift

Longitudinal air drag (Px)

The longitudinal component of the resultant of pressure distribution is called longitudinal air drag. The magnitude of this component can be represented by,

$$Px = Cx\, \rho\, A\, v^2 / 2$$

Where,

Cx - Longitudinal wind force dimensionless co-efficient

ρ - Air density in kg/m^3

v - Velocity of wind in m/s

A - Cross sectional area of the vehicle viewed from the front in m.

Cross wind force (Py)

It is formed by the asymmetric flow of air around the vehicle body when the wind angle is not equal to zero. The cross wind force can be given as

$$Py = Cy\, \rho\, A\, v^2 / 2$$

Where,

Cy - Cross wind force dimensionless co-efficient

Aerodynamic lift (Pz)

It is the vertical component of the resultant of the pressure distribution over the vehicle body due to flow of air around it. The aerodynamic lift can be represented as

$$Pz = Cz\, \rho\, A\, v^2 / 2$$

Where,

Cz - Lift co-efficient

The lift will tend to reduce the pressure between the wheels and the ground, which causes losses of steering on the front axle and the loss of friction on the rear axle. The magnitude of this lift and its distribution over the front and rear is a function of ground clearance, the contours of the body and the underbody and the angle of attack of the air on the vehicle body.

Since these factors are not acting at the CG of the vehicle body but at the centre of pressure, they create the following three aerodynamic moments:

Mx - Rolling moment

My - Pitching moment

Mz - Yawing moment

Rolling moment (Mx)

This moment is caused by the cross wind force Py about the longitudinal axis. This magnitude of this rolling moment is given by

$$Mx = Py\ a = Cmx\ \rho\ A\ L\ v^2 / 2$$

Where,

a - Height of centre of thrust above CG

Cmx - Rolling moment coefficient

L - Reference length

The rolling moment effects the weight distribution on the wheels. This effect is dangerous for tall vans where the side force acts much above the CG. The only near solution to reduce rolling moment is to increase the wheel track.

Pitching moment (My)

This moment is caused about Y-axis by cross wind force Py or the longitudinal force Px. The pitching moment My is given by

$$My = Px\ b = Cmy\ \rho\ A\ L\ v^2 / 2$$

Where,

b - Distance between CG and CP

Cmy - Pitching moment coefficient

L - Reference length of the wheel base

The pitching moment is usually negative i.e., nose down and this moves. The rear axle lifts off the ground and further reduces the available traction.

Yawing moment (Mz)

This moment is caused about Z-axis by cross wind force Py. The yawing moment Mz is given by

$$Mz = Py\ c = Cmz\ \rho\ A\ L\ v^2 / 2$$

Where,

c - Distance between CG and CP

Cmz- Yawing moment coefficient

L - Reference length

These moments adversely affects the directional stability of the vehicle at high speed. The use of stabilizer fins at the rear of the vehicle gives a very good reduction in yawing moment.

Both aerodynamic lift and pitching moment have undesirable effects. The lift will lend to reduce the pressure between the wheels and the ground, which causes loss of steering on the front axle and loss of traction on the rear axle. Pitching moment is usually negative that is nose down and this makes the rear axle lift off the ground and further reduce the available traction.

Note:

CG – is the point where the whole mass of a system is assumed to be act.

CP – is the point where the total pressure acts on the system.

DRIVER'S SEAT

One of the most important factors in relaxed, stress free driving is ergonomically optimized seating for the driver and co-driver.

Not only the pneumatic seat springing but also, in particular, seat position and convenient adjustment are important. It is of fundamental importance too that all the control elements should be easy to reach.

Geometrical relations to driver's seat

A correct driving position is important in the vehicle layout and the seat position in relation to the steering wheel, foot controls and other secondary controls is of fundamental importance in body design. The following points are to be considered in designing the driver's seat.

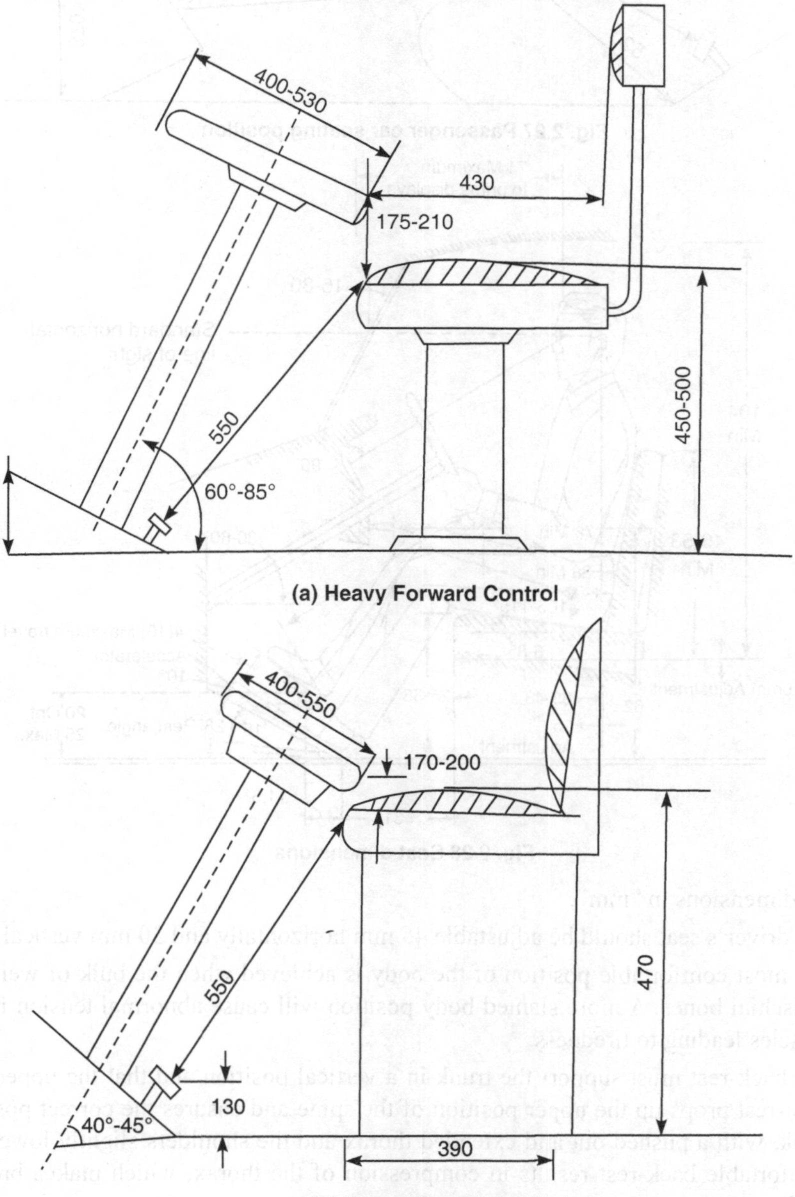

(b) Heavy Normal Control

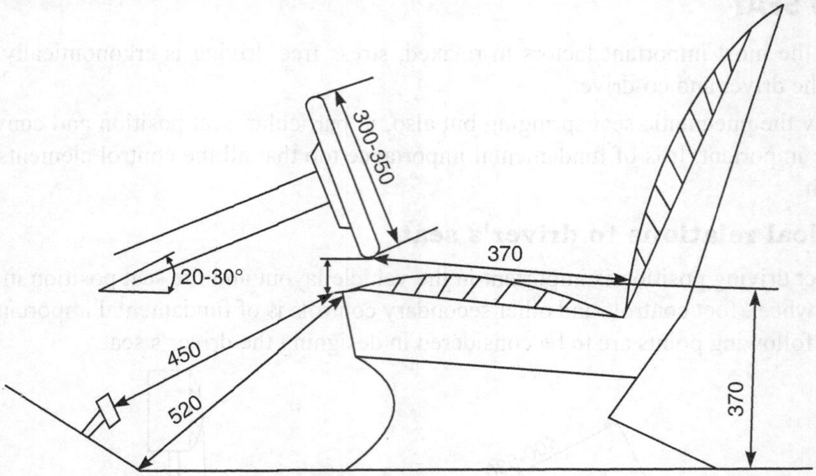

Fig. 2.27 Passenger car seating position

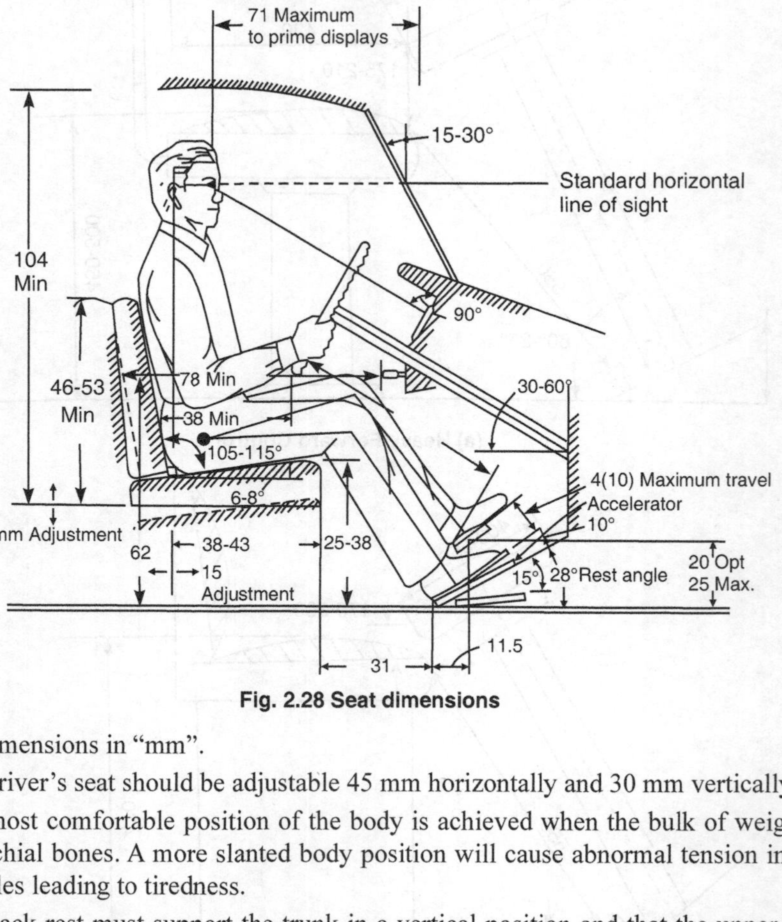

Fig. 2.28 Seat dimensions

- All dimensions in "mm".
- The driver's seat should be adjustable 45 mm horizontally and 30 mm vertically.
- The most comfortable position of the body is achieved when the bulk of weight is taken by ischial bones. A more slanted body position will cause abnormal tension in the pelvis muscles leading to tiredness.
- The back-rest must support the trunk in a vertical position and that the upper part of the back-rest props up the upper position of the spine and ensures the correct position of the trunk, with a pushed out and extended thorax and the shoulders slightly lowered. An uncomfortable back-rest results in compression of the thorax, which makes breathing difficult.

- A good back-rest relieves the neck and shoulder muscles and must therefore, depend on the size of the individual. Thus it is advisable to use an adjustable back rest.
- The angle between the seat and back-rest must be obtuse, although less for the driver than for the passenger seats.
- Arm rests reduce tiredness if their position does not cause the track to bend or stretch.
- It is important to avoid acute angles between the truck and pelvis, since the knees become raised and the thighs press on the stomach. This can be caused by any of the following:
  (*a*) The seat being tilted too much
  (*b*) Insufficient room for the legs
  (*c*) An unsuitable angle between the seat and the back-rest
- The seat cushions should be fairly rigid and must have sufficient shock absorbing qualities to prevent resonance of spring.
- Numbness in the calves of the legs and in the feet is caused by the front edge of the seat exerting too great pressure on the lower part of the thigh. This results from excessive height of the seat or a hollow seat.

Inclination of the steering column has a direct influence on the force which can be applied by the driver.

(*a*) Vertical steering column allows the driver to use the maximum force because the whole body is involved in turning the wheel.

(*b*) In horizontal steering column a little force is applied by the shoulders.

Forces of varying magnitude can be exerted on the foot pedals, depending on the angles of the inclination of the seat and back-rest. The distance between the floor and the seat also has some influence on these forces.

Modern driver's seats can be adjusted to suit almost any driver. Given the predominantly stationary body position when driving, it is important to maintain the 'comfort angles' that is the angular ranges which are comfortable for human joints. The seats that are now usually fitted, some of which are pneumatically sprung, provide all the adjustment necessary. Good lateral support against lateral acceleration makes driving easier while restraint systems improve safety.

VISIBILITY

A good view of everything around the vehicle is likewise an integral aspect of the ergonomics of the driver's working area. Good visibility should be incorporated at the design stage (pillars, window frame members etc.) and maintained during driving by efficient ventilation and heating systems that keep the windows clear.

In daylight colour is probably the most important characteristic in making cars more easily seen and work is now going on to establish what colours are best from this point of view. Glitter also makes a car more visible as well as more attractive. Requirements, however, now demand visibility over considerable angles, in addition to front and rear visibility, Fig.2.30.

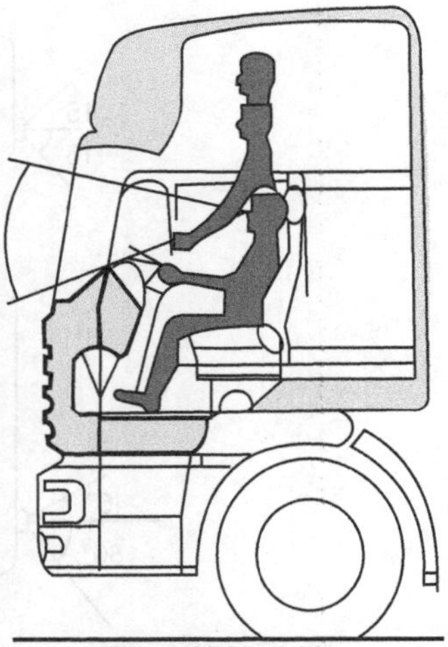

Fig. 2.29 Visibility

Good all round visibility is now one of the main requirements of body design. This clearly depends on the size of the window openings and their position relative to the occupants. Fig.2.30 shows the improvement of forward visibility. For example, if the occupant is placed close to the windscreen, the forward visibility is considerably improved. On the other hand, the problem of comfortable entry is increased. Since the dimension "a" between the pillar and the scat is decreased. Ease of entry is possible by suitably shaping the door as shown by the dotted line at the expense of a more complicated structure. In military vehicles the downward visibility is important and the driver must be positioned as high as possible in relation to the lower edge of the windscreen. There are no strict regulations regarding visibility. It is assumed that the upward angle of vertical visibility should be such as to enable driver to see the traffic lights etc. and this must be taken into consideration at the design stage. Rearward visibility has assumed considerable importance in modern traffic conditions and the increase in glass area required to maintain a given rear view vertical angle with a "fast-back" window is shown in Fig.2.31.

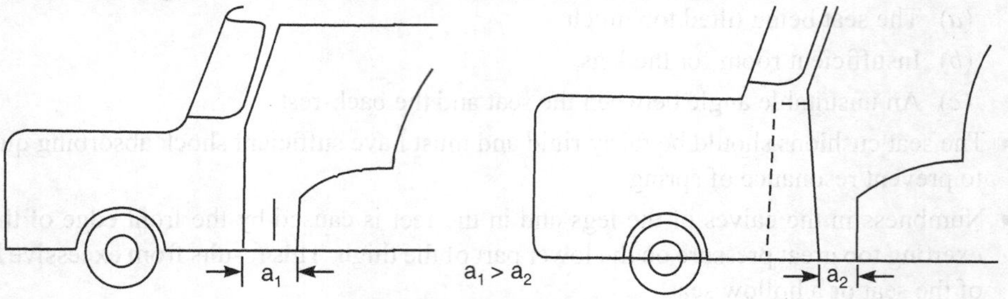

Fig. 2.30 Forward visibility

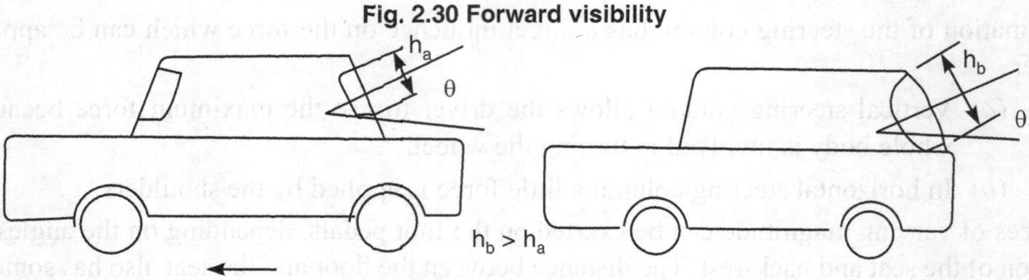

Fig. 2.31 Rearward visibility

Requirements, however, now demand visibility over considerable angles, in addition to front and rear visibility. Fig.2.32 shows the legal requirements and recommendations for positional lamps for indicators. Repeated flashers on the side must considerably increase the chance of seeing the vehicle sideways on.

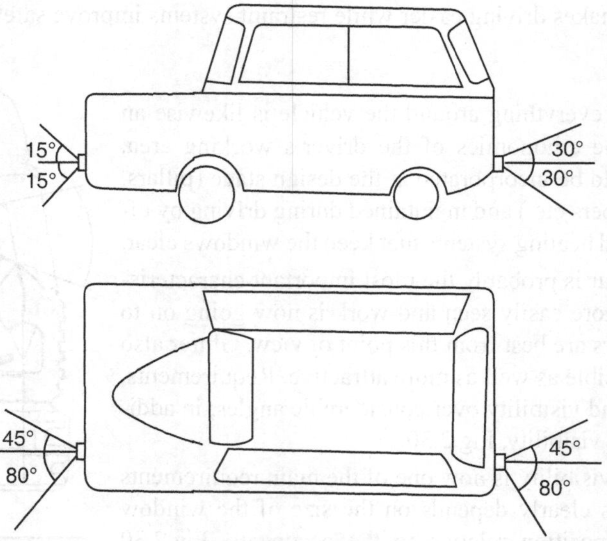

Fig. 2.32 Position of lamps

Solid particles dirty the outer surfaces of the driver's cab due to turbulence, particularly in the wet. On the windows and mirrors, this can sometimes lead to dangerous impairment of vision. Air guide elements in the area of the front corner radii underneath the windows create an air flow which keeps spray away from the side areas. Together with aerodynamic side fairings, profiled mats in the wheel housings can limit spray in an effective manner. This improves both the driver's visibility and that of overtaking drivers.

Review Questions

1. What is a frame? What are its functions?
2. What are the essential characteristics of an automobile frame?
3. Why is the frame narrowed at the front?
4. What are the types of frames?
5. What is the purpose of the X or K members of a frame?
6. What is a backbone frame?
7. What are the types of sections used to make the frame?
8. Why are box and I-sections normally used for frame construction?
9. List the characteristics of I-section frames.
10. What is called chassis of an automobile?
11. What is meant by unitary construction in automobile body?
12. Give another name for integral construction.
13. What are the advantages of integral frame body construction?
14. What is a stressed panel?
15. Why are sub frames used with integral bodies?
16. Differentiate unitized body construction from conventional frame construction.
17. Explain how strength is obtained in unitized body construction.
18. With sketches, explain how frames are tested.
19. How is noise of friction between members reduced to a minimum and absorbed?
20. Sketch and explain a typical passenger car frame. State the functions of various members.
21. What are the usual faults and damages occurring in the car frame? How are they rectified?
22. Discuss the various loads acting on automobile frames.
23. What are the aspects considered in the body design?
24. What is the difference between normal control and forward control in commercial vehicles?
25. Why vehicle body design is important?
26. What is meant by aerodynamic drag?
27. What is aerodynamic lift?
28. What is the effect of aerodynamic lift?
29. What are the three moments caused by aerodynamic forces acting on a vehicle?

3
CHAPTER

ENGINE

The wheels of an automobile must be powered externally for the vehicle to be able to overcome the resistance of the road, air resistance, etc., and move forward. The external source of power is called an engine.

An engine is a device that converts the energy of heat, electricity, wind, atomic power, etc., into mechanical energy. An engine that changes the energy of heat (thermal energy) into power is called a thermal engine or a heat engine.

Gasoline engines (petrol engines), diesel engines, turbine engines, etc., which produce thermal energy internally, are called Internal Combustion (IC) engines. Steam engines, steam turbine engines, etc., which produce thermal energy externally, are called External Combustion (EC) engines.

Gasoline engines and diesel engines for automobiles

Engines that are used to power automobiles must be compact and lightweight as they are mounted in a limited space. They must be able to generate great speed and high power output. They must be easy to operate and their noise must be kept minimal. For these reasons, gasoline engines and diesel engines are used more often than other types of engines for automobiles.

IC ENGINE TERMINOLOGIES (or ENGINE PARAMETERS)

The following are some of the important terms used in specifying an IC engine.

(*i*) Bore: The inside diameter of the engine cylinder and is usually expressed in millimeter.

(*ii*) TDC (Top Dead Centre): It is the extreme position reached by the piston on the top of the cylinder. At this position the piston just begins to come down.

(*iii*) BDC (Bottom Dead Centre): It is the bottom most position reached by the piston inside the cylinder. At this position the cylinder volume is at a maximum.

(*iv*) Stroke: The distance between TDC and BDC of the piston travel.

(*v*) Capacity, CC: Engine capacity is also called stroke volume, swept volume or piston displacement. The volume covered by the piston as it moves from BDC to TDC is engine capacity and indicated in CC or litres.

(*vi*) Clearance volume: The volume of the cylinder when the piston is at TDC. In fact, clearance volume is the combustion chamber volume.

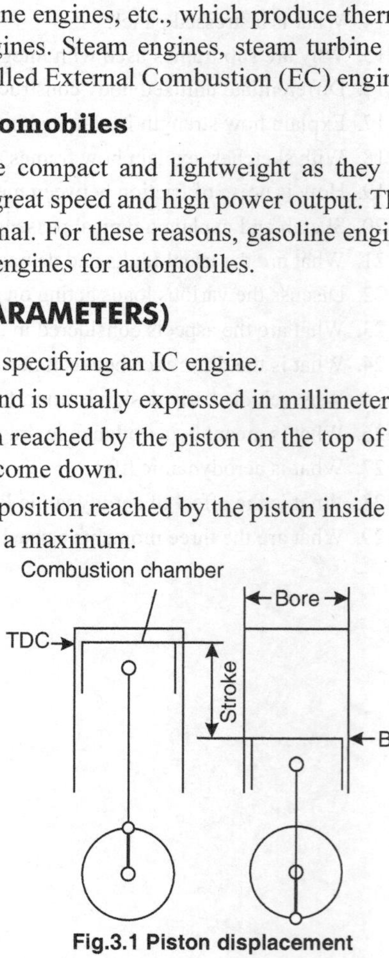

Fig.3.1 Piston displacement

(*vii*) Compression ratio: It is the ratio between total volume and clearance volume. To a certain extent, a higher the compression ratio creates a higher combustion gas pressure, resulting in higher output. This value is calculated as follows:

$$\text{Compression Ratio} = \frac{\text{Total volume}}{\text{Clearance volume}}$$

$$= \frac{\text{Swept volume} + \text{Clearance volume}}{\text{Clearance volume}}$$

Generally the compression ratio is between 8:1 and 11:1 in the gasoline engine and between 16:1 and 24:1 in the diesel engine.

As a general rule, small engines require a higher compression ratio than larger engines.

CONSTRUCTIONAL DETAILS OF ENGINES

An engine consists of the engine proper and various auxiliary devices. The engine proper consists of the cylinder block, cylinder head, piston, crankshaft and valve mechanism. Auxiliary devices of the engine are designed to help the operation of the engine. They include lubrication, cooling, intake and exhaust, fuel, and electrical systems.

This section provides a brief constructional details of engines. The **cylinder block** contains one or more cylinders in which each piston is located and guides the piston movement. It also provides mounting points for the crankshaft and on some engine, for the camshaft too. On water-cooled engines it also incorporates a jacket for cooling water to flow round.

The *piston* and its seals, the *piston rings*, transmit the force of the expanding gas to the connecting rod. The *connecting rod* connects the piston to the crankshaft and has two bearings. It is attached to the piston by the *gudgeon pin*, which runs in a bearing called the small end. The other, larger end of the connecting rod is connected to the crankshaft by means of the big end bearing.

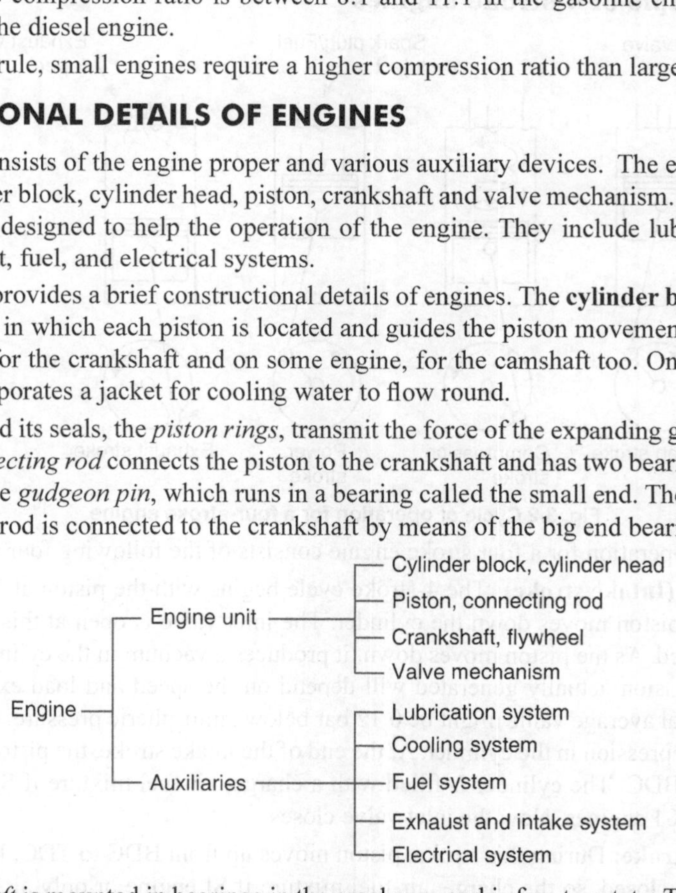

The *crankshaft* is mounted in bearings in the crankcase and is free to rotate. The crankshaft and connecting rod convert the linear or up-and-down motion of the piston to rotary motion. One end of the crankshaft has an attachment that drives the camshaft.

The *flywheel* is fastened to one end of the crankshaft. It is relatively heavy, in order to provide the momentum that keeps the engine turning between power strokes. **Valves** open and close the inlet and exhaust valves at predetermined times to control the entry of the fresh charge of fuel and the exit of burnt exhaust gases. They are often called poppet valves.

The *camshaft* is mounted in bearings and is driven by the crankshaft. It has a number of lobes called cams protruding along its length but spaced at intervals around the circumference. The cams open and close each valve in sequence for a set angle of crankshaft rotation. On a four stroke engine the camshaft rotates at half the speed of the crankshaft.

ENGINE OPERATING CYCLES

The two main types of piston or reciprocating engine are two-stroke and four stroke engines.

Four-stroke engines

Basically every engine has to repeat the four operations, namely suction, compression, power and exhaust. If the four operations are completed in four strokes of the piston or two revolutions of the crankshaft, the engine is said to be four stroke engines.

Each stroke of the piston consists of 180° of crank rotation and hence a four-stroke cycle is completed through 720° of crank rotation.

Working principle of 4-stroke engines

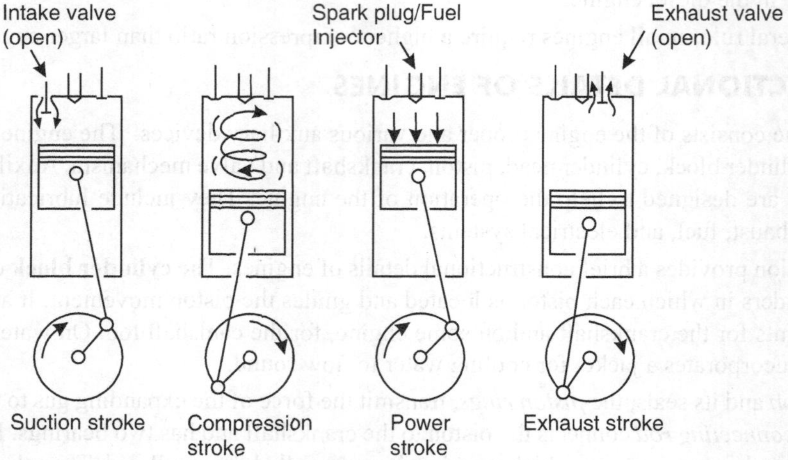

Fig. 3.2 Cycle of operation for a four-stroke engine

The cycle of operation for a four stroke engine consists of the following four strokes.

1. Suction stroke (Intake stroke): The 4-stroke cycle begins with the piston at TDC. To start the intake stroke, the piston moves down the cylinder. The inlet valve is open at this time and the exhaust valve is closed. As the piston moves down, it produces a vacuum in the cylinder. The pressure reduction or depression actually generated will depend on the speed and load experienced by the engine, but a typical average value might be 0.12 bar below atmospheric pressure. Fresh charge will rush in to fill the depression in the cylinder. At the end of the intake stroke, the piston is at the bottom of the cylinder at BDC. The cylinder is filled with a charge, air-fuel mixture if SI engines or only atmospheric air if CI engines. Now the inlet valve closes.

2. Compression stroke: During this stroke, piston moves up from BDC to TDC. Both the inlet and exhaust valves are closed, so the charge, air-fuel mixture if SI engine or only air if CI engine, has no place to go. It is pushed or compressed into the clearance volume (charge is progressively compressed to one-eighth to one-tenth of the cylinder's original volume). This compression squeezes the air and atomized fuel molecules closer together and increases the charge pressure and temperature. At the end of the compression stroke, the air-fuel mixture is ignited with the help of spark plug in SI engines. Similarly in CI engines just before the piston reaches the TDC, diesel is injected into the hot compressed air in the cylinder in the form of fine spray. The fuel gets vapourized and self-ignited due to the heat of compressed air.

On completion of this stroke, the crankshaft completes one full revolution.

3. Power stroke (Combustion & Expansion): The pressure and temperature of the product of combustion (due to the expansion of charge) suddenly go up. When the piston begins to move down the cylinder again, the power stroke begins. This downward movement is due to the combustion pressure. During this stroke also, both the valves remain closed. The high pressure of the burnt gases forces the piston towards the BDC. Thus, power is obtained during this stroke. Both pressure and temperature decrease during expansion.

By now, the crankshaft has completed one and a half revolutions.

4. Exhaust stroke: At the end of expansion stroke the exhaust valve opens and the inlet valve remains closed. At this instant, the pressure of the gas is higher than atmospheric pressure. This high pressure forces about 60% of the burnt gases into the atmosphere through exhaust valve. The remainders of the burnt gases are forced out when the piston moves from BDC to TDC.

The crankshaft by now has completed two revolutions.

Each cylinder of a four-stroke engine completes the above four operations in two crank revolutions, one revolution of the crankshaft occurs during the suction and compression strokes and the second revolution during the power and exhaust strokes. Thus, for one complete cycle there is one power stroke in a four stroke engine.

Two-stroke engines

Basically every engine has to repeat the four operations, i.e., suction, compression, power and exhaust. If the four operations namely suction, compression, power and exhaust are completed in two strokes of the piston or one revolution of the crankshaft, the engine is said to be two stroke engines.

Each stroke of the piston consists of 180° of crank rotation and hence a two-stroke cycle is completed through 360° of crank rotation.

Working principle of 2-stroke engines

The cycle of operation for a two stroke petrol engine consists of the following two strokes of a piston.

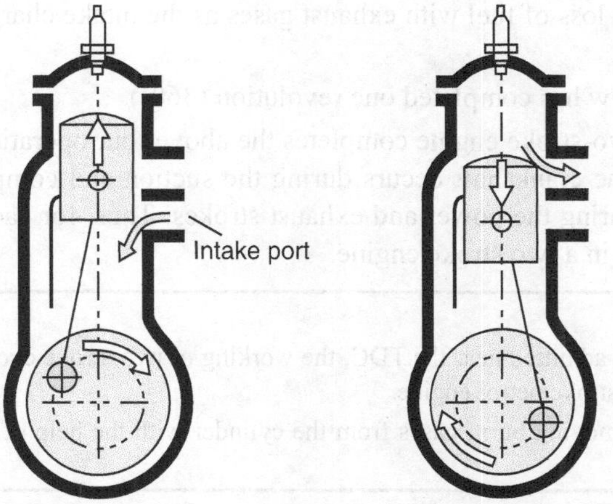

Fig. 3.3 Cycle of operation for a two-stroke engine

1. Upward Stroke (Suction and Compression): This stroke begins with the piston at BDC. The upward motion of the piston during this stroke lowers the pressure in the crankcase below atmosphere pressure. At the same time, the inlet port is uncovered first by the moving piston and, therefore, a fresh charge is drawn into the crankcase through the inlet port. The crankcase is filled with a charge, air-fuel mixture if SI engines or atmospheric air if CI engines. As the piston moves upward further, it covers the transfer port stopping the flow of fresh charge into the cylinder. A little later, the piston covers the exhaust port and actual compression of the charge begins. The compression of the charge is continued until the piston reaches to its TDC position. Both the inlet and exhaust ports are covered, so the charge has no place to go. The charge is now compressed into the clearance volume. At the end of the compression stroke, the air-fuel mixture is ignited with the help of spark plug in SI engines. Similarly in CI engines just before the piston reaches the TDC, diesel is injected into the hot compressed air in the cylinder in the form of fine spray. The fuel gets vapourized and self-ignited due to the heat of compressed air.

In this stroke of the piston, the following processes are completed:

- Fresh charge is sucked in the crankcase.
- Compression of the charge is completed.
- Partly scavenging takes place as the piston moves from BDC until it covers exhaust port.

On completion of this stroke, the crankshaft completes a half revolution (180°).

2. Downward Stroke (Power and Exhaust): During this stroke, piston moves down from TDC to BDC. The pressure and temperature of the gases increase and the gases push the piston downward producing the power stroke. When the piston uncovers the exhaust port during the downward stroke, the expanded burnt gases leave the cylinder through the exhaust port. A little later, the piston uncovers the transfer port. In this position, the crankcase is directly connected to the cylinder through the transfer port. When the piston moves down, the charge is partially compressed in the crankcase by the underside of the piston to a pressure of 1.4 bar. This compression is known as crankcase compression. At this position, the partially compressed charge is transferred through the transfer port to the upper part of the cylinder. The exhaust gases are swept out with the help of fresh charge entering the cylinder. The top of the piston is made of a deflected shape, called deflector, so the fresh charge entering the cylinder is deflected upward in the cylinder. This serves the double purpose of scavenging the upper part of the cylinder of combustion products and minimizing the escape of fresh charge (short circuit) along with the exhaust gases. The same objective can be achieved without piston deflector by proper shaping of the transfer port. The two-stroke diesel engine does not suffer from these defects. There is no loss of fuel with exhaust gases as the intake charge in diesel engine is air only.

The crankshaft by now has completed one revolution (360°).

Each cylinder of a two-stroke engine completes the above four operations in one crank revolution, half revolution of the crankshaft occurs during the suction and compression strokes and the second half revolution during the power and exhaust strokes. Thus, for each crankshaft revolution there is one power stroke in a two stroke engine.

Note:

- Except that fuel is admitted near the TDC, the working of two-stroke cycle diesel engine is similar to that of the two-stroke petrol engine.
- The process of removing burnt gases from the cylinder with the help of fresh charge is known as scavenging.

DIFFERENCE BETWEEN 4-STROKE AND 2-STROKE CYCLE ENGINES

S. No.	4 – Stroke Engine	2 – Stroke Engine
1.	The cycle is completed in 4 strokes of the piston or in two revolutions of the crankshaft. Thus one power stroke is obtained in every two revolutions of crankshaft.	The cycle is completed in 2 strokes of the piston or in one revolution of the crankshaft. Thus one power stroke is obtained in every revolution of crankshaft.
2.	Because of only one power stroke in every two revolutions of the crankshaft, turning movement is not so uniform. So heavier flywheel is needed.	Because of one power stroke for one revolution of the crankshaft, turning movement is more uniform. So lighter flywheel is needed.

3.	Because of only one power stroke in every two revolutions of the crankshaft, for the same power the engine is heavy and bulky.	Because of one power stroke for one revolution of the crankshaft, for the same power the engine is light and compact.
4.	Because of one power stroke in two crank revolutions lesser cooling and lubrication requirements. Lesser rate of wear and tear.	Because of one power stroke in one crank revolution greater cooling and lubrication requirements. Greater rate of wear and tear.
5.	Valves are provided.	Ports are provided.
6.	Because of the heavy weight and complicated valve mechanism, higher in initial cost.	Because of light weight and simplicity due to the absence of valve mechanism, cheaper in initial cost.
7.	Volumetric efficiency is more due to greater time for induction of fresh charge.	Less volumetric efficiency due to lesser time for induction of fresh charge.
8.	Thermal efficiency is more.	Less thermal efficiency. Due to short circuit, some part of fuel is exhausted which results in higher fuel consumption and lower thermal efficiency.
9.	Mostly liquid cooling system is used.	Mostly air cooling system used.
10.	Used where efficiency is important. Ex: cars, buses, locomotives, etc.	Used where low cost, compactness and light weight important. Ex: motorbikes, scooters, mopeds, etc.

DIFFERENCE BETWEEN SI AND CI ENGINES

S. No	Spark Ignition Engines	Compression Ignition Engines
1.	Operates on the principle of Otto cycle.	Operates on the principle of Diesel cycle.
2.	Gasoline (petrol) as fuel. High self-ignition temperature desirable.	Diesel as fuel. Lower self-ignition temperature desirable.
3.	Fuel and air introduced as a gaseous mixture in the suction stroke.	Fuel is injected directly into the cylinder at the end of compression stroke.
4.	Fuel is ignited by spark plug.	Fuel is ignited by hot compressed air.
5.	Low compression ratio (6 to 11). Upper limit of compression ratio fixed by antiknock quality of fuel.	High compression ratio (14 to 22). Upper limit of compression ratio is limited by the rapidly increasing weight of the engine structure as the compression ratio is further increased.
6.	Operates at high speed due to lighter weight.	Operates at low speed due to more weight.
7.	Maximum efficiency is lower due to low compression ratio.	Maximum efficiency is higher due to high compression ratio.
8.	Lighter in weight.	Heavier in weight. Due to high compression ratio, operating pressure is more. To withstand such pressure, it has to be stronger.
9.	Less vibration.	More vibration.
10.	Gasoline is highly volatile. So, handling is more risky.	Diesel is less volatile. So, handling is not risky.
11.	Less maintenance.	More maintenance.
12.	Initial cost is less due to lighter in construction and less costly fuel system. Operating cost (running cost) is more because of higher gasoline price.	Initial cost is more. Operating cost is less due to less price of diesel.

ENGINE PARTS, MATERIALS AND PRODUCTION METHODS

Component	Materials	Production Method
Cylinder block	Alloy cast iron, Aluminium alloy	Casting
Cylinder head	Alloy cast iron, Aluminium alloy	Casting
Cylinder liner	Alloy cast iron, Nickel alloy steel, Aluminium alloy	Casting
Engine gasket	Soft copper, Asbestos sheet, Synthetic rubber cork, Treated paper	Rolling
Piston	Aluminium alloy, Semi-steel, Cast iron	Casting
Piston rings	Alloy cast iron	Casting
Gudgeon pin	Alloy steel, Nickel or Vanadium steel for high speed engines	Forging, Extrusion
Connecting rod	High grade nickel alloys, Plain carbon steel, Duralumin	Forging
Crankshaft	Alloy cast iron, Forged steel, Plain carbon steel	Forging, Casting
Crankcase	Grey cast iron, Aluminium alloy, Aluminium-copper-zinc alloy	Casting
Oil sump	Pressed steel, Cast iron, Aluminium	Casting, Stamping
Camshaft	Alloy steel, Alloy cast iron, Forged steel	Forging
Engine valves	Austenitic steel, Precipitation hardening steel, Low alloy steels (Cr-Ni steel, Cr-Ni-Mo steel)	Forging
Manifolds	Alloy cast iron, Alloy steel, Aluminium alloy	Casting
Flywheel	Cast iron	Casting

ENGINE PERFORMANCE

To enable intelligent comparisons to be made between different engines' ability to pull or operate at various speeds, we shall now consider engine design parameters and their relationship in influencing performance capability.

Piston displacement or Swept bolume

When the piston moves from one end of the cylinder to the other, it will sweep or displace air equal to the cylinder volume between TDC and BDC. Thus the full stroke movement of the piston is known as either the swept volume or the piston displacement.

In general, the larger the displacement the greater the amount of air-fuel mixture drawn in the cylinder and since the combustion pressure would also increase, greater output becomes possible.

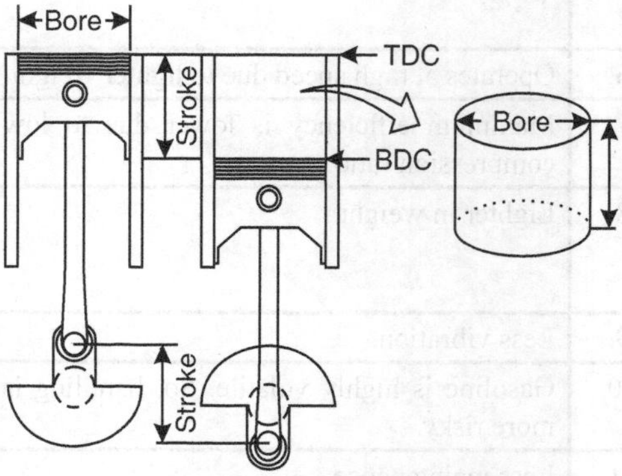

Fig. 3.4 Piston displacement

The total piston displacement of an engine can be calculated as follows:

$$V = \frac{\pi}{4} D^2 \times L \times N$$

$$= 0.7854 \times D^2 \times L \times N$$

V : Piston displacement

π : Ratio of the circumference of a circle to its diameter (= 3.14159)

D : Cylinder bore

L : Piston stroke

N : No. of cylinders

Mean effective pressure

Mean effective pressure (P_m) is defined as a hypothetical pressure which is thought to be acting on the piston throughout the power stroke.

The cylinder pressure varies considerably while the gas expands during the power stroke. Peak pressure will occur just after TDC, but this will rapidly drop as the piston moves towards BDC. When quoting cylinder pressure, it is therefore more helpful to refer to the average or mean effective pressure throughout the whole power stroke.

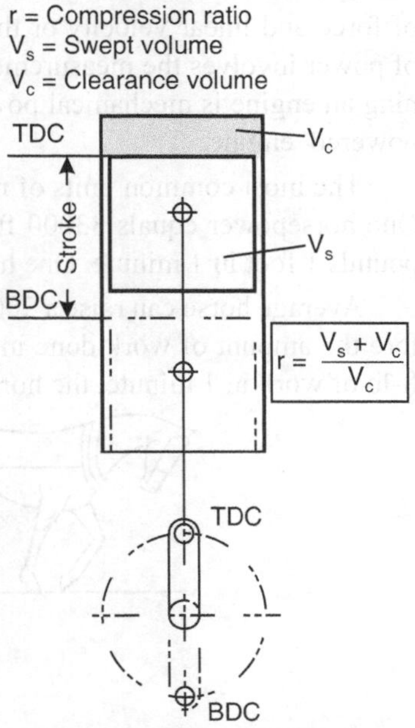

Fig. 3.5 Compression ratio

Compression ratio

The compression ratio shows how far the intake air-fuel mixture taken in during the intake stroke is compressed in the cylinder during the compression stroke. In other words, it is the ratio of the cylinder volume (V_2) when the piston is at BDC and combustion chamber volume with the piston at TDC (V_1). This value is calculated as follows:

$$\text{Compression ratio} = \frac{V_2}{V_1} = \frac{V_s + V_c}{V_c}$$

To a certain extent, a higher the compression ratio creates a higher combustion gas pressure, resulting in higher output. If the displacement is made larger, there would be danger of increasing the fuel consumption. Thus, the trend in engines in recent years is to improve the combustion chamber head shape together with raising the compression ratio, but there is a limit to this as raising it too high would create knocking which tends to lower the output.

Engine torque

Ordinarily, pushing and pulling forces are merely called forces, but in contrast, a force that turns or twists is called torque. For example, in tightening a bolt with a wrench, the force used to turn the bolt is torque.

In this case, the torque tending to turn the bolt is the product of the force and the distance from the center of bolt to the point where the force is applied. If the radius on which the forces acts is "r" and the force applied is "F" N, the torque "T" will be,

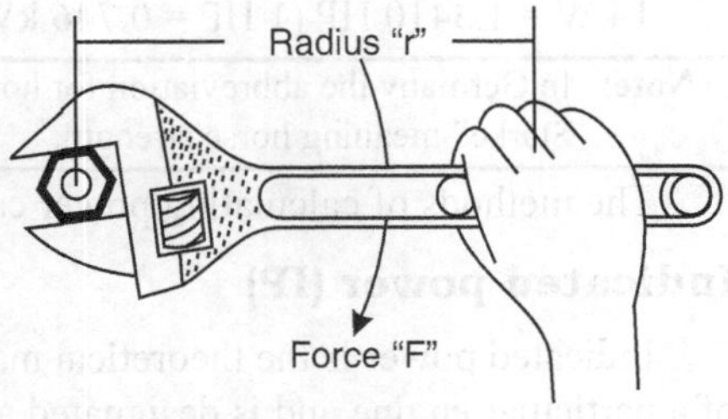

Fig. 3.6 Torque

$$T = F \times r \text{ Nm}$$

Therefore, if greater torque is desired, a longer wrench should be used or more force applied. (1/2 the piston stroke).

Engine torque comes from the pressure of the burning gases in the cylinders. This force pushes down on the pistons and causes the crankshaft to turn. The greater the force, the greater the torque. Torque is the twisting force that the pistons apply to the crankshaft. In practice, the amount of torque developed depends upon the pressure exerted on the piston and the length of the crank arm. It is the torque of the engine that provides acceleration and "performance". Engine torque is expressed in Nm (Newton-metre).

Engine power

Engine power is the power available from the crankshaft to do work. Work can be done slowly or it can be done rapidly. The rate at which work is done is called power and is equal to the product of force and linear velocity or the product of torque and angular velocity. Thus, the measurement of power involves the measurement of force (or torque) as well as speed. The main purpose of running an engine is mechanical power. An engine that can do a lot of work in a short time is a 'high-powered' engine.

The most common units of measure for power are the horsepower (hp) and the kilowatt (kW). One horsepower equals 33000 ft-lb of work per minute. It is the power necessary to raise 33000 pounds 1 foot in 1 minute. One horsepower equals 746 watts.

Average horse can raise a 200 pound weight a distance of 165 feet in 1 minute (by walk). Therefore the amount of work done in 1 minute is 200 × 165 = 33,000 ft-lb. When a horse does 33,000 ft-lb of work in 1 minute, the horse is working at the rate of 1 hp.

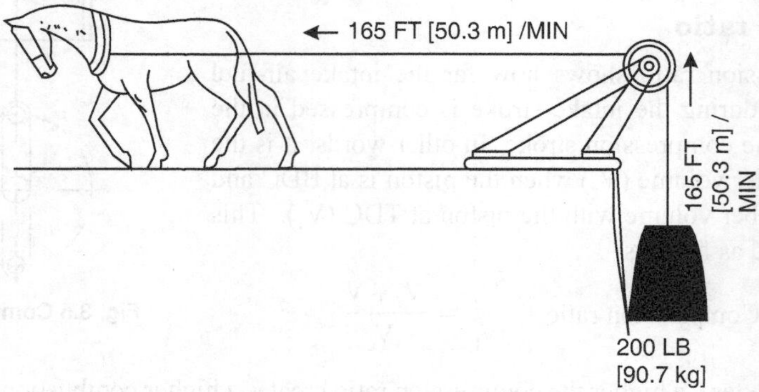

Fig. 3.7 Engine torque

The international unit for power is the watt (W) or more usually the kilowatt (kW), although other units such as horsepower (HP) and German horsepower (PS) are commonly used also. These conventional units have the following relationship with the kW unit:

1 kW = 1.3596 PS (1 PS = 0.736 kW)

1 kW = 1.3410 HP (1 HP = 0.746 kW)

Note: In Germany the abbreviation for horsepower is PS derived from the translation of the words "Pferd-Stärke" meaning horse strength.

The methods of calculating power can be expressed as follows:

Indicated power (IP)

Indicated power is the theoretical maximum power that could be produced inside the cylinders of a particular engine and is designated as IP. Engineers measure indicated power with instruments that measure gas pressures in the cylinders through all four strokes of an operating cycle. The IP developed by the engine is given by

Indicated power **per cylinder**

$$IP = P_m A L \frac{N}{n} \text{ Watts}$$

Where, P_m = Indicated mean effective pressure, N/m^2

L = Length of the stroke, m

A = Area of the piston, m^2

N = Rotational speed of the engine, rev/s

n = Number of revolutions required to complete one engine cycle

= 1 for 2-stroke engine

= 2 for 4-stroke engine

Brake power (BP)

The net power available at the crankshaft is called the brake power. It is called 'brake' power because some type of brake is used to measure it. The brake places a load on the engine crankshaft. Today most measurements of engine power are made with a dynamometer. It can measure the power that a running engine is producing. If the engine is out of the car, an engine dynamometer is used. A chassis dynamometer can measure the engine power reaching the drive wheels.

The amount of power that an engine produces depends on its torque and speed. As speed goes up, horsepower goes up. And as torque goes up, horsepower goes up.

The brake power of the engine is given by

$$BP = \frac{2\pi NT}{60} \text{ Watts}$$

Where, T = Torque in Nm

N = Engine rpm

Friction power (FP)

Friction is heat energy and a lot of engine power is used to overcome the friction of its own moving parts such as piston and cylinder, crankshaft and bearings and gears and valve mechanism, some of the power is used in the process of inducting the air and exhausting the products of combustion from the engine cylinder and for running the fuel pumps, lubricating oil pumps and water pumps for cooling system. This lost power is friction power. The difference between IP and BP will give friction power.

$$FP = IP - BP$$

Engine capacity

A method of indicating the capacity of an engine is to state the theoretical volume of fuel and air or in the case of a CI engine air only, which can be taken into the engine on its suction stroke. This is the volume of cylinder 'displaced' or 'swept' by a single stroke of the piston. Engine sizes are compared on the basis of total cylinder swept volume, which is known as cylinder capacity. Thus engine capacity is equal to the piston displacement of each cylinder times the number of cylinders.

Engine capacity, $$V_E = \frac{Vn}{1000} \text{ in litres}$$

Where, V = Piston displacement, cm^3 (cc)

n = Number of cylinders

Fuel consumption rate

In engine performance, fuel consumption rate is not the commonly called fuel consumption that means how many kilometers the car will run on a litre of fuel. Instead, it is the amount of fuel consumed by one horsepower in one hour and expressed in grams.

Whether the fuel consumption rate is good or bad will be determined by the relation between the amount of fuel supplied and the horsepower produced at that time. Therefore, unlike the running fuel consumption, it cannot always be said that larger displacement cars will always higher fuel consumption.

The following factors are concerned with this unit.

$$\text{Fuel consumption rate} = \frac{\text{Grams (amount of gasoline consumed)}}{\text{PS} - \text{hours (one horse} - \text{power, one hour)}}$$

ENGINE PERFORMANCE CURVES

Power, torque and fuel consumption can be said as being important factors of engine performance. In regard to these three factors, curves are plotted to determine how they vary with the engine speed. These curves are known as the engine performance curves.

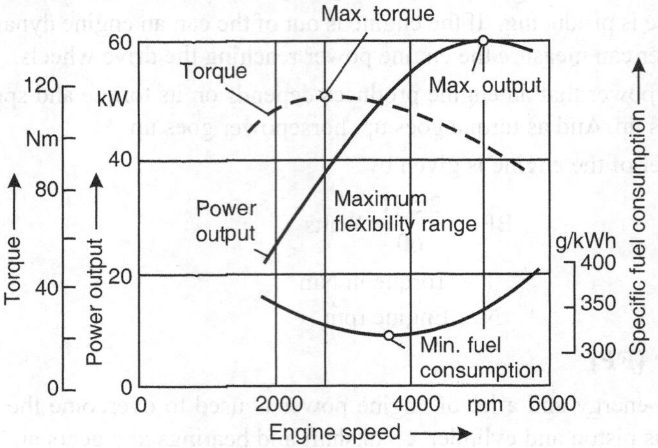

Fig. 3.8 Engine performance curves

The brake power is always less than the indicated power, due to frictional and pumping losses in the cylinders and the reciprocating mechanism of the engine.

Since the rate of doing work increases with piston speed, the engine's power will tend to rise with crankshaft speed of rotation and only after about two thirds of the engine's speed range will the rate of power rise drop off. The slowing down and even decline in power at the upper speed range is mainly due to the very short time available for exhausting and for inducting fresh charge into the cylinders at very high speeds, with a resulting reduction in the cylinders' mean effective pressures.

The torque that an engine can develop changes with engine speed. An engine can develop more torque at intermediate speeds than at high speeds. This is because there is more time for air-fuel mixture to enter the cylinders. Volumetric efficiency is high. There will be a greater amount of air-fuel mixture to burn during the power stroke and higher combustion pressures will develop. This means, in turn, that greater torque will be applied to the crankshaft.

The specific fuel consumption is lowest at the mixture ratio nearer to chemically correct mixture. If the mixture is richer or leaner than this, fuel consumption will be higher. A 4-stroke engine consumes less fuel in the medium engine speed. The specific fuel consumption rises at low speeds because of incomplete fuel-air mixing, but also at high engine speeds as a result of incomplete combustion.

MULTI-CYLINDER ARRANGEMENTS

Although there are many single-cylinder engines, they are generally small and limited in their application. They are frequently used for motor cycles, water pumps, generators and boats. To increase the power of an engine the cylinder can be made larger.

It would seem logical to develop a large single cylinder engine, as there would be fewer parts. But the disadvantage of one power stroke in every four means that there are considerable out-of-balance forces because of the heavy reciprocating parts such as the piston. The resulting roughness and vibration must be smoothed away with a large flywheel, as is often the case with stationary and marine engines.

The car needs instant response as well as smooth running. A large flywheel gives reasonably smooth running, but it absorbs a great deal of energy and takes a long time to build up speed. The reverse is also true. The kinetic energy takes a long time to dissipate. Other components must also be heavier in construction to take the load on them. This would result in a very poor power-to-weight ratio (this is the ratio that compares the power produced by an engine and its weight).

Economy and good performance require engines to be light in weight but produce a lot of power. This is best achieved by increasing the number of cylinders. The engine will run more smoothly, will have a better power-to-weight ratio and will be more responsive to required changes in speed and torque. For example, the firing intervals of a four-cylinder engine can be arranged to give a power stroke every 180° of crankshaft rotation, giving four power strokes for every two crankshaft revolutions.

The disadvantage is that multi-cylinder engines are more complicated and costly, because of the number of parts.

Cylinder layout

Generally, the following cylinder arrangements are used:

(*i*) **In-line type:** Cylinders are arranged in a single row. This type is used most frequently because it provides the simplest construction. In-line engines may have 2 to 6, or even 8 cylinders mounted in a straight line, one after the other to obtain smoother performance. Light and heavy motor vehicles usually have in-line engines.

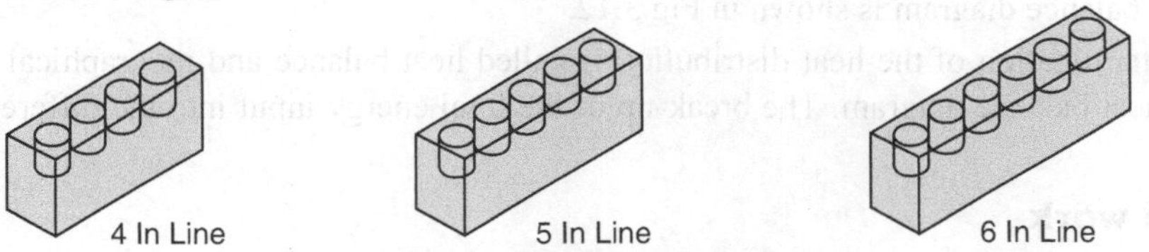

Fig. 3.9 In-line engines

(*ii*) **V-type:** Space considerations often demand that multiple cylinders are mounted into two banks arranged as a "vee", but operating a common crankshaft. This type allows the overall engine height and length to be reduced. Sport car and bike engines are examples of V-type engines.

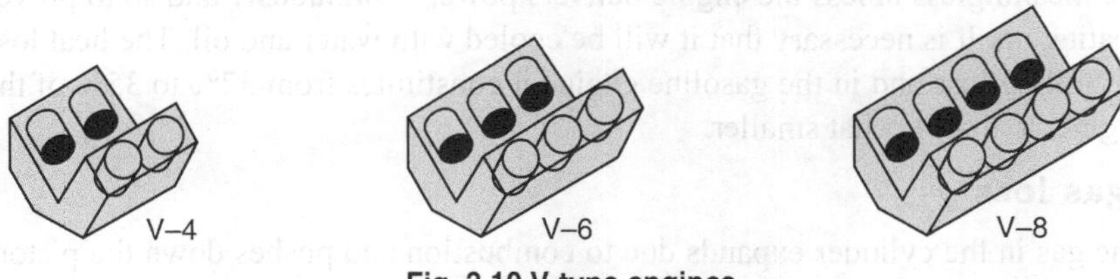

Fig. 3.10 V-type engines

(*iii*) **Horizontally opposed type:** Cylinders are set horizontally opposing each other. This arrangement reduces the engine height. The pistons move inwardly and outwardly together providing excellent balance and regular firing intervals. Such engines can be housed below the floor line to increase the space available for people or luggage.

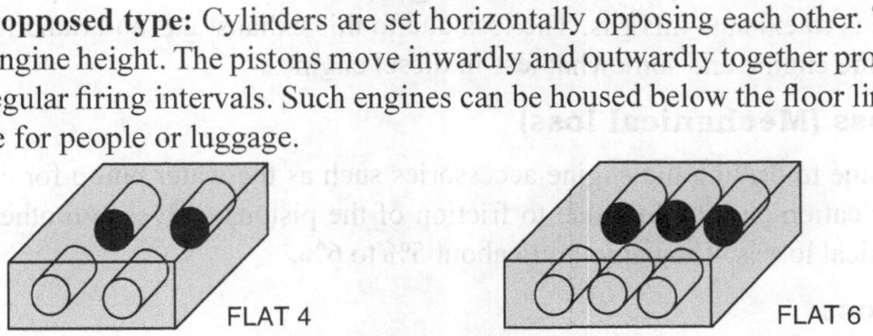

Fig. 3.11 Horizontally opposed engines

The most notable design was 4-cylinder, opposed piston, air-cooled Volkswagen engine.

HEAT BALANCE (ENGINE LOSSES)

Only a part of the total fuel energy supplied to the internal combustion engine is converted into useful work. The work is delivered at the crankshaft and rest of the fuel energy is rejected as follows:

- Heat from the engine boundaries due to radiation, convection and to a small extent, conduction.
- Exhaust heat
- Heat rejected to coolant

The engine burns fuel in the cylinder to transform its thermal energy (heat energy) into a driving power. But the thermal energy of the fuel is not converted into power entirely. It can be stated that approximately 25 per cent of the energy contained in the fuel is converted into useful work, 45 per cent passes away in the hot exhaust gases frictional losses and pumping losses, and the remaining 30 per cent has to be removed by the cooling system not to increase the engine temperature beyond working temperature of an engine.

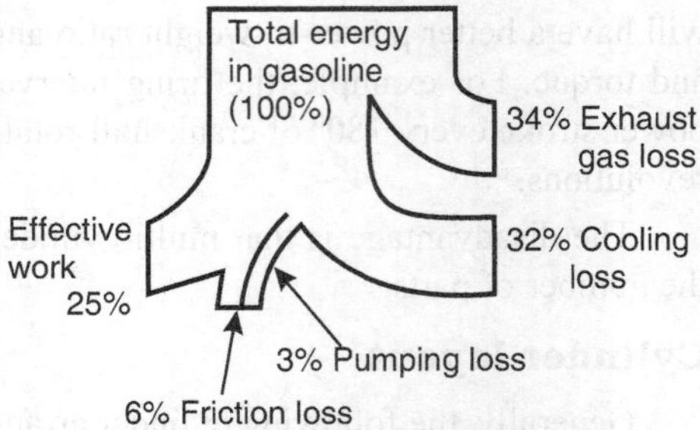

Fig. 3.12 Heat balance diagram

Whatever may be the exact amount of heat carried away by the coolant be, it must be noted that it is a dead loss because not only no useful work can be obtained from it, but a part of engine power is also used to remove this heat. Therefore, this heat loss must be kept minimum by the designer. The typical heat balance diagram is shown in Fig.3.12.

The determination of the heat distribution is called heat balance and its graphical representation is the heat balance diagram. The break-up of the total energy input into the different losses as follows:

Effective work

This is the amount that can be obtained from the crankshaft and is from 23% to 28% in gasoline engines and from 30% to 34% in diesel engines.

Cooling loss

It will be meaningless unless the engine delivers power continuously and so to prevent the engine from heating up. It is necessary that it will be cooled with water and oil. The heat lost in doing this is called cooling loss and in the gasoline engine it constitutes from 32% to 35% of the total. In the diesel engine, it is somewhat smaller.

Exhaust gas loss

When the gas in the cylinder expands due to combustion and pushes down the piston to BDC, this gas connot be utilized any further even though it still has some heat and pressure left. The only thing possible is to exhaust this gas. The loss due to this exhaust gas and radiation is from 33% to 38% in gasoline engine and somewhat less in diesel engines.

Friction loss (Mechanical loss)

The loss due to driving the engine accessories such as the water pump for cooling and the oil pump for lubrication and the loss due to friction of the pistons, valves and other engine parts are called mechanical losses. They amount to about 5% to 6%.

Pumping loss

When the piston travels downward and a vacuum is created to draw in the air-fuel mixture, this becomes negative work. The same thing can be said in the case of compressing the fresh air-fuel mixture induced in the cylinder. The losses resulting from drawing in and compressing the air-fuel mixture are called pumping losses. They amount to about 3%.

Note: 1. For diesel engines: 33% Exhaust gas loss
31% Cooling loss
36% Heat to IP
10% Friction and Pumping losses
26% Heat to BP
2. Top fuel conversion efficiencies are now approaching
45% in gasoline engine applications and
50% in diesel engine applications.

Heat balance sheet

The main components in a heat balance are brake output, coolant losses, heat going to exhaust, radiation and other losses. Preparation of heat balance sheet gives us an idea about the amount of energy wasted in various parts and allows us to think of methods to reduce the losses so incurred.

FIRING ORDER

Engines are designed to deliver the power strokes to the crankshaft in a certain pattern. Two adjacent cylinders are usually not allowed to fire one after the other. When an end cylinder fires, the next cylinder to fire should be near the center or toward the other end of the crankshaft. The purpose of carefully scattering the power strokes along the crankshaft is to avoid stress on any one part of the crankshaft. If two or three adjacent cylinders are fired one after the other, this places a strain on the crankshaft. It may break. A proper firing order prevents this.

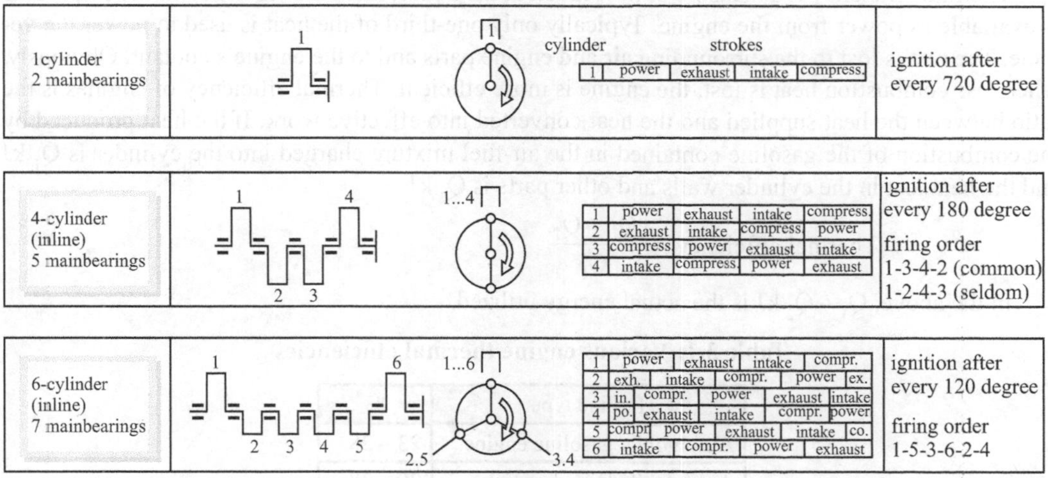

Fig. 3. 13 Firing orders

ENGINE EFFICIENCIES

One of the dominating trends in automotive design is increasing an engine's efficiency. Efficiency is simply a measure of the relationship between the amount of energy put into an engine and the amount of energy available from the engine.

Mechanical efficiency

Mechanical efficiency is a measure of how much power is available once it leaves the engine compared to the amount of power that was exerted on the pistons during the power stroke. Power losses occur because of the friction generated by the moving parts. Minimizing friction increases mechanical efficiency. Brake power divided by indicated power is a measure of an engine's mechanical efficiency. For example, if brake power is 100 hp and indicated power is 125 hp, the mechanical efficiency is: 100/125 = 0.8, or 80% efficiency.

Volumetric efficiency

It was previously explained that the cylinder volume displaced by the piston in moving from BDC to TDC is called stroke volume. Theoretically, it can be considered that power is produced by the combustion of the air-fuel mixture drawn into this stroke volume, but in practice, the amount of air-fuel mixture drawn in the engine differs due to various factors such as pressure, temperature, residual gas and valve timing. Therefore, in order to designate the actual intake performance volumetric efficiency is used as measurement means.

Assume any desired condition. If the absolute temperature and pressure are T and P respectively and the standard conditions $T_o = 15°C$ and $P_o = 760$ mmHg, volumetric efficiency would be as follows:

$$\text{Volumetric efficiency} = \frac{\text{Volume of air - fuel mixture drawn in at P and T}}{\text{Stroke volume}}$$

It is also defined as the ratio of actual mass of air inducted by the engine during the suction stroke to the theoretical mass of air that should have been inducted to fill the piston displacement volume with air at atmospheric temperature and pressure.

$$\text{Volumetric efficiency} = \frac{\text{Weight of air - fuel mixture drawn in at P and T}}{\text{Weight of air - fuel mixture in stroke volume at P and T}}$$

Thermal efficiency

Thermal efficiency is a measure of how much of the heat formed during the combustion process is available as power from the engine. Typically only one-third of the heat is used to power the vehicle. The rest is lost to the surrounding air and engine parts and to the engine's coolant. Obviously, when less combustion heat is lost, the engine is more efficient. Thermal efficiency of engines is the ratio between the heat supplied and the heat converted into effective work. If the heat produced by the combustion of the gasoline contained in the air-fuel mixture charged into the cylinder is Q_1 kJ and the heat lost in the cylinder walls and other parts is Q_2 kJ,

$$\text{Thermal efficiency} = \frac{Q_1 - Q_2}{Q_1}$$

In the above, $Q_1 - Q_2$ kJ is the actual energy utilized.

Table 3.1: Various engine thermal efficiencies

Engine type	%
Automobile gasoline engine	23 – 28
Automobile Diesel engine	29 – 38
Airplane gasoline engine	21 – 31
Steam locomotive	5 – 10
Marine steam engine	10 – 15
Marine steam turbine	12 – 20

VEHICLE PERFORMANCE

Maximum speed

An item that represents the vehicle's traveling performance. The maximum speed is measured with the vehicle in the G.V.W. condition on a flat and paved road without wind. It is indicated in terms of the distance traveled per hour (km/h or mph).

Fuel consumption

Fuel consumption is a measure of how much fuel an engine or vehicle uses per unit distance and is thus an indication of how economical that engine or vehicle is in regards to fuel consumption.

To show vehicle fuel consumption, two different methods are used. In the first method, a vehicle is run over a certain distance and the amount of fuel is measured. The units used to express this are liters per 100 km (l/100 km). The method that is more familiar to most of us is that in which the distance a vehicle can travel on a certain amount of fuel is measured. This is measured in km per liter (km/l) or in miles per gallon (mpg).

These values l/100 km, km/l or mpg are used to compare fuel consumption of vehicles under various driving conditions.

Maximum gradeability

Ability of the vehicle to climb a given grade at a specified G.V.W. The maximum grade that a vehicle can climb is found by the formula shown below, which shows the height (B) a vehicle climbs in terms of a horizontal distance (A) it travels.

The grade θ is expressed as B/A. if

$A = 100 \text{ and } B = 20, \text{ then } \theta = \frac{B}{A} = \frac{20}{100} = 0.2,$

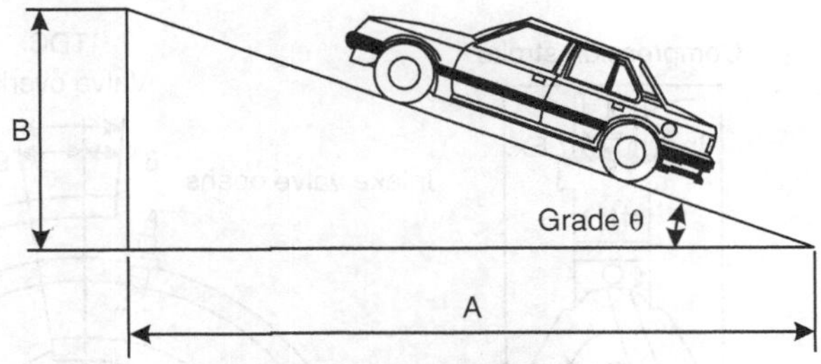

Fig. 3.14 Gradeability

which is equal to the vehicle's maximum gradeability.

The maximum gradeability is a theoretical ability. In reality, friction between the tyre and road may be insufficient and the vehicle may not be able to climb this grade.

Minimum turning radius

This is the smallest radius in which a vehicle can make a turn. It is equal to the radius of a circle drawn by the center of the outermost tyre or the outermost part of the vehicle's body as it turns slowly on a flat pavement with the steering wheel turned completely in either direction.

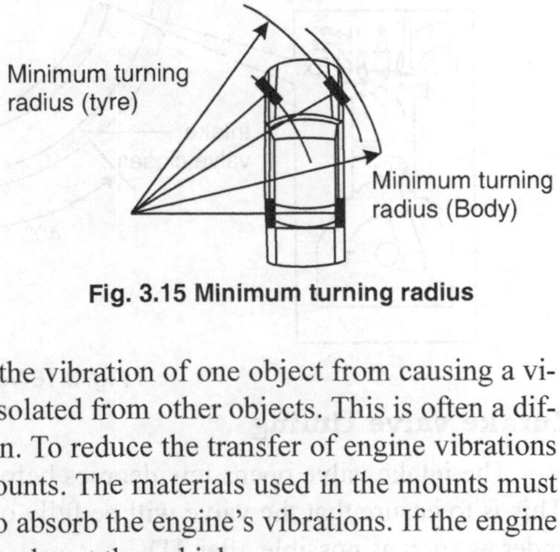

Fig. 3.15 Minimum turning radius

ENGINE MOUNTING

When an object oscillates, it vibrates. To prevent the vibration of one object from causing a vibration in other objects, the oscillating mass must be isolated from other objects. This is often a difficult task. For example, all engines vibrate as they run. To reduce the transfer of engine vibrations to rest of the vehicle, the engine is held by special mounts. The materials used in the mounts must keep the engine in place and must be elastic enough to absorb the engine's vibrations. If the engine was mounted solidly, the vibrations would be felt through-out the vehicle.

The engine mounting system is important as it supports the weight of the engine in the vehicle. In addition, it counteracts the torque reaction under load conditions. The mounting system has to isolate the vehicle from the engine vibrations. The engine mounts consist of steel plates with a rubber sandwich between to provide the vibration isolation. The mountings have appropriate brackets and fittings to fix to the engine and vehicle frame.

For a front-engine, rear-drive powertrain layout, the engine mounts are often at the centre position of the engine side, approximately at the engine centre of gravity. The engine mounts bear compression and shear forces in supporting the engine weight and torque. The rear of the engine is bolted to the transmission, which in turn is supported at the rear end via a rubber mounting system. This three-point mounting is very common for this powertrain configuration.

For a front-wheel drive, transverse powertrain layout, the mounting system has to cope with weight of the engine, plus the torque reaction of the wheel torque. The mounting system therefore includes mountings to support weight and counteract torque separately. These are mounted at the top or bottom of the engine respectively.

VALVE TIMING AND PORT TIMING DIAGRAMS

Valve timing diagram

In the ideal cycle inlet and exhaust valves open and close at dead centres, but in actual cycles they open or close before or after dead centres.

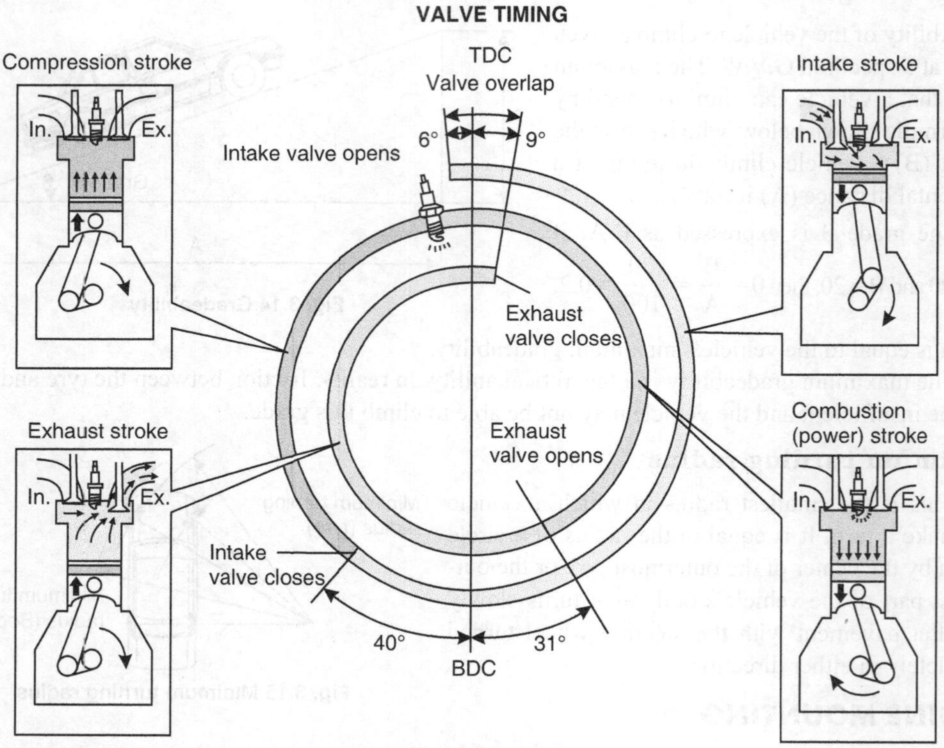

Fig. 3.16 Valve timing diagram

Intake valve timing

The intake valve opens few degrees before the arrival of piston at TDC on the exhaust stroke. This is to ensure that the valve will be fully open and the fresh charge starting to flow into the cylinder as soon as possible after TDC.

As the piston comes down in the suction stroke, the fresh charge is drawn in through the intake valve. When the piston reaches the BDC and starts to move in the compression stroke, the inertia of the entering fresh charge tends to cause it to continue to move into the cylinder. To take advantage of this, the intake valve is closed after TDC so that maximum air or air-fuel fuel mixture is taken in. This is called **ram effect**. The kinetic energy of the charge produces this ram effect which packs more charge into the cylinder during this additional valve opening. Therefore, the intake valve closing is delayed.

However, if the intake valve is to remain open for too long time beyond BDC, the up moving piston on the compression stroke would tend to force some of the charge back into the intake manifold.

The time the intake valve should remain open after TDC is decided by the speed of the engine. At low engine speed the charge speed is low and so the air inertia is low and hence the intake valve should close relatively early after BDC for a slow speed engine. In high speed engines the charge speed is high and consequently the inertia is high and hence to induct maximum quantity of charge due to ram effect the intake valve should close relatively late after BDC.

Exhaust valve timing

The exhaust valve is set to open before BDC and close few degrees after TDC. Complete clearing of the exhaust from the cylinder is necessary to take in more charge. Earlier opening of the exhaust valve facilitates the removal of burnt gases by virtue of the pressure at this point. The kinetic energy of the fresh charge may also assist the removal of the burnt gases.

It is obvious from the valve timing diagram that both the intake and exhaust valves are open at the same time for some period. This is called valve overlap. This overlap should not be excessive otherwise it will allow the burned gases to be sucked into the intake manifold or the fresh charge to escape through the exhaust valve.

Overlapping of the valves makes possible the scavenging of the clearance space, resulting in an increased output.

Port timing diagram

In a two-stroke engine, the inlet, exhaust and transfer ports open at precisely the same number of degrees of crankshaft rotation before top or bottom dead centre as they close. The resulting timing chart is therefore symmetrical.

As the piston moves up toward TDC, the transfer port closes first, followed by the exhaust port. This can allow fresh mixture to escape through the exhaust.

As the piston moves down towards BDC, the exhaust port opens first, followed by the transfer port. The pressure drop when the exhaust port opens is so severe that the remaining burnt gas cannot flow back so strongly into the crankcase and mix there with the precompressed fresh mixture.

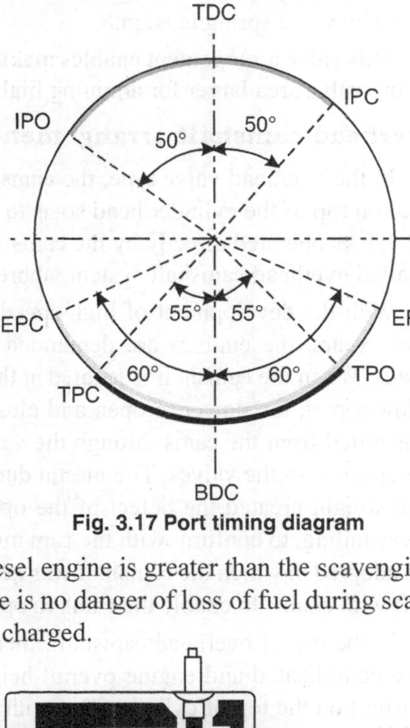

Fig. 3.17 Port timing diagram

The charging and scavenging period of two stroke diesel engine is greater than the scavenging period of two-stroke gasoline engine. This is because, there is no danger of loss of fuel during scavenging (due to short circuit) of diesel engine as only air is charged.

VALVE ACTUATING MECHANISM

In a four-cycle engine, each cylinder is equipped with an intake valve and an exhaust valve to charge the air-fuel mixture into the cylinder and to discharge the burnt gas to the outside. The series of parts that open and close the valves at proper intervals is called the valve mechanism. The valve mechanism can be classified by the method of valve arrangement into side valve and overhead valve types.

Side valve arrangement

As shown in Fig. 3.18, the valves are pushed up directly by the cam shaft located at crankcase side and

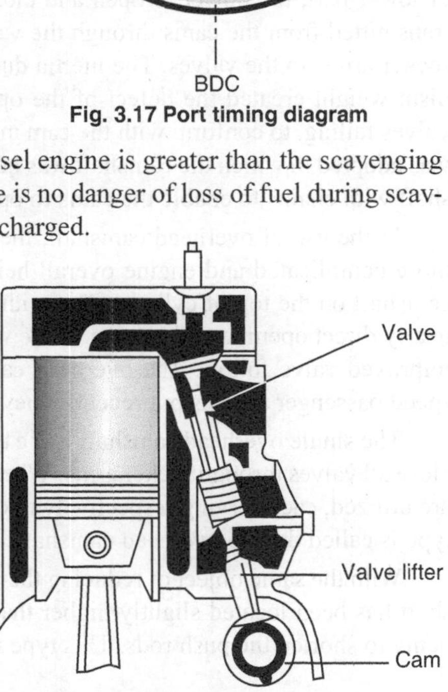

Fig. 3.18 Side valve arrangement

acting on the valve lifters. In this arrangement there are no valves in the cylinder head, so that compared to the overhead valve type, the cylinder head construction is simpler. The valve mechanism is also less complicated, has fewer parts, and creates less noise. But the shape of combustion chamber becomes bad and prevents attaining high performance and because of this disadvantage, this type is hardly in use today.

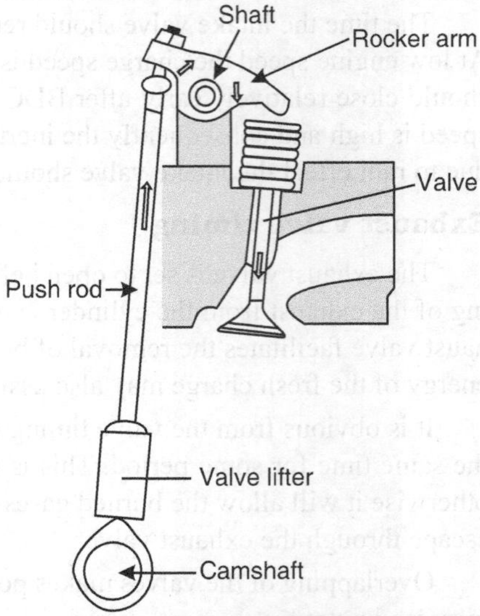

Fig. 3.19 Overhead valve arrangement

Overhead valve arrangement

As shown in Fig. 3.19, the overhead valve system is comprised mainly of the camshaft, valve lifters, push rods, and rocker arms. In operation, when the camshaft cam lobe comes under the valve lifter, the push rod is forced up by the valve lifter. When the push rod lifts up one end of the rocker arm, the other end pushes down the valve and causes it to open. When the cam turns further, the valve is closed by valve spring tension.

This valve arrangement enables making the combustion chamber more compact as well as making the valve area larger for attaining high performance.

Overhead camshaft arrangement

In the overhead valve type, the camshaft is sometimes located on top of the cylinder head so as to have the rocker arms and valves operated directly by the cams. Such an arrangement is called overhead camshaft system, abbreviated OHC.

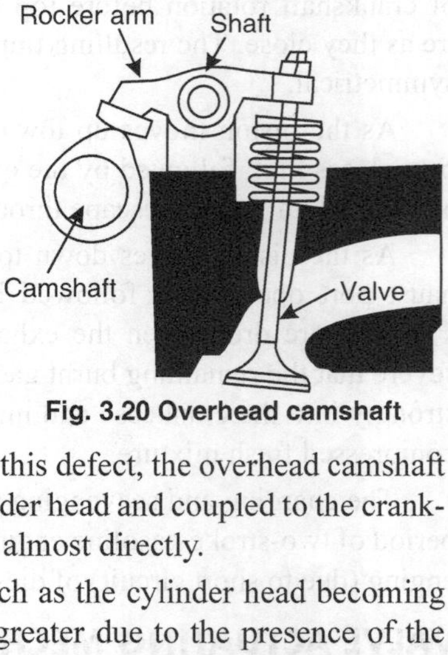

Fig. 3.20 Overhead camshaft

With the development of high-speed automobile roads in recent years, the engines are demanded to operate at higher speeds. When the camshaft is located at the cylinder block side or lower part, the power to open and close the valves must be transmitted from the cams through the valve lifters, push rods, rocker arms, to the valves. The inertia due to the valve mechanism weight created the defect of the opening and closing of valves failing, to conform with the cam movements. To eliminate this defect, the overhead camshaft was adopted in which the camshaft was brought to the top of cylinder head and coupled to the crankshaft with chains to enable the cams to open and close the valves almost directly.

In the use of overhead camshaft, there are disadvantages such as the cylinder head becoming more complicated and engine overall height becoming slightly greater due to the presence of the camshaft on the top of cylinder. But with the elimination of the push rods and valve lifters and the nearly direct opening and closing of the valves by the cams, there is the advantage of getting vastly improved valve follow. The overhead camshafts were limited in use to sport cars and other high speed passenger models but recently they have found widespread use in ordinary passenger cars.

The single overhead camshaft is the type in general use, where one camshaft serves to open and close all valves through rocker arms. Where specially high performance is demanded, two camshafts are utilized, each serving respectively to open and close the intake and exhaust valves directly. This type is called double overhead camshaft.

With the same object of reducing the valve mechanism weight, there is a type in which the camshaft has been located slightly higher than the in the common overhead valve engine, the purpose being to shorten the push rods. This type is called high camshaft which is used in Toyota corolla.

COMBUSTION CHAMBERS

Combustion chambers for gasoline engines

It is necessary that the combustion chamber be formed to allow good combustion of the air-fuel mixture, but this shape will be dependent on factors such as type of valves and location of valve mechanism.

The location of valve especially have large effects on the chamber shape. Through the arrangement of valves in the combustion chamber, classification can be made into overhead valve type, side valve type, and F head type.

Combustion chamber shapes for overhead valve arrangement

In this arrangement, both the intake and exhaust valves are positioned on the top part of combustion chamber. When in this position, it is generally possible to make the combustion chamber more compact and most effective. Even though the valve mechanism will become more complicated, this arrangement is used in practically all engines today. In the combustion chambers for the overhead valves, the following three shapes are most commonly used.

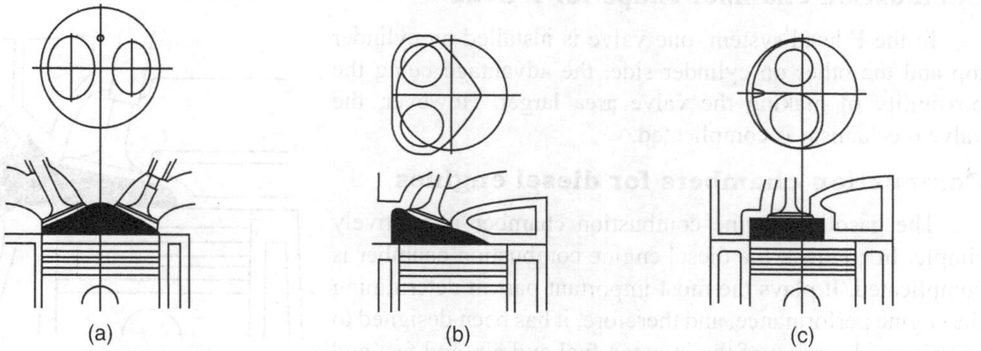

Fig. 3.21 (a) Hemispherical type (b) Wedge type (c) Bathtub type

(*a*) **Hemispherical type:** This has the smallest surface per unit volumes so its loss is small. The valves can also be made larger for better charging efficiency, making this the most ideal combustion chamber. Its disadvantage is that among the three shapes, the valve mechanism required is the most complicated and difficult to manufacture.

(*b*) **Wedge type:** The valves are tilted from the vertical so that the bending in the intake and exhaust ports have been reduced. This allows the gas to flow smoother and also makes it easier to develop better turbulent flow for fast combustion rate, making the wedge type combustion chamber the next best to the hemispherical type. Because of these features, the wedge type is used to a considerable extent.

(*c*) **Bathtub type:** When the piston compresses the air-fuel mixture, pushing-in turbulence is created to result in fast combustion rate. The construction cost is also lower so that this is the type most commonly used. However, the main trend today is toward the adoption of the wedge type.

Combustion chamber shape for side valve arrangement

In the side valve system, the intake and exhaust valves are positioned on the side of the cylinder, with the camshaft located under the valves. This arrangement has the advantage of simpler valve mechanism. Since the cylinder head construction is also simple, the engine overall height can be lowered. However, the combustion chamber cannot be made compact so that thermal efficiency is bad and in the present day engines where largest output possible is demanded, the side valve arrangement cannot be used. In this system, there is the L-head where the valves are located on one side of the cylinder and the T-head type where the valves are positioned on both sides of the cylinder.

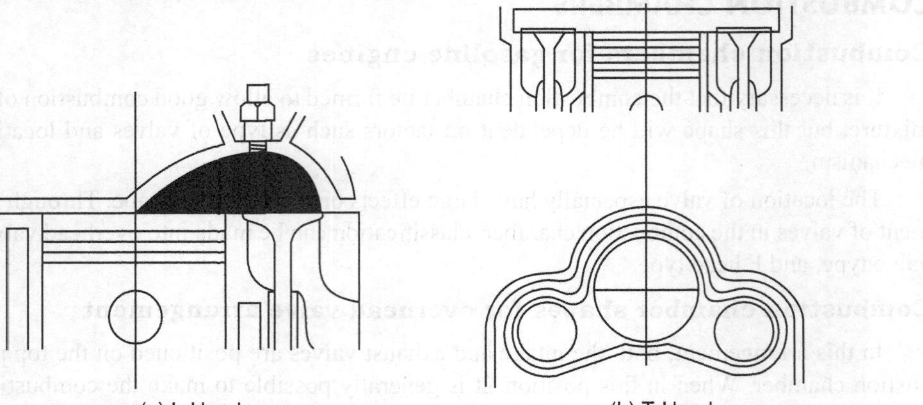

(a) L-Head (b) T-Head

Fig. 3.22 (a) L-Head (b) T-Head

Combustion chamber shape for F-head

In the F-head system, one valve is installed on cylinder top and the other on cylinder side, the advantage being the possibility of making the valve area larger. However, the valve mechanism is complicated.

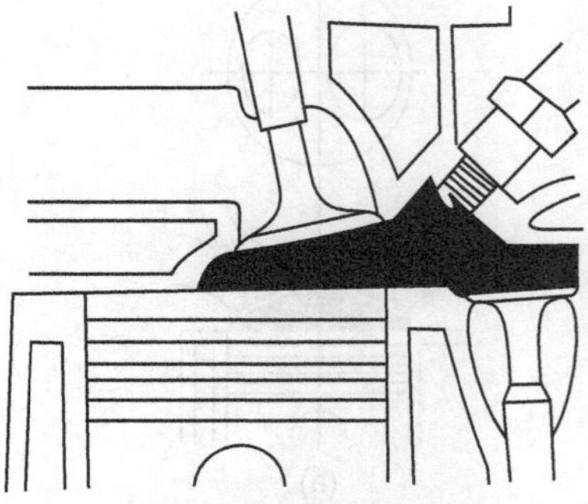

Fig. 3.23 F-head type

Combustion chambers for diesel engines

The gasoline engine combustion chamber is relatively simple. In contrast, the diesel engine combustion chamber is complicated. It plays the most important part in determining the engine performance, and therefore, it has been designed to permit good mixing of the injected fuel and air, and fast and uniform combustion of the mixture.

The following types of combustion chambers are used in automotive diesel engines today:

- Diesel combustion chambers
  - Direct combustion chambers — Direct injection type
  - Auxiliary combustion chambers
    - Precombustion chamber type
    - Swirl chamber type

Direct injection combustion chamber

This type of combustion chamber is formed between the top of the cylinder and piston head and the fuel injected directly into the combustion chamber with the fuel nozzle.

In order to attain the best fuel mixture with this direct injection combustion chamber, the nozzle shape, nozzle orifice diameter and injection direction become important factors.

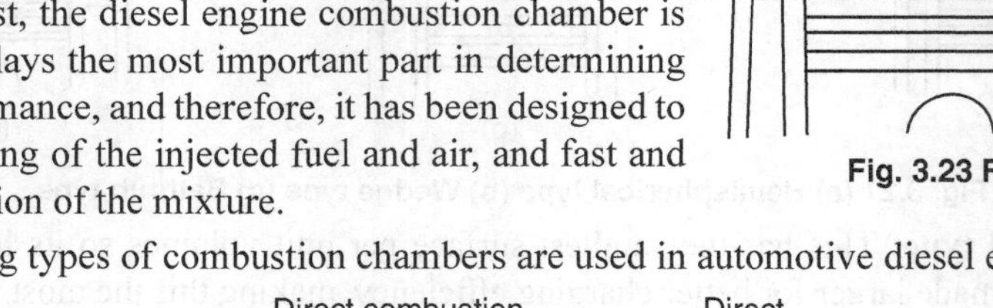

(A) Heart type (B) Semi spherical type (C) Spherical type

Fig. 3.24 Direct injection combustion chambers

Advantages

- Combustion chamber shape is simple so that thermal efficiency is high and fuel consumption is low.
- Starts readily from cold state without using special starting aids (glow plugs), even in the case of small engines with compression ratio of around 15.
- Suited for high power engines due to simplicity of cylinder head construction and small heat distortion.

Disadvantages

- Sensitive to fuel quality and requires good grade fuel.
- Higher fuel injection pressure required.
- Nozzle troubles frequent and nozzle life shorter due to use of multiple-orifice nozzle. Spray condition has larger effect on engine performance.
- When compared to auxiliary chamber type, turbulence is weaker so that high speed operation is difficult.

Auxiliary combustion chamber

(*a*) Precombustion chamber type

As shown in Fig. 3.25, the fuel is sprayed in the precombustion chamber by the injection nozzle. Partial combustion of the fuel discharges the unburnt fuel through the small passageways between the precombustion chamber and main chamber, where the fuel is broken up into fine particles for complete combustion in the main chamber.

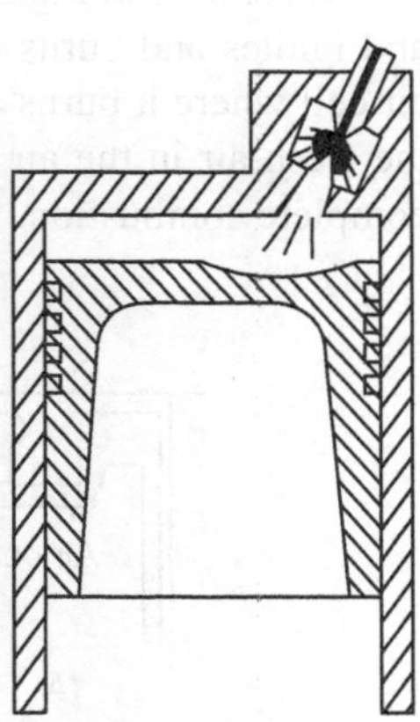

Fig. 3.25 Precombustion chamber type

As two combustions occur in this system, the temperature of the precombustion chamber is low when the engine is to be started. Since compression temperature is high enough to ignite the injected fuel cannot be attained, a glow plug is provided in the precombustion chamber to heat the air in the chamber by passing a 40 ampere current through the glow plug nichrome wire.

Advantages

- Wide range of fuel can be used. Relatively poor fuel can be used with practically smokeless combustion.
- Easy to maintain as the fuel injection pressure is relatively low and the engine is comparatively insensitive to changes in injection timing.
- Due to use of throttle nozzles, diesel knock is reduced and engine operates more quietly.

Disadvantages

- Construction cost is higher due to complicated cylinder design.
- Larger starter is required. Starting performance is bad and glow plugs must be used.
- Fuel consumption rate is higher.

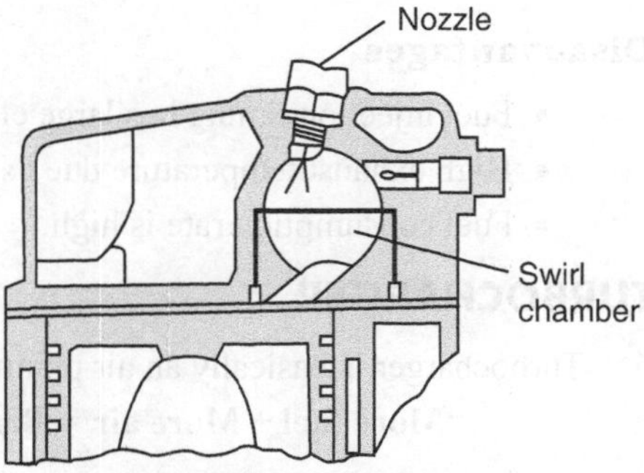

Fig. 3.26 Swirl chamber type

(*b*) Swirl chamber type

As shown in Fig. 3.26, the swirl chamber is of spherical shape. The air compressed by the piston enters into the swirl chamber and produces turbulent flow. The fuel is injected into this swirling air. Most of the fuel is burnt in the swirl chamber but a part of the unburnt fuel passes through the transfer passage into the main combustion chamber for complete combustion.

Advantages

- High engine speed can be attained due to utilization of large compression turbulence.
- Small nozzle troubles due to use of pin type nozzles.
- Wide engine speed range possible and smoother operation, making this type suited for automotive use.

Disadvantages

- Complicated cylinder head or cylinder block construction.
- Thermal efficiency and fuel consumption rate are both inferior to those of direct injection system.
- Glow plugs are required but are not very effective due to the large size of the swirl chamber.
- Diesel knock is relatively greater at low speed.

(*c*) Air cell type

As shown in Fig.3.27, the fuel injected from the nozzle is directed toward the air cell opening, and ignites and burns in the main combustion chamber. A part of the sprayed fuel enters into the air cell where it burns and increases the pressure inside the cell. When the piston starts to descend, the fresh air in the air cell discharges into the main combustion chamber to aid in accomplishing complete combustion.

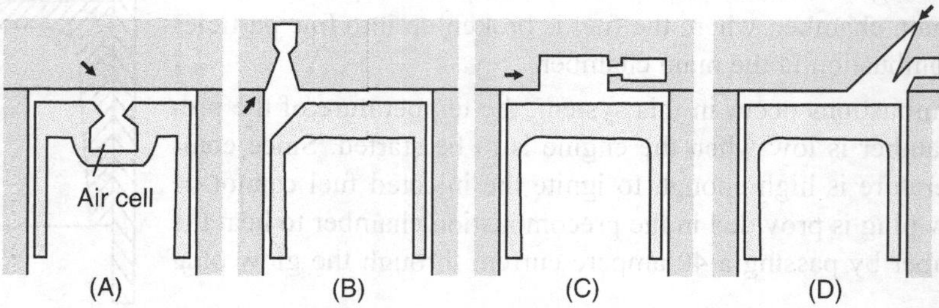

Fig. 3.27 Air cell type combustion chamber

In this type, the ignition is performed in the main combustion chamber so that glow plugs are generally not required.

Advantages

- Engine operation is quieter as the combustion takes place more gradually.
- Fuel is injected directly into the combustion chamber so that ease of starting is next to direct injection system, and glow plugs are not used in many of the cases.
- Less nozzle trouble due to use of pin type nozzle.

Disadvantages

- Fuel injection timing has large effect on engine performance.
- High exhaust temperature due to large amount of after burning.
- Fuel consumption rate is high.

TURBOCHARGER

Turbocharger is basically an air pump driven by the exhaust gas from the engine.

"More fuel + More air = Bigger explosion = Greater power"

Purpose

Turbocharger forces an additional amount of air or air-fuel mixture into the engine cylinder. With more air-fuel to burn, the engine produces more combustion pressure and hence more engine power. On many turbocharged engines, *power output is boosted 30% or more* (for example, a 100 horsepower engine could produce 130 horsepower with a turbocharger).

Construction

The turbocharger consists of the turbine housing, compressor housing, center housing, turbine wheel, compressor wheel, full floating bearings, waste gate valve, actuator, etc.

The turbine wheel and the compressor wheel are mounted on the same shaft. When the engine is running, the exhaust gases flow from the exhaust manifold to the turbine wheel. They strike the blades of the turbine, spinning it up to 100,000 rpm or higher. Since the compressor is on the same shaft, it also spins at high speed. As the compressor spins, it forces the intake air into the engine cylinders.

Since the turbine and compressor wheels turn at very high speed, full floating bearings are used to ensure the absorption of vibrations from the shaft and lubrication of the shaft and bearings.

Operation

The turbocharger has two operating phases, the atmospheric phase and the boost phase. During light-load and cruising conditions, the compressor is almost idling. It is rotating too slowly to pressurize the intake air. The engine operates about the same as an engine of similar size without a turbocharger. As the engine is accelerated for more power, the combustion of more air-fuel mixture, thereby increasing the flow of exhaust gas. This speeds up the turbine and compressor. Now additional air-fuel mixture is delivered to the cylinders and the engine delivers more power. A turbocharged engine operates in the atmospheric phase most of the time. The turbocharger does not add power during cruising at normal highway speeds. It usually provides boost only when acceleration or full power is required.

As the compressor begins to force additional air-fuel mixture into the cylinders, a pressure develops in the intake manifold. The amount of pressure increase is called the *manifold pressure (or) boost pressure.*

The turbocharger can raise boost pressure high so that detonation and engine damage occur. To limit boost pressure and prevent over boost, most turbochargers have *actuator and waste gate valve.*

Boost pressure is low (normal)

As long as the boost pressure inside the intake manifold is normal, the actuator does not operate and the waste gate valve remains closed. All exhaust gas is therefore routed into the turbine housing.

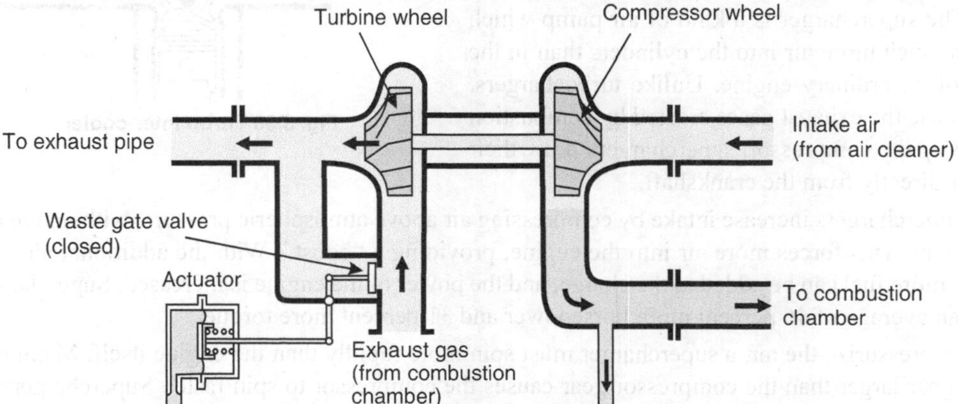

Fig. 3.28 Turbocharger operation: Boost pressure is low

Boost pressure is high

As the accelerator pedal is depressed (fuel volume increases), the exhaust gas pressure increases, thus increasing the boost pressure.

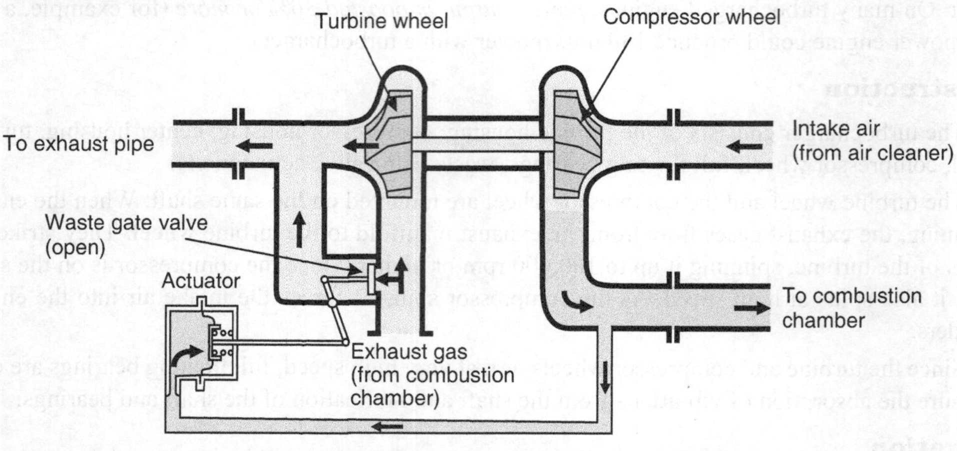

Fig. 3.29 Turbocharger operation: Boost pressure is high

When the boost pressure reaches high, the waste gate valve is opened by the actuator and part of the exhaust gas is diverted around the turbine wheel. As a result, the turbine speed is kept within the optimal range to prevent the boost pressure from rising excessively.

Intercooler

Air gets hot when it is compressed. This causes the air to expand and become less dense. Heated air contains less oxygen to support combustion. To cool the air and increase its density, most turbocharged engines have a *charge air cooler or intercooler* which is either of the air-cooled type or water-cooled type. This is a radiator like heat exchanger that cools the air after it has been pressurized. At the same time, by lowering the temperature of the air-fuel mixture, knocking is suppressed, giving improved driveability and fuel economy.

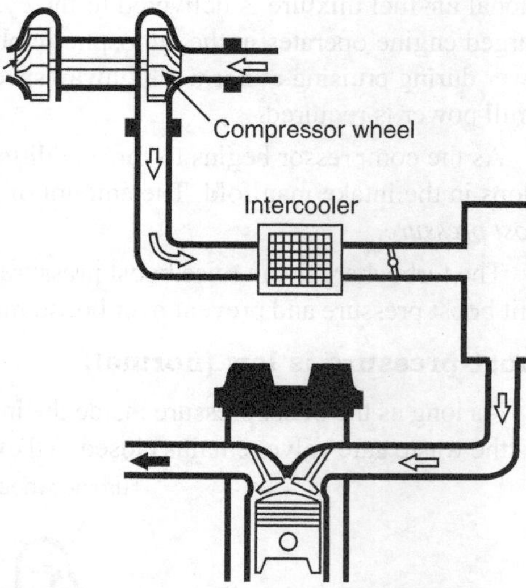

Fig. 3.30 Turbo Inter-cooler

SUPERCHARGER

The supercharger is a kind of air pump which forces much more air into the cylinders than in the case of an ordinary engine. Unlike turbochargers, which use the exhaust gases created by combustion to power the compressor, superchargers draw their power directly from the crankshaft.

Superchargers increase intake by compressing air above atmospheric pressure, without creating a vacuum. This forces more air into the engine, providing a "boost." With the additional air in the boost, more fuel can be added to the charge, and the power of the engine is increased. Supercharging adds an average of 46 percent more horsepower and 31 percent more torque.

To pressurize the air, a supercharger must spin more rapidly than the engine itself. Making the drive gear larger than the compressor gear causes the compressor to spin faster. Superchargers can spin at speeds as high as 50,000 to 65,000 rpm.

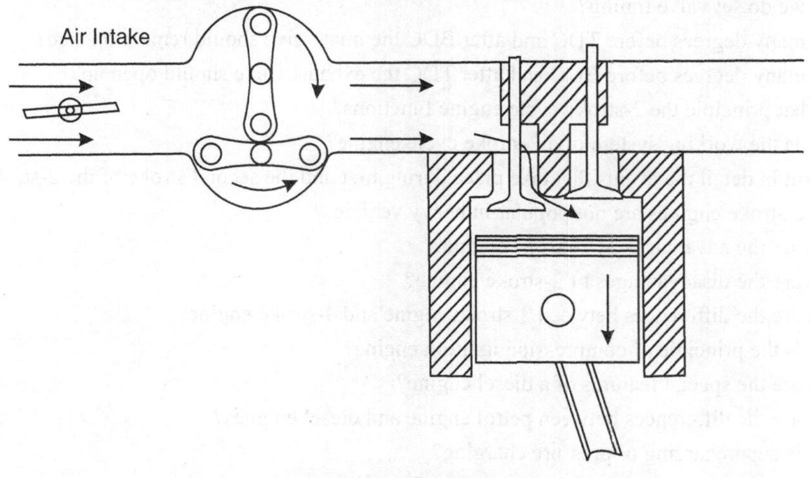

Fig. 3.31 Supercharger

Review Questions

1. What is an engine?
2. What is meant by heat engine?
3. How heat energy is converted into mechanical energy?
4. How many types of heat engines are there?
5. What is meant by external combustion engine?
6. What is meant by internal combustion engine?
7. In what ways could we classify the internal combustion engines?
8. What is the working principle of the petrol engine?
9. Name the prominent motor vehicles manufactured in India and also indicate whether these have a 4-stroke or 2-stroke engine.
10. What is meant by TDC and BDC?
11. What is a stroke?
12. What is clearance volume?
13. What is swept volume?
14. What is meant by compression ratio?
15. What is a bore?
16. Describe the construction of an engine?
17. What are the strokes that occur under the engine cycle?
18. How does 4-stroke cycle petrol engine function?
19. Explain the happenings that take place in each stroke of an engine cycle.
20. What is meant by valve timing?
21. What are the advantages of opening an inlet valve widely?
22. At what degrees the inlet valve and the exhaust valve open in valve timing? Also indicate the overlapping degrees in these valves.
23. Why the inlet valve is opened before TDC and after BDC?
24. Why the exhaust valve is opened before BDC and even after TDC?
25. How do the valves open?
26. What is the connection between camshaft and the crankshaft?
27. What are the ways in which connection between cam shaft and crankshaft can be established?

28. How we do set valve timing?
29. How many degrees before TDC and after BDC the inlet valve should remain opened?
30. How many degrees before BDC and after TDC the exhaust valve should open up?
31. On what principle the 2-stroke cycle engine functions?
32. What is the working system of a 2-stroke cycle engine?
33. Explain in detail the events that take place during first and the second stroke of the 2-stroke engine.
34. Why 2-stroke engines are not popular in heavy vehicles?
35. What are the advantages of 2-stroke engine?
36. What are the disadvantages of 2-stroke engine?
37. What are the differences between 2-stroke engine and 4-stroke engine?
38. What is the principle of compression ignition engine?
39. What are the special features of a diesel engine?
40. What are the differences between petrol engine and diesel engines?
41. What is supercharging or pressure charging?
42. What are the advantages and disadvantages of super charger?
43. What are the different types of engines on the basis of cylinder?
44. Why do we use cylinder liners?
45. What is the difference between dry and wet cylinder liners?
46. What is the function of cylinder head?
47. What is the function of piston?
48. Why rings are provided in the pistons?
49. Describe the kinds of piston rings and their functions.
50. How many rings are mounted on a piston?
51. What do you understand by ring end gap? Why and how much is kept?
52. What do you understand by piston ring groove clearance and how much it is kept?
53. What are the functions of crankshaft?
54. What do you understand by the words 'Firing Order'?
55. Indicate the different firing orders of 4-cylinder, 6-cylinder and 8-cylinder engines?
56. Why is the firing order of V-8 type engines arranged differently from the in-line engines?
57. How can the firing order of an unfamiliar engine be found?
58. What are the functions of camshaft?
59. Why it is necessary to have valve clearance and how much clearance is kept?
60. Which parts are included in the valve operating mechanism?
61. What is the function of flywheel?
62. Which bearings are fitted in an internal combustion engine and where?
63. Of which metal main bearings and the big end bearing are made?
64. What is the use of gasket?
65. What is the function of exhaust pipe and silencer?
66. What are the different types of combustion chamber for SI engines?
67. How does a solid or open combustion chamber function? What is the drawback?
68. What are the special features of pre-combustion chamber?
69. What are the salient features of swirl chamber?
70. What are the possible faults in the injection system?
71. Why air bleeding is done in diesel fuel supply system?
72. What is the use of heater plug (glow plug) in a diesel engine?
73. What is meant by a transverse engine?

74. What is the advantage of a horizontally opposed engine?
75. Is a flat engine the same as an in-line engine?
76. Where are horizontally opposed engines used?
77. What is meant by the critical speed of an engine?
78. What is known as rated horse power (road horse power)?
79. What is meant by a quench area in combustion chambers?
80. What is mono block cylinder?
81. Why is a single cylinder engine not being used widely in vehicles?
82. What is meant by cylinder or piston scoring?
83. Why is the cylinder head cast as a separate piece?
84. Why are copper-asbestos gaskets preferable to plain copper gaskets?
85. Which side of the piston is the major thrust side?
86. What is a piston skirt?
87. What is meant by piston seizure?
88. What serious damage can result because of piston seizure?
89. What is the cause of piston seizure or scuffing?
90. How are pistons cooled?
91. Why are piston pins made hollow?
92. What are the different methods by which pistons may be expanded?
93. What is heat dam in a piston?
94. What is meant by piston relief? Why is it provided?
95. Why are pistons dished or somewhat hollowed at the top?
96. What is meant by blow by?
97. What is squish?
98. Why are T slots provided in a piston?
99. Why is crank case ventilation employed in an automobile?
100. What is positive crankcase ventilation system?
101. Why a long chain is not used in camshaft drive?
102. What is DOHC engine?
103. What is the effect of too much valve clearance?
104. What are the reasons for less compression pressure in one of the cylinders?
105. What modifications that could increase volumetric efficiency?
106. What methods are used to have equal mixture distribution?
107. How does the flywheel stores energy?
108. What is the difference between static and dynamic balancing?
109. What is power balance and mechanical balance?
110. What are the properties of gasoline?
111. What characteristic of the fuel affects easy starting?
112. What is meant by unleaded gasoline?
113. How does gum like deposits affect engine operation?
114. What is octane rating of fuel?
115. How can octane rating be increased?
116. What is true diesel engine?
117. What is a semi diesel engine?
118. What are the methods employed for starting diesel engines?
119. How does high altitude affect the operation of diesel engines?

120. What does the cetane number of the diesel fuel indicate?
121. What is a dual-fuel engine?
122. How is an engine supercharged?
123. What is meant by turbulence as applied to diesel engine operation?
124. What methods are used to provide air turbulence?
125. What is the advantage of fitting inlet and exhaust manifolds together?
126. What are the two main classes of carburetor?
127. What is a constant choke carburetor?
128. What is a constant vacuum carburetor?
129. Why do most engines use down draft carburetors?
130. What is meant by a submerged jet and why it is used?
131. What is a choke?
132. What is another name for the choke?
133. What is meant by carburetor icing?
134. How carburetor icing is eliminated?
135. What is the theoretical air-fuel ratio for complete combustion?
136. Give suitable ratios of air to petrol for (a) starting from cold (b) economy at part loads (c) maximum power.
137. What is a lean mixture?
138. What is a rich mixture?
139. What is meant by compensation and why it is necessary?
140. What are the reasons for the engine missing with reference to petrol flow?
141. What is an engine misfire?
142. What are the causes for misfires at slow speed?
143. What are the causes for misfires at high speed?
144. What are the reasons for misfires in a scooter?
145. What are the limitations or disadvantages of a conventional carburetor?
146. What are the advantages of petrol injection in a carburetor engine?
147. What are the usual methods of fuel injection?
148. What is meant by air-injection fuel system?
149. What is a unit injector?
150. What are the advantages of the unit injector?
151. What is bleeding in injection system?
152. Where is the Pintle nozzle used?
153. To what type of cylinder head is Pintaux nozzle?
154. What is the speciality of a Pintaux nozzle?
155. How can we verify whether all the cylinders in an engine are getting fuel and are firing?
156. What four major parts form an exhaust system in an automobile system?
157. What effect does backpressure have in the operation of the engine?
158. Name the three systems of airflow scavenging in common use for 2-stroke engine.
159. What is air lock?
160. What is pre-ignition?
161. State the causes of pre-ignition.
162. What do you understand by detonation?
163. What are the causes of detonation?
164. What is the probable fault of an engine misfire and how can it be located?
165. What is turbocharger? What are the advantages?

166. What are the causes of diesel knock?
167. For the same power diesel engine is bigger in size compared with petrol engine -Justify.
168. What factors make the running cost of CI engines much less than SI engines?
169. What is Lean Burn Engine? What are the advantages?
170. What are the losses of heat from the engine?
171. What factors to be considered while designing the combustion chamber?
172. What types of combustion chambers are considered good for diesel engines?
173. What is meant by octane number rating?
174. What is meant by cetane number rating?
175. What is the function of timing gear?
176. Why diesel engines are not so popular in passenger cars?
177. What is meant by specific fuel consumption?
178. Why are mufflers necessary?

4 CHAPTER

FUEL SYSTEM

AUXILIARY SYSTEMS

The spark ignition and compression ignition engines consist of number of systems and they serve different purposes. The major systems from this subject point of view are:

1. Fuel system
2. Lubrication system
3. Cooling system
4. Intake and exhaust system
5. Electrical system

FUEL SYSTEM

The purpose of the fuel supply system for an engine is to store, transfer and filter the fuel required by the carburetor or injection system. The most important components of this system are:

- Air cleaner
- Fuel filter
- Fuel tank
- Fuel line
- Charcoal canister (some models only)
- Carburetor/Electronic fuel injection system
- Fuel pump
- Fuel pump

In fuel supply system, *air cleaners or air filters* remove dust, dirt and other foreign particles present in the air and send clean air into engine cylinder. *Fuel filters* filter foreign particles that may be present in the fuel. A *fuel pump* lifts fuel from the *fuel tank* and supplies the same to the carburetor through tubes and hoses (*fuel lines*). Correct quantity of air fuel mixture is supplied to the cylinder by *carburetor or electronic fuel injection system*. On some models, the HC (Hydrocarbon) gas generated in the fuel tank is temporarily absorbed in the *charcoal canister* and is burned in the engine. As a result, the amount of HC gas which leaks out of the fuel tank is reduced.

CARBURETORS AND THEIR SYSTEMS

CARBURETION & CARBURETOR

The process of preparing combustible air fuel mixture in the petrol engine is called carburetion. A device which does this process is called carburetor. The carburetor atomizes the fuel and mixes it with air in correct proportions according to the engine operating conditions.

MIXTURE STRENGTH: AIR-FUEL RATIO

Air fuel ratio is the ratio of the weight of air to the weight of fuel supplied to an engine cylinder during a cycle of operations.

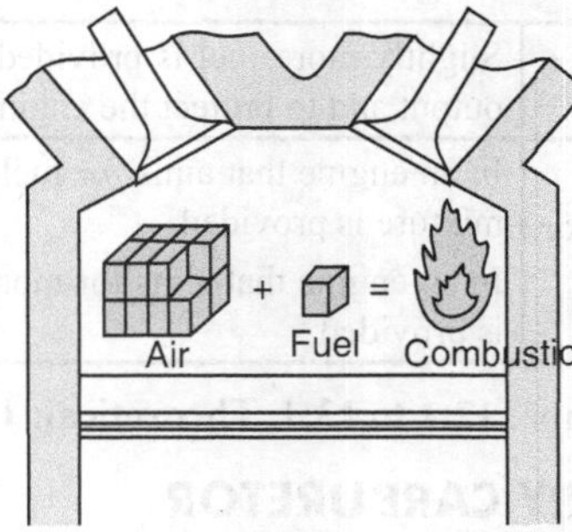

Fig. 4.1 Combustion in internal combustion engines

Chemically correct (or) Stoichiometric air-fuel mixture

A mixture that contains just enough air for complete combustion of the fuel is called a stoichiometric air fuel ratio. This value is normally 14.7:1 for petrol engines (approximately 15:1-15 parts of air to 1 part of fuel). This ratio also known as theoretical at actual or ideal air-fuel ratio.

Rich mixture

A mixture is said to be rich if it contains more fuel than the fuel quantity in the chemically correct mixture. For example: 12:1

Lean mixture

A mixture is said to be lean if it contains more air than the air quantity in the chemically correct mixture. For example: 17:1

Desirable mixture strength

The approximate proportions of air to fuel (petrol by weight) for different engine operating conditions are:

Driving conditions and Air-fuel ratio

Driving condition	Air-fuel ratio	Remarks
Normal operation after warm-up	Theoretical	The theoretical air-fuel ratio is used because the fuel and air mix well at this temperature.
Cold engine	Richer (depending on engine tempera-ture)	When the engine is cold, fuel does not vaporize well and often clings to the walls of the intake manifold and combustion chambers without mixing properly with air. Thus, in order for the actual combustion mixture to approach as close as possible to the theoretical ratio, a larger amount of fuel must be provided.
During starting	Richer	Since the engine cranks at a very low rpm during starting, the air flows at an extremely low speed. For this reason, the fuel and air do not mix well, thus requiring more fuel.
During idling	Slightly richer	Since the engine runs at a low speed at idle, the air also flows at a low speed, slowing the mixing of fuel and air. Slighlty more fuel must therefore be supplied in order to decrease the disparity of air-fuel mixtures supplied to the cylinders.
During acceleration	Additional fuel injected	Because fuel is heavier than air, the flow of fuel cannot keep up with the airflow at the begining of acceleration. This results in a leaner mixture. An additional amount of fuel is therefore injected from the acceleration pump in order to prevent the mixture from becoming too lean.

Under high loads	Slightly richer	Slightly more fuel is provided in order to obtain a higher power output and to protect the engine parts.
Cruising (light load)	Slightly leaner or theoretical	In an engine that aims for fuel economy, a slightly leaner air-fuel mixture is provided. In an engine that aims for more power, a theoretical air-fuel ratio is provided.

Richer: about 9:1, Slightly richer: 12:1 to 13:1, Theoretical: 15:1, Slightly leaner: about 16:1

A SIMPLE (OR) ELEMENTARY CARBURETOR

To understand a modern carburetor, which is a complicated one, it is helpful to first study a simple or elementary carburetor. It consists of a float chamber, venturi, discharge jet or main nozzle, choke valve and throttle valve.

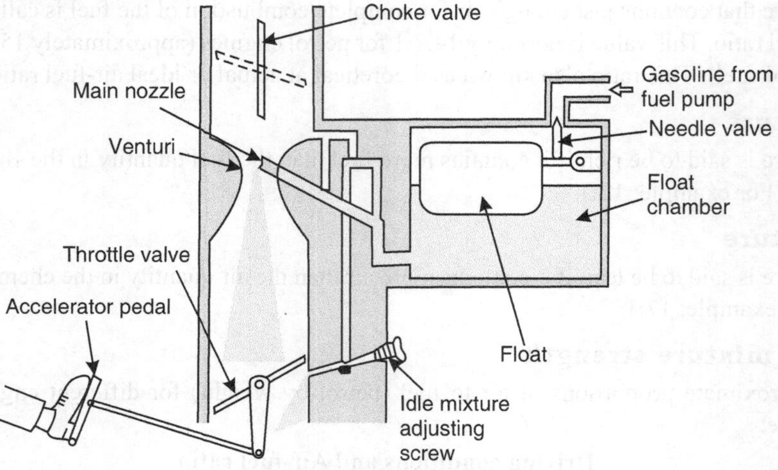

Fig. 4.2 Simple carburetor

Float chamber (or) Float bowl

It consists of a float and needle supply valve. This system maintains a constant petrol level in the float chamber. If the fuel level is too high, fuel will continue to flow from the main nozzle. The air fuel mixture will become too rich. This result in wastage of fuel, engine stall or poor running and the pollutant exhaust emissions such as hydrocarbons and carbon monoxide. If the fuel level in the float chamber is too low, the vacuum in the venturi will not pull enough fuel out of the float chamber. The air fuel mixture will become too lean. This will results in engine stall or poor running. If the amount of fuel in the float chamber falls below the desired level, the float lowers, thereby opening the needle of fuel supply valve and admit fuel into the chamber. When the desired level has been reached, the float closes the needle valve, thus stopping additional fuel flow from the supply system. Float chamber is vented to the atmosphere.

Venturi (or) Choke tube

Venturi is a tube of decreasing cross section which reaches a minimum at the throat. During suction stroke air is drawn through the venturi. The air passing through the venturi increasing in velocity and the pressure in the venturi throat decreases.

Main nozzle (or) Discharge jet

From the float chamber, the fuel is fed to a main nozzle. The tip of the main nozzle is located in the throat of the venturi.

Throttle valve

The throttle valve is a round disc located between the venturi and the intake manifold. The throttle is connected to the accelerator pedal by a flexible cable. Depressing the accelerator pedal opens the throttle valve and permits an increased amount of air fuel mixture to reach the engine cylinders. This will increase the power output of the engine and hence the vehicle speed.

Choke valve

It is a valve which is used for controlling the amount of air passing to the venturi and is used when starting a cold engine.

Principle

As the air flows through the venturi, its velocity increases and hence pressure decreases. Now the pressure in the float chamber is atmospheric pressure and at the venture throat is below the atmospheric pressure. Because of the pressure difference (called **carburetor depression**) the fuel is discharged through the main nozzle into the air flow of the venturi. Now the fuel particles get mixed with air and the mixture is supplied to the engine cylinder.

TYPES OF CARBURETORS

Based on the direction of air flow

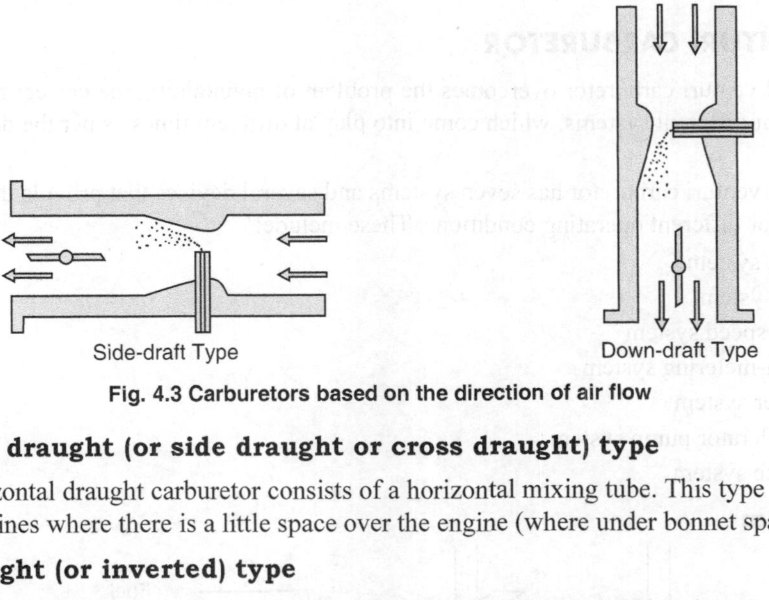

Fig. 4.3 Carburetors based on the direction of air flow

Horizontal draught (or side draught or cross draught) type

The horizontal draught carburetor consists of a horizontal mixing tube. This type of carburetor is used in engines where there is a little space over the engine (where under bonnet space limited).

Down draught (or inverted) type

In the down draught carburetor, air fuel mixture flows downward. This mixture will reach the engine, even when the velocity is low. This is because the mixture flow is assisted by gravity. Carburetor throat and inlet manifold can therefore be made larger. This in turn makes high speed and high output possible. Down draught carburetor is preferred for high output engines.

Based on the venturi

Fixed venturi (or) Constant choke carburetor

In this carburetor, the venturi area is always maintained to be constant. But the depression or vacuum which cause flow of fuel and air are being varied as per the demand on the engine. Solex, Carter, Stomberg, Weber, and Zenith carburetors are examples of this type.

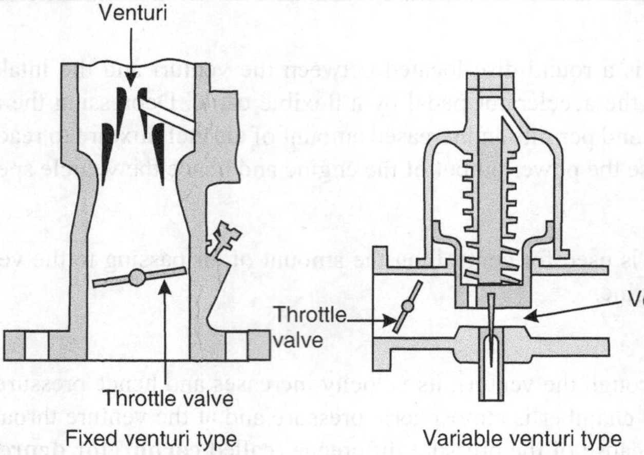

Variable venturi (or) Constant vacuum carburetor

In this carburetor, the venturi area is being varied as per the demand on the engine, while the vacuum or depression is maintained to be always constant.

This is currently the most commonly used type of carburetors in two-wheelers. SU carburetor is of this type.

FIXED VENTURI CARBURETOR

The fixed venturi carburetor overcomes the problem of maintaining the correct mixture by an arrangement of different systems, which come into play at different times as per the demand on the engine.

The fixed venturi carburetor has seven systems and several devices that provide the correct air-fuel mixture for different operating conditions. These include:

1. Float system
2. Idle system
3. Low speed system
4. Main-metering system
5. Power system
6. Accelerator pump system
7. Choke system

Float system

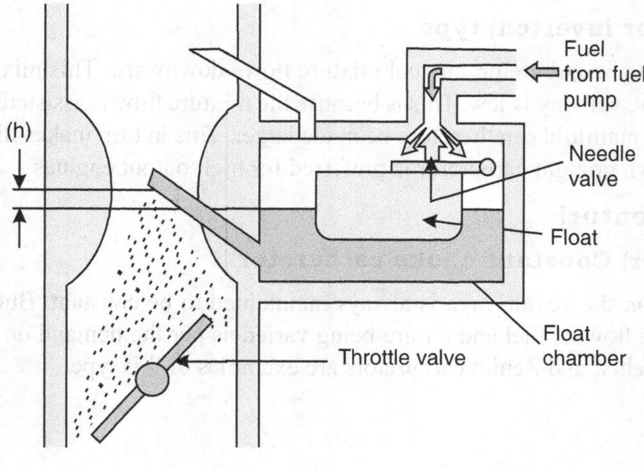

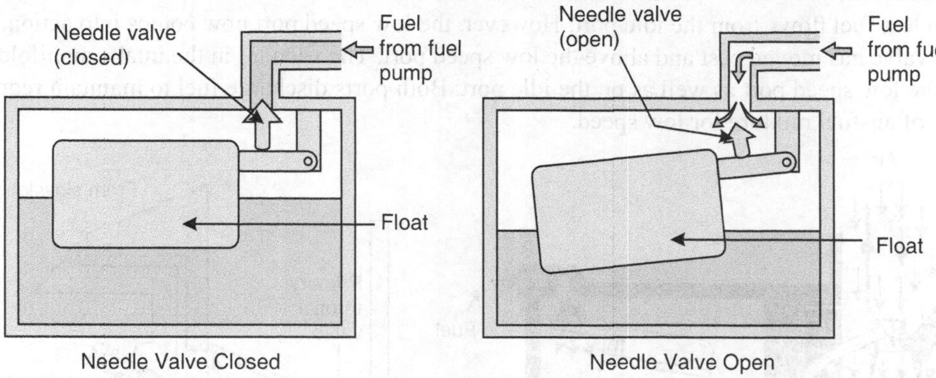

Fig. 4.5 Float system

Idle system

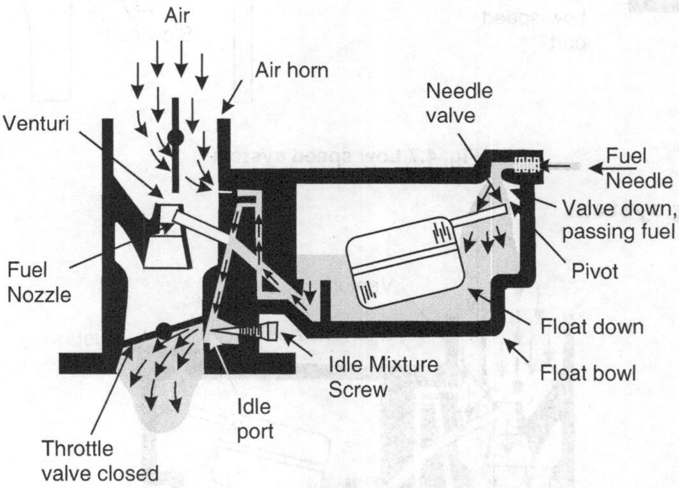

Fig. 4.6 Idle system

When the throttle valve is closed or slightly open, only a small amount of air can pass through the air horn. With low air speed, there is very little vacuum in the venturi. No fuel will feed from the main nozzle. To supply fuel during idle, an idling system is built into the carburetor. This system has an opening below the throttle valve. This hole is called idle port. The port is connected by a passage to the float chamber. In addition to the idle port, there is an idle-mixture screw located behind the idle port to control the amount of mixture discharge through it.

When the throttle valve is closed and the engine is running, a high vacuum develops in the intake manifold. The pistons are repeatedly moving down on their suction strokes, which mean they are demanding air-fuel mixture. If the pistons do not get enough air-fuel mixture, then a vacuum develops. This vacuum is great enough, when the throttle valve is closed, to cause fuel to flow through the fuel passage from the float chamber to the idle port.

Air flows down through a passage in the side of the air horn. The air mixes with the petrol flowing out of a connecting passage from the float chamber. This mixture moves down to the idle port and discharges in the lower part of the carburetor. This mixture goes to the cylinders.

Low speed system

If the throttle valve is open just a little for low speed, the edge of the throttle valve moves past the idle port. More air can flow past the throttle valve now, reducing the vacuum in the intake manifold. So less fuel flows from the idle port. However, the low speed port now comes into action. The throttle valve has moved past and above the low speed port. The vacuum in the intake manifold can act on the low speed port as well as on the idle port. Both ports discharge fuel to maintain required amount of air-fuel mixture for low speed.

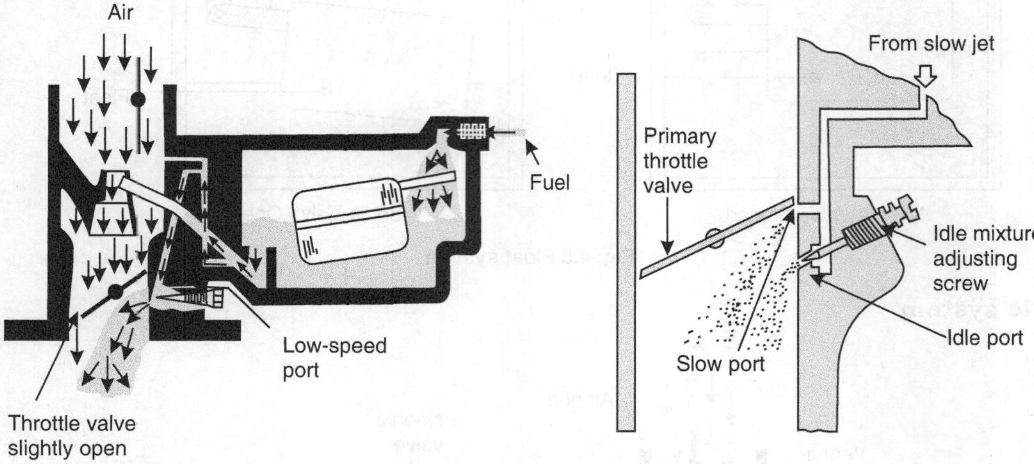

Fig. 4.7 Low speed system

Main-metering system

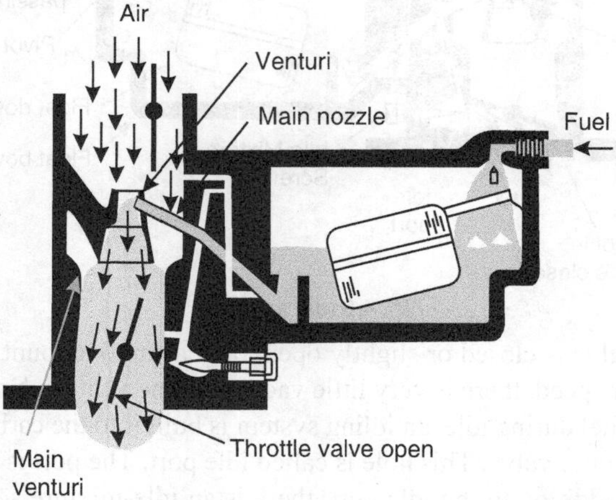

Fig. 4.8 Main-metering system

If the throttle valve is opened farther, more air will flow through. This means that there will be less vacuum in the intake manifold. As a result, the idle and low speed ports stop discharging fuel. However, with more air flow, there is a vacuum in the venturi. This causes the main nozzle to discharge fuel. Therefore, fuel gets mixed with the air passing through.

Power system

When a driver wants full power, the accelerator pedal is pushed to the floor (i.e. to the maximum position). This causes the throttle valve to open wide. Another system in the carburetor comes into action to add fuel. This system is called power system. It includes a power piston, power valve and a power jet. The power valve is tapered at its lower end. This restricts the fuel flow by partly blocking the jet. However, enough fuel flows to provide the proper air-fuel mixture ratio during part-throttle operation (normal running condition).

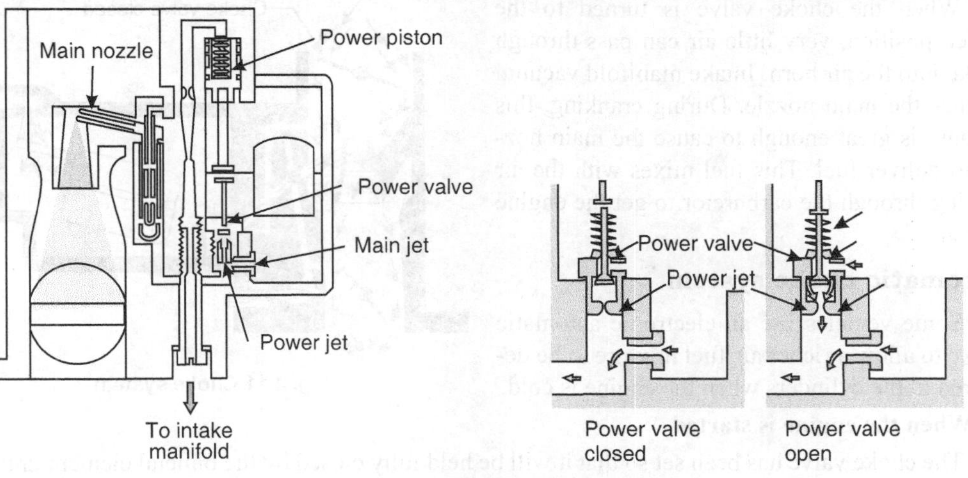

Fig. 4.9 Power system

In piston type, a power piston is used to push the power valve to open power jet. The space above the piston is connected to the inlet manifold vacuum. When there is vacuum in the inlet manifold, the vacuum holds the piston up. In this position the power valve is up and the additional fuel flow is restricted.

However, when the throttle is opened wide, the vacuum is lost and can no longer hold the piston up. A spring pushes the piston down. This lowers the power valve so that additional fuel can flow into the carburetor. So that a rich mixture is formed and is delivered to the engine for full power operation.

Acceleration pump system

There is another operating condition that needs a rich mixture. This condition occurs when the accelerator pedal is pushed down suddenly to increase the speed. To get the power needed, the engine has to be supplied rich mixture immediately. This is done by the accelerator pump system. The system includes a pump that is operated when the accelerator pedal is depressed. The movement causes the pump plunger to be pushed down. Pushing the pump plunger down suddenly, forces the fuel to flow out through the pump jet. The fuel discharges into the air-fuel mixture that is moving through the carburetor. This further enriches the air-fuel mixture.

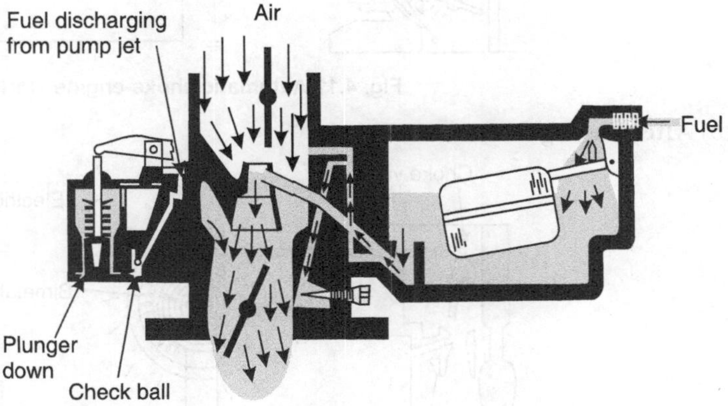

Fig. 4.10 Acceleration pump system

Choke system

When a cold engine is being cranked for starting, extra fuel must be delivered to the engine. The choke valve does this job.

When the choke valve is turned to the closed position, very little air can pass through choke into the air horn. Intake manifold vacuum reaches the main nozzle. During cranking, this vacuum is great enough to cause the main nozzle to deliver fuel. This fuel mixes with the air passing through the carburetor to get the engine started.

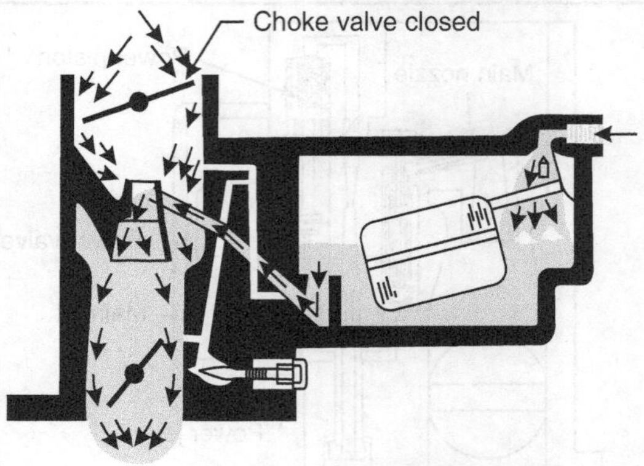

Fig. 4.11 Choke system

Automatic choke system

Some vehicles use an electronic automatic choke to allow a richer air-fuel mixture to be delivered to the cylinders when the engine is cold.

(*a*) When the engine is started

The choke valve has been set so that it will be held fully closed by the bimetal element until the ambient temperature reaches 30°C (86°F).

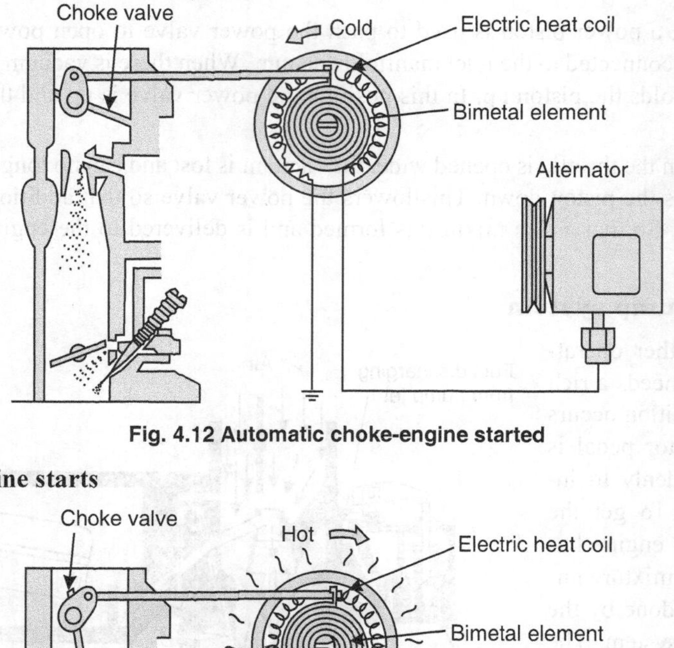

Fig. 4.12 Automatic choke-engine started

(*b*) After the engine starts

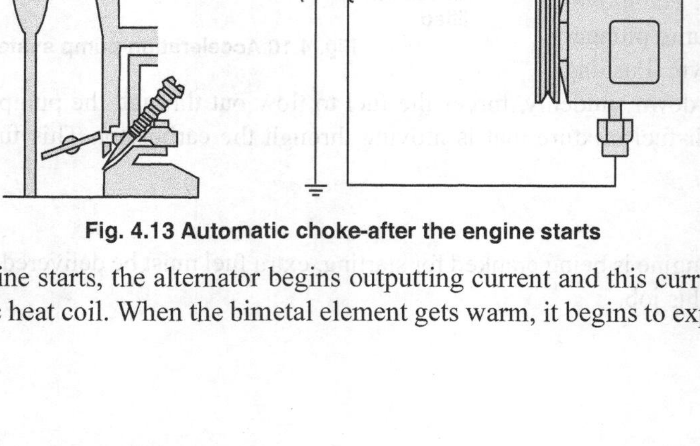

Fig. 4.13 Automatic choke-after the engine starts

When the engine starts, the alternator begins outputting current and this current is directly applied to the electric heat coil. When the bimetal element gets warm, it begins to expand, opening the choke valve.

SINGLE AND MULTI BARREL CARBURETORS

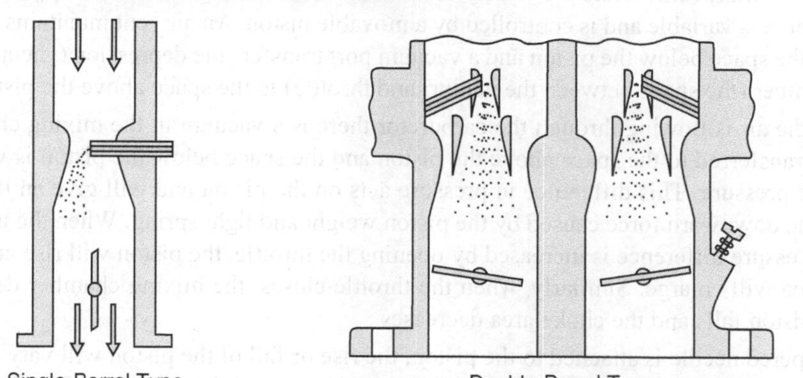

Fig. 4.14 Single and multi-barrel carburetors

Many four-cylinder engines use single-barrel carburetors. For better performance, many six-cylinder and all eight-cylinder engines use two or four barrel carburetors. Adding the extra barrel allows more air-fuel mixture to enter the engine to improve engine volumetric efficiency. This improves engine performance and drivability. One barrel is the primary barrel which takes care of the air-fuel mixture for all cylinders during idle, low speed and normal running operation. When the throttle is opened wide for high-speed operation, the secondary barrel comes into operation. Then it supplies the additional air-fuel mixture for full power and hence high speed.

VARIABLE VENTURI CARBURETOR

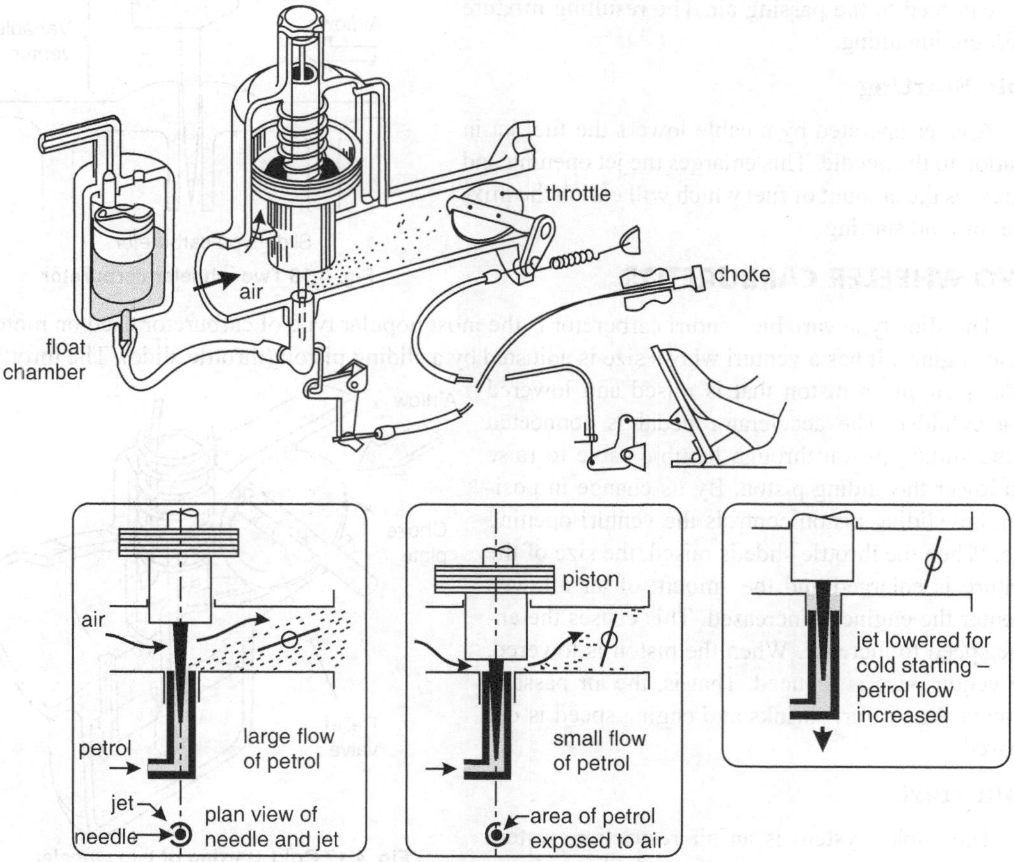

Fig. 4.15 Variable venturi carburetor

Variable venturi carburetors are widely used in two wheeler engines. In this type of carburetor, the venturi area is variable and is controlled by a movable piston. An air vent maintains atmospheric pressure in the space below the piston and a vacuum port transfers the depression (vacuum) from the mixing chamber (the space between the venturi and throttle) to the space above the piston.

When the air is flowing through the carburetor there is a vacuum in the mixing chamber. This vacuum is transferred to the space above the piston and the space below the piston is vented to the atmospheric pressure. This difference in pressure acts on the piston and will give an upward force to oppose the downward force caused by the piston weight and light spring. When the upward force due to air pressure difference is increased by opening the throttle, the piston will rise and the choke (venturi) area will enlarge. Similarly, when the throttle closes, the mixing chamber depression reduces, the piston falls and the choke area decreases.

As a tapered needle is attached to the piston, the rise or fall of the piston will vary the effective area of the petrol jet. By altering the taper of the needle it is possible to vary the fuel flow to suit the quantity of the air being supplied at any speed.

Idling

When the throttle valve is closed so that the engine is idling, there is very little vacuum on the throttle valve side. So the piston spring pushes the piston down to its lowest side. The space between it and the lower floor of the throttle body is small. Only a little air can pass through. At the same time, the tapered needle valve is well down in the fuel jet so only a little gasoline can feed to the passing air. The resulting mixture is for engine idling.

Cold Starting

A lever operated by a cable lowers the fuel jet in relation to the needle. This enlarges the jet opening and increases the amount of fuel which will enrich the mixture for cold starting.

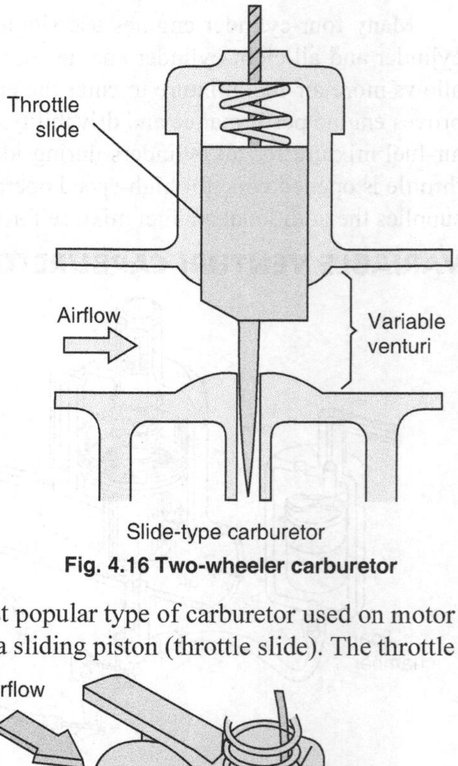

Fig. 4.16 Two-wheeler carburetor

TWO WHEELER CARBURETOR

The slide type variable venturi carburetor is the most popular type of carburetor used on motor cycle engines. It has a venturi whose size is adjusted by a sliding piston (throttle slide). The throttle slide is simply a piston that is raised and lowered in a cylinder. The accelerator pedal is connected to the sliding piston through flexible cable to raise and lower the sliding piston. By its change in position, the sliding piston controls the venturi opening size. When the throttle slide is raised, the size of the venture is enlarged and the amount of air allowed to enter the engine is increased. This causes the engine speed to increase. When the piston is lowered, the venturi size is reduced. That is, the air passage through the venturi shrinks and engine speed is decreased.

Cold start

The choke system is an air restriction system that controls the amount of air available during a

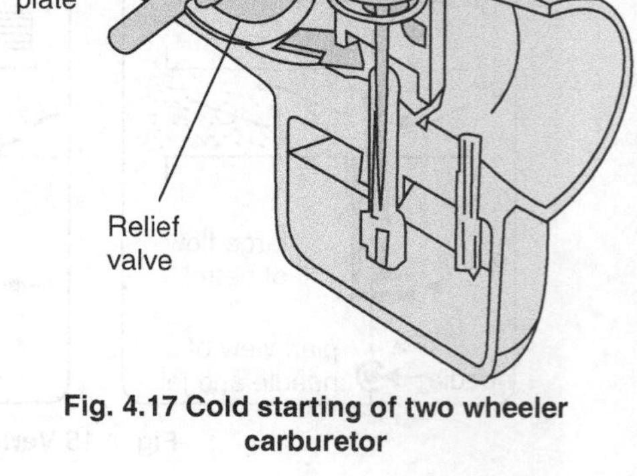

Fig. 4.17 Cold starting of two wheeler carburetor

cold engine start. This system uses a rider-controlled plate, called a choke valve, to block air to the carburetor venturi at all throttle openings. This plate has either a small hole cut into it or a spring-loaded relief valve, to allow some air into the carburetor venturi. This gives the engine enough air to run but creates a very rich mixture in comparison to the mixture created if the plate were in the open position. The choke valve is located on the air filter side of the carburetor.

ELECTRONICALLY CONTROLLED GASOLINE INJECTION SYSTEM

In trying to keep up with emissions and fuel efficiency laws, the fuel system used in modern cars has changed a lot over the years. Fuel injection is not a new development. Fuel injection has been around since the 1950s, and electronic fuel injection was used widely on European cars starting around 1980. Now, almost all the cars sold all over the world have fuel injection systems.

There are practical difficulties faced in the carburetors for switching over to electronic fuel injection system. A carburetor is a mechanical device. It is neither totally accurate nor particularly fast at responding to changing engine needs. The intake manifold is also a mechanical device and usually the following problems occur.

- Intake manifold distribution problems. Intake manifold supplies different mixture strength to the engine cylinders for the same operating condition called 'maldistribution'.
- Intake manifold is to be designed for the smooth flow of both fuel and air, which is very difficult.

The result, when these two devices are used together, is an engine that does not run efficiently at low and high speeds.

If the air-fuel mixture can be precisely controlled and the distribution to the cylinders can be made more efficient, then today's strict emissions standards can be met, while at the same time the engine will run better and consume less fuel. Fuel injection is one of the best ways to get this precise control.

TYPES OF ELECTRONIC FUEL INJECTION SYSTEM

There are two basic types of gasoline fuel-injection systems, Throttle body injection and multi-point injection. At first, carburetors were replaced with throttle body fuel injection (TBI) systems. Gradually, as new engines were designed, throttle body fuel injection was replaced by multi point fuel injection (MPFI).

The difference is in how many places fuel (under pressure) is injected into the engine. In single-point system, fuel enters the intake air at only one place. This is usually the throttle body on the intake manifold. In the multi-point system, fuel is injected into the intake air for each cylinder.

Single-point injection system

It is also known as throttle body injection (TBI), central fuel injection (CFI) or digital fuel injection (DFI). In 1980, this system was introduced. The system has one or two small injection valves positioned just above the throttle valves in the throttle body. The throttle body is similar to the carburetor throttle body. There they spray fuel into the air stream passing through.

The drawback of this system is maldistribution is not eliminated totally.

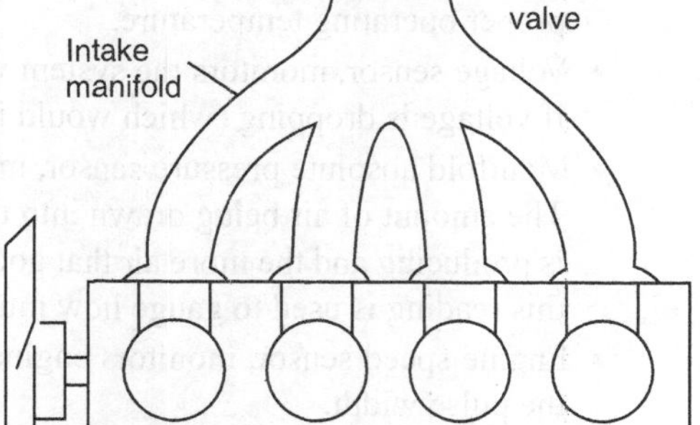

Fig. 4.18 Single-point injection

Multi-Point Fuel Injection system (MPFI)

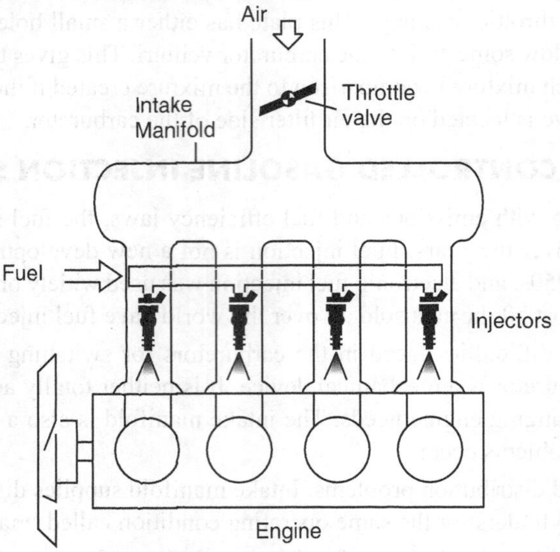

Fig. 4.19 Multi-point fuel injection

It is also known as port injection or sequencial injection. Multi-point injection systems have a fuel injector for each cylinder. Each injector is placed so that it points at the intake valve for the cylinder. The injectors are connected to fuel rails that are connected through a fuel filter to an electric fuel pump. Only air enters the intake manifold. Then as the air approaches the intake valves, injection valves open to spray fuel into the air stream. The maldistribution problem is completely eliminated with MPFI systems. These systems provide more accurate fuel metering and quicker response.

Engine sensors in MPFI system

In order to provide the correct amount of fuel for every operating condition, the engine control unit (ECU) has to monitor a huge number of input sensors. Here are a few:

- Mass airflow sensor, signals the ECU the mass of air entering the engine.
- Oxygen sensor, monitors the amount of oxygen in the exhaust so the ECU can determine how rich or lean the fuel mixture is and make adjustments accordingly.
- Throttle position sensor, monitors the throttle valve position (which determines how much air goes into the engine) so the ECU can respond quickly to changes, increasing or decreasing the fuel rate as necessary.
- Coolant temperature sensor, allows the ECU to determine when the engine has reached its proper operating temperature.
- Voltage sensor, monitors the system voltage in the car so the ECU can raise the idle speed if voltage is dropping (which would indicate a high electrical load).
- Manifold absolute pressure sensor, monitors the pressure of the air in the intake manifold. The amount of air being drawn into the engine is a good indication of how much power it is producing and the more air that goes into the engine, the lower the manifold pressure, so this reading is used to gauge how much power is being produced.
- Engine speed sensor, monitors engine speed, which is one of the factors used to calculate the pulse width.

Working principle of MPFI

In MPFI system, a high-pressure electric fuel pump is located in or near the fuel tank. The pump sends fuel from the tank through the fuel-pressure regulator to the injectors at constant high pressure all the time the engine runs. Injector is operated by a small electric solenoid. When the solenoid is connected to the battery, it pulls back on the nozzle needle, opening the valve. Now fuel can spray out of the valve. Various sensors located on the engine detect the operating mode of the engine and signal this condition to the electronic control unit (ECU). It processes the information. Then the ECU computes when and for how long the injectors should be opened. The ECU sends a voltage pulse to the injectors. The voltage pulse causes the injectors to remain open for the required time. To increase engine speed, the pulse width increases so that injectors stay open longer. If less fuel is needed, the pulse width decreases. Therefore the injectors close earlier and engine speed decreases.

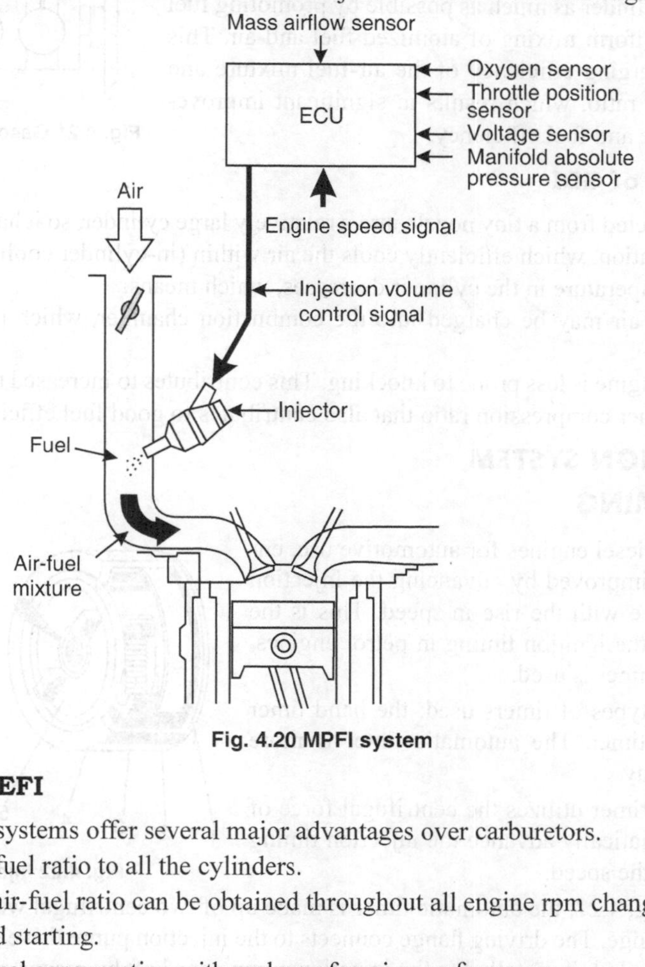

Fig. 4.20 MPFI system

Advantages of EFI

Fuel injection systems offer several major advantages over carburetors.

- Equal air-fuel ratio to all the cylinders.
- Accurate air-fuel ratio can be obtained throughout all engine rpm changes.
- Better cold starting.
- Reduces fuel consumption with no loss of engine performance.
- 10% advance of fuel economy over carbureted systems.
- Quick response.
- Reduce pollution levels.
- Precise control of engine operation.
- Reduce design consideration in the manufacture of inlet manifold.
- Earlier default detection.

Gasoline Direct Injection (GDI)

Gasoline direct-injection engines generate the air/fuel mixture in the combustion chamber. During the suction stroke, only the air flows through the intake valve. The fuel is injected directly into the combustion chamber at high pressure by special fuel injectors. As in a diesel engine, air-fuel mixture formation takes place inside the combustion chamber.

The electric fuel pump delivers fuel to the high-pressure pump at a pre-supply pressure of 3-5 bar. The highly pressurized fuel flows into and is stored in the fuel rail. The high-pressure fuel injectors are mounted on the fuel rail, also known as the "common rail". These injectors are actuated by the engine ECU and spray the fuel into the cylinder combustion chambers.

In developing the gasoline direct injection, it is aimed to cool the interior of the cylinder as much as possible by promoting fuel vaporization and uniform mixing of atomized fuel and air. This produces a high charging efficiency of the air-fuel mixture and a high compression ratio, which results in significant improvements in both torque and fuel efficiency.

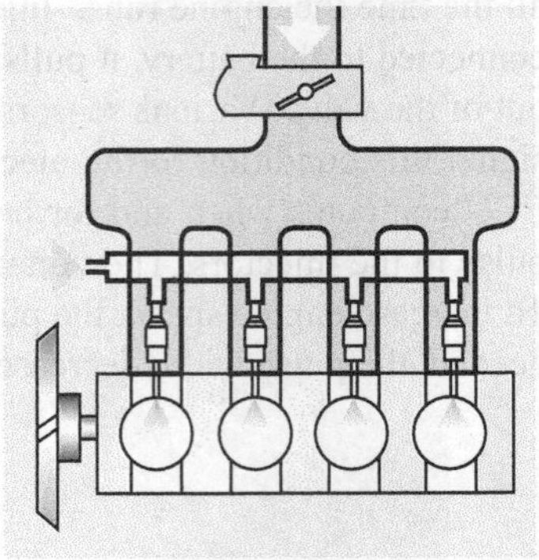

Fig. 4.21 Gasoline direct injection

Characteristics of GDI

1. Fuel is injected from a tiny nozzle into a relatively large cylinder, so it has a high latent heat of vaporization, which efficiently cools the air within (in-cylinder cooling effect).
2. The air temperature in the cylinder decreases, which means:
   - more air may be charged into the combustion chamber, which produces increased torque.
   - the engine is less prone to knocking. This contributes to increased torque, and enables a higher compression ratio that also contributes to good fuel efficiency.

DIESEL INJECTION SYSTEM

INJECTION TIMING

In high speed diesel engines for automotive use, engine output can be improved by advancing the injection timing in accordance with the rise in speed. This is the same as advancing the ignition timing in petrol engines. For this purpose, a timer is used.

There are two types of timers used: the hand timer and the automatic timer. The automatic timer is more commonly used today.

The automatic timer utilizes the centrifugal force of its rotation to automatically advance the injection timing in accordance with the speed.

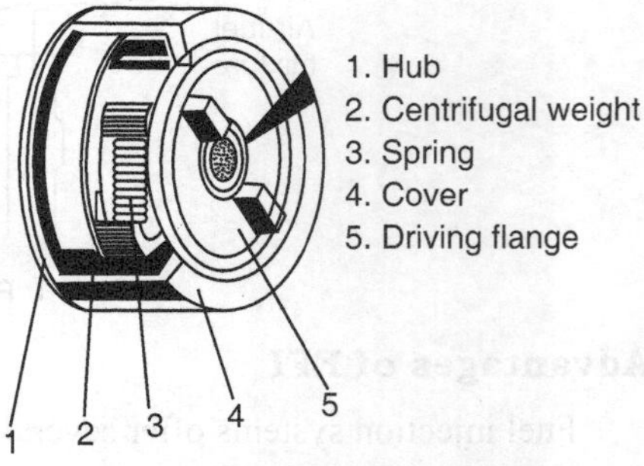

Fig. 4.22 Injector timer

As shown in Fig. 4.22, the automatic timer is made up of two centrifugal weights, two springs, cover and driving range. The driving flange connects to the injection pump drive shaft by the protrusions on its face. The hub is installed to the injection pump camshaft by means of key and nut.

The springs fit in between the journals installed to the flange and the bolts installed to the hub. The weights are attached to the bolts. The torque driving the injection pump is transmitted from the driving flange, through the journals, weights, and hub to the camshaft. Therefore, reducing the distance between the journals and bolts will advance the timing.

INJECTION SYSTEM

The fuel from the fuel tank is compressed by the injection pump and injected into the cylinder through the nozzle. All parts concerned with this operation constitute the fuel system. At present two different systems are used.

1. Independent system

In this system, an injection pump is provided for each cylinder and is used in automotive engines and high speed engines for passenger train service.

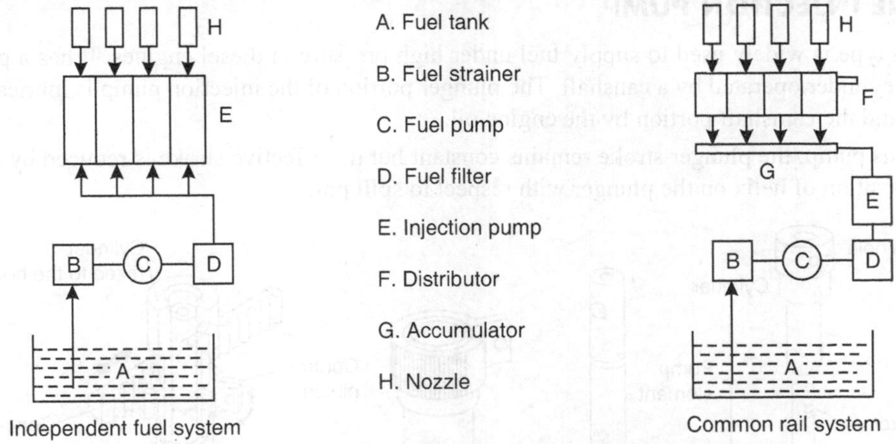

Fig. 4.26 (a) Independent system (b) Common rail system

2. Common system

In this system, only one injection pump is used, which sends the oil under high pressure to the accumulator (common rail). From here the distributor which controls the amount and timing of the high pressure oil sends the oil to the various nozzles. The accumulator is provided with a safety valve to maintain its internal pressure constant. Due to the long distance from the injection pump to the nozzles and the large amount of oil contained in the accumulator, there is considerable oil inertia and this makes the system unsuited for high speed operation.

COMPONENTS OF INJECTION SYSTEM

In this system, the fuel is supplied at a very high pressure (around 150 bar) from the fuel pump to the fuel injector and then it is injected to the combustion chamber with the help of an injector. The main parts of this system are fuel filters, fuel transfer pump, fuel injection pump, fuel injector, and governor.

Air cleaner

Fresh air naturally contains dust. If dust enters the cylinders with intake air, it will wear out the cylinders and contaminate the lubricating oil. The engine life will be shortened as a result. Therefore, dust must be removed from the intake air before it reaches the cylinders. In automobiles, the intake air is cleaned by an air cleaner.

Fuel filters

Since the injection pump and the injectors are manufactured to very high standards of precision (1/1000 mm (1/40 in.)), even the smallest particle of dirt or other foreign body would cause severe wear or damage within a short time, and make parts unserviceable. It is therefore more economical in the long run to keep the fuel filter in good working order than to renew expensive pump elements or injectors.

Fuel lift or transfer pump

A fuel pump lifts fuel from the fuel tank and supplies the same to the injection pump.

Injection pump

The injection pump pressurizes and supplies fuel sent by the feed pump to the nozzles according to the firing order. The injection pump is usually located on the side of the engine. It is driven by the crankshaft via timing gears or a timing belt.

There are two types of injection pumps: the distributor type and the in-line type.

IN-LINE INJECTION PUMP

This type is widely used to supply fuel under high pressure in diesel engines. It has a plunger for each cylinder operated by a canshaft. The plunger portion of the injection pump is lubricated by the fuel and the camshaft portion by the engine oil.

In this pump, the plunger stroke remains constant but the effective stroke is reduced by changing the position of helix on the plunger with respect to spill port.

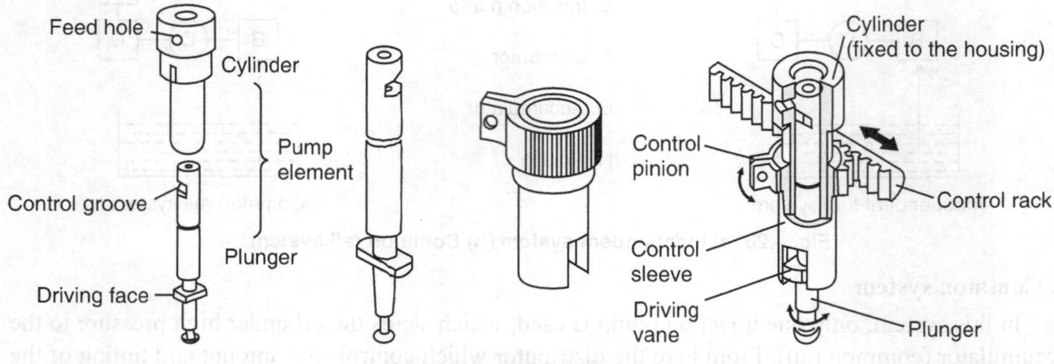

Fig. 4.23 In-line injector pump

Pumping element

It has a cylindrical plunger which is fitted into the barrel. The plunger has a constant stroke and reciprocating motion of the plunger is given by the cam. The plunger is partly machined away to produce a control helix and vertical groove. The vertical groove extends from the top of the plunger to control helix. An inlet and spill port in the barrel communicates with a gallery fed from the fuel tank.

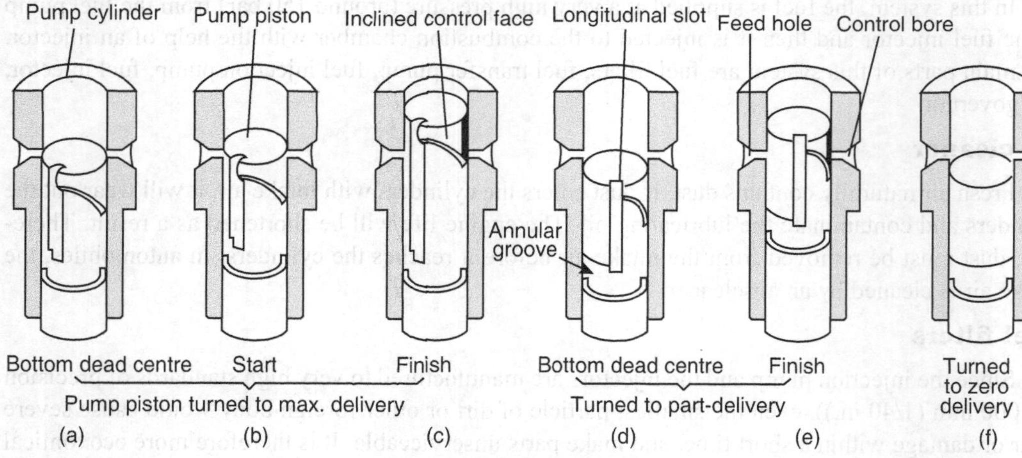

Fig. 4.24 Pump element

Partial rotation of the plunger varies the output from zero for stopping the engine, to maximum for starting. Between these limits a variable supply of fuel is necessary to meet the engine power and speed requirements.

The operation of the pumping element is as follows:

- When the plunger is at BDC (Fig. a) the depression in the pump chamber causes fuel to enter both ports.
- This position (Fig. b) is known as the point of port closure (or spill cut-off), i.e. theoretical point of injection. Both ports have been covered and so the upward movement of the plunger raises the pressure of the fuel to produce injection.

- Injection stops when the edge of the helix uncovers the spill port (Fig. c). Pressure is relieved by fuel passing down the vertical groove, around the waist of the plunger and out of the spill port.
- Rotation of the plunger causes the helix to uncover the spill port either earlier or later, to give less or more fuel respectively.
- Moving the plunger to make the vertical groove coincide with the spill port means that the port will remain open (Fig. f). Therefore no fuel will be delivered and the engine will come to rest.

Plunger control

Two lugs on the plunger fits into slots in a control sleeve. Pinion is clamped on to control sleeve. This pinion engages a control rack which is actuated by accelerator pedal. By moving the control rack, the plunger can be rotated. Rotation of the plunger causes the helix to uncover the spill sport either earlier or later, to give less or more fuel respectively.

ROTARY DISTRIBUTOR TYPE PUMP

This type of injection pump is compact, light weight and has fewer parts. The internal parts of the injection pump are lubricated by the fuel.

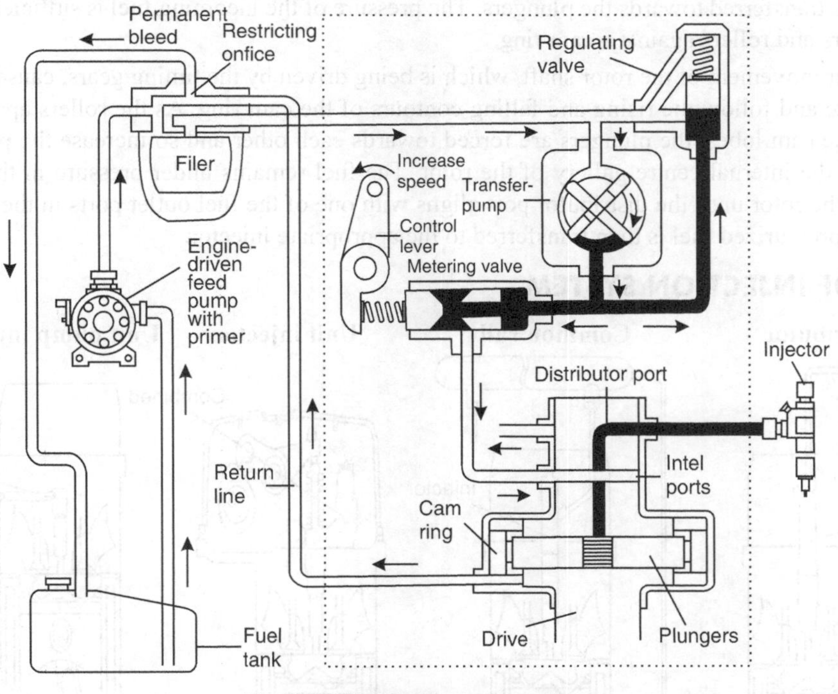

Fig. 4.25 Distributor pump system

The rotary distributor pump has a set of plungers located within a centrally mounted rotor shaft, which is driven by and timed to the engine. Behind the plungers is a set of rollers, which are mounted on a cam ring. The main purpose of the rotor is to transport fuel towards the plungers, and then to distribute the fuel to each of the injector outlet ports in the appropriate sequence. The cam ring has a number of cam lobes machined at equally spaced distances from each other. There are as many cam lobes as the engine has cylinders.

The main steel body of the distributor pump is called the hydraulic head. This contains a set of internal drillings, which allow the fuel into the pump. Then, in conjunction with the rotor, the pressurized fuel is distributed to each of the injector outlet pipes in the appropriate sequence. To control and regulate the pressure of the fuel accurately, a transfer pump and a regulator valve are fitted inside the injection pump. These two components ensure that the line pressure of the fuel is kept within specified tolerances. To measure the quantity of fuel entering the injection pump precisely under all operating conditions, a metering valve is built into the pump.

In order to provide the pump with a means by which the fuel injection phase can be progressively advanced or retarded with engine speed and load changes, an automatic advancement mechanism is fitted.

Operation

When the fuel is delivered to the distributor injection pump by the fuel lift pump, a sliding vane-type transfer pump raises the fuel's pressure still further. The purpose of the transfer pump is to create a transfer pressure, so that the injection pump can supply all of the engine's fuel requirements under varying operating conditions. To prevent the transfer pressure inside the pump from exceeding certain design tolerances, a spring-loaded regulator valve is fitted.

The position of the fuel-metering valve is controlled by a combination of throttle lever movement and the action of the governor. From the metering valve, the pressurised fuel is transferred to the metering port in the hydraulic head. When the charging port on the rotor aligns with the metering port, fuel is transferred towards the plungers. The pressure of the incoming fuel is sufficient to force the plungers and rollers against a cam ring.

Further movement of the rotor shaft, which is being driven by the timing gears, causes the rollers to rotate and follow the rising and falling contours of the cam ring. As the rollers approach the peaks of the cam lobes, the plungers are forced towards each other and so increase the pressure of the fuel in the internal centre gallery of the rotor. The fuel remains under pressure in the internal gallery of the rotor until the distributor port aligns with one of the fuel outlet ports in the hydraulic head. The pressurized fuel is then transferred to the appropriate injector.

TYPES OF INJECTION SYSTEM

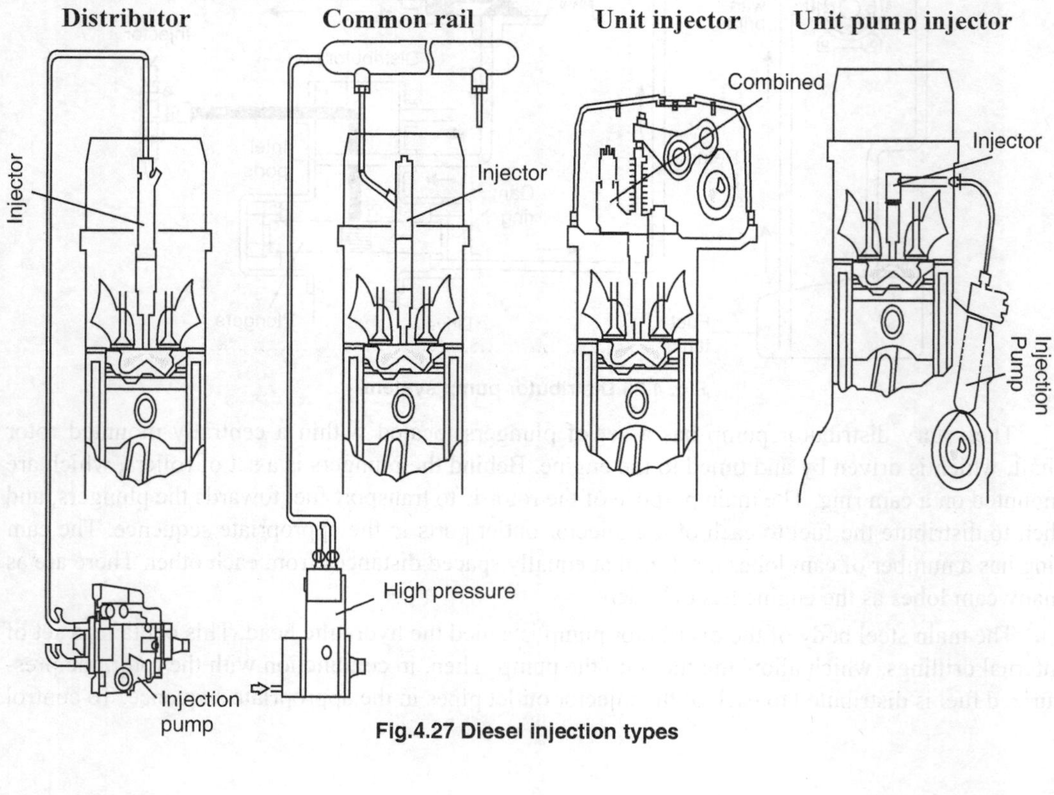

Fig.4.27 Diesel injection types

Common Rail Direct Injection (CRDI)

This technology has turned diesel engines into fuel efficient, clean, high torque and quieter engines. CRDI is an intelligent way of controlling a diesel engine with use of modern computer systems. So it helps to improve the power, performance and reduce harmful emissions from a diesel engine. Conventional diesel engines (non-CRDI engines) are sluggish, noisy and poor in performance compared to a CRDI engine. CRDI system is also sometimes referred to by many similar or different names. Some brands use name CRDe / DICOR / Turbojet / DDIS / TDI etc. All these systems work on same principles with slight variations and enhancements here and there.

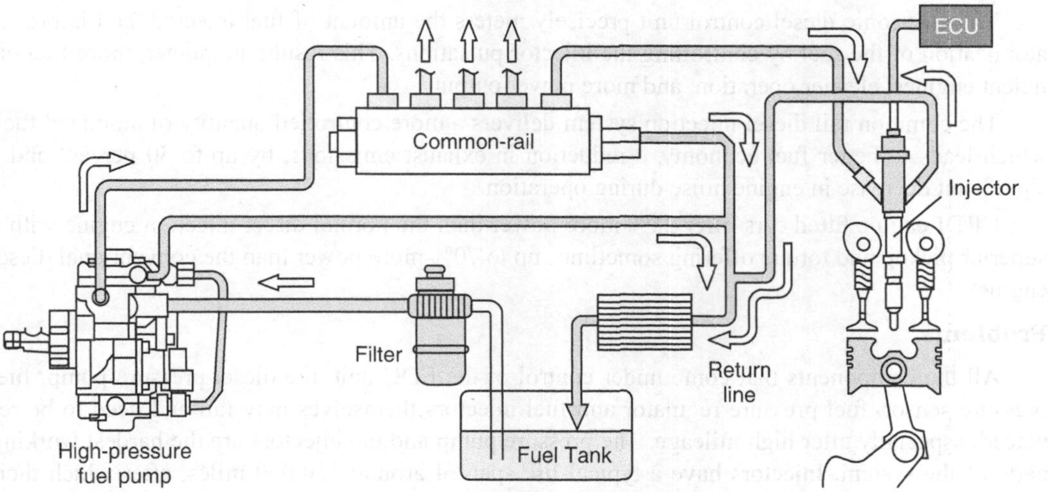

Fig. 4.28 Common rail direct injection

Construction 2

A common rail diesel fuel injection system consists of a high pressure fuel pump driven by the engine of a vehicle, a thick-walled steel tube known as an accumulator or rail that runs alongside the cylinder head, and electrically operated injectors. The rail creates a reservoir of fuel "common" to all the fuel injectors, hence the name. Unlike conventional fuel injectors, which are controlled by the position and speed of the camshaft, common rail diesel injectors are controlled by an external Electronic Diesel Control, (EDC), unit, which regulates fuel pressure and the timing and duration of fuel injection.

A high-pressure pump increases the fuel pressure in the accumulator up to 1,800 bar. The pressure is set by the engine control unit and is independent of the engine speed and quantity of fuel being injected into any of the cylinders. The fuel is then transferred through rigid pipes to the fuel injectors, which inject the correct amount of fuel into the combustion chambers.

In conventional diesel engines, there will be as many pumps and fuel rails as there are cylinders. As an example, for a conventional 4 cylinder diesel engine there will be 4 fuel-pumps, 4 fuel rails each feeding to one cylinder. In CRDI, there will be one fuel rail for all 4 cylinders so that the fuel for all the cylinders is pressurized at same pressure. This high pressure in the common rail ensures that when injected, the fuel breaks up into small particles and mixes evenly with the air.

The injectors used in common rail systems are triggered externally by an Electronic Diesel Control, (EDC) unit. Some common rail diesel injectors are controlled by a solenoid, which is a coil of wire wrapped around an iron core that becomes magnetic when electric current is passed through the coil, triggered by the EDC unit, while others employ piezoelectric ceramic crystals, which expand and contract in response to an electric field.

Working principle

To run a CRDI system, the microprocessor works with input from multiple sensors which include throttle position sensor, crank position sensor, pressure sensor, lambda sensor, etc. Based on the input from these sensors, the microprocessor can calculate the precise amount of diesel and the timing when the diesel should be injected inside the cylinder. Using these calculations, the CRDI control system delivers the right amount of diesel at the right time to allow best possible output with least emissions and least possible wastage of fuel.

Advantages

The electronic diesel control unit precisely meters the amount of fuel injected, and improves atomization of the fuel by controlling the injector pulsations. This results in quieter, more fuel efficient engines, cleaner operation, and more power output.

The common rail diesel injection system delivers a more controlled quantity of atomized fuel, which leads to better fuel economy, a reduction in exhaust emissions, by up to 30 percent and a significant decrease in engine noise during operation.

CRDI engine fitted cars offer 25% more power than the normal direct injection engine with a superior pickup and torque offering sometimes up to 70% more power than the conventional diesel engines.

Problems

All the components that come under control of the EDC unit, the diesel pressure pump, fuel pressure sensor, fuel pressure regulator and fuel injectors themselves may fail and need to be replaced, especially after high mileage. The pressure pump and the injectors are the hardest working parts of the system. Injectors have a typical life span of around 150,000 miles, after which their deterioration may cause difficulty in starting the engine, low power and emissions of black or white smoke.

CRDI engines are at least 25% more costly than the conventional engines. They also require a higher degree of maintenance and spares are not cheap also.

Unit-Injector System (UIS)

Unit Injector System (UIS) is an integrated direct fuel injection system for diesel engines, combining the injector nozzle and the injection pump in a single component. The pump is usually driven by a shared camshaft. The unit injector is fitted into the engine cylinder head, where the fuel is supplied via integral ducts machined directly into the cylinder head. Each injector has its own pumping element, and in the case of electronic control, a fuel solenoid valve as well.

As unit injection uses a combined injection pump and nozzle for each cylinder, it eliminates long, high pressure pipelines from pump to injector, and thereby the compressibility and wave effects associated with them. Consequently, it is possible to attain very high injection pressure (up to 2000 bar) so that smoke can be reduced. Also by reducing the degree of air swirl needed, high pressure improves volumetric efficiency and reduces heat loss to coolant. Therefore, unit injection also offers a reduction in fuel consumption. The unit injector system allows accurate injection timing, and amount control as in the common rail system. Servicing is also simplified. The high pressure ducts used in this system are very short, of equal length, and are drilled in the body of the injector. As a result, the rate of delivery of fuel is consistent from cylinder-to-cylinder, chances of leakage is practically eliminated, any wave effects if occur are at very high frequencies and low amplitudes, and injection timing can be more accurate and consistent.

Operation principle

The basic operation can be described as a sequence of four separate phases: the filling phase, the spill phase, the injection phase, and the pressure reduction phase.

The fuel system is divided into the low pressure fuel supply system and the high pressure injection system. A low pressure fuel delivery pump supplies filtered diesel fuel into the cylinder head fuel ducts, and into each injector fuel port of constant stroke pump plunger injector, which is overhead camshaft operated.

(i) Fill phase: The constant stroke pump element on the way up draws fuel from the supply duct in to the chamber, and as long as electric solenoid valve remains de-energized fuel line is open.

(ii) Spill phase: The pump element is on the way down, and as long as solenoid valve remains de-energized the fuel line is open and fuel flows in through into the return duct.

(iii) Injection phase: The pump element is still on the way down, the solenoid is now energized and fuel line is now closed. The fuel cannot pass back into return duct, and is now compressed by the plunger until pressure exceeds specific opening pressure, and the injector nozzle needle lifts, allowing fuel to be injected into the combustion chamber.

(iv) Pressure reduction phase: The plunger is still on its way down, the engine ECU de-energizes the solenoid when required quantity of fuel is delivered, the fuel valve opens, fuel can flow back into return duct, causing pressure drop, which in turn causes the injector nozzle needle to shut, hence no more fuel is injected.

Unit pump system

The unit pump system is a modular high-pressure diesel injection system, which is closely related to the unit injector system, and is designed for use in commercial vehicle diesel engines.

The systems use an individual injection pump mounted on the engine block for each cylinder so it is primarily designed for OHV or "cam in the block" engines. The fuel pumps are driven by an extra camshaft lobe where each pump unit is connected to the injector via a short precise length high-pressure fuel line.

This system also feature electronically controlled fuel solenoids for precise timing and the injection of fuel quantity is variably adjusted for each cylinder.

FUEL INJECTORS

The purpose of the injector is to break up the fuel (atomization) to the required degree and deliver it to the combustion chamber. This atomization and penetration is done by using a high pressure to force the fuel through a small orifice.

The complete injector, shown in figure, consists of a nozzle needle and body, which is clamped to form a gas tight seal in the cylinder head. A spring, compressed to give the correct opening pressure (breaking pressure), thrusts the needle on to its conical seat. Fuel flows through an annular groove and thrust caused by fuel acting on the conical face in the pressure chamber, will overcome the spring and lift the needle when the pressure exceeds the opening pressure. The opening of the valve permits discharge of fuel until the pressure drops to the lower limit.

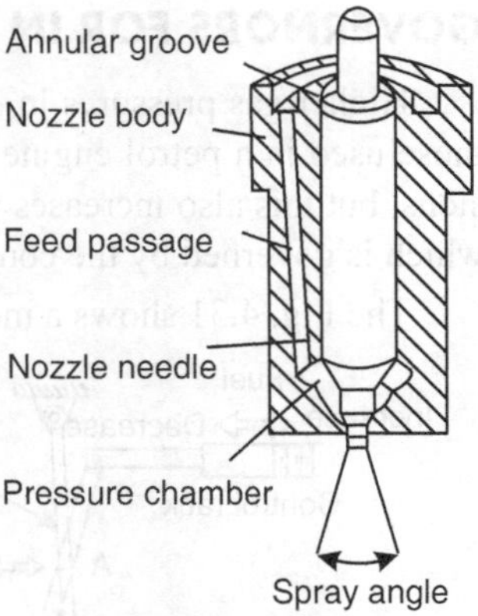

Fig. 4.29 Diesel fuel injector

NOZZLES

There are three main types of nozzle:

- Single-hole
- Multi-hole
- Pintle

A single hole, which may be as small as 0.2 mm (0.008 in) is drilled in the nozzle to give a single jet form of spray. When this nozzle is used, a comparatively low injection pressure of 80-100

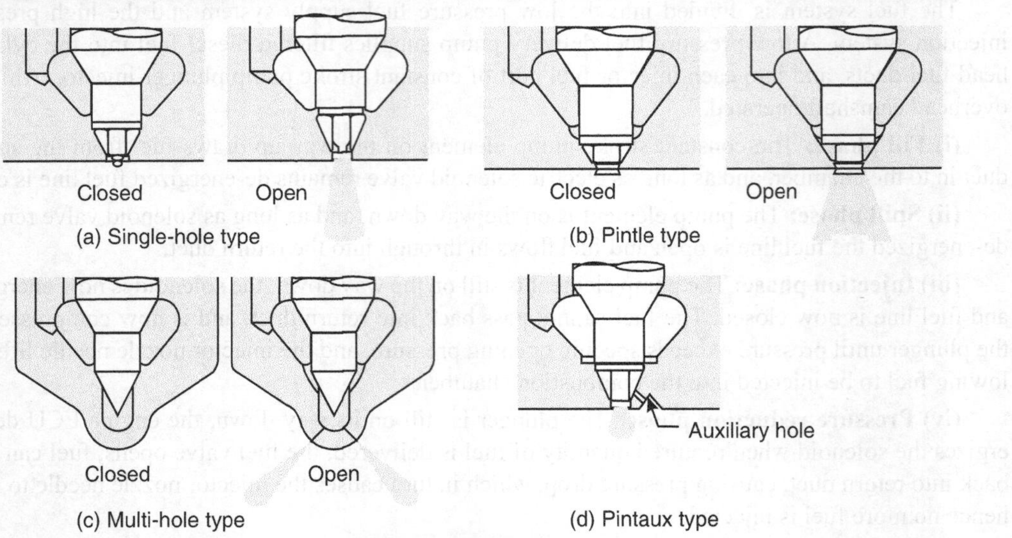

Fig. 4.30 Injection nozzles

bar is used. In multi-hole nozzle two or more small orifices, drilled at various angles to suit the combustion chamber, produced a highly atomized spray form. Many engines use a four-hole nozzle with a high operating pressure of 150-250 bar. Pintle type of nozzles set to operate at a low injection pressure of 110-135 bar. A small cone extension on the end of the needle produces a conical spray pattern and increases the velocity of the fuel as it leaves the injector.

The elimination of heater plugs on some light indirect injection engines has been made by the invention of a special pintle nozzle known as the pintaux type, shown in Fig. 4.30 Starting conditions produce a small needle lift, and so fuel passes through the small auxiliary hole and is directed to the hottest part of the chamber. Under normal running pressures, the full lift of the needle discharges the fuel through the main orifice.

GOVERNORS FOR IN LINE INJECTION PUMPS

Higher gas pressures in the cylinder of a CI engine usually demand stronger components than those used in a petrol engine. Strength is normally improved by increasing the component dimensions, but this also increases weight and leads to engine damage if the speed exceeds a given value which is governed by the component's strength/weight ratio.

The Fig. 4.31 shows a mechanical governor which is often used on heavy vehicle engines.

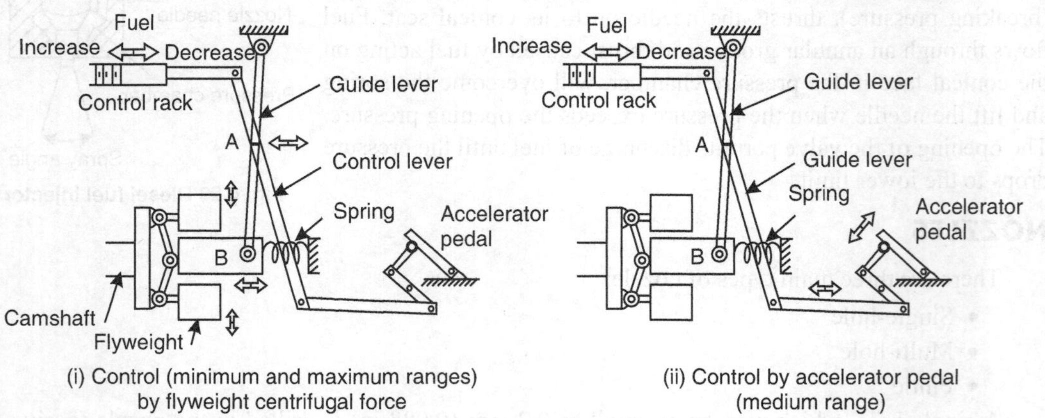

Fig. 4.31 Governor operation

To control the injection volume, a mechanical governor uses the centrifugal force that is generated by a rotating flyweight. The flyweights are rotated by the pump camshaft. A mechanical governor consists of a flyweight and various levers and springs.

Control by flyweight centrifugal force

When the engine is running close to its maximum speed, if the engine speed exceeds a prescribed maximum speed, the centrifugal force that is generated in the flyweight becomes greater than the spring force pushing the control block B. Thus, control block B moves to the right, and together with this movement, the guide lever A also moves to the right. This movement is transmitted via the control lever to pull the control block towards the "fuel decrease" direction, thus decreasing the injection volume. As a result, the engine speed decreases to prevent the engine from overrunning.

Control by accelerator pedal

The driver's movement of the accelerator pedal, which is linked to the control lever, controls the injection volume as needed by the driver. If the driver presses the accelerator pedal, the control lever pushes the control rack towards the "fuel increase" direction, thus increasing the injection volume. When the accelerator pedal is released, the control lever pulls the control rack back, thus reducing the injection volume.

Thus, to control engine output at maximum engine speed range, conventional mechanical governors regulate the fuel injection volume by using the centrifugal force that is generated by the flyweight and in the medium-speed range. It relies on the movement of the accelerator pedal.

COLD START DEVICES

Cold starting

Cold starting of compression-ignition engines can be a problem because of initial heat losses. This is particularly so with the indirect injection type. The difficulty can be overcome in several ways.

Need for cold starting devices

Although a diesel engine is inherently more difficult to start from cold than its petrol engine counterpart, various measures can be taken in practice to minimize the problem. The basic reason why a diesel engine should pose this problem at all is that even under normal air temperature conditions, there is a greater loss of heat from the more highly compressed air for combustion to the cylinder and combustion chamber walls. This is, of course, the effect of the physical principle that the greater their difference in temperature the more rapidly is heat transferred from a hotter to a colder region. Therefore if the final temperature of the compressed air for combustion remains below the self-ignition temperature of the injected fuel oil, the engine will not start. Furthermore, the situation can be aggravated by too slow a cranking speed for starting, which only serves to encourage heat loss in the manner described. The fact that a diesel engine may eventually start with prolonged slow cranking is explained by the engine warming itself up by its own heat loss.

Glow plug

When a diesel engine is cold-started, the combustion chamber is still cold and the compressed air sometimes does not become hot enough to ignite the injected fuel. This problem happens more often with diesel engines having an auxiliary chamber due to the larger overall surface areas in the combustion chamber.

For this reason, glow plugs are needed in the combustion chambers of auxiliary chamber type diesel engines. An electric current is supplied to the glow plugs before and during the engine cranking to heat the combustion chamber and thus maintain the temperature of the compressed air at a sufficiently high level for ignition.

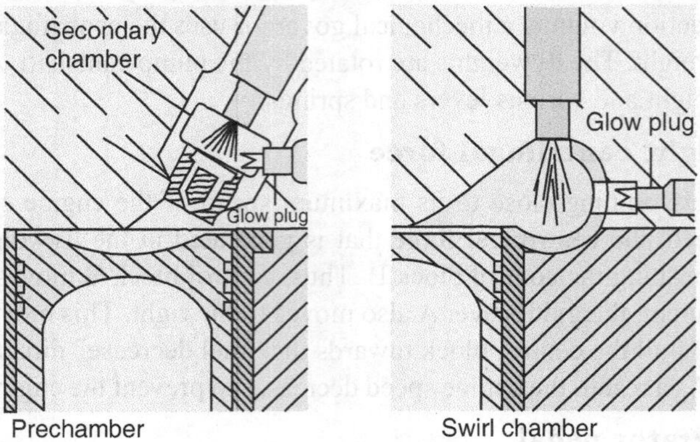

Fig. 4.32 Glow plug

Most direct injection systems have no glow plugs because their combustion chambers have small surface areas and are less subject to heat losses. In cold areas, however, the temperature of the outside air is often very low and the engine cannot be started easily. For this reason, some diesel engines have an intake air heater to increase the temperature of the intake air.

There are several types of glow plug. The three that have been used most commonly up to the present are:

- The conventional type
- The self-temperature controlling type, and
- The low-voltage type for conventional super-glow system

A glow plug is screwed into the wall of each combustion chamber. The glow plug housing contains a heat coil inside a tube. Electrical current flows through the heat coil, heating the tube. The tube has a large surface area to yield greater heat energy. The space inside the tube is filled with an insulating material to prevent the heat coil from contacting the inner surface of the tube when it vibrates.

The glow plug control unit governs the preheating period. The unit monitors the engine temperature via the coolant temperature sensor and will alter the pre-heat time to suit the conditions. Turning the ignition key to the second position most commonly triggers the preheat cycle. On some vehicles opening and closing the driver's door triggers the system.

Excess fuel device

Multi-element injection pumps are normally fitted with an excess fuel device which, when operated, allows the pumping elements to deliver fuel in excess of normal maximum. This ensures that the delivery pipes from the injection pump to the injectors are quickly primed if the engine has not been run for some time or if assistance is needed for easy starting in cold conditions. When the device is operated (with the engine stationary), the rack or control rod of the fuel injection pump moves to the excess position under the pressure of the governor spring. On operating the starter, excess fuel is delivered to the engine. As soon as the engine starts, governor action moves the control rod towards the minimum fuel position making the device inoperative.

Review Questions

1. What are the ways of delivering petrol from the petrol tank to the carburetor?
2. How does gravity feed system function?
3. Why is gravity feed system not suitable for cars and other heavy vehicles?
4. What arrangement is made for filtering the petrol?

5. Why a hole is made in a fuel pump tank or cap?
6. What is the function of carburetor?
7. What are the different proportions of the mixture of air and petrol?
8. What is the working principle of carburetor?
9. What will be the effects if the level of petrol in the float chamber is high or low?
10. What are the different types of carburetor?
11. What are the characteristics of a down-draft carburetor?
12. What are the characteristics of a horizontal carburetor?
13. What are the main circuits of the carburetor?
14. What is the use of venturi in a carburetor air horn?
15. What are the different makes of carburetors that are used in the motor vehicle?
16. What do you understand by carburetor flooding? Why does it happen?
17. Why carburetor is generally fitted near exhaust manifold?
18. What is the difference between butterfly and choke valves?
19. How is (i) the airflow controlled (ii) the air intake measured, on an electronic fuel injection system?
20. How does an ECU control the quantity of fuel injected?
21. What are the main types of electronically controlled fuel injection system?
22. In what respect is single-point injection no better than a carburetor?
23. What will happen, if the air cleaner is not cleaned?
24. What are the main parts in fuel system of a diesel engine?
25. What is the capacity of an ordinary diesel tank?
26. How many types of fuel filters? Of what material fuel filters are made?
27. What is the function of fuel transfer pump?
28. How many types of fuel injection pumps are there?
29. What is the type of individual pump?
30. What is the meaning of injection?
31. At what pressure diesel is injected by the injector?
32. Why it is necessary to inject diesel at high pressure?
33. How many types of injector nozzles are?
34. What are the merits and demerits of pintle nozzle?
35. What is the speciality of pintle nozzle?
36. What are the merits and demerits of pintaux nozzle?

5
CHAPTER

LUBRICATION SYSTEM

The engine has many moving parts. All the moving parts are operating at high temperatures and at high speeds and most of these components are subjected to very high pressures. If the parts rub against one another, they will wear out quickly due to friction. It becomes essential to reduce this friction. The lubricating system performs this job by supplying oil to prevent metal-to-metal contact.

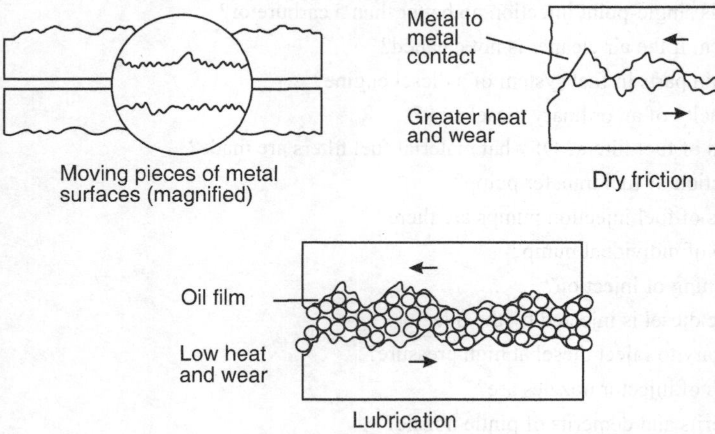

Fig. 5.1 Friction between the metal parts

It also performs the following tasks:

- **Act as a seal** and prevent leakage between the parts such as pistons, rings and cylinders.
- **Remove the heat** generated by friction. This keeps down the temperature of the moving parts and thus prevents seizure.
- **Act as a cleaning agent**. Wash away dirt, carbon particles and abrasive metal worn from the friction surfaces.
- **Absorbs shock** between bearings and other engine parts, thus reducing engine noise and extended engine life.

ENGINE LUBRICATION

The principal friction surfaces in an engine are piston, cylinder, crankshaft, camshaft, main bearings, valves and valve operating mechanism. Friction between moving surfaces can be reduced by interposing a lubricant between them. The lubricant actually replaces dry friction with a fluid friction.

The various frictional parts of the engine are lubricated by oil, which is pumped to them from the oil pan (or) sump. The oil reaches those parts through smaller pipes, passages, drilled holes and grooves. These together with oil pump, oil filter, oil pressure controls and oil sump form a lubricating system. The main parts of the engine such as crankshaft bearings are provided with positive lubrication, receiving oil directly under pressure (pressure feed). The other parts that are not heavily loaded are lubricated with oil that is sprayed on to the moving parts through a hole or jet. The cylinder walls and pistons are lubricated in this way. Some parts of the engine do not require pressure lubrication, but must still be lubricated in this way. These parts receive lubrication oil on its way back to the oil pan. The push rods, cam followers and cams on some engines are lubricated in this manner. Some parts depend on the oil mist that is present in the crankcase when the engine is operating. Oil thrown from the other parts (for example connecting rod bearing) creates a general spray or mist of oil within the crankcase.

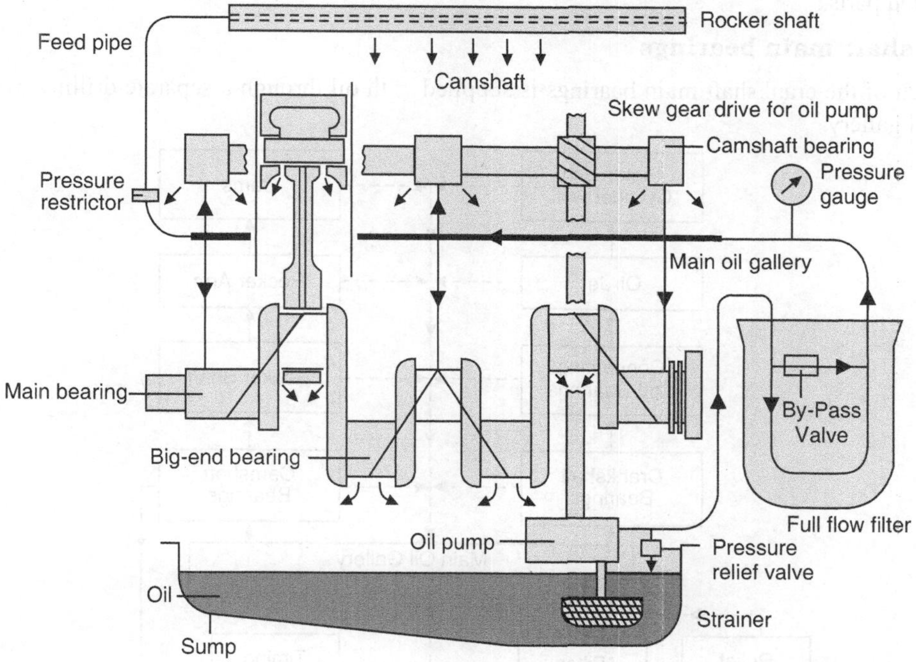

Fig. 5.2 Pressurized engine lubrication

In the lubrication system, oil is delivered to the various parts of the engine by the oil pump and after performing its functions, returns to the oil sump. Oil circulates through the systems as follows:

Oil pump

The pump is driven by the engine and takes oil from the oil sump through the strainer and pickup pipe. The strainer is provided to prevent any foreign matter present in the oil from reaching the pump. Oil leaving the pump is directed to the filter. The three main types of oil pumps are the *gear oil pump, rotor oil pump* and *crescent pump*. Oil pumps can be driven by gears or by a chain with the drive being taken from camshaft or crankshaft.

Relief (or) Regulator valve

This valve regulates pressure in the system. As the engine speed increases, pump output increases and this must be controlled to prevent excessive pressure in the system. When the specified pressure for the engine is reached, the relief valve opens to regulate the pressure. Excess oil from the relief valve is then bypassed to the intake side of the pump.

Oil filter

This is a full flow oil filter (commonly used type) which means all the oil entering the engine is filtered. The filter also includes a relief or bypass valve which will open if the filter becomes blocked. This will allow unfiltered oil to be circulated in the system, thus preventing the damage to the engine that would occur if were being starved of oil.

Main oil gallery

The main oil gallery is a passage that runs full length of the crankcase. A number of drillings and passages from the gallery to other parts of the lubrication system. Fig. 5.2 shows two passages from the gallery, one to the crankshaft and its associated parts, and the other to the camshaft and its associated parts.

Crankshaft main bearings

Each of the crankshaft main bearings is supplied with oil through a separate drilling from the main oil gallery.

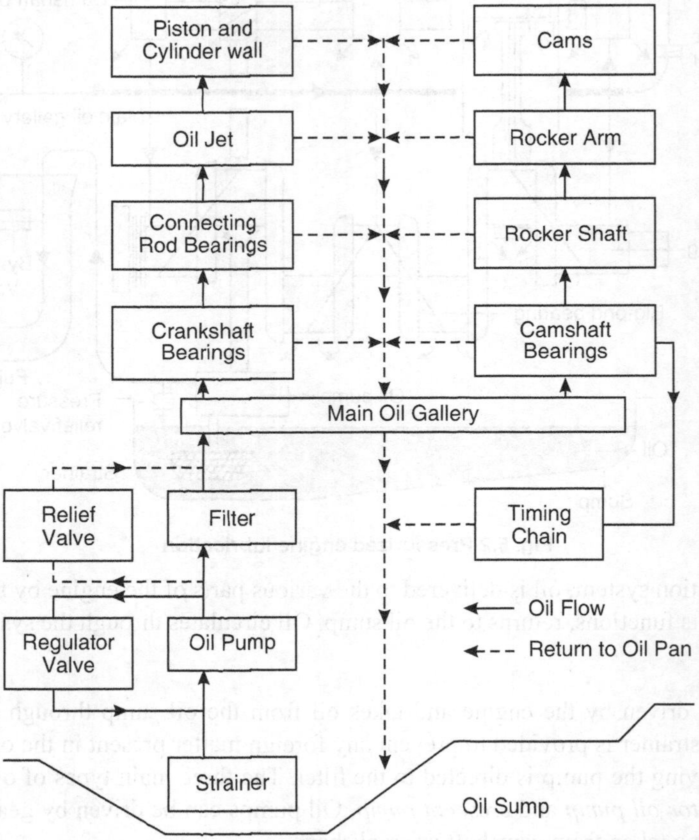

Fig. 5.3 Flow diagram for a pressurized lubrication system

Connecting rod bearings

Oil from the drillings in the crankshaft lubricates the connecting rod bearings.

Oil jet

An oil jet is used to lubricate the cylinder walls and pistons. A small hole in the side of the connecting rod is arranged to line up with the oil drilling in the crankpin journal. As this occurs, a stream of oil is directed onto the cylinder walls as a mist to provide lubrication. This happens once in each crankshaft revolution.

Camshaft bearings

The camshaft receives its oil supply from the main oil gallery. The oil to lubricate the camshaft bearings is carried through the hollow rocker shaft to the camshaft bearing caps where drillings take it to the camshaft bearings.

Rocker shafts

Drillings in the rocker shafts provide oil to the rocker arms and these inturn have a small drilling to provide lubrication to the cams.

Cams

After receiving oil directly from the rocker arms, the cams and the other parts are lubricated by splash. The cylinder head under the camshaft is shaped to form an oil reservoir, from which oil is splashed by the cams to lubricate the cam surface, valve stems and valve springs.

Timing chain

Where a timing chain is fitted, oil is provided from the end of camshaft bearing or similar source to that the chain and sprockets are lubricated.

Return oil

After lubricating the various components, oil from the cylinder head drains back to the oil sump through oil drain holes provided for this purpòse. Oil from the camshaft drops directly back to the oil sump.

BOUNDARY LUBRICATION AND HYDRODYNAMIC LUBRICATION

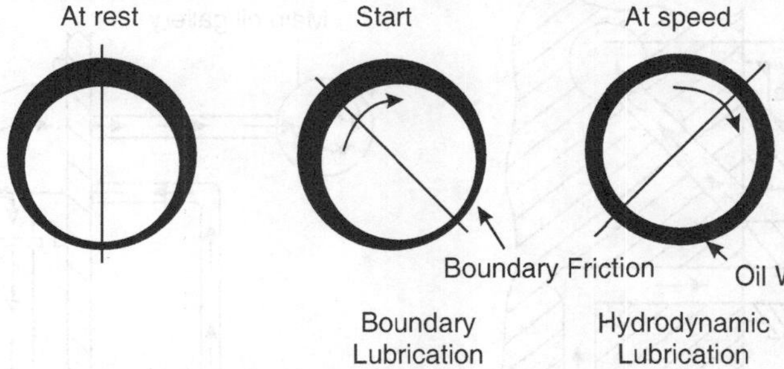

Fig. 5.4 Boundary and hydrodynamic lubrication

Boundary lubrication

Dry friction occurs between unlubricated clean surfaces. Fluid friction occurs because of the internal friction of the lubricant separating the moving surfaces. Boundary friction refers to a condition between the dry friction and fluid friction where the surfaces are almost unprotected, being coated only by a greasy lubricant film. These surfaces are therefore actually in contact and not separated by a layer of lubricant oil. If we consider a crankshaft bearing, when the shaft comes to rest any lubricant that is in the bearing will be forced out due to the load of the shaft. This is particularly true if the shaft remains stationary for quite some time. When the shaft starts to rotate, then several revolutions occur before the lubricant circulates completely around the bearings (and then shaft is floating on the oil). During this time, *boundary friction occurs and bearing wear takes place*. Chemical additives in the oil can assist in protecting the parts against the effects of boundary friction. The term boundary lubrication may be used in relation to very small amount of lubricant (oil film) on the shaft and bearing under these conditions. All engine parts rely on boundary lubrication alone when the engine is first started. This is the critical period that is responsible for most engine parts wear.

Hydrodynamic lubrication (Oil-wedge principle)

Oil supplied under pressure from a pump to bearings does not, as might at first be imagined, merely force the shaft off the bearing and cause it to float on the oil. The rotation of the shaft is responsible for this. It collects layers of the oil delivered to a bearing and carries them around with it. These layers of oil are wedged between the shaft and the bearing, so that the shaft is forced to rise (or float) on the oil. Thus prevents metal-to-metal contact. This is known as hydrodynamic lubrication.

OIL FILTERS

Sources of lubricating oil contamination: Abrasive and corrosive particles such as

- carbon particles due to incomplete combustion
- acids and varnishes formed from condensed crankcase vapours
- metal particles from the wear of the metal surfaces
- silica or dust enter through the crankcase or carburetor intake

become mixed with the lubricating oil. After 10,000 km (6000 miles) of continuous vehicle use, a high proportion of abrasive and corrosive contaminates would be found. The oil filter keeps the oil clean by removing these impurities, which would otherwise find their way through the oil passages to the bearings and other surfaces. The pleated paper filter element is porous to allow oil flow without restriction, but the pores are fine enough to filter out the impurities in the oil. There are two general types of filters: full-flow filters and bypass filters.

Full-flow filters

All the oil delivered from the pump passes through the filter on its way to the bearings and other engine parts, so that only filtered oil is used for lubrication, provided the filter is in good condition.

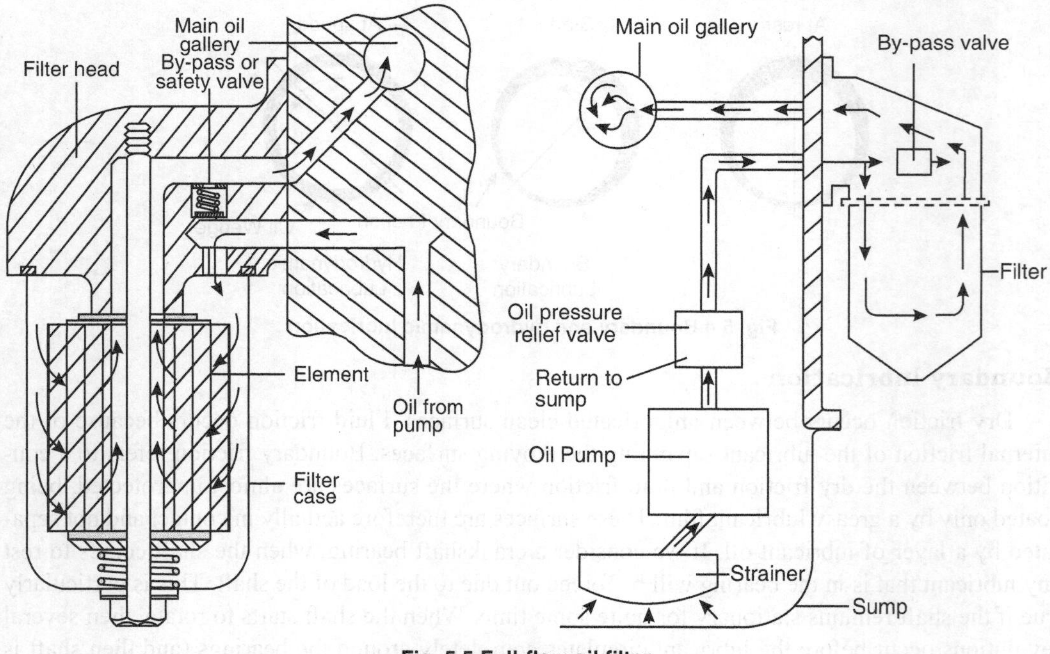

Fig. 5.5 Full-flow oil filter

A relief valve is located in the filter so that if the filter becomes clogged, the relief valve will open and continue to supply oil to the system. Full-flow filter operate at a higher pressure than bypass filters, and attention should be paid to renewing seals and applying correct torque to the bolt or filter during servicing, so that oil leaks do not occur.

2. Bypass filters

In this type of filters only a portion of the oil delivered from the pump to the oil ways of the engine. An oil line is tapped into the oil gallery and a restricted amount of oil (5-10%) is allowed to flow to the filter and then back to the oil sump. This oil is not delivered into the engine oil ways as clean oil, but it bypasses the engine, to be returned as clean oil to the oil pan, again ready for the pump. In this way some oil is always being filtered though not directly on its way to the engine parts.

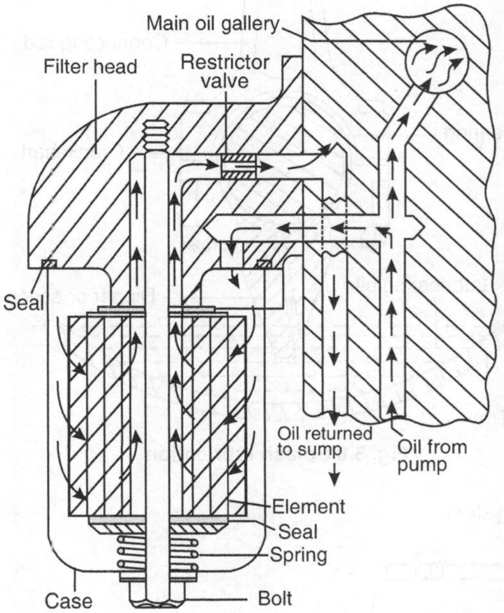

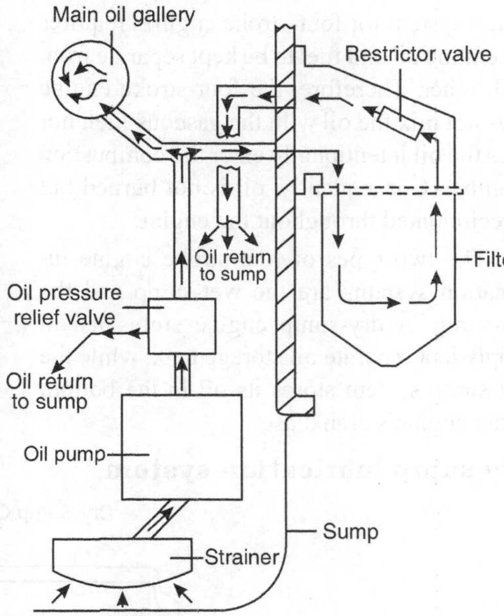

Fig. 5.6 Bypass oil filter

PETROIL (or) MIST LUBRICATION

Include a clicfrom

In the small two-stroke engine, the air-fuel mixture passes through the crankcase on its way from the carburetor to the engine cylinders. For this reason it is not possible to maintain a reservoir of oil in the crankcase. The oil would be picked up by the passing air-fuel mixture, carried to the engine cylinders and burned. Therefore, to provide lubrication of two-stroke engine parts, the oil is mixed with the fuel (petroil). As the air and oil-fuel mixture enters the crankcase, the fuel, being more volatile, evaporates and passes on to the engine as an air-fuel mixture. Some of the oil is carried along with the air-fuel mixture and is burned, but enough oil is left behind to keep the moving parts coated with oil and thus adequately lubricated. The oil and fuel are mixed together in proportion by volume. Different proportions are recommended by different engine manufactures which vary from 16:1 to 50:1.

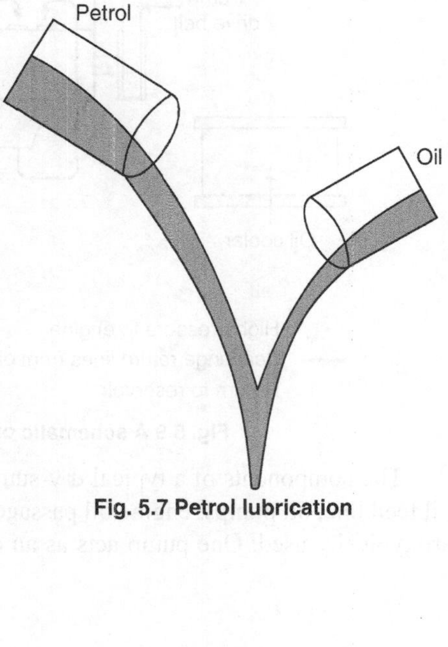

Fig. 5.7 Petrol lubrication

SPLASH LUBRICATION

Small four-stroke engines of the type used in motor bikes and for small stationary engines, use a splash system of lubrication, although a small pump may be used as well. Oil is held in the crank-case and a dipper on the bottom of the connecting rod bearing cap is used to pick up oil for the bearings. The dipper also splashes oil into the upper parts of the engine to lubricate the valve mechanism.

PRESSURE LUBRICATION SYSTEMS

Unlike the two-stroke engine, the lubrication system for four-stroke engines requires the engine oil and fuel to be kept separate from each other. Therefore, the four-stroke engine does not mix the oil with the gaseous fuel, nor does the oil intentionally enter the combustion chamber. Consequently, oil is not burned but is recirculated throughout the engine.

The two types of four-stroke engine lubrication systems are the wet-sump and the dry-sump. A dry-sump engine stores its oil supply in a separate oil storage tank, while the wet-sump system stores its oil in the bottom of the engine's crankcase.

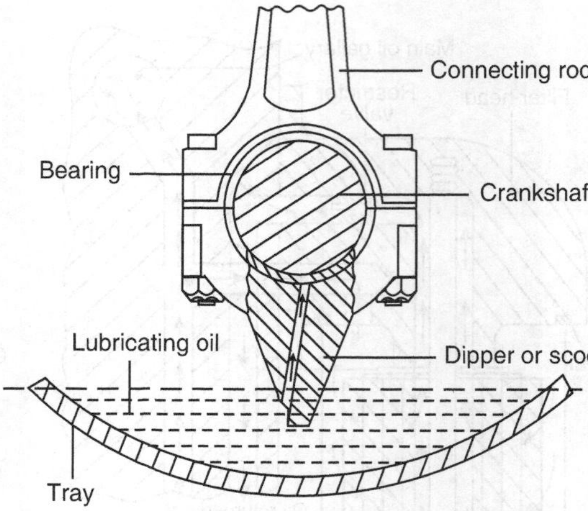

Fig. 5.8 Splash lubrication

Dry sump lubrication system

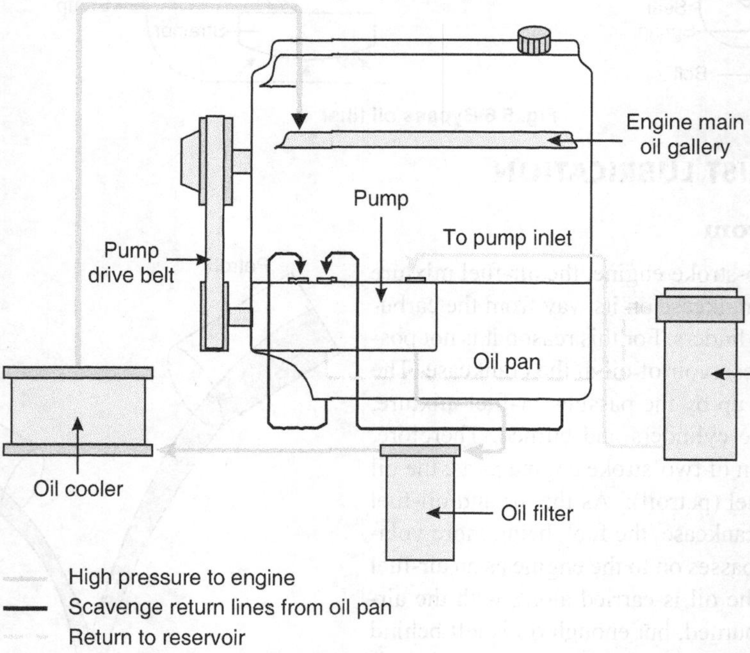

Fig. 5.9 A schematic of a typical dry sump lubrication system

The components of a typical dry-sump lubrication system are the oil storage tank, oil strainer, oil feed line, oil pumps, engine oil passageways and an oil return line. In this system, two oil pumps are typically used. One pump acts as an oil pressure feed. The other is an oil return pump. Oil in the oil storage tank is gravity-fed to the pressure-feed side of the oil pump. The oil strainer keeps relatively large pieces of dirt and debris from entering the feed line. The pump then forces oil, under pressure, through oil passes in the engine. This lubricates the moving internal engine components. Oil that is thrown off the pressure-fed parts lubricates other internal engine components using the splash lubrication method. Finally, the excess oil collects in the sump and is returned to the oil storage tank by the oil return pump.

One advantage of the dry-sump lubrication system in four-stroke engines is that the oil has a better place to cool by being stored in a separate storage tank away from the hot engine. A one-way check valve prevents the oil in the storage tank from leaking back into the sump.

Wet sump lubrication systems provide sufficient oiling in most cases, but dry sump systems are needed when engines are used in extreme conditions. They are used on race cars and high performance production cars like the Audi A8, Corvette ZR1 and Porsche 911. Dry sumps are also used in airplanes and in large diesel engines found in bulldozers and earthmovers.

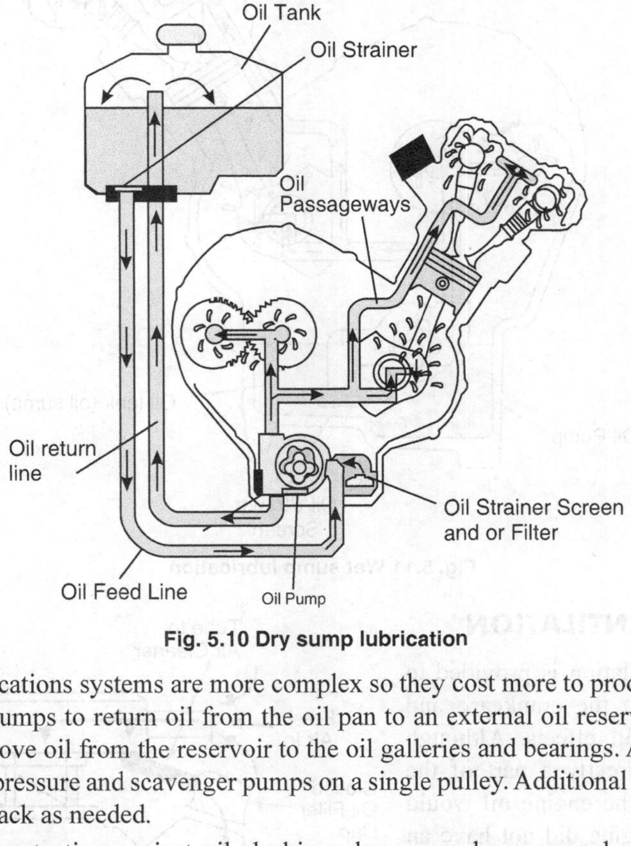

Fig. 5.10 Dry sump lubrication

Dry sump lubrications systems are more complex so they cost more to produce. They have one or more scavenge pumps to return oil from the oil pan to an external oil reservoir (oil tank) and a pressure pump to move oil from the reservoir to the oil galleries and bearings. A typical system has stacked belt driven pressure and scavenger pumps on a single pulley. Additional pumps can be added to the back of the stack as needed.

In addition to protecting against oil sloshing, dry sumps have several advantages over wet sumps. When an engine's oil capacity is increased, cooler oil results. The dry sump oil tank reservoir can be made as large as necessary and it can be located anywhere on the vehicle. The oil pan is no longer a reservoir for oil so it can be made smaller, lowering a race car's center of gravity.

Wet sump lubrication system

Wet-sump lubrication systems differ from dry-sump lubrication systems in two major ways. First, in wet-sump lubrication systems, oil is stored in the engine crankcase, not in a separate oil tank. Second, only one oil pump is used in wet-sump four-stroke engines. Similarly to dry-sump lubrication systems, oil is pressure-fed to all areas in need of lubrication. Examples of areas needing lubrication are cam bearing areas, pistons and cylinders and main crankshaft bearing areas. The oil that is pressure-fed to these areas is thrown off the rotating components and drained back to the sump, where the oil pump picks it up once again and recirculates it to those high-friction areas that need lubrication.

One advantage of a four-stroke wet-sump lubrication system is that is has fewer components and no external oil lines carrying the major supply of engine oil. This results in the wet-sump system being less prone to oil leaks. Another advantage of wet-sump systems is a lower center of gravity, because the engine oil is contained in the bottom of the engine. This helps to improve the handling of the vehicles.

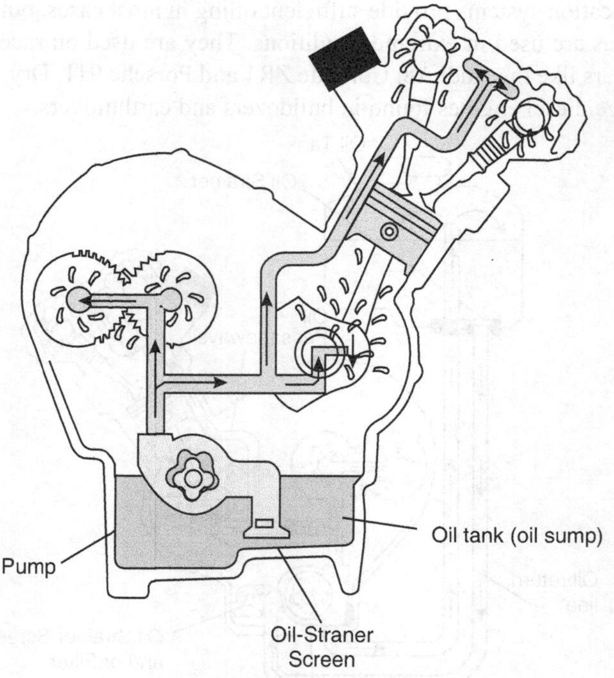

Fig. 5.11 Wet sump lubrication

CRANKCASE VENTILATION

Crankcase ventilation is provided to remove vapors from the crankcase and prevent their harmful effects. Although ventilation is not directly a part of the lubricating system, the engine oil would deteriorate if the engine did not have an effective ventilating system. During normal engine operation, some combustion gases leak past the piston rings (blowby) and tend to pressurize the crankcase. In addition, traces of water appear, and some unburned fuel may reach the crankcase. Without ventilation, all these would have a deteriorating effect on the engine oil and also on mechanical parts. Earlier ventilation systems merely vented the crankcase

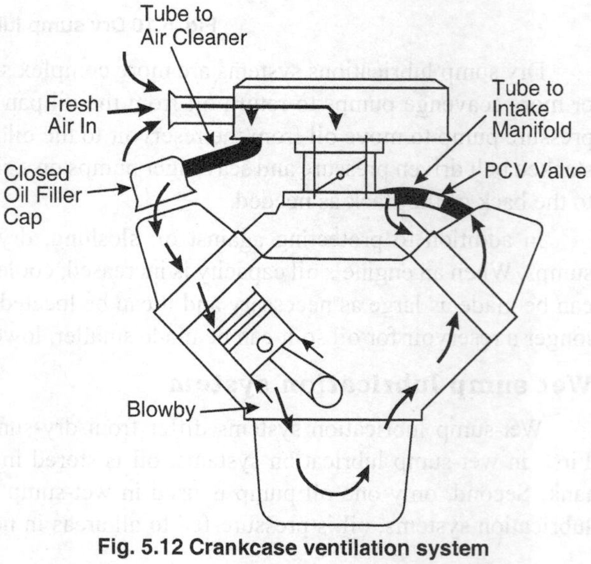

Fig. 5.12 Crankcase ventilation system

to the atmosphere, but this contributed to air pollution. It was also a rather inefficient method of ventilation and did not keep dust out. Closed-crankcase ventilation systems were therefore developed.

Closed-crankcase ventilation

This type of system is referred to as closed crankcase ventilation or positive crankcase ventilation (PCV). Clean air is drawn in through the filter in the air cleaner, where it mixes with the blowby gases in the crankcase. The gases are then drawn from the crankcase through a flow control valve (PCV valve) into the intake manifold and then to the combustion chambers, where they are burned.

PCV VALVE

This is fitted between the crankcase and the manifold. It controls the air entering the manifold at idling speed, so that excessive air cannot upset idling of the engine. If this valve does not seal properly, the engine will idle badly. If the valve is stuck closed, harmful vapours will remain in the crankcase to form acids, sludge, etc., and give poor lubrication. Correct operation of this valve is essential. If it sticks either open or closed, it should be cleaned or replaced.

CLASSIFICATION OF LUBRICATION OILS

The lubricating oils used in automotive vehicles are usually petroleum base and a variety of additives. Some are made from a synthetic base.

Requirements

The following properties are required of engine lubricating oil:

- It must have an appropriate viscosity. If it is too low, the oil film will be broken easily and seizure of parts will occur. If it is too high, it will create additional resistance in parts movement and cause hard engine starting and loss of power.
- The viscosity level must remain relatively stable regardless of changes in temperature.
- Engine oil must be suitable for use with metals.
- It must not corrode or rust parts.
- It must not foam.

Liquid lubricants

Lubricating oils form a highly adhesive, pressure resistant film of lubricant between sliding metal surfaces. If this function is performed correctly, friction occurs only within the actual lubricant. Since this is a liquid, the level of friction is extremely low.

Classification by viscosity

To simplify the overall range of engine oil viscosities, the American Society of Automotive Engineers (SAE) has drawn up a table of SAE viscosities classes. SAE indexes are usually determined according to the temperature at which a particular oil may be used. But engine oil must be selected carefully not only according to the expected ambient temperatures but also to the expected operating conditions of the vehicle.

Viscosity of an oil is expressed by a number called the viscosity index. The lower the index, the thinner the oil. The higher the index, the thicker the oil.

Oil whose viscosity indexes are indicated as a range (10 W-30, 15 W-40, etc) are called "multi-grade" oils. Since their viscosity is not affected much by a change in temperature, they are usually used throught the year. These oils are easier starting in cold weather and stability at high temperatures.

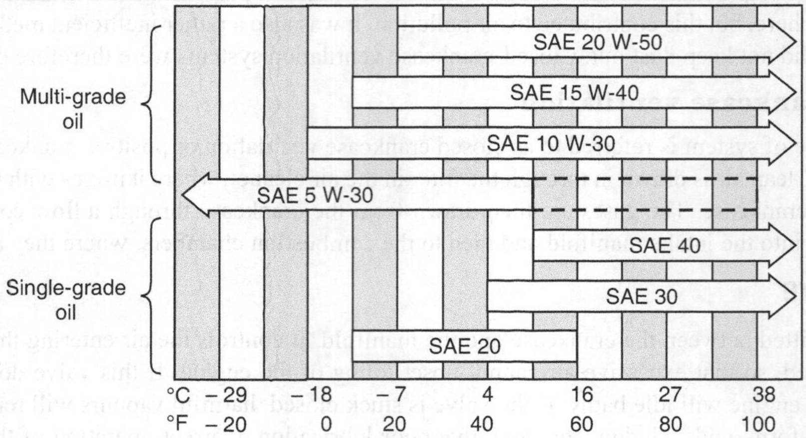

Fig. 5.13 Lubrication oil grades

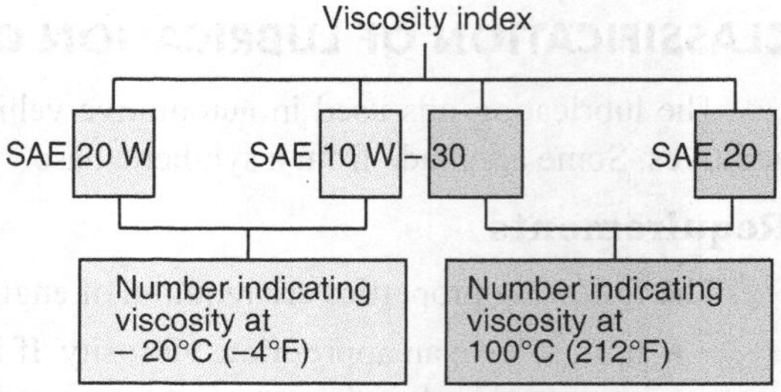

Fig. 5.14 Viscosity index

Viscosity indexes followed by the letter E (10 W, etc) indicate oil's viscosity measured at –20°C (–4°F). Using a low viscosity oil helps to start the engine more easily in cold climates. Viscosity numbers after a "W" indicate the viscosity at 100°C (212°F). For example, "SAE 10 W–30" means that the engine oil meets standards for SAE10 oil at –20°C (–4°F) and standards for SAE30 oil at 100°C (212°F).

2. Classification by quality

Engine oil is classified by quality according to standards set by American Petroleum Institute (API) and by test methods also set by API.

API classification	Service and oil description
SD	For use in engines operating under extreme temperatures or other severe conditions; contains detergent-dispersant, wear-resisting agent, anti-oxidant, etc.
SE	For use in engines operating under more extreme or severe conditions than those in SD; contains large amounts of detergent-dispersant, wear-resisting agent, anti-oxidant, etc.
SF	Superior to SE, the SF type oil offers outstanding wear resistance and durability.
SG	This oil offers better performance than SF to prevent oxidation, wear and rust.
SH	The top-most category, this oil is superior to SG.

Semi-solid lubricants

Greases are semi-solid (plastic) lubricants. Greases have a high viscosity or waxy consistency (density). The principal automobile grease categories are calcium soap greases (for general lubrication), sodium soap greases (for anti-friction bearings) and lithium soap greases (multipurpose greases).

Solid lubricants

Solid lubricants are extremely resistant to temperature change and possess a high load capacity when exposed to high pressures. The most frequently used solid lubricants are molybdenum sulphide and graphite.

LUBRICATION - POSSIBLE FAULTS & LOGICAL TROUBLESHOOTING

Problem	Possible cause	Remedy
Oil leakage	Cylinder head, cylinder block or oil pump body damaged or cracked Oil seal faulty Gasket faulty	Repair as necessary Replace oil seal Replace gasket
Low oil pressure	Oil leakage Relief valve faulty Oil pump faulty Engine oil poor quality Crankshaft bearing faulty Connecting rod bearing faulty Oil filter clogged	Repair as necessary Repair relief valve Repair oil pump Replace engine oil Replace bearing Replace bearing Replace oil filter
High oil pressure	Relief valve faulty	Repair relief valve

Review Questions

1. What will happen, if lubrication is not done?
2. What are the advantages of lubrication?
3. What is lubrication?
4. What are the different devices used for lubrication of motor vehicles?
5. What are the different systems of lubrication?
6. What is meant by forced lubrication system?
7. What is meant by splash lubrication system?
8. Name the different types of oil pumps.
9. To which parts the oil reaches from the mail oil gallery and through which passage?
10. What is lubricant?
11. What are the different types of lubricants?
12. What do you understand by viscosity of lubricant?
13. What do you understand by the term SAE number?
14. Indicate the SAE number of oils used in motor vehicles?
15. What are the sources of lubricants?
16. What should be the qualities in a good lubricant?
17. Which are the parts in motor vehicles where grease is applied?
18. When do we change oil of an engine?
19. What is the need for oil filter?
20. What are the different types of oil filters?
21. Which are the different ways of fitting filters?
22. What is sludge formation?
23. What do you understand by crank case ventilation?
24. What are the reasons for excess engine oil pressure?
25. What are the reasons for heavy consumption of lubrication oil?
26. When does the periodic care take place?
27. State whether petrol engine and diesel engines make use of the same lubricating oil.

6 CHAPTER

COOLING SYSTEM

The burning of fuel in an internal combustion engine produces heat, which is sufficient to melt the metal of the cylinder. If the engine operating temperature were allowed to go unchecked, it would burn and dry up the lubricating oil film, so that the pistons would seize in their cylinders and distortion would result from over-expansion of metals. It is the function of the cooling system to prevent the engine overheating but it must also allow it to operate at a temperature high enough to assist in effective combustion.

NEED FOR COOLING

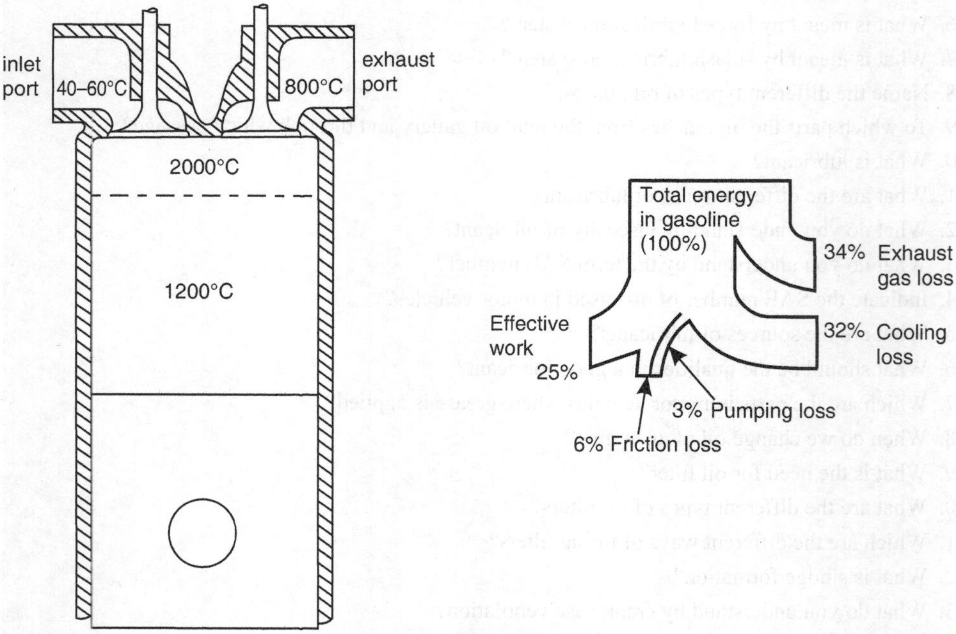

Fig. 6.1 Need for cooling

The engine burns fuel in the cylinder to transform its thermal energy (heat energy) into a driving power. But the thermal energy of the fuel is not converted into power entirely. It can be stated that approximately 25 per cent of the energy contained in the fuel is converted into useful work; 30 per cent is absorbed by the engine itself, and the remaining 45 per cent passes away in the hot exhaust gases, frictional losses and pumping losses. The heat that is absorbed by the engine must be discharged to the atmosphere because the engine will become overheated and eventually seize up. Therefore a cooling system is built into the engine to cool it and prevent overheating.

The temperature attained during combustion in the cylinder of a petrol engine may be as high as 2000°C. These temperatures are considerably higher than the melting points of the materials used in the construction of the engine. Therefore, it is essential that excessive heat is removed quickly and efficiently to avoid serious damage to the engine. To ensure that the engine operates efficiently it must be kept within a given range of temperatures. In the case of a normal water-cooled engine this would be in the region of 75°C–90°C; for air-cooled engines this range would be higher.

Effects of increased working temperature (Overheating)

- Operation at high temperatures, high loads, or extremely high speeds without adequate cooling, results in oxidation of the lubricating oil. This, in turn, may result in high temperature varnish and sludge deposits being formed, also piston ring sticking. Ring scuffing may follow ring sticking. In some cases, oil oxidation may cause corrosion of some types of bearings.
- If working temperatures are too high, excessive expansion will take place in the pistons and the crankshaft journals, causing them to exceed their running tolerances and, as a result, they may seize into their bearings.
- Areas within the combustion chamber such as the exhaust valve seats, spark plugs, etc., may become overheated and ignite the fresh charge of mixture before the spark occurs. This condition is known as 'pre-ignition' and may result in permanent damage to the engine if allowed to continue.
- If the fresh charge of mixture entering the cylinder is overheated, its density will be reduced and a loss of power will result.

Effects of reduced working temperature (Overcooling)

- Excessive cooling may result in lower thermal efficiency, which prevents proper vaporization of the fuel, leading to dilution of the engine oil by the unvapourized fuel, which gets past the piston.
- Unvapourized fuel tends to remove the oil film from the cylinder walls and therefore increases cylinder bore wear.
- The engine lubricating oil is unable to maintain its correct working temperature and will not flow freely, resulting in greater frictional losses and inefficiency.
- In general, overcooling causes loss of power, poor fuel economy, and reduced engine life.

Since excessive undercooling and overcooling can cause a number of problems, there is an optimum working temperature, and as the ambient air temperature varies considerably, the amount of cooling should be controllable.

AIR COOLING

If the engine is air-cooled, excess heat is radiated from the cylinder bores and head directly into the surrounding air. In order to increase the surface area exposed to the cooling effect of the air, fins are formed on the external surfaces of the engine. The fins are cast integrally with the cylinder and cylinder head and act as a means of increasing the amount of radiation surface presented to the cooling air stream. Heat produced by the combustion process passes through the walls of the cylinder and cylinder head to the fins, where it is dissipated into the passing air.

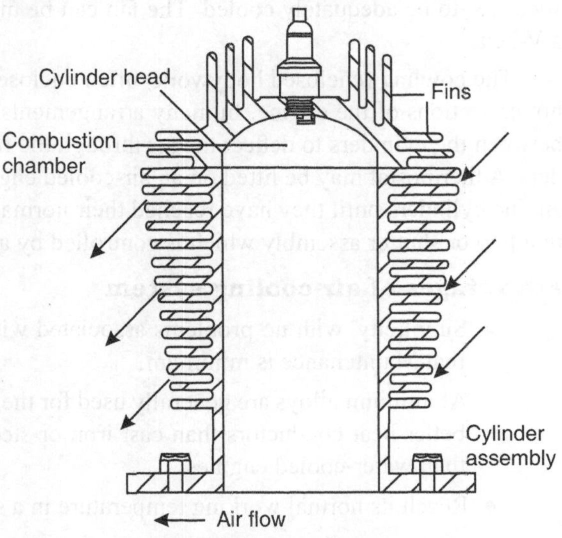

Fig. 6.2 Direct air cooling

Direct cooling

It is the most straightforward method and normally used on *motorcycles* which have an engine exposed to the air stream on its forward motion and no surrounding bodywork. To improve the thermal conductivity of cylinders and cylinder heads, they are usually alloy castings with cooling fins (in some cases the crankcase also) to maximize the cooling effect.

Drawback: Cooling effect depends on vehicle speed and outside temperature.

Fan (or) Blower cooling

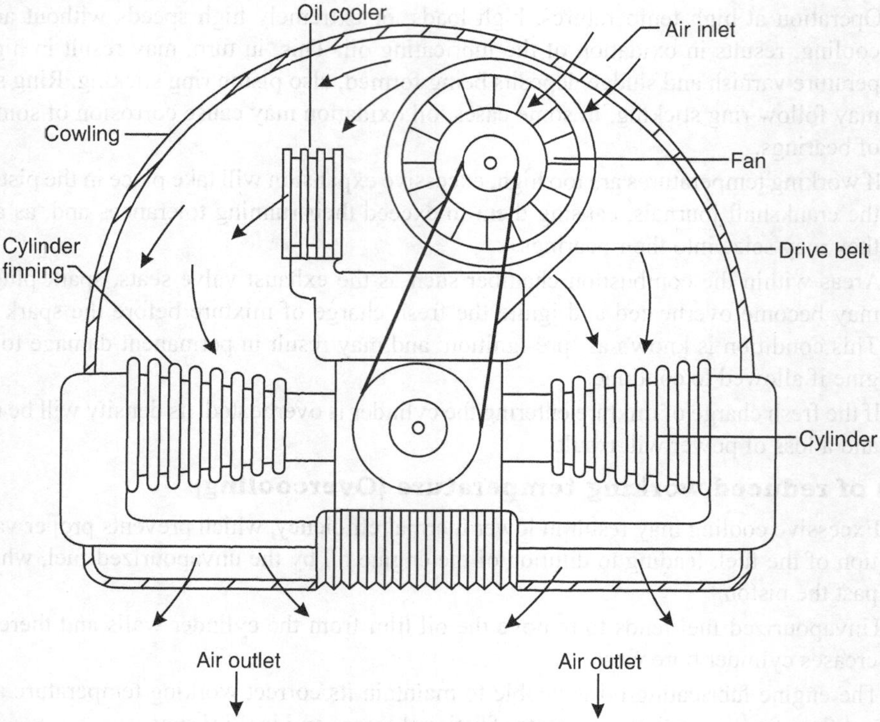

Fig. 6.3 Blower air cooling

Fan cooling enables engines enclosed within bodywork, for instance in *autoricksaws and scooters,* to be adequately cooled. The fan can be mounted directly on the crankshaft or driven by a V-belt.

The cowling (enclosed bodywork) often encloses the engine to control the flow of air over the hotter sections of the engine. In many arrangements, baffles or deflector plates are located near or between the cylinders to deflect the air through the finning and around the rear of the engine cylinders. A thermostat may be fitted on an air-cooled engine to prevent the fan from forcing air past the engine cylinders until they have reached their normal working temperature. This will take the form of a flap or shutter assembly which is controlled by a thermostatically operated valve.

Advantages of air-cooling system

- Simplicity, with no problems associated with water leaks, radiators, water pumps, etc. so that Maintenance is minimum.
- Aluminium alloys are generally used for the construction of engine components as they are better heat conductors than cast iron or steel. This ensures air-cooled engines are lighter than water-cooled engines.
- Reach its normal working temperature in a shorter period than a water-cooled engine.

- Able to operate at a higher temperature than a water-cooled engine.

Disadvantages of air-cooling system

- Absence of a sound-muffling water jacket results in noisy engine operation.
- Variations in engine operating temperatures are very difficult to control and lead to temperature variations between different parts of the engine which may result in distortion of major components.
- In most cases it is necessary to cast each cylinder separately to ensure proper formation of the fins. The cylinders must also be a considerable distance apart to accommodate the depth of fins between each cylinder. Therefore, multi-cylinder air-cooled engines tend to be arranged in a "vee" or "horizontally opposed layout", which is more expensive than a simple "in-line layout".
- Since it operates at higher temperatures than other types of engine, greater clearances must be provided between moving parts to allow for expansion.
- Improved grade of lubricating oil may be required as a result of the higher operating temperature.
- A large fan must be provided. Fans of this type absorb engine power when driven by the engine and therefore reduce its effective output.

The disadvantages of air-cooled engines can be overcome or minimized by careful design. That is why, there are still very few vehicle and all the motorcycles preferred to employ this type of cooling medium. Air-cooling is not generally used for the larger and more highly rated, high-speed engines.

WATER COOLING (INDIRECT AIR-COOLING)

The term 'indirect air cooling' refers to the conventional liquid-or water-cooled engine. In a water-cooled system the heat from the cylinders is transferred to the coolant contained in jackets surrounding the cylinders. This coolant then passes through a radiator which transfers heat to the cool air flowing around it.

In the modern internal combustion engine, the rate of coolant circulation must be rapid enough to ensure that localized pockets of relatively stagnant water are not formed, otherwise local overheating will take place even though the coolant may be at a comparatively low temperature. If local overheating does occur, the area affected will rise to a temperature considerably higher than the general temperature of the surrounding metal and this results in heavy localized 'heat stress' which may eventually cause the metal to crack. It is therefore very important that the rate of coolant circulation is controlled to ensure adequate cooling throughout the complete system.

For the efficient and successful operation of a liquid cooling system it is necessary to maintain constant circulation of the coolant under all operating conditions. The simplest method of coolant circulation is the 'thermo-syphon' system which depends upon the natural circulation of heated water. An improvement on this basic method of circulation can be found in the modern 'forced circulation (or) pump assisted' cooling system which ensures a more positive circulation of the coolant.

Thermo-syphon cooling system

In this simple cooling system, which is rarely used in modern vehicle engines, movement of the coolant depends upon the natural circulation. The water surrounds each of the cylinders, combustion chambers, valves, etc. As the water in these areas absorbs heat it expands, becomes less dense, and so rises to the top of the radiator, thus making room for cold water from the bottom of the radiator to take its place and so maintain circulation by natural means.

The cooling efficiency of this system can be improved by increasing the speed of air passing through the radiator. This is achieved by a fan located between the engine and radiator, and usually driven by a belt from the engine crankshaft. The cooling fan is essential when the vehicle is moving at *low speeds or is stationary (engine idling).*

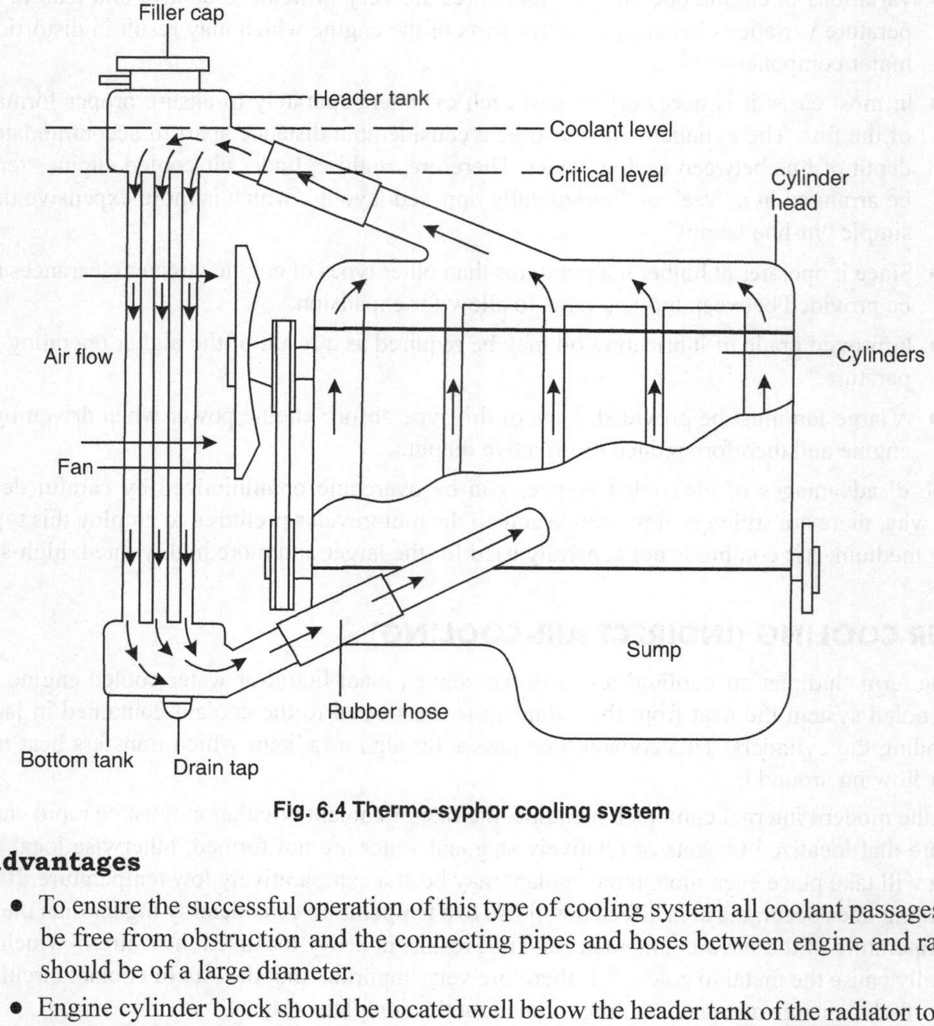

Fig. 6.4 Thermo-syphor cooling system

Disadvantages

- To ensure the successful operation of this type of cooling system all coolant passages must be free from obstruction and the connecting pipes and hoses between engine and radiator should be of a large diameter.
- Engine cylinder block should be located well below the header tank of the radiator to assist the convection action.
- Coolant level is not allowed to fall below the level of the delivery pipe to the radiator header tank. If the water level should fall, circulation will cease.
- Speed of circulation is dependent upon coolant temperature, i.e., the hotter the coolant the faster it circulates.
- Overall circulation efficiency is relatively low and consequently this method of cooling is unsuitable for modern high-speed engines.

Although the thermo-syphon system of coolant circulation has the advantage of being simple and relatively efficient in small, low-speed engines, it is seldom used in modern vehicle design because of the above mentioned disadvantages.

Forced circulation (or) Pump assisted pressurized cooling system

As a result of the disadvantages associated with the thermo-syphon system, it has been replaced by a pump assisted cooling system. The pump provides for more positive circulation of the coolant and is essential for powerful engines and complex cooling systems. The modern water-cooled engine can be divided into a number of separate elements or components that function together to maintain the engine at its normal operating temperature.

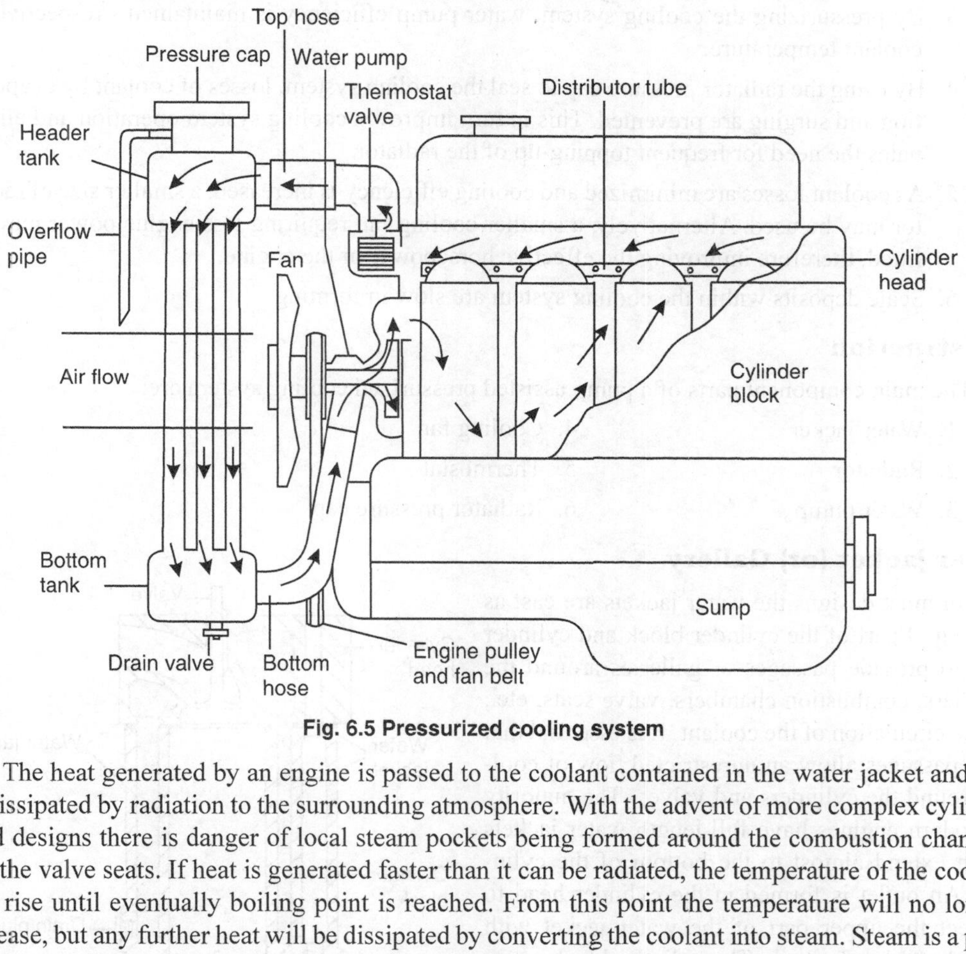

Fig. 6.5 Pressurized cooling system

The heat generated by an engine is passed to the coolant contained in the water jacket and can be dissipated by radiation to the surrounding atmosphere. With the advent of more complex cylinder head designs there is danger of local steam pockets being formed around the combustion chamber and the valve seats. If heat is generated faster than it can be radiated, the temperature of the coolant will rise until eventually boiling point is reached. From this point the temperature will no longer increase, but any further heat will be dissipated by converting the coolant into steam. Steam is a poor conductor of heat and should therefore be removed from the engine cooling system as efficiently as possible.

Water which is subjected to atmospheric pressure boils at 100°C (212°F). However, when a cooling system is pressurized, the engine is able to operate at higher and more efficient working temperatures with less risk of local overheating occurring. The greater the pressure acting on the surface of the coolant, the higher the temperature at which it boils. For every 10 kPa increase in pressure, the boiling point of water is raised by approximately 2.5°C. If the cooling system is sealed off and therefore not influenced by atmospheric pressure, the expanding water will increase the pressure of air within the header tank of the radiator. The pressure increase will also be assisted by any steam which is formed. The result is to increase the temperature at which the water boils. A radiator pressure cap is used to seal off the cooling system in order to pressurize the coolant and thereby improve the overall efficiency of the cooling system.

Advantages of a pressurized cooling system

1. The engine is able to operate at a higher, more efficient temperature without the coolant boiling and producing dangerous steam pockets.
2. The actual cooling efficiency of the system is increased by 2.5 per cent for each 6.9 kPa increase in pressure since heat dissipation is proportional to the difference between the coolant temperature and the external air temperature.
3. By pressurizing the cooling system, water pump efficiency is maintained irrespective of coolant temperature.
4. By using the radiator pressure cap to seal the cooling system, losses of coolant by evaporation and surging are prevented. This in turn improves cooling system operation and eliminates the need for frequent topping-up of the radiator.
5. As coolant losses are minimized and cooling efficiency is increased, a smaller size of radiator may be used. Alternatively, a smaller cooling fan requiring less engine power may be fitted, therefore improving the effective horsepower of the engine.
6. Scale deposits within the cooling system are slow in forming.

Construction

The main component parts of a pump assisted pressurized cooling system are:

1. Water jacket
2. Radiator
3. Water pump
4. Cooling fan
5. Thermostat
6. Radiator pressure cap

Water jacket (or) Gallery

In most designs the water jackets are cast as an integral part of the cylinder block and cylinder head to provide passages or galleries around the cylinders, combustion chambers, valve seats, etc., for the circulation of the coolant. It is essential that these passages allow an unrestricted flow of coolant around the cylinders and valves. The majority of modern engines have full-length water jackets which extend almost to the bottom of the cylinders. An outlet is formed in the cylinder head to connect the upper part of the water jacket with the radiator header tank. The cylinder block water jacket is connected to the radiator bottom tank via the inlet connection on the water pump. A drain plug or valve should also be provided in the cylinder block at the lowest point in the water jacket so that the coolant may be drained from the jackets.

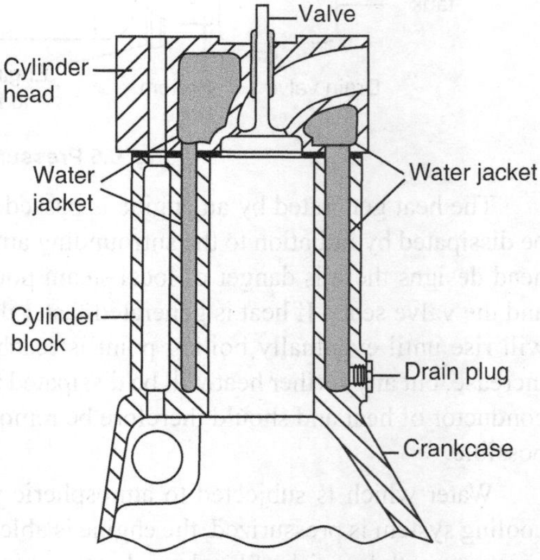

Fig. 6.6 Water jacket

Radiator

The function of the radiator is to transfer heat from the coolant to the surrounding air stream.

The radiator consists of two storage tanks; the top tank which is called a header tank, and the bottom tank. These two tanks are connected by a series of brass or copper tubes fitted with finning to increase their surface area and thereby improve the cooling effect. This group of tubes between the two tanks is known as the radiator core. As the coolant passes through the radiator core it dissipates its heat through the tubes into the air steam flowing around the core.

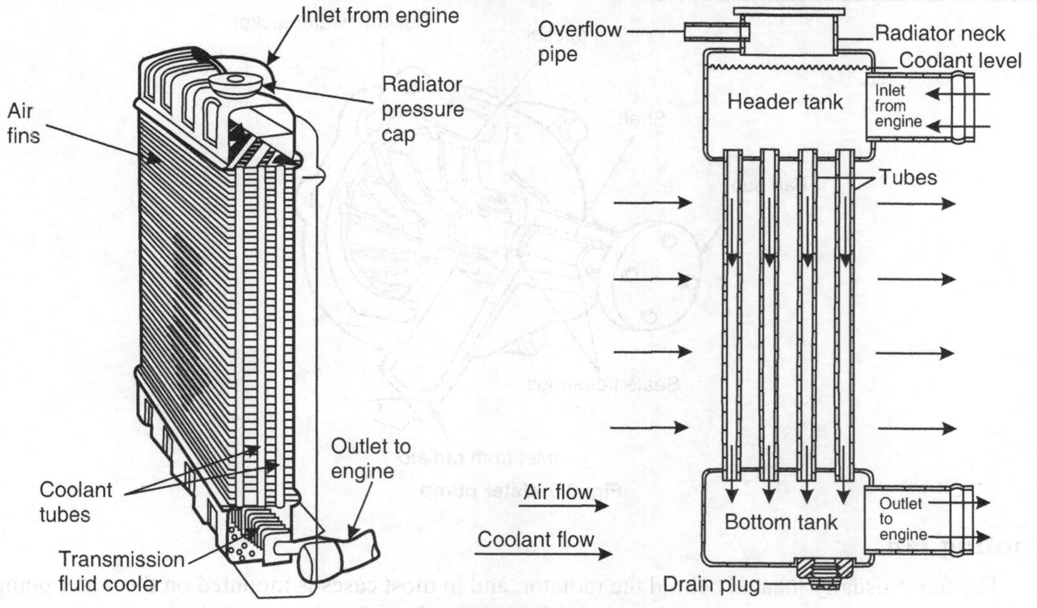

Fig. 6.7 Radiator construction

Expansion tank

The expansion tank (or reservoir tank or overflow tank) is connected to the radiator by the overflow hose.

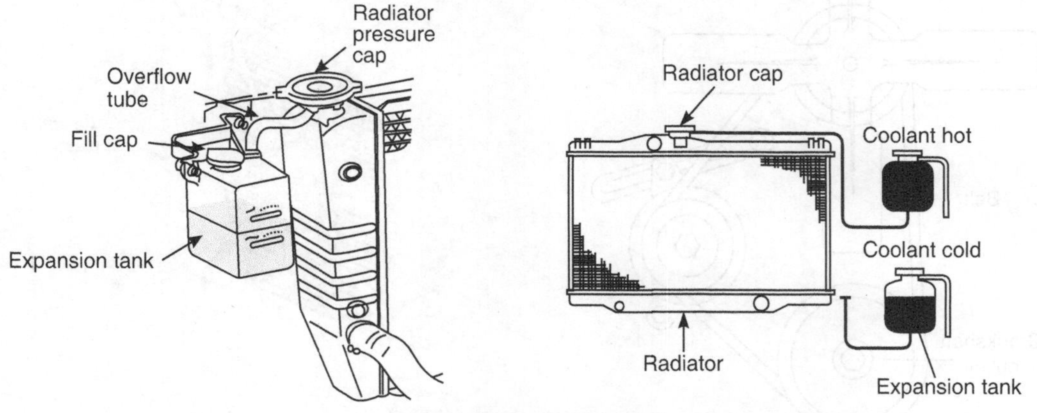

Fig. 6.8 Expansion tank

When the coolant volume expands due to a rise in temperature, the excess coolant is sent to the expansion tank. When the temperature drops, the coolant in the expansion tank returns to the radiator. This prevents wasteful discharge of the coolant and eliminates the need for constant replenishment of the coolant supply.

Water pump

To provide effective cooling in modern engines, it is necessary to incorporate a water pump to assist and maintain circulation. The water pump is mounted centrally at the front of the engine cylinder block and is usually driven by a belt from the crankshaft.

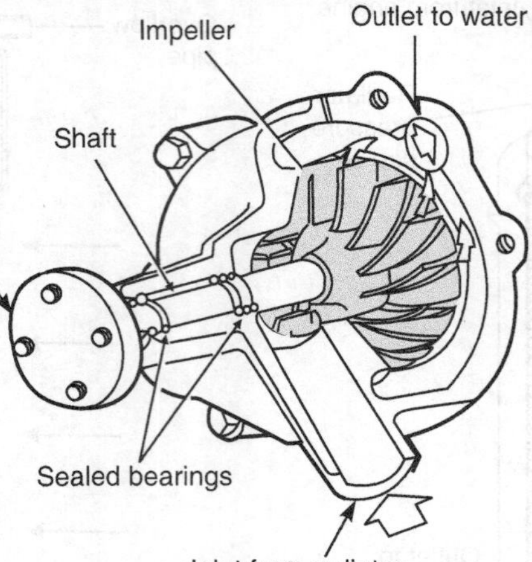

Fig. 6.9 Water pump

Cooling fan

The fan is usually located behind the radiator, and in most cases is mounted on the water pump drive flange. A vee belt may be employed to drive the fan from the crankshaft.

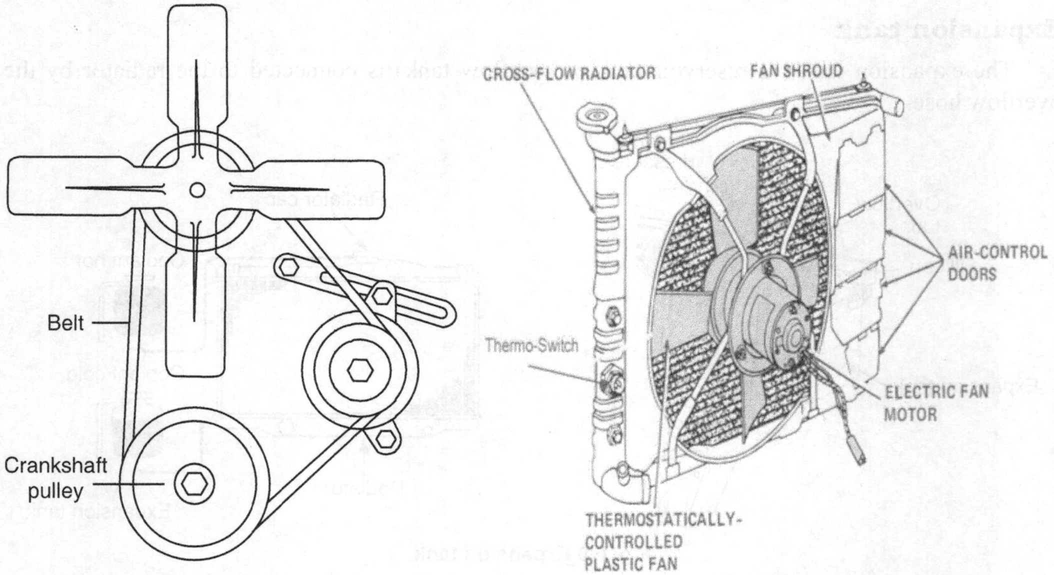

(a) Mechanical belt driven fan (b) Electric fan

Fig. 6.10 Cooling fan

The fan consists of a number of blades constructed from metal or a plastic such as nylon. In the case of a vehicle travelling at a relatively high speed, a great deal of air flows through the radiator core, but when the engine is idling or travelling at low speed in heavy traffic on a hot day, the flow of air would be insufficient to provide effective cooling. Therefore, the purpose of the cooling fan is to maintain an adequate flow of air through the radiator, particularly at low road speeds and under engine idling conditions. Air flowing through the radiator assists in dissipating the heat of the coolant flowing through the radiator core. Care must be taken with the design of the fan, as the amount of power absorbed in driving the fan increases with engine speed. Furthermore, by increasing the number of blades the fan size can be reduced and improvements in efficiency obtained.

Thermostat

The thermostat is usually located between the cylinder head (water jacket outlet) and the header tank of the radiator. Its exact location varies with engine application.

Internal combustion engines are designed to operate most efficiently at a particular temperature (operating or working temperature) and it is most important that this temperature should be attained as soon as possible after starting the engine, and then maintained. The thermostat continues to control the flow of coolant to prevent overheating or overcooling and ensure that the engine will operate at its most efficient temperature. Therefore the function of a thermostat is to maintain ideal engine working temperature, which it does by controlling the rate of coolant flow through the radiator according to engine operating conditions.

The opening and closing of the thermostat is controlled by the temperature of the coolant in the system. When the coolant is cold and during the 'warm-up' period, the thermostat remains closed and the water pump circulates the coolant through the cylinder block and cylinder head only. As the normal operating temperature is reached, the valve opens to allow the coolant to circulate throughout the entire system. The thermostat is usually marked with the temperature at which the valve begins to open. A standard temperature range used in modern engines may be in the region of 80°C to 90°C and the valve should be fully opened at 93°C. However, this range will be recommended by the manufacturers. Thermostats are of the bellows type and wax type.

Bellows type thermostat

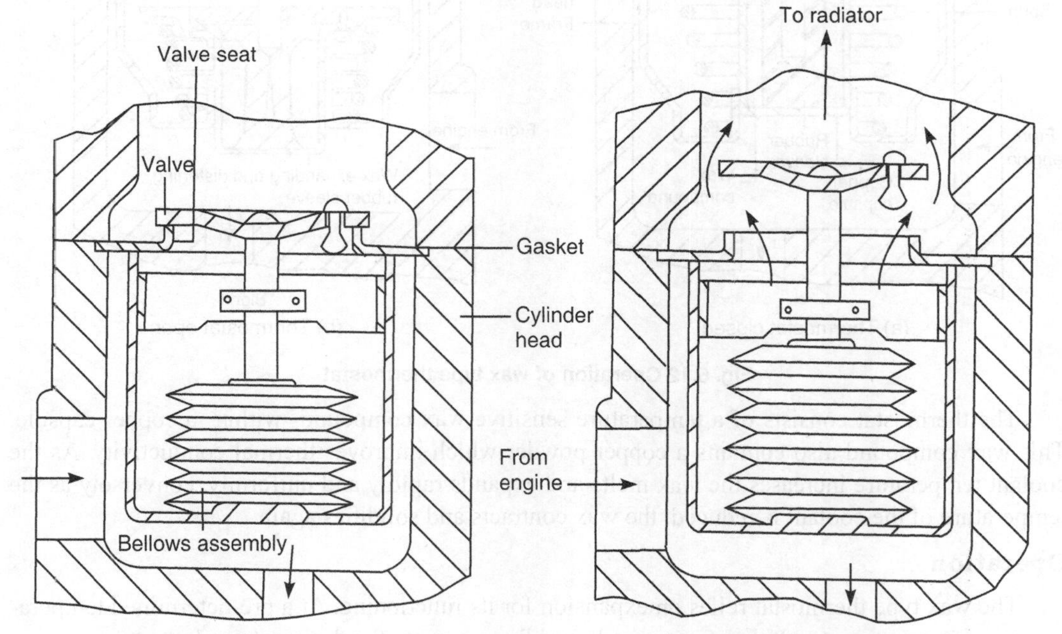

Fig. 6.11 Operation of Bellows type thermostat

The unit comprises a disc valve and seat with the valve attached to a brass bellows. These bellows contain a volatile liquid, which is usually a mixture of methyl alcohol and water, in a partial vacuum.

Operation

The thermostat is a heat-sensitive valve, which opens and closes according to the temperature of the coolant acting upon it.

Engine cold: When the engine is cold, the disc valve of the thermostat is held on its seating by the contraction of the bellows. In this situation there can be no flow of coolant between the cylinder head and the radiator.

Engine hot: As the engine warms up, the coolant in the jacket is heated, which in turn heats the volatile liquid contained within the bellows. This increase in pressure causes the bellows to expand and lift the valve off its seat. The coolant is then free to flow through the open valve and circulate through the radiator to be cooled.

Wax type thermostat

In most engines the wax thermostat has almost completely superseded the bellows type. The wax type thermostat has a stronger action and is more reliable in service. It is not affected by normal coolant pressures and is particularly suitable for cooling systems where the operating pressures are in excess of 48 kPa.

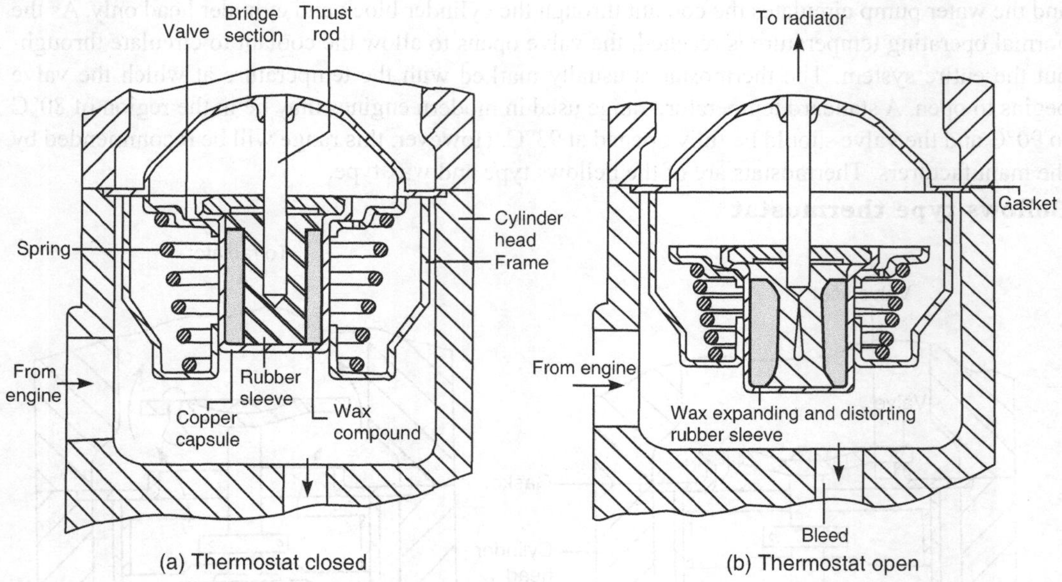

Fig. 6.12 Operation of wax type thermostat

The thermostat consists of a temperature sensitive wax compound within a copper capsule. This wax compound also contains a copper powder which improves thermal conductivity. As the coolant temperature increases the wax melts and expands rapidly and uniformly, conversely as the temperature of the coolant is reduced, the wax contracts and solidifies again.

Operation

The wax type thermostat relies on expansion for its functioning. At a pre-determined temperature (working temperature), the wax expands rapidly to operate the thermostat valve.

Engine cold: At lower temperatures the thermostat valve is held in the closed position by spring pressure so that the coolant may only circulate around the engine cylinder block. There is no flow of coolant between the radiator and engine.

Engine hot: As the coolant in the engine begins to absorb heat and reaches a pre-determined temperature, the small quantity of wax contained in the capsule melts and begins to expand rapidly. Due to the construction of the capsule, the expansion force of the wax exerts pressure through the synthetic rubber sleeve on to the thrust rod which is located at the top by the bridge section. As the rod is retained by the bridge section and cannot move, the capsule is gradually forced downwards against spring pressure, opening the valve which is attached to it, and allowing the flow of coolant between the engine and radiator. Once the coolant temperature is reduced, the wax contacts and solidifies and the spring closes, preventing the flow of coolant.

ANTI-FREEZE AND INHIBITING SOLUTIONS

Anti-freeze

Although water is coolant used in a liquid cooling system, there is a major disadvantage in its use. When cooled to 0°C, it freezes. When water is frozen, the solid mass expands and exerts a force against the internal surfaces of the cooling system, so that the cylinder block casting may be damaged and cracked. Furthermore, radiator tubes and connections may split if the water contained within them freezes. Adequate protection must be provided for the engine during the cold winter months to ensure that damage does not occur as a result of the effects of frost.

Anti-freeze lowers the freezing point of water and gives a margin of safety in cold operating conditions.There are two anti-freezes in common use:

Methyl alcohol (methanol): When mixed with water in correct proportions, methanol will provide adequate protection at very low temperatures. It is least favoured because of the following reasons:

Lower boiling point (approx. 82°C) which causes it to evaporate after long engine operating periods.

Inflammable which increases the risk of fire in the engine compartment.

Ethylene glycol: Most modern anti-freeze solutions are based upon either ethylene glycol or propylene glycol. The following table shows coolant mixture for different freezing points.

5 liters of Coolant		Ratio of water To ethylene glycol	Freezing point (in degree centigrade)
Quantity of water	Quantity of ethylene glycol		
3.75	1.25	3:1	– 10
3.3	1.9	2:1	– 20
3.0	2.0	3:2	– 30
2.5	2.5	1:1	– 35

Inhibiting solutions

- Corrosion inhibitors such as benzotriazole or tolytriazole are added which prevent corrosive attack on the internal components of the cooling system.
- Other compounds such as phosphoric acid and sodium tetraborate may be added to improve the quality of the anti-freeze solution.
- A dye stuff like fluorescein may be used to give the solution an identifying colour.

Cooling system - Possible faults & logical troubleshooting

Problem	Possible cause	Remedy
Engine overheats	Fan belt loose or missing	Adjust or replace belt
	Dirt, leaves or insects on radiator or condenser	Clean radiator or condenser
	Hoses, water pump, thermostat housing, radiator, heater, core plugs or head gasket leakage	Repair as necessary
	Thermostat faulty	Check thermostat
	Ignition timing retarded	Set timing
	Radiator hose plugged or rotted	Replace hose

	Water pump faulty Radiator plugged or cap faulty Cylinder head or block cracked or plugged	Replace fluid coupling Check radiator Repair as necessary

Review Questions

1. Why it is necessary to keep on cooling the internal combustion engine?
2. What are the different methods of cooling the engine?
3. How does air cooling system cools the engine?
4. How the hot water of engine comes back into the radiator?
5. What is the process of water getting cool in a radiator?
6. What are the advantages and disadvantages of air cooling system?
7. What are the advantages and disadvantages of water cooling system?
8. What is the function of thermostat valve in water cooling system? How does it work?
9. What measures can be taken to ensure that in the cold region the water does not freeze in the radiator?
10. What are the contents of the anti-freeze lotion?
11. What are the possible reasons because of which the engine gets excessively hot?
12. What are the indications of an overheated engine?
13. Why should not an engine be allowed to run over cool?
14. Explain why anti freeze solution is added in the liquid cooling system?

7

CHAPTER

ELECTRICAL SYSTEM

BATTERY (ELECTROCHEMICAL CELL) AND ITS TYPES

A storage battery is an electrochemical device that converts chemical energy into electric energy. It does not store electricity. The energy stored is chemical energy, which is transformed into electric energy when a circuit is completed across the terminals of the battery. There are two types of batteries used to produce electric energy: Dry cells or Primary cells and Wet cells or Secondary cells.

Dry cell (or) Primary cell

The batteries which use electrolyte as paste are called dry cells or primary cells. These are used in flashlights, cameras, portable radios, etc. A major disadvantage of dry cells is that they are not rechargeable. Once the chemical energy is exhausted, the cell must be replaced.

Wet cell (or) Secondary cell

The batteries which use liquid electrolyte are called wet cells or secondary cells. Automotive batteries are of these types. A major advantage of wet cells is that they are rechargeable. Discharged wet cells may be recharged to their original state by forcing an electric current from some other source through the cell in the direction opposite to that of discharge.

AUTOMOTIVE BATTERIES

The battery is the heart of the electrical system of an automobile. An automotive battery is an electrochemical secondary cell capable of producing electric energy. The automotive battery produces direct current electricity that flows in only one direction. When discharging (current flowing from the battery), the battery changes chemical energy into electrical energy. It means battery releases stored energy. During charging (current flowing through the battery from the charging system), electrical energy is converted into chemical energy.

The batteries used in automotive applications are lead-acid battery, nickel-alkaline battery, nickel-iron battery, nickel-cadmium battery, aluminium-air battery, zinc-air battery, sodium-nickel chloride battery, sodium-lithium battery and sodium-sulphur battery. Although there are many types of storage batteries, the lead-acid is most commonly used for automotive service because it has been found to be the most practical and economical type. This battery can be charged and discharged continuously throughout its life.

The main functions of a battery in automobile are as follows:

- It supplies a high value of current to the starter motor and a low value of current to the ignition system when the engine is being started.

- It intermittently supplies current to the electrical units (lights, radio and other electrical accessories) when the total demand exceeds the power output of the alternator (when the alternator fails to supply the electrical load).
- It controls the voltage of the electrical system (stabilizes over voltage).

Some of the batteries for automotive use are highlighted below:

Lead-acid battery

It is called lead-acid battery because its active ingredients are the metal lead and sulphuric acid. The difference in voltage between the positive plate (lead peroxide) and the negative plate (spongy lead) is 2.13 V when a sulphuric acid solution of 1.265 – 1.280 specific gravity is added, and the temperature is 68°F – 80°F.

Alkaline battery

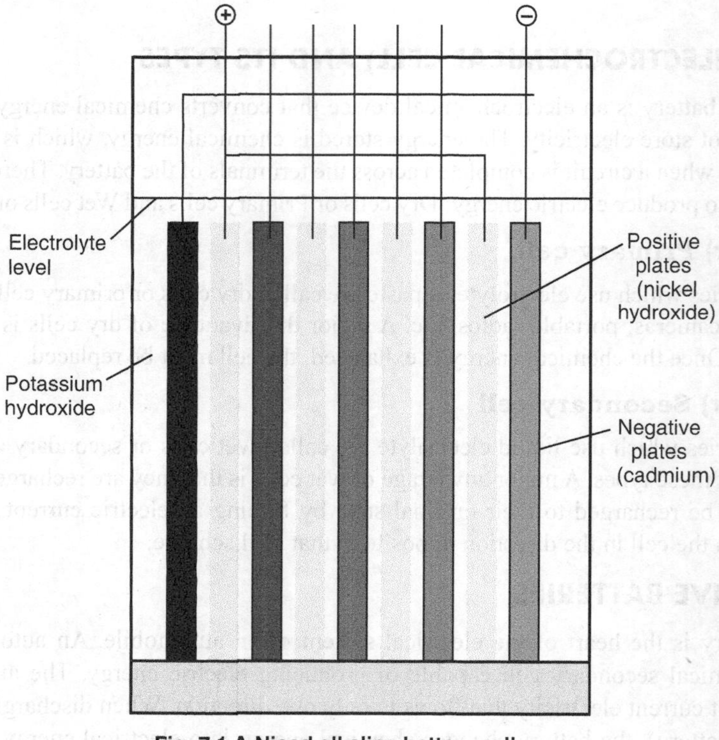

Fig. 7.1 A Nicad alkaline battery cell

Lead-acid batteries traditionally required a considerable amount of servicing to keep them in good condition, although this is not now the case with the advent of sealed and maintenance-free batteries. However, when a battery is required to withstand a high rate of charge and discharge on a regular basis, or is left in a state of disuse for long periods, the lead-acid cell is not ideal. Alkaline cells on the other hand require minimum maintenance and are far better able to withstand electrical abuse such as heavy discharge and over-charging. The disadvantages of alkaline batteries are that they are more bulky, have lower energy efficiency and are more expensive than a lead-acid equivalent. When the lifetime of the battery and servicing requirements are considered, the extra initial cost is worth it for some applications. Bus and coach companies and some large goods-vehicle operators have used alkaline batteries.

Alkaline batteries used for vehicle applications are generally the nickel-cadmium type, as the other main variety nickel-iron is less suited to vehicle use. The main components of the nickel-cadmium or Nicad cell for vehicle use are as follows:

- Positive plate – nickel hydrate (NiOOH)
- Negative plate – cadmium (Cd)
- Electrolyte – potassium hydroxide (KOH) and water (H_2O)

The process of charging involves the oxygen moving from the negative plate to the positive plate, and the reverse when discharging. When fully charged, the negative plate becomes pure cadmium and the positive plate becomes nickel hydrate. A chemical equation to represent this reaction is given below but note that this is simplifying a more complex reaction.

$$2NiOOH + Cd + 2H_2O + KOH \leftrightarrow 2Ni(OH)_2 + CdO_2 + KOH$$

The $2H_2O$ is actually given off as hydrogen (H) and oxygen (O_2) as gassing takes place all the time during charge. It is this use of water by the cells that indicates they are operating. The electrolyte does not change during the reaction. This means that a relative density reading will not indicate the state of charge. These batteries do not suffer from over-charging because once the cadmium oxide has changed to cadmium, no further reaction can take place.

The cell voltage of a fully charged cell is 1.4V but this falls rapidly to 1.3 V as soon as discharge starts. The cell is discharged at a cell voltage of 1.1V. Fig. 7.1 shows a simplified representation of a Nicad battery cell. Ni-MH or (nickel-metal-hydride) batteries show some promise for electric vehicle use.

ZEBRA battery

The Zero Emissions Battery Research Activity (ZEBRA) has adopted a sodium-nickel-chloride battery for use in its electric vehicle. This battery functions on an electrochemical principle. The base materials are nickel and sodium chloride. When the battery is charged, nickel chloride is produced on one side of a ceramic electrolyte and sodium is produced on the other. Under discharge, the electrodes change back to the base materials. Each cell of the battery has a voltage of 2.58V. The battery operates at an internal temperature of 270–350°C, requiring a heat-insulated enclosure. The whole unit is 'vaccum packed' to ensure that the outer surface never exceeds 30°C. The ZEBRA battery has an energy density of 90 Wh/kg, which is more than twice that of a lead-acid type. When in use on the electric vehicle (EV), the battery pack consists of 448 individual cells rated at 289V. The energy density is 81 Wh/kg. It has a mass of 370 kg (over 1/4 of the total vehicle mass) and measures $993 \times 793 \times 280$ mm^3. The battery pack can be recharged in just one hour using an external power source. It is currently in use/development on the Mercedes A-class vehicle.

Sodium sulphur battery

The sodium-sulphur (NaS) battery consists of a cathode of liquid sodium into which is placed a current collector. This is a solid electrode of alumina. A metal can that is in contact with the anode (a sulphur electrode) surrounds the whole assembly. The major problem with this system is that the running temperature needs to be 300-350°C. A heater rated at a few hundred watts forms part of the charging circuit. This maintains the battery temperature when the vehicle is not running. Battery temperature is maintained when in use due to I^2R losses in the battery. Each cell of this battery is very small, using only about 15g of sodium. This is a safety feature because, if the cell is damaged, the sulphur on the outside will cause the potentially dangerous sodium to be converted into polysulphides, which are comparatively harmless. Small cells also have the advantage that they can be distributed around the car. The capacity of each cell is about 10 Ah. These cells fail in an open circuit condition and hence this must be taken into account, as the whole string of cells used to create the required voltage would be rendered inoperative. The output voltage of each cell is about 2V. Fig. 7.2 shows a representation of a sodium-sulphur battery cell.

A problem still to be overcome is the casing material, which is prone to fail due to the very corrosive nature of the sodium. At present, an expensive chromized coating is used. This type of battery, supplying an electric motor, is becoming a competitor to the internal combustion engine.

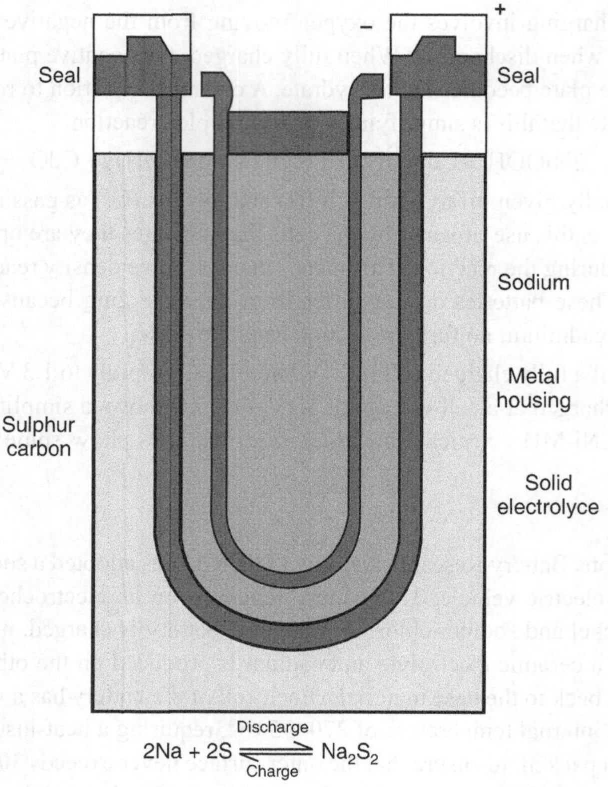

Fig. 7.2 Sodium sulphur battery

Swing battery

Some potential developments in battery technology are major steps in the right direction but many new methods involve high temperatures. One major aim of battery research is to develop a high performance battery that works at a normal operating temperature. One new idea is called the 'Swing battery'. Fig. 7.3 shows the chemical process of this battery.

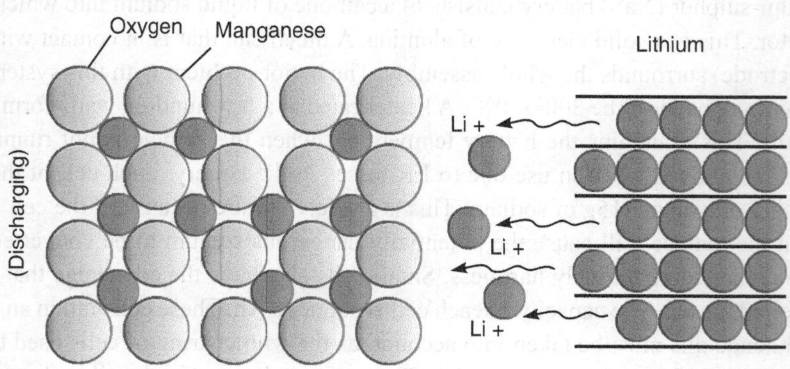

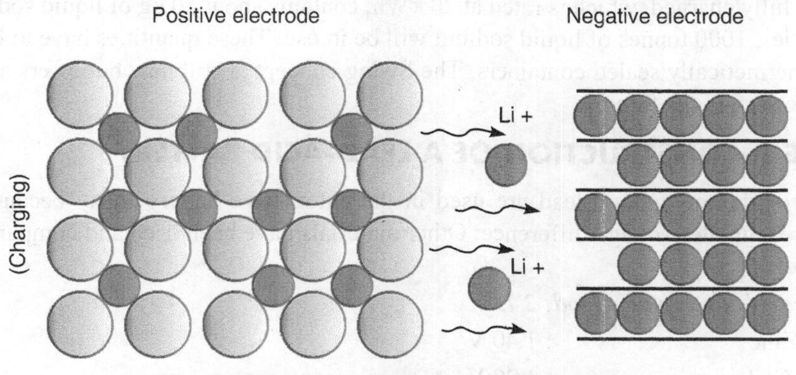

Fig. 7.3 Chemical process of the swing battery

The Swing concept batteries use lithium ions. These batteries have a carbon anode and a cathode made of transition metal oxides. Lithium ions are in constant movement between these very thin electrodes in a non-aqueous electrolyte. The next step is the development of swing bettery is to use a solid polymer electrolyte, based on polyethylene oxide instead of the liquid electrolyte.

The Swing process takes place at normal temperatures and gives a very high average cell voltage of 3.5V, compared with cell voltages of approximately 1.2V for nickel-cadmium and about 2.1V for lead-acid or sodium-sulphur batteries. Tests simulating conditions in electric vehicles have demonstrated specific energies of about 100 Wh/kg and 200 Wh/l.

The complexity of the electrical storage system increases with higher operating temperatures, an increased number of cells and with the presence of agitated or recycled electrolytes. To ensure reliable and safe operation, higher and higher demands will be made on the battery management system. This will clearly introduce more cost to the vehicle system as a whole. Consideration must be given not only to specific energy storage but also to system complexity and safety. Fig. 7.4 is a comparison of batteries considering energy density and safety factors.

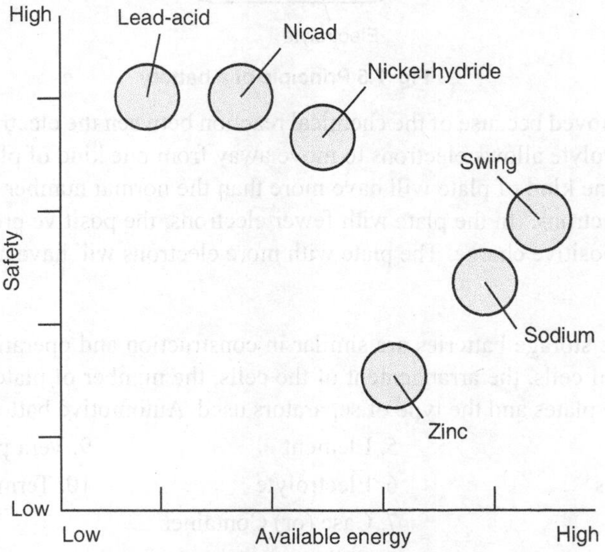

Fig. 7.4 Comparison of battery technologies

The high temperature systems have, however, proved their viability for use in vehicles. They have already passed a series of abuse tests and other systems are in preparation. A sodium-sulphur battery when fully charged, which is rated at 20 kWh, contains about 10 kg of liquid sodium. Given 100000 vehicles, 1000 tonnes of liquid sodium will be in use. These quantities have to be encapsulated in two hermetically sealed containers. The Swing concept is still new but offers a potentially safe system for use in the future.

PRINCIPLE & CONSTRUCTION OF A LEAD-ACID BATTERY

Lead peroxide and spongy lead are used in the automotive battery today because no other materials have a greater voltage difference. Other materials have been used and compared with the load-acid type.

Lead peroxide and spongy lead: *2.13 V*
Silver – Zinc : 1.40 V
Nickel – Cadmium : 1.20 V

Principle

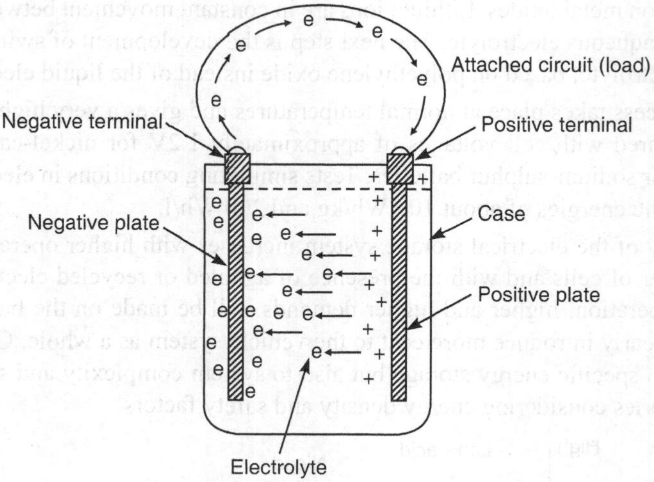

Fig. 7.5 Principle of a battery

Electrons are moved because of the chemical reaction between the electrolyte and the two kinds of plates. The electrolyte allows electrons to move away from one kind of plate and build up on another. As a result, one kind of plate will have more than the normal number of electrons. The other plate with fewer electrons. In the plate with fewer electrons, the positive protons will predominate giving that plate a positive charge. The plate with more electrons will have a negative charge.

Construction

All Automotive storage batteries are similar in construction and operation but their difference lies in the number of cells, the arrangement of the cells, the number of plates in each cell, the size and thickness of the plates and the type of separators used. Automotive batteries consist of:

1. Cells
2. Grid & Plates
3. Plate groups
4. Separator
5. Element
6. Electrolyte
7. Case (or) Container
8. Cell cover
9. Vent plug & Vent hole
10. Terminal posts

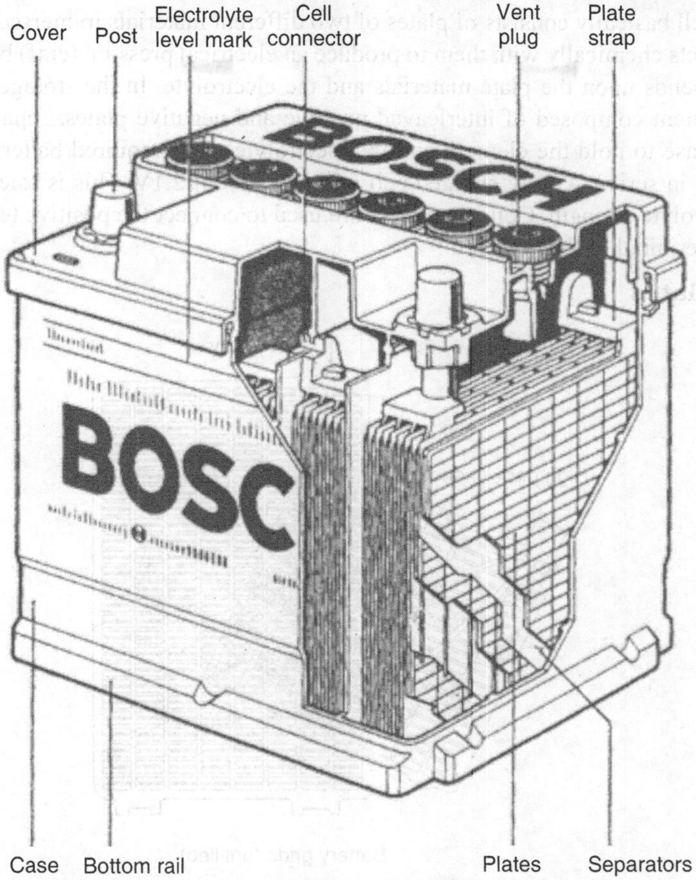

Fig. 7.6 Parts of a lead-acid battery

(a) Cells

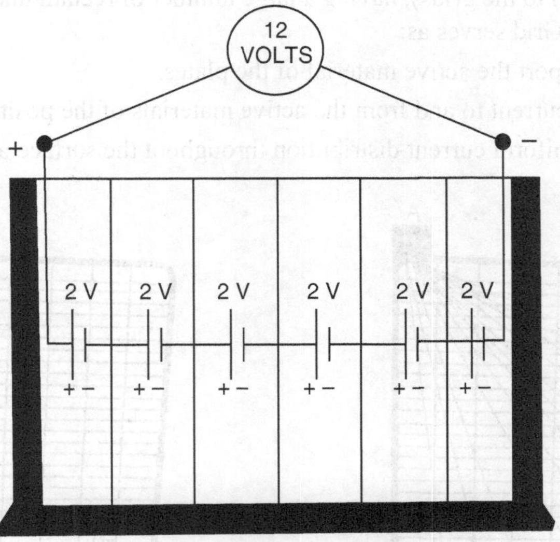

Fig. 7.7 Battery cell

A battery cell basically consists of plates of two different materials immersed in an electrolytic solution that reacts chemically with them to produce an electrical pressure (emf) between the plates. The voltage depends upon the plate materials and the electrolyte. In the storage battery each cell includes an element composed of interleaved positive and negative plates, separators to keep the plates apart, a case to hold the element and the electrolyte. The required battery size is made by connecting cells in series. A fully charged cell will have about 2.1V. This is true regardless of the size or the electrolyte strength. Cell connectors are used to connect the positive terminal of one cell to the negative terminal of the next cell.

(b) Grids & Plates

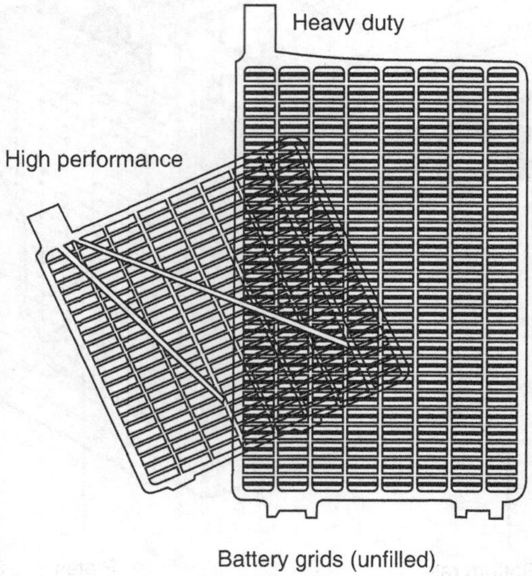

Fig. 7.8 Grids

The positive and negative plates consist of a grid made of hard lead-antimony alloy (antimony stiffens and adds strength to the grids), having a large number of rectangular openings, in which active materials are filled. Grid serves as:

(1) to hold and support the active material of the plates.

(2) to conduct the current to and from the active materials of the positive and negative plates.

(3) to maintain a uniform current distribution throughout the surface area of the active materials.

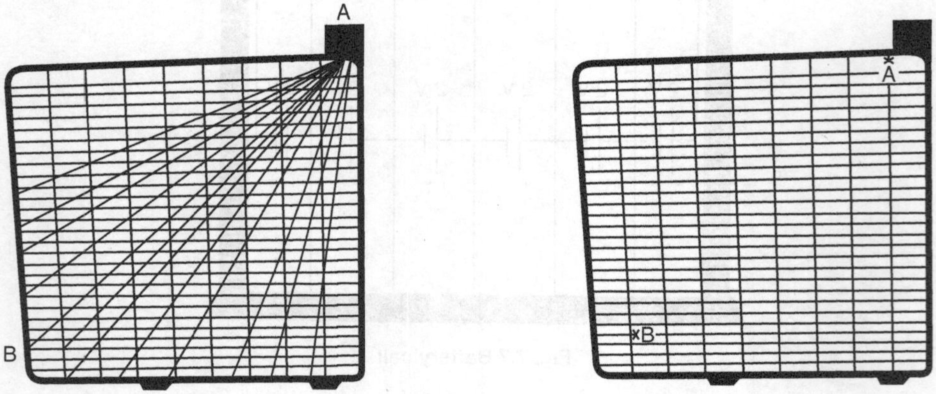

Fig. 7.9 Grid design

The active materials, which make chemical reaction to produce electricity, are stored on the plates in the form of paste. The positive plate's grids are filled with a lead peroxide paste, and negative plate grids are filled with spongy lead.

Some batteries use a grid design with only vertical and horizontal strips. The battery plate creates electrical energy from chemical energy, and this current must flow from where it is generated (for example, location B) to where it is connected to the outside battery post indicated by point A. The current must move over and up along the grid strips to reach point A.

With a radial grid design ("radial" means branching out from a common center), the current generated near point B in figure can travel directly to point A. Therefore, a grid with a radial design has lower resistance and can provide more current more rapidly than can conventional non-radial grid design batteries. The radial spokes act as a superhighway system for the current to travel from all areas of the grid to the battery post.

(c) Plates & Plate group

The positive plates are filled with lead peroxide active materials. This is a dark brown crystalline material which consists of very small grains or particles, arranged so as to provide a high degree of porosity in order to allow the electrolyte to penetrate the plate freely. The negative plates are filled with a porous mass of lead, in spongy form, which the electrolyte can penetrate freely.

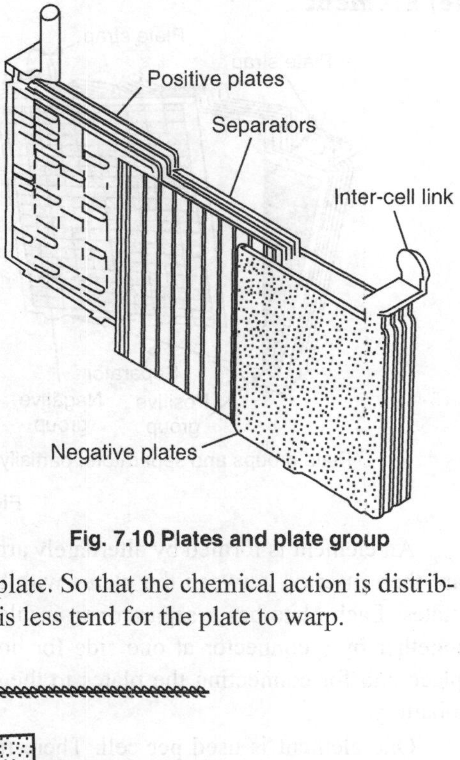

Fig. 7.10 Plates and plate group

Single positive and Negative plates of the size used in automobile will not create enough reaction to start the engine. So that a number of plates are connected together by their lug ends to form a plate group. Each group is made by welding, called lead burning, the plate lugs to a lead alloy plate strap. Thus each cell is composed of a positive plate group and a negative plate group. The negative group always contains one more plates than the positive plate group so that there is always a negative plate on both sides of each positive plate. So that the chemical action is distributed evenly on both sides of the positive plate and there is less tend for the plate to warp.

(d) Separators

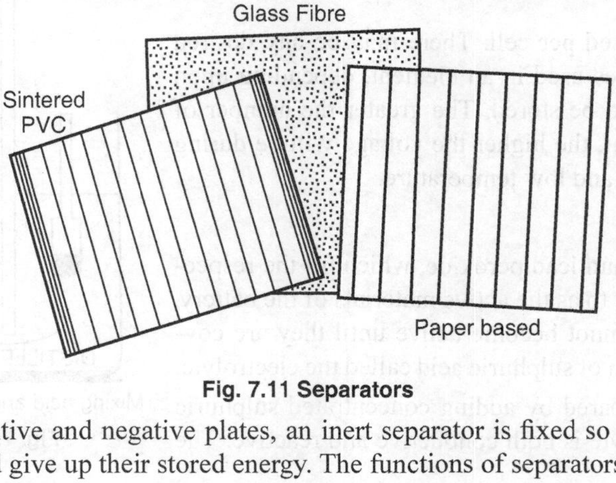

Fig. 7.11 Separators

Between the positive and negative plates, an inert separator is fixed so that the plates cannot touch one another and give up their stored energy. The functions of separators are to:

- insulate positive and negative plates from physical contact
- acts as packaging material
- provide passage for transport of irons

The positive and negative plates are always interleaved and separators are placed between each plate. The plates insulated by the separators electrically and the separators are porous for the passage of electrolyte between them. One face of the separator is grooved vertically to allow for free circulation of electrolyte within the cell and to permit loosen active material to fall to the sediment chamber at the bottom of the battery case.

Separators are non-electrical conducting materials that resist heat and acid. Treated wooden separators were used in the past, however, resin impregnated cellulose fibre types are used nowadays. Micro-porous rubber and plastic are used alone or a combination with glass fibre mats and also flat glass sheets with a micro-porous backing are used.

(e) Element

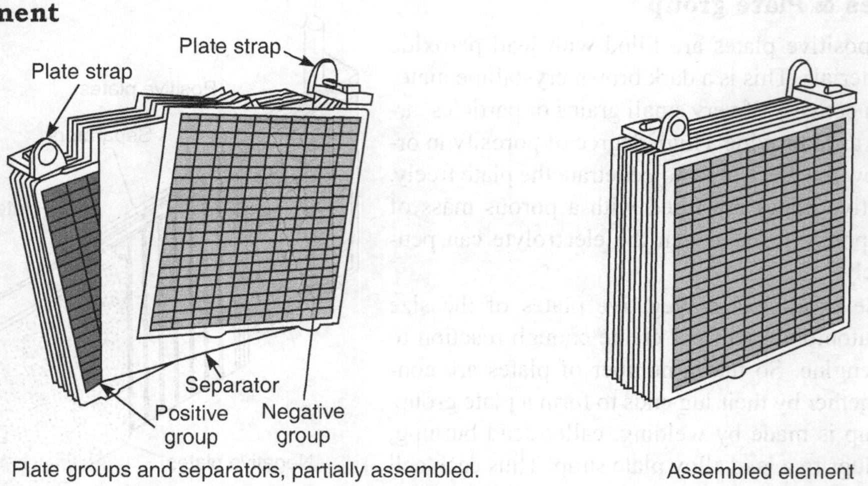

Fig. 7.12 Element

An element is formed by alternately arranging a positive and a negative plate group. Separators are then inserted between the plates with the grooved faces of the separators next to the positive plates. Each plate has a separator to insulate the adjacent plates and each group of plates is held together by a connector at one side for holding the plates in place and for connecting the plates to the cells in making up a battery.

One element is used per cell. There may be any desired number or size of plates used in an element, depending upon how much energy is to be stored. The greater the number of plates used per element, the higher the voltage will be during discharge at high rates and low temperature.

(f) Electrolyte

The spongy lead and lead peroxide, which fill the respective plates, are referred to as the active materials of the battery. But these materials cannot become active until they are covered by a water solution of sulphuric acid called the electrolyte.

Electrolyte is prepared by adding concentrated sulphuric acid to water. Electrolyte is both conductive and reactive. The

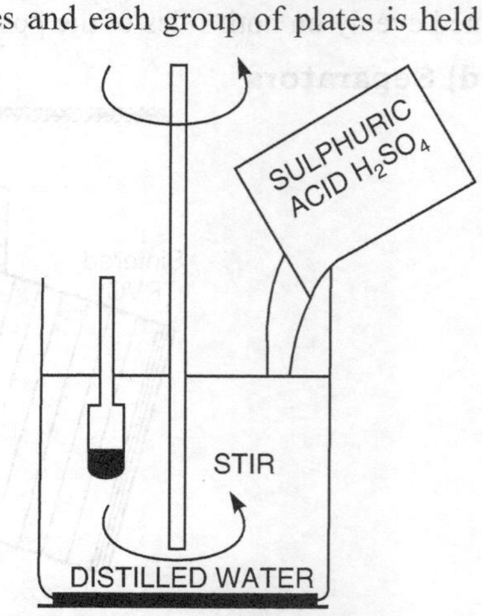

Fig. 7.13 Electrolyte

purpose of the distilled water is to give freedom for the ions to move freely. The electrolyte reacts chemically to combine with the active materials on the plates to form new compound and release electrons at the same time.

The correct concentration of water and sulphuric acid is usually contains about 38% sulphuric acid and 62% water by weight (fully charged condition). This corresponds to a specific gravity of about 1.280 at 80°F.

The following table shows the specific gravity of batteries used in different climates.

State of charge	Specific gravity		
	In cold climate	In temperate climate	In tropical climate
Fully charged	1.280	1.260	1.225
75% charged	1.260	1.215	1.180
50% charged	1.220	1.170	1.135
25% charged	1.190	1.120	1.090
Discharged	1.110	1.070	1.045

(g) Case (or) Container

The battery case is a one-piece moulded box with open at the top, made from hard rubber or plastic material, which is shock and acid resistant, and mechanically strong. They must also withstand extremes of heat and cold. Case has as many as the number of cell in the battery. In the bottom of each cell of a case, there are four-moulded narrow elements rest (or bridge) on which the elements sits and sediment chamber to collect the materials that slowly wear away from the plates and thus prevents short-circuiting.

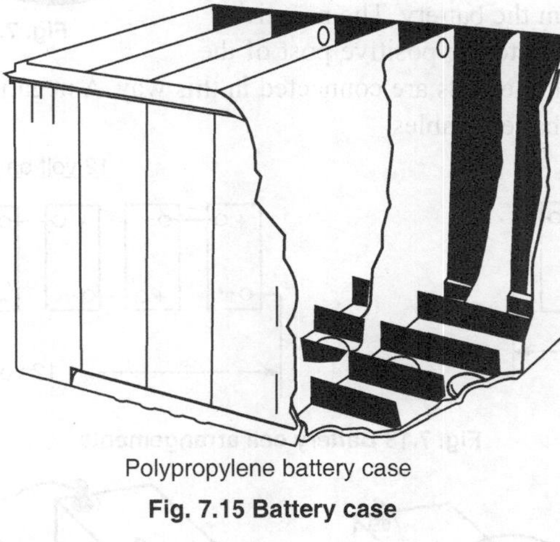

Polypropylene battery case

Fig. 7.15 Battery case

(h) Cell cover & Vent plug

Cell cover is also made of hard rubber. It has holes for terminal posts and for vent plug. Vent plugs are provided in the cell cover to facilitate the checking of electrolyte and pouring distilled water. Vent plugs either push into the plain holes or screw into threaded holes in the cell cover. The plugs can be removed so that water can be added to the cell when necessary. Water is lost during battery charging. Some evaporates and some is converted into hydrogen and oxygen gases. The plug has a vent hole to permit these gases to escape and prevents battery explosion. Perforated baffle plates are usually included in the plug. When the battery is being charged, the outgoing gases will often contain droplets of electrolyte. The baffle plates tend to trap these droplets so that the electrolyte is returned to the cell instead of escaping with the gases.

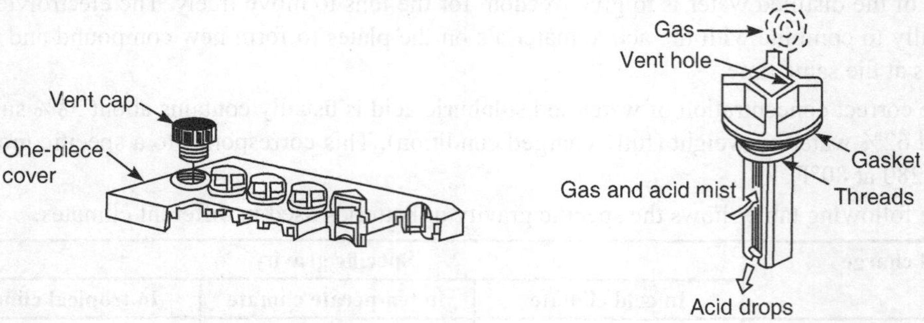

Fig. 7.16 Cell cover and vent plug

(i) Terminal posts

The battery has top mounted terminal posts. The plate strap has a round post which protrudes through a hole in the cell cover and becomes cell terminal. The positive post is larger than the negative post to help correct installation of the batter cables. Some batteries have terminal posts on the side of the battery case. This type of battery is called a side terminal battery.

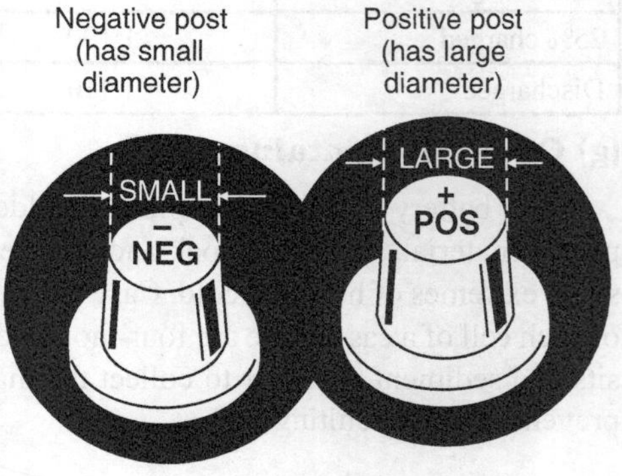

Fig. 7.17 Terminal post

Cell and battery arrangements

Storage batteries are made up of a number of cells. The number and dimensions of the cells depend on the service required from the battery. The negative post of one cell is connected to the positive post of the adjacent cell (in series). All the cells are connected in this way. A negative post and a positive post are left for connecting the battery cables.

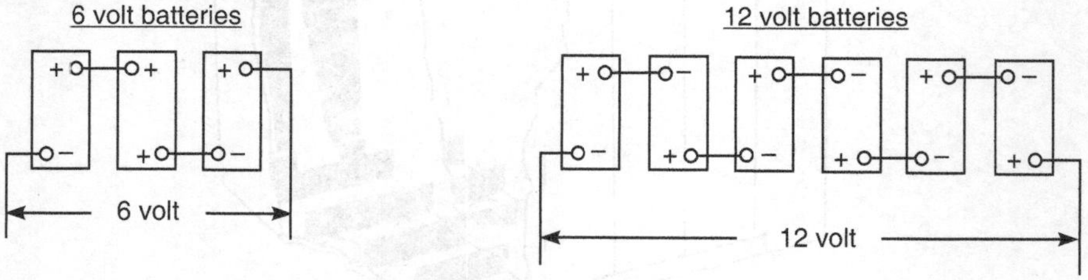

Fig. 7.18 Battery cell arrangements

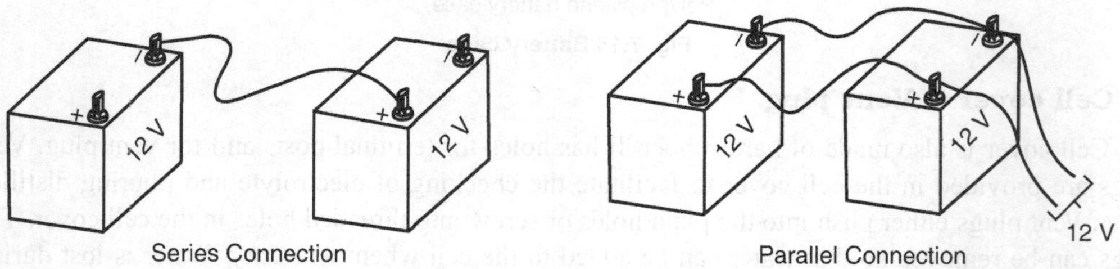

Fig. 7.19 Battery connections

Voltage of the two batteries can be added if they are connected in series. For example, two 12 V batteries connected in series provides a 24 V supply. Two batteries connected in parallel provide the same voltage but can deliver larger currents. For example, two 12 V batteries connected in parallel provides same 12 V supply but this arrangement will double the Ah capacity.

NON-SEALED & MAINTENANCE FREE BATTERIES

There are two types of automotive batteries: Maintenance free (sealed batteries) and non sealed batteries. Sealed batteries have vent caps which cannot be removed. This means there is no provision for the addition of water to the cells since the battery is sealed. On non sealed batteries, the vent caps can be removed. Both types of batteries are similar in internal construction, but they differ slightly in materials.

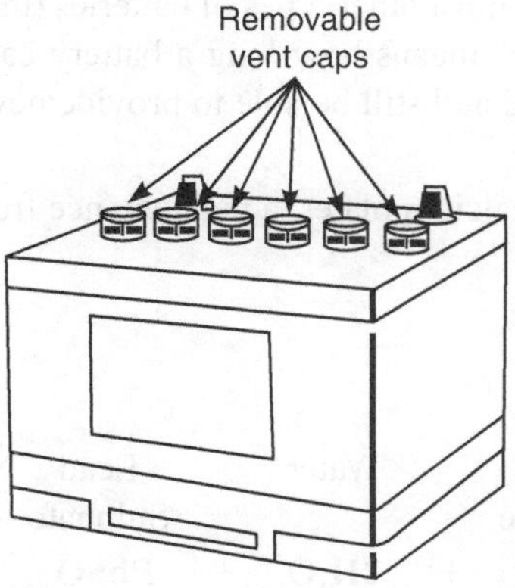

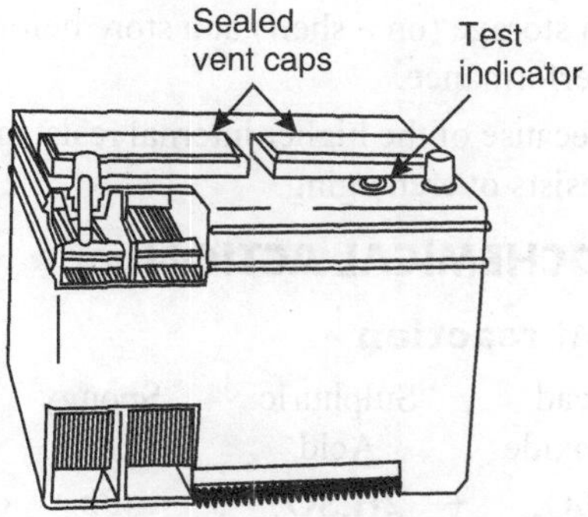

Fig. 7.20 Maintenance free batteries

Sealed batteries have a much longer storage life than non-sealed batteries. They never need water. They contain a lifetime supply of water, which is put in during manufacturing. The reason that the batteries do not require water during their lifetime is that the plate grids are made of a special lead alloy and calcium, strontium or cadmium, which greatly reduces gassing. The gases come from the split-up of water into hydrogen and oxygen. Because there is less of this, there is less water loss. However, one or more small vent openings are provided to release any pressure formed by gassing. Also, these batteries are materials of a higher purity. The Maintenance free batteries are also called *"low water loss" batteries.*

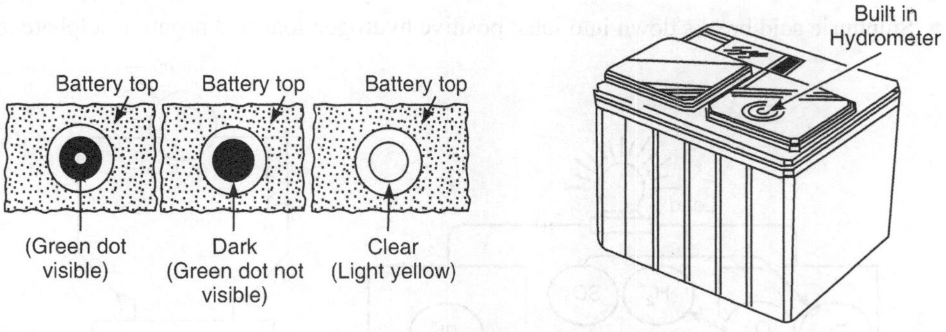

Fig. 7.21 Charge indicator

Many maintenance free batteries have a charge indicator (built-in-hydrometer) built into the cover. The indicator shows the state of charge of the battery (actually only one cell). If the dot that is at the bottom of the indicator is green, then the battery is charged (more than 65% charged). If the dot is black, the battery state of charge is low. If the dot is yellow or clear, do not attempt to recharge the battery. A yellow or clear eye means the electrolyte is low and the battery must be replaced.

A normal battery uses up to 5% antimony in the construction of the plate grids to add strength. However, the greater the amount of antimony, the greater the amount of gassing and therefore the more water the battery will use. Maintenance free batteries use calcium instead of antimony because 0.2% calcium has the same strength as 6% antimony. A typical lead-calcium grid use only 0.09–0.12% calcium.

Advantages of maintenance free batteries

- Generally do not use water during normal usage.
- Reduce the corroding of battery cables, terminals, and battery trays because lead-calcium cells do not "gas" until the cell voltage exceeds 2.15 V (12.9 battery voltage), whereas non-maintenance free (lead-antimony) batteries start to gas at 2.0 V per cell (12.0 battery voltage).
- A lead-calcium battery has a longer shelf life than most other types of batteries (three times longer than a lead-antimony battery), "Shelf life" means how long a battery can remain in storage (on a shelf) at a store before being sold and still be able to provide new-battery performance.
- Because of the higher internal resistance of lead-calcium plates, a maintenance free battery resists overcharging.

ELECTROCHEMICAL ACTION

Chemical reaction

Lead Peroxide		Sulphuric Acid		Spongy Lead		Lead Sulphate		Water		Lead Sulphate
PbO_2	+	$2H_2SO_4$	+	Pb	↔	$PbSO_4$	+	$2H_2O$	+	$PbSO_4$
Positive Plate		Electrolyte		Negative Plate		Positive Plate		Electrolyte		Negative Plate

Discharge process

The term discharge means to use a battery to provide electric energy. If the two terminals of a lead storage cell are connected to each other through an electric load, electrons flow from the negative electrode through the load to the positive electrode because of the difference in potential. When a battery is being discharged, electrons (given the symbol e^-) leave the negative terminal. The battery produces electrons by means of chemical reactions. In the reactions the following changes take place:

- Sulphuric acid breaks down into ions: positive hydrogen ions and negative sulphate ions.

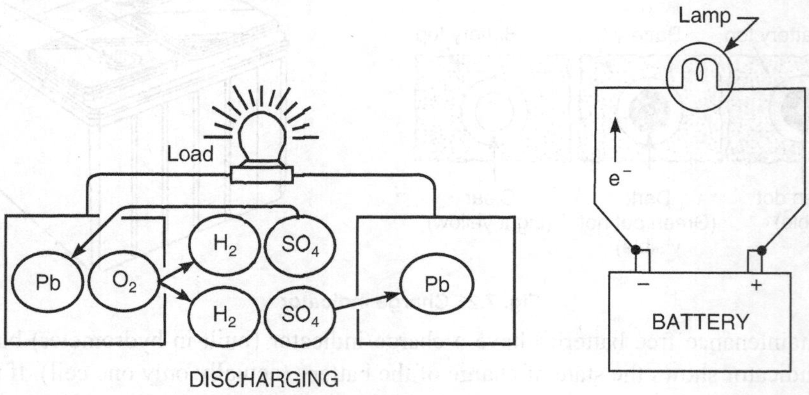

Fig. 7.22 Discharging process

- Lead molecules change into positive lead ions and in doing so release electrons. The electrons build up on the spongy lead plates, which become the negative plates of the battery.
- Lead peroxide also breaks down into positive lead ions and oxygen. The oxygen reacts with the positive hydrogen ions to form water. When water is formed, the positive charges of the hydrogen ions draw electrons away from the lead peroxide plates. Because electrons are

removed from the lead peroxide plates, they become positively charged and become the positive plates of the battery.

- The positive lead ions react with the sulphate ions to form lead sulphate.

As the battery discharges, the plate materials and the sulphuric acid are decreasing quantity. The amount of water is increasing. If the discharge reactions were allowed to continue, the battery would become completely discharged. Much of the active material in the positive and negative plates would become lead sulphate. The electrolyte would become very weak in acid. The lead sulphate coats the plates and becomes a barrier to further chemical action. When the electrolyte is weak in acid, it is no longer effective as a supply of ions. Therefore, the battery no longer produces electric current.

Charging process

To charge a battery, electrons must be made to flow into the negative terminal. This reverses the chemical reactions. In the automobile, the alternator charges the battery by forcing a flow of electrons into the negative terminal of the battery. In the charging reactions, the following changes occur:

- Lead sulphate on the plates reacts with the water in the electrolyte to form sulphuric acid.
- Lead sulphate on the plates is also converted into spongy lead on the negative plates and lead peroxide on the positive plates.

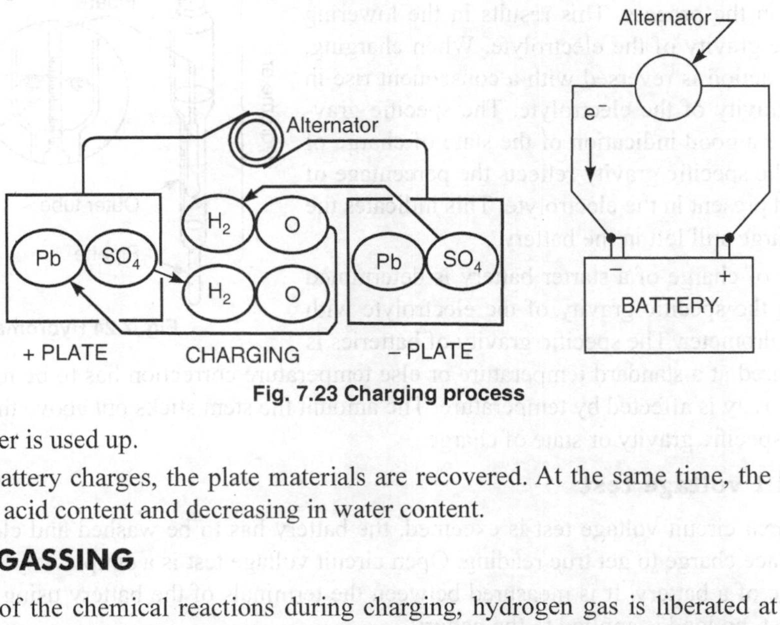

Fig. 7.23 Charging process

- Water is used up.

As the battery charges, the plate materials are recovered. At the same time, the electrolyte is increasing in acid content and decreasing in water content.

BATTERY GASSING

As part of the chemical reactions during charging, hydrogen gas is liberated at the negative plates and oxygen gas is liberated at the positive plates. This is known as gassing and it causes water loss in the battery. The higher the rate of charge, the greater the gassing. Vent holes are provided to prevent pressure build up in the battery and hence prevent battery explosion. Gassing causes the battery to release the above mentioned gases and sulphuric acid fumes. Which can cause corrosion to the battery terminals, battery tray and other areas surrounding the battery.

TESTING OF A BATTERY

The purpose of testing a battery is to determine whether it:

- is in good condition
- needs recharging

- is defective and must be discarded

There are the following tests to test the battery:

Leakage test

The outer surface of the battery is covered with dirt, moisture or electrolyte (contaminated with adverse impurities, especially with iron or copper), which result in a discharge through battery cover surface (external leakage).

Dirt and the effects of acid fumes on the top surface of the battery can result in conducting film paths between the positive and negative battery posts. This trouble can be minimized by periodic cleaning of the battery top. Sediment paths at the bottom of the battery case can also lead to leakage paths.

Battery external leakage is measured with the help of voltmeter. This is executed by connecting the voltmeter positive probe to the positive terminal post of the battery, and slides the negative probe against the battery cover towards the negative terminal post side. Leakage voltage should be $V \leq 0.1$ volt. If not, clean the top cover and make again a test.

Hydrometer (or) Specific gravity test

During discharge, chemical reaction converts the active material of both plates to lead sulphate, water being liberated in the process. This results in the lowering of the specific gravity of the electrolyte. When charging, this chemical action is reversed with a consequent rise in the specific gravity of the electrolyte. The specific gravity is therefore a good indication of the state of charge of the battery. The specific gravity reflects the percentage of sulphuric acid present in the electrolyte. This indicates the amount of charge still left in the battery.

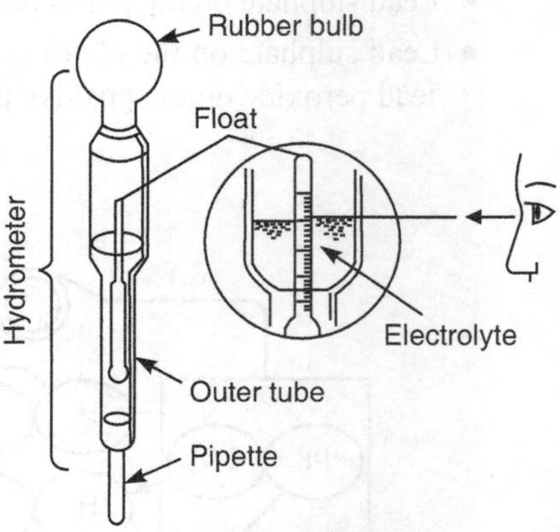

Fig. 7.24 Hydrometer

The state of charge of a starter battery is determined by measuring the specific gravity of the electrolyte with the help of hydrometer. The specific gravity of batteries is usually measured at a standard temperature or else temperature correction has to be made because the specific gravity is affected by temperature. The amount the stem sticks out above the electrolyte gives battery specific gravity or state of charge.

Open circuit voltage test

Before open circuit voltage test is executed, the battery has to be washed and cleaned dry to eliminate surface charge to get true reading. Open circuit voltage test is a simple way of testing the state of charge of a battery. It is measured between the terminals of the battery using a voltmeter. During this test, no load is applied to the battery.

The voltmeter reading can be compared with state of charge table below in order to determine the condition of the battery. The voltages shown are for batteries at or near room temperature (20°C – 27°C).

Battery voltage (Volts)	State of battery charge (%)
12.6 V (or) Higher	100% Charged
12.4 V	75% Charged
12.2 V	50% Charged
12.0 V	25% Charged
11.9 V (or) Below	Discharged

Peak load test

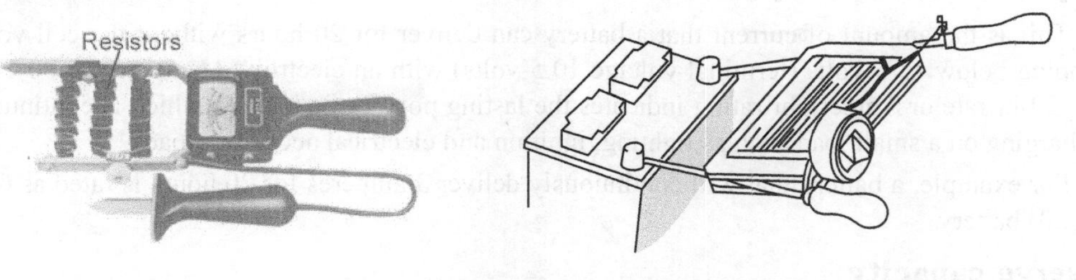

Fig. 7.25 Peak load tester

This unit is provided with a voltmeter and has a measuring scale of 12-0-12 volts and 6-0-6 volts and coloured dial. It is used for measuring the total battery voltage with load applied to the battery.

- Green colour indicates good battery condition
- Red colour indicates weak (or) poor battery condition

During peak load test, the battery should be in a good state of charge to three fourth (3/4) or better charged, preferably fully charged. This is because a run down battery does not accurately reflect its condition. The test should be done within 5 to 10 seconds. This load placed on the battery during this test is approximately the same as that of the starter motor.

During this test, the voltmeter reading should not drop below 9.6 Volt

$V \geq 9.6 \rightarrow$ battery is in good condition

$V < 9.6 \rightarrow$ battery is defective

Simple battery tests (without testing instruments)

Possible compliant: The starter motor doesn't crank properly or not at all when the engine is cold. This could be a flat (discharged or run down) battery. Therefore the following tests can give whether it is due to battery failure or not.

- Check the cables for loose or defective connections
- Turn on the head lights
- With the headlight on operate the starter motor.

Observation

- If the head light gets dim, the defect is not by the battery
- If the head light gets dark or off, the problem might be flat battery

BATTERY RATING

The capacity or rating is a measure of the energy stored in it and is expressed as the period during which the battery will give the rated current before reaching the specified final voltage. The battery must provide good cranking power for the vehicle's engine and adequate reserve power for the electrical system in which it is used. The factors that influence battery capacity include:

- the number of plates per cell,
- the size and thickness of plates, and
- the amount and strength of electrolyte.

No matter how many plates are put into a cell of this type, its voltage will remain at 2.1 V. The type of plate material used determines the voltage. The number of plates per cell determines amperage. The more plates per cell, the longer the battery will be able to produce electricity. The starting current of a fully charged battery is roughly proportional to the plate area. Consequently, automotive batteries are generally built with thin plates to provide a large area (by increasing the plates) so the acid can have access to as much active material as possible. The ratings most commonly used are:

Ampere-hour capacity

This is the amount of current that a battery can deliver for 20 hours without the cell voltage dropping below 1.75 volts (terminal voltage 10.5 volts) with an electrolyte temperature 80°F. The SAE 20-hr rate or Ampere-hr rating indicates the lasting power of a battery, which is continuously discharging on a small load such as lighting, ignition and electrical accessory loads.

For example, a battery that will continuously deliver 3 amperes for 20 hours is rated as 60 Ah (3 × 20) battery.

Reserve capacity

The reserve capacity rating is the time in minutes a vehicle can be driven after the charging system fails. This is roughly equivalent to the conditions after the alternator fails while the vehicle is being driven at night with the head lights on. The battery alone must supply current to the headlights and the ignition system. The assumed battery load is a constant discharge current of 25A. It is the length of time in minute that a fully charged battery at 80°F can deliver 25 amperes without the cell voltage dropping below 1.75 volts. This shows for how long the battery can deliver the electrical operating load, if the alternator fails to supply current.

Cold cranking rate

Large engines require that a starter motor deliver a large amount of cranking torque. Smaller engines require less torque. The greater the torque supplied by a starter motor, the more current it draws from the battery. As a rough guide, a starter motor requires approximately 1A of current for each cubic inch (in^3) of engine displacement. Therefore, a 350 in^3 engine would require a battery with a cold cranking rating of approximately 350 amperes. This rating indicates the power a battery can supply for engine cranking under low temperature conditions. It is the number of amperes that a battery delivers for 30 seconds at 0°F without the cell voltage falling below 1.2 volts. The ampere values may be listed as 305, 315, 350 or 440.

Cranking power available from a fully charged battery based on temperature is:

Temperature	Cranking power (percent)
80°F (26.7°C)	100
32°F (0°C)	65
0°F (–17.8°C)	40

BATTERY CHARGING

Charging a battery means causing electrons to flow into the negative terminal. On the car, this job is performed by the alternator. Usually the batteries do not require charge from the external source provided the charging system of the vehicle is working efficiently. In the case of less charging or fault in the system, it becomes necessary to recharge the battery by means of battery chargers. Since most commercially available electricity is alternating current (AC) the charger consists of a transformer to reduce the voltage to a usable value and a rectifier to change the alternating current to direct current. The battery charger has a control switch and an ammeter so the charging rate can be adjusted. The battery chargers are categorized as slow charger and fast charger.

Slow charger

In this method, battery is removed from the vehicle and connected to a slow charger to recharge it. Slow chargers are usually constant current machines which use a rectifier to convert AC to DC and a rheostat to adjust current flow to the battery. Slow battery chargers operate at low rate and take considerably longer time to charge a battery. Slow charging permits the battery to be completely charged. The charging rate is one ampere for each positive plate in a cell. For example, a battery having four positive plates in a cell should be charged at a rate of 4 amps. Batteries of different size can be charged at the same time. But the charging rate is determined by the smallest battery. Batteries are safely charged at a high rate if the temperature is below 113°F. The length of time required to recharge a good battery to fully charged condition is 12 to 16 hours at normal rates.

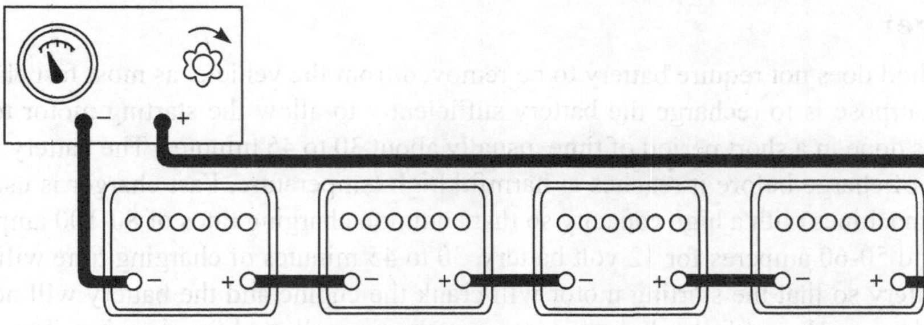

Fig. 7.26 Slow charger

During slow charging the maximum charging current should be less than 1/10th of the battery capacity. For example, the battery capacity is 40 Ah, and then the charging current is 1/10th of 40 Ah.

i.e., 40/10 = 4 amps or less

Slow charging time can be calculated by the following formula:

$$\text{Charging time (h)} = \frac{\text{State of discharge capacity (Ah)}}{\text{Charging current (A)}} \times (1.2 \text{ to } 1.5)$$

Problem. *The battery capacity is 60Ah and specific gravity is 1.16, find the charging current and charging time.*

Solution. From the graph for specific gravity 1.16, state of discharge is about 50%.

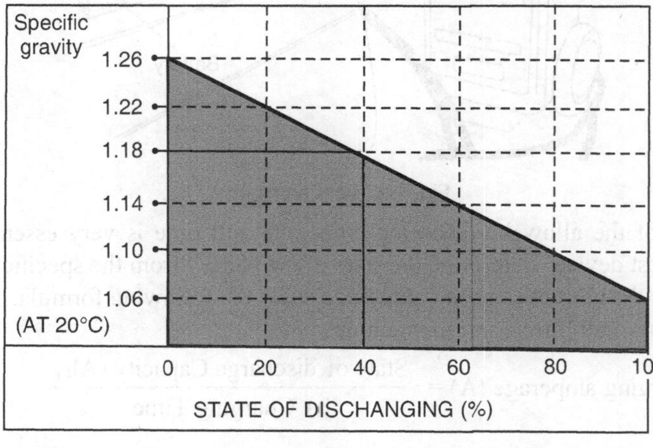

$$\text{Charging current} = \frac{1}{10} \text{ of battery capacity}$$

$$= \frac{1}{10} \times 60$$

$$= 6 \text{ A}$$

$$\therefore \quad \text{State of discharge capacity} = 50\% \text{ of battery capacity}$$

$$= 50\% \text{ of } 60 \text{ Ah}$$

$$= 30 \text{ Ah}$$

$$\text{Charging time} = \frac{30}{6} \times (1.2 \text{ to } 1.5)$$

$$= 6 \text{ to } 7.5 \text{ hours}$$

Fast charger

This method does not require battery to be removed from the vehicle, as most fast chargers are portable. Its purpose is to recharge the battery sufficiently to allow the starting motor to start the engine. This is done in a short period of time, usually about 30 to 45 minutes. The battery is brought to a fair state of charge before it reaches at harmful high temperature. Fast charger is usually constant voltage machines with a high capacity so that common charging rates of 80-100 amperes for 6 volt battery and 50-60 amperes for 12 volt battery. 30 to 45 minutes of charging time will normally charge the battery so that the starting motor will crank the engine and the battery will not be over heated. Fast chargers do not fully charge a battery in the time allotted for charging. The remaining recharge is done by the alternator when the engine is operating. Some fast chargers have controls for finishing the charging cycle at low rate so the battery can be brought up to a full charge.

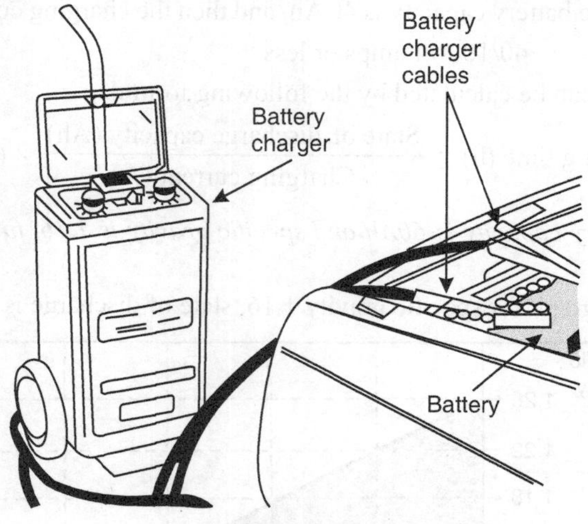

Fig. 7.27 Fast charger

Determination of the allowable charging amperage and time is very essential if the battery chargers have no a test device. Determine the state of the battery from the specific gravity, using the graph, then calculate the correct charging amperage using the following formula. The charging time for quick charging is usually from half to one hour.

$$\text{Correct charging amperage (A)} = \frac{\text{State of discharge Capacity (Ah)}}{1 + \text{Charging Time}}$$

Problem: The battery capacity is 40 Ah specific gravity at 20°C (or 68°F) is 1.18. What would be the charging current for half an hour?

From the chart, the specific gravity 1.18 tells us it is 40% discharged,

$\therefore$ State of discharge capacity = 40% of battery capacity

= 40% of 40 Ah

= 16 Ah

To charge the battery for half an hour, the correct charging amperage would be:

$$\text{Charging current} = \frac{16}{1 + 0.5} \cong 10 \text{ amps}$$

BOOST CHARGING

The fast charger can also be used to give a battery an emergency boost when a customer is in a hurry or in some other emergency requiring quick service. The battery is charged at the normal fast charging rate for one-third to one-half the normal charging time. This puts back sufficient current for starting the engine. The vehicle should be operated for a long enough time so the car's generator or alternator can complete recharging the battery.

OVER CHARGING

Batteries that are completely charged need not be charged furthermore. Because the current that is applied to charge the battery makes electrolysis of water and the water will be broken into oxygen (O) and hydrogen (H_2) gasses. Oxygen find no Pb and hydrogen find no SO_4 to combine with and they bubble out of the electrolyte through vent holes (battery gassing). Since oxygen and hydrogen are constituent parts of water, water is rapidly lost from the battery cells.

The effects of overcharging are as follows:

- **Plates loose their ability to take charge:** As a result of water loss, the electrolyte level falls down which makes plates exposed to air. The dry plates get hard and loose their ability to take charge.
- **Plates deteriorate rapidly:** Due to water loss, the acid at the lower parts of plates becomes more thick or concentrated. Due to concentrated acid the plates deteriorate rapidly.
- **Separators loose their insulating properties:** The upper part of the separators is also exposed to air due to fall in electrolyte level. Hence separators dry out and crack at the top and loose their insulating properties.
- **Short circuit between the plates:**
    1. The high temperature developed in the battery cells during overcharging cause the plates to buckle. The buckling plates crush the separators and makes short circuit between the positive and negative plates.
    2. During overcharging, some of the oxygen gathering at the positive plates attacks the grid structure of the plates causing them to oxidize. This result in swelling of the plates resulting in pushing up of cell covers. Too much swelling causes the upper edges of positive plates to be pushed against the negative plate straps. This results in direct short circuit and hence battery failure.

SULPHATION

During discharging process the active materials of the plate is converted into lead sulphate and restored back into the active material by the charging process. This is a normal cycle which is continually repeated in the battery. However, if the battery stands for long periods in a discharged condition, the lead sulphate changes into a hard crystalline substance. As it forms, the crystalline sulphate tends to break the plate grids. It is very difficult to reconvert hard crystalline lead sulphate into active materials by normal charging process. Such a battery should be charged at half the normal rate for 60 to 100 hours. Batteries that are heavily sulphated generally cannot be restored to a serviceable condition.

IGNITION SYSTEM

An internal combustion engine like the automobile engine operates by the force of expansion obtained through combustion of the air-fuel mixture in the cylinders. However, the mixture will not ignite by itself. Therefore, in petrol engines, some means must be provided to ignite the mixture to start it burning. This function is performed by the ignition system. This system serves to distribute the ignition at the proper time to the proper cylinder in correct time relationship with the piston position and start of ignition.

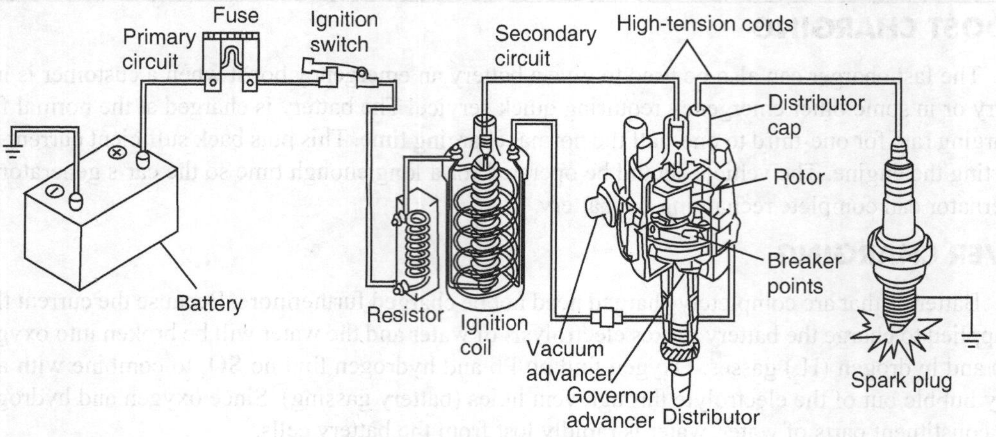

Fig. 7.29 Ignition system

FUNCTIONS AND REQUIREMENTS

The basic function of the ignition system is to generate sparks that can ignite the air-fuel mixture in the cylinders, so the following conditions must be satisfied:

A strong spark

When the air-fuel mixture is compressed in the cylinders, it becomes difficult for the spark to pass through the air. This is because even air has electrical resistance and this resistance rises as the air is compressed. For this reason, the voltage that is supplied to the plugs must be high enough to ensure the generation of a powerful spark between the electrodes of the spark plug.

Proper ignition timing

In order to obtain the most effective combustion of the air-fuel mixture, there must be some means of varying the ignition timing in accordance with engine speed and load. That is, of varying the crankshaft angle at which each plug fires.

Sufficient durability

If the ignition system fails, the engine will stop running. The ignition system must therefore have sufficient reliability to endure the vibration and heat generated by the engine, as well as the high voltage in the ignition system itself.

IGNITION ENERGY

Approximately 0.2 mJ of energy is required per individual ignition for igniting an air-fuel mixture by electric spark, providing the mixture (static, homogeneous) has a stoichiometric composition. Rich and lean mixtures (turbulent) require over 3 mJ. This amount of energy is the ignition energy. If insufficient ignition energy is available, ignition does not occur. The mixture cannot ignite and there are combustion misses.

PRINCIPLE OF HIGH VOLTAGE GENERATION

Self-induction effect

A magnetic field is generated when a current flows through a coil. As a result, an EMF (electromotive force) is generated which creates a magnetic field in a direction which impedes (obstruct) the generation of magnetic field in the coil. Therefore, current does not flow immediately when it is first introduced in the coil, but a certain period of time is required for the current to rise.

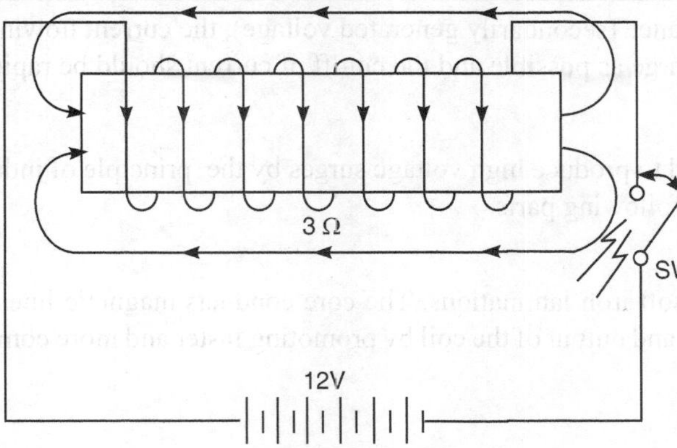

Fig. 7.30 Self-induction

When current starts to flow in a coil or when current is cut off, the coil generates EMF which acts to impede changes in the coil's magnetic field. This is called the "self-induction effect".

Mutual induction effect

When two coils are arranged in a line and the amount of current flowing in one of the coils (the primary coil) is changed, an EMF is generated in the other coil (the secondary coil) in a direction which impedes the change in the primary coil's magnetic field. This is called the "mutual induction effect".

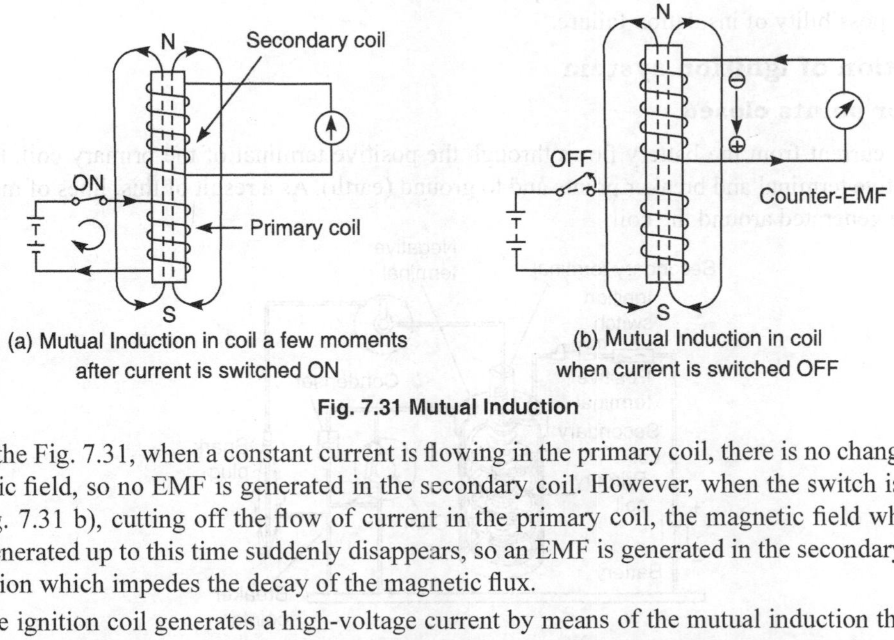

Fig. 7.31 Mutual Induction

In the Fig. 7.31, when a constant current is flowing in the primary coil, there is no change in the magnetic field, so no EMF is generated in the secondary coil. However, when the switch is turned off (Fig. 7.31 b), cutting off the flow of current in the primary coil, the magnetic field which has been generated up to this time suddenly disappears, so an EMF is generated in the secondary coil in a direction which impedes the decay of the magnetic flux.

The ignition coil generates a high-voltage current by means of the mutual induction that takes place between the primary coil and the secondary coil when the primary current is suddenly cut off by the opening of the breaker points.

The amount of EMF is determined by the following three factors:

- Amount of magnetic flux: The more magnetic flux generated in a coil, the higher the amount of induced voltage.
- Number of coil windings: The more turns in a coil, the higher the induced voltage.
- Rate at which magnetic flux changes: The faster the change in the amount of magnetic flux generated in a coil, the higher the induced voltage. In order to obtain a large EMF due to

mutual inductance (secondarily generated voltage), the current flowing in the primary coil should be as large as possible and the cutoff of current should be rapid.

Ignition coil

Ignition coil is used to produce high voltage surges by the principle of induction in the secondary winding. It has the following parts.

Core

It consists of thin soft iron laminations. The core conducts magnetic lines of forces. Hence, it increases the efficiency and output of the coil by promoting faster and more complete coil saturation.

Windings

Primary winding

It consists of approximately 250 turns of relatively heavy wire and wound around the core. It is insulated with special varnish.

Secondary winding

It consists of approximately 20,000 turns of very fine varnished wire. It is wound inside the primary winding around the same iron core. The layers of the secondary windings are insulated from each other by high dielectric paper.

Oil in the coil

Oil may be added in the coil to dissipate heat rapidly, to provide greater insulation, and to reduce the possibility of insulation failure.

Operation of ignition system

Breaker points closed

The current from the battery flows through the positive terminal of the primary coil, through the negative terminal and breaker points and to ground (earth). As a result of this, lines of magnetic force are generated around the coil.

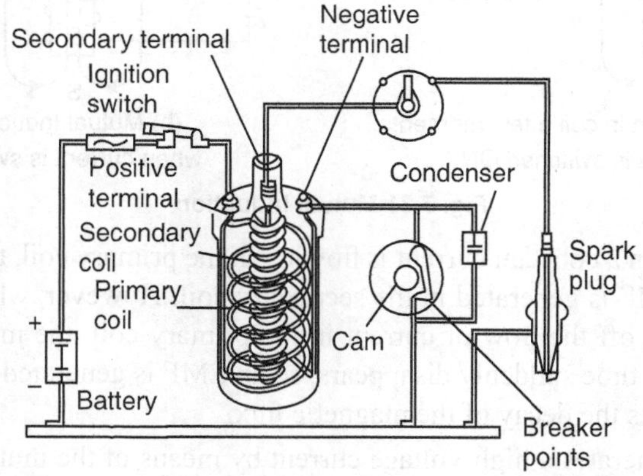

Fig. 7.32 (a) Operation of ignition system: Breaker points closed

Breaker points open

As the crankshaft rotates the camshaft, the distributor cam opens the breaker points, causing the current flowing through the primary coil to be suddenly interrupted. As a result, the magnetic flux generated in the primary coil starts to decrease. Because of the self-induction of the primary coil and mutual induction of the secondary coil, EMF is generated in each coil, preventing the reduction of the existing magnetic flux.

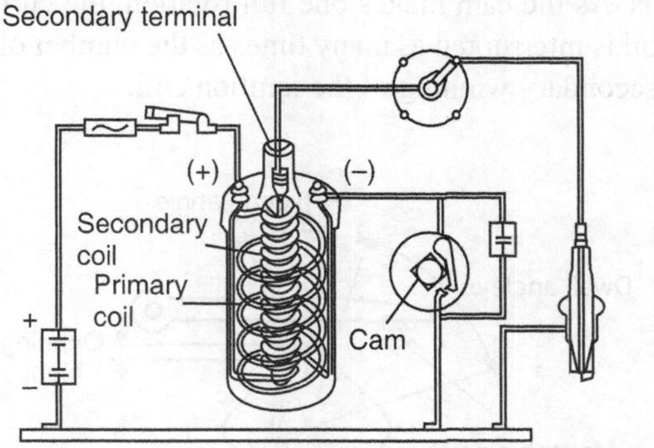

Fig. 7.32 (b) Operation of ignition system: Breaker points open

The self-induced EMF rises to about 500 V, while the mutually-induced EMF rises to about 20,000 V, causing discharge by spark generation at the spark plug.

Distributor

The distributor consists of the following component parts:

1. Breaker section: Breaker points
2. Distributor section: Distributor cap and rotor
3. Ignition advancer: Governor advancer, Vacuum advancer and Octane selector
4. Condenser (Capacitor)

Breaker section

Breaker points

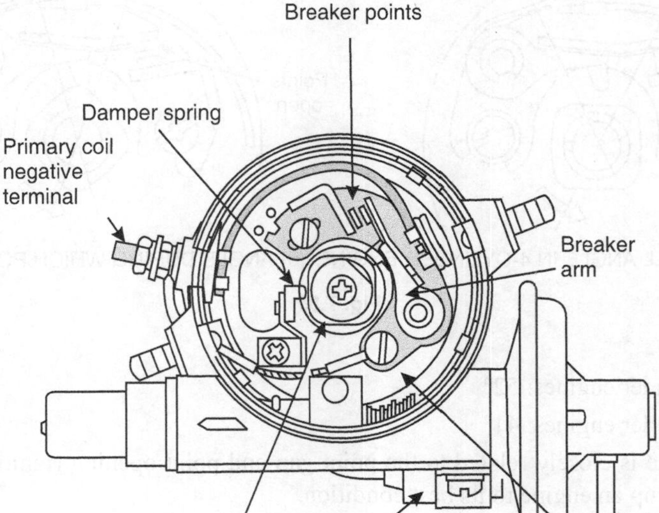

Fig. 7.33 Breaker points

The breaker points are opened and closed by the cam installed on the governor shaft. The governor shaft is driven by the camshaft at half the engine speed. The cam has cam lobes identical in number to the engine cylinders. As the cam rotates, each cam lobe pushes the breaker arm to open the breaker points. As the cam rotates further, the breaker arm is returned by the breaker arm spring to close the breaker points. As the cam makes one full rotation, the current flowing in the primary winding of the ignition coil is interrupted as many times as the number of engine cylinders to generate a high voltage in the secondary winding of the ignition coil.

Dwell angle

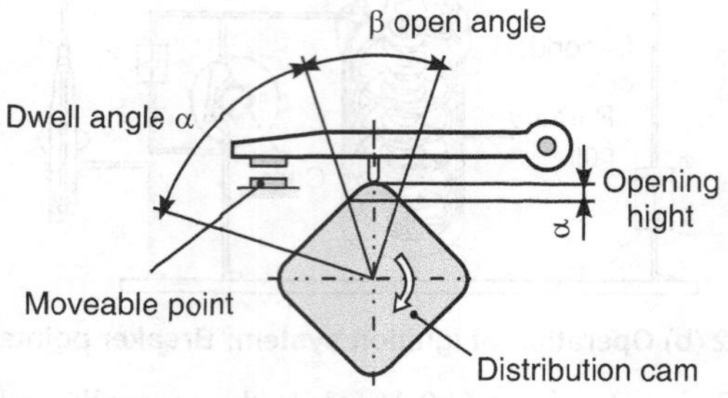

Fig. 7.34 Dwell angle

The dwell angle refers to the angle of distributor shaft (cam) rotation between the time that the breaker points are closed by the breaker arm spring and the time that they are opened by the next cam lobe. If the gap of a 4-cylinder engine has been adjusted correctly to the standard value, the points should remain closed while the cam rotates 52° ± 6°.

Furthermore, the points should stay open until the cam rotates another 38° ± 6°. Since the combination of the point closing angle and opening angle is 90° (52° + 38°), the breaker points are opened and closed by every ¼ turn of the cam.

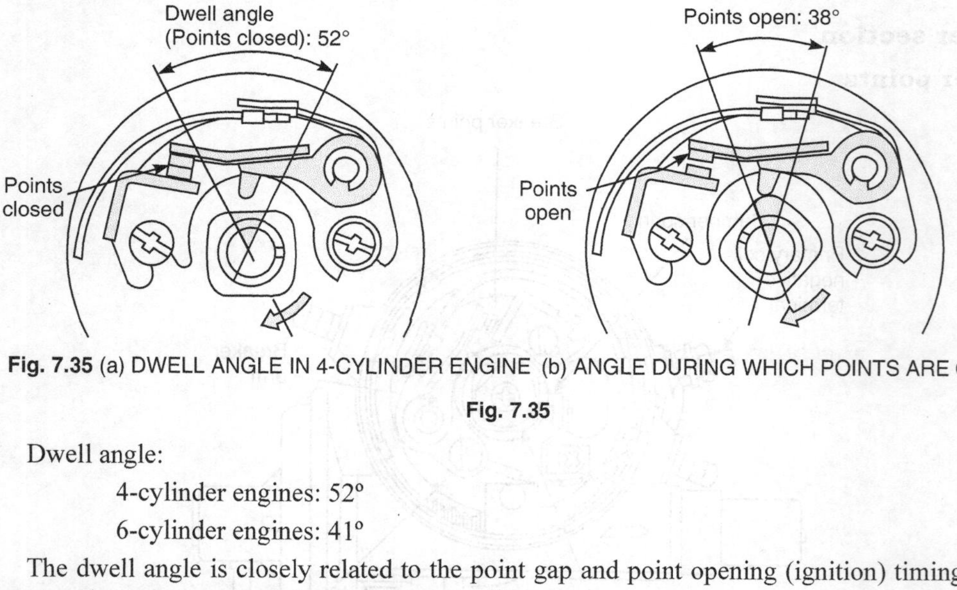

Fig. 7.35 (a) DWELL ANGLE IN 4-CYLINDER ENGINE (b) ANGLE DURING WHICH POINTS ARE OPEN

Fig. 7.35

Dwell angle:

4-cylinder engines: 52°

6-cylinder engines: 41°

The dwell angle is closely related to the point gap and point opening (ignition) timing and is important in tuning up an engine to its best condition.

Distributor section

The high-tension current generated in the secondary winding of the ignition coil passes from the secondary terminal of the ignition coil to the center electrode of the distributor cap via a high-tension cord.

The high-tension current then passes from the center electrode via the center contact piece, to the side electrodes in the form of an electric spark via the rotor, which rotates at half the crankshaft speed. The high-tension current then passes from a side electrode to the spark plug of the corresponding cylinder via another high-tension cord.

The distributor is comprised of a distributor cap with terminals and a rotor.

Since ozone is generated due to ionization during high-tension discharge across these air gaps, small air vent holes are provided in the cap and housing for ventilation.

Distributor cap and rotor

The rotor is mounted to turn with the camshaft and its center is made to contact with the terminal from the ignition coil. The cap has a center terminal that connects to the ignition coil and terminals that connect to the spark plugs. The turning of the rotor distributes the high voltage to the spark plugs in firing order.

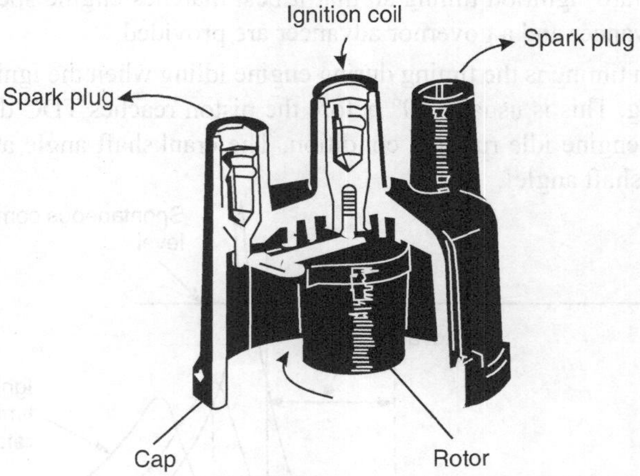

Fig. 7.36 Distributor cap and rotor

IGNITION ADVANCER

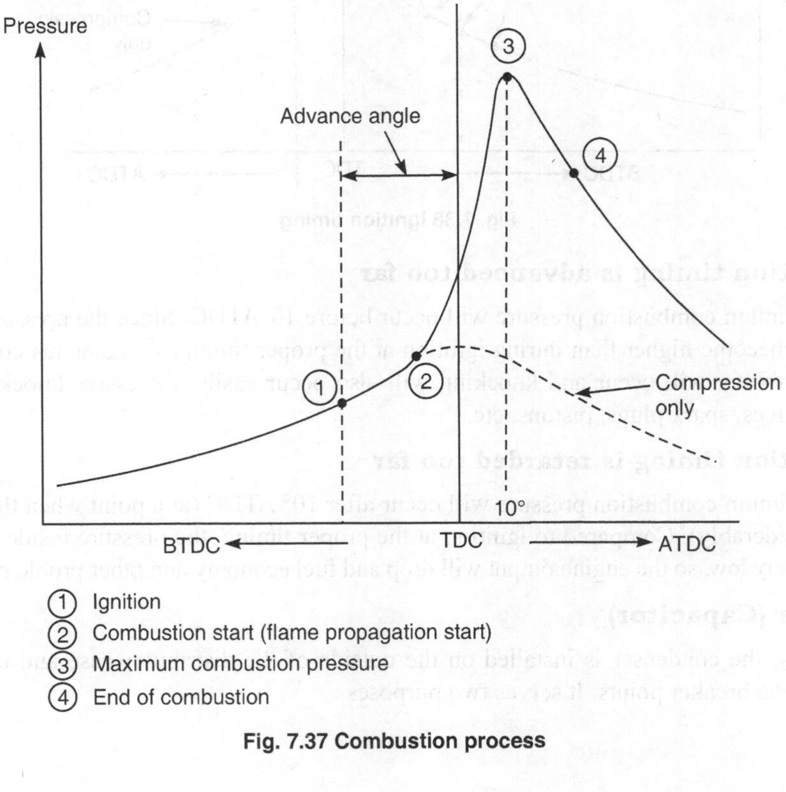

Fig. 7.37 Combustion process

After the air-fuel mixture is ignited by a spark, a certain amount of time is required for the flame to propagate throughout the combustion chamber. For this reason, there is slight delay between the time of the first ignition and the attainment of maximum combustion pressure. This means that, because engine output is maximized when the pressure in the combustion chamber is at its greatest (at about 10° after TDC), the flame propagation period must be taken into account when determining what the ignition timing shall be.

Due to the time lag needed for flame propagation after ignition, the mixture must actually be ignited before TDC. This timing is called 'ignition timing'. It is necessary to have some means to change (advance or retard) ignition timing so that it best matches engine speed, load, etc. For this purpose, a vacuum advancer and a governor advancer are provided.

The initial ignition timing is the timing during engine idling when the ignition advancer mechanisms are not operating. This is usually 10° before the piston reaches TDC during its compression stroke. This is during engine idle running condition. The crankshaft angle at which this occurs is called the 'basic crankshaft angle'.

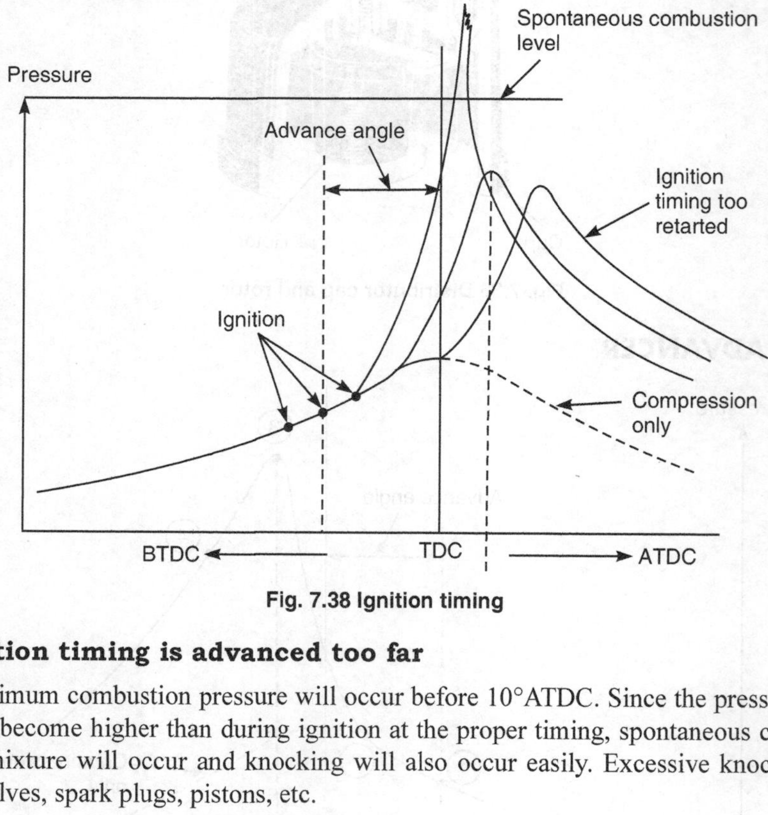

Fig. 7.38 Ignition timing

If the ignition timing is advanced too far

The maximum combustion pressure will occur before 10°ATDC. Since the pressure inside the cylinder will become higher than during ignition at the proper timing, spontaneous combustion of the air-fuel mixture will occur and knocking will also occur easily. Excessive knocking leads to burning of valves, spark plugs, pistons, etc.

If the ignition timing is retarded too far

The maximum combustion pressure will occur after 10° ATDC (at a point when the piston has dropped considerably). Compared to ignition at the proper timing, the pressure inside the cylinder will be relatively low, so the engine output will drop and fuel economy and other problems will occur.

Condenser (Capacitor)

Generally, the condenser is installed on the outside of the distributor case and connected in parallel with the breaker points. It serves two purposes :

- It reduces arcing of the contacts.
- It ensures a quick-collapse of the magnetic field.

The sudden breaking of the primary current through the opening of the contact points induces high voltage, causing a spark to jump across the points. The spark prevents quick breaking of the current and also produces heat to melt the point faces. The condenser temporarily stores the high voltage tending to produce the spark discharge across the points and sends it back to the primary circuit when the points close. As a result, the current flow in the primary circuit is increased so that the ignition coil self induction becomes stronger to enable inclucing higher voltage in the secondary coil.

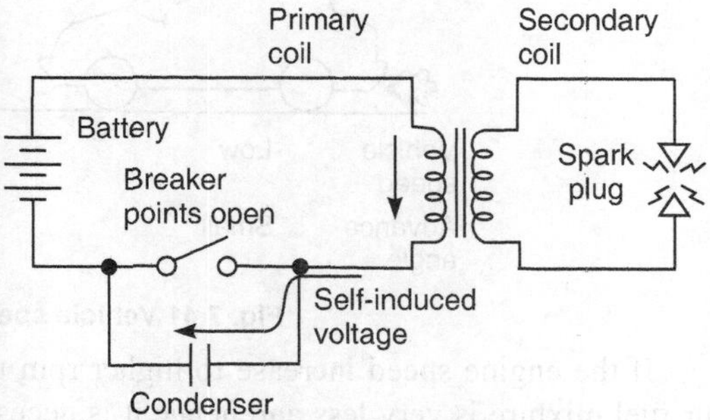

Fig. 7.39 Condenser connection

Ignition advance mechanisms

The governor advancer adjusts the ignition timing based on the engine speed. Since the flame propagation time is almost constant irrespective of the engine speed (as long as the air-fuel ratio is constant), the crankshaft angle during the flame propagation period increases as the engine speed rises. In other words, the flame propagation time gets relatively longer ($\theta_1 < \theta_2$) as the engine speed rises, so the curve indicating the crankshaft angle at maximum combustion pressure shifts to the right as shown below. The governor therefore advances the ignition timing as the engine speed rises so that the maximum combustion pressure will always occur at a position 10° after TDC.

The distributor is therefore provided with an advancer section, which consists of a governor advancer for controlling the ignition timing in accordance with engine speed and a vacuum advancer for controlling ignition timing according to the engine load.

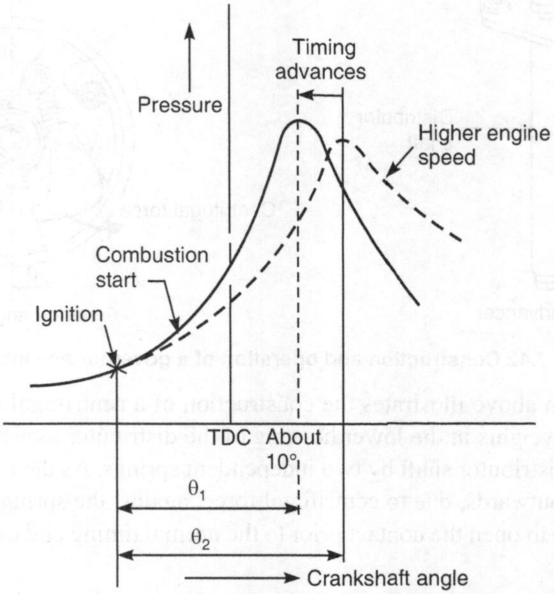

Fig. 7.40 Advanced Ignition timing

Centrifugal (or) Governor advance mechanism

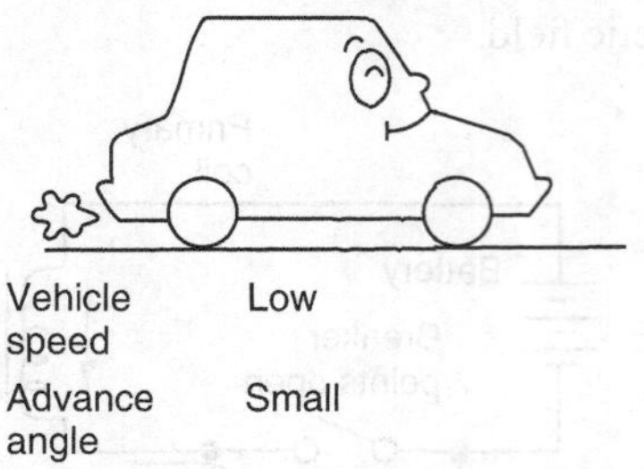

Fig. 7.41 Vehicle speed Vs Advance angle

If the engine speed increase to higher rpm the time required for complete combustion of the air-fuel mixture is very less and hence it is necessary to increase the time to burn air fuel mixture. The spark advance during engine high speeds can be achieved by a centrifugal or governor advance mechanism.

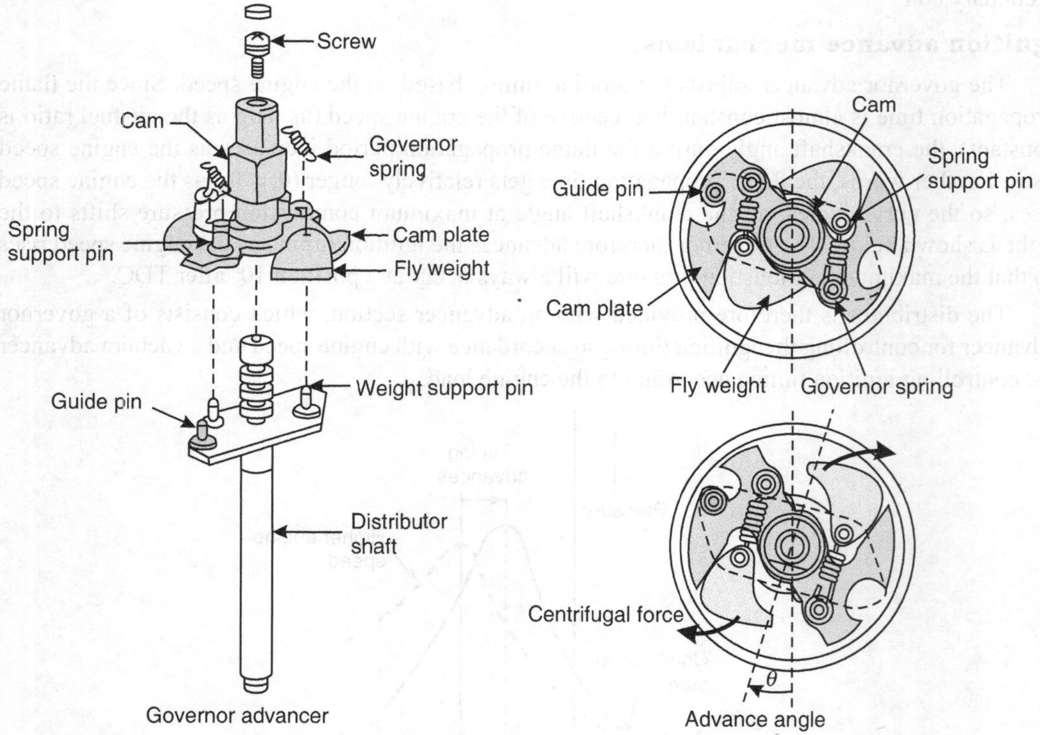

Fig. 7.42 Construction and operation of a governor advancer

The Fig. 7.42 shown above illustrates the construction of a centrifugal advance mechanism. It consists of two pivoted weights in the lower housing of the distributor assembly. These are held towards the center of the distributor shaft by two independent springs. As the rotation speed increases, the weights are thrown outwards, due to centrifugal force, against the spring tension. This will turn the center shaft cam lobe to open the contact prior to the normal timing and cause the advance sparking.

As the speed reduces to idle running, the centrifugal forces also reduce, thus the weights are pulled back to their original position by the springs tension. Thereby the distributor shaft lobe turns back to the original position to provide the ignition at initial timing.

Vacuum spark advance mechanism

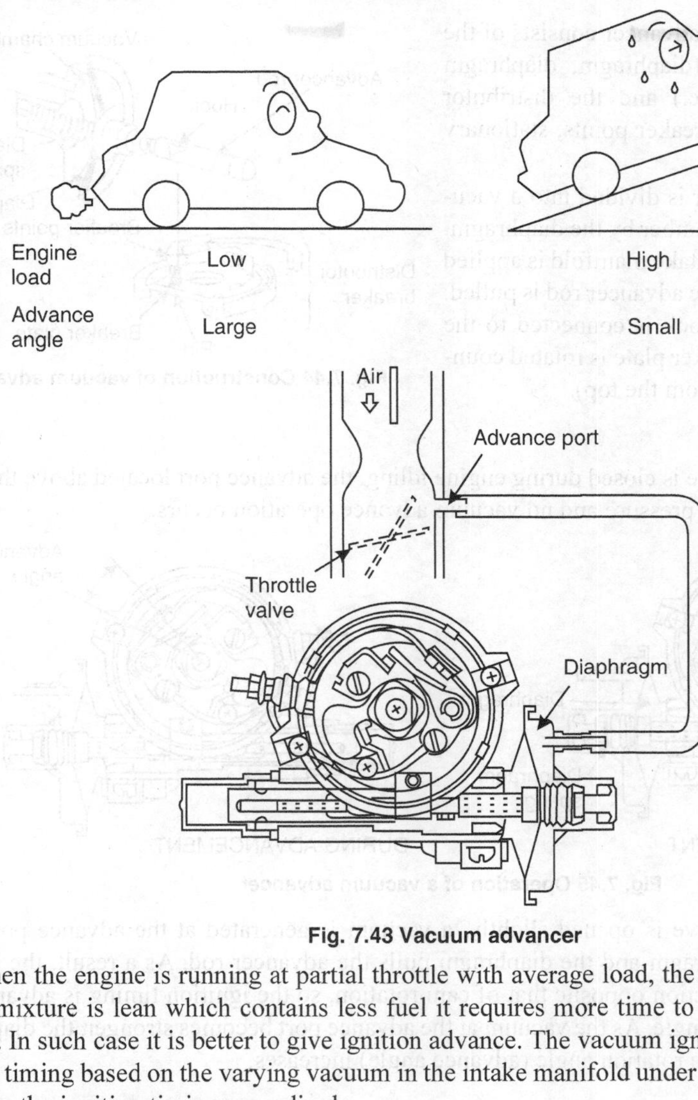

Fig. 7.43 Vacuum advancer

When the engine is running at partial throttle with average load, the air fuel ratio is very lean. As the mixture is lean which contains less fuel it requires more time to complete the combustion process. In such case it is better to give ignition advance. The vacuum ignition advancer adjusts the ignition timing based on the varying vacuum in the intake manifold under varying engine loads, and advances the ignition timing accordingly.

When the load on the engine is light, the throttle valve opening is also small, so the vacuum in the intake manifold increases. A strong vacuum in the intake manifold lowers the air-fuel mixture intake efficiency, causing little air-fuel mixture to be drawn into the cylinders. This results in lowered flame propagation speed after ignition. However, when the load on the engine increases, the vacuum in the intake manifold decreases, improving the air-fuel mixture intake efficiency and resulting in an increase in the flame propagation speed after ignition.

The vacuum ignition advancer therefore advances the ignition timing when the load is light to in sure that the maximum combustion pressure will always occur at 10° after TDC.

Note: Since the vacuum outlet port is above the throttle valve when the throttle is fully closed, the vacuum advancer does not advance during idling.

Construction

The vacuum ignition advancer consists of the vacuum advancer itself (diaphragm, diaphragm spring, advancer rod, etc.) and the distributor breaker (breaker plates, breaker points, stationary plate, etc).

The vacuum advancer is divided into a vacuum chamber and an air chamber by the diaphragm. When the vacuum in the intake manifold is applied to the vacuum chamber, the advancer rod is pulled. Since the advancer rod hook is connected to the breaker plate pin, the breaker plate is rotated counterclockwise (as viewed from the top).

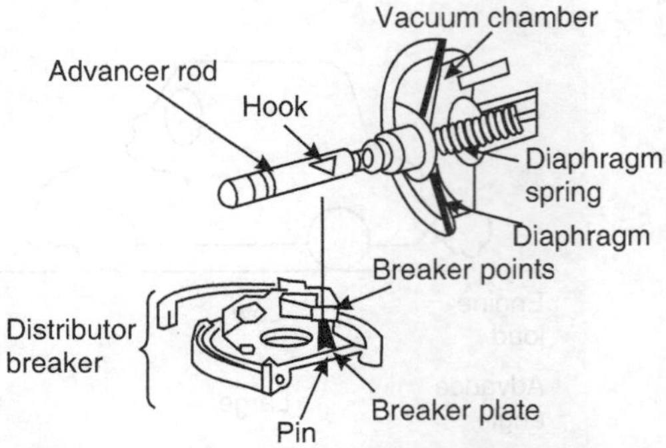

Fig. 7.44 Construction of vacuum advancer

Operation

Since the throttle valve is closed during engine idling, the advance port located above the throttle valve is at atmospheric pressure and no vacuum advance operation occurs.

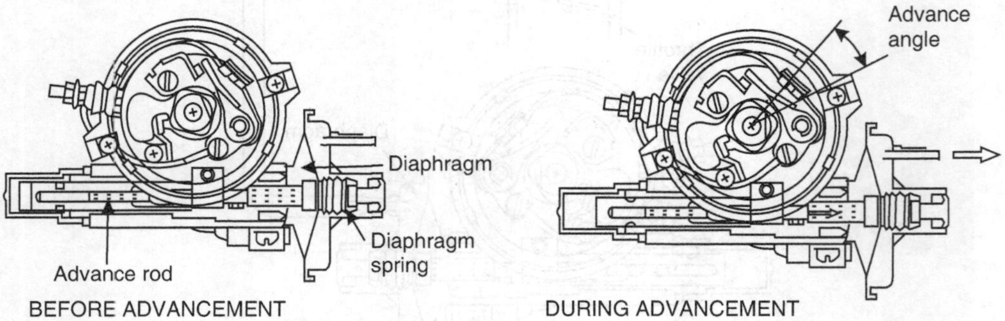

Fig. 7.45 Operation of a vacuum advancer

When the throttle valve is opened slightly, a vacuum is generated at the advance port. This vacuum acts on the diaphragm and the diaphragm pulls the advancer rod. As a result, the breaker plate is rotated in the direction opposite that of cam rotation, so the ignition timing is advanced by the breaker plate rotation angle. As the vacuum at the advance port becomes stronger, the diaphragm travel i.e., the breaker plate rotation angle (advance angle) increases.

SPARK PLUG

The high-voltage current from the distributor generates a high-temperature spark between the center and ground (earth) electrodes of the spark plug to ignite the compressed air-fuel mixture.

Although the spark plug construction is simple, the conditions under which it operates are very severe. The temperature of the electrodes of spark plugs rises as high as 2000°C in the power stroke, but quickly drops in the suction stroke because of cooling by the mixture. This rapid heating and cooling are repeated at the rate of once per two engine revolutions. Furthermore the pressure in the cylinder is less than 1 bar in the suction stroke, but rises to 45 bar in the power stroke. The spark plugs must be able to maintain their ignition performance for long periods of time while being exposed to such high temperatures and pressure changes, and while maintaining insulation resistance against voltages of as high as 10,000 to 30,000 Volts.

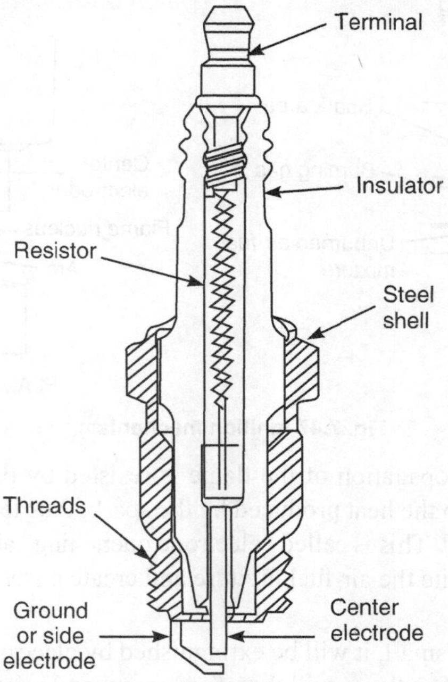

Fig. 7.46 Components of a typical spark plug

Construction

The spark plug consists mainly of the insulator, casing and center electrode.

1. Ceramic insulator

The ceramic insulator holds the center electrode and serves as the insulation between the center electrode and casing. The insulator is made of high-purity alumina porcelain having excellent heat resistance, mechanical strength, dielectric strength at high temperatures, and thermal conductivity.

2. Casing

The casing supports the ceramic insulator while at the same time serving as the means for mounting the spark plug to the engine.

3. Center electrode

The center portion of the spark plug consists of the terminal, upper stem, glass seal, resistor, copper core and center electrode. The center electrode generates the spark with the ground electrode.

4. Ground electrode

The ground electrode is made of the same material as the center electrode.

Ignition mechanism

The explosion of the air-fuel mixture by a spark from the spark plug is generally called combustion. Combustion, however, does not occur in a moment but proceeds as described below.

As the spark travels through the air-fuel mixture from the center electrode to the ground electrode as shown in the illustration 7.47 the air fuel mixture along the path of the spark is activated and a so-called "flame nucleus" is formed. The molecules of the air-fuel mixture in the immediate vicinity of this flame nucleus are activated by the propagation of the heat of the spark and are pushed outward away from the nucleus by the shock wave created by the spark, activating the molecules further out from the center of combustion. These molecules then become part of the flame nucleus, which now has enough energy to continue to propagate outwards in this way by itself.

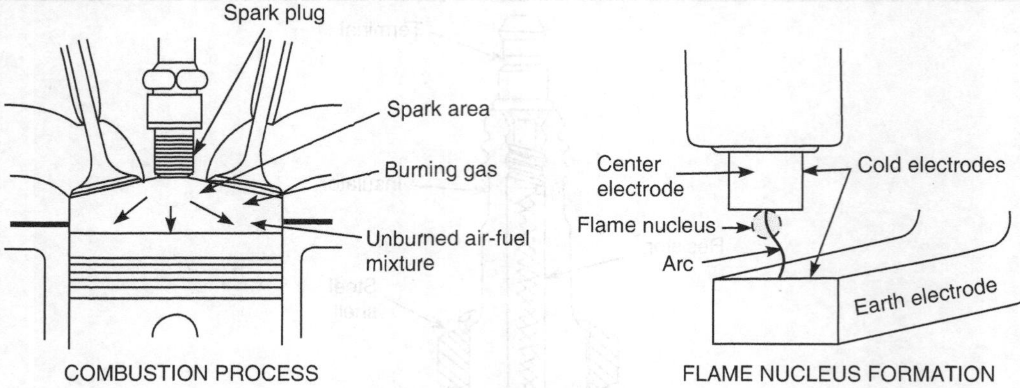

Fig. 7.47 Ignition mechanism

However, this outward propagation of the flame is resisted by the relatively low temperature of the electrodes, which absorb the heat produced by the spark, thus tending to extinguish the flame nucleus before it can get started. This is called "electrode quenching" and must be overcome by each new spark as it attempts to ignite the air-fuel mixture and create a steadily propagating flame in the combustion chamber.

If the flame nucleus is too small, it will be extinguished by electrode quenching and the air-fuel mixture will not be activated. The flame will therefore go out and misfiring will occur. Suppressing electrode quenching and facilitating flame nucleus expansion and growth will enhance flame nucleus heat generation and flame propagation, thus improving combustion of the mixture.

Nose length and Heat range

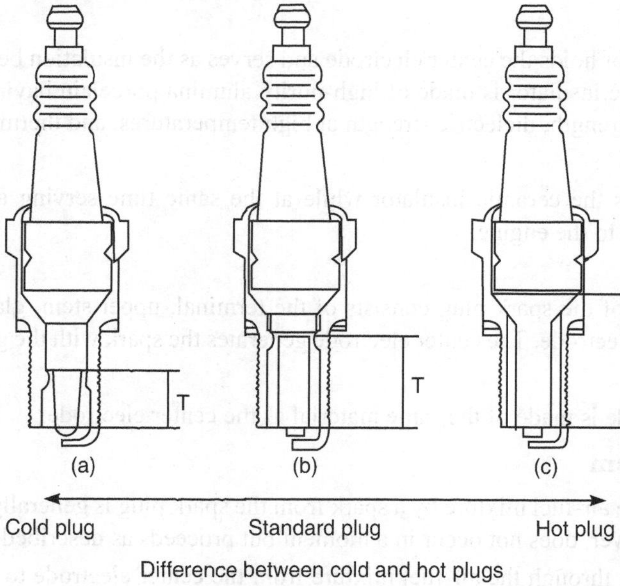

Fig. 7.48 Difference between cold and hot plugs

The heat range of a spark plug refers to amount of heat radiated by the spark plug. Spark plug that radiates move heat is called "cold plug" because the plug itself stays cooler while one that radiates less heat is called a "hot plug", because it keeps its heat in.

The insulator nose length (T) of cold and hot type plugs differs as shown in Fig. 7.48. The cold plug has a shorter insulation nose as shown in Fig. 7.48 (a) below. Since the surface area exposed to the flame is small and the heat radiation route is short, heat radiation is excellent and the center electrode temperature does not rise very high. For this reason, if the cold spark plug is used, it is more difficult for pre-ignition to occur.

On the other hand, since the hot type plug has a longer insulator nose, the surface area exposed to the flame is large, the radiation route is long and heat radiation is small. As a result, the center electrode temperature rises fairly high and the self-cleaning temperature can be attained more quickly in the low-speed range than in the case of the cold type.

Note:

a. The 'Hot' Plug is used in cold running engines.

b. The 'Cold' Plug is used in hot running engines.

c. The lower operational limit of a spark plug is the self-cleaning temperature (450°C), while the pre-ignition temperature is the upper limit. Spark plugs perform best when the center electrode temperature is between about 450 and 950°C.

TYPES OF IGNITION SYSTEMS

A normal gap is about 0.6 mm and although only a small charge of about 600 V is required to produce a spark across this gap in the open air, it will take 10-50 times this voltage to fire a plug that is under pressure in an engine. A high-voltage spark can be generated by a magneto or battery ignition system.

Compared with a magneto system, the battery ignition system makes engine starting much easier. Also it is simpler to control the maximum voltage to suit the conditions.

Magneto ignition system

This is a small self-contained ignition unit which generates pulses of high-tension current and distributes them to the appropriate cylinders at the correct time.

Motor cycles and small single-cylinder engines use this system on account of their compact construction, but it is not used on modern cars.

They consist of a rotating pole wheel carrying a number of permanent magnets, the ignition armature with primary and secondary windings, the contact breaker points, the ignition condenser and a cam rotating at crankshaft speed.

The alternating north and south poles of the rotating permanent magnets induce an alternating current in the primary winding. When the contact breaker points are closed, a current flows in the primary winding of the ignition armature and generates a magnetic field as shown in the Fig. 7.49. The points are opened at the moment when the current flow is at its greatest, that is to say when the magnetic field in the primary winding has reached a maximum. This is the case when the pole wheel position causes the direction of the magnetic field in the ignition armature to change suddenly (Fig. 7.49 c). This sudden reversal of the magnetic field induces a high voltage in the secondary winding. The ignition condenser, which is wired in parallel with the contact breaker, suppresses spark formation and encourages the magnetic field to decay rapidly. Since the cam revolves at crankshaft speed, a spark is produced during each revolution of the engine. This is ideal for the requirements of a single-cylinder two-stroke engine. In a single-cylinder four-stroke engine, a 'false spark' occurs every second revolution of the crankshaft, but takes place during the exhaust stroke and therefore has no effect on the engine's actual performance.

To avoid backfiring when the engine is started, the ignition is often retarded. The movable cam is turned by a manual or automatic device in the direction of crankshaft rotation. This has the effect of retarding the ignition.

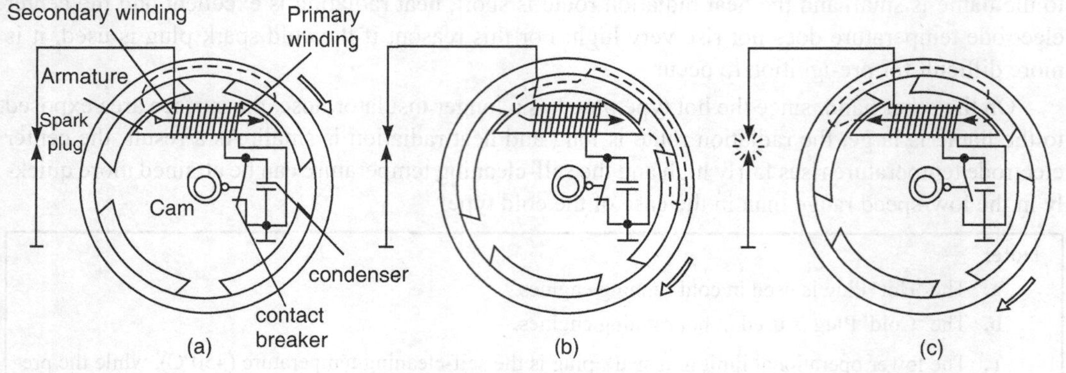

Fig. 7.49 Magneto

Battery ignition system

This system uses electrical energy produced by a battery or alternator to supply the low-tension ignition current. The ignition coil transforms the voltage to that required to produce a high-voltage spark.

Principle of operation

The layout of battery ignition system is shown in Fig. 7.50. The system consists of two circuits: primary and secondary.

Primary circuit is one that wound around a soft iron core in the coil are several turns of comparatively heavy enameled wire. This is arranged in series with a battery, ammeter, switch and contact breaker. A capacitor is connected in parallel with the contact breaker.

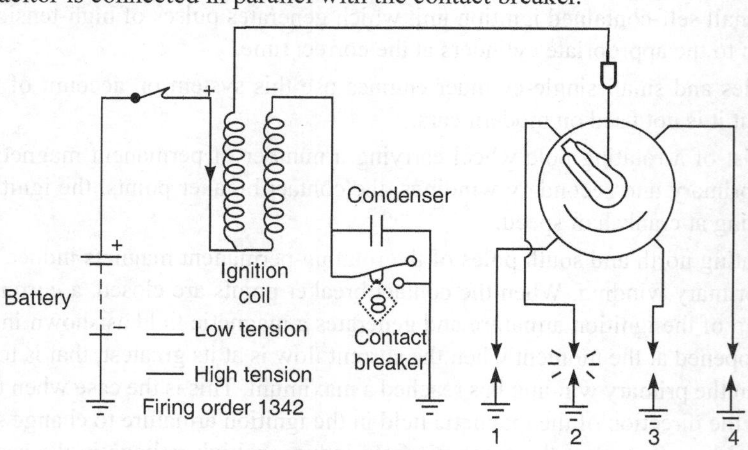

Fig. 7.50 Battery ignition system

A secondary circuit coil winding, consisting of several thousand turns of fine enameled wire, is wound under the primary. One end of this winding is joined to the contact breaker terminal and the other end is connected in series with the distributor and spark plugs. A return path from the plug, via earth, passes through the battery and primary winding and so e.m.f. induced in the primary winding is added to the large e.m.f. produced in the secondary winding. This gives higher coil efficiency.

When the ignition is switched on and the contacts are closed, the current flowing in the primary winding sets up a magnetic field around the iron core of the coil. Opening the contacts, at a time when the spark is required, interrupts the current flowing in the primary circuit and causes the magnetic field to collapse. During this collapse, the lines of force cut the secondary winding and induce e.m.f. in the secondary. A higher e.m.f. than that acting in the primary is obtained, since the secondary contains more turns. The HT current is conveyed from the coil to the rotor arm which should be pointing to the correct distributor segment. This is the segment connected to the plug of the cylinder that requires ignition of the charge.

ELECTRONIC IGNITION SYSTEM

In case of conventional contact breaker point ignition system, large amount of current is allowed to pass through the contacts. Thereby there is a chance of spark (arcing) at contacts causing damage to the contacts and also loss of high amount of current through the contacts. The spark produced also not powerful to ignite the lean mixture. The coil used in such a system has to carry high amount of current to produce a powerful spark. This makes the size of the coil bulky and heavy. Later the electronic ignition has been introduced to avoid the problems in the conventional type of ignition.

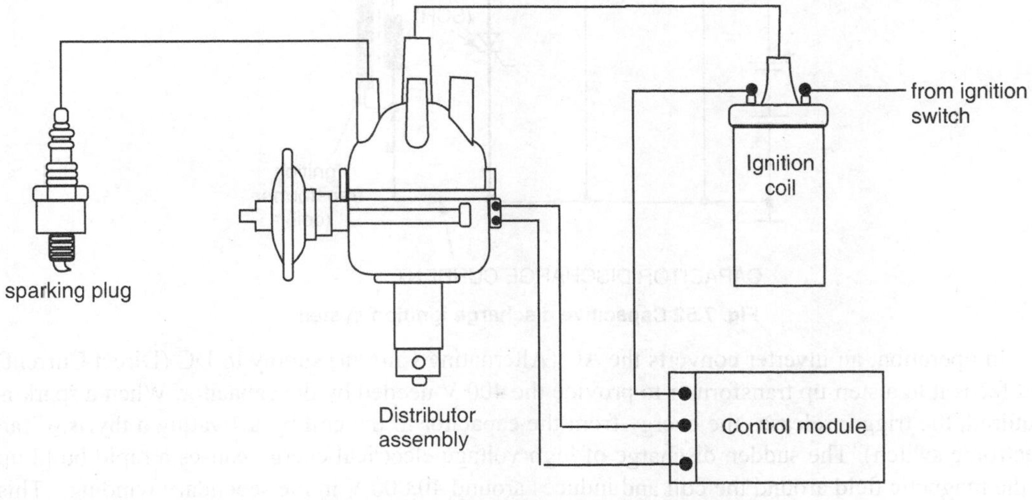

Fig. 7.51 A layout of electronic ignition system

Electronic ignition system uses electronic switching devices instead of mechanical contact breaker points to send a spark to the spark plug.

The advantages of electronic ignition are:

1. It is small and light weight
2. It gives higher ignition voltage
3. It gives longer duration of spark
4. It has very accurate control of timing
5. Less maintenance
6. Longer service life
7. It helps vehicles meet exhaust emission regulations and reduces fuel consumption.

Electronic ignition systems may be categorized as capacitor discharge or transistorized or distributor less.

Capacitive discharge ignition System

This system is not widely used and differs considerably from the standard and inductive systems. One of the problems with using a coil to provide the high voltage is the time required to build up and collapse the magnetic field before a spark can be produced. On eight or twelve cylinder engines this can be a major problem.

In the capacitor discharge system the supply to the coil is stored in a capacitor inside an electronic control unit. An electronic 'trigger' releases the charge stored in the capacitor suddenly to the primary winding of the coil.

Operation

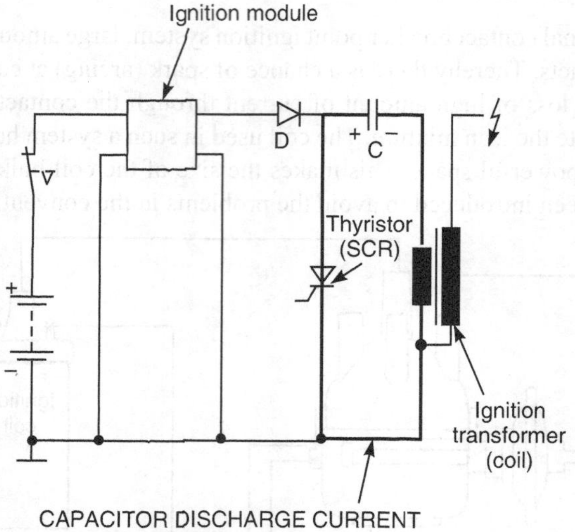

Fig. 7.52 Capacitive discharge ignition system

In operation, an inverter converts the AC (Alternating Current) supply to DC (Direct Current) and feeds it to a step-up transformer to provide the 400 V needed by the capacitor. When a spark is required, the trigger releases the energy from the capacitor to the coil by activating a thyristor (an electronic switch). The sudden discharge of high voltage electrical energy causes a rapid build-up of the magnetic field around the coil and induces around 40,000 V in the secondary windings. This results in a spark of high intensity but short duration. Voltage transformation time is about one hundredth of the time taken by the standard system. This allows a much higher rate of sparks per second. However, the short duration of each individual spark renders the system unsuitable for most engines.

Transistorized ignition system

This is widely used type of electronic ignition system. It is similar to the conventional system but the big difference is that the primary current is switched on and off by a transistor (an electronic switch) or other electronic device. It therefore eliminates the problems associated with contact breaker points. The system does, however, still use the mechanical centrifugal advance mechanism to sense engine speed and a vacuum advance to sense engine load.

The breaker points of an ordinary ignition system require periodic maintenance because they are oxidized by sparks with use. The solid state transistorized ignition system (hereafter called the transistorized ignition system) has been developed to eliminate the need for such maintenance, thus reducing the user's maintenance costs.

In the transistorized ignition system, a signal generator is provided in the distributor in place of the cam and breaker points. It generates a voltage, switching on the transistors in the igniter to interrupt the primary current in the ignition coil. Since the transistors that are used for interruption of the primary current do not involve mechanical metal-to-metal contact, there is no wear or consequent secondary voltage drop.

Operation

(i) Engine stopped: A voltage is applied to point 'P' when the ignition switch is turned on. The voltage at point 'P' is kept below the base voltage required for transistor operation through voltage division by resistors R_1 and R_2. As a result, the transistor remains off while the engine is stopped, so no primary current flows in the ignition coil.

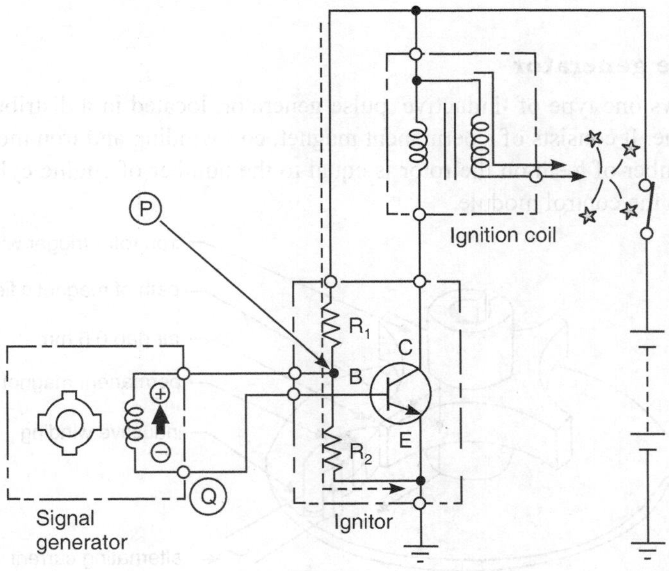

Fig. 7.53 Transistorized ignition system

(ii) Engine running (positive voltage generated in pick-up coil): When the engine is cranked, the signal rotor of the distributor rotates, generating an AC voltage in the pick-up coil. If the generated AC voltage is positive, it is added to the voltage from the battery (applied to point 'P'), raising the voltage at point 'Q' (base voltage) above the transistor operating voltage, thus turning on the transistor.

As a result, the ignition coil primary current flows through the transistor from the collector (C) to the emitter (E).

(iii) Engine running (negative voltage generated in pick-up coil): When the AC voltage in the pick-up coil is negative, this voltage is added to the voltage at point 'P', so the voltage at point 'Q' decreases below the transistor operating voltage, turning off the transistor. As a result, the ignition primary current is turned off and a high voltage is induced in the secondary coil.

Triggering devices

All ignition systems use some type of triggering devices to turn the primary coil winding on and off. A triggering device works much like a switch. The ignition system's circuit is closed when the switch closes. When the switch closes, current flows from the power source to the transformer. When the switch opens, the circuit is opened and the flow of current immediately stops. When the current stops, the magnetic field in the transformer collapses, producing the voltage needed to fire the spark plug.

The triggering device is connected to one end of the ignition coil's primary winding. Each time the triggering device stops the current flow in the primary winding, the spark plug fires. The spark plug keeps firing continually, about 1,800 times per minute, so the engine keeps running.

In electronic ignition system, the distributor unit is similar to a conventional unit with the exception that the contact breaker is replaced by a sensor called a pulse generator. This device generates an electrical pulse to signal to the 'control module' when a spark at the plug is required. When the trigger produces a pulse, the control module breaks the primary circuit, which causes the ignition coil to produce the HT voltage. The three main types of pulse generators are:

- Inductive
- Hall
- Optical

Inductive pulse generator

Fig. 7.54 shows one type of 'inductive' pulse generator, located in a distributor suitable for a four-cylinder engine. It consists of a permanent magnet, coil winding and iron motor, which acts as a reluctor. The number of teeth on the rotor is equal to the number of engine cylinders. Two leads connect this unit to the control module.

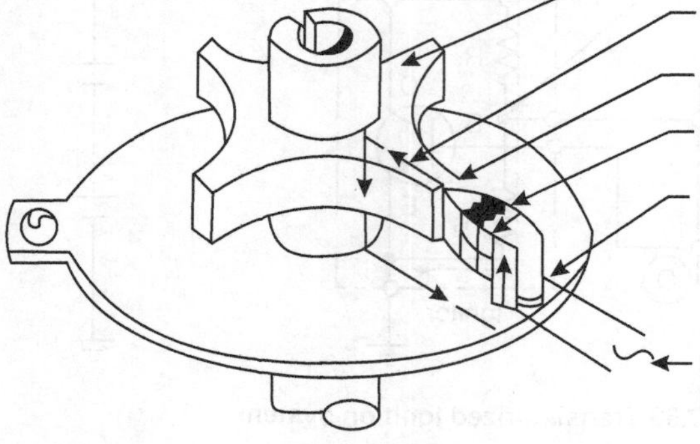

Fig. 7.54 An inductive pulse generator

A magnetic flux field surrounds the permanent magnet. When the reluctor rotates, the tooth of the reluctor passes the permanent magnet and the air gap decreases. The reluctor rotates further and the air gap increases. The movement of the reluctor changes the magnetic flux and induces an emf in the coil. Since this emf varies between 0.5V and 100V (the output depending on the speed of the reluctor), the voltage variation together with the frequency provides a sensing signal.

Hall generator

Fig. 7.55 shows a distributor unit fitted with a Hall generator. It gets this name because the system is based the "Hall effect".

The unit consists of a permanent magnet, vanes and semi-conductor chip (Hall IC), which is supplied with a voltage. A three-core cable connects the hall generator with the control module, hall IC supply voltage, hall output signal and earth.

The hall IC is located adjacent to the magnet. The vane is connected to the distributor shaft, which passes between the hall IC and magnet. When the shaft rotates the vane also rotates. The vane has a number of gaps equal to the number of engine cylinders.

When the vane passes between the magnet and Hall IC, the vanes divert the magnetic flux from the magnet away from the hall IC. The change in magnetic flux causes the hall IC to switch the sensor on and off. A signal voltage is passed to the control module. The control module is therefore able to detect the engine speed and position from the hall IC-generated signal. The signal for the spark occurs the instant the vane leaves the air gap.

Note: With the ignition switched on, the hall generator produces a signal, which will trigger a spark, even when the engine is being turned over by hand. Extreme care should be exercised when handling this system owing to the risk of receiving an electric shock.

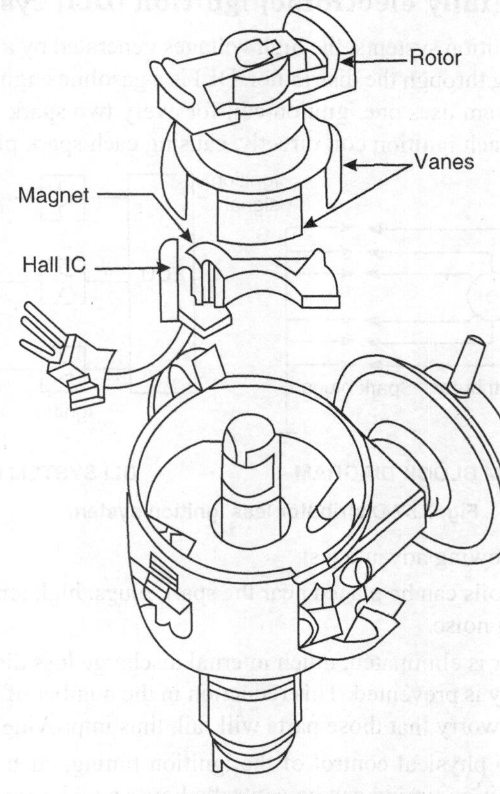

Fig. 7.55 Hall generator

Optical pulse generator

Fig. 7.56 shows a conventional distributor unit with an optical trigger. The optical system consists of a shutter (chopper), which is connected to the distributor shaft cam. Either side of the shutter is a light-emitting diode (LED) and a phototransistor (a semiconductor switch that is sensitive to light intensity).

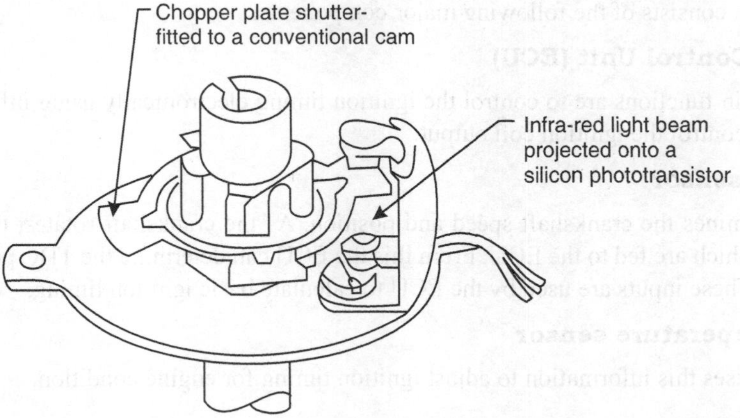

Fig. 7.56 An optical trigger system

When the distributor rotates, the shutter passes between the LED and the phototransistor and the projected beam of light is interrupted. The on and off signal voltage that is produced by this action is passed to the control module and used to determine the engine speed and position.

(iii) Distributor Less (fully electronic) Ignition (DLI) system

In past transistorized ignition systems, the high voltages generated by a single ignition coil were distributed to each spark plug through the distributor. DLI is a gasoline engine ignition system which uses no distributor. This system uses one ignition coil for every two spark plugs. The ECU distributes the primary current to each ignition coil directly, causing each spark plug to spark.

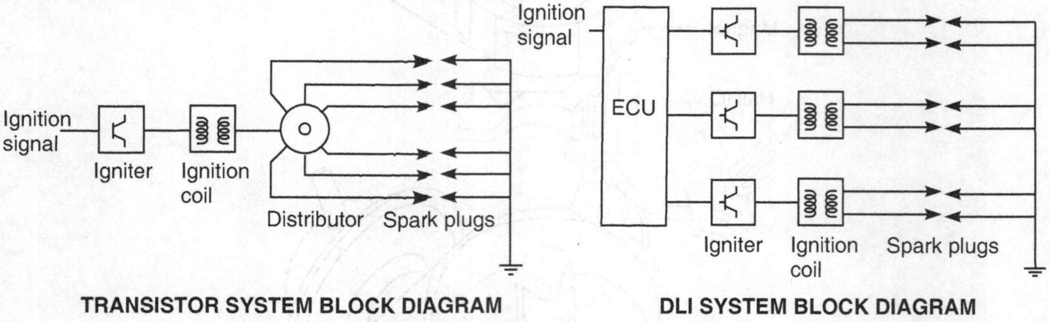

Fig. 7.57 Distributor less ignition system

This system has the following advantages:

(*a*) Since the ignition coils can be placed near the spark plugs, high tension cords can be shortened, thus reducing noise.

(*b*) Since the distributor is eliminated, much internal discharge loss disappears and the generation of noise thereby is prevented. This reduction in the number of mechanical components also eliminates the worry that those parts will fail, thus improving reliability.

(*c*) Because there is no physical control of the ignition timing, such as of the side electrode dimensions, the ignition timing can be controlled over a wider range.

To further improve the control of the ignition system a powerful microcomputer called an electronic control unit (ECU) is used. This system is similar to the electronic system outlined above. The main difference is that the ignition timing is controlled by the ECU instead of the centrifugal and vacuum advance mechanisms. The ECU operates as a pre-programmed computer. It gathers information from a variety of sensors interprets that information and adjusts the ignition timing accordingly.

The system consists of the following major components.

Electronic Control Unit (ECU)

Its two main functions are to control the ignition timing electronically using information from sensors and to control the ignition coil output.

Crankshaft sensor

This determines the crankshaft speed and position. As the crankshaft rotates, the sensor produces pulses, which are fed to the ECU. From this the ECU can determine the TDC position and the engine speed. These inputs are used by the ECU to calculate basic ignition timing.

Coolant temperature sensor

The ECU uses this information to adjust ignition timing for engine condition.

Knock sensor

This provides a small input voltage to the ECU, which is proportional to the vibration sensed in the engine block. The vibrations set up by combustion detonation are detected by the sensor and the information is fed to the ECU. The ECU responds by retarding the ignition timing until the knocking stops. The timing is then advanced again, in steps, up to the setting programmed into the ECU. This process of sensing and adjusting is carried out for each individual cylinder all the time the engine is running. It enables the engine to be run with the maximum possible advance setting to give optimum efficiency, without the risk of damage caused from detonation.

Ignition coil

This acts very like a normal coil. The only difference is that the primary resistance has been lowered in order to ensure that the HT output is reached faster and is maintained constantly throughout the speed range. It is important that the correct coil is used, as a coil from a contact breaker type of ignition system is not suitable.

STARTING SYSTEM

The internal combustion engines are not capable of self-starting. Early cars were cranked by hand, but as engines became larger, the starting system replaced the hand crank. The starting system includes the battery, the ignition switch, the starter solenoid or relay, the neutral safety switch and the starter motor.

This system cranks the engine by a small but powerful electric motor when it is being started. The battery sends current to the starter motor when the driver turns the ignition switch to start. This causes a pinion gear in the starter motor mesh with teeth on the ring gear around the engine flywheel. Then the starter motor rotates the crankshaft for starting.

The starting system can be separated into two circuits: the control circuit and the motor circuit. The motor circuit is the direct circuit path from the battery positive terminal to the starter motor. The motor circuit carries the starter motor current, which can be approximately 150 to 400 A. This current is too large to be carried by the small ignition switch contacts. Solenoids, and some relays, have large contacts capable of carrying a large amount of current. The control circuit controls the operation of the solenoid (or relay), which in turn switches current to the starter motor.

When starting, starter motor gets a heavy dose of current from the battery. Normally high current creates more heat. If the starter motor cranks the engine for long time, more heat will be generated. This results in damage of the motor. For this reason, the starter motor must never be used for more than 30 seconds continuously when starting. Also cranking should not be repeated without a pause of at least 2 minutes. During the first start, heat will be induced and it should be dissipated. Two minutes gap should be given between the one start and the subsequent start to allow the heat dissipation.

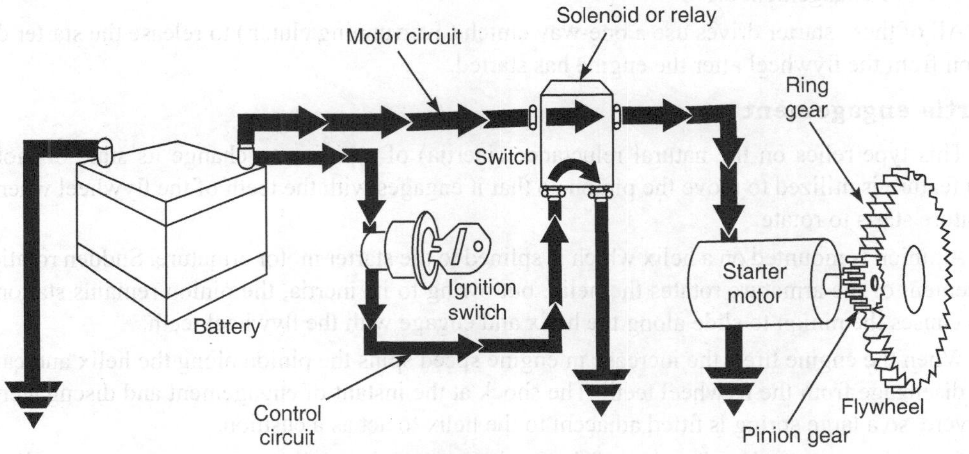

Fig. 7.58 Starting system

STARTER REQUIREMENTS

The requirements of a starting system are:

- Continuous readiness for starting
- Sufficient starter power at different temperatures
- Long service life for a high number of starts
- Robust design (to withstand meshing, cranking, high temperature, etc)
- Compact and light weight – helps mounting easier
- Longest possible maintenance free service life

STARTER DRIVE MECHANISM

A typical ratio of ring-gear teeth to pinion-gear teeth is 20 to 1. This gear ratio means that the starter motor rotates 20 times faster than the flywheel (and engine crankshaft). This ratio also means that there is a mechanical advantage of 20. It is 20 times easier for the motor to turn the crankshaft by driving the flywheel gear than for the motor to turn the crankshaft directly. This feature permits a relatively small starter motor to crank the engine.

Because the starter motor turns 20 times faster than the engine, the pinion and ring gears cannot be meshed together permanently. At high engine speeds, the starter motor shaft would be driven so fast that the armature windings would be thrown outward and the motor would be damaged. Therefore, provision must be made to engage the pinion gear into the ring gear when the engine is being cranked and to disengage the gears after the engine has started. This function is performed by the starter drive mechanism.

Generally speaking, these are two advantages from the starter drive mechanisms.

- When starting, it transmits motor torque to the engine flywheel and disconnects the starter motor from the flywheel after the engine has started.
- Provide gear reduction between the starter motor and the engine. Hence there will be sufficient torque to overcome the cranking resistance.

Almost all late-model starters use a positive-engagement drive mechanism to engage the motor pinion with the flywheel ring gear. There are two common kinds of starter drives used on light vehicles:

1. Inertia drive
2. Pre-engagement drive

All of these starter drives use a one-way clutch (overrunning clutch) to release the starter drive pinion from the flywheel after the engine has started.

Inertia engagement

This type relies on the natural reluctance (inertia) of a pinion to change its state of motion. This feature is utilized to move the pinion so that it engages with the teeth of the flywheel when the armature starts to rotate.

A pinion is mounted on a helix which is splined to the starter motor armature. Sudden rotational movement of the armature rotates the helix, but owing to its inertia, the pinion remains stationary. This causes the pinion to slide along the helix and engage with the flywheel teeth.

When the engine fires, the increase in engine speed spins the pinion along the helix and causes it to disengage from the flywheel teeth. The shock at the instant of engagement and disengagement is severe, so a large spring is fitted adjacent to the helix to act as a cushion.

On some systems the vibration of the engine causes the pinion to move along the helix and touch the flywheel. On some models the 'tinkling noise' given from this contact is prevented by using a light spring to hold the pinion away from the flywheel.

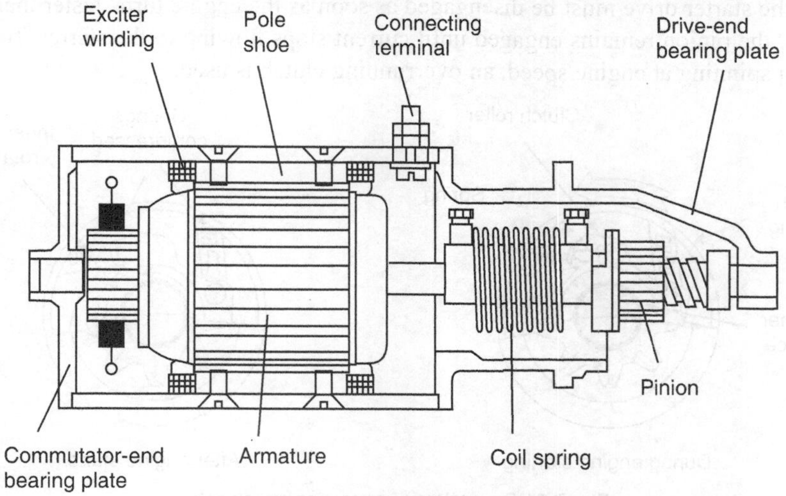

Fig. 7.59 Bendix inertia drive

Pre-engagement

This type was originally confined to diesel engines, but nowadays it is often used on petrol engines. The change from the inertia type to a pre-engaged drive on petrol engines was due to the difficulty of maintaining pinion engagement with an inertia drive when an engine 'part-fires' during the cranking period.

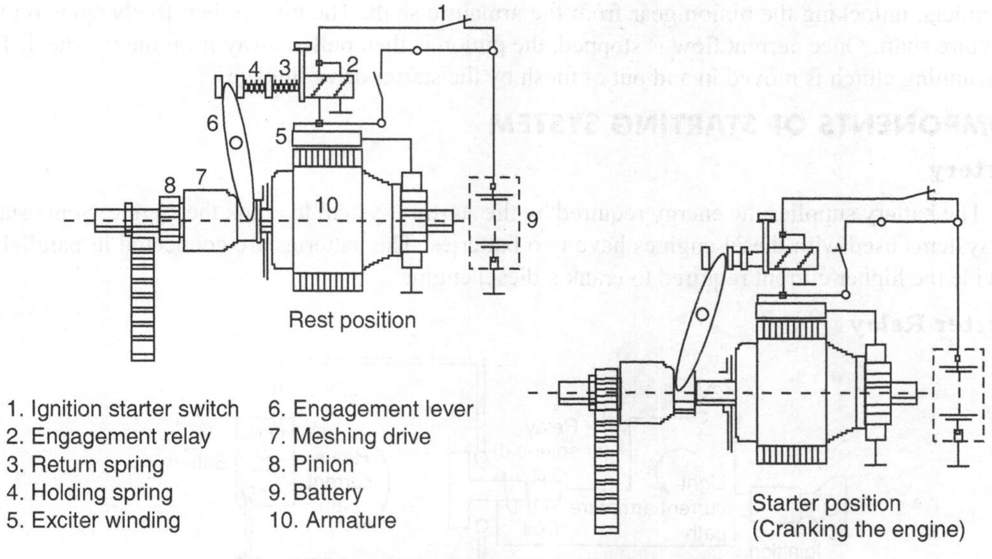

Fig. 7.60 Operation of pre-engagement type drive

In this arrangement the drive pinion on the starter motor shaft is pushed axially into mesh with the flywheel ring gear before the starter motor is switched on. When the pinion meshes with flywheel ring gear, the starter motor is switched on by engagement raky. A Solenold is usually employed to move the lever and close the switch contacts. This method is quite simple and having the advantage not to change gear teeth.

OVERRUNNING CLUTCH

Once the engine starts, its speed increases. If the starter motor remains connected to the engine through the flywheel, it will spin at very high speeds, destroying the armature and other parts. To prevent this, the starter drive must be disengaged as soon as the engine turns faster than the starter. In most cases, the pinion remains engaged until current stops flowing to the starter. To prevent the armature from spinning at engine speed, an overrunning clutch is used.

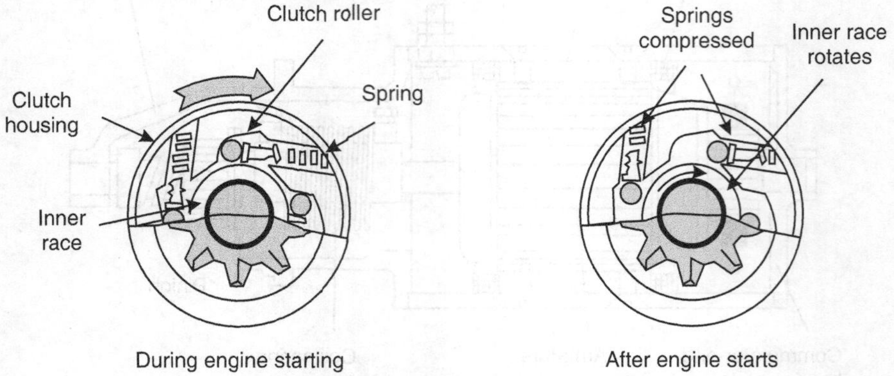

Fig. 7.61 Operation of overrunning clutch

The clutch housing is internally splined to the armature shaft. The drive pinion turns freely on the armature shaft within the clutch housing. When the clutch housing is driven by the armature, the spring loaded rollers are forced into the small ends of their tapered slots and wedged tightly against the pinion barrel. This locks the pinion and clutch housing solidly together, permitting the pinion to turn the flywheel and, thus, crank the engine.

When the engine starts, the flywheel spins the pinion faster than the armature. This releases the rollers, unlocking the pinion gear from the armature shaft. The pinion then freely spins on the armature shaft. Once current flow is stopped, the pinion is then pulled away from the flywheel. The overrunning clutch is moved in and out of mesh by the starter drive linkage.

COMPONENTS OF STARTING SYSTEM

Battery

The battery supplies the energy required by the starting system to crank the engine. Some starting systems used with diesel engines have two batteries. The batteries are connected in parallel to provide the higher current required to crank a diesel engine.

Starter Relay

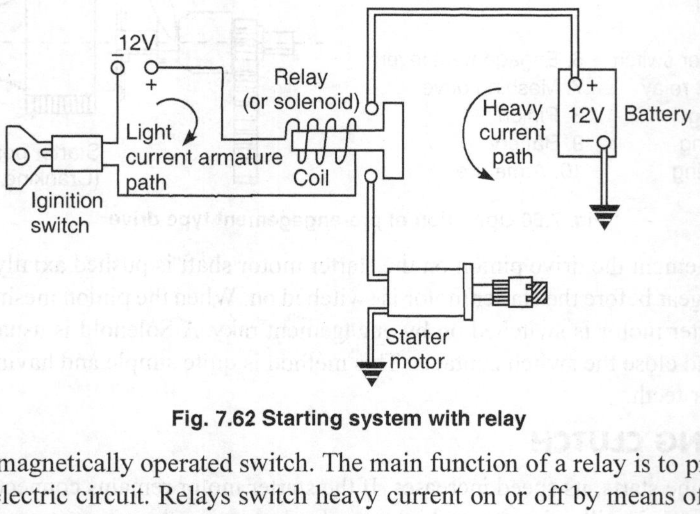

Fig. 7.62 Starting system with relay

A relay is a magnetically operated switch. The main function of a relay is to provide switching operation in an electric circuit. Relays switch heavy current on or off by means of a much smaller control current. The ignition switch controls the relay.

Relays are often used in starting circuits because of the large starter motor current draw. The ignition switch contacts are not large enough to carry the starter motor current. They would overheat and burn. To design an ignition switch to carry this current would be impractical (the switch would be too large). Instead, the relay contacts are made large enough to carry the starter motor current. By using a relay, the small current to energize the relay coil can control the large starter motor current. Therefore, the ignition switch contacts that carry the current to control the relay can be small. Therefore, ignition switch is protected from being damaged.

Ignition switch

The ignition switch is the key switch operated by the driver to start the engine. In the START position, current is supplied to the ignition system and to the starting system to operate the starter motor. The start position of the ignition switch is a momentary contact. In the start position, battery voltage is switched to the starter relay to operate the starter motor. When the engine starts, the driver releases the key and the switch automatically returns to the run position.

Starter motor

The starter motor is a small, but powerful, electric motor which operates when the ignition switch is turned to the START position. The starter motor has a small gear, called a pinion gear, mounted on the end of the armature shaft. The pinion gear engages a large ring gear mounted on the outside edge of the flywheel.

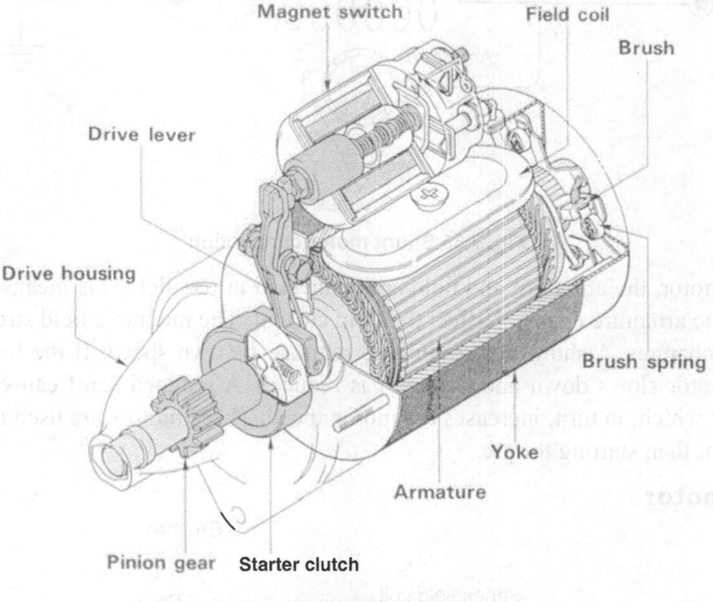

Fig. 7.63 Starter motor

MOTOR CONNECTIONS

Three common motor connections are series, shunt, and compound.

Series motor

In a series motor, the field and armature windings are connected in series. This means that all the armature current must pass through the field winding. When the armature of a motor is rotating, a voltage (called a counter electromotive force, or cemf) is induced in the armature. This occurs because whenever a conductor moves through a magnetic field, a voltage (and current) is generated in the conductor. This is the basic principle of electric current generation.

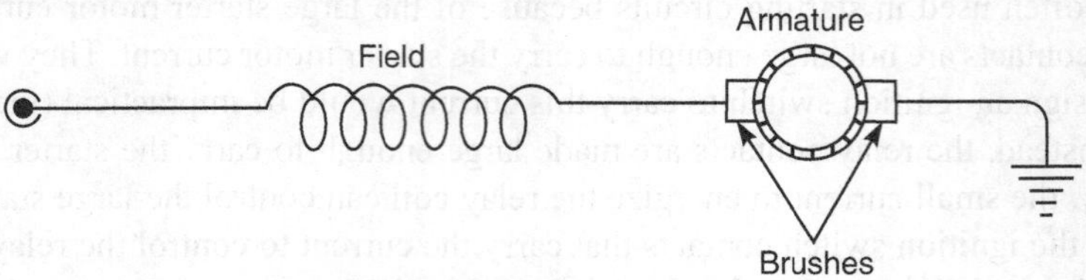

Fig. 7.64 Series motor connection

The cemf opposes the voltage that is being applied to the armature. Because the armature and field are in series, the effect of the cemf is to reduce the field and armature current. The faster the motor armature rotates the greater the cemf. Therefore, at low rpm, the field current is high (low cemf) and at high rpm, the field current is low (high cemf). The torque produced by a motor is directly related to its magnetic-field strength. A series motor can produce a large torque at low rpm because this is when its field current and magnetic-field strength are greatest. At higher speeds, the torque output of the motor is reduced. This is an ideal characteristic for a starter motor. When the starter motor first begins to crank the engine, a large amount of torque is required to overcome the inertia of the engine at rest. Series motors are commonly used as automotive starter motors.

Shunt motor

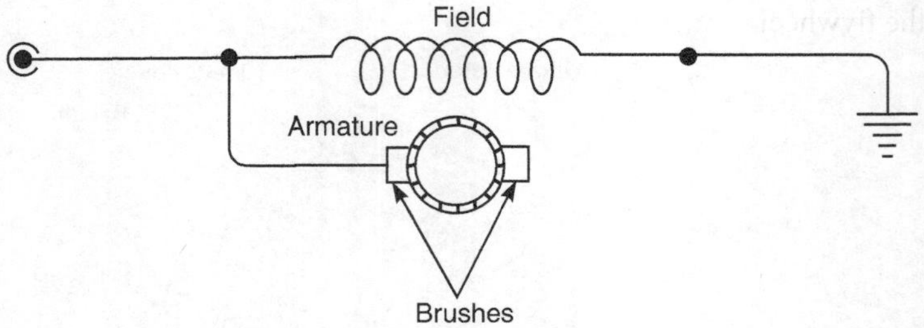

Fig. 7.65 Shunt motor connection

In a shunt motor, the armature and field are connected in parallel. This means the cemf which is generated in the armature does not affect the field current. The magnetic field strength is constant as motor speed changes. A shunt motor tends to regulate its own speed. If the load on the motor increases, the motor slows down and the cemf is reduced. A reduced cemf causes an increase in armature current which, in turn, increases the motor speed. These motors are used if constant speed is more important than starting torque.

Compound motor

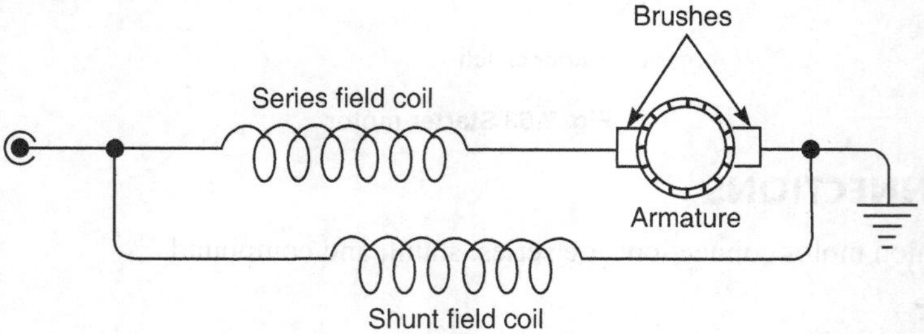

Fig. 7.66 Compound motor connection

In a compound motor, some of the field windings are in series, and some of the windings are in parallel or shunt. This type of motor combines the characteristics of the series motor and the shunt motor. The compound motor has a high starting torque and a fairly constant speed. Compound motors are also used as automotive starter motors.

CHARGING SYSTEM

The storage battery is a necessary source of power for the ignition of the air-fuel mixture, lighting, starting of engine and other duties, but the amount of energy which it can store is limited so that it cannot supply the power required by the automobile continuously.

The charging system serves to supply power to the various electric parts while the automobile is in operation and with the reserve power, charges the battery so that the battery will always be in the state to supply power when required. The charging system is comprised essentially of the generator, regulator, and battery.

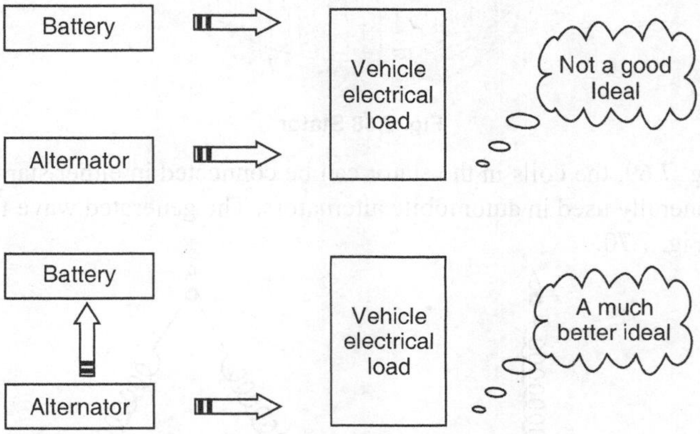

Fig. 7.67 Vehicle charging system

GENERATOR

The generator is driven by the V-belt which gets drive from the crankshaft. It converts mechanical energy obtained from the engine into electrical energy. Generators can be DC (dynamo) or AC (alternators).

All power required while the automobile is in operation is supplied by the generator, but when this is not enough, the battery also serves as the power source. In the reverse case, when the generator is producing more power than is required, the surplus power goes to charge the battery. The generator is, therefore, the power source when the vehicle is in operation and at the same time, it serves to charge the battery.

All charging circuits operate in three stages:

- During starting, battery supplies all load current
- During normal operation, generator supplies all current and recharges the battery
- During peak operation, battery helps generator supply current

ALTERNATOR

With the traffic growing heavier in recent years, the necessity for making frequent stops has increased engine idling time. The increasing numbers of accessories also consume a larger amount of power. Due to these causes, the output capacity of the direct-current generator is beginning to be over strained and tends to leave the battery in a discharged state.

To withstand the heavier electric loads and to enable charging the battery while idling, the alternator has been selected as being better suited for present day needs.

Construction

The alternator is comprised primarily of the stator, rotor, bracket, rectifier (silicon diodes) and brushes.

Stator

The stator has three sets of armature coils wound on it to induce a three-phase current.

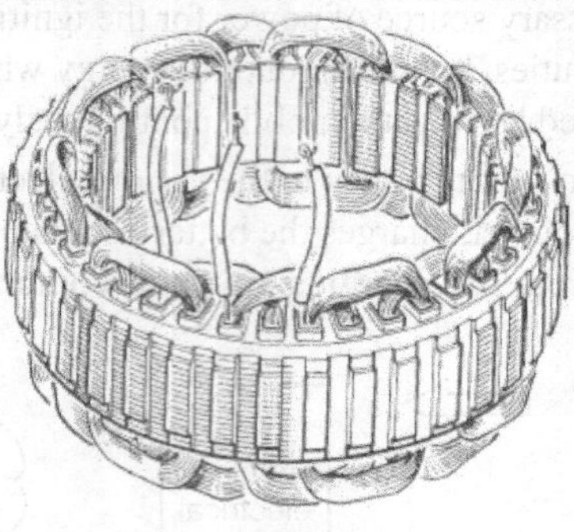

Fig. 7.68 Stator

As shown in Fig. 7.69, the coils in the stator can be connected in either star or delta form. The star connection is generally used in automobile alternators. The generated wave forms, phased 120° apart, are shown in Fig. 7.70.

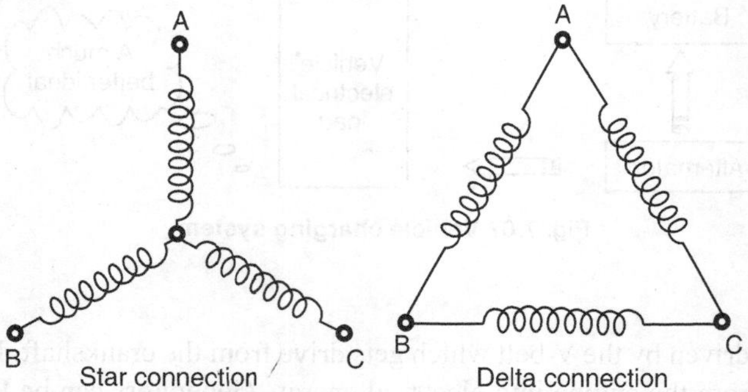

Fig. 7.69 Stator coil connection method

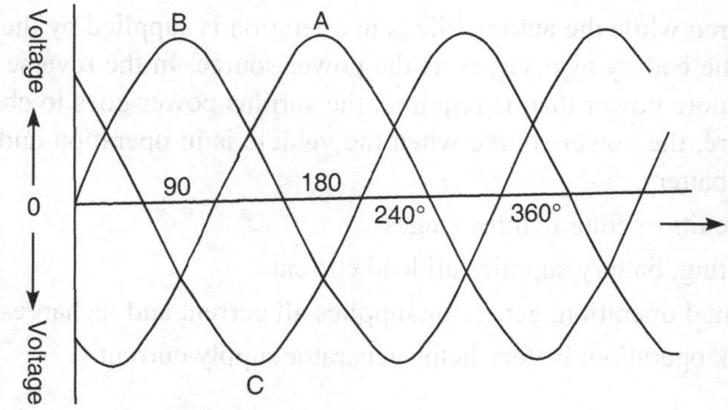

Fig. 7.70 Three-phase AC voltage wave forms

The stator coils are so fixed that they are not subject to centrifugal force. Thus, these stationary coils insure longer life, as there is less danger of the insulation becoming damaged and developing short circuits.

Rotor

Rotors can be classified into the salient pole type and Randell type. At present, the Randell type is mostly used in automotive alternator rotors. In this type, the number of poles is equal to the number of fingers and range from a few poles to more than a dozen poles.

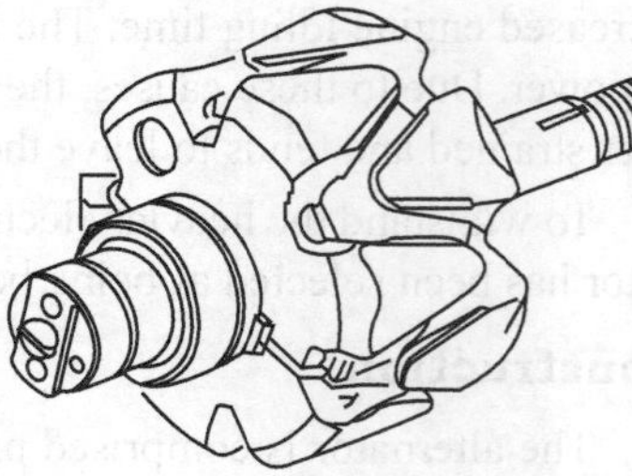

Fig. 7.71 Rotor

When the current flows through the coils, all fingers at one side of the disk become N poles and all those at the other side become S poles, resulting in the N and S pole to be arranged alternately. The features of this type are simplicity of construction and high strength against centrifugal force.

Bracket

The end bracket opposite to the pulley side has six diodes assembled into it that serve to rectify all of the three-phase alternating current generated.

Rectifier (Silicon diodes)

When voltage is impressed on the alternator silicon diodes from the reverse side, hardly any current will flow through. But when the voltage is impressed from the regular side, a large current will flow even if the impressed voltage is small. The silicon diodes must be cooled as the passage of current through them causes their temperatures to rise. When the diodes heat up to above 150ºC, they will no longer be able to rectify. Therefore, they are under forced cooling by the fan on the pulley to prevent them from heating over the specified temperature.

Brushes

The brushes serve to pass a current of 2 to 3 amperes to the rotor coils. As the main current does not flow through these brushes, the brushes have much longer life and hardly require replacement.

Principle of alternator

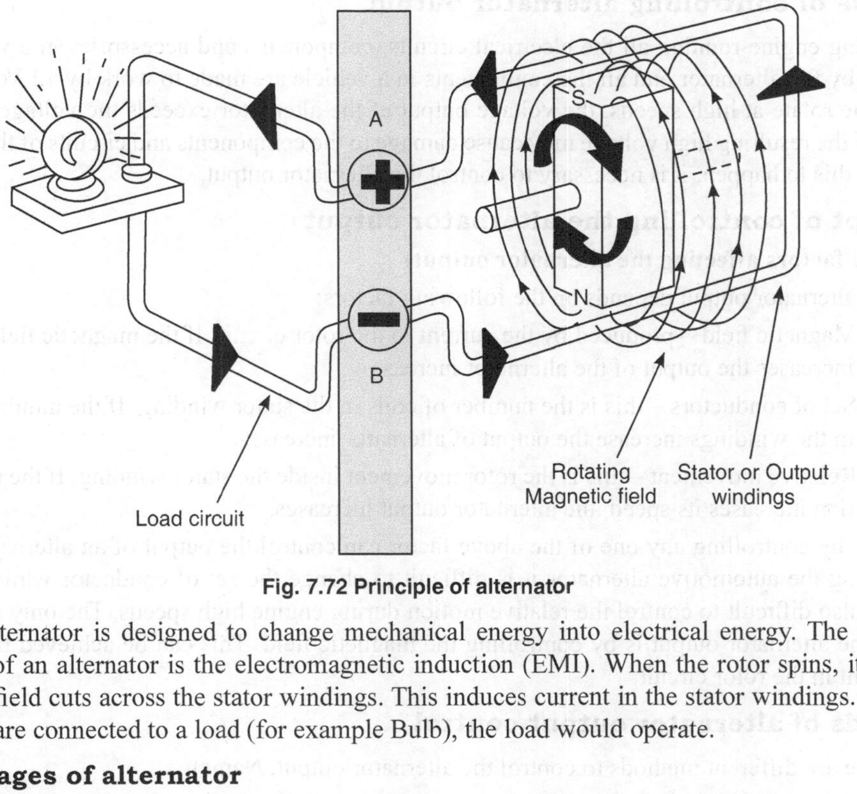

Fig. 7.72 Principle of alternator

An alternator is designed to change mechanical energy into electrical energy. The working principle of an alternator is the electromagnetic induction (EMI). When the rotor spins, its strong magnetic field cuts across the stator windings. This induces current in the stator windings. If stator windings are connected to a load (for example Bulb), the load would operate.

Advantages of alternator

1. The brushes contact on slip rings so that there is no sparking to shorten the brush life. In the alternator, the field coils (rotor coils) rotate so that the brushes are required to pass only a small current, and moreover there are no commutator grooves to wear out the brush.
2. **Rotor has high strength against speed**

   Only the field coils are wound on the rotor so that there are a small number of windings, which makes the rotor lighter and also stronger against high speed operation. In the Randell type rotor, the coils are wound in the direction of rotation which gives them high strength against centrifugal forces.

3. **Good rectifying characteristics**

   Six diodes are used to perform full-wave rectification of the three-phase alternating current generated. Compared to the commutator, higher efficiency rectification can be performed at high speeds without trouble.

4. **Current limiter not required, depending on the design**

   Due to the inductance resistance of the stator coil, the current produced by the alternator will not increase even if the output speed rises above the specified value.

5. **Cut-out relay not required**

   The rectifying diodes have the property of preventing the current from flowing in the reverse direction.

6. **Charging is possible while idling**

   The pulley ratio can be made longer since the strength is high and generating characteristics good at high speed.

ALTERNATOR OUTPUT CONTROL

Purpose of controlling alternator output

During engine running all the electrical circuits, components and accessories in a vehicle are supplied by the alternator and all the components in a vehicle are made to work by 12 Volts. When the engine rotate at high speeds, the voltage output of the alternator exceeds the voltage above 14 Volts and the resulting high voltage may cause damage to the components and circuits of the vehicle. To avoid this to happen, it is necessary to control the alternator output.

Concept of controlling the alternator output

(The factors affecting the alternator output)

The alternator output depends on the following factors:

1. Magnetic field – produced by the current in the rotor circuit. If the magnetic field strength increases the output of the alternator increases.
2. Set of conductors – this is the number of coils in the stator winding. If the number of coils in the windings increase the output of alternator increases.
3. Relative movement – this is the rotor movement inside the stator winding. If the rotor rotation increases its speed, the alternator output increases.

Thus by controlling any one of the above factor can control the output of an alternator. When considering the automotive alternator it is difficult to change the set of conductor while working and it is also difficult to control the relative motion during engine high speeds. The only method to control the alternator output is by controlling the magnetic field. This can be achieved by varying the current in the rotor circuit.

Methods of alternator output control

There are different methods to control the alternator output. Namely

1. Constant current type: In this method the output of the alternator is measured in terms of ampere current and the output is controlled to maintain the constant current output.
2. Constant voltage type: In this method the output of the alternator is measured in terms of voltage and the output is controlled to maintain constant voltage output.

In case of motor vehicles the alternator is controlled by using the voltage regulators. These regulators use the criteria of controlling the current flow to the rotor to vary the magnetic field in order to control the alternator output.

The regulator increases and decreases the amount of field current to the rotor in order to control the amount of voltage produced by the alternator. When the voltage rises, a resistance is inserted in series with the field coil circuit to limit current flow through the field coils and lower the generated voltage. When the voltage drops, the resistance is removed from the field coil circuit to allow the generated voltage to build up again. The repetition of this action maintains the voltage at a constant value. Voltage regulators can be classified into the contact point type and the IC type.

Point (vibrating contact) type of voltage regulator

Point type voltage regulator composed of points, a magnetic coil and a resistor. The regulator controls the supply of current to the rotor coil by pulling and releasing the moving point in accordance with the voltage applied to the regulator coil.

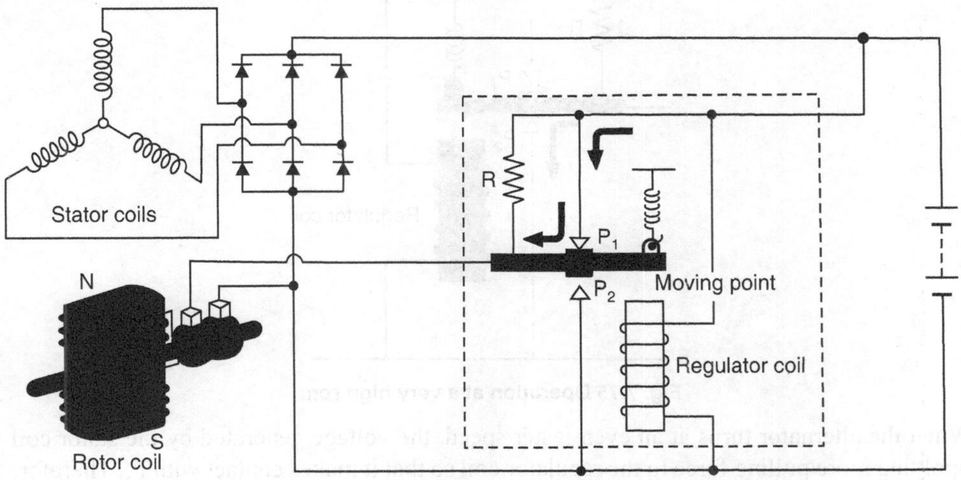

Fig. 7.73 Point type voltage regulator

When the alternator is turning at a low rpm and a heavy load is applied, the voltage at the stator coil will become lower than the regulating voltage (approximately 14 V) at the regulator. Accordingly, the moving point will make contact with P_1, thus allowing the battery current to flow to the rotor coil through P_1.

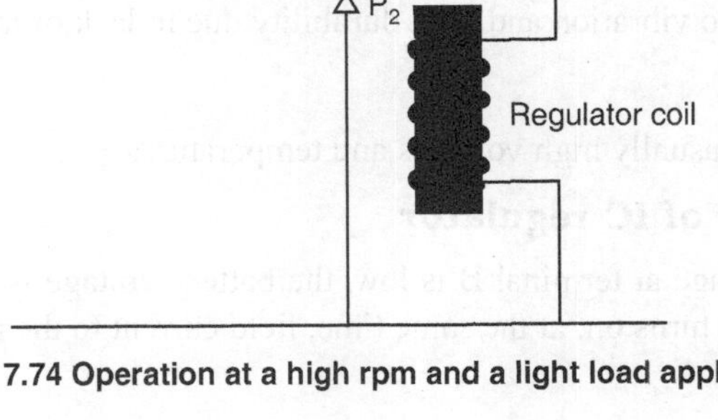

Fig. 7.74 Operation at a high rpm and a light load applied

When the alternator is turning at a high rpm and the voltage of the stator coil rises above that of the regulating voltage (approximately 14 V) at the regulator, this voltage is applied to the regulator coil so it is affected by a greater pulling force which separates it from P_1.

When the moving point moves away from P_1, the current flowing to the rotor coil passes through resistor R and therefore is reduced in intensity. Less current to the rotor coil will cause the stator coil to generate less voltage and there will be reduced pulling force on the coil, so the moving point will return and make contact with P_1. This, in turn, causes a rise in the current to the rotor coil and the moving point again moves away from P_1.

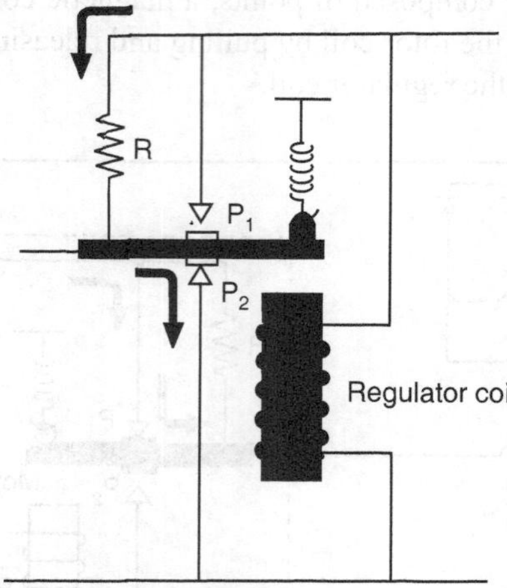

Fig. 7.75 Operation at a very high rpm

When the alternator turns at an even faster speed, the voltage generated by the stator coil will rise, applying more pulling force to the regulator coil so that it makes contact with P_2. Therefore, the current through resistor R will then flow to P_2 and not to the rotor coil.

When there is no longer any current to the rotor coil, the stator cannot generate electromotive force, so the voltage of the alternator drops and the moving point moves away from P2. Thus, once again the alternator voltage will rise and the moving point will be pulled.

IC voltage regulator (pointless type)

In IC regulator, Integrated Circuit (IC) is used instead of relay as in the point type regulator. An IC is a miniaturized circuit composed of many small electronics and electrical components (transistors, diodes, resistors, capacitors, etc) built into a circuit board or silicon chip.

Advantages

- Compact and light weight
- Excellent reliability due to its lack of mechanical points.
- Good resistance to vibration and high durability due to lack of moving parts.

Disadvantages

- Susceptible to unusually high voltages and temperatures.

Operating principle of IC regulator

When the output voltage at terminal B is low, the battery voltage is applied to the base of Tr_1 through resistor R, and Tr_1 turns on; at the same time, field current to the rotor coil flows from B ⇒ rotor coil ⇒ F ⇒ Tr_1 ⇒ E.

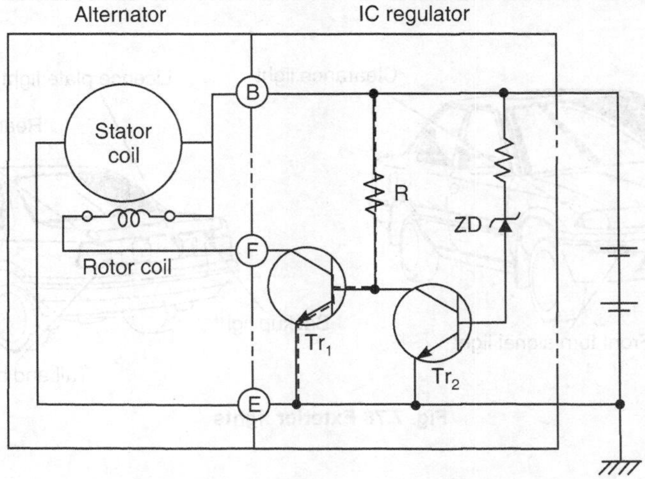

Fig. 7.76 Operation at a low rpm and heavy load applied

When the output voltage at terminal B is high, a higher voltage is applied to the Zener diode (ZD) and when this voltage reaches the Zener voltage, the ZD becomes conductive. Accordingly, as Tr_2 turns on, Tr_1 turns off. This interrupts the field current, regulating the output voltage.

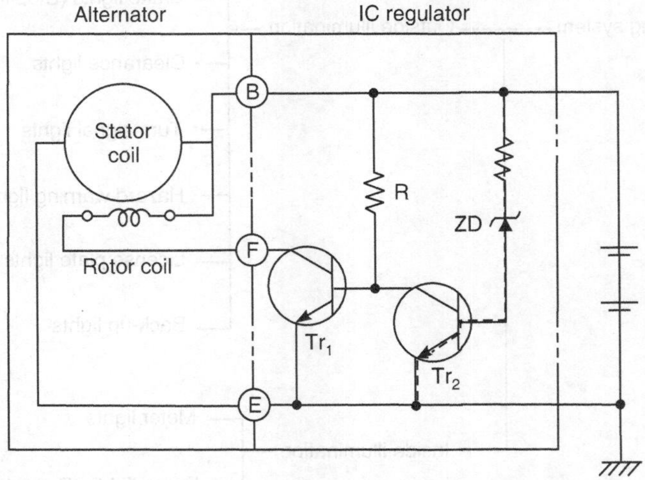

Fig. 7.77 Operation at a high rpm and a light load applied

> **Note:** The difference between the Zener diode and a normal diode is that when any voltage more than a certain level is applied in the reverse direction, the Zener diode will become conductive and will allow a current to flow.

LIGHTING SYSTEM

The lighting system in automobiles includes exterior lights such as head lights, parking lights, turn signals, back up lights, tail lights, number plate lights and interior lights such as instrumental-panel lights, map lights, various warning and indicator lights and courtesy lights, which turn on when the car door is opened.

This system is regulated by federal law. For this reason, all vehicles have standardized lighting systems and use similar circuit arrangements. The entire lighting circuit is made up of a series of individual circuits each having its own switch and earth return connection.

Exterior lights

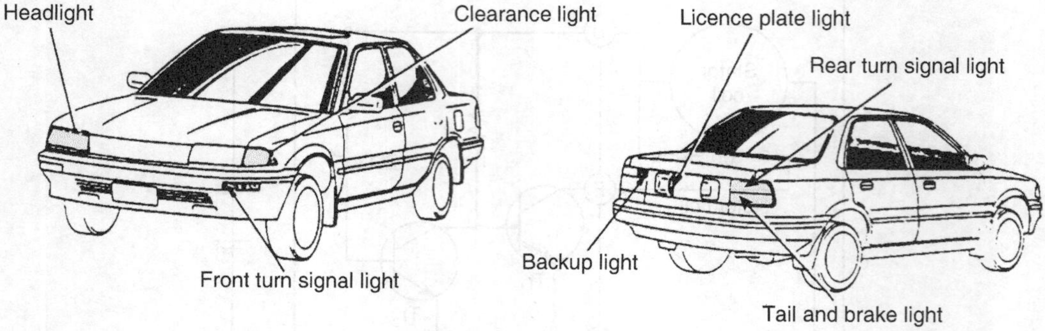

Fig. 7.78 Exterior lights

Headlight

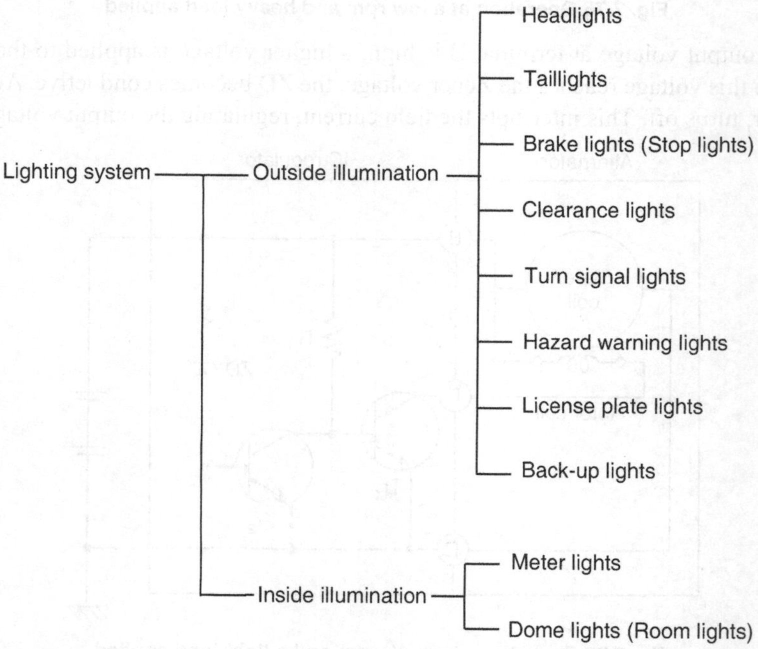

The headlight system is a lighting system to illuminate the road in front of the vehicle. Generally, high-beam and low-beam lights are provided and can be switched from one to the other by the dimmer switch. Halogen headlights are used on some vehicles. This improves visibility on high beam by 25 percent. Halogen headlamps require about 40 percent less power on low beam. This allows the car to have a smaller and lighter weight alternator.

Signal light systems

(a) Clearance lights and tail lights

These are low-intensity lights to indicate the presence and width of a vehicle at night to other vehicles in the front or behind. Those in the front are called clearance-lights and those in the back are called taillights. The power rating of these lights is 5 watts.

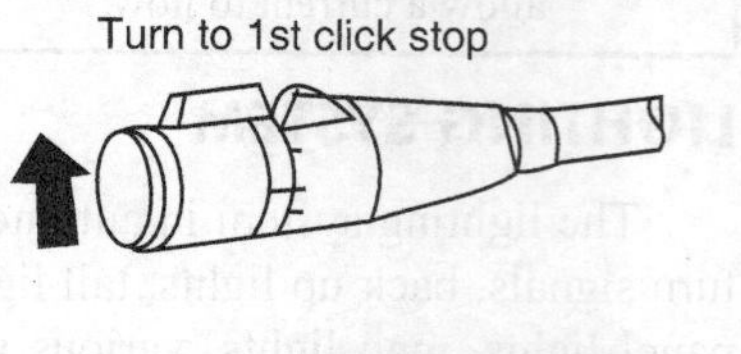

Fig. 7.79 Clearance and tail lights

(b) Brake lights (Stop lights)

Brake lights are installed at the rear of the vehicle to prevent rear-end collisions by indicating to following vehicles that the vehicle is braking. Brake lights come on when the driver presses the brake pedal. The movement of the brake pedal closes a switch. This sends electrical current to the brake lights and they glow behind the red plastic lanes in the taillight.

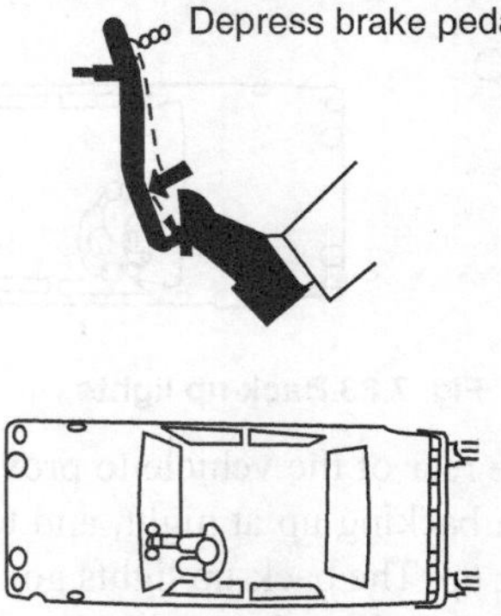

Fig. 7.80 Brake lights

The stoplights are about three times as bright as taillight. This makes sure that any driver behind you can see your car parking even in the daytime. The stoplights have power rating of 21 watts.

In some cars, the brake light and taillights are combined into one double filament bayonet base bulb. In some other cars, a separate bulb is used for each light.

(c) Turn signal lights

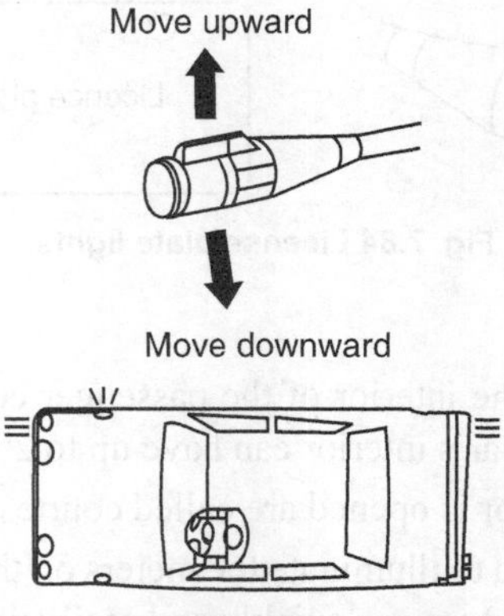

Fig. 7.81 Turn signal lights

Turn signal lights are used to let other drivers know that you are about to make a turn. They flash 60 to 120 times per minute. This blinking (flashing) controlled by a flasher unit in the circuit. Bulb rating should be within the range of 15 to 36 watts for each of the front and rear lamps, and the side mounted repeater lamp is about 6 watts.

(d) Hazard warning lights

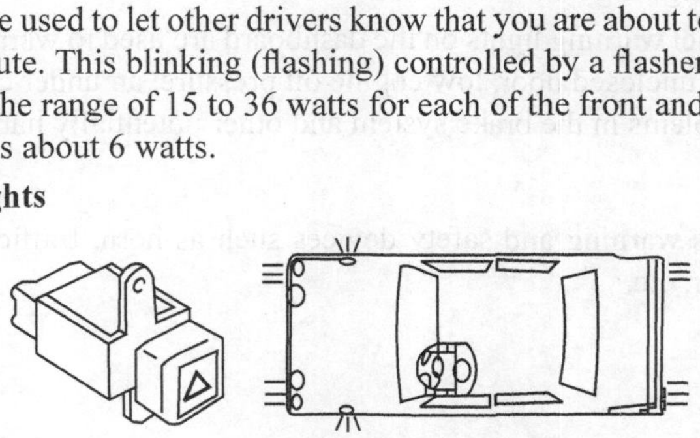

Fig. 7.82 Hazard warning lights

In the event of an emergency, such as a roadside breakdown, all the lamps should be capable of working simultaneously, when they are called "hazard warning lights". The hazard warning lights indicate the existence of the vehicle to the front, rear and both sides during emergency stopping or parking. The emergency warning lights are turned on with a separate switch that causes all four turn signals to flash at once. The power rating of turn signal lights is 21 watts.

(e) Back-up lights

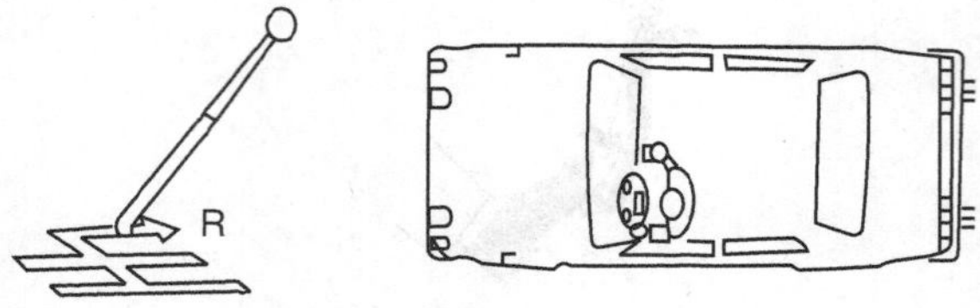

Fig. 7.83 Back-up lights

Back-up lights are installed at the rear of the vehicle to provide extra illumination to allow the driver to see behind the vehicle when backing up at night, and to warn following vehicles that the driver intends to back up or is backing up. The back-up lights go on when the transmission is shifted into reverse with the ignition switch on. It is activated by the switch located on the transmission. Their power rating is 21 watts.

(f) License plate lights

These lights illuminate the rear license plate. The license plate lights go on when the taillights go on.

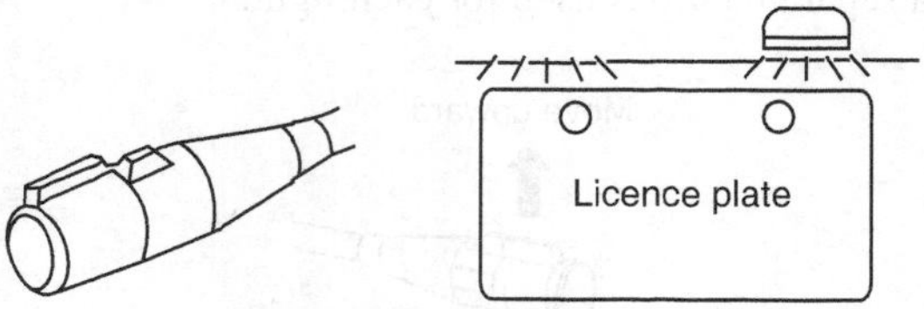

Fig. 7.84 License plate lights

Interior lights

The interior light illuminates the interior of the passenger compartment, but is designed so as not to dazzle the driver at night. A car's interior can have up to 20 lamps.

The bulbs that light when a door is opened are called courtesy lights.

Instrument panel lights are used to illuminate the meters on the instrument panel at night, to enable the driver to read the meters and gauges quickly and easily while driving. The instrument panel lights go on when the taillights go on.

The instrumental panel warning lights on the dashboard are used to warn the driver of a car with problem. These indicates unclosed door, low engine oil pressure, an under charging alternator, high coolant temperature, problems in the brake system and other potentially harmful situations.

Accessories

This system includes warning and safety devices such as horn, trafficator (or) flasher, windshield wiper, speedometer, etc.

Review Questions

1. What is meant by ignition timing?
2. What are the classifications of an ignition system?
3. Why is a resistor used in the primary ignition circuit?
4. How does ignition take place in a petrol engine?
5. How many Volts of current reaches at the spark plug?
6. What are the special features of the magneto ignition system?
7. Where magneto ignition system is being used?
8. What is the principle of current generation?
9. What other functions are performed by magneto except ignition?
10. What is battery ignition system?
11. What is the function of a distributor?
12. Which are the main parts of a distributor?
13. What is the function of contact breaker point?
14. How much gap is maintained between contact breaker points?
15. What will happen if the contact breaker points gap is less or more?
16. What is the function of condenser?
17. What do you understand by advance or retard of the ignition system?
18. What is the main benefit of advance ignition?
19. What are the different types of advance or retard mechanisms?
20. What is the function of spark plug?
21. Which are the main parts of a spark plug?
22. What should be the characteristics of a good spark plug?
23. What is the importance of spark plug gap? How much gap should be maintained?
24. What will be the effects if the spark plug gap is less or excess?
25. How many types of spark plugs are there?
26. What could be the possible faults in a spark plug?
27. What should be done for the maintenance of the spark plug?
28. Why is the spark advance mechanism provided in the distributor?
29. What are the causes of the engine backfire?
30. What is meant by reach of the spark plug?
31. What is a hot plug?
32. What is a cold plug?
33. What will happen if a long reach plug is replaced with a short reach plug by mistake?
34. What will happen if a short reach plug is replaced with a long reach plug by mistake?
35. What are the reasons for no spark?
36. What happens when the condenser gets discharged?
37. What is the essential difference between the magneto and the coil ignition system?
38. Why is it necessary to retard the spark for full throttle operation under load?
39. Why is it desirable to advance the ignition timing when the engine speed increases?
40. What is referred to as vacuum advance? How does this mechanism works?
41. What is referred to as centrifugal advance? How does this mechanism works?
42. When does a condenser get charged?
43. What are the advantages of electronic ignition?
44. Which component feeds the battery with current?
45. Why are nearly all automobile electrical components wired on the earth return system?
46. Why is a relay used to operate the starter?

47. What is a hydrometer used for?
48. What is a high rate discharge tester used for?
49. What are the main circuits in an auto electrical system?
50. Which is the source of electric energy in an automobile?
51. What is the purpose of the voltage regulator?
52. What is the purpose of the current regulator?
53. What is the approximate wattage of the headlamp?
54. What is a self-starter?
55. What is the approximate gear ratio between the cranking motor pinion and the engine flywheel ring gear?
56. Why is it necessary for the starter pinion to disengage from the flywheel as soon as the engine starts?
57. What are the reasons for the failure of a starting motor to crank an engine?
58. Sometimes the starter motor spins but does not crank the engine, Why?
59. For what purpose is the solenoid used in a starting circuit?
60. What is Bendix drive in a starting system?
61. Is electricity generated by a battery?
62. What is a cell?
63. How are the cells of a battery grouped?
64. What is the difference between series and parallel cell connection?
65. Name the materials for separators.
66. Why battery is called storage battery?
67. What is a primary cell?
68. What is a secondary cell?
69. On what factors the power of a battery depends?
70. What does the capacity of a battery indicate?
71. How many cells are there in a 12 volt storage battery?
72. How are positive and negative plates identified in a battery?
73. What type of battery is used in automobiles?
74. What is an electrolyte?
75. Why ordinary water is not used in an electrolyte?
76. How is the electrolyte prepared for a battery?
77. The specific gravity of a battery should not vary more than ---------- between the cells.
78. What will happen when the specific gravity of the electrolyte is more than 1.31?
79. What is meant by a grid in a battery?
80. Why does the terminal of a battery get corroded? How these are cleaned?
81. What is the effect of neglecting to top up the battery?
82. Why is distilled water added in the battery?
83. If the specific gravity of the acid in a battery is low, is it desirable to add some more acid?
84. If the specific gravity reading of a storage battery is 1.29 at 90°F, what is the correct specific gravity?
85. What is the specific gravity for (1) fully charged (2) fully discharged battery and (3) dead battery?
86. What is ampere-hour rating?
87. What is known as cold cranking amperes of a battery?
88. What is reserve capacity of a battery?
89. What are the methods of battery testing?
90. What do you understand by battery sulphation?
91. What instrument is used to measure the specific gravity of a liquid?
92. What precautions to be taken before the battery is put in charge?
93. What are the gauges fitted on the instrument panel?
94. Why do we prefer series motor as automotive starter motor?

8

CHAPTER

CLUTCH

CLUTCH

The clutch is a device used to connect and disconnect engine torque to the gearbox. There are friction clutches and various types of fluid or hydrodynamic coupling. If the vehicle has a manual-shift gearbox, a friction clutch normally has to be operated.

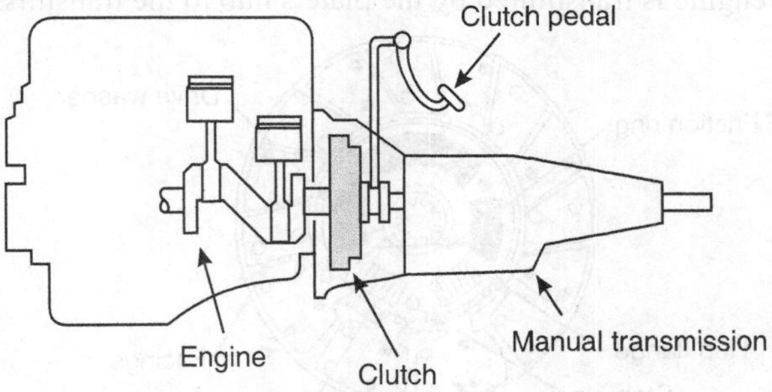

Fig. 8.1 Clutch location

The friction clutch is a link between the engine and the transmission which can be disengaged (separated) by a pedal-operated mechanism. The normal condition of the clutch is engaged, with the friction surfaces pressed together. When it is disengaged, the friction surfaces are moved apart. The clutch is usually disengaged,

- when starting the engine
- when shifting the gears
- when stopping the vehicle, and
- when idling the engine

FUNCTIONS

The functions of clutches are:

- transmits power gradually from the engine to the drive wheels in order to start the vehicle smoothly from a stop.
- smoothly change the transmission gears (i.e. without gear clashing) when shifting gears.

COMPONENTS

The clutch consists of a number of parts: Clutch Palte, clutch shaft (or input shaft), pressure plate assembly, release bearing and clutch linkages.

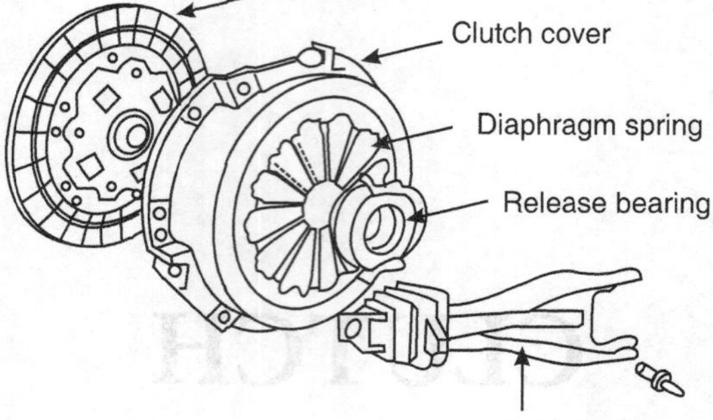

Fig. 8.2 Components of a clutch

Clutch Plate

The clutch plate is a steel plate covered with frictional material that fits between the flywheel and the pressure plate. In the center of the plate is the hub, which is splined to fit over the splines of the input shaft.

When the clutch is engaged, the disc is firmly squeezed between the flywheel and pressure plate. So the power from the engine is transmitted by the plate's hub to the transmission's input shaft.

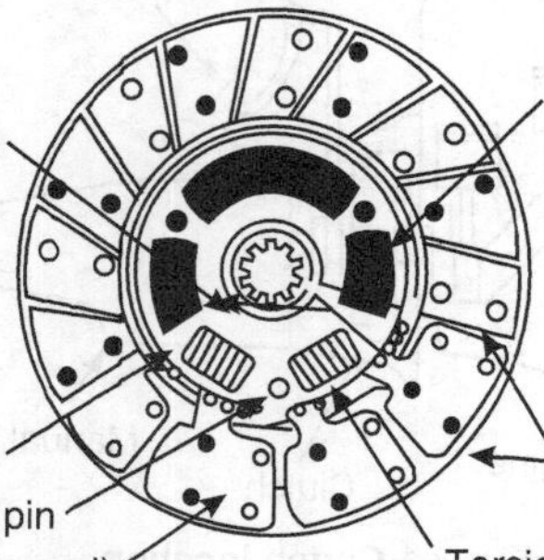

Fig. 8.3 Clutch disc

A clutch plate has frictional material riveted or bonded to both sides. Grooves are cut across the face of the friction facings to allow for smooth clutch action, increased cooling and a place for the dust to go as the clutch plate wears.

Asbestos wire-woven material was the most common facing for clutch plates. Due to recent awareness of the health hazards resulting from asbestos, new lining materials such as paper based and ceramic materials that are strengthened by the addition of cotton and brass particles and wire. These increase the torsional strength of the facings and prolong the life of the clutch plate. The torsional dampener springs circle the center hub. This type of clutch plate is called "flexible clutch plate". When the clutch is engaged, the springs cushion the sudden loading by flexing and allowing some twist between the hub and plate. Stop pins limit this torsional movement to approximately $\frac{3}{8}$ inch.

Clutch shaft (or Input shaft)

The clutch shaft projects from the front of the transmission. The clutch plate will be splined to the clutch shaft. When the clutch is engaged, the clutch plate drives the transmission's input shaft through these splines.

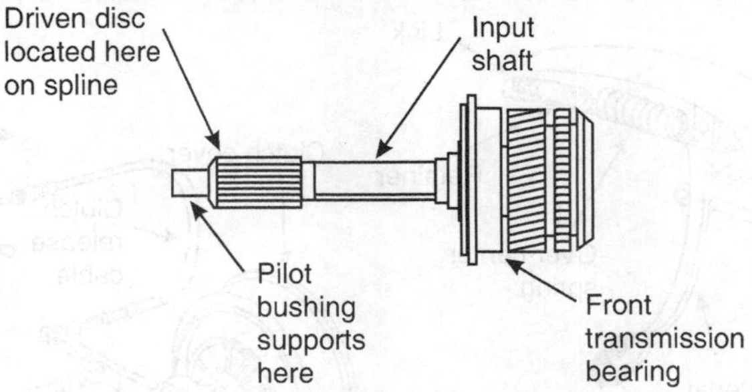

Fig. 8.4 Clutch shaft

Pressure plate assembly

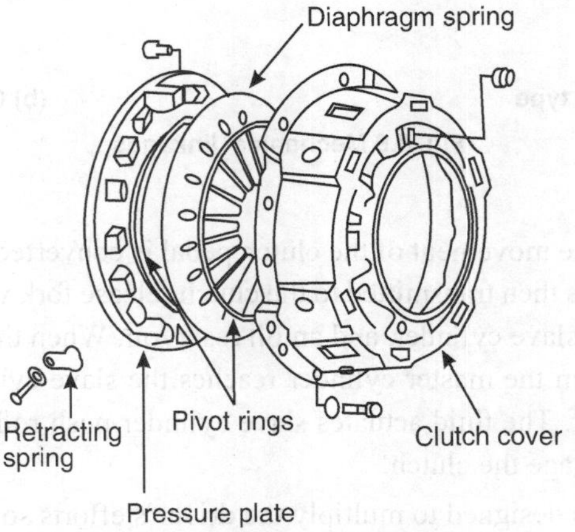

Fig. 8.5 Pressure plate assembly

The pressure plate squeezes the clutch plate onto the flywheel when the clutch is engaged and moves away from the plate when the clutch is disengaged. These actions allow the clutch plate to transmit or not transmit the engine's torque to the transmission.

A pressure plate assembly includes a clutch cover (or clutch housing), release bearing, a pressure plate and a spring. The spring used in most pressure plates is a single Belleville spring or diaphragm type spring, however a few use multiple coil springs. The clutch cover is a large bell-shaped metal casting that is fitted to the flywheel of the engine and rotates with the flywheel.

Release bearing (or) throw-out bearing

The clutch release bearing is a ball type bearing and is usually sealed and prelubricated to provide smooth and quiet operation as they move against the pressure plate to disengage the clutch.

Clutch linkages

Clutches are normally operated by either mechanical or hydraulic linkages.

(a) Mechanical linkages

Two types of mechanical linkages are used: the cable type and the shaft and lever type. The shaft and lever clutch linkage has many parts and pivot points and transfers the movement of the clutch pedal to the release bearing via shafts, levers, and bell cranks. This action causes the release bearing to move against the pressure plate.

A cable-type clutch linkage is simple and lightweight. However, cables will gradually stretch and can break due to electrolysis. When the clutch pedal is depressed, the cable pulls on the clutch fork, which causes the release bearing to move against the pressure plate.

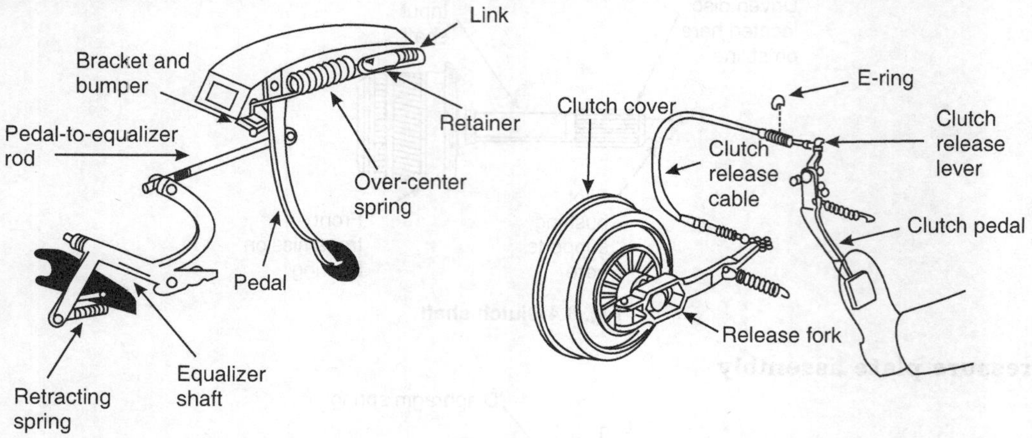

(a) Lever type (b) Cable type

Fig. 8.6 Mechanical linkages

(b) Hydraulic linkage

In this type of clutch, the movement of the clutch pedal is converted by the master cylinder into a hydraulic pressure which is then transmitted to the clutch release fork via the slave cylinder. It consists of a master cylinder, a slave cylinder, and an oil reservoir. When the clutch pedal is depressed, the fluid under pressure from the master cylinder reaches the slave cylinder. The slave cylinder is mounted on the clutch itself. The fluid actuates slave cylinder push rod which further operates the clutch release fork to disengage the clutch.

The hydraulic system is designed to multiply the driver's efforts so that a light force applied to the foot pedal produces a much greater force on the clutch fork. A small piston in the master cylinder travels a relatively long distance with only a low input force. This moves larger piston in the slave cylinder a relatively small distance but produces a greater force to disengage the clutch .

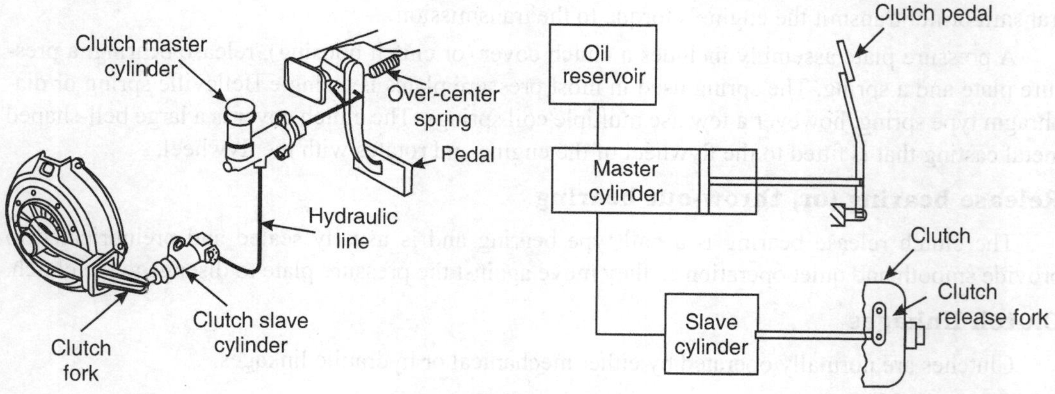

Fig. 8.7 Hydraulic linkage

TYPES OF A CLUTCH

There are different types of friction clutches, either running dry or in oil. The clutches discussed here are dry friction types, which are common practice in today's vehicle.

Cone clutch

The cone clutch was used in the early days of vehicles because of its mechanical simplicity.

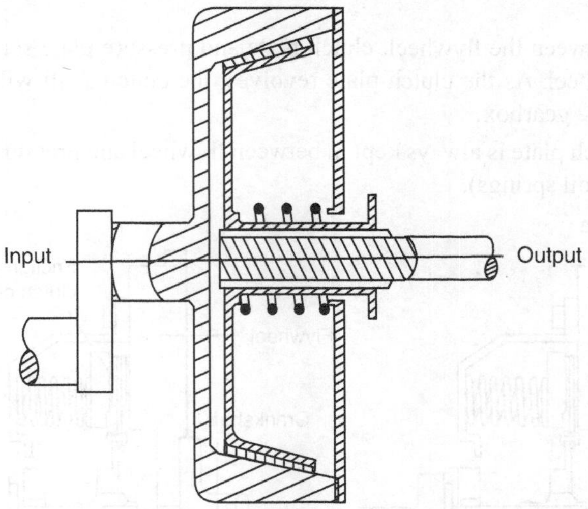

Fig. 8.8 Cone clutch

The cone clutch is so called because each of its two friction faces is a frustrum of a cone, one male and the other female. The clutch uses these two conical surfaces to transmit torque by friction. The female cone is keyed to the crankshaft, whereas the male cone is free to axially slide on the output shaft. A clutch pedal is used to engage and disengage the clutch, by bringing the two conical surfaces in contact. Leather, cork, asbestos or brass is generally used as friction material.

Torque is transmitted due to the frictional forces set up at the contact. With a correct choice of cone angle the clutch is free from slip as long as the friction linings remain in good condition. The axial force required to engage the clutch is provided by a helical compression spring. A short rearward displacement of the male member against helical compression spring is needed to disengage the clutch completely. This is done by the driver through clutch operating mechanism.

The cone clutch transfers a higher torque than plate or disk clutches of the same size due to the wedging action and increased surface area.

Limitations

The major limitation of cone clutches is that the conical alignment of the cones is critical. Deviations would lead to rapid wear of the friction lining. Besides that in case of conical clutches, a larger force is required to engage a clutch than that required during operation when both the cones rotate at the same speeds.

Applications

Cone clutches are generally now only used in low peripheral speed applications although they were once common in automobiles and other combustion engine transmissions. This is because the clutch does not have to be pushed in all the way and the gears will be changed quicker. They are now confined to very specialist transmissions in racing, rallying, or in extreme off-road vehicles, although they are common in power boats.

The cone clutch, although sometimes used in the early days, is not now considered suitable as a dry clutch for this application due to its tendency towards sticking, harshness and inconsistency in operation. Small cone clutches, however, employed in transmission systems, generally in oil, and particularly in synchromesh mechanisms.

Single plate clutch

It is most commonly used in motor vehicles such as cars, buses, trucks and tractors. The clutch consists of a number of parts: Clutch plate, clutch shaft (or input shaft), pressure plate assembly, release bearing and clutch linkages.

Operation

Due to friction between the flywheel, clutch plate and pressure plate surfaces, the clutch plate revolves with the flywheel. As the clutch plate revolves, the clutch shaft will also revolve. Clutch shaft is connected to the gearbox.

Normally, the clutch plate is always kept in between flywheel and pressure plate by the pressure spring (diaphragm or coil springs).

(i) Coil spring type

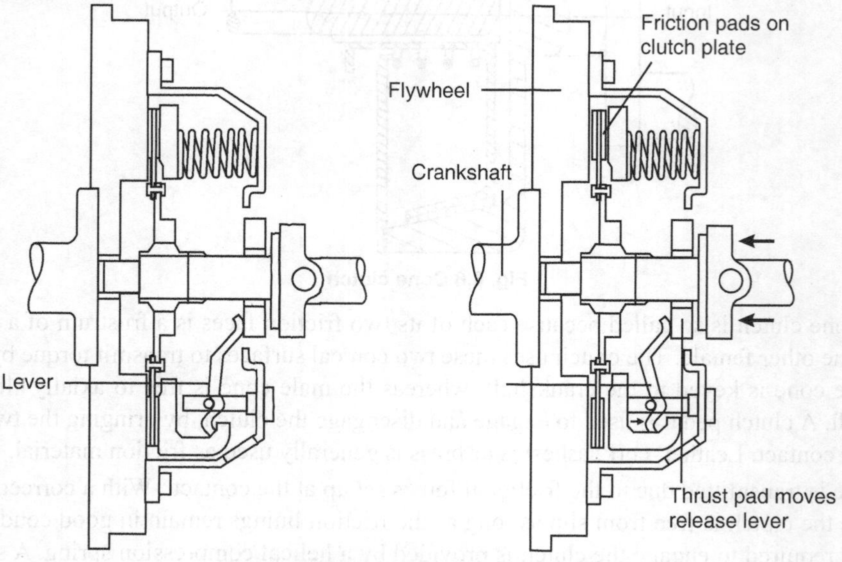

Fig. 8.9 Single plate coil spring clutch

When the clutch pedal is depressed, the pressure plate moves out against the pressure springs. The gap between pressure plate and flywheel increases. Now, the clutch plate is free to rotate. Thus power is not transmitted. This position is called *clutch release* or *declutching*.

(ii) Diaphram spring type

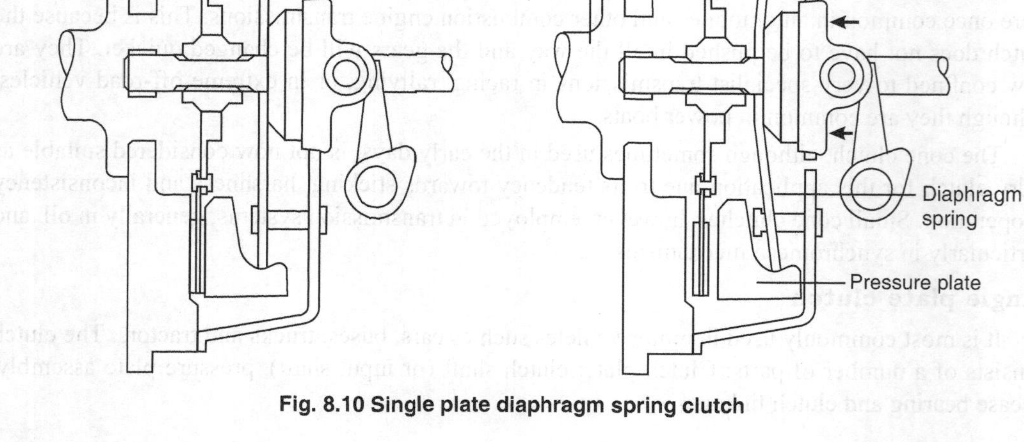

Fig. 8.10 Single plate diaphragm spring clutch

In the diaphragm type, a diaphragm spring is used instead of a number of coil springs. When the clutch is engaged the spring is almost flat and its outer rim exerts pressure against the clutch plate. To disengage the clutch, the clutch pedal is depressed. This causes the linkage to move the throwout bearing against the inner portion of the diaphragm spring. This in turn causes the rim of the diaphragm spring away from the flywheel. The gap between pressure plate and flywheel increases. Now, the clutch plate is free to rotate. Thus power is not transmitted.

As soon as the pedal is released, the pressure spring forces the pressure plate towards the flywheel. The clutch plate is gripped between the flywheel and pressure plate. This is called clutch engaging. At this position, the power is transmitted to the gearbox.

Advantages

1. It makes easy to change gears.
2. It is reliable.

Disadvantages

Space required to accommodate the clutch is more as compared to multi plate clutch.

Multi-plate clutch

Some high performance clutch assemblies use multiple clutch plates. A separator plate is used in these assemblies to separate the clutch plates and it is fitted to the flywheel by a driving pin. When the clutch is engaged, the first clutch plate is held between the clutch pressure plate and seperator plate and the second clutch plate is held between the seperator plate and the flywheel. When disengaged, the seperator plate, flywheel and pressure plate assembly rotate as a unit while the clutch plates which are not in contact with the pressure plates do not transmit power to the transmission.

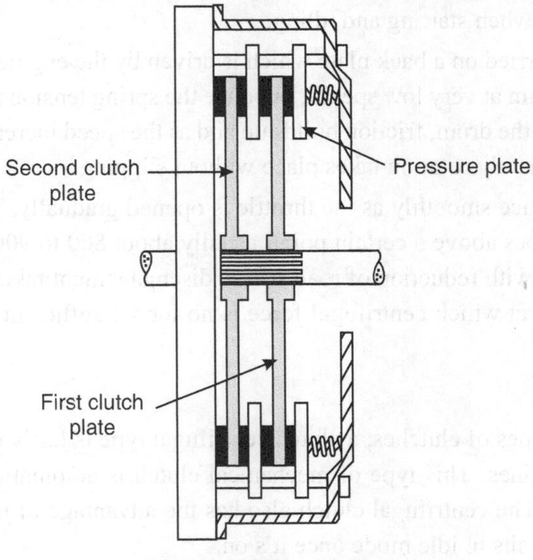

Fig. 8.11 Multiplate clutch

Multiplate clutches are preferred in vehicles, where

- high torque is to be transmitted
- space available is limited

Centrifugal clutch

Centrifugal clutch is the common name given to a clutch which uses centrifugal forces to engage. This type of mechanical clutch is fully automatic, and works depending on the speed of the engine. If the engine is turning over very slowly, then the centrifugal clutch is disengaged, and the vehicle comes to a stop. If the engine speeds up then the automatic clutch will engage, and the vehicle will move forward. The centrifugal clutch and the drive axle have sprockets which spin a chain, which will spin the wheels.

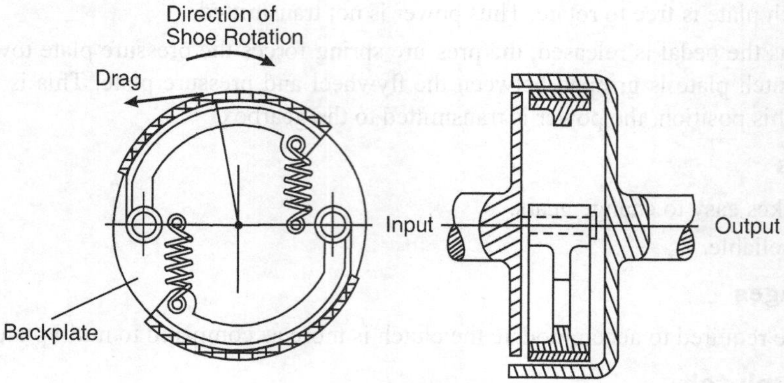

Fig. 8.12 Centrifugal clutch

Centrifugal clutches are often used in mopeds, lawn movers, go-karts, chainsaws, and mini bikes to:

- keep the internal combustion engine from stalling when the vehicle is stopped abruptly; and,
- disengage loads when starting and idling.

The two shoes are carried on a back plate which is driven by the engine. Springs hold the shoes out of contact with the drum at very low speeds, but once the spring tension is overcome by centrifugal force the shoes rub on the drum, friction builds up and as the speed increases the drum is dragged round by the shoes. Ultimately rotation takes place without slipping.

Engagement takes place smoothly as the throttle is opened gradually. The springs expand outward when engine rpm goes above a certain point, usually about 800 to 900 rpm's. As the speed of the driven member drops with reduction of road speed, disengagement takes place when the engine reaches the critical speed at which centrifugal force is no longer sufficient to overcome the spring tension.

Advantages

Compared to other types of clutches, a clutch centrifugal type is fairly cheap, which is why it's popular among small engines. This type of mechanical clutch is automatic, so no kind of control mechanism is necessary. The centrifugal clutch also has the advantage of not needing to be turned off and on. Instead, it just sits in idle mode once it's on.

> **Note:** **Centrifugal force** usually refers to a fictional force that seems to give an outward "center-fleeing" acceleration to an object traveling in a circle. Centrifugal forces come into effect when an object is continuously going around in a circle.

Review Questions

1. What is the function of a clutch?
2. When a clutch is used in a motor vehicle?
3. What are the features of a good quality clutch?
4. Why is multiplate clutches sometimes used in heavy vehicles?
5. What are the shortcomings in the cone clutch because of which it is not being used these days?
6. Why do we call single plate clutch, a dry disc clutch?
7. What is meant by a wet clutch?
8. Why are clutch plates perforated?
9. What is a clutch grab?
10. What is a clutch drag?
11. Why are coil springs installed in a clutch plate?
12. Should all clutch springs in a multispring clutch be of the same length and strength? If not what will happen?
13. What is Belliville spring in a clutch assembly?
14. How can the driver identify that a conical spring is installed in the clutch simply by operating the clutch?
15. What is free play in a clutch? Why is it provided?
16. What is clutch chattering? What causes it?
17. Why is it considered a bad practice to rest the foot on the clutch pedal while driving?
18. What is clutch slippage? What causes it?
19. What is the objection in allowing the clutch to slip when rounding a corner?
20. What item should first be checked when clutch slip occurs?
21. What are the main causes of clutch noise?
22. Hydraulic clutches are used in ------------------.
23. A hydraulic clutch does not incorporate a ---------------- plate.
24. What are the common defects of clutch?
25. What is the other name of hydraulic clutch?

9 CHAPTER

GEARBOX

GEARBOX

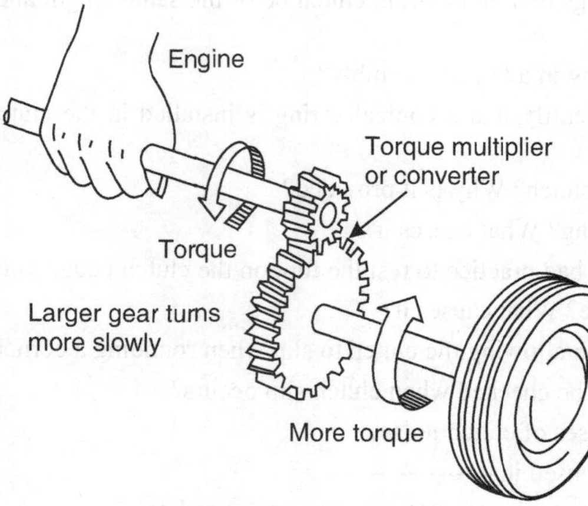

Fig. 9.1 Torque multiplication

The engine produces very little power at low speeds. If the engine were permanently connected through the clutch directly to the propeller shaft, it would not be possible to move easily from the stationary position.

A vehicle requires a large torque to start off or to climb a hill or to pull a heavy load. However, a large torque is not necessary during high speed travel when the wheels need to be driven at a high speed. It should also be noted that any increase in engine speed would be of no advantage, as this would increase power but decrease the torque developed by the engine and in turn, the torque at the road wheels.

The transmission is provided to handle this problem by changing gear combinations (gear ratios) to change the engine output into a torque that suits the travel condition of the vehicle.

PURPOSE

In simple terms, the purpose of a gearbox is summarized as follows:

- To multiply engine torque.
- To provide a definite break in the transmission system so that the engine may run with the vehicle stationary (neutral position).
- To provide a means of reversing the drive to the road wheels, thus enabling the vehicle to move backwards.

TRACTIVE EFFORT

The torque available on the wheel produces a driving force which is parallel to the road known as tractive effort. The traction between the tyres and the road determines how fast a car can accelerate, brake and/or corner or how well it sticks to the ground.

TRACTIVE RESISTANCE

When a vehicle is travelling at a constant speed along a road, the resistance to its forward motion is termed "tractive resistance", which consists of:

(i) Rolling resistance

In general, this depends upon the nature of the ground. A vehicle travelling off the road on the rough ground will obviously have a greater rolling resistance to overcome than a vehicle travelling on the hard smooth surface of a well-maintained road. The weight of the vehicle, friction between the tyres and the road surface and even the speed, may influence the rolling resistance. Furthermore, transmission friction may also be included in rolling resistance.

(ii) Gradient resistance

This is dependent upon the steepness of the hill and the overall weight on the vehicle.

(iii) Wind (or) Air resistance

This depends upon the actual shape and size of the vehicle. A degree of control can be exercised over wind resistance by careful design of the vehicle and by improved streamlining techniques.

If a vehicle is to travel at a uniform speed, the tractive resistance must be balanced by the tractive effort produced at the tyre-tread contact area. During acceleration, the driving force must be greater than the total tractive resistance in order to overcome the inertia of the vehicle.

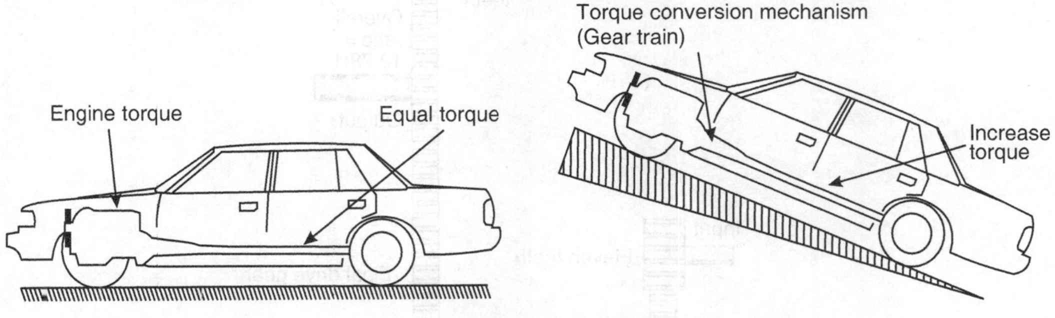

Fig. 9.2 Wind resistance

When a car is travelling on level road, engine torque is enough to keep car moving. If the vehicle should meet a hill, the torque at the road wheels required to propel the vehicle will have to increase to overcome the tractive resistance to motion. If there is no increase in torque, the speed of the vehicle will decrease, as will both the speed and power of the engine.

GEAR RATIO

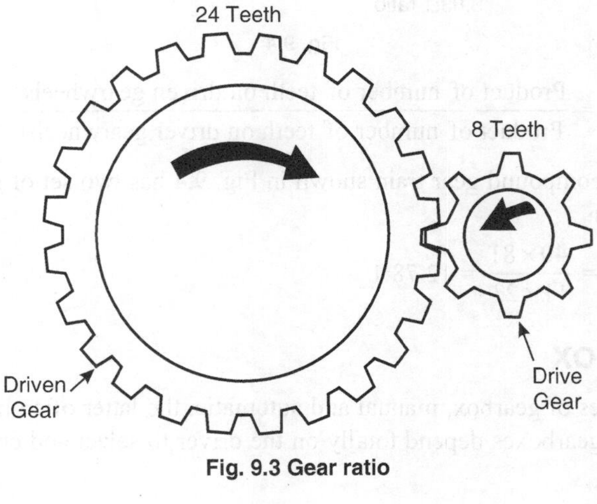

Fig. 9.3 Gear ratio

A gear ratio is a measure of the relationship between two or more gearwheels that are in meshed contact with each other.

$$\text{Gear ratio} = \frac{\text{Number of teeth on driven gear wheel}}{\text{Number of teeth on driver gear wheel}}$$

For example, in Fig. 9.3 two gearwheels are meshed in contact with each other. The drive gear has 8 teeth and the driven gearwheel has 24 teeth.

$$\text{Gear ratio} = \frac{24}{8} = 4:1$$

To provide a vehicle with a suitable set of gear ratios, manufacturers use gearboxes that contain several set of gears. These are called compound gears. To calculate a compound gear ratio or overall gear ratio, we use the formula,

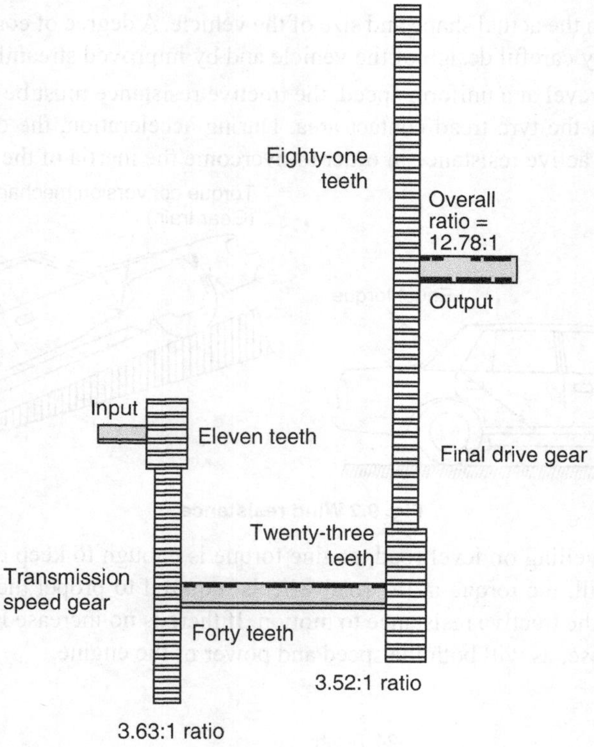

Fig. 9.4

$$\text{Overall gear ratio} = \frac{\text{Product of number of teeth on driven gearwheels}}{\text{Product of number of teeth on driver gearwheels}}$$

For example, the compound gear train shown in Fig. 9.4 has two set of gearwheels meshed in contact with each other.

$$\text{Overall gear ratio} = \frac{40 \times 81}{11 \times 23} = 12.78:1$$

MANUAL GEARBOX

There are two types of gearbox, manual and automatic, the latter often being called automatic transmission. Manual gearboxes depend totally on the driver to select and change gear. Automatic gearboxes can change gear according to engine load, road speed, driver's demand and in the latest computer controlled units, according to the style of driving. There are three types of manual gearbox:

1. Sliding mesh gearbox
2. Constant mesh gearbox
3. Synchromesh gearbox

Today the synchromesh is the most common type in use.

Sliding mesh gearbox

Sliding mesh type gearbox is the oldest type of manual transmission used in automobiles. Among the manual gear transmission, this sliding mesh type is the simplest in construction.

However, in this type the mechanical efficiency is very low and the noise level is quite high. Moreover the driver required considerable skill in changing the gears.

Construction

The Fig. 9.5 below shows the construction of a sliding mesh type transmission having three forward and one reverse speeds. There are two gears (6 and 5) attached on the main shaft and four gears (2, 3, 4 and 7) on the counter shaft. The two gears on the main shaft can slide and can mesh with the gears on counter shaft. Therefore, it is called sliding mesh gearbox. In this gearbox, spur gears are used because of the sliding action. A separate gear is mounted on the idler shaft (8). The gears 1 and 6 are mounted on the splined main shaft. These gears can be slided by a shifting yoke.

Power flow of 3-speed sliding mesh gearbox

(i) Gears in neutral

When the engine is running and the clutch is engaged, the counter shaft is driven by the clutch gear. The low speed and high speed gears are fitted on the transmission main shaft which does not rotate.

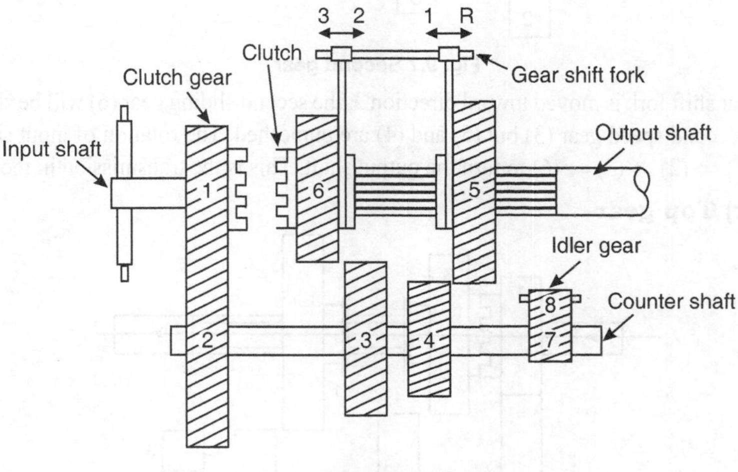

Fig. 9.5 Gears in neutral

At the same time, they are not engaged with any driving gears. Therefore, there is no motion transmitted from engine to the wheels. Hence, the vehicle is stationary.

(ii) First (or) Low speed gear

When the gear shift fork moves towards direction (1) by operating the gear shift lever, the sliding gear (5) on the output shaft will be shifted forward to mesh with low speed gear (4) on the countershaft. It results the rotations of input shaft being transmitted in the order (1) ⇒ (2) ⇒ (4) ⇒

(5) to turn the output shaft. This gear combination is the one that produces the lowest speed from the input shaft and low transmission. In this case the torque output from the gearbox will be as geart as that applied at the input.

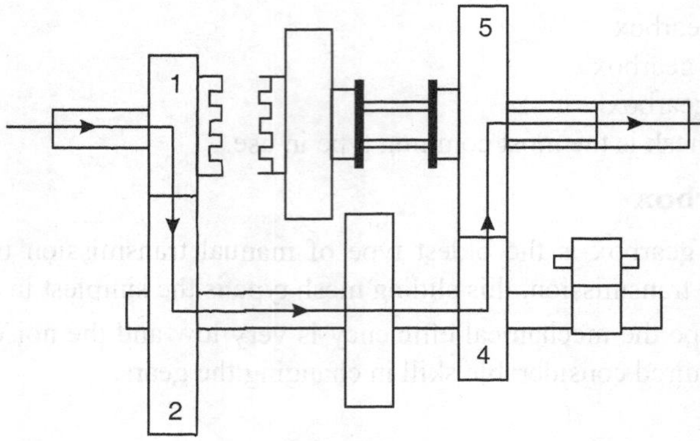

Fig. 9.6 First gear

(iii) Second gear

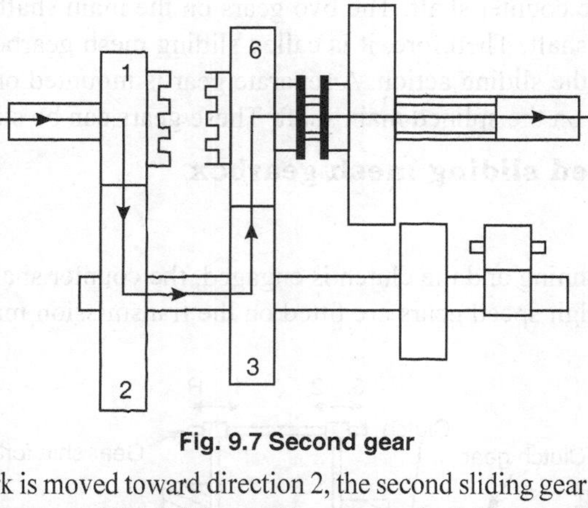

Fig. 9.7 Second gear

When the gear shift fork is moved toward direction 2, the second sliding gear (6) will be shifted backward to mesh with the second speed gear (3) but (5) and (4) are unmeshed. The rotation of input shaft is transmitted in the order (1) ⇒ (2) ⇒ (3) ⇒ (6) to turn the output shaft. This is the transmission in the second speed.

(iv) Third (or) Top gear

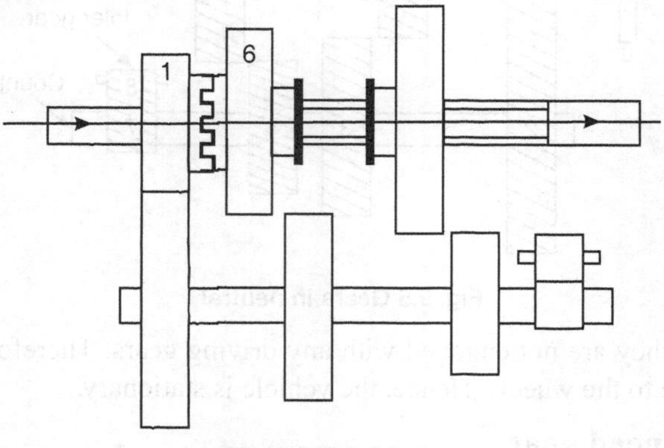

Fig. 9.8 Third gear

When the gear shift fork is moved toward direction 3, the clutch will be meshed but gears (6) and (3) are unmeshed. Due to this, both the input and output shafts are coupled and rotated together with the same speed. This is the transmission in the third or top speed that gives a ratio of 1:1.

(v) Reverse gear

When the gear shift fork is moved toward direction R, the sliding gear (5) will be shifted backward to mesh with the reverse idler gear (8). Then the rotation of input shaft is transmitted in the order (1) ⇒ (2) ⇒ (7) ⇒ (8) ⇒ (5) to turn the output shaft in reverse direction. This is the transmission in reverse speed.

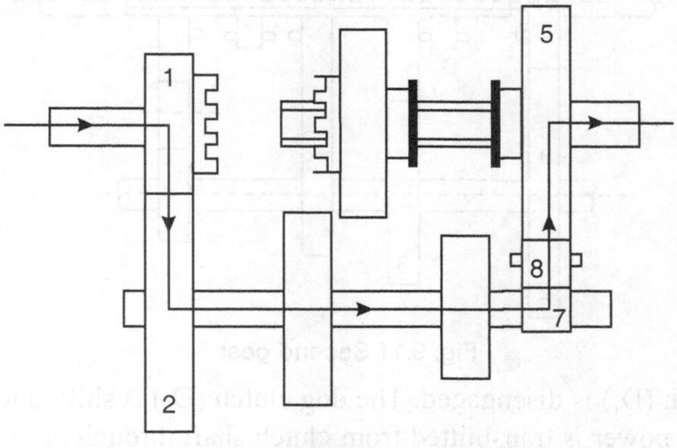

Fig. 9.9 Reverse gear

This is the same ratio as for the first gear and irrespective of the size of the idler gear it will be seen that the ratio always remains the same. For this reason it is called an idler – it changes the direction, but does not alter the ratio.

Constant mesh gearbox

In this type of gearbox, all the gears are in constant mesh having dog clutches for engaging and disengaging the gears. The gears on the splined main shaft are free. The dog clutches are provided which are free to slide on the main shaft. The gears on the counter shaft are fixed. Only reverse gears are spur gear type and all other are helical gears. As the gears are always in mesh, helical gears are used which are quiter running.

Power flow of 3-speed constant mesh gearbox

(i) Neutral

When the gear lever is in neutral position, the two dog clutches D_1 and D_2 are not in contact with any of the gears and cannot transmit torque to the main shaft.

(ii) First gear

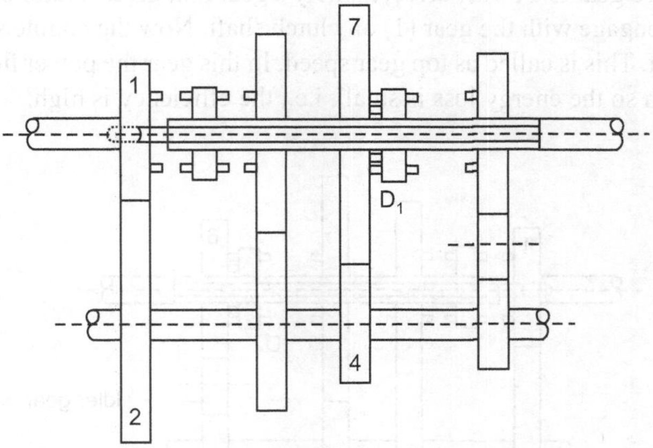

Fig. 9.10 First gear

The dog clutch (D_1) is shifted to left to make engage on (7). Now the power is transmitted through the gear (1) ⇒ (2) ⇒ (4) ⇒ (7) and dog clutch D_1, transmits to the main shaft. Hence, the first gear speed is obtained.

(iii) Second gear

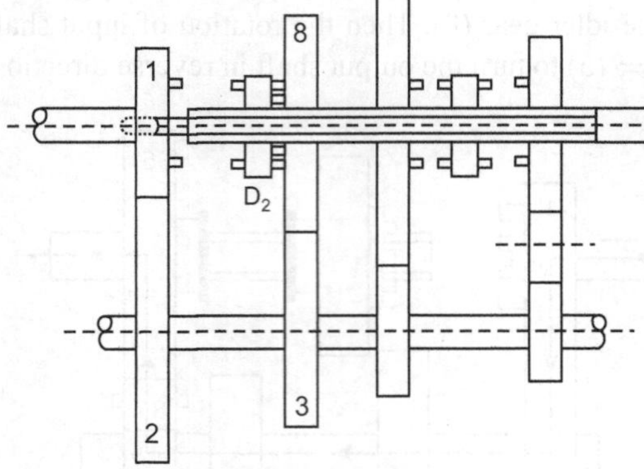

Fig. 9.11 Second gear

Now, the dog clutch (D_1) is disengaged. The dog clutch (D_2) is shifted to right to lock with the gear (8). Therefore, the power is transmitted from clutch shaft through (1) ⇒ (2) ⇒ (3) ⇒ (8) and dog clutch (D_2) to the main shaft. So, the main shaft rotates with the second gear speed.

(iv)Third (or) top gear

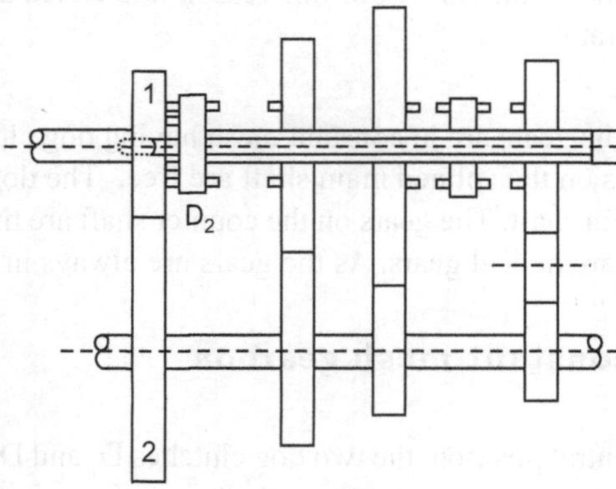

Fig. 9.12 Third gear

In this layout, third gear is a direct drive; namely a gear that gives a ratio of 1:1. The dog clutch (D_2) is moved left to engage with the gear (1) on clutch shaft. Now the engine speed is directly supplied to the main shaft. This is called as top gear speed. In this gear the power flow is not transmitted through any gear teeth so the energy loss is small, i.e., the efficiency is high.

(v) Reverse gear

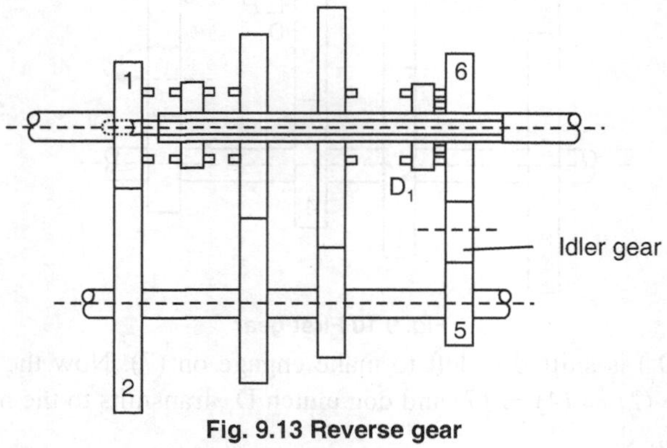

Fig. 9.13 Reverse gear

First the dog clutch D_2 is disengaged. Then the dog clutch D_1 is shifted to right to engage with the gear (6). The idler gear causes the main shaft to rotate in the opposite direction.

Synchromesh gearbox

This is similar to constant mesh gearbox and dog clutch is replaced by synchronizer unit. In the simplest type of constant mesh gear box, which is now absolute, gears could be engaged by snatching the gear lever from one position to the next as fast as possible. This was noisy and jerky. There will still be noise if the dog teeth are not rotating at the same speed when the engagement is made. To do the job more quietly and smoothly without clashing, the gears were synchronized by ***double de-clutching*** i.e., engaging the clutch with the gearbox in neutral and accelerating the engine to speed up the input component, then disengaging the clutch again and engaging the appropriate gear. Drivers today are relieved from the need for double de-clutching by a synchronizing device built into the sliding collars in the gearbox. This synchromesh device is usually fitted to all forward gears.

Synchronizers

Synchronizers equalize the speed of the shaft and gear before they are engaged. They use friction to synchronize the speed of the gear and the shaft before the connection is made.

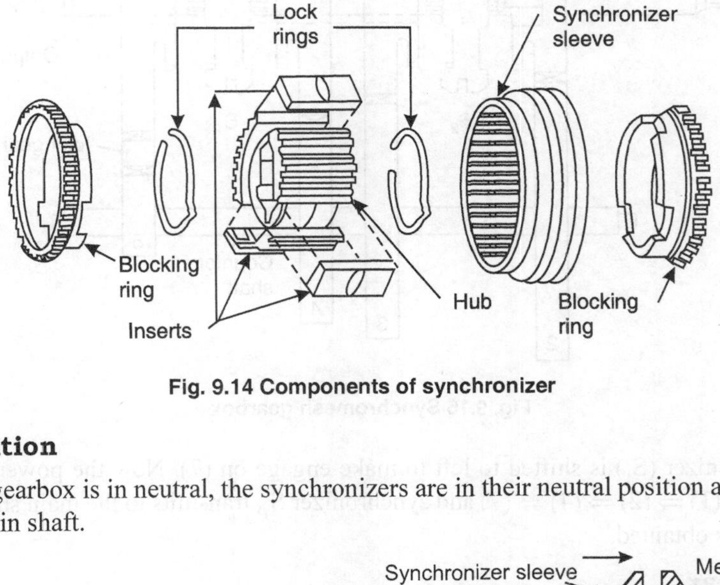

Fig. 9.14 Components of synchronizer

Neutral position

When the gearbox is in neutral, the synchronizers are in their neutral position and are not rotating with the main shaft.

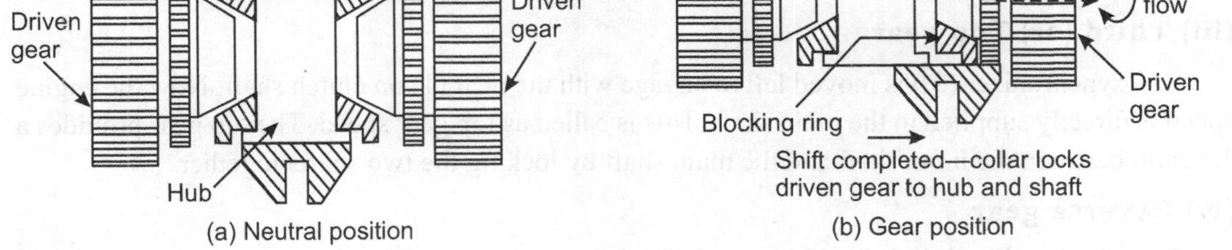

Fig. 9.15 Synchronizer operation

Gear position

When a gear is selected, the shifting fork forces the sleeve toward the selected gear. As the sleeve moves, inserts also moves because they are locked in the sleeve. The movement of the inserts pushes the blocking ring into contact with the shoulder of the gear. When this contact is made, there is a metal to metal contact and begins to rotate.

As the components reach the same speed, the synchronizer sleeve can now slide over the external dog teeth on the blocking ring and then over the dog teeth on the gear's shoulder. This completes the engagement of the synchronizer and the gear is locked to the main shaft. Power now flows as follows:

Input gear ⇒ Counter gear ⇒ Gear selected ⇒ Synchronizer ⇒ Main shaft

Power flow of 3-speed synchromesh mesh gearbox

(i) First gear

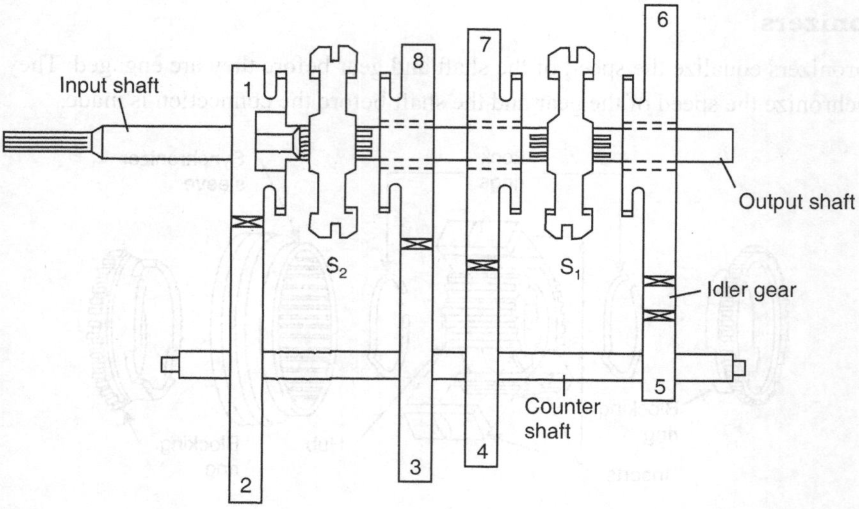

Fig. 9.16 Synchromesh gearbox

The synchronizer (S_1) is shifted to left to make engage on (7). Now the power is transmitted through the gear (1) ⇒ (2) ⇒ (4) ⇒ (7) and synchronizer S_1, transmits to the main shaft. Hence, the first gear speed is obtained.

(ii) Second gear

Now, the synchronizer (S_1) is disengaged. The synchronizer (S_2) is shifted to right to lock with the gear (8). Therefore, the power is transmitted from clutch shaft through (1) ⇒ (2) ⇒ (3) ⇒ (8) and synchronizer (S_2) to the main shaft. So, the main shaft rotates with the second gear speed.

(iii) Third (or) Top gear

The synchronizer (S_2) is moved left to engage with the gear (1) on clutch shaft. Now the engine speed is directly supplied to the main shaft. This is called as top gear speed. The top gear provides a 1:1 ratio between the input shaft and the main shaft by locking the two shafts together.

(iv) Reverse gear

First the synchronizer S_2 is disengaged. Then the synchronizer S_1 is shifted to right to engage with the gear (6). The idler gear causes the main shaft to rotate in the opposite direction.

GEAR SELECTOR MECHANISM

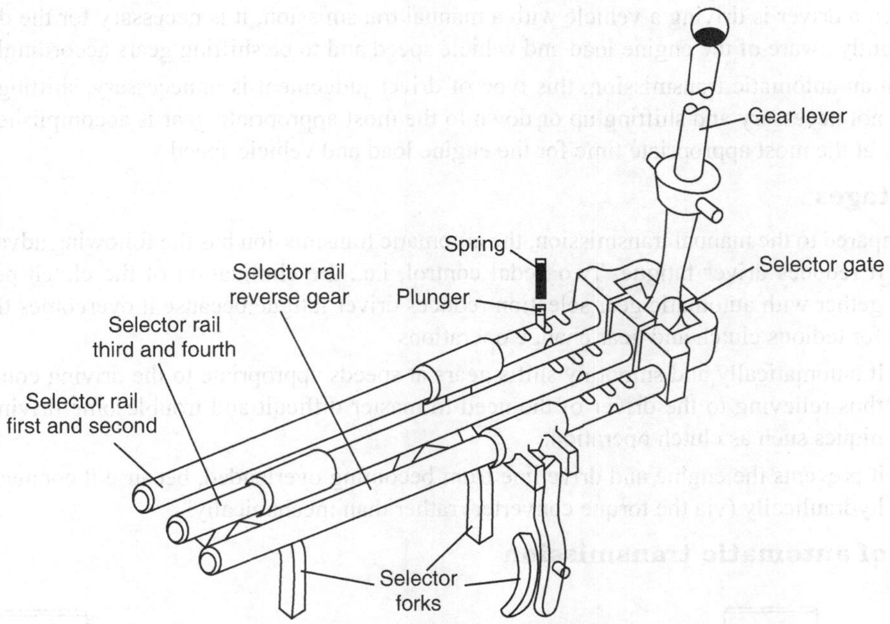

Fig. 9.17 Gear selector mechanism

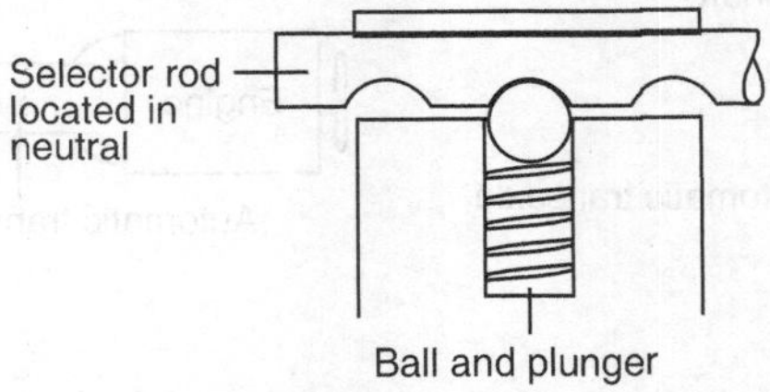

Fig. 9.18: Gear Locating Device

To allow the driver to select the most suitable gear ratio, manual gearboxes are fitted with a gear lever and selector mechanism. The main components of such a selector mechanism are shown in Fig. 3.4. When the driver uses the gear lever to select a particular gear, the movement is transmitted along the appropriate selector rail to the gearwheel. Selector-locking or gear-locating device hold a gear engaged when it has been selected as shown in Fig. 9.21.

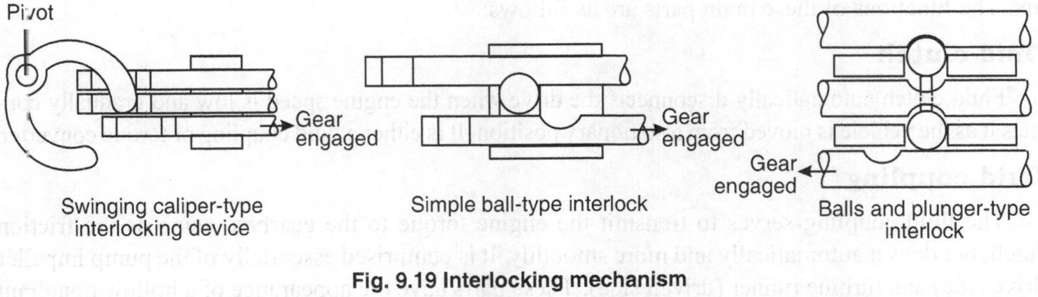

Fig. 9.19 Interlocking mechanism

To ensure that only one gear can be selected at a time, an interlocking mechanism is incorporated into the gearbox selectors. A selection of interlocking mechanisms is shown in Fig. 9.22.

AUTOMATIC TRANSMISSION

When a driver is driving a vehicle with a manual transmission, it is necessary for the driver to be constantly aware of the engine load and vehicle speed and to be shifting gears accordingly.

With an automatic transmission, this type of driver judgement is unnecessary, shifting by the driver is not necessary and shifting up or down to the most appropriate gear is accomplished automatically at the most appropriate time for the engine load and vehicle speed.

Advantages

Compared to the manual transmission, the automatic transmission has the following advantages:

- It reduces driver fatigue. Two pedal control, i.e., the elimination of the clutch pedal together with automatic gear selection reduces driver fatigue because it overcomes the need for tedious clutch and gear change operations.
- It automatically and smoothly shifts gears at speeds appropriate to the driving conditions, thus relieving to the driver of the need to master difficult and troublesome driving techniques such as clutch operation.
- It prevents the engine and drive line from becoming overloaded, because it connects them hydraulically (via the torque converter) rather than mechanically.

Types of automatic transmission

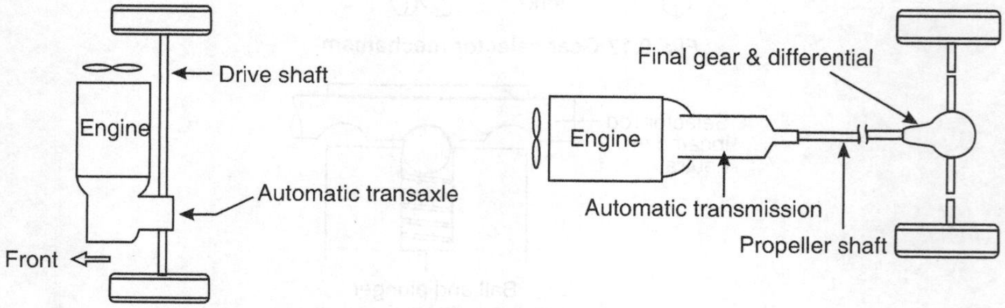

Fig. 9.20 Automatic transmission

Automatic transmissions can be basically divided into two types, those used in FF (Front-engine, Front-wheel drive) vehicles (automatic transaxle) and those used in FR (front-engine, Rear-wheel drive) vehicles.

MAJOR COMPONENTS

Most modern automatic transmissions consist of two main units: a fluid clutch and a main gearbox. The functions of these main parts are as follows:

Fluid clutch

Fluid clutch automatically disconnects the drive when the engine speed is low and gradually connects it as the vehicle is moved from a stationary position. It is either a fluid coupling or torque converter.

Fluid coupling

The fluid coupling serves to transmit the engine torque to the gearbox, same as the friction clutch, but does it automatically and more smoothly. It is comprised essentially of the pump impeller (drive side) and turbine runner (driven side). These parts have the appearance of a hollow doughnut sliced vertically into to equal halves.

Both of these parts are provided with radiating out from the center. These parts are contained in a housing filled with oil and installed facing each other, with very little clearance provided between them. The pump impeller is installed on the engine crankshaft and the turbine runner coupled to transmission input shaft.

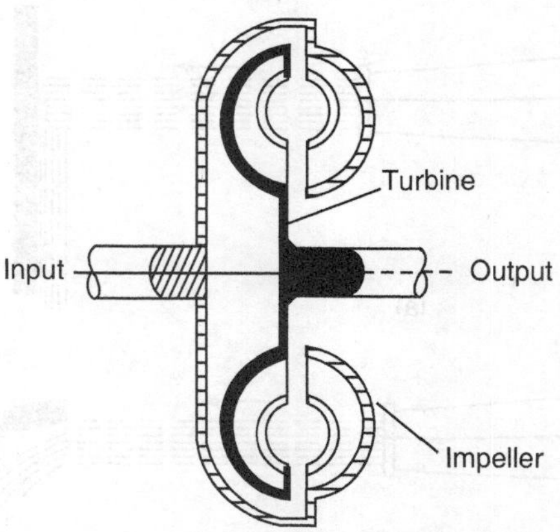

Fig. 9.21 Fluid Coupling

When the engine rotates, the pump impeller provides motion to the oil in between the blades to turn the turbine runner and transmit the engine power to the transmission. When the engine speed drops, the turbine runner will turn faster than the pump impeller so that the turbine runner will now be working as a pump impeller and exert a braking action to the engine.

At idling, the pump impeller is rotating slowly and since the oil pressure is low, the turbine runner receiving the oil does not turn. The oil merely circulates between the opposing blades and there is no transmission of engine power to the propeller shaft. This is because the oil pressure generated by the pump impeller is not large enough to overcome the resistance of the drive wheels.

Torque converter

Torque converters, in its simple form, can double the output torque from the engine. In addition the converter is able to reduce the torque amplification gradually as the output speed of the converter increases.

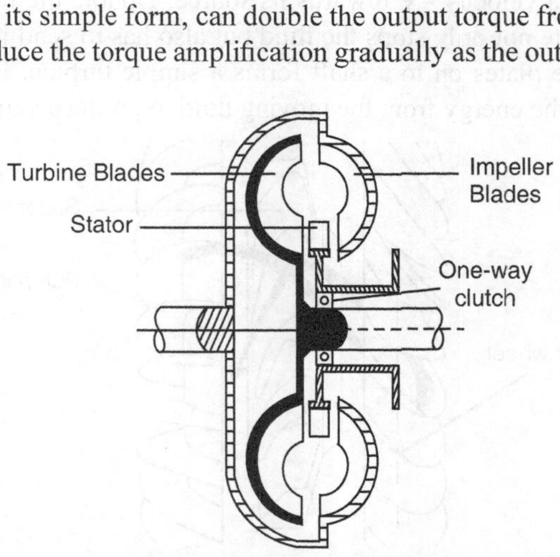

Fig. 9.22 Torque Converter

Principle

A moving fluid possesses energy and this means that it is capable of doing work. Directing a fluid from a nozzle on to a plate causes the fluid direction to change and exerts a force on the plate. The force of impact can be varied by moving the plate with the fluid direction. During this movement the speed of the fluid relative to the plate is slower than in the previous case, so the impact force will be less. If it is possible to move the plate at the same speed as the fluid is moving, then no impact will take place, consequently no force will be produced on the plate.

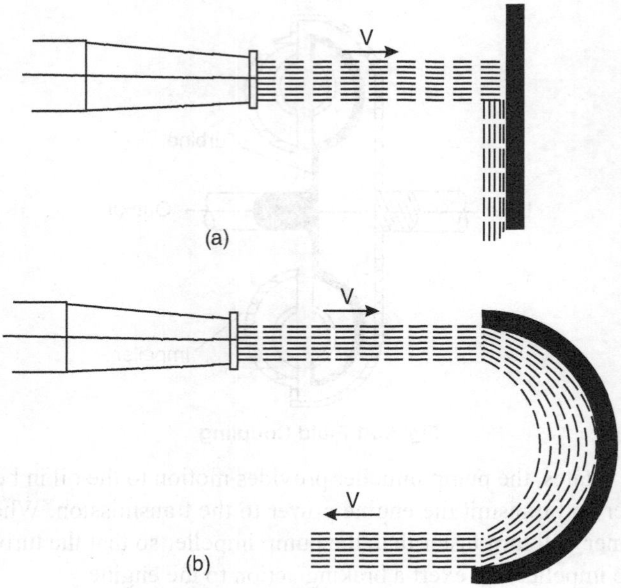

Velocity changes
(a) When fluid strikes a flat plate
(b) When fluid strikes a curved plate

Fig. 9.23 Principle of a torque converter

In the case of curved plate, the fluid strikes the plate with a velocity V and the curved surface redirects the fluid back at a velocity –V towards its source. Double the force is obtained with this arrangement, since the plate not only stops the fluid but also has to send it back at the same speed. Mounting a series of these plates on to a shaft forms a simple turbine. Each plate, which is now called a vane, will extract the energy from the moving fluid to produce a turning action on the shaft.

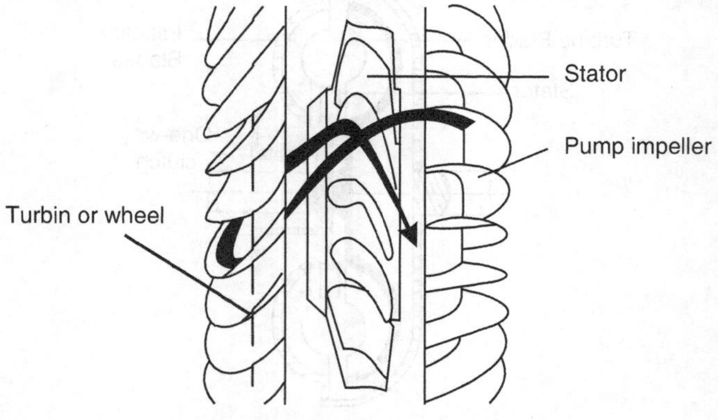

Fig. 9.24 Stator action

Applying the analogy of the nozzle-plate would indicate that when the turbine is turning slower than the pump, the force of impact of the fluid striking the turbine vanes should give a torque increase. This would be true if the fluid did not have to return to the pump, but since this fluid has to recirculate then the speed of the fluid compared to the speed of the pump vane must be considered. To give a high impact force on the output member, the pump must be turning at a higher speed than the turbine, so when the fluid is returned to the pump it is travelling slower than the pump vane. In this condition the vane will strike the slower moving fluid particle and this will give a force which is acting against the motion of the pump, i.e., the fluid will tend to act as a brake on the pump. The greater the speed difference between pump and turbine, the greater will be the impact force on the turbine but this will also result in a larger braking action on the pump. To obtain a torque multiplication, this braking action must be eliminated. This is achieved by fitting a separate member called a stator (stationary member) between the turbine and the pump. The stator consists of a number of vanes which are shaped in the manner to redirect the fluid returning to the pump such that it now enters the pump at a suitable speed and direction.

Roles of a torque converter

The roles of a torque converter are:

- Multiplying the torque generated by the engine.
- Serving as an automatic clutch which transmits (or does not transmit) the engine torque to the transmission.
- Driving the oil pump of the hydraulic control system.

Torque converter operation

When the engine is running, the oil inside the blades of the pump is flung out (throw forcefully) by centrifugal force and deflected by blade curvature into the turbine blades. Oil returned from turbine blades attempts to rotate the stator in the opposite direction to the pump and turbine rotation, but this movement is prevented by the stator free wheel. The oil is therefore deflected by the stator blades such that it now enters the pump at a suitable speed and direction and thus complete the oil circuit.

As the turbine speeds up, the difference between its speed and that of the pump decreases, so that the oil flow strikes the stator blades at a different angle. This in turn reduces the additional forces on the turbine blades, so that the torque is reduced.

The stator then begins to turn slowly in the oil flow, when the pump impeller and turbine speeds are almost identical, the oil flow striking the stator blades has changed its angle to such that torque at the turbine is almost the same as the torque input from the engine. In other words, no further torque conversion takes place at this speed and the unit acts as a fluid coupling.

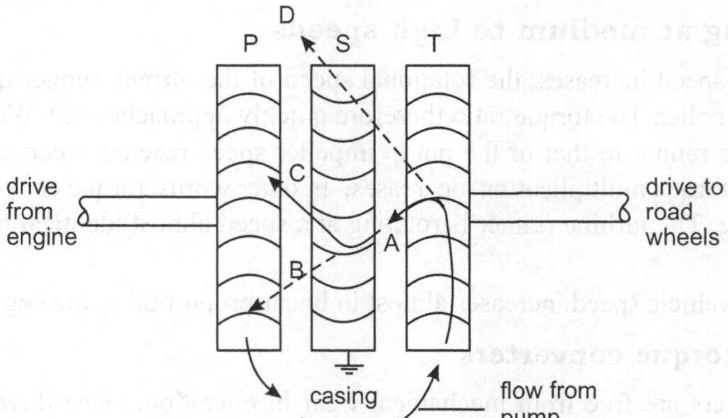

Fig. 9.25 Operation of torque converter

At this stage in vehicle operation, the ratio of impeller to turbine speed is about 0.86 to 0.91. This is described as the *coupling point*. At this point, the stator is revolving at almost the same speed as the other two wheels and therefore has no effect on torque conversion.

Depending on the design of the torque converter, engine torque as the vehicle is started can be multiplied by between 2 and 4.5 times. As the impeller and turbine speeds coincide more and more closely, this torque multiplication ratio drops steplessly to 1:1, so that the vehicle moves away and accelerates absolutely smooth.

Fluid from the pump acts on the turbine T, but if the turbine is turning slower than the oil, then the oil will be deflected in the path A, the stator will act as a reaction member and will direct the fluid from path B to path C, a suitable direction for the pump to receive the fluid. As the turbine speed is increased the fluid path A will gradually change until it is taking path D. Fluid attempting to flow in path D will now be obstructed by the stator vanes and the disturbance caused by this obstruction would give a considerable drop in efficiency. To limit this drawback a unidirectional clutch (free wheel) is fitted in the stator. As soon as the fluid strikes the back of the stator vanes the clutch will unlock and the fluid will then pass along path D to the pump. Once this occurs the unit will act as a fluid coupling (1:1 drive).

Fig. 9.25 shows the arrangement of a three-element single stage converter. This type is quite common and is used in conjunction with many different types of automatic gearbox. A general description of torque converter operation is given below.

Vehicle stopped, engine idling

When the engine is idling, the torque generated by the engine itself is at a minimum. If the brakes are applied, the load on the turbine runner is great because it cannot rotate.

Since the vehicle is stopped, the speed ratio of the turbine runner to the pump impeller is zero while the torque ratio is at maximum. Therefore, the turbine runner is always ready to be rotated with a higher torque than the torque generated by the engine.

Vehicle starting off

When the brakes are released, the turbine runner is able to rotate with the transmission input shaft.

Depressing the accelerator pedal therefore causes the turbine runner to rotate with a torque greater than that generated by the engine, so the vehicle begins moving.

Vehicle running at low speeds

When the vehicle is running with low speed, torque converter multiplies the necessary torque to move the vehicle.

Vehicle running at medium to high speeds

As the vehicle speed increases, the rotational speed of the turbine runner quickly approaches that of the pump impeller. The torque ratio therefore quickly approaches 1.0. When the ratio of the speed of the turbine runner to that of the pump impeller speed reaches a certain value, the stator begins rotating and torque multiplication decreases. In other words, torque converter starts to operate as fluid coupling. The turbine runner is rotating at a speed almost identical to that of the pump impeller.

Therefore, the vehicle speed increases almost in linear proportion to the engine speed.

Advantages of torque converters

Torque converters are free from mechanical wear in operation, since there is no direct contact between moving parts or those transmitting the torque. Engine vibration and torque peaks are damped by the hydraulic fluid. The engine cannot be stalled, since only a very small amount of torque is transmitted at idle speed.

> **Note:** The fluid for the converter is normally supplied by the automatic gearbox and it is generally a low viscosity mineral oil which contains additives to improve lubrication and resist frothing. Cavitation noise caused by air in the converter is minimized by pressurizing the fluid to about 1.38 bar.

Automatic gearbox

Up to about the mid 1970s, the majority of automatic gearboxes used on light vehicles were made by Borg Warner. This company offered a range of units to suit engine sizes between 1.5 and 5 litres. Based on production numbers, one of the most successful gearboxes was the Model 35 and its derivatives.

Today, most vehicle manufacturers produce a gearbox either of their own design or made under license to some other manufacturer.

This gearbox automatically provides a series of stepped ratios to enable the vehicle to overcome road conditions needing a large driving effort. Also it allows the vehicle to operate over a wide road speed range.

Power flow

P - Park
R - Reverse
N - Neutral
D - Drive
2 – Second gear
1 or L– First (or) Low gear

R is reverse and backward movement of the vehicle is achieved in this position. P is parking position. In neutral (N) no drive is applied. This gear position is used when the vehicle is being towed. D is the normal automatic mode which covers the full range of forward gears (1-2-3 or 3-2-1 according to the engine load and vehicle speed).

Planetary gear set

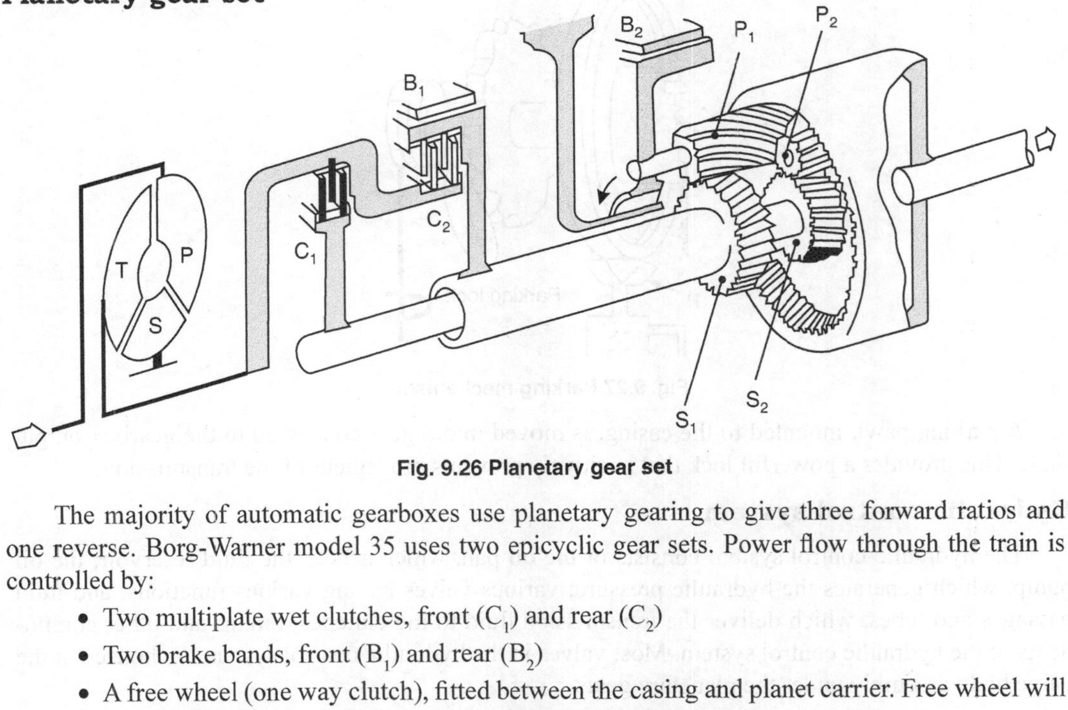

Fig. 9.26 Planetary gear set

The majority of automatic gearboxes use planetary gearing to give three forward ratios and one reverse. Borg-Warner model 35 uses two epicyclic gear sets. Power flow through the train is controlled by:

- Two multiplate wet clutches, front (C_1) and rear (C_2)
- Two brake bands, front (B_1) and rear (B_2)
- A free wheel (one way clutch), fitted between the casing and planet carrier. Free wheel will unlock if planet carrier rotates in the forward direction.

The front set does not have an annulus. Instead it uses a compound planet arrangement in which the front planet P_1 mesh with three gear members: the sun S_2, annulus and planet P_2. This combination is known as a *Ravigneaux gearbox* set.

First (or) low gear (1 or D1)

Front clutch C_1 is applied and drive is applied to sun S_2. The free wheel (fully automatic) or rear band brake B_2 (first gear selected by the driver) holds the planet carrier. Forward motion of sun S_2 transmits the drive through planets P_1 & P_2, which act as idlers, to the annulus and output shaft. Now annulus rotates slower and gives first gear.

Second gear (D2)

Front clutch C_1 is applied and drive is applied to sun S_2. The sun S_1 is held by the front band brake B_1. Rotation of P_1 by P_2 causes it to roll around the fixed sun S_1 and drive the planet carrier in the forward direction. This drives the annulus faster (compared to first gear) and gives second gear. Since the planet carrier is moving in a forward direction, the free wheel offers no resistance.

Direct drive (D3)

Drive is applied to S_1 and S_2 by locking both clutches C_1 and C_2. This action causes the annulus and both sets of planets to rotate as one unit and give direct drive (1:1).

Reverse (R)

Rear clutch C_2 is applied and drive is applied to sun S_1. The rear band brake B_2 is applied which holds the planet carrier. The locked planet carrier causes the planets to act as idlers, so the forward moving sun S_1 moves the annulus in the reverse direction.

Neutral (N)

All clutches and brake bands are released, so no drive is transmitted.

Park (P)

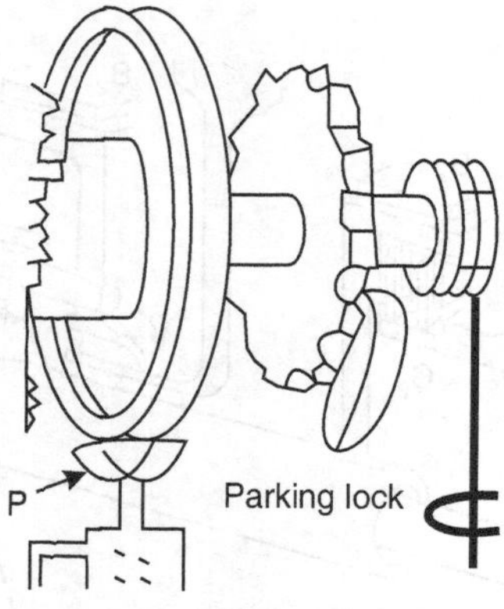

Fig. 9.27 Parking mechanism

A parking pawl, mounted to the casing, is moved into a gear connected to the gearbox output shaft. This provides a powerful lock that positively prevents movement of the transmission.

Hydraulic control system

The hydraulic control system consists of the oil pan, which acts as the fluid reservoir; the oil pump, which generates the hydraulic pressure; various valves having various functions; and fluid passages and tubes, which deliver the transmission fluid to the clutches, brakes and other components of the hydraulic control system. Most valves in the hydraulic control system are housed in the valve body assembly under the planetary gears.

Manual shift valve

This valve is located in the hydraulic control unit and actuated by the driver's selector lever. It determines which gear ratio is to be selected. The position of the selector lever can be used to vary the working pressure in the shift valves. Operation of the lever moves the valve and uncovers the fluid port that supplies hydraulic pressure to the clutches and brake bands to obtain the desired gear position.

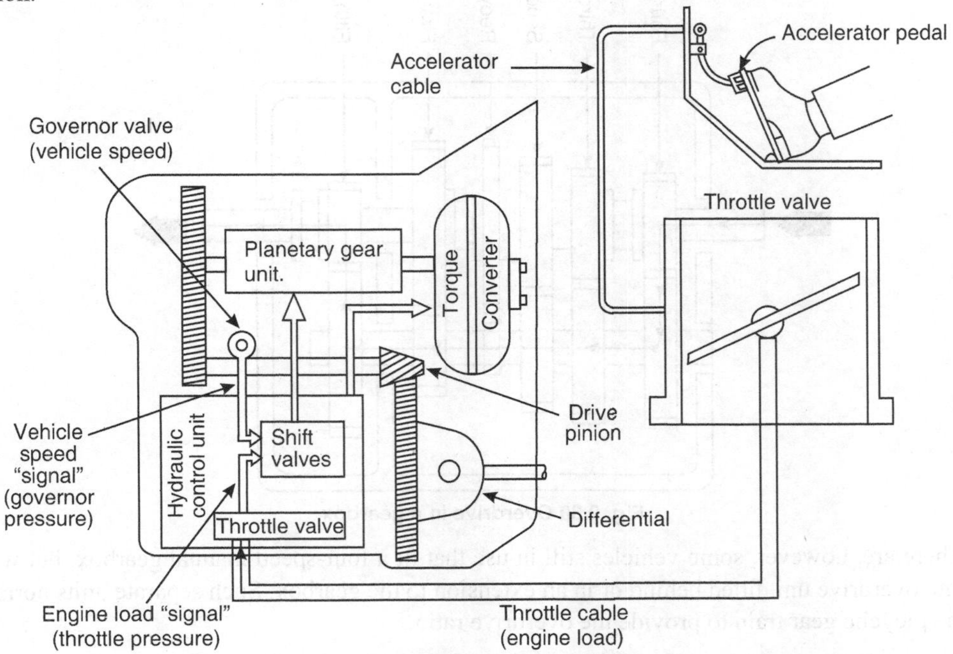

Fig. 9.28 Hydraulic control system

Speed sensing

The centrifugal governor is mounted on the transmission output shaft and supplies a governor pressure dependent on road speed, which increases with the speed of rotation. This pressure is applied to one side of the spool shift valves in the valve body. Above a certain road speed, governor pressure rises and accordingly the shift valves supply pressure to the clutches and brake bands which cause the next higher gear to be selected. If road speed drops, governor pressure also falls and the drive shifts to the next lower gear.

Load sensing

The function of the regulating valve is to control, in a separate line, the fluid pressure that increases as the accelerator pedal is depressed. This throttle pressure applied to the shift valves and as a result alters the position of the shift valves with respect to governor pressure.

OVERDRIVE

An overdrive is a gear ratio in which the speed of the output shaft is greater than that of input shaft. This principle is put to good use on motor vehicles to reduce engine wear and fuel consumption.

Almost all early cars had four-speed gearboxes with a straight-through or 1:1 drive in fourth gear. Nearly all modern cars have five-speed gearboxes, with fifth gear being an overdrive ratio. Similarly, most modern automatic transmission units have their epicyclic gearing so arranged that their top gear, usually fourth, is an overdrive.

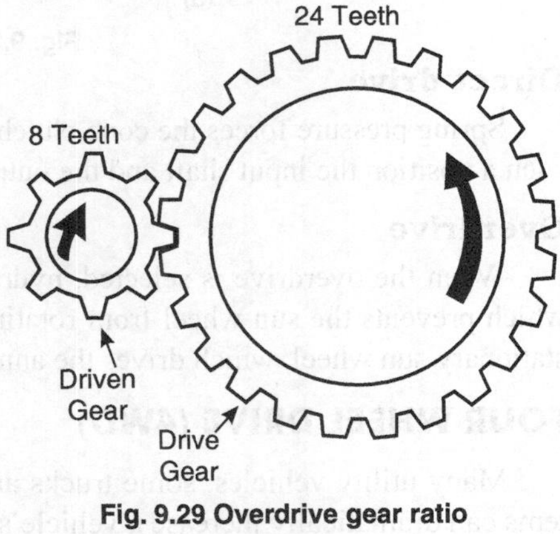

Fig. 9.29 Overdrive gear ratio

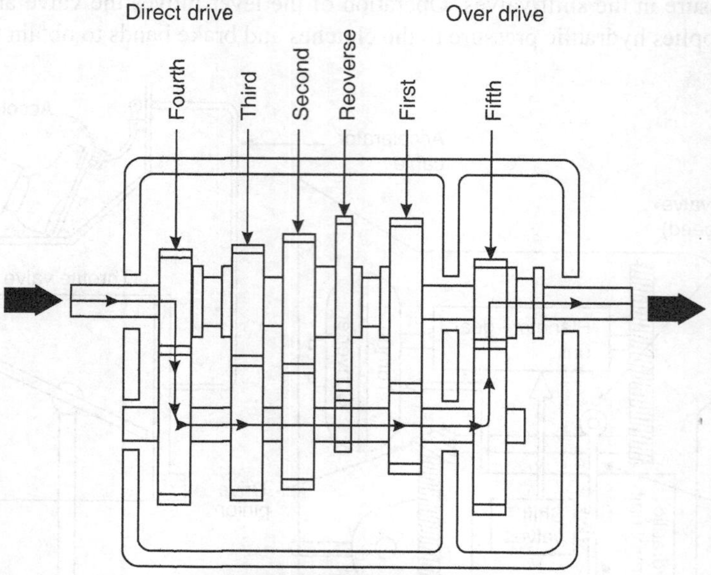

Fig. 9.30 Overdrive in a gearbox

There are, however, some vehicles still in use that fit a four-speed manual gearbox, but with a separate overdrive unit fitted behind or in an extension to the gearbox. Such separate units normally use an epicyclic gear train to provide the overdrive ratio.

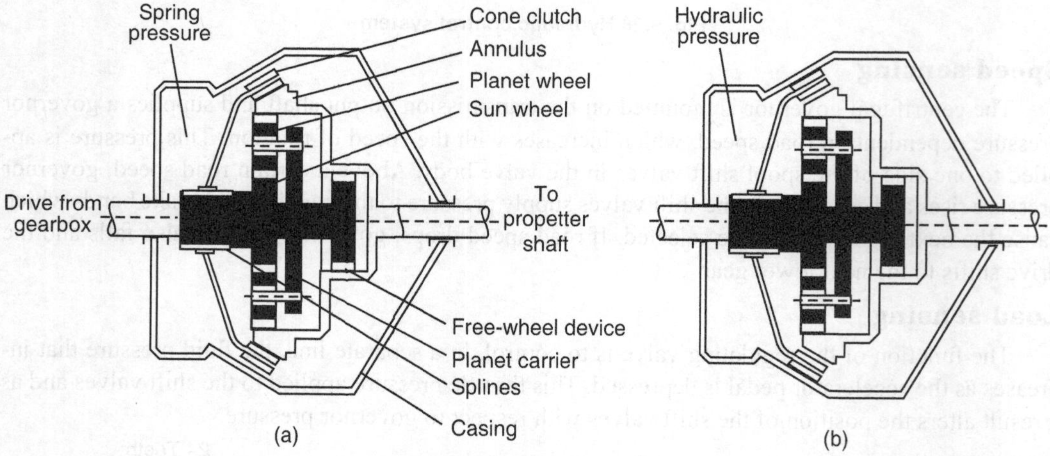

Fig. 9.31 Epicyclic overdrive

Direct drive

Spring pressure forces the cone clutch mounted on the sun wheel firmly against the annulus. In such a position the input shaft and the output shafts both rotate at the same speed.

Overdrive

When the overdrive is selected, hydraulic pressure forces the cone clutch against the casing, which prevents the sun wheel from rotating. The planet carrier and planet gears rotate around the stationary sun wheel, which drives the annulus and output shaft at a higher rotational speed.

FOUR WHEEL DRIVE (4WD)

Many utility vehicles, some trucks and a few cars have four wheel drive (4WD). 4WD systems can dramatically increase a vehicle's traction and handling ability in rain, snow, and off-road driving (driving over uneven mountain terrain and through riverbeds). Consider that the vehicle's only contact with the road is the small area of the tyres. Driving and handling is vastly improved if the workload is spread out evenly among four wheels rather than two. 4WD systems add initial cost and weight. With most passenger cars, the weight problem is minor. A typical 4WD system adds approximately 80 kg to a passenger car. An AWD system adds even less weight. The additional weight in larger 4WD trucks can be as much as 180 kg or more. Vehicles equipped with 4WD require special service and maintenance not performed on 2WD vehicles. However, the slight disadvantages of 4WD are heavily outweighed by the traction and performance these systems offer.

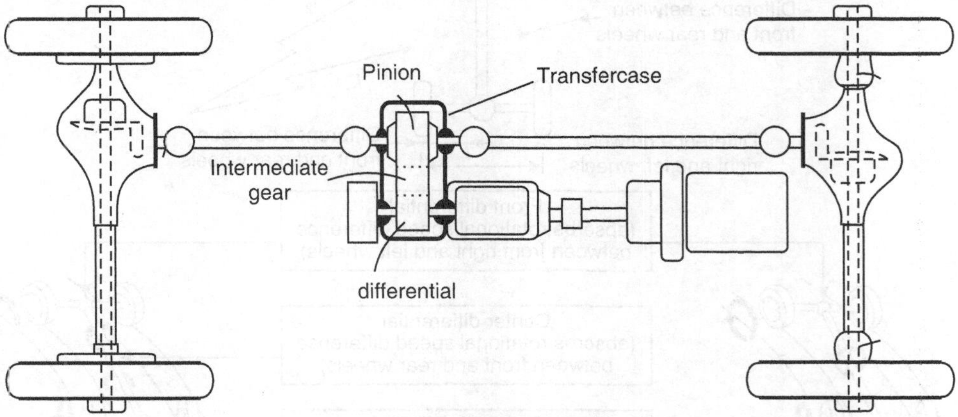

Fig. 9.32 Four wheel drive

Factors such as the side forces created by cornering and wind gusts have less effect on vehicles with four driving wheels. The increased traction also makes it possible to apply greater amounts of energy through the drive system. Vehicles with 4WD and AWD can maintain control while transmitting levels of power that would cause two wheels to spin either on take off or while rounding a curve. The improved traction of 4WD and AWD systems allows the use of tyres narrower and less expensive than those used on similar 2WD vehicles. They also tend to cut through snow and water rather than hydroplane over it.

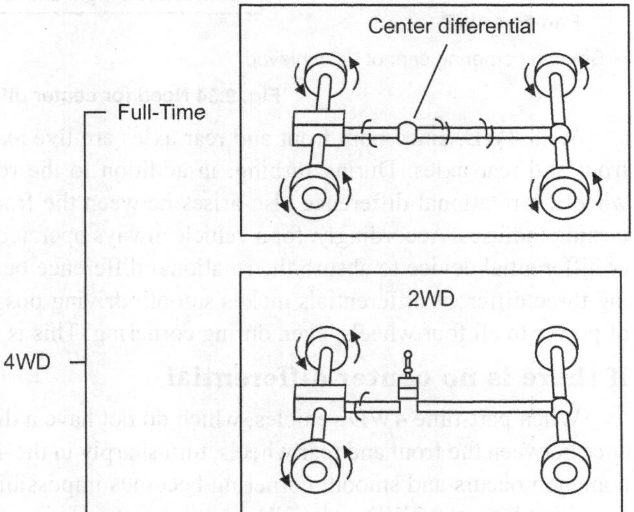

Fig. 9.33 4WD types

Differences between full-time 4WD and part-time 4WD

Besides these different uses, there are two types of basic 4WD mechanism. These are part-time 4WD, which is usually driven in the 2WD (2-wheel drive) mode and is only switched to 4WD by the driver when it is necessary and full-time 4WD, which is always driven in 4WD.

The difference between them is that the part-time 4WD has only one differential device each for the front and rear axles, while the full-time 4WD has an extra differential device (a center differential device).

Center differential

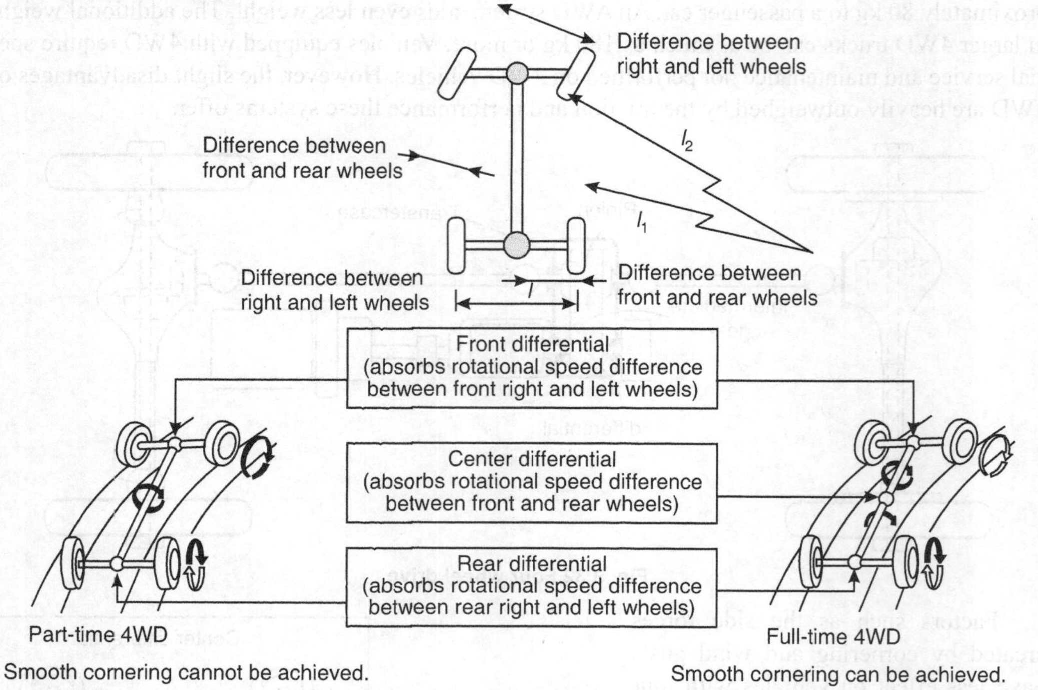

Fig. 9.34 Need for center differential

With 4WD, since both front and rear axles are live axles, a differential device is fitted to both front and rear axles. During turning, in addition to the rotational difference of the left and right wheels, a rotational difference also arises between the front and rear wheels due to their different turning radiuses. Accordingly, for a vehicle always operated in 4WD, it is necessary to install a center differential device to absorb the rotational difference between the front and rear wheels. Providing three different differentials makes smooth driving possible by ensuring the equal transmission of power to all four wheels, even during cornering. This is the major advantage of full-time 4WD.

If there is no center differential

When part-time 4WD vehicles, which do not have a differential to absorb the rotational difference between the front and rear wheels, turn sharply in the 4WD mode, the tight corner braking phenomenon occurs and smooth cornering becomes impossible. For this reason, with part-time 4WD, switching between 2WD and 4WD in response to driving conditions becomes necessary.

Advantages and disadvantages

Advantages

- Excellent drive-through performance on snowy roads
- Excellent drive-through performance on rough roads
- Excellent hill-climbing performance
- Excellent cornering stability
- Excellent starting and acceleration performance
- Excellent straight-line stability

Disadvantages

- Construction is complex
- Weight is increased
- Cost is increased
- Sources of vibration and noise increase

TRANSFER CASE

A transfer case is required on vehicles with four-wheel drive. A transfer case is an auxiliary transmission mounted behind the main transmission used to divide engine power and transfer it to both front and rear differentials, either full or part time.

With a full-time transfer case, the front axle is engaged automatically as soon as the rear wheels begin to spin. With part-time four-wheel drive, the transfer case shift lever must be moved to engage or disengage the front differential.

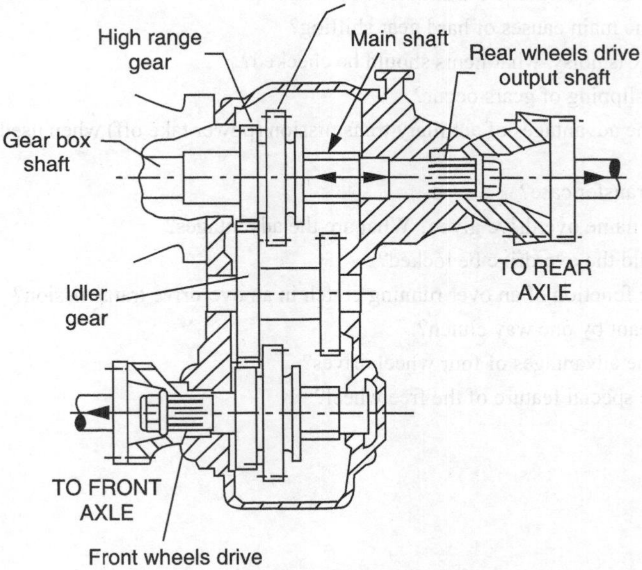

Fig. 9.35 Transfer case

Review Questions

1. Why is a gearbox necessary in an automobile?
2. What are the different types of gearboxes used in automobiles?
3. What is tractive effort?
4. Why are helical gears preferred in transmission?
5. What is meant by sliding mesh gearbox?
6. Why is sliding mesh gearbox not preferred?
7. Why is oil of high viscosity used in the gearbox?
8. How often should the oil be changed in (1) a new engine and (2) an old engine?
9. What is a constant mesh gearbox?
10. What do you understand by double declutch? Why is it necessary?
11. What is the principle of a synchromesh gearbox?
12. How does the synchromesh gear differ from the sliding mesh type?
13. What are the advantages of the synchronizing mechanism?

14. How does the synchronizing unit function in a synchronizing gear box?
15. How is the gear ratio in the gearbox obtained?
16. What are the common faults of a gear box?
17. Why does a gear miss?
18. What are the main characteristics of epicyclic gearbox?
19. Why is automatic transmission preferred for commercial vehicles?
20. Why is the fluid flywheel provided in automatic transmission?
21. What is a torque converter?
22. What are the 3 major elements in a torque converter?
23. What is the function of the stator in the torque converter?
24. What are the advantages of torque converter?
25. Under what condition does the stator function as a free wheel?
26. What does the hydromatic transmission constitute?
27. What are the main causes of hard gear shifting?
28. If a gearbox is noisy, what items should be checked?
29. Why does slipping of gears occur?
30. What are the advantages of auxiliary transmission (power take off) when used along with the conventional one?
31. What is a transfer case?
32. Why is the name overdrive given? What are the advantages?
33. When should the overdrive be locked?
34. What is the function of an over running clutch in an overdrive transmission?
35. What is meant by one way clutch?
36. What are the advantages of four wheel drives?
37. What is the special feature of the free wheel?

10

CHAPTER

PROPELLER SHAFT ASSEMBLY

In the front-engine rear-drive automobiles, the gearbox rotations are transmitted to the rear axles by means of the propeller shaft assembly. It consists of propeller shaft, universal joints, slip joint, etc.

DRIVING THRUST AND TORQUE REACTION

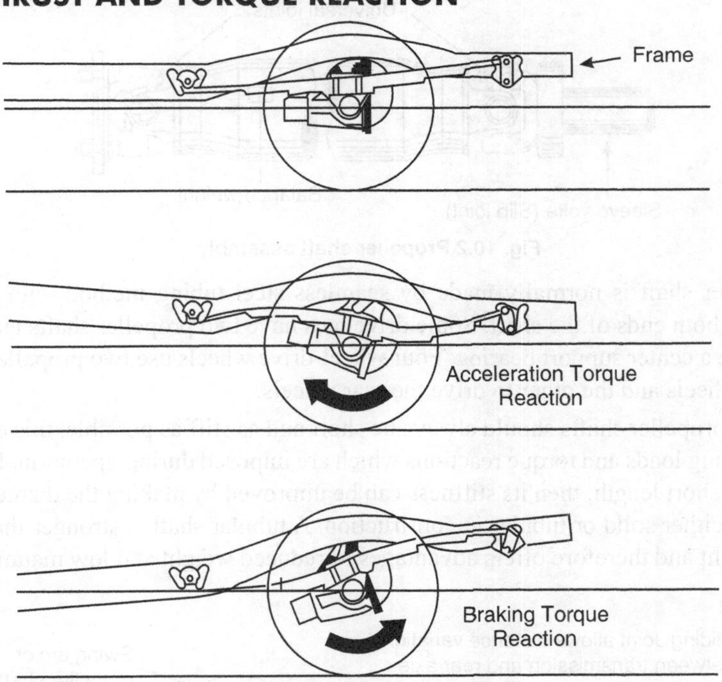

Fig. 10.1 Effect of torque reaction

Driving thrust

Driving torque produced in the engine causes the thrust to be produced in the road wheels, which has to be transmitted from the axle housing to the frame and the body of the vehicle. This is most conveniently done by some form of member connecting the axle casing and the frame or body of the vehicle in the longitudinal direction. Such members are either leaf springs or radius rods (or strut rods).

Torque reaction

If the road wheels are prevented from rotation with the propeller shaft rotating, it is seen that the bevel pinion will tend to roll round the crown wheel. This tendency is also present when the vehicle is running so that the bevel pinion always tends to climb round the crown wheel. Thus there is a force on the axle casing to rotate. This is called torque reaction. In the same way, the braking torque on the axle casing is opposite in direction to the torque reaction.

PROPELLER SHAFT

Where the engine and axles are separated from each other, as on four-wheel-drive and rear-wheel-drive vehicles, it is the propeller shaft that serves to transmit the drive force generated by the engine to the axles.

The propeller shaft is normally a carbon steel tube having a high resistance against torsional or bending forces. A balance weight is installed outside the tube to balance out rotational weight. The duties of the propeller shaft assembly are:

- to transmit torque
- to allow different drive shaft angles
- to allow changes in length
- to reduce rotary vibrations

Construction

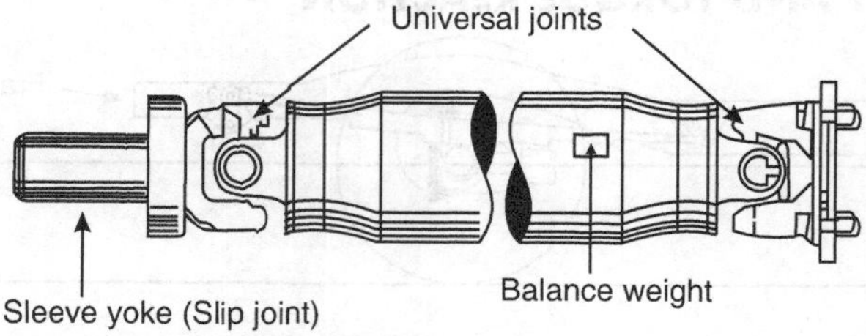

Fig. 10.2 Propeller shaft assembly

The propeller shaft is normally made by seamless steel tubing method with universal joint yokes welded to both ends of the shaft. Some drivelines have two propeller shafts and three universal joints and use a center support bearing. Four wheel-drive wheels use two propeller shafts, one to drive the front wheels and the other to drive the rear wheels.

In practice, propeller shafts should always be short and as stiff as possible, this enable the shaft to resist the bending loads and torque reactions which are imposed during operation. If the shaft cannot be made in a short length, then its stiffness can be improved by making the diameter larger. Propeller shafts are either solid or tubular in construction. A tubular shaft is stronger than a solid shaft of the same weight and therefore offers advantages of reduced weight and low manufacturing costs.

Components

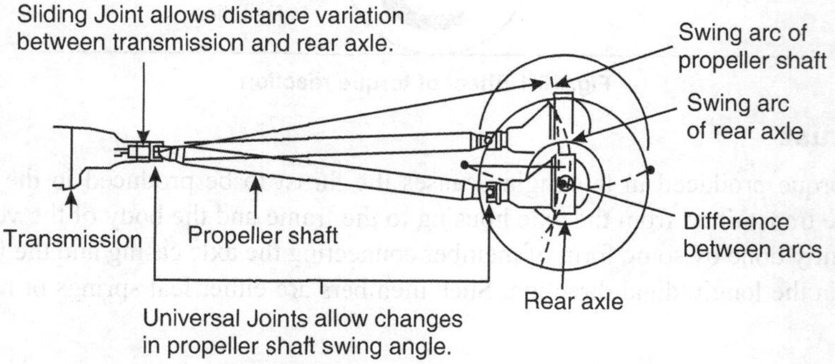

Fig. 10.3 Components of a propellershaft assembly

Universal joint

A universal joint, sometimes called a Carden joint, forms a mechanical connection between the two shafts and allows angular movement of one or both shafts. Also it transmits power smoothly from the gearbox to the differential.

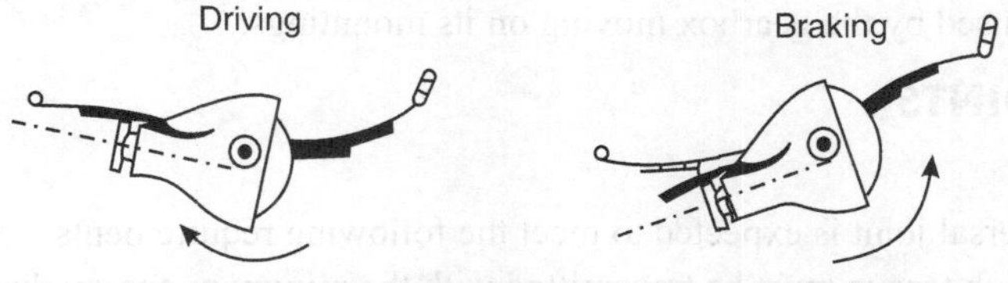

Fig. 10.4 Deflection of spring due to road shocks

Road shocks will deflect the springs to the position shown in Fig. 10.4. This will alter the angle of the propeller shaft, relative to the gearbox and final drive and unless a universal joint is fitted to each end of the propeller shaft, the shaft will bend and fracture.

Slip joint (or Sliding joint)

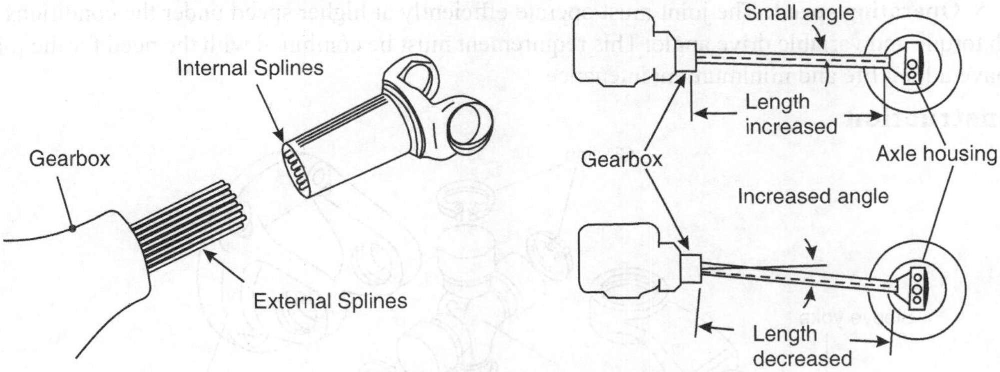

Fig. 10.5 Slip Joint and its function

Propeller shafts use a slip joint at one end, which allows it to lengthen or shorten. It permits the effective length of the propeller shaft to change due to the up and down movement of the wheels.

Center bearing

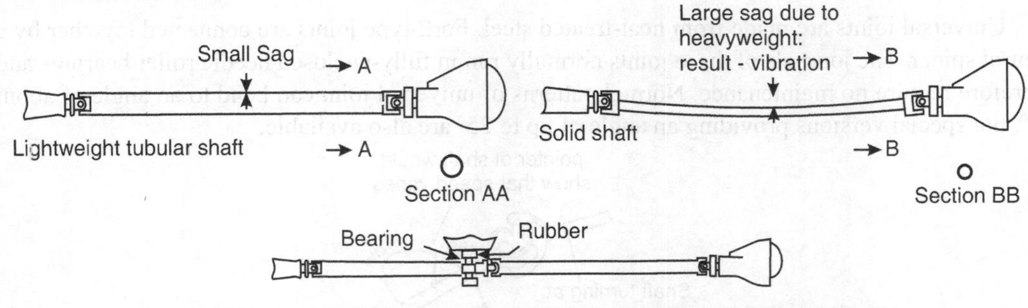

Long or high-speed shafts require a center bearing to avoid vibration due to whip

Fig. 10.6. Centre bearing

Long-wheelbase vehicles (trucks) often have a propeller shaft in two sections; a two-piece, three-joint type propeller shaft incorporates a rubber-mounted center bearing which is designed to support the shafts at the middle and to reduce torsional vibration and noise. For its usage, the optimal shaft is a short, bar-like product. The longer the bar, the more liable it is to sag and sagging is further promoted when rotation is applied. Sagging causes vibration and results in an increase in noise, to such an extent that the shaft is likely to break when the critical speed is exceeded.

It consists of a rubber collar contained within a steel casing, which is mounted on the vehicle's chassis. The centre bearing normally uses self-aligning bearings, which allow for slight misalignment of the shaft caused by the gearbox moving on its mountings.

UNIVERSAL JOINTS

Requirements

A modern universal joint is expected to meet the following requirements:

1. **Strength:** High torque must be transmitted with the minimum energy due to friction.
2. **Compactness:** Space is limited so the joint must be small and robust.
3. **Large drive angle:** Modern road springs allow large wheel deflections so the joint must be able to accommodate the large drive angle given by this movement.
4. **Shaft balance:** Severe vibration occurs if the shaft runs out-of-true, so the joint must maintain good alignment.
5. **Operating speed:** The joint must operate efficiently at higher speed under the conditions of high torque and variable drive angle. This requirement must be combined with the need for the joint to have a long life and minimum maintenance.

Construction

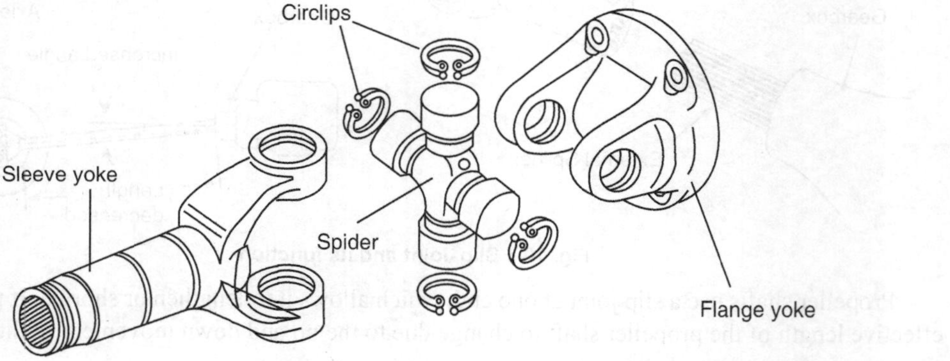

Fig. 10.7 Parts of a universal joint assembly

Universal joints are made from heat-treated steel. Fork-type joints are connected together by a central spider. The journals of these joints normally run in fully-enclosed needle roller bearings and therefore require no maintenance. Normal patterns of universal joint can bend to an angle of about 15°, but special versions providing an angle of up to 25° are also available.

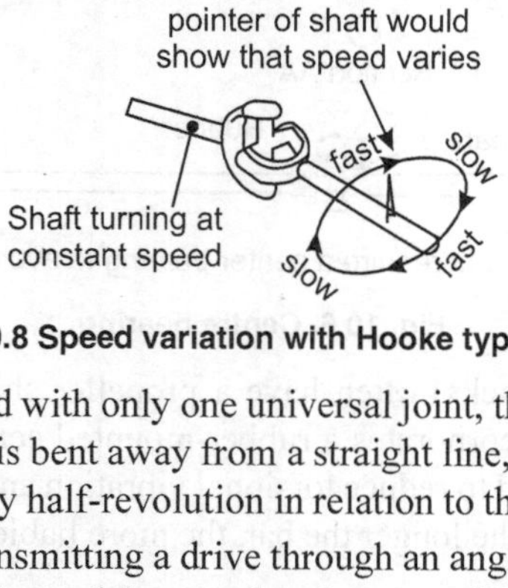

Fig. 10.8 Speed variation with Hooke type joint

If a propeller shaft is provided with only one universal joint, the shaft will only run uniformly if the joint is not bent. As soon as it is bent away from a straight line, the section of shaft after the joint will speed up and slow down every half-revolution in relation to the section of shaft before the joint.

When a hook-type joint is transmitting a drive through an angle, the output shaft does not rotate through 360° at a constant speed. Instead the speed varies every 90° of rotation and the rate of movement for one revolution is fast, slow, fast and slow. This cyclic speed variation and its associated vibration is insignificant when the drive angle is less than about 5°. This vibration increases with increasing angle.

Two universal joints on a shaft have the effect of cancelling out non-uniform rotation. The front and rear sections of the shaft then run at a uniform speed and only the center section varies in speed.

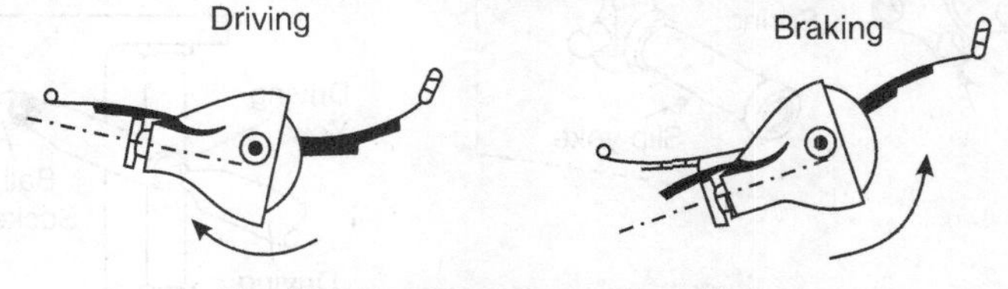

Fig. 10.9 Need for rear universal joint

Another reason for using two universal joints is shown in Fig.10.9. Due to torque reaction, the spring deflects. Thus torque reaction is taken up by the springs. Similarly, to take up the braking torque the springs would deflect in the opposite direction. When the springs deflect, the bevel pinion shaft also changes its position. Therefore if there is only one universal joint at the front end of the propeller shaft, it will bend under this condition. To avoid this, another universal joint at the rear end of the propeller shaft is used.

Universal joints are usually pre-greased by the manufacturer whereas some are having a nipple for further greasing. In case of failure the spider and all collars with needle rollers have to be replaced.

The merits of this type of joint are:

1. Compactness.
2. High mechanical efficiency.
3. Ability to drive through a large occasional bump angle (maximum about 25°).
4. Accurate centering of shaft, hence the joint is suitable for high speed operation.

CONSTANT VELOCITY (CV) JOINTS

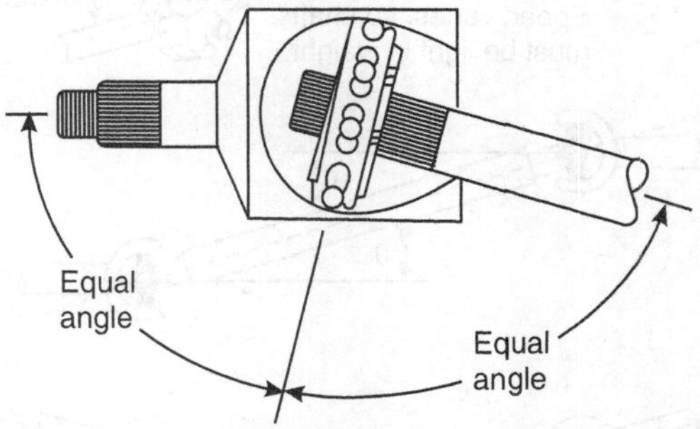

Fig. 10.10 Constant velocity joint

A constant velocity joint is a type that provides an output shaft speed equal to that of the input in all shaft positions within the working range of the joint. Constant-velocity conditions are achieved when the connecting device between the driving and driven yokes is positioned in a plane that bisects the angle of drive.

Constant velocity universal joints

One method of achieving a constant speed output from the propeller shaft is to mount two universal joints back-to-back (double Carden type) or positioned in a certain way at each end of the propeller shaft. In both configurations the relative positions of each joint must be arranged so that the speed change of one joint is counteracted by the other.

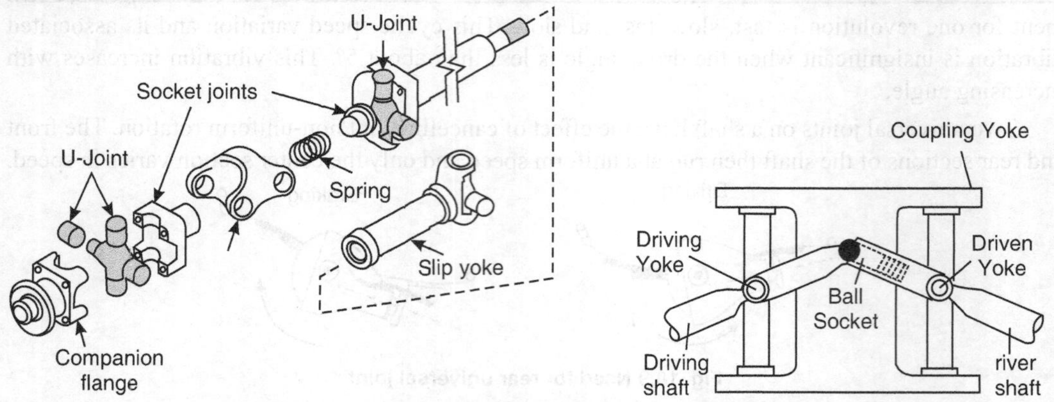

Fig. 10.11 Double Carden constant velocity universal joints

A constant velocity universal joint (double Carden type) used in front engine rear wheel drive is shown in Fig. 10.11. It consists of two universal joints linked by a ball and socket. The ball and socket splits the angle of the drive and driven shafts between the two universal joints of the constant-velocity unit. Because the two universal joints operate at the same angle, the speed-up and slow-down action is cancelled out. The speed-up resulting at any instant from the action of one universal joint is cancelled out by the slow-down of the other. Therefore no speed change occurs between the two shafts connected to a constant-velocity universal joint.

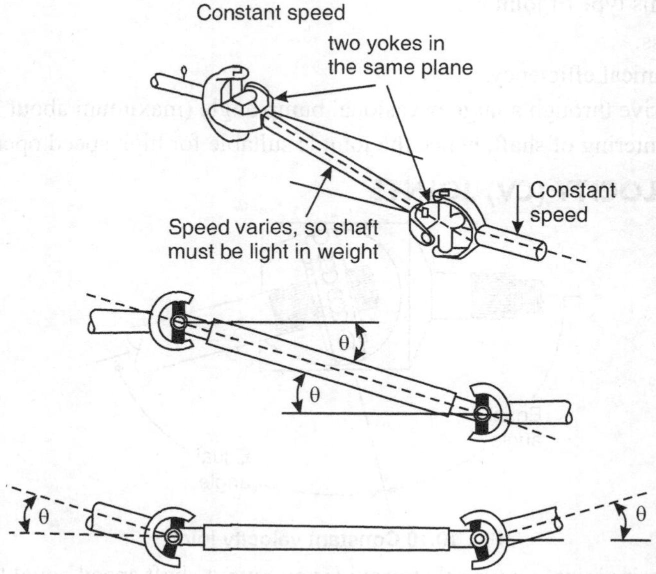

Fig. 10.12 Driving through an angle. Both angles are equal and giving no variation between input and output

The phasing of universal joints, as applied to two separate driveline layouts, is shown in Fig. 10.12. This diagram shows that to restore a constant speed, two conditions must be satisfied:

- yokes at each end of the propeller shaft must be positioned in the same plane.
- drive angle of each coupling must be equal.

Constant velocity joints

In the front-wheel drive vehicles, one end of the driveshaft is connected to a fixed transaxle assembly and the other end is attached to a wheel hub that moves up and down with the suspension spring. In addition to giving flexibility in this direction (plane), the outer joint must allow the road wheels to be steered through a large angle of about 25°.

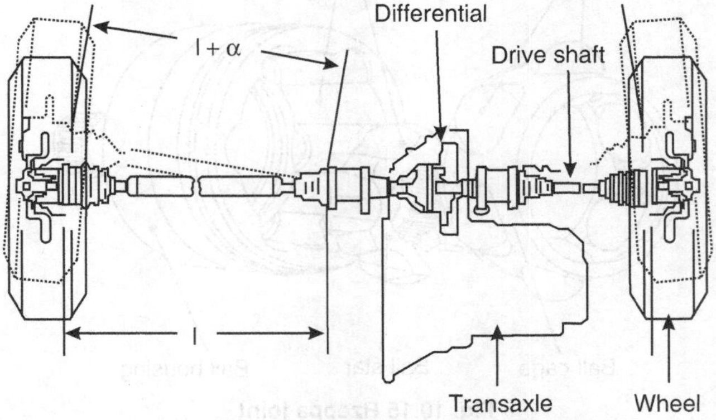

Fig. 10.13 CV joints in front-wheel drive vehicles

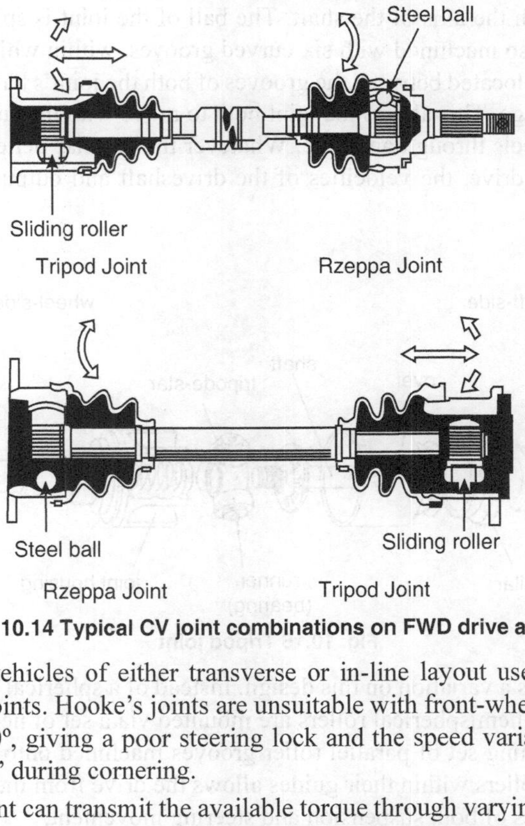

Fig. 10.14 Typical CV joint combinations on FWD drive axles

Front-wheel drive vehicles of either transverse or in-line layout use similar shafts but with constant velocity (CV) joints. Hooke's joints are unsuitable with front-wheel drive because they are limited to an angle of 20°, giving a poor steering lock and the speed variations would give rise to some steering 'twitching' during cornering.

In contrast, a CV joint can transmit the available torque through varying angles without any noticeable difference in the speeds of the two shafts. This results in the vehicle's having an acceptable steering lock, but without the vibration associated with other designs of coupling.

Front wheel drive cars use CV joints of either Birfield type (Rzeppa joint) or Tripod type or both. CV-joints don't show rotary vibrations even at a big drive shaft angle of up to 44°.

Rzeppa (Birfield) joint

The Birfield joint is one of the most popular CV joints fitted to front-wheel-drive vehicles. It consists of a specially designed ball and socket to which both the driveshaft and the output shaft are fitted.

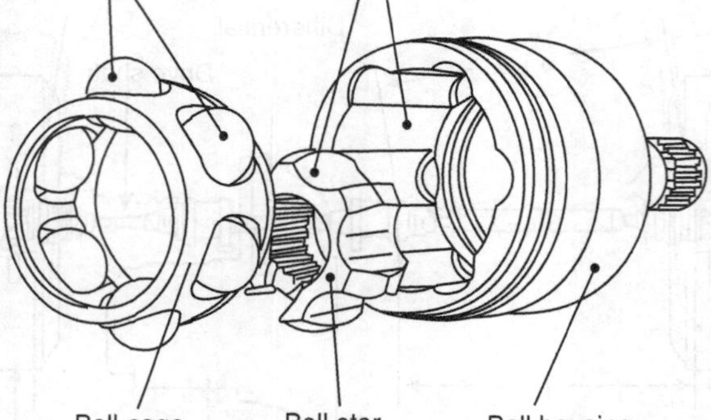

Fig. 10.15 Rzeppa joint

The part of the output shaft that forms the socket of the joint is machined with six curved grooves, which align with the axis of the shaft. The ball of the joint is splined onto the end of the driveshaft. This ball is also machined with six curved grooves, within which six smaller steel balls move. These six balls are located between the grooves of both the joint's ball and socket and are held in place by a steel ring cage. This allows the joint both to move with the suspension and to transmit power to the steered wheels through an angle. Whatever the angular deflection through which the joint has to transmit the drive, the velocities of the driveshaft and output shaft are the same and hence the name.

Tripod joint

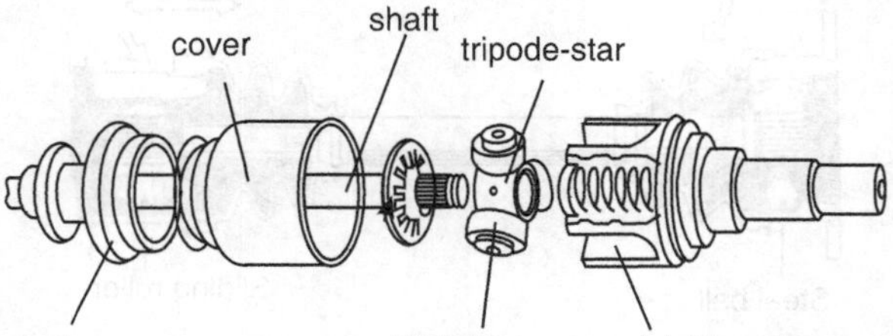

Fig. 10.16 Tripod joint

The tripod CV joint is a variation on this design. Instead of a spherical ball it uses a splined spider hub onto which three hemispherical rollers are mounted via a set of needle roller bearings. The rollers align with a matching set of parallel roller grooves machined onto the socket of the output shaft. Movement of the rollers within their guides allows the drive from the gearbox to be transmitted through varying angles of both suspension and steering movement.

TYPES OF DRIVE ARRANGEMENT

Propeller shafts are either solid or tubular and are employed in two main types of drive arrangements: Hotchkiss drive and torque tube drive.

Hotchkiss drive (or Open shaft drive)

This system employs a tubular or hollow propeller shaft and is the simplest type of drive. In this case the suspension springs besides taking weight of the body, also take the torque reaction, driving thrust and the side thrust.

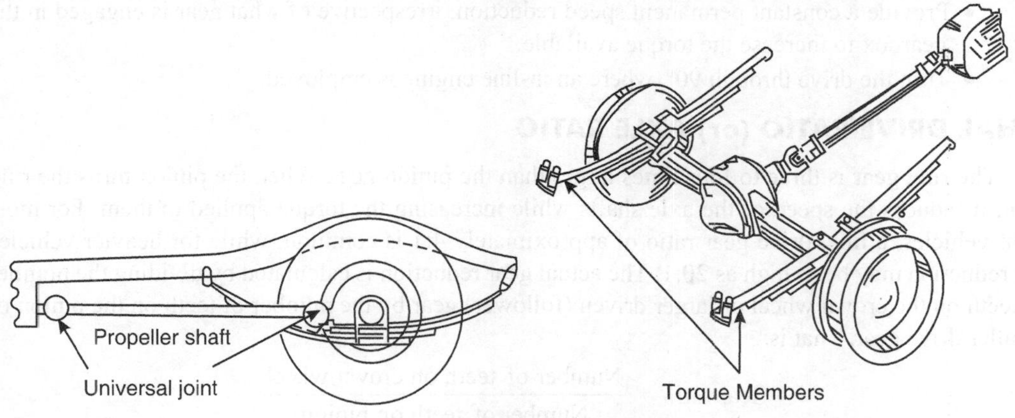

Fig. 10.17 Hotchkiss drive

Application

This system is more commonly used in all types of passenger cars and commercial vehicles.

Torque tube drive

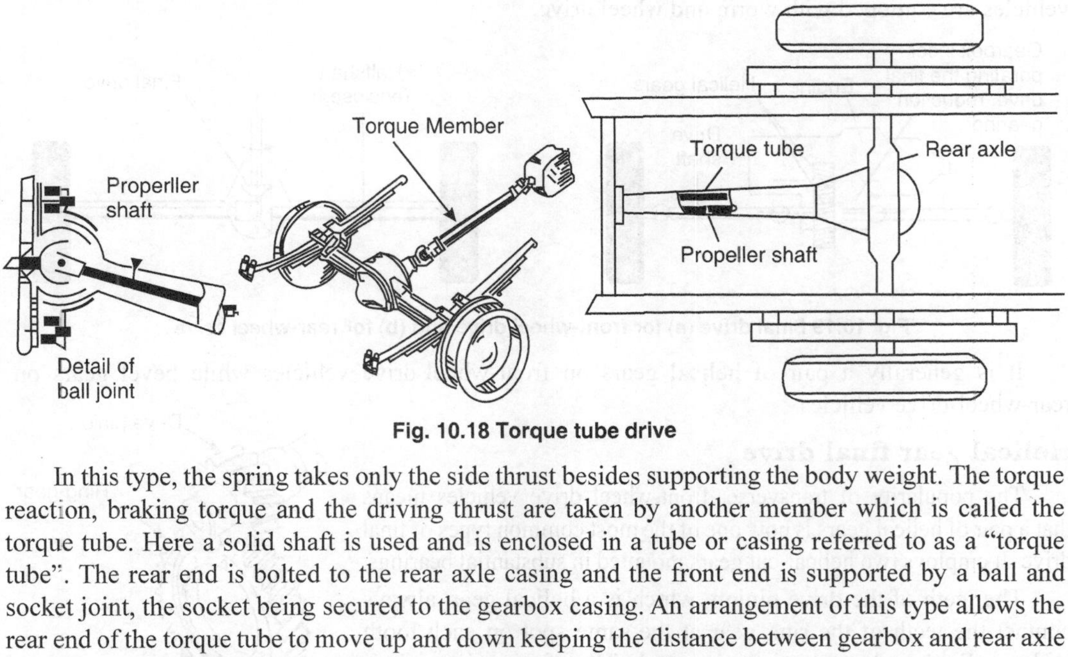

Fig. 10.18 Torque tube drive

In this type, the spring takes only the side thrust besides supporting the body weight. The torque reaction, braking torque and the driving thrust are taken by another member which is called the torque tube. Here a solid shaft is used and is enclosed in a tube or casing referred to as a "torque tube". The rear end is bolted to the rear axle casing and the front end is supported by a ball and socket joint, the socket being secured to the gearbox casing. An arrangement of this type allows the rear end of the torque tube to move up and down keeping the distance between gearbox and rear axle constant. One universal joint is fitted to the front of the propeller shaft connecting it to the gearbox main shaft.

Application

Although the torque tube drive system was used extensively on early vehicles, it is rarely employed in modern vehicle design.

FINAL DRIVE, DIFFERENTIAL AND REAR AXLE ASSEMBLY

FINAL DRIVE

The final gear of the differential assembly consists of the drive pinion and ring gear (crown wheel). The purpose of final drive is to:

- Provide a constant permanent speed reduction, irrespective of what gear is engaged in the gearbox to increase the torque available.
- Turn the drive through 90°, where an in-line engine is employed.

FINAL DRIVE RATIO (or) AXLE RATIO

The ring gear is three to four times larger than the pinion gear. When the pinion turns the ring gear, it reduces the speed of the axle shafts while increasing the torque applied to them. For most light vehicles, a final drive gear ratio of approximately 4:1 is common, while for heavier vehicles the reduction may be as high as 20:1. The actual gear reduction is calculated by dividing the number of teeth on the crown wheel or larger driven (follower) gear by the number of teeth on the pinion or smaller drive gear. That is:

$$\text{Gear ratio} = \frac{\text{Number of teeth on crown wheel}}{\text{Number of teeth on pinion}}$$

TYPES OF FINAL DRIVE

The position and type of final drive varies according to the vehicle's layout. With a transverse engine the final drive is driven directly from the gearbox output shaft and is known as reduction gearing. When an in-line engine layout is employed, a crown wheel and pinion is used. Some heavy vehicles are equipped with worm and wheel drive.

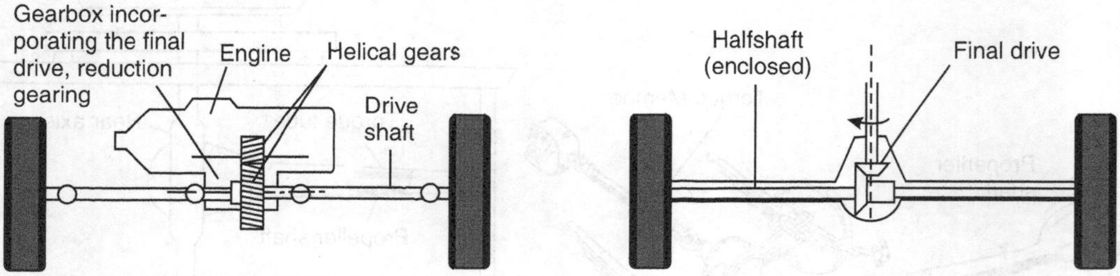

Fig. 10.19 Final drive (a) for front-wheel drive and (b) for rear-wheel drive

It is generally a pair of helical gears on front-wheel-drive vehicles while bevel gears on rear-wheel-drive vehicles.

Helical gear final drive

The popularity of transverse, front-wheel drive vehicles means that a pair of helical gears is now one of the most common types of final drive. It employs two helical-cut gears mounted in substantial bearings.

The teeth of the drive pinion, which is a helical gear, always contact the teeth of the ring gear at the same spot on each tooth without slipping along the opposing teeth. Therefore, noise and vibration are kept to a minimum, and torque is transmitted smoothly.

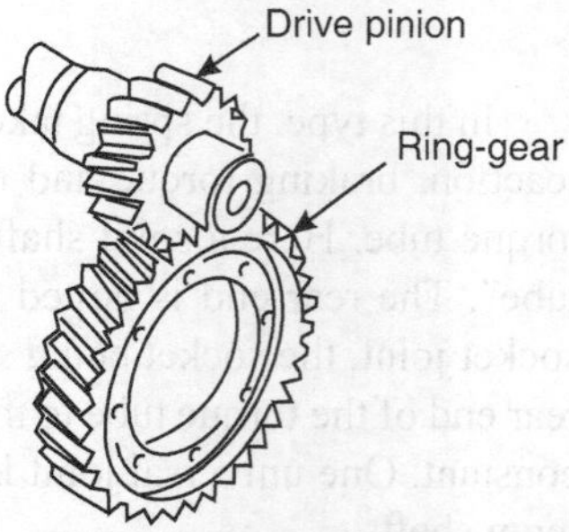

Fig. 10.20 Helical gear final drive

Hypoid final drive

This is the type of bevel drive most likely to be found on current front-engine rear-drive vehicles. One of its main features is that the centerline axis of the pinion is offset relative to the centreline axis of the crown wheel. An offset of one-fifth of the crown wheel diameter is common.

The pinion offset may be used to improve body design. By lowering the propeller shaft level it enables the vehicle body floor to be dropped. This allows the vehicle to be designed with a body having normal ground clearance which helps to improve stability of the vehicle. Gears are meshed at a larger meshing ratio and the gear operation is very quiet. It also allows more teeth to be in contact to carry the load.

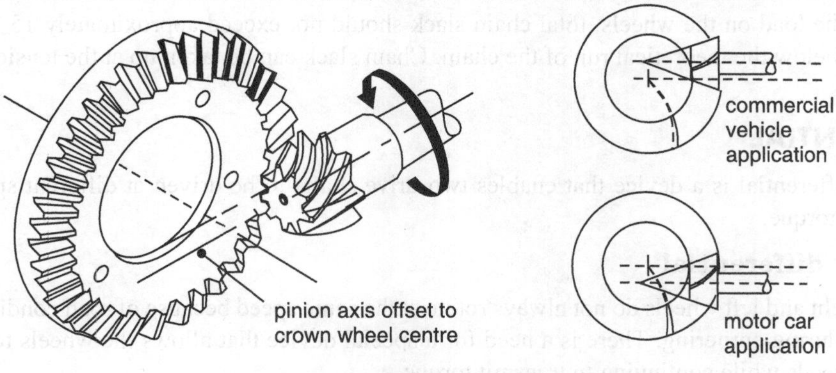

Fig. 10.21 Hypoid final drive

Since these gears are constantly sliding and rolling against each other, the hypoid bevel gear must be lubricated with hypoid gear oil (extreme pressure oil), which has a high oil film strength. Additives such as chlorine and sulphate prevent the gear teeth from 'scuffing' as well as providing adequate lubrication at all likely temperatures.

Chain-sprocket final drive

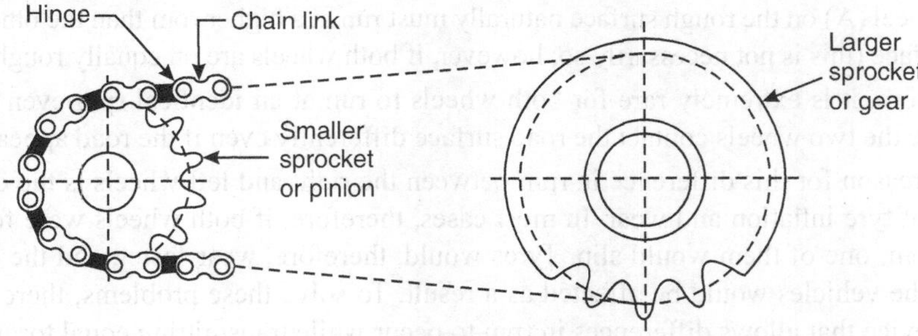

Fig. 10.22 Chain final drive

Chain final-drive is perhaps motor cycling's most common system used for transferring mechanical energy to the rear wheel.

Power is transmitted from the engine via a roller chain and a pair of toothed wheels, or sprockets, one each on the countershaft and on the rear wheels. As the chain is drawn around the countershaft sprocket by that sprocket's rotation, the gear teeth mesh with each link. This action pulls the chain, which rotates the sprocket on the rear wheel in the same fashion. That is, the chain meshes with the rear wheel sprocket's teeth, turning it, and the entire rear wheel, around.

These days, there are two types of roller chains for motorcycles: O-ring and non O-ring. O-ring chain can be a bit of a misnomer. Rather than O-rings, manufacturers are using X and Z shape rings that help keep special, installed at the factory lubricant inside the chain and water, dirt and other nasties out. Note that most high-quality chains used on motorcycles are O-ring (or X or Z ring) chains.

There are several good reasons why motorcycles prefer chain drives. To begin with, chain final-drive systems are lighter than their other two counter parts, belt and shaft drives. They are more efficient, too, than big, heavy, power-snapping shaft final drives and narrower than belt final drives. Moreover, chain drives allow owners to alter their overall gearing with relative ease.

Chain drive has its disadvantages too. Chain drive is noisy. It requires the most maintenance such as periodic cleaning, lubrication and adjustment, as well as replacement. Indeed, when a chain and/or sprockets are worn out, you need to replace all three-chain, countershaft sprocket and rear wheel sprocket. Otherwise the remaining part(s) will wear out the new one(s) quickly.

With the load on the wheels, total chain slack should not exceed approximately 15 to 20 mm above and below the theoretical run of the chain. Chain slack can be taken up at the tensioning nuts or adjusters.

DIFFERENTIAL

The differential is a device that enables two drive shafts to be driven at different speeds, but with equal torque.

Need for differential

The right and left wheels do not always rotate at the same speed because of road conditions, and especially during cornering. There is a need for a special device that allows the wheels to rotate at different speeds while continuing to transmit torque.

In comparing the path of the inside wheel (A) with the path of the outside wheel (B) of a vehicle when it turns along a curve, as illustrated in Fig. 10.23*a*, the outside wheel (B) draws an arc whose radius is the distance O-B, while the inside wheel (A) draws an arc whose radius is the distance O-A. Therefore, the distance of travel of the outside wheel is longer than that of the inside wheel. For this reason, the outside wheel is forced to move faster and rotate more than the inside wheel.

If one of the wheels is on a flat surface and the other on a rough surface, as illustrated in Fig. 10.23b, the wheel (A) on the rough surface naturally must run at a higher rpm than the other wheel (B) on the flat surface (this is not necessarily so, however, if both wheels are on equally rough surfaces).

Furthermore, it is extremely rare for both wheels to run at an identical rpm even on ordinary roads, because the two wheels contact the road surface differently even if the road appears to be flat.

Another reason for this difference in rpm between the right and left wheels is the difference in the amounts of tyre inflation and wear. In most cases, therefore, if both wheels were forced to run at the same rpm, one of them would slip. Tyres would, therefore, wear faster, and the driving performance of the vehicles would be affected as a result. To solve these problems, there is needed a differential device that allows differences in rpm to occur while transmitting equal torque.

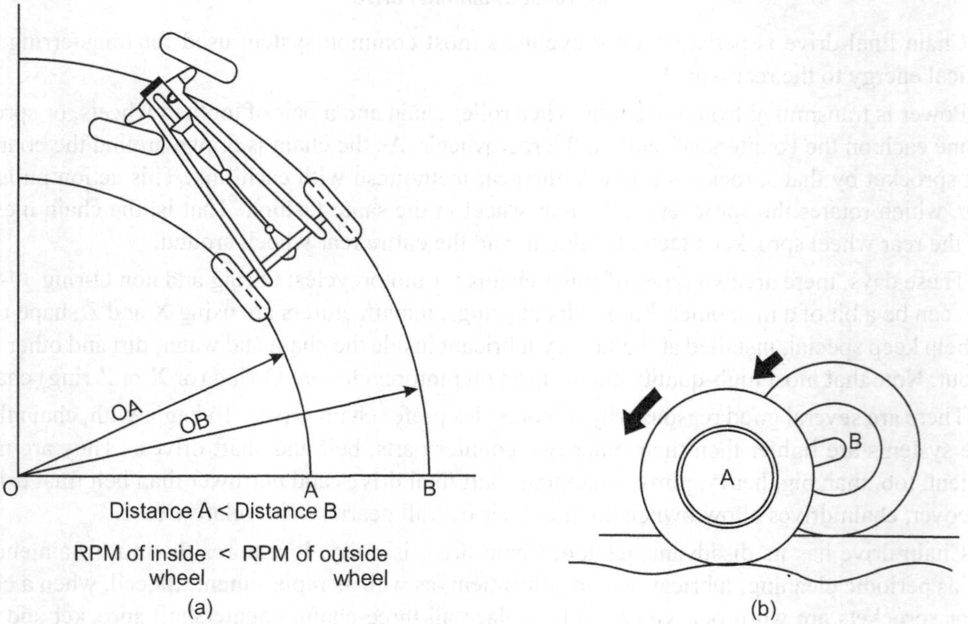

Fig. 10.23 Need for differential unit

Construction

The general constructional detail of the final drive and differential assembly is shown in Fig.10.24.

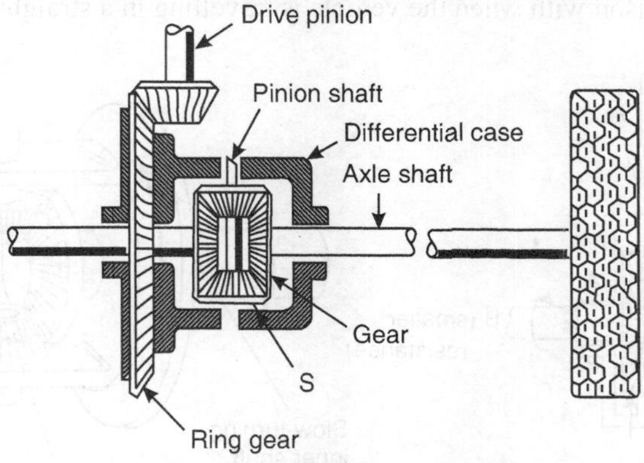

Fig. 10.24 Differential assembly

The ring gear (crown wheel) of the final drive is attached to a differential case which contains four bevel-type gear pinions all facing inwards, meshing with each other in the form of a box. Two of the bevel pinions opposite each other are splined to the half shafts and are referred to as the sun gears. The other opposed pair of pinions are free to rotate upon a pinion shaft and are known as pinion gears. The pinion shaft which acts as a pivot for the pinion gears is mounted in the differential housing which is driven by the ring gear. There is no direct connection between the ring gear and the half shafts.

The final drive gears must function precisely in correct relationship with each other. At the same time they will be transmitting very high torque. For this reason, the final drive and differential assembly is located in the axle casing and supported on taper roller bearings.

Operation

Straight-ahead travel

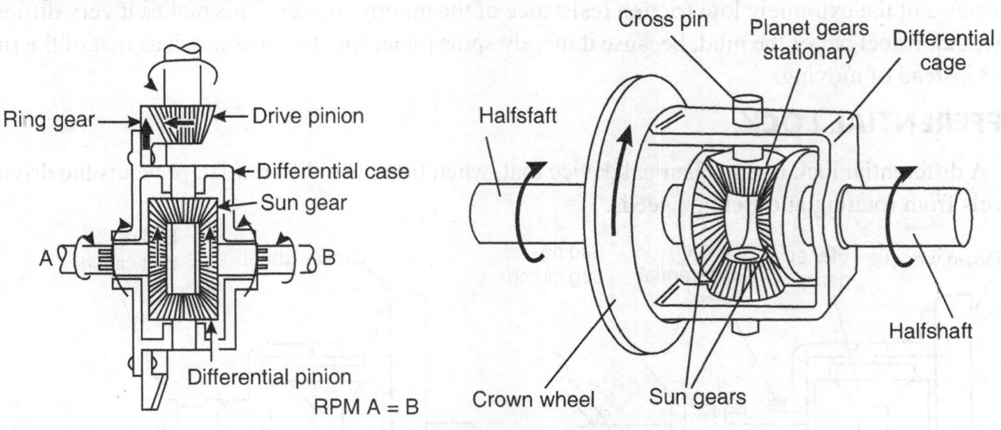

Fig. 10.25 Straight-ahead

The rolling resistances of the two drive wheels are almost identical when the vehicle is travelling straight ahead on a level road. When resistance is equal in both axle shafts, the differential pinions themselves do not rotate but turn as a unit with the ring gear, differential case and pinion shafts. In this case, the differential pinions only function to connect the right and left sun gears. As a result, the two sun gears rotate as a unit with the revolution of the differential pinions, causing both drive wheels to turn at an equal rpm.

Turning

When the vehicle is turning, the inside wheel travels less distance (i.e., in a shorter arc) than the outside wheel in comparison with when the vehicle is travelling in a straight line.

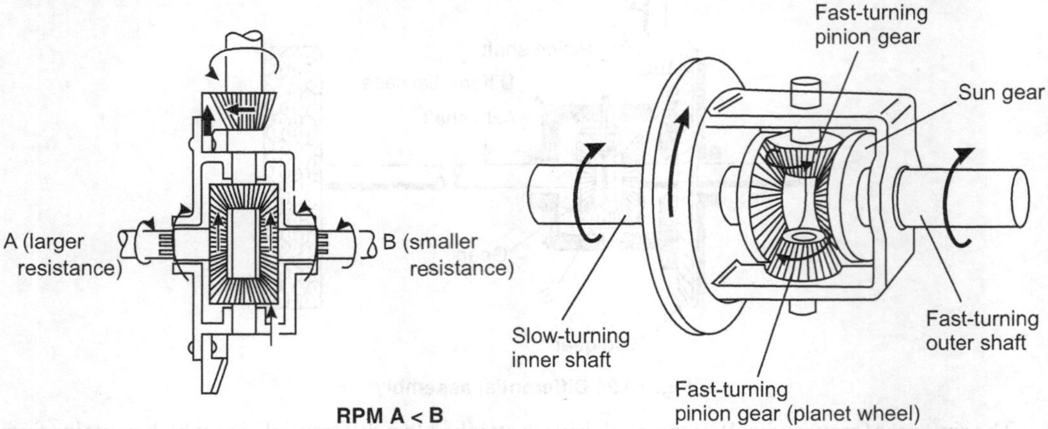

Fig. 10.26 Cornering

Since a resistance is therefore applied to the left-hand sun gear, as illustrated above in Fig. 10.26, each differential pinion rotates around its own shaft and also revolves around the rear axle. The rpm of the right-hand sun gear increases as a result.

One wheel on a muddy surface

The differential described above is a standard or open differential. It delivers the same torque to each wheel. If one tyre begins to slip and spin, the open differential divides the rotary speed unequally. The tyre with good traction slows and stops. This may also stop the vehicle or prevent it from moving.

If one of the wheels gets in the mud it will start to spin if the accelerator pedal is pressed. This is because of the extremely low friction resistance of the muddy surface. This makes it very difficult to get that wheel out of the mud, because it merely spins (at an rpm twice as much as that of the ring gear) instead of moving.

DIFFERENTIAL LOCK

A differential lock is a mechanical device that, when fitted to a differential, prevents the driving wheels from rotating at different speeds.

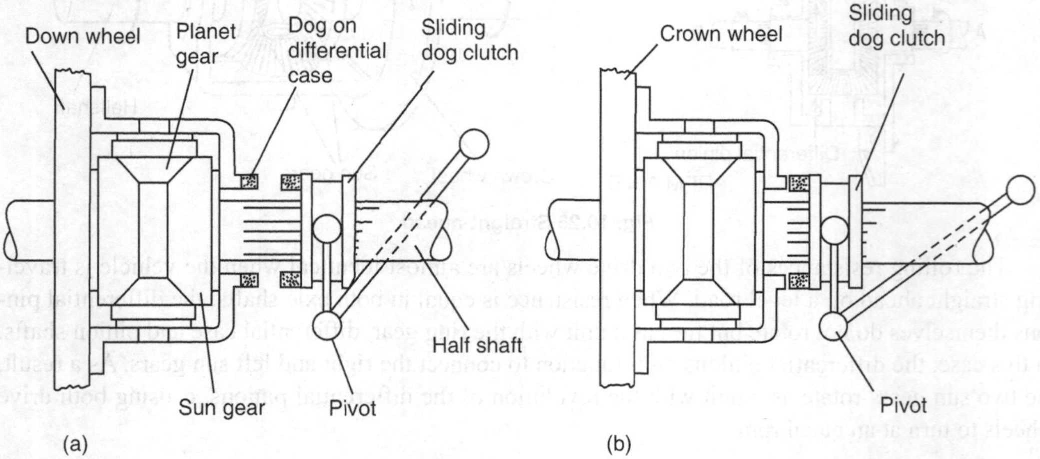

Fig. 10.27 Differential lock: (a) disengaged and (b) engaged

One of the most common types of differential lock consists of a sliding dog clutch, which is moved by an electrically operated solenoid unit or by compressed air. When engaged, the sliding dog clutch meshes with a similar set of dog teeth machined onto the differential cage. This prevents the planet gears from driving the sun gears at different speeds. It is important to remember that a differential lock must not be selected for normal road use, as this can cause serious damage to the final drive and differential.

LIMITED SLIP DIFFERENTIAL

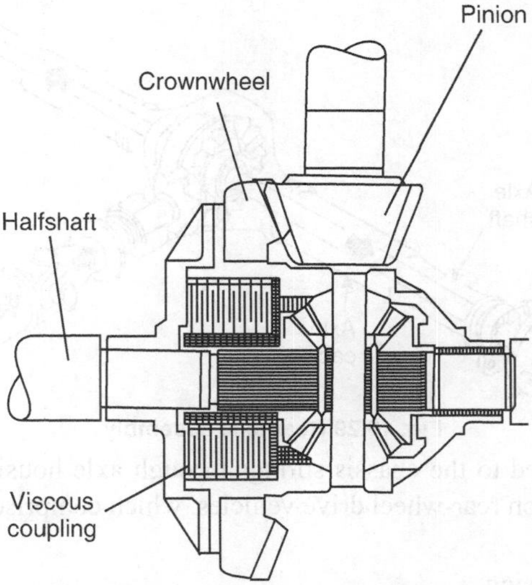

Fig. 10.28 Viscous coupling limited-slip differential

In any vehicle, if any one of the wheels gets slipped due to slippery surface, its traction will be lost. In order to restrict this drawback, the differential action is controlled by multi-plate clutch between the sun gear and differential cage (or case). Differentials having this feature are called Limited Slip Differentials (LSD) and are available in a number of designs. One of them is the limited-slip viscous coupling type shown in Fig. 10.28.

The driving plates of a multi-plate clutch are attached to the differential case and driven plates are attached to the sun gear axle shaft. The space between the closely fitted plates is filled with silicon fluid. When there is limited variation between the speed of the input member and output member, the silicon fluid remains viscous. If the speed of the two components begins to change too much, the fluid effectively solidifies and the plates are locked together. Normal cornering speed variations within the differential are acceptable as there is limited slip. As soon as one wheel starts to spin, the coupling locks up. When the speed and torque difference returns to an acceptable level, the silicon becomes fluid again and there is limited slip.

REAR AXLE

The axle supports the wheels as well as the drive shaft. The rear axle serves purposes which can vary according to vehicle design. Axles are usually classified under two headings:

Live axle

A live axle is one that drives the vehicle. This consists of a hollow axle casing through which drive is transmitted, passing from the final drive to the differential, to the half shafts and finally to the road wheels. The axle rotates with the road wheels and is supported in bearings mounted in or on the axle casing.

Dead axle

A dead axle does not rotate. It merely supports the vehicle load and provides a mounting place for the wheels. The rear axle of a front-wheel drive vehicle is a dead axle, as are the axles used on trailers.

Construction

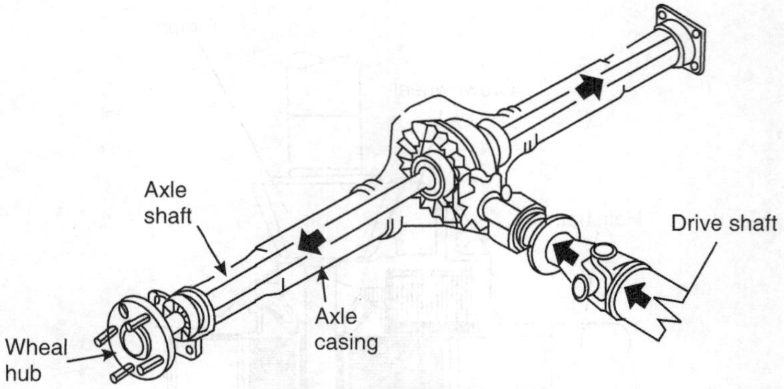

Fig. 10.29 Rear axle assembly

The rear axle is installed to the chassis springs through axle housings. The basic layout of a conventional live axle used on rear-wheel drive vehicles, which comprises the following main components:

(*a*) Axle housing or casing
(*b*) Final drive
(*c*) Differential unit
(*d*) Half shaft to each road wheel
(*e*) Support bearings
(*f*) Two hub assemblies

The axle housing is a single-piece construction and has the brakes installed at both ends. The centre part of the axle housing is made to allow installing the differential and also serve as an oil well. Drive from the propeller shaft is transmitted via the crown wheel and pinion, to both rear wheels by means of the half shafts. The axle housing itself acts as a beam to support the weight of the rear of the vehicle and provide a mounting for the final drive and differential gears. The axle housing must also act as a reservoir for lubrication purposes. Each half shaft is supported at its inner end by the differential sun wheel and bearing while their outer ends are carried in hub bearings. An oil seal is provided on the outer end of each axle shaft to prevent the oil from leaking into the brakes.

On front-wheel drive vehicles, the rear axle is considered a dead axle. In a dead axle, bearings are used to support the vehicle. However, since there is no differential, the axle is not connected to a differential and is not used to transmit power.

Types of rear axle

The driving axles are grouped by the bearing mounting method into the full-floating type, the three-quarter floating type and the semi-floating type. All three use axle shafts that are splined to the differential sun gears. At the wheel ends, the axles can be attached in any one of a number of ways. This attachment defines the type of axle it is and the manner in which the shafts are supported by bearings.

Semi-floating type

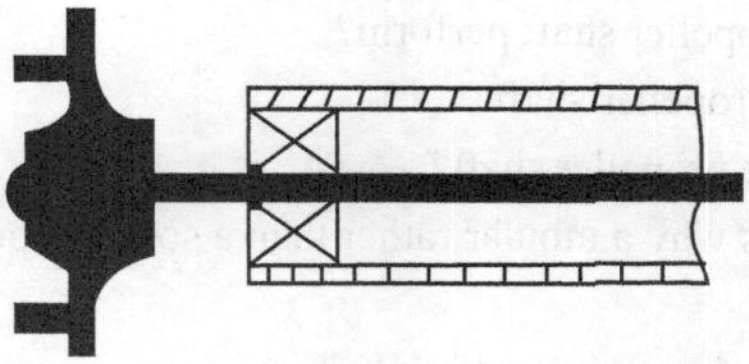

Fig. 10.30 Three-quarter floating rear axle

Bearings are installed between the axle housing and the axle shaft and the wheel is fitted directly to the shaft. For this reason, the shaft is required to support all of the vehicle weight as well as lateral loads during turning. Since it is simple in construction, this type is used with most passenger cars.

Three-quarter floating type

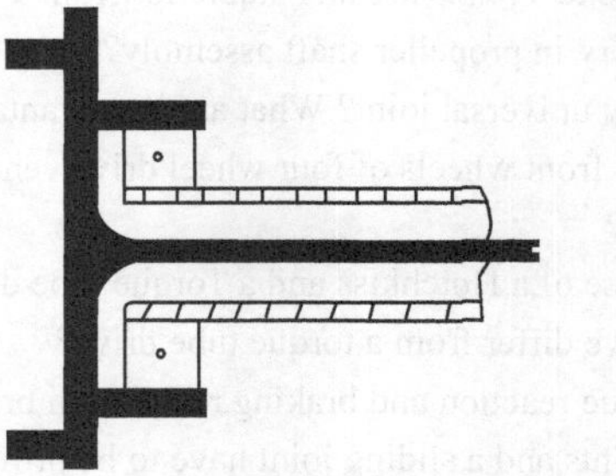

Fig. 10.31 Three-quarter floating rear axle

A single bearing is installed between the axle housing and the wheel hub and the wheel is fitted directly to the shaft. Most of the vehicle weight is supported by the housing, although lateral loads during turning are applied to the axle shaft.

Full-floating type

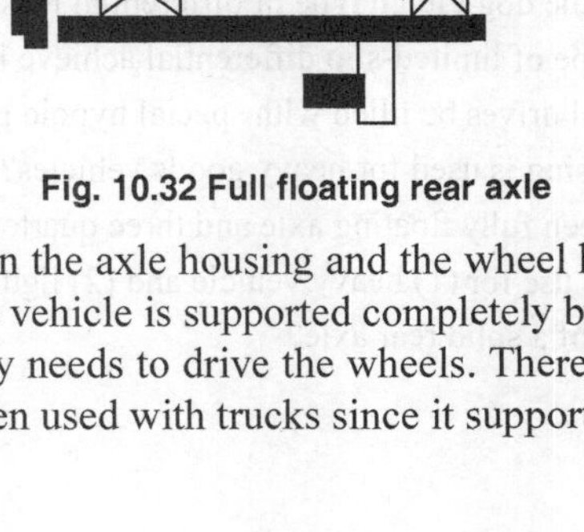

Fig. 10.32 Full floating rear axle

Bearings are placed between the axle housing and the wheel hub and the wheel is fitted to the wheel hub. Since the load of the vehicle is supported completely by the axle housing in this type of suspension system, the axle only needs to drive the wheels. Therefore, the shaft is prevented from excessive force. This type is often used with trucks since it supports heavy loads well.

Review Questions

1. What functions does the propeller shaft perform?
2. What are the two types of propeller shaft?
3. What faults are found in the propeller shaft?
4. State the three main reasons why a tubular rather than a solid propeller shaft is fitted to a vehicle.
5. What is an universal joint?
6. What is the special feature of an universal joint?
7. Universal joints work satisfactorily up to --------------.
8. What are the various universal joints in use?
9. How many universal joints are there in the torque tube transmission and why?
10. What is the major drawback of Hooke's type of universal joint?
11. Why must Hooke's joints be properly aligned with each other?
12. State two reasons why Hooke's joints are unsuitable for front-wheel drive shafts.
13. Why is a slip joint necessary in propeller shaft assembly?
14. What is a constant velocity universal joint? What are its advantages?
15. How axles are fitted in the front wheels of four wheel drive vehicles?
16. What is a Hotchkiss drive?
17. What is the specific purpose of a Hotchkiss and a Torque tube drive?
18. How does a Hotchkiss drive differ from a torque tube drive?
19. Discuss the effects of torque reaction and braking reaction in brief.
20. When do two universal joints and a sliding joint have to be provided?
21. How does imbalance affect the propeller shaft?
22. What is a final drive?
23. Why is final drive called as such?
24. What are the different types of final drive?
25. What is hypoid gear drive? Why are these gears preferred in final drive?
26. What is meant by backlash?
27. Give two reasons for using a final drive in a vehicle transmission system.
28. Why does a motor vehicle need a differential?
29. Which types of differential are used on motor vehicles?
30. How does the differential function when driving in a straight line and when cornering?
31. When can the automatic differential action prove to be a disadvantage?
32. Which vehicles need a differential lock?
33. What are the limitations on the dog-clutch type of differential lock?
34. How does the multi-plate type of limited-slip differential achieve its differential locking action?
35. Why must hypoid-bevel final drives be filled with special hypoid gear oils?
36. Which type of rear axle housing is used for heavy goods vehicles?
37. What is the difference between fully floating axle and three quarter floating type rear axle?
38. Which type of rear axle is in use for (1) heavy vehicle and (2) light vehicle?
39. What are the disadvantages of a solid rear axle?

11 CHAPTER

FRONT AXLE & STEERING

FRONT AXLE

The front axle supports the front of the vehicle and is also used for steering. It also absorbs shocks due to road irregularities. This usually takes the form of an I-section beam which is machined from a heat-treated steel forging. The beam is provided with spring seats for mounting the front road springs. Both ends of the beam are upswept and of oval section to resist the action of the braking torque which attempts to turn the axle with the road wheel. To keep the chassis height low the center portion of the front axle is given a downward sweep as shown in the Fig. 11.1. A stub axle or swivel pin assembly is secured to each end of the beam by means of a king pin.

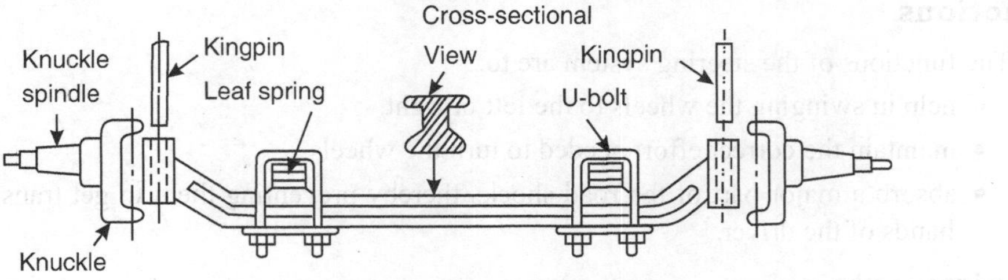

Fig. 11.1 Front axle of commercial vehicles

Simple tubular type non-driving axles are also sometimes used on commercial vehicles. In this type the centre section of the axle is manufactured from tempered seamless steel tube. The stub axle eyes and spring seats are electrically welded into position on the tube and become integral parts of the axle assembly.

STUB AXLE

Vehicles are equipped with stub axles mounted on kingpins or steering knuckles. The stub axle of the steered wheel is pivoted round the steering axis. The wheelbase remains more or less the same. As a result, the vehicle remains stable even at the maximum steering lock angles.

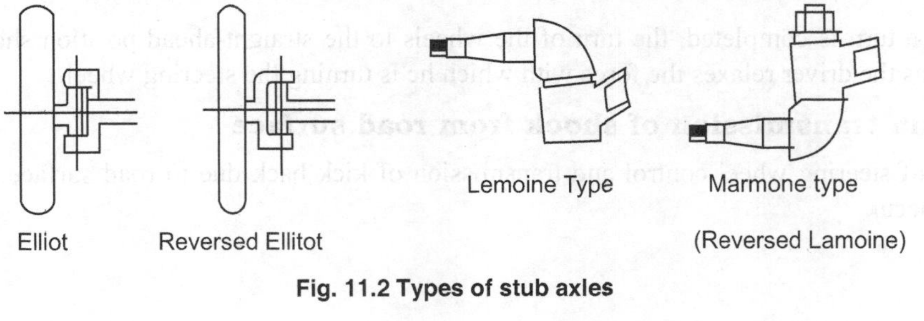

Fig. 11.2 Types of stub axles

The stub axle pivots on the king pin which is mounted at the correct angle for the steering geometry. Phosphor-bronze bushes are fitted between the king pins and stub axle to provide a bearing surface. These bushes are a press fit into the stub axle trunnion eyes and are reamed to be sliding fit to the actual king pin, which must pass through the three eyes to provide a firm but free swivel action. The vertical load is taken on a hardened-steel thrust washer or ball-thrust bearing which is located on the underside of the axle eye.

Each stub axle is machined to accommodate the steering arms. These are connected by a track rod to ensure that each road wheel is turned through the correct angle. On right-hand drive vehicles the offside stub axle carries an intermediate steering arm which is connected to the drag link. Each end of the track rod and drag link must be fitted with a ball joint to allow the wheels to turn.

To prevent the road wheels from being turned through too great an angle, steering stops are mounted on each stub axle. In practice these restrict the steering movement to prevent the wheels fouling the chassis on full lock.

Stub axles that are used on motor vehicles can be grouped into several types as shown above in the Fig. 11.2. The most popular is reversed Elliot type.

STEERING SYSTEM

The purpose of a steering system is to control the direction in which a vehicle travels. Movement of the steering wheel by the driver should cause an accurate response of the road wheels. Control of the vehicle should be maintained with safety throughout the speed range with little effort and over a wide range of road surfaces under all conditions.

Functions

The functions of the steering system are to:

- help in swinging the wheels to the left or right.
- maintain the correct effort needed to turn the wheels.
- absorb a major part of the road shocks thereby preventing them to get transmitted to the hands of the driver.

Requirements

The main requirements of a steering system are:

Excellent maneuverability

When the car is cornering on a narrow, twisting road, the steering system must be able to turn the front wheels sharply yet easily and smoothly.

Proper steering effort

In order to obtain easier steering and better feel of the road, the steering should be made lighter at low speeds and heavier at high speeds.

Smooth recovery

After a turn is completed, the turn of the wheels to the straight-ahead position should occur smoothly as the driver relaxes the force with which he is turning the steering wheel.

Minimum transmission of shock from road surface

Loss of steering wheel control and transmission of kick back due to road surface roughness must not occur.

COMPONENTS

The steering system generally consists of three main sections: steering column, steering gear and steering linkage.

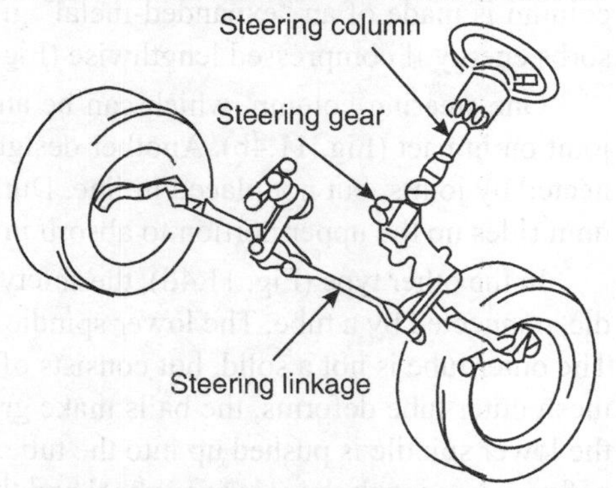

Fig. 11.3 Components of a steering system

STEERING COLUMN

The steering column consists of the main steering shaft which transmits the steering wheel rotation to the steering gear and the column tube which fixes the main steering shaft to the body. The top end of the main steering shaft is fitted to steering wheel by a nut.

The bottom end of the main steering shaft is connected to the steering gear, generally by way of a flexible joint or universal joint to minimize the transmission of road shock from the steering gear to the steering wheel.

Collapsible steering column

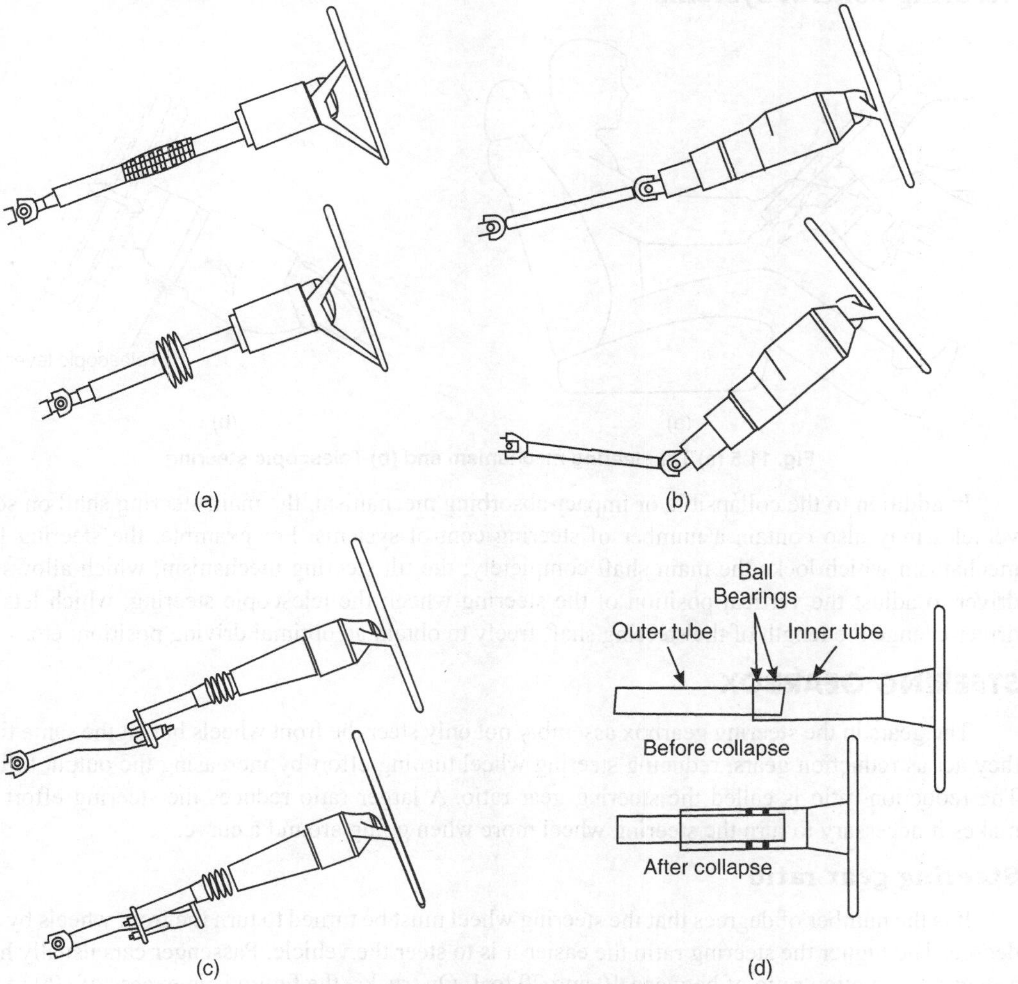

Fig. 11.4 Collapsible steering columns

The steering column can be designed to collapse on impact. In the event of collision, the driver is exposed to the risk of injury from the steering wheel and steering column. The tubular steering column is made of an "expanded-metal" grid so that, although strong in twist, it collapses and absorbs energy if compressed lengthwise (Fig. 11.4a).

One steering column, which can be angled to suit the driver's needs, collapses at a universal joint on impact (Fig. 11.4b). Another design divides the steering shaft into sections which are connected by joints, but not placed in line. During the front-end collision, the lower portion of the column rides up the upper portion to absorb impact energy (Fig. 11.4c).

In the other type (Fig. 11.4d), the safety steering column has an upper and a lower steering spindle, connected by a tube. The lower spindle is secured in the tube by a ball bearing or a plastic rivet. The outer tube is not a solid, but consists of an expanded metal mesh. In the event of a collision the mesh outer tube deforms, the balls make grooves in the tubes or the plastic rivet is sheared off and the lower spindle is pushed up into the tube. Deformation of the outer tube absorbs the impact force before it can reach the steering wheel and the spindle sliding in the tube avoids the risk of injury.

The steering wheel is "dished" and provided with a large boss and wide spokes in order to spread the load of impact over the driver's chest. The wheel or boss can also be designed to collapse when under a pre-determined load.

Steering control systems

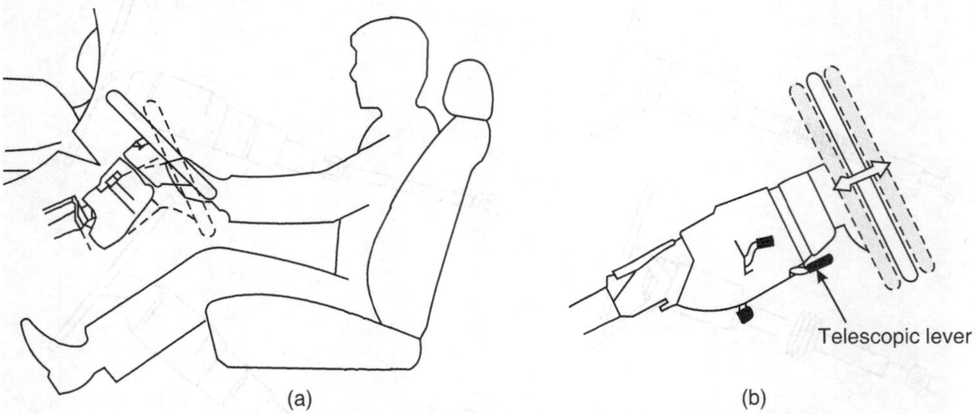

Fig. 11.5 (a) Tilt steering mechanism and (b) Telescopic steering

In addition to the collapsible or impact-absorbing mechanism, the main steering shaft on some vehicles may also contain a number of steering control systems. For example, the steering lock mechanism which locks the main shaft completely; the tilt steering mechanism, which allows the driver to adjust the vertical position of the steering wheel; the telescopic steering, which lets the driver change the length of the steering shaft freely to obtain an optimal driving position; etc.

STEERING GEARBOX

The gears in the steering gearbox assembly not only steer the front wheels but, at the same time, they act as reduction gears, reducing steering wheel turning effort by increasing the output torque. The reduction ratio is called the steering gear ratio. A larger ratio reduces the steering effort but makes it necessary to turn the steering wheel more when going around a curve.

Steering gear ratio

It is the number of degrees that the steering wheel must be turned to turn the front wheels by one degree. The higher the steering ratio the easier it is to steer the vehicle. Passenger cars usually have a steering reduction ratio of between 10 and 20 to 1. On trucks, the figure is in excess of 20 to 1.

In the case of the recirculating-ball type, the steering gear ratio is found by dividing the amount of steering wheel rotation by the amount of pitman arm movement.

$$\text{Steering gear ratio} = \frac{\text{amount of steering wheel rotation (in degrees)}}{\text{pitman arm movement (in degrees)}}$$

For the rack-and-pinion type, the steering gear ratio is found by dividing the amount of steering wheel rotation by the front wheel steering angle.

$$\text{Steering gear ratio} = \frac{\text{amount of steering wheel rotation (in degrees)}}{\text{front wheel steering angle (in degrees)}}$$

Types of steering gearbox

Over the years a number of different types of steering gearbox have been used. These include:

1. Worm and sector
2. Screw and nut
3. Worm and peg
4. Worm and roller
5. Recirculating ball
6. Rack and pinion

Worm and sector

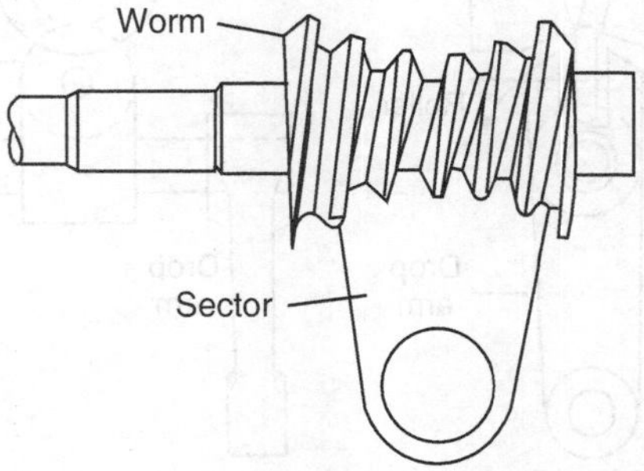

Fig. 11.6 Worm and sector

This type has been developed from a worm and wheel which was one of the earliest designs of box. A case-hardened steel worm and sector are located by bearings in a malleable iron or light alloy casing.

Screw and nut

Threads are cut on the lower end of main shaft and a nut screwed into it. Nut end is provided with a protrusion which fits into a lever installed on the housing. Turning the steering wheel moves the nut up and down, imparting a swinging motion to the lever and causing the pitman arm connected to the lever to rotate.

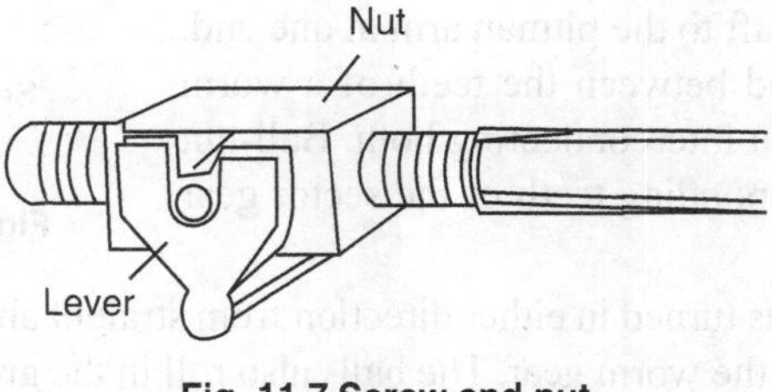

Fig. 11.7 Screw and nut

Worm and peg

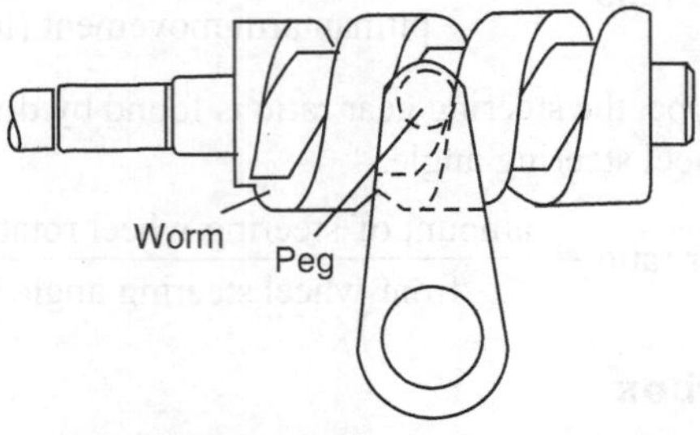

Fig. 11.8 Cam and peg steering gear

This type of steering gearbox is used widely in lighter cars. A cone shaped peg travels along the worm gear as the steering shaft is rotated. Peg is mounted on a lever which drives the drop arm via a shaft.

Worm and roller

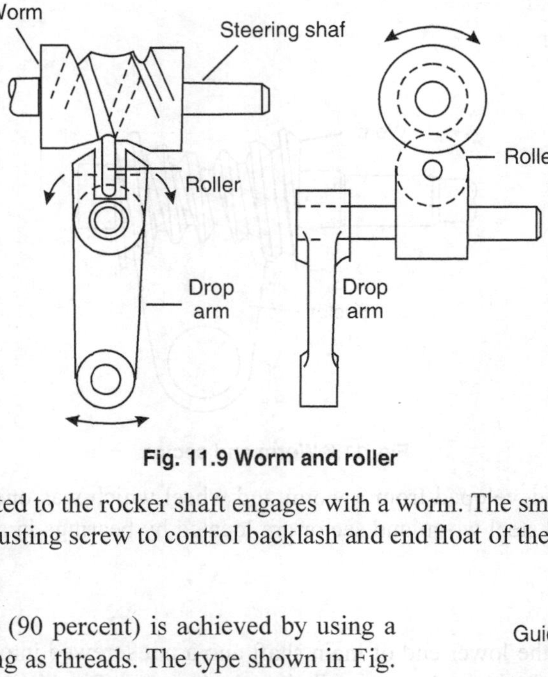

Fig. 11.9 Worm and roller

A roller follower fitted to the rocker shaft engages with a worm. The small offset of the roller to the worm enables an adjusting screw to control backlash and end float of the rocker shaft.

Recirculating ball

A higher efficiency (90 percent) is achieved by using a nut with steel balls acting as threads. The type shown in Fig. 11.10 uses a half nut with a transfer tube which feeds the balls back to the nut.

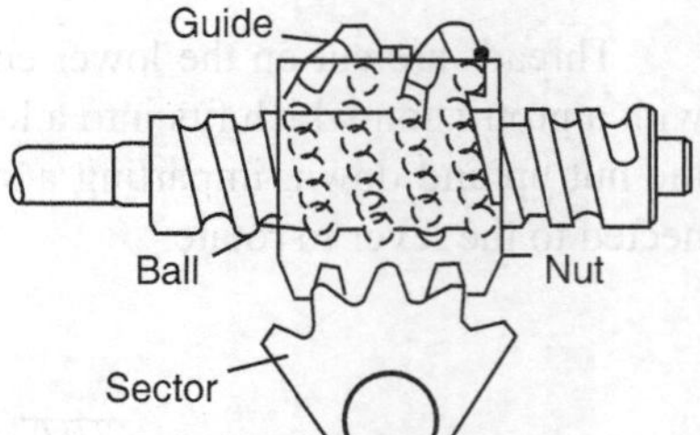

Fig. 11.10 Recirculating ball

Worm shaft is connected to the steering wheel via main shaft at one end and sector shaft to the pitman arm at one end. Steel balls with guides placed between the teeth of a worm shaft and grooves of a ball-nut interconnecting both. Ball-nut has teeth matching the corresponding teeth of the sector gear connected to the sector shaft.

When the steering wheel is turned in either direction from straight ahead, the rotation of the worm gear causes the balls to roll in the worm gear. The balls also roll in the grooves cut in the inner face of the ball nut. Therefore, as the worm shaft rotates, the balls cause the ball nut to move up or down along the worm. The up and down motion is carried to the gear sector by the ball nut teeth forcing the gear sector and cross shaft to rotate. Turning of the sector shaft turns the pitman arm and causes the complete steering linkage to move in one direction, with the result that the front wheels turn in the same direction as the steering wheel. The balls are called recirculating balls because they can continuously recirculate from one end of the ball nut to the other through a pair of ball return guides.

Rack and pinion

The rack and pinion steering gear, used mostly on smaller cars, has pinion connected to the lower end of the steering main shaft. The pinion is meshed with a rack of gear teeth cut on the underside of the major cross member of the steering linkage. When the steering wheel is turned, the pinion turns. This moves the rack to the left or right. The movement of the rack is transmitted through the tie rods and spindle arms to steer the front wheels.

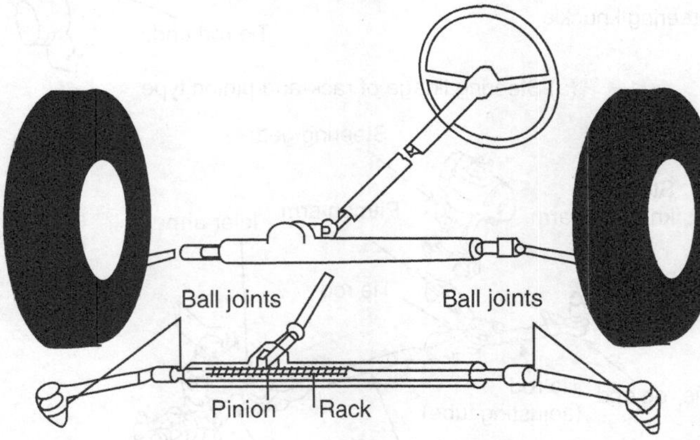

Fig. 11.11 Rack-and-pinion steering gear

Advantages

- Construction is compact, simple and light in weight since the gearbox is small, and the rack itself acts as the steering linkage, the relay rods used on the recirculating ball type are not necessary.
- Gear meshing is direct, so steering response is very sharp.
- There is little sliding and rotational resistance, and torque transmission is better, so steering is very light.
- The steering gear assembly is completely sealed, so it needs no maintenance.

Although there are various types of steering gear systems, the recirculating-ball type and the rack-and-pinion type are most commonly used on current vehicles.

STEERING LINKAGES

A steering linkage consists of rods and arms that transmit the movement of the steering gear to the front wheels. It is crucial that the steering wheel movement be transmitted very accurately to the front wheels at all times despite up-and-down movements of the car.

There are various types of steering linkage and joint constructions designed for this purpose. The appropriateness of the design greatly affects driving stability.

Steering linkage for independent suspension system

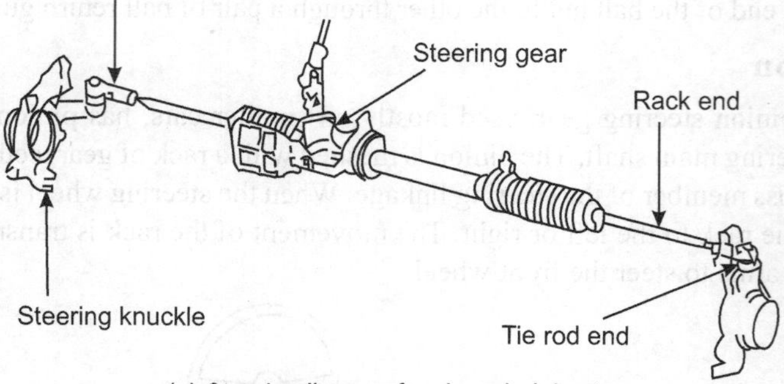

(a) Steering linage of rack-and-pinion type

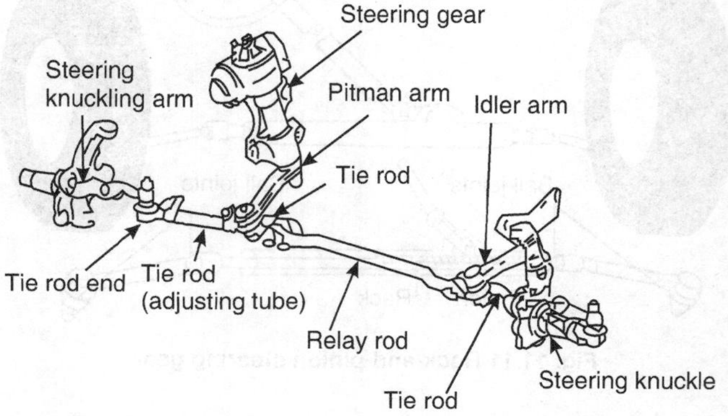

(b) Steering linkage of recirculating ball type

Fig. 11.12 Linkages for independent suspension system

This type of steering linkage has a pair of tie rods that are connected by a relay rod (the rack of a rack-and-pinion type steering system acts as the relay rod). A tube is fitted between the tie rod and a tie rod end for adjusting the rod length.

Steering linkage for rigid-axle suspension system

This type of steering linkage consists of pitman arm, drag link, knuckle arms, tie rod and tie rod ends. This linkage also has a tube for adjusting the tie rod length.

Fig. 11.13 Linkage for rigid axle suspension

Pitman arm

It is connected between the steering gear sector shaft by tapered spline and the steering linkage by a ball joint. It moves in an arc and pushes or pulls the relay rod.

Relay rod

It is attached at one end to the pitman arm by a ball and socket joint. The idler arm supports the opposite end. It moves back and forth.

Idler arm

It is mounted on the frame so that moves in the same plane as the pitman arm and thus parallels its motion. The other end of the arm is connected to the relay rod by ball studs. It merely supports the end of the relay rod and keeps the relay rod aligned. It duplicates the length of the pitman arm.

Steering knuckle

It is supported by upper and lower ball joints and by the wheel. It is the part on which a front wheel is mounted. It is turned for steering. It is forged with spindles upon which the front wheel hubs are mounted.

On cars with front wheel drive the steering knuckles do not have spindles. The end of the drive axle passes through a hole in the steering knuckle.

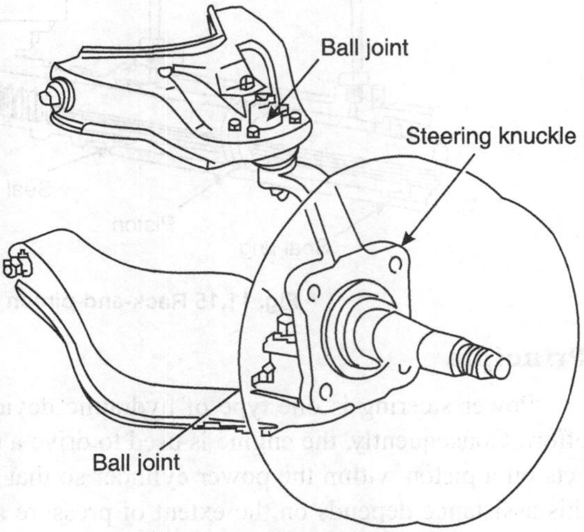

Fig. 11.14 Steering knuckle

Tie rod ends

They are ball and socket joints provided with threaded stems. The threaded stems fit into the rod adjusting sleeves. The tapered ball stud fits into a matching hole in the steering arm.

POWER-ASSISTED STEERING (POWER STEERING)

The purpose of power-assisted steering is to reduce driver's effort at the steering wheel. To improve driving comfort, most modern automobiles have wide low-pressure tyres, which increase the tyre to road contact area. As a result of this, more steering effort (the effort required by the driver to operate the steering wheel) is required. Steering effort can be decreased by increasing the gear ratio of steering gear. However, this will cause a larger rotary motion of the steering wheel when the vehicle is turning, making sharp turns impossible. The power steering system provides automatic power assistance to the turning effort applied to the manual steering system.

A power-assisted steering system has a hydraulic booster to reduce the steering effort. The steering effort is normally 20-39 N. A power steering system is designed to reduce the steering effort when the vehicle is moving at a low speed and to adjust it to an appropriate level when the car is moving at medium to high speeds.

Advantages of power steering

The power assistance arrangement has the following advantages:

- The driver's effort is substantially reduced while he can easily get the 'feel' of the road.
- When the vehicle suddenly meets a bump or the front tyre bursts there is no coming back of the steering wheel as in the case of conventional steering. The driver can easily control the vehicle.
- Even if the hydraulic power system fails, the vehicle can be maneuvered easily by the help of manual steering.

HYDRAULIC POWER STEERING

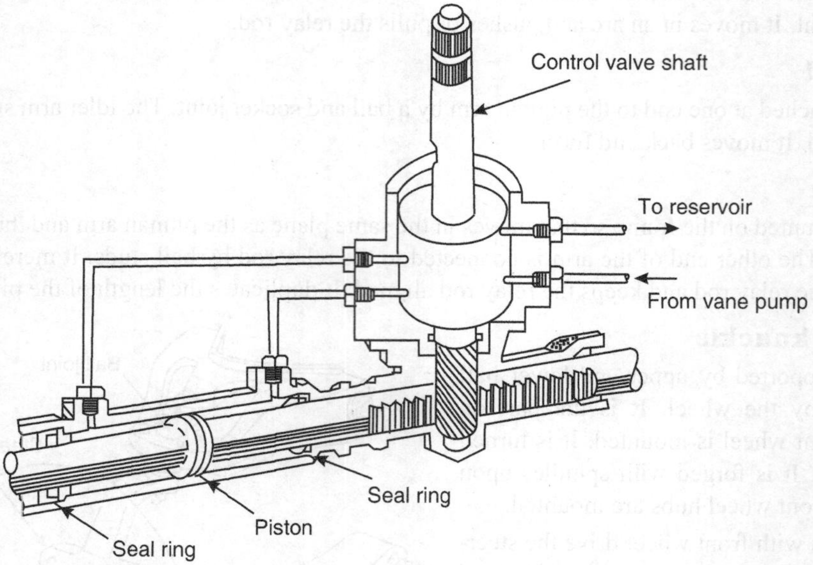

Fig. 11.15 Rack-and-pinion hydraulic power steering

Principle

Power steering is one type of hydraulic device for utilizing engine power to reduce steering effort. Consequently, the engine is used to drive a pump to develop fluid pressure and this pressure acts on a piston within the power cylinder so that the piston assists the rack effort. The amount of this assistance depends on the extent of pressure acting on the piston. Therefore, if more steering force is required, the pressure must be raised. The variation in the fluid pressure is accomplished by a control valve which is linked to the steering main shaft.

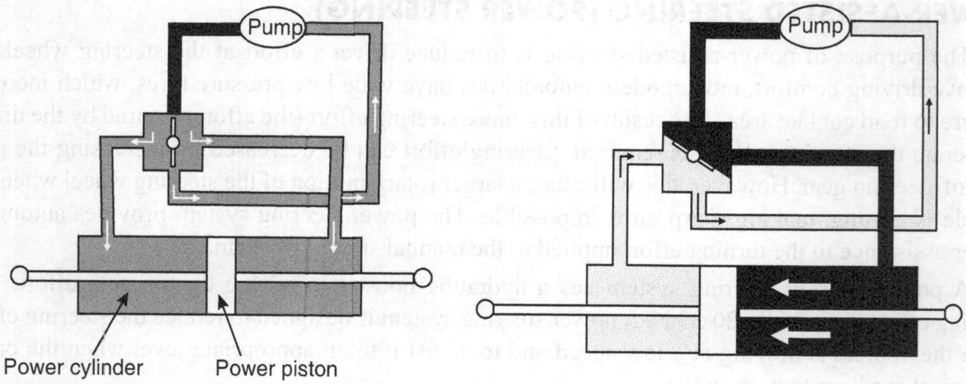

(a) Neutral (b) Turning

Fig. 11.16 Principle of hydraulic power steering

Neutral (straight-ahead) position

Fluid from the pump is sent to the control valve. If the control valve is in the neutral position, the fluid will flow through the control valve into the relief port and back to the pump. At this time, hardly any pressure is created and because the pressure on the cylinder piston equal on both sides, the piston will not move in either direction.

When turning

When the steering main shaft is turned in either direction, the control valve also moves, closing one of the fluid passages. The other passage then opens wider, causing a change in fluid flow volume and, at the same time, pressure is created. Consequently, a pressure difference occurs between both sides of the piston and the piston moves in the direction of the lower pressure so that the fluid in the cylinder is forced back to the pump through the control valve.

Components

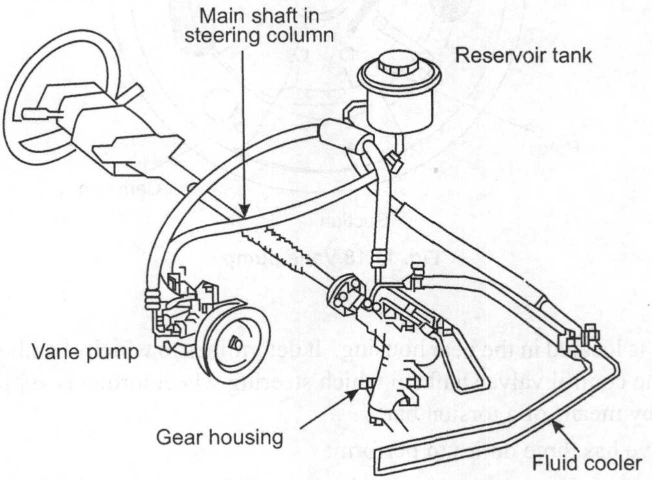

Fig. 11.17 Components of hydraulic power steering (Recirculating type)

The power steering system includes a control valve assembly and a power cylinder. In addition, the system has fluid reservoir, hydraulic pump, and control hoses. The reservoir may be attached to the pump or separately mounted. A filter may be located in the reservoir or hose to remove dirt and particles from the fluid. Some power steering systems also have a fluid cooler.

Fluid reservoir

The reservoir controls and supplies the power steering fluid. It is installed either directly to the pump body or separately. If not installed to the pump body, it is connected to it by two hoses. Normally, the reservoir tank cap has a level gauge for checking the fluid level. If the fluid in the reservoir falls below the standard level, the pump will suck in air, causing faulty operation.

Power steering pump

The pump usually mounts at the front of the engine and is driven by a belt from the engine crankshaft pulley or electric motor. The pump can produce high pressure, up to 2000 psi (140 bar) in some systems. It is the vane pump, which produces this pressure. The rotor turns in an oval cam ring inside the pump housing. As the rotor turns the clearance between the rotor and cam ring increases and decreases in size. The vane plate partitions off this clearance to form a fluid chamber. The capacity of this fluid chamber is increased or decreased as the rotor rotates to operate the pump. In other words, the capacity of the fluid chamber increases at the suction port so that reservoir fluid is drawn into the fluid chamber from the suction port. The volume of the fluid chamber is decreased on the discharge side and when it reaches zero, the fluid previously drawn into the chamber is forced out through the discharge port.

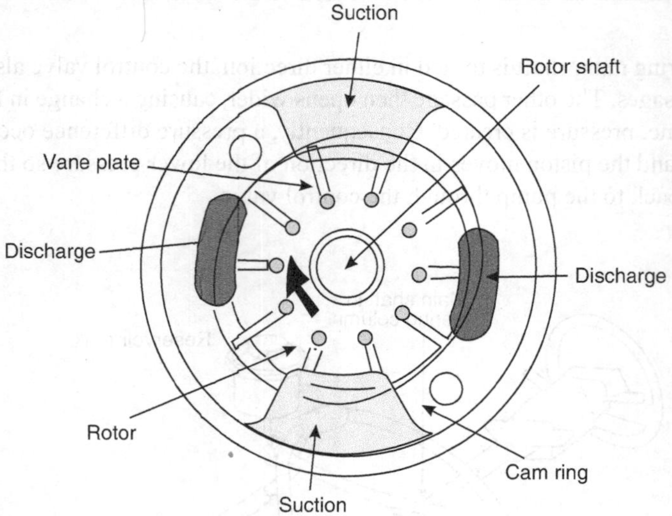

Fig. 11.18 Vane pump

Control valve

A control valve is located in the gear housing. It determines to which chamber the fluid from the vane pump goes. The control valve shaft (to which steering wheel torque is applied) and the pinion gear are connected by means of a torsion bar.

The control valve has three duties to perform:

- When there is no demand for power assistance and the valve remains in its neutral position, it must allow the fluid being delivered by the pump to be recirculated via the valve to the reservoir.
- In response to an increasing steering effort, the movement of the control valve must be such as to redirect the fluid being delivered by the pump to the appropriate side of the power piston in the power cylinder, and simultaneously it must allow fluid displaced on the other side of the power piston to be returned via the valve to the reservoir.
- The control valve according to type must contrive to give either a natural or an artificial steering feel to the driver, by providing a proportional increase in steering effort as the demand for power assistance is increased.

Power cylinder

This is double acting and provides a means of utilizing the available hydraulic energy to produce force and travel at some point in the steering system. The cylinder contains a piston that has a pressure chamber at each end. Oil enters one chamber to aid in right turns and the other chamber for left turns. Fluid pressure leakage is prevented by a seal ring on the piston. Also, there is an oil seal on both sides of the cylinder to prevent external leakage of the fluid.

Hoses and fittings

Most power steering systems have a pressure hose and a return hose. The hoses and fittings provide the fluid path between the power steering pump and the control valve. They are made to take high pressures, temperature extremes and continual stretching and flexing. The hose also help reduce noise from pump pulsations.

Fluid cooler

Some vehicles with air conditioning and high under hood temperatures have a small power steering fluid cooler. It prevents excessive fluid temperature that could damage seals, vanes, and other parts. The fluid cooler may simply be a loop in the tubing or a small heat exchanger at the front of the vehicle.

Power steering fluid

Several hydraulic fluids are used as power steering fluid. Normally a low-viscosity mineral oil similar to the type used in an automatic transmission. It is made to take high temperatures and pressures. Only the fluid recommended by the vehicle manufacturer should be used in a power steering system.

ELECTRIC/ELECTRONIC POWER STEERING

Today a number of manufacturers use electric power steering. Electric power steering (EPS) or Electric power assisted steering (EPAS) is designed to use an electric motor to reduce effort by providing steering assist to the driver of a vehicle. This steering uses an electric motor to drive either the power steering hydraulic pump or the steering linkage directly. The power steering function is therefore independent of engine speed, resulting in significant energy savings.

Principle

Sensors detect the motion and torque of the steering column, and a computer module applies assistive torque via an electric motor coupled directly to either the steering gear or steering column. This allows varying amounts of assistance to be applied depending on driving conditions.

Operation

A steering sensor is located on the input shaft where it enters the gearbox housing. The steering sensor is actually two sensors in one: a torque sensor that converts steering torque input and its direction into voltage signals, and a rotation sensor that converts the rotation speed and direction into voltage signals. An interface circuit that shares the same housing converts the signals from the torque sensor and rotation sensor into signals the control electronics can process.

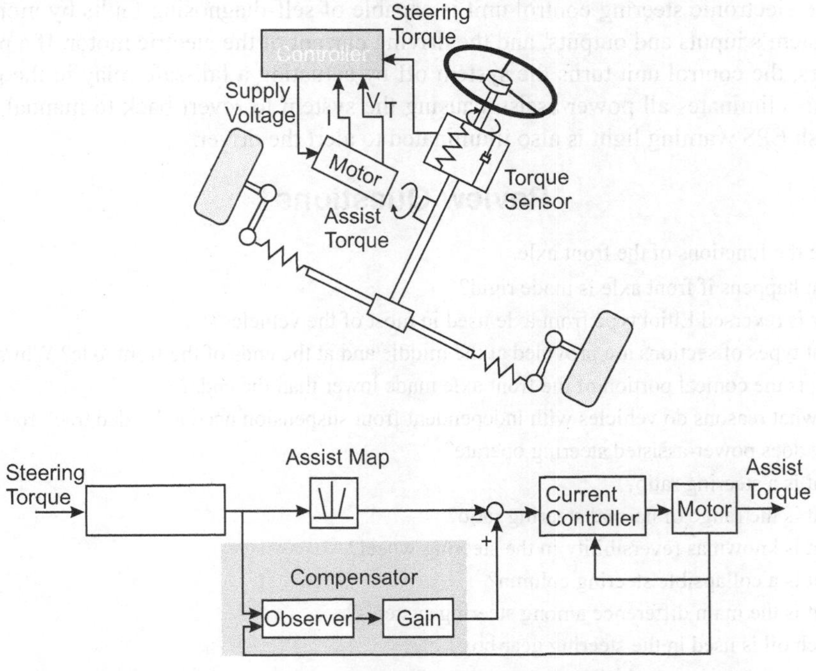

Fig. 11.19 Electric/electronic power assisted steering

Inputs from the steering sensor are digested by a microprocessor control unit that also monitors input from the vehicle's speed sensor. The sensor inputs are then compared to determine how much power assist is required according to a preprogrammed force map in the control unit's memory. The control unit then sends out the appropriate command to the power unit which then supplies the electric motor with current. The motor pushes the rack to the right or left depending on which way the voltage flows (reversing the current reverses the direction the motor spins). Increasing the current to the motor increases the amount of power assist.

The system has three operating modes: a normal control mode in which left or right power assist is provided in response to input from the steering torque and rotation sensor's inputs; a return control mode which is used to assist steering return after completing a turn; and a damper control mode that changes with vehicle speed to improve road feel and dampen kickback.

Advantages

Electric power steering has the following advantages:

- A slight advantage in fuel efficiency because there is no belt-driven hydraulic pump constantly running, whether assistance is required or not.
- Another major advantage is the elimination of a belt-driven engine accessory, and several high-pressure hydraulic hoses between the hydraulic pump, mounted on the engine, and the steering gear, mounted on the chassis. This greatly simplifies manufacturing and maintenance.
- By incorporating electronic stability control electric power steering systems can instantly vary torque assist levels to aid the driver in evasive maneuvers.
- If the steering wheel is turned and held in the full-lock position and steering assist reaches a maximum, the control unit reduces current to the electric motor to prevent an overload situation that might damage the motor. The control unit is also designed to protect the motor against voltage surges from a faulty alternator or charging problem.
- The electronic steering control unit is capable of self-diagnosing faults by monitoring the system's inputs and outputs, and the driving current of the electric motor. If a problem occurs, the control unit turns the system off by actuating a fail-safe relay in the power unit. This eliminates all power assist, causing the system to revert back to manual steering. A dash EPS warning light is also illuminated to alert the driver.

Review Questions

1. State the functions of the front axle.
2. What happens if front axle is made rigid?
3. Why is reversed Elliot type front axle used in most of the vehicles?
4. What types of sections are provided at the middle and at the ends of the front axle? Why?
5. Why is the conical portion of the front axle made lower than the ends?
6. For what reasons do vehicles with independent front suspension need a divided track rod?
7. How does power-assisted steering operate?
8. What is a steering ratio?
9. What is the range of normal steering ratio?
10. What is known as reversibility in the steering wheel?
11. What is a collapsible steering column?
12. What is the main difference among steering systems?
13. Which oil is used in the steering gear box?
14. What is a steering knuckle?
15. What is a pitman arm (or drop arm)?
16. What is known as power steering? What are the advantages?
17. What types of power steering are normally in use?
18. What are the different types of steering gear box exist?
19. What is known as excessive play in the steering system? What are the causes of it?

12 CHAPTER

WHEEL ALIGNMENT

WHEEL ALIGNMENT (OR) STEERING GEOMETRY

The driver can turn the automobile in any direction he desires by turning the steering wheel. However, if the driver manipulates the steering wheel continuously to keep the vehicle running in a straight line when travelling on a straight road or if he is required to expend a lot of energy to turn the vehicle on curves, he would be under a great physical and mental strain.

The wheels are installed on the body (or chassis) at certain angles in accordance with certain requirements to eliminate these problems, as well as to prevent early wearing of tyres. These angles, in combination, are called "wheel alignment".

Steering is easy as long as the wheels are aligned properly, because the steering wheel will remain in a straight-ahead position on straight roads with little help from the driver and will require little efforts to turn on curves. But if even one of these angles is incorrect, the following problems can occur:

- difficult steering
- poor steering stability
- poor recovery on curves
- shortened tyre life

Wheel alignment refers to positioning of the front wheels and steering mechanism in such a way that the geometry may impart:

- good directional stability
- steering ease
- minimum tyre wear
- reversibility of steering, and
- durability of the component parts

FRONT-WHEEL GEOMETRY

The term 'front-wheel geometry' or 'steering geometry' refers to the various angles between the front wheels, the frame, and the attachment parts. The angles include:

1. Camber
2. Steering Axis Inclination (SAI)
3. Caster
4. Toe angle, and
5. Turning radius

CAMBER

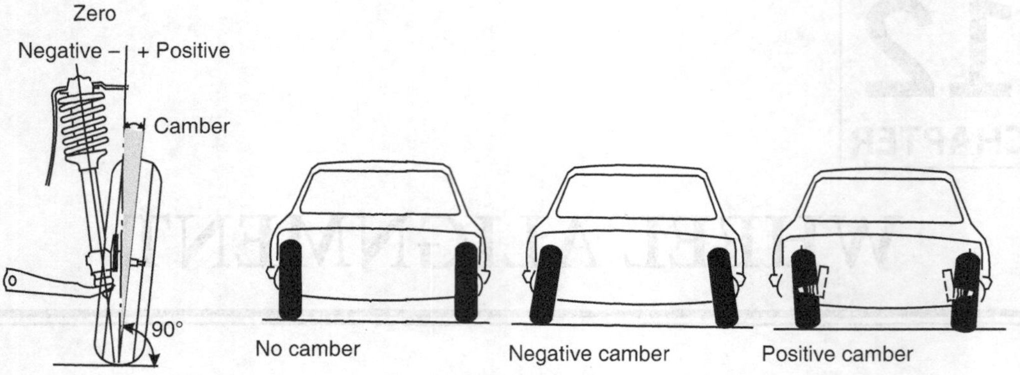

Fig. 12.1 Camber angle

Camber is the tilt of the car wheels from the vertical when viewed from the front of the vehicle. Camber is "positive" if the tilt is outwards at the top and is "negative" if it tilts inwards at the top. If the top of a wheel is not tilted in either direction, it is called "zero camber". Camber is also called wheel rake and is measured in degrees which is normally up to 2°.

If the camber on the two front wheels is not equal, the vehicle will try to pull towards the side where the camber is higher.

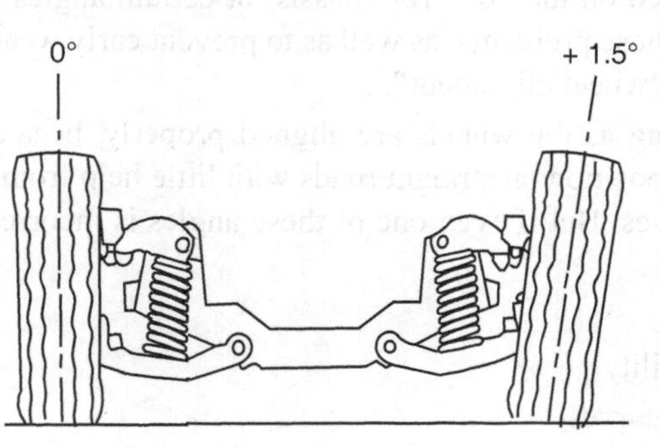

Fig. 12. 2 Unequal camber angle

On the conventional rigid axle, the camber remains almost fixed.

Effects of positive camber

The effects of positive camber are as follows:

- Reduction of vertical load
- Prevention of wheel slip-off
- Prevention of undesirable negative camber due to load
- Reduction of steering effort

Effects of negative camber

Some vehicles (frequently travel in hills) are being given negative camber to improve cornering performance.

Effects of zero camber

The main reason for adopting zero camber is that it prevents uneven wear of tyres. It is always desirable that tyres should roll on the ground vertically so that the wear is uniform. The tyre life will be maximum when the camber angle in running condition is zero with average load.

If while running, the tyres are inclined from the vertical either inward or outward, they will wear more on one side than the other.

CASTER AND CASTER TRAIL

Caster is the forward or backward tilt of the steering axis as veiwed from the side. Caster is measured in degrees from the steering axis to vertical.

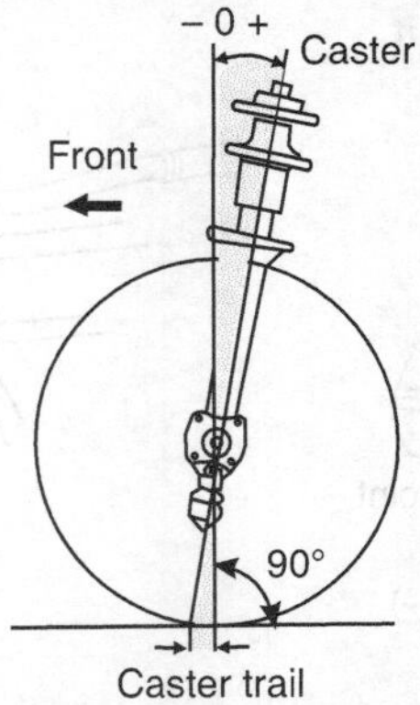

Fig. 12.3 Caster and caster trail

The distance from the intersection of the steering axis centerline with the ground, to the center of the tyre-to-road contact area is called "caster trail".

Backward tilt from the vertical line (steering axis meets the ground at a point in front of the wheel centerline) is called "positive caster", while forward tilt (steering axis meets the ground at a point behind the wheel centerline) is called "negative caster".

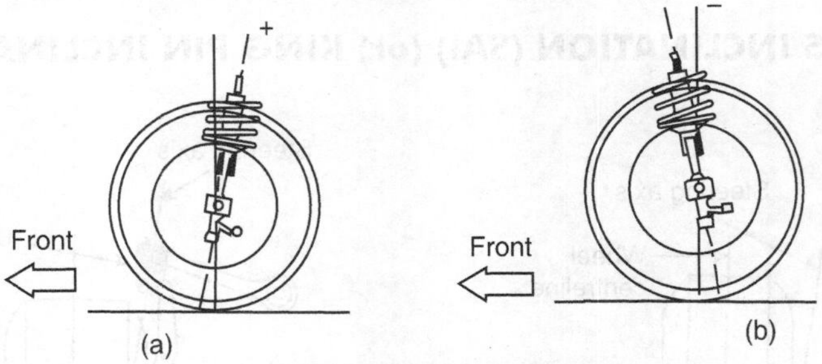

Fig. 12.4 (a) Positive caster and (b) Negative caster

If the caster on the two front wheels is not equal, the vehicle will try to pull towards the side where the caster is least.

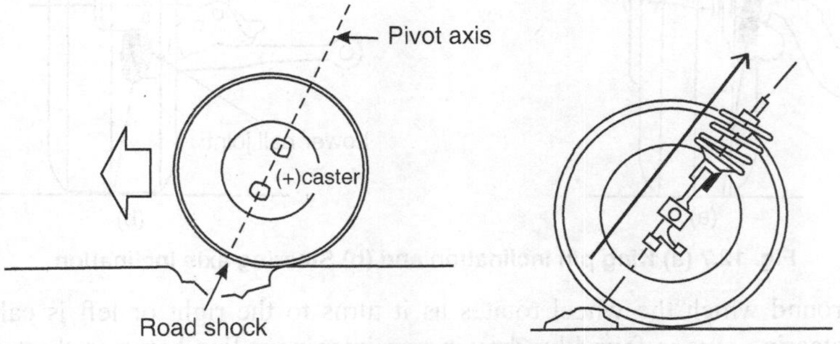

Fig. 12.5 Excessive positive caster

Excessive caster provides a road shock path to the vehicle.

Effects of caster

Caster angle is the stability angle. It provides directional stability while taking a turn or while cruising in straight ahead position.

Positive caster puts the point of intersection (lead point) of the steering axis and the road surface a little ahead of the tyres point of contact. While going straight straight ahed, the wheel follows the lead point which always lies in front of it.

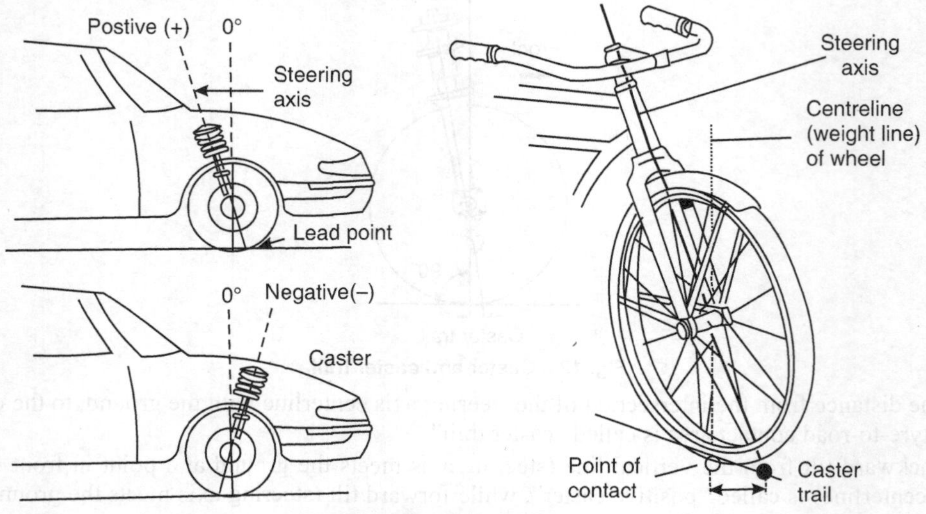

Fig. 12.6 Effect of positive caster

STEERING AXIS INCLINATION (SAI) (or) KING PIN INCLINATION (KPI)

Steering axis

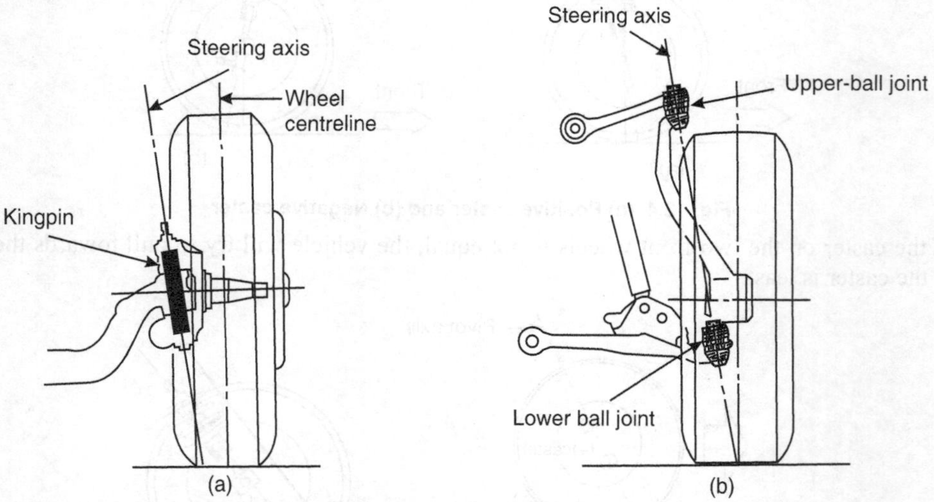

Fig. 12.7 (a) King pin inclination and (b) Steering axis inclination

The axis around which the wheel rotates as it turns to the right or left is called the "steering axis". The steering axis is found by drawing an imaginary line between the top of the shock absorber's upper support bearing and the lower suspension arm ball joint in the case of strut type suspensions. With rigid-axle suspensions, a part called a kingpin is included at each end of the axle. The kingpin axis is equivalent to the steering axis of other types of suspension. In the case of the double wishbone suspension, the line connecting the upper ball joint and the lower ball joint forms the steering axis.

Steering Axis Inclination (SAI)

The steering axis is tilted inward as viewed from the front of the car and is called the "steering axis inclination (SAI)" (for an independent suspension) or "kingpin angle" (for a rigid axle suspension). This angle is measured in degrees.

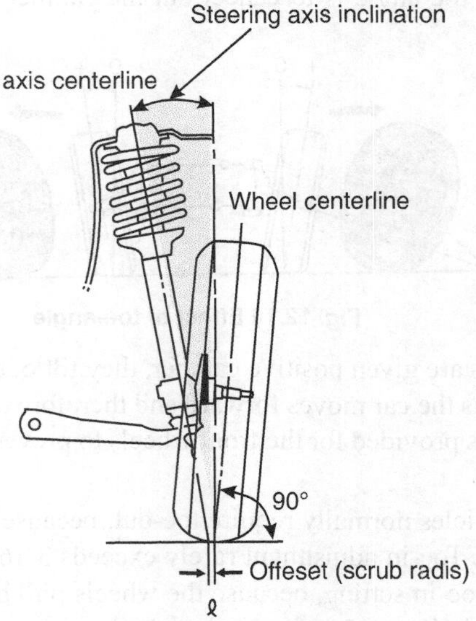

Fig. 12.8 Steering axis inclination

Furthermore, the distance "*l*" from the intersection of the steering axis with the ground to the intersection of the wheel centerline with the ground is called the "offset" or "scrub radius".

SAI is non-adjustable, since it would change only if the wheel spindle or steering knuckle is bent.

Effects of SAI

The effects of SAI are as follows:

- Reduction of steering effort
- Reduction of kickback and pulling to one side
- Improving straight-line stability

TOE-ANGLE (TOE-IN (or) TOE-OUT)

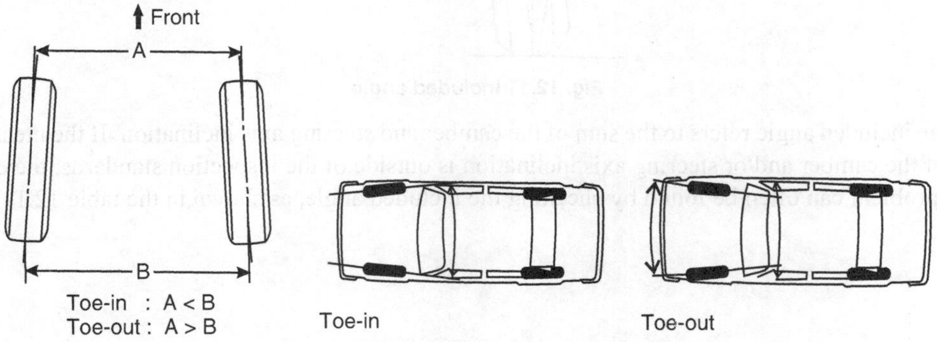

Fig. 12.9 Toe-angle: toe-in and toe-out

It is the difference in distance between the front wheels of a car as measured at the front and at the rear as viewed from the top when the vehicle is stationary. Toe angle is usually expressed by a distance (B-A). Toe-in is amount by which the front wheels are set closer together at the front than at the rear. On the other hand, the wheel may be set closer at the rear than at the front in which case the difference of the distances between the front wheels at the front and at the rear is called toe-out.

Effect of toe-angle

The main function of toe angle is to cancel out the camber thrust generated when camber is applied.

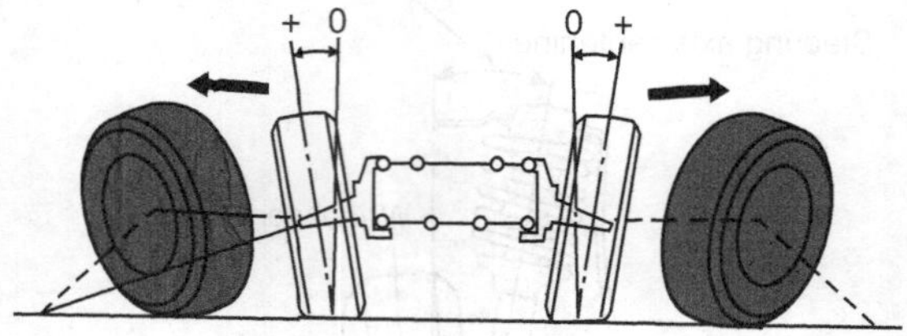

Fig. 12.10 Effect of toe-angle

When the front wheels are given positive camber, they tilt outward at the top. This causes them to attempt to roll outward as the car moves forward and therefore to side-slip. This subjects the tyres to wear. Therefore, toe-in is provided for the front wheels to prevent this by cancelling outward rolling due to camber.

Front-wheel drive vehicles normally require toe-out, because the wheels pull inwards to a parallel position under power. Toe-in adjustment rarely exceeds 3/16 in. Conversely, rear-wheel drive vehicles commonly use a toe-in setting, because the wheels pull back when the vehicle moves forwards. This adjustment is similar to that for toe-in, which rarely more than 3/16 in.

INCLUDED ANGLE

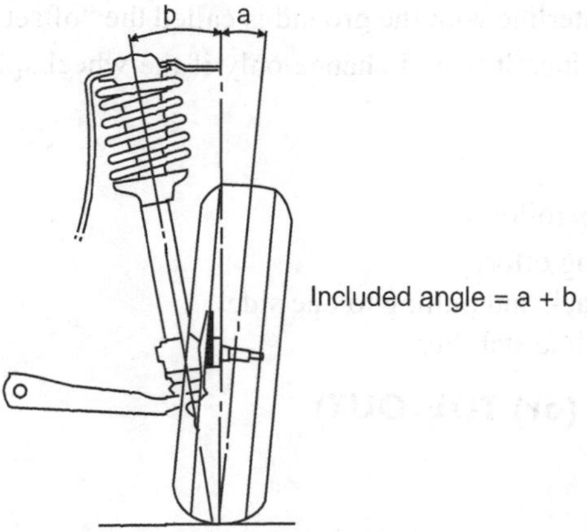

Fig. 12.11 Included angle

The included angle refers to the sum of the camber and steering axis inclination. If the measurement of the camber and/or steering axis inclination is outside of the inspection standards, the cause of the problem can often be found by checking the included angle, as shown in the table 12.1.

Table 11.1

ALIGNMENT ANGLES			PROBLEM
S.A.I.	**Camber**	**Included Angle**	
Correct	Less than specification	Less than specification	Bent spindle
Less than specification	Greater than specification	Correct	Bent lower control arm
Greater than specification	Less than specification	Correct	Bent upper control arm
Less than specification	Greater than specification	Greater than specification	Bent lower control arm and spindle

TURNING RADIUS

When a car turns a corner, the wheel on the inside must always turn more than the wheel on the outside. This increases the distance between the wheels at the front so that they actually toe-out with respect to each other.

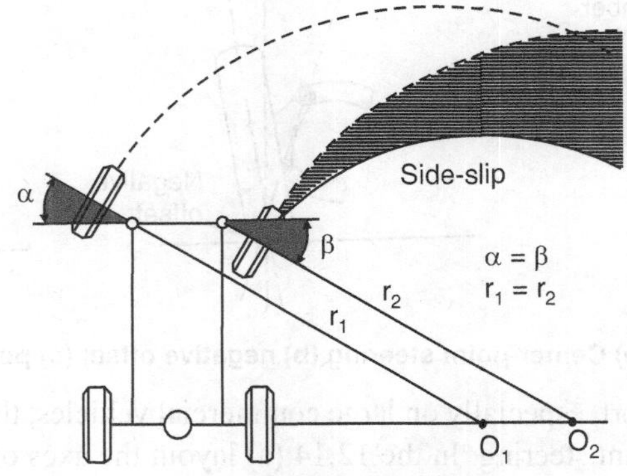

Fig. 12.12 Side slip

If the right and left front wheels were both to turn by exactly the same amount (*i.e.* $\alpha = \beta$), they would have the same turning radius ($r_1 = r_2$), but each wheel would turn around a different center (O_1 and O_2). Smooth turning would therefore be impossible due to side slipping of the tyres. The result is that, irrespective of correct tyre inflation and wheel alignment factors, the tyre would undergo unusual wear.

Turning radius in actual cases

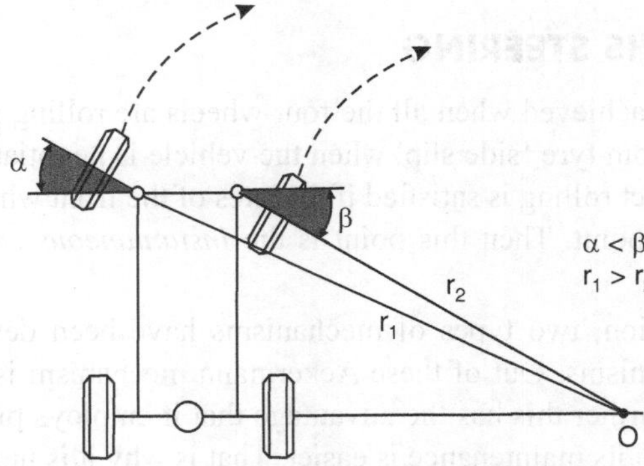

Fig. 12.13 Turning radius in actual cases

In an actual vehicle, the steering linkage is modified in such a way that the inner road wheel will move through a greater angle than the outer ($\alpha < \beta$) to achieve the desired turning radii. The difference between them is called toe-out on turn which is normally between 2° and 3°.

Side-slip

Side-slip is the total distance that the right and left tyres slip to the side while the vehicle is in motion. Side-slip is measured with a side-slip tester during staright-ahead driving at a very low speed.

Side-slip is generally expressed as the amount of sideway slippage, in mm, per 1 m of forward motion. The general guideline is 0-3 mm (0-0.118 in).

The cause of side-slip is mainly incorrect camber or toe-in, but it is also important to pay attention to caster and steering axis inclination.

Centre-point steering and scrub (or roll) radius

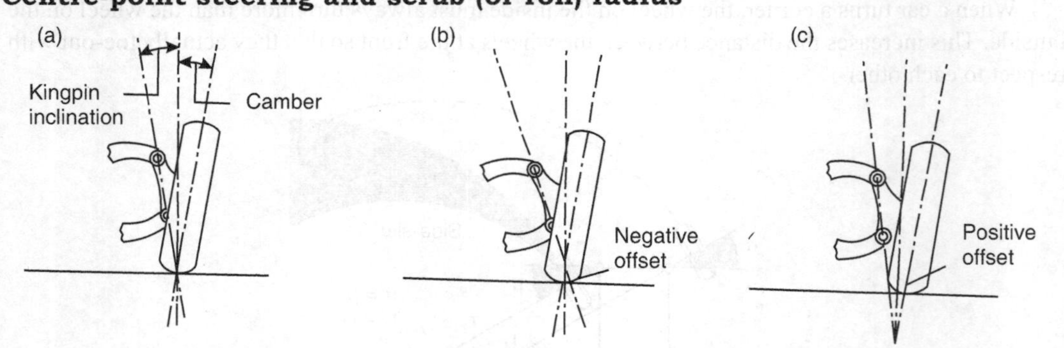

Fig. 11.14 (a) Center-point steering (b) negative offset (c) positive offset

To reduce steering effort, especially on large commercial vehicles, the steering geometry can be arranged to give centre-point steering. In the 12.14 (a) layout the axes of the road wheel and of the steering axis intersect where the tyre touches the road.

In the layout 12.14b, the axis of the road wheel and the steering axis intersect slightly above ground level. It has been found that this arrangement improves stability and reduces the pull on the steering wheel if there is a tyre blow-out or front brakes become unbalanced. It is now widely used on cars. It is called negative scrub radius.

In another layout, the axis of the road wheel and the steering axis meet below ground level as shown in Fig. 12.14c. It is called positive scrub radius and gives plenty of "feel" to the steering, but can make it heavy.

ACKERMANN & DAVIS STEERING

The perfect steering is achieved when all the four wheels are rolling perfectly under all conditions of running *i.e.*, free from tyre 'side slip' when the vehicle is negotiating a bend. While taking turns, the condition of perfect rolling is satisfied if the axes of the front wheels when produced meet the rear wheel axis at one point. Then this point is the *instantaneous centre* about which all the wheels must rotate.

To achieve this condition, two types of mechanisms have been devised: the Davis and the Ackermann steering mechanisms. Out of these Ackermann mechanism is almost universally used because of its simplicity. Further this has the advantage that it employs pivots and not sliding constraints, due to which reason its maintenance is easier. That is why it is universally employed.

The Ackermann principle

A motor vehicle is steered by the side swiveling action of the front wheels. In order to provide effective control of the steering of the vehicle, it is important that the wheels rotate on their axles with a true rolling motion.

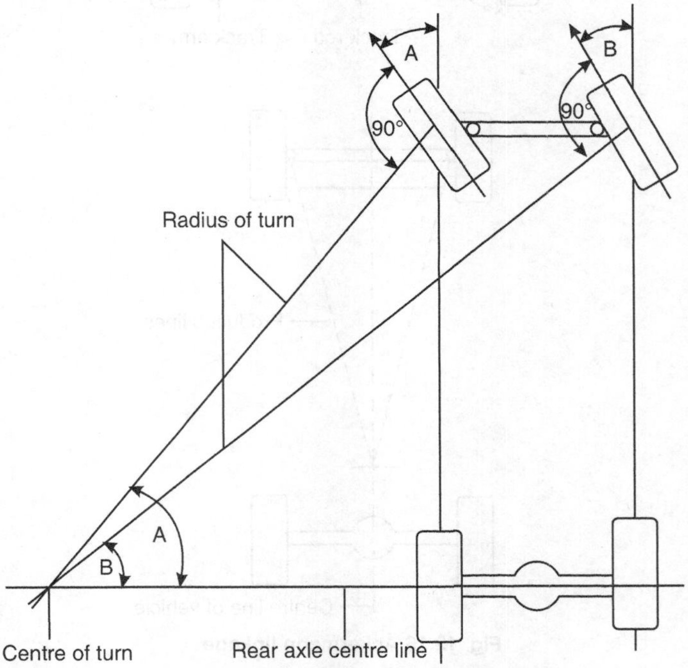

Fig. 12.15 Ackermann principle

When the vehicle is making a turn, true rolling motion must be obtained without sliding. Therefore each road wheel should roll round the centre point of the curve. Each wheel must lie at right angles (90°) to a radius drawn to this centre. As the rear wheels of a conventional vehicle cannot swivel, this centre must be on a line drawn through the axis of the rear axle. Therefore, the rear wheels will always roll true as they are fixed at 90° to the rear axle. If, however, both front wheels must align themselves at 90° to their radius of turn, they must be turned at different angles from the straight-ahead position.

The front wheel on the inside of the corner has therefore to be turned through a greater angle than the outer wheel and this is obtained by the use of the 'Ackermann' steering principle.

Ackermann linkage

The differnce in movement of the inner and outer wheels is obtained by inclining the steering arms. In the straight-ahead position, the steering arms are arranged so that their centre lines, if produced, would meet on the centre line of the vehicle on or near the nose of the rear axle. The track rod is therefore shorter than the distance between the kingpin axes if it lies behind the axle beam.

When the vehicle is travelling in the straight-ahead position, the track rod is parallel to the axle beam but, as it moves the steering arms, the inner end moves nearer to the axle than the outer end (as indicated by the dotted lines in Fig. 12.16). The result of this action is that the inner steering arm and road wheel are turned through a greater angle than the outer arm and wheel. It should be noted that the differencd between these two angles is not constant but is automatically corrected to maintain the front wheels at 90° to any radius of turn.

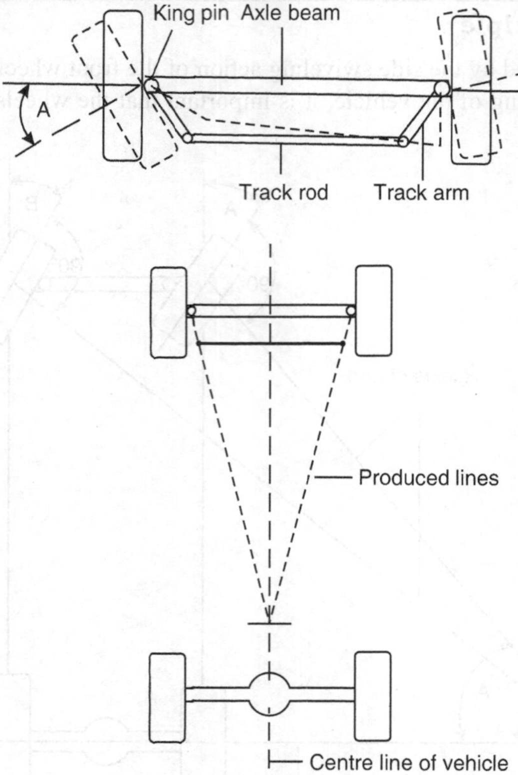

Fig. 12.16 Ackermann linkage

Oversteer and Understeer

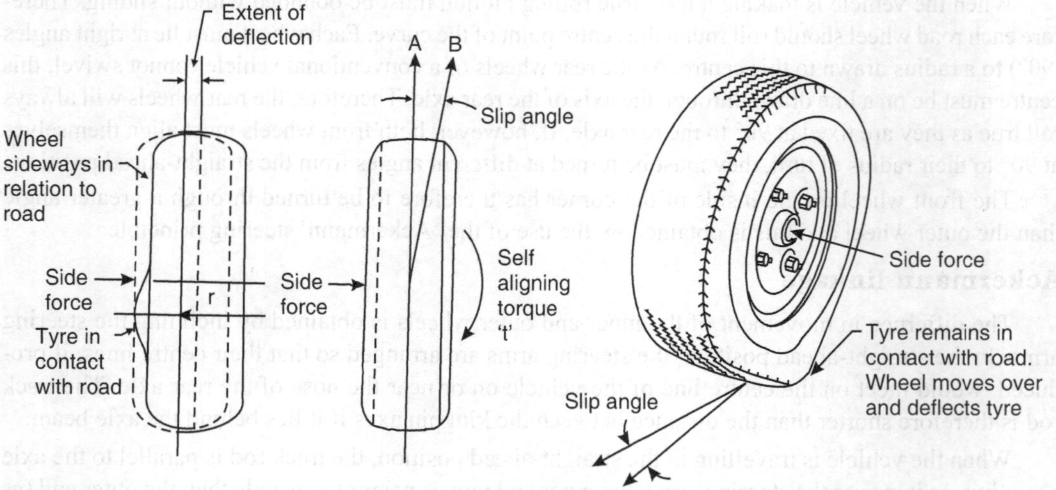

Fig. 12.17 Causes of slip angle

Low-pressure tyres, used on modern vehicles, take a different path when subjected to a side force. A side force caused by wind, road camber or cornering forces produces a slip angle at each tyre. Fig. 12.17 shows a top view of a wheel travelling in the direction of A. If a side force acts on the wheel, tyre deflection will cause the wheel to take the path B, although the wheel is still pointing in the original direction. The angle between the path that the wheel is actually taking and the plane of the wheel (AB) is termed the slip angle. The slip angle caused by the deflection of the side wall of a given tyre is proportional to the side force acting on the tyre.

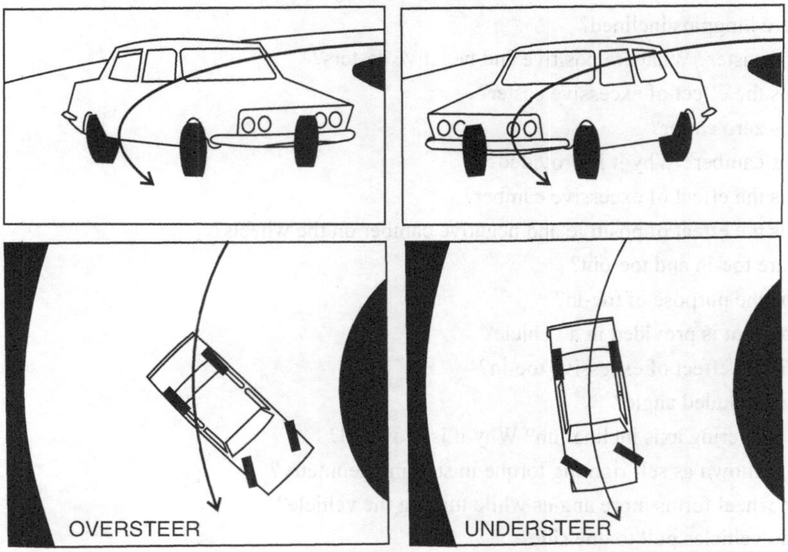

Fig. 12.18 Oversteer and understeer

Tyre slip angles affect the steering characteristics of a vehicle by causing either oversteer or understeer. When the rear slip angles are greater than the front, the vehicle will turn more sharply than normal-conditions called oversteer. To correct for this, the driver has to straighten up the steering wheel, a difficult feat under cornering conditions, and when this is linked with the fact that the sharper turn causes a further increase in the cornering force, then it will be apparent why oversteer is regarded as dangerous. A mixed tyre arrangement which uses radial ply on the front and diagonal ply on the rear increases the oversteer effect, so for safety reasons it is made illegal to use this tyre arrangement. Over steer can also be caused by:

(*a*) moving the centre of gravity towards the rear by increasing the load on the rear of the vehicle.

(*b*) lower tyre inflation pressure at the rear than front is recommended.

(*c*) large load transference from inner rear wheel to outer rear wheel when cornering.

Understeer is produced when the front slip angles are greater than the rear. This tends to cause the vehicle to move away from the side force and makes the vehicle take a path of larger radius than normal. A reasonable degree of understeer is desirable, but if it becomes excessive, hard steering results.

Review Questions

1. What is centre point steering?
2. What is termed as cornering force?
3. What is known as turning radius?
4. What is referred to as wheel alignment?
5. What is the condition necessary to achieve true rolling of the wheels?
6. What is known as steering geometry?
7. Why are camber and kingpin inclination needed?
8. How is caster produced?

9. Why do cars with rear-wheel drive have toe-in?
10. Why do cars with front-wheel drive have zero or negative toe-in (toe-out)?
11. Why are kingpins inclined?
12. What is caster? What are positive and negative casters?
13. What is the effect of excessive caster?
14. What is zero caster?
15. What is camber? Why it is provided?
16. What is the effect of excessive camber?
17. What is the effect of positive and negative camber on the wheels?
18. What are toe-in and toe-out?
19. What is the purpose of toe-in?
20. Why toe-out is provided in a vehicle?
21. What is the effect of excessive toe-in?
22. What is included angle?
23. What is steering axis inclination? Why it is provided?
24. What is known as self righting torque in steering geometry?
25. Which wheel forms more angles while turning the vehicle?
26. Why do vehicles pull to one side?
27. Why do vehicles wander on either side?
28. What are the causes of hard steering?
29. What is known as steering shimmy?
30. What do you understand by steering wheel wobbling? What are the causes of it?

13 CHAPTER

SUSPENSION SYSTEM

A suspension system supports the frame on a vehicle. It acts an intermediary between the axles and the frame. The job of a vehicle suspension is to maximize the friction between the tyres and the road surface, to provide steering stability with good handling and to ensure the comfort of the passengers.

A vehicle with a solid suspension or no suspension would bounce off the ground when the tyres hit a bump. If the tyres are off the ground, even for a fraction of a second, loss of control is possible. The axles are subject to whatever forces they encounter when running down the highway. With no suspension, these forces would be transferred directly to the frame.

FUNCTIONS

The suspension system carries out the following functions:

- During running, it acts together with the tyres to absorb and damp the various vibrations, oscillations and shocks received by the vehicle due to irregularities of the road in order to protect the passengers and cargo, and improve driving stability.
- It transmits the driving and braking forces, which are generated due to friction between the road surface and the wheels, to the chassis and body.
- It supports the body on the axles and maintains the proper geometrical relationship between the body and wheels.

REQUIREMENTS

The main functional requirements of a suspension system are:

- Minimum deflection consistent with required stability
- Low maintenance operating costs
- Minimum weight
- Strong and durable
- Minimum tyre wear

SPRUNG AND UNSPRUNG WEIGHTS

The weight of the body, engine, transmission, etc., which is supported by springs is called the sprung weight. On the other hand, the wheels and axles and other parts which are not supported by springs, make up the unsprung weight.

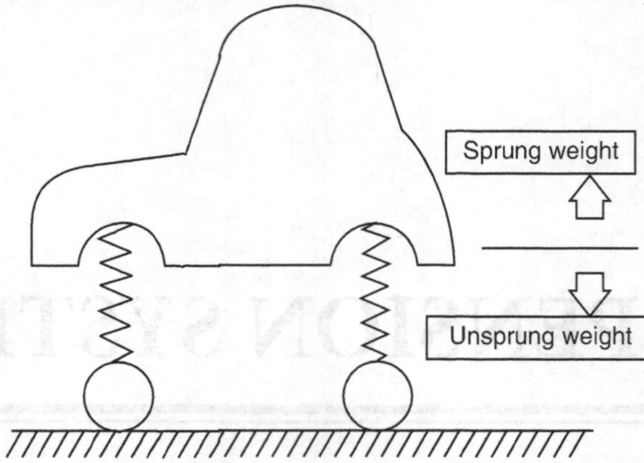

Fig. 13.1 Sprung weight and unsprung weight

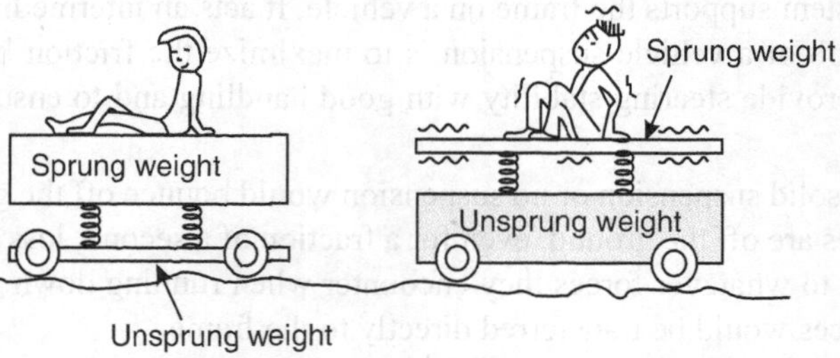

Fig. 13.2 Effect of sprung and unsprung weights

If the unsprung weight is less, the riding comfort is better because of the tendency of the body to be jolted decreases.

OSCILLATION OF THE SPRUNG AND UNSPRUNG WEIGHTS

Oscillation and jolting of the sprung and unsprung parts of the vehicle have a particularly great effect on riding comfort. This oscillation and jolting can be classified as follows:

Oscillation of sprung weight

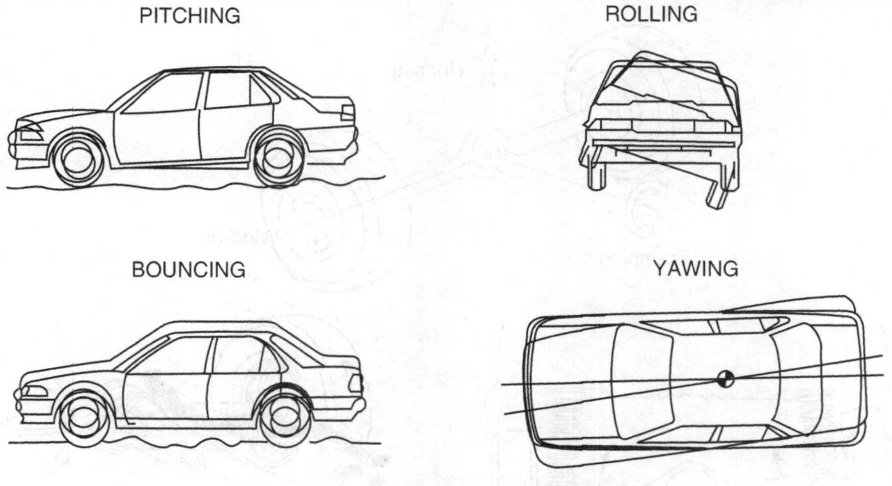

Fig. 13.3 Oscillation of sprung weight

Pitching

Pitching is the up-and-down oscillation, in relation to the car's centre of gravity, of the front and back of the car. This happens especially when the car goes over large ruts or bumps in the road or when driving over an unpaved road which is rough and full of potholes. Also, pitching occurs more easily in vehicles with softer (easily compressed) springs than in those with harder springs.

Rolling

When turning or when driving on a bumpy road, the springs on one side of the vehicle expand, while those on the other side contract. This results in body rolling in the lateral (side-to-side) direction.

Bouncing

Bouncing is the up-and-down movement of the auto body as a whole. When a car is running at high speeds on an undulating surface, bouncing is likely to occur. Also, it occurs easily when the springs are soft.

Yawing

Yawing is the movement of the car's longitudinal centerline to the right and left, in relation to the car's center of gravity. On roads where pitching occurs, yawing is also likely to occur.

Oscillation of unsprung weight

Hopping

Hopping is the up-and-down bouncing of the wheels which usually occurs on corrugated roads while driving at medium and high speeds.

Tramping

Tramping is the up-and-down oscillation in opposite directions of the left and right wheels, causing the wheels to skip over the road surface. This occurs more easily in vehicles with rigid axle suspension.

Wind-up

Wind-up is the phenomenon in which the leaf springs attempt to wind themselves around the axle due to the driving torque.

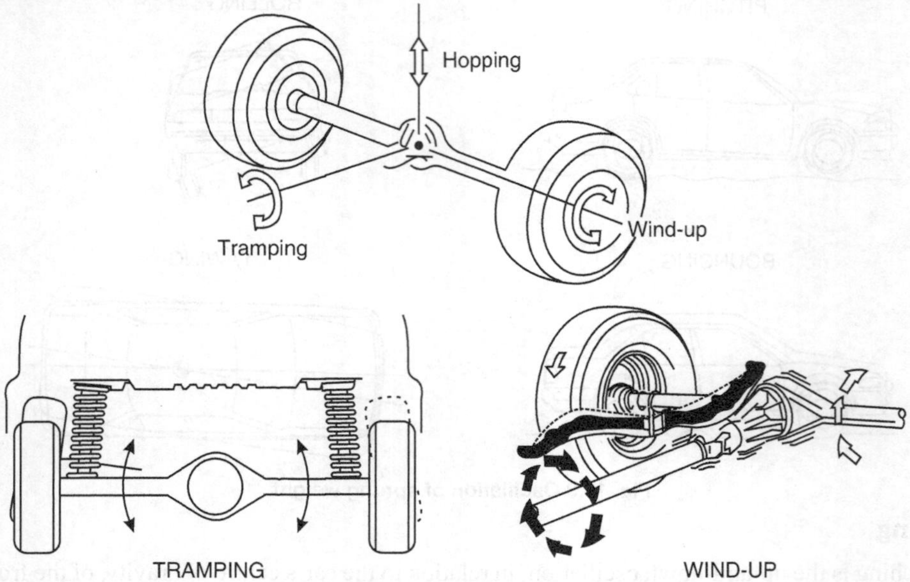

Fig. 13.4 Oscillation of unsprung weight

COMMON SUSPENSION TERMS

Before we begin looking as the different suspension categories used on vehicles, here are some suspension terms that we will be using:

Bounce

The vertical (upward and downward) movement of the suspension system is called bounce.

Jounce

Jounce literally means 'bump'. In suspension terminology, it is the most compressed condition of a spring due to the upward movement of the suspension system.

Rebound

The downward movement of the tyre and wheel that extends the spring is called rebound.

Dive

The lowering of the front end of the vehicle along with a raising of the rear end during braking is known as dive.

COMPONENTS OF A SUSPENSION SYSTEM

It consists of the following principle components:

1. Springs, which neutralize the shocks from the road surface.
2. Shock absorbers (dampers), which act to improve riding comfort by limiting the free oscillation of the springs.
3. Stabilizer (sway or anti-roll bar), which prevents lateral swaying of the car.
4. A linkage system, which acts to hold the above components in place and to control the longitudinal and lateral movements of the wheels.

SUSPENSION SPRINGS

A suspension spring serves two purposes:

- Its acts as a buffer between the suspension and frame to absorb vertical wheel and suspension movement without passing it onto the frame.

- Each spring transfers part of the vehicle weight to the suspension component it rest on, which transfers it to the wheels.

The basic method by which springs absorb road shocks varies according to the type of spring. Simply stated, leaf springs flatten, coil springs and air springs compress and torsion bar twist.

SPRING MATERIALS

Most springs are made of a tempered steel alloy known as spring steel, usually chrome silicon or chrome-vanadium alloy. Tempering is a process of heating and cooling metal under controlled conditions, which increases the resilience of the metal. Resilience is the ability of the metal to return to or spring back to its original shape after being twisted or compressed.

CHARACTERISTICS OF SUSPENSION SPRINGS

Elasticity

If a force (load) is applied to an object made of a material such as rubber, it will create stress (deformation) in that object. When that force is removed, the stress will disappear and the object will return to its original shape. We call this characteristic elasticity. The springs of a vehicle use the principle of elasticity to cushion the body and occupants of a vehicle from road shocks and in so doing, temporarily store the energy created by the applied stress.

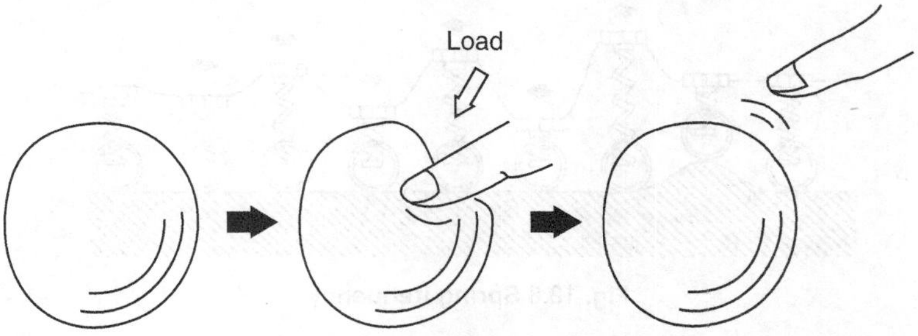

Fig. 13.5 Elasticity

Steel springs store this energy by bending (as in the case of leaf springs) or twisting (as in the case of coil springs or torsion bar springs). The energy is released when the spring resumes its normal state.

Spring rate (or spring constant)

Spring rate is the system used to measure spring strength. It is the amount of weight that is required to compress the spring a certain distance (deflection).

Spring rate $K = \frac{W}{a}$

Where,

W = external load, N

a = amount of deflection, mm

If the loads applied to the springs are equal, the spring with the low spring rate will contract more than the spring with the high spring constant. A spring with a low spring constant is said to be "soft", while a spring with a high spring constant is said to be "firm".

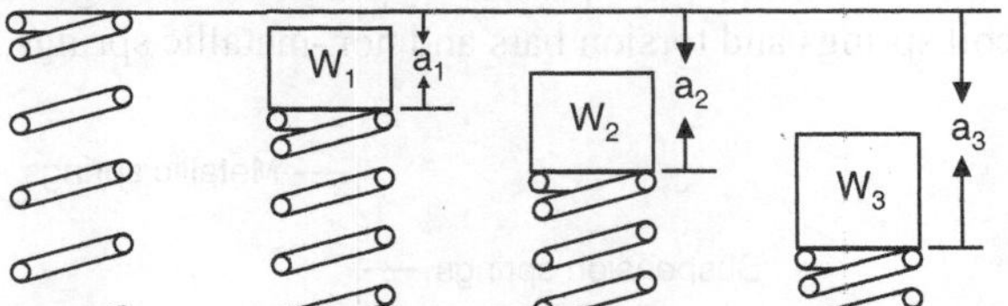

$\frac{W_1}{a_1} = \frac{W_2}{a_2} = \frac{W_3}{a_3} = k$ (constant)

Fig. 13.6 Spring constant

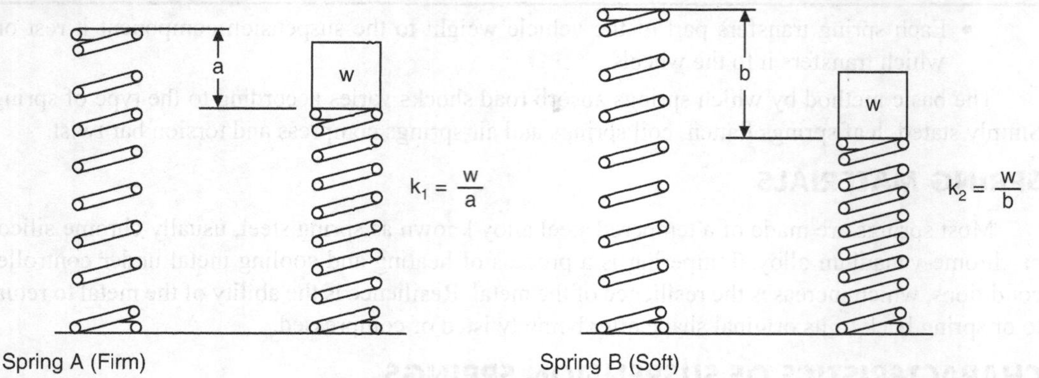

Fig. 13.7 Firm and soft springs

Spring frequency

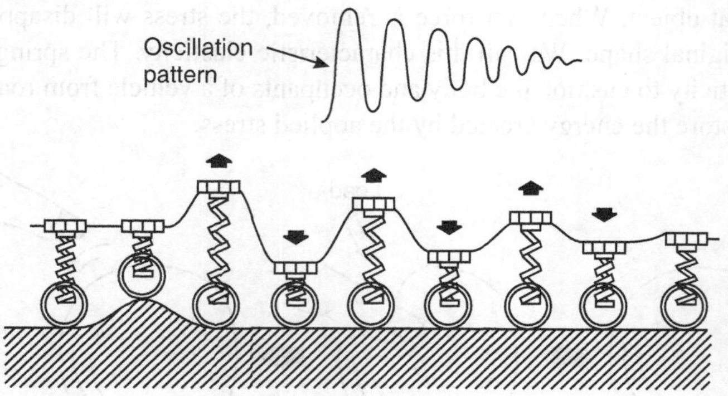

Fig. 13.8 Spring frequency

Frequency refers to the speed of the natural oscillations of a spring. Each travel period from the upper most point to the lowest point and back to the highest point is called a cycle. The number of cycles completed in one second is called cycles per second (CPS). This is the normal spring frequency measuring system. There is a direct correlation between spring rate and spring frequency: the higher the spring rate, the higher the spring frequency. This means that stiffer springs bounce at a much higher rate while softer springs bounce more slowly.

TYPES OF SPRINGS

In automotive suspension systems, the springs used are metallic springs, such as leaf springs, coil springs and torsion bars and non-metallic springs, such as rubber springs and air springs.

- Suspension springs
  - Metallic springs
    - Leaf springs
    - Coil springs
    - Torsion bar springs
  - Non-metallic springs
    - Rubber springs
    - Air springs

LEAF SPRING

Leaf springs are made of a number of curved bands of spring steel called "leaves", stacked together in order from shortest to longest. Stack of leaves is fastened together at the center with a center bolt or a rivet. To keep the leaves from slipping out of place, they are held at several places with clips. Both ends of the longest (main) leaf are bent to form spring eyes, used to attach the spring to the frame or structural member of a body.

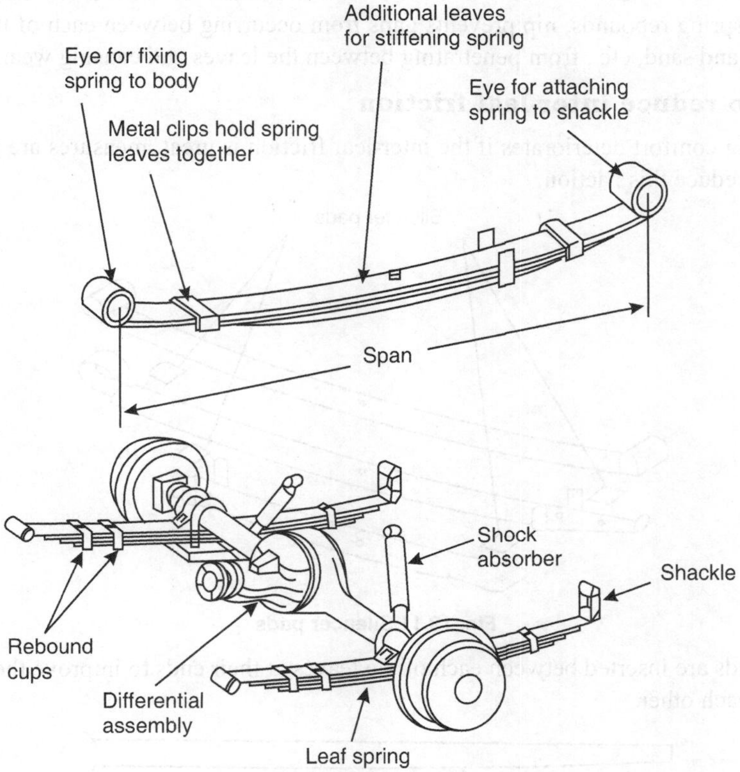

Fig. 13.9 Parts of a leaf spring

Generally, the longer a leaf spring, the softer it will be. Also, the more leaves in a leaf spring, the greater the load they will withstand. But on the other hand, the spring will become firmer and riding comfort will suffer.

Greatest feature of a leaf spring

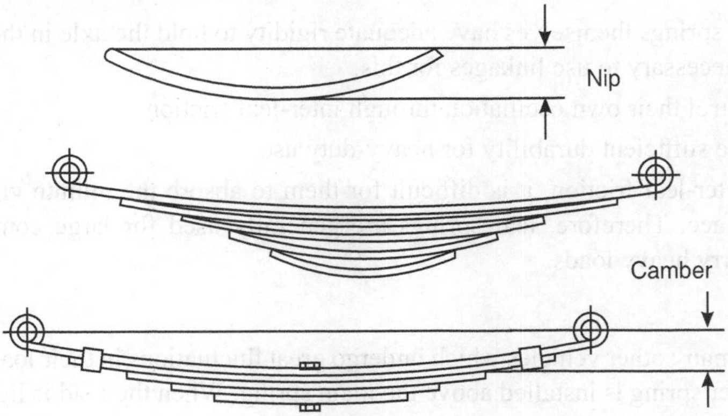

Fig. 13.10 Nip and Camber

The curvature of each leaf is called "nip". The overall curvature of the leaf spring is called 'camber". When a spring is flexed, nip causes the leaves in the spring to rub against together and the friction created by this rubbing quickly damps the oscillations of the spring. This friction is called inter-leaf friction and is one of the greatest features of the leaf spring. However, this friction also causes a decrease in riding comfort, since it prevents the spring from flexing easily.

When the spring rebounds, nip prevents gaps from occurring between each of the leaves, thus preventing dirt and sand, etc., from penetrating between the leaves and causing wear.

Measures to reduce inter-leaf friction

Since riding comfort deteriorates if the inter-leaf friction is great, measures are taken in actual leaf springs to reduce this friction.

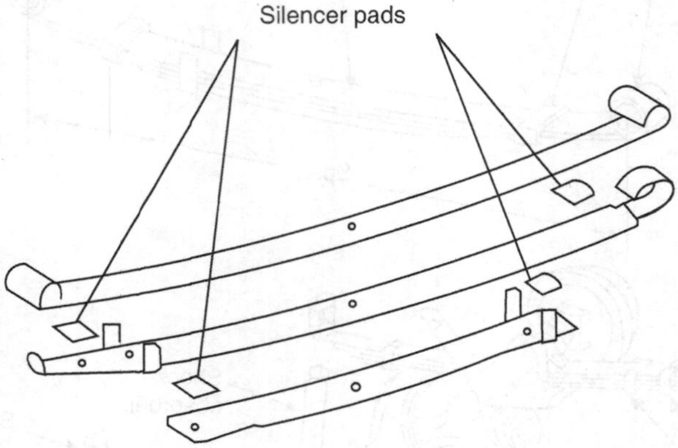

Fig. 13.11 Silencer pads

Silencer pads are inserted between each of the leaves at their ends to improve the sliding of the leaves against each other.

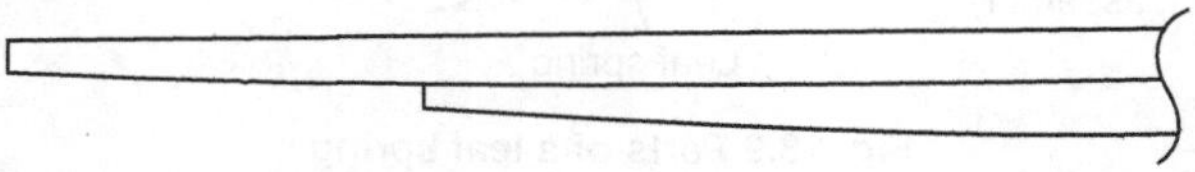

Fig. 13.12 Leaves tapered at the ends

Each of the leaves is also tapered at the ends so that they exert the proper amount of pressure when they come in contact with each other.

Characteristics

- Since the springs themselves have adequate rigidity to hold the axle in the proper position, it is not necessary to use linkages for this.
- They control their own oscillation through inter-leaf friction.
- They have sufficient durability for heavy-duty use.
- Due to inter-leaf friction, it is difficult for them to absorb the minute vibrations from the road surface. Therefore, leaf springs are generally used for large commercial vehicles which carry heavy loads.

Helper spring

In trucks and many other vehicles which undergo great fluctuations in their loads, helper springs are used. The helper spring is installed above the main spring. When the load is light, only the main spring operates, but when the load exceeds a certain value, both the main and helper springs come into operation.

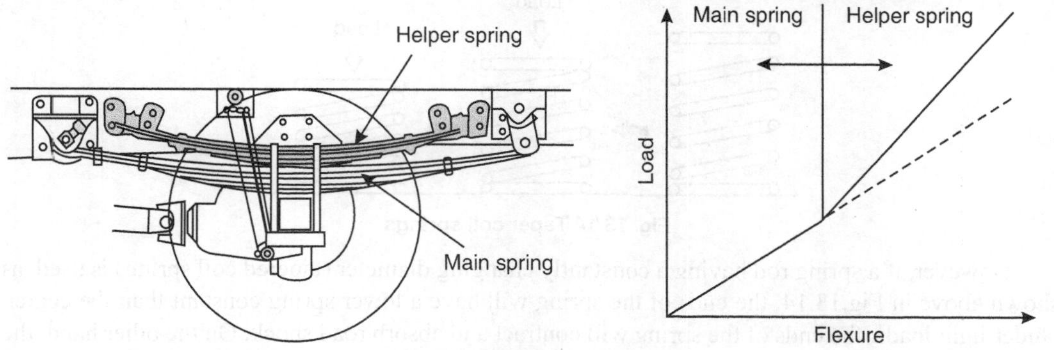

Fig. 13.13 Helper spring

COIL SPRING

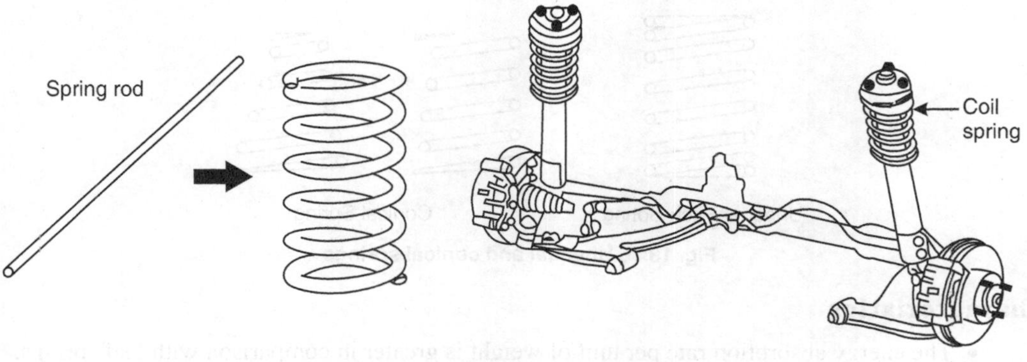

Fig. 13.14 Coil springs

Coil springs are made from rods of special spring steel formed into the shape of a coil. When a load is placed on a coil spring, the entire rod is twisted as the spring contracts. In this way, the energy is stored and shock is cushioned.

Progressive coil springs

If a coil spring is made from a rod of spring steel having a uniform diameter, the entire spring will flex uniformly in proportion to changes in the load. This means that if a soft spring is used, it will not be stiff enough to handle heavy loads, while if a hard spring is used, it will give a rough ride when only lightly loaded.

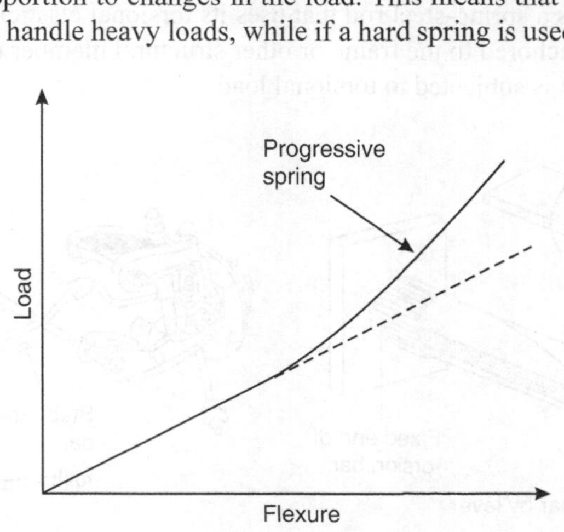

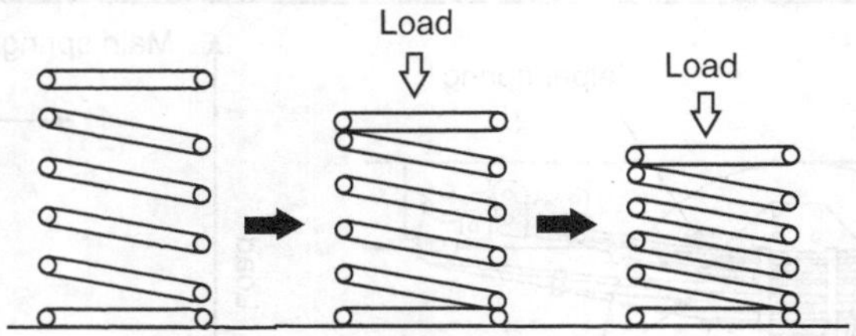

Fig. 13.14 Taper coil springs

However, if a spring rod having a constantly changing diameter (tapered coil spring) is used, as shown above in Fig.13.14, the ends of the spring will have a lower spring constant than the center. Under light loads, the ends of the spring will contract and absorb road shock. On the other hand, the center part of the spring will be stiff enough to handle heavy loads. Hence these springs are sensitive to both light and heavy loads.

The following types of springs can also be used to achieve the same effect.

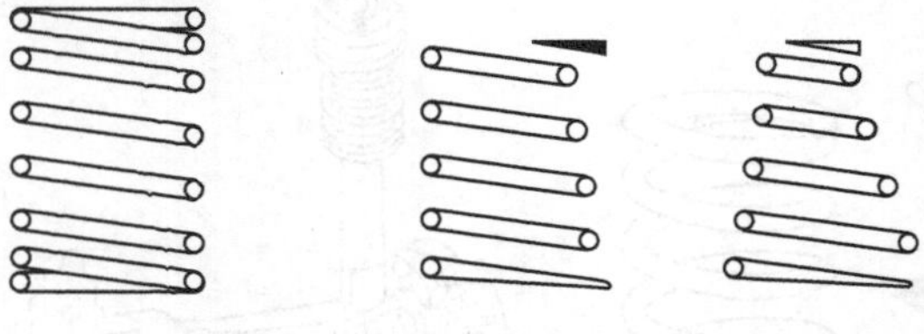

Fig. 13.15 Unequal and conical springs

Characteristics

- The energy absorption rate per unit of weight is greater in comparison with leaf springs.
- Soft springs can be made.
- Since there is no inter-leaf friction, there is no control of oscillation by the spring itself. So it is necessary to use shock absorbers along with them.
- Since there is no resistance to lateral forces, linkage mechanisms to support the axle (suspension arms, lateral control rod, etc.) are necessary.

TORSION BAR SPRING

A torsion bar spring is a spring-steel rod that uses its torsional elasticity to resist twisting. One end of the torsion bar is anchored to the frame or other structural member of the body and the other end to suspension arm that is subjected to torsional load.

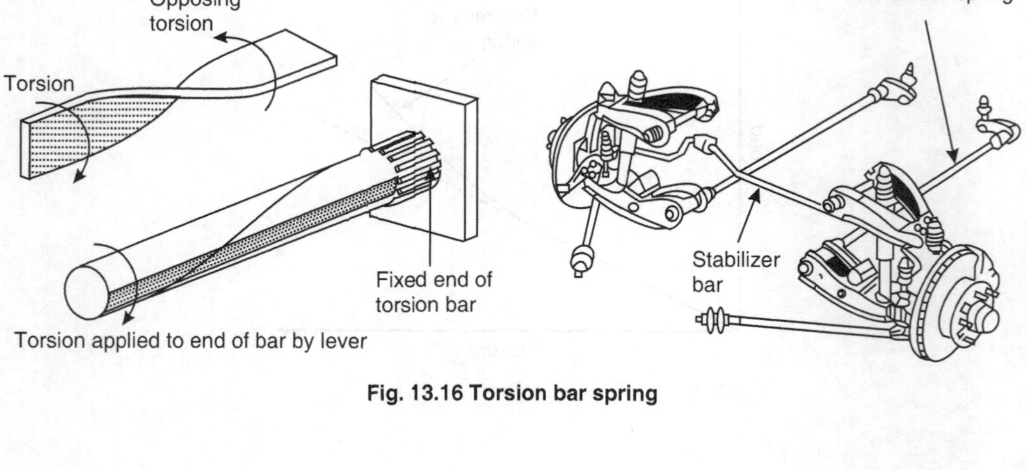

Fig. 13.16 Torsion bar spring

Characteristics

- Since the energy absorption rate per unit weight is great as compared to other springs, the suspension can be lightened.
- The layout of the suspension system is simplified.
- As with coil springs, torsion bar springs do not control oscillation, so it is necessary to use shock absorbers along with them.

RUBBER SPRING (RUBBER SUSPENSION)

Rubber springs absorb oscillations through the generation of internal friction when they are deformed by an external force. Some advantages of rubber springs are that

- they can be made in any shape
- they are silent during use, and
- they do not need to be lubricated

However, they are not appropriate for use in supporting heavy loads. Therefore, rubber springs are used mainly as auxiliary springs or as bushings, spacers, cushions, stoppers and other supports for the suspension components.

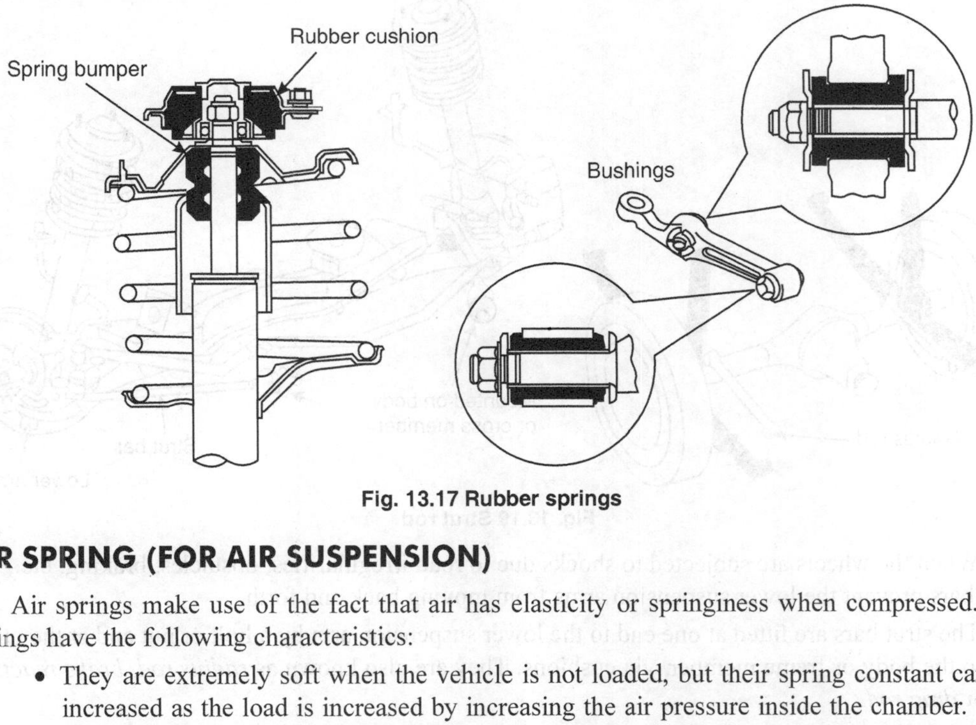

Fig. 13.17 Rubber springs

AIR SPRING (FOR AIR SUSPENSION)

Air springs make use of the fact that air has elasticity or springiness when compressed. Air springs have the following characteristics:

- They are extremely soft when the vehicle is not loaded, but their spring constant can be increased as the load is increased by increasing the air pressure inside the chamber. This provides optimum riding comfort both when the vehicle is lightly loaded and when it is fully loaded.
- The height of the vehicle can be kept constant, even if the load changes, by adjusting the air pressure.

However, in air suspensions using air springs, devices for controlling the air pressure and compressors for compressing air, etc, are necessary, so the suspension becomes complex.

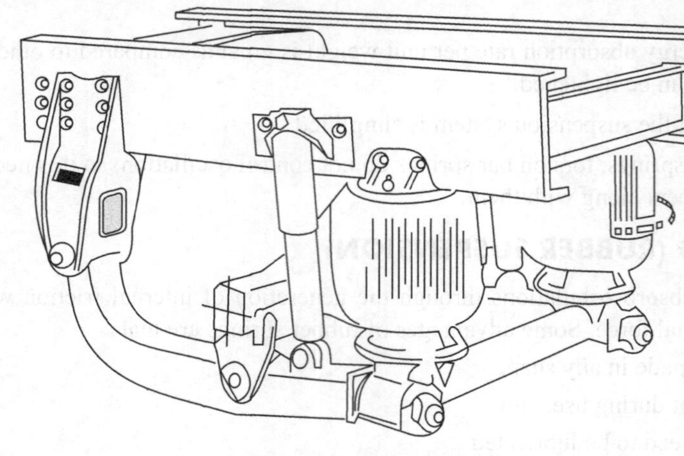

Fig. 13.18 Air suspension

STRUT BAR

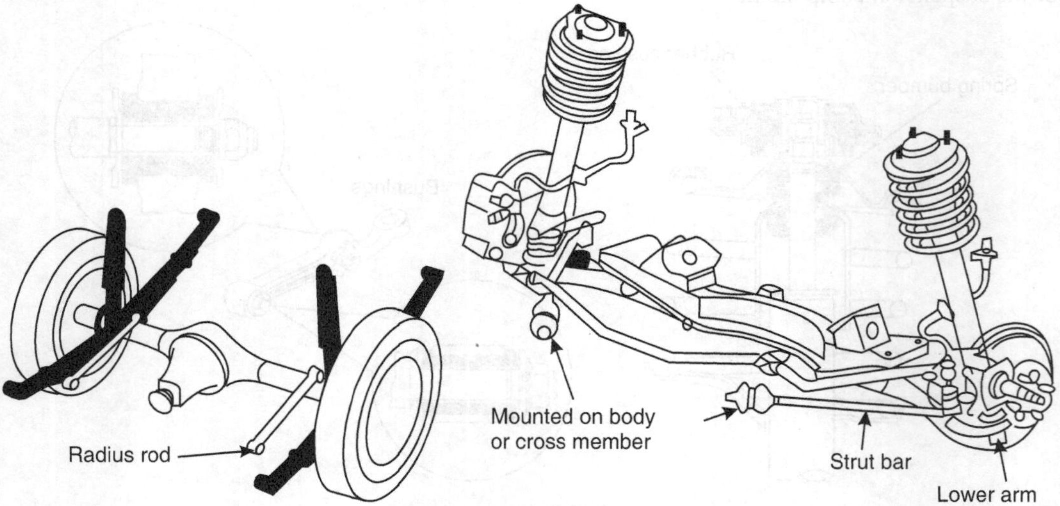

Fig. 13.19 Strut rod

When the wheels are subjected to shocks due to road irregularities, obstacles, braking, etc., the strut bars prevent the lower suspension arms from moving back and forth.

The strut bars are fitted at one end to the lower suspension arm by a bolt or nut and at the other end to the body or frame member, via cushions. They are also known as *radius rod, brake reaction rod* or *drag rod.*

LATERAL CONTROL ROD

In order to bear forces in the lateral direction and to help position the axle so that it is not displaced in the lateral direction, a lateral control rod is used, mainly on the rear suspension. The lateral control rod is mounted transversely between the axle and a structural member of the body. It is also called *panhard rod* or *track bar*.

There are alternative systems of lateral location. A popular one giving perfect lateral location over a limited range, is that invented by James Watt. The Fig. 13.21 explains the principle of this linkage. With such excellent axle location, one can replace the heavy semi-elliptic spring with the lighter, less expensive coil spring.

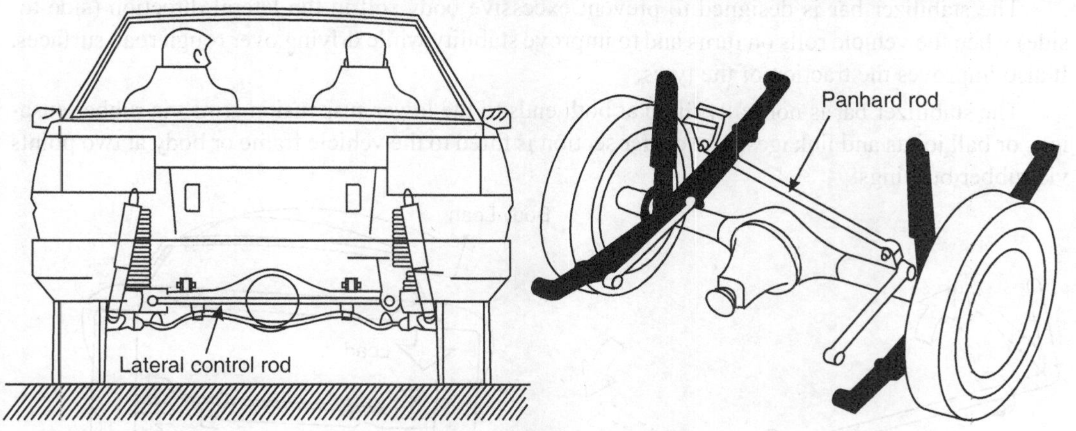

Fig. 13.20 Panhard rod

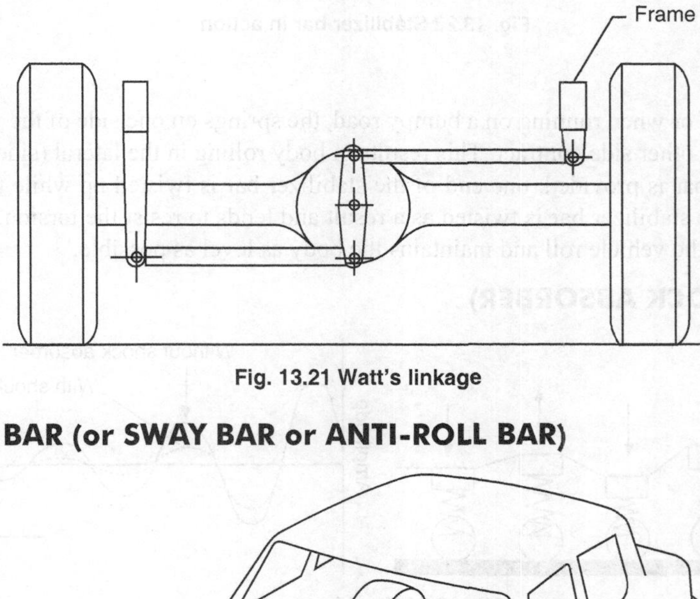

Fig. 13.21 Watt's linkage

STABILIZER BAR (or SWAY BAR or ANTI-ROLL BAR)

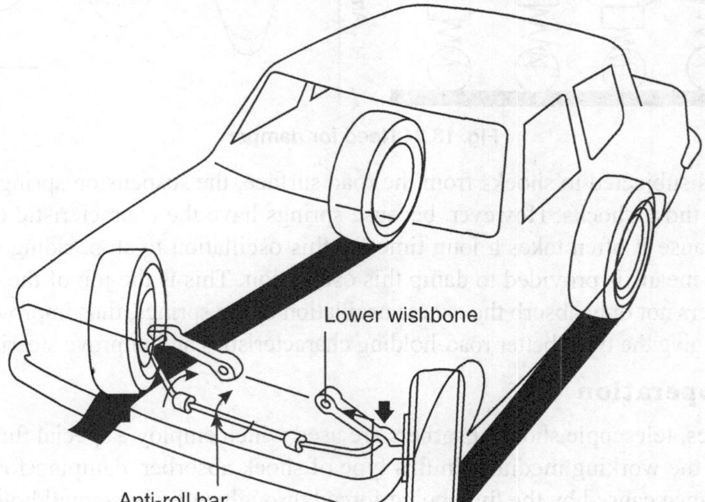

Fig. 13.22 Stabilizer bar

The stabilizer bar is designed to prevent excessive body roll in the lateral direction (side-to-side) when the vehicle rolls on turns and to improve stability while driving over rough road surfaces. It also improves the traction of the tyres.

The stabilizer bar is normally fitted at both ends to the lower suspension arms via rubber cushions or ball joints and linkages. The center section is fitted to the vehicle frame or body at two points via rubber bushings.

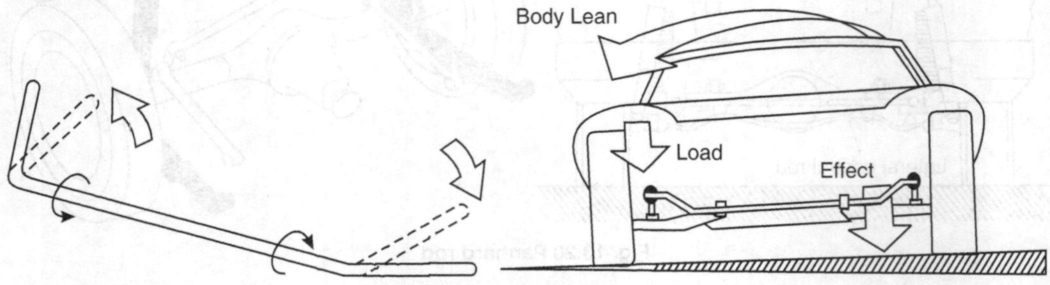

Fig. 13.23 Stabilizer bar in action

Operation

When turning or when running on a bumpy road, the springs on one side of the vehicle expand, while those on the other side contract. This results in body rolling in the lateral (side-to-side) direction. If stabilizer bar is provided, one end of the stabilizer bar is twisted up while the other end is twisted down. The stabilizer bar is twisted as a result and tends to resist the torsion. It is the resistance that reduces the vehicle roll and maintains the body as level as possible.

DAMPER (SHOCK ABSORBER)

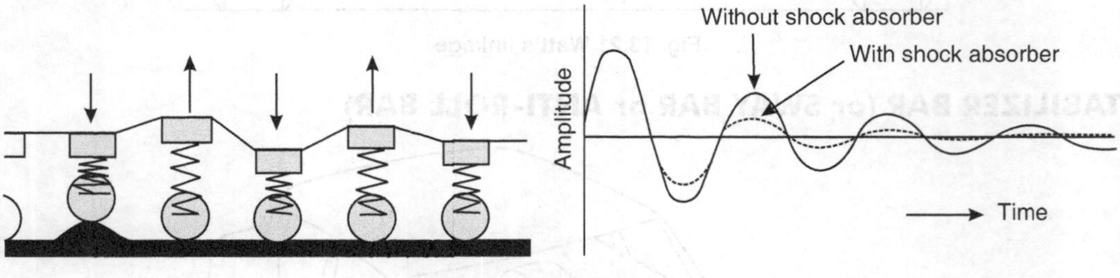

Fig. 13.24 Need for damper

When a car is subjected to shocks from the road surface, the suspension springs compress and expand to absorb those shocks. However, because springs have the characteristic of continuing to oscillate, and because it often takes a long time for this oscillation to stop, riding comfort will be poor unless some means is provided to damp this oscillation. This is the job of the shock absorber. The shock absorbers not only absorb the excess oscillation of the springs, thus improving riding comfort, but they also give the tyres better road-holding characteristics and improve steering stability.

Principle of operation

In automobiles, telescopic shock absorbers are used which employ a special fluid, called shock absorber fluid, as the working medium. In this type of shock absorber, damping force is generated by the flow resistance caused by the fluid being forced through an orifice (small hole) by the movement of a piston.

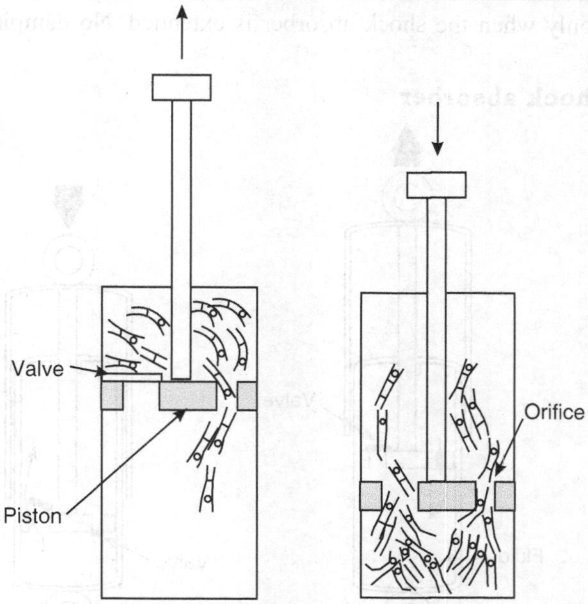

Fig. 13.25 Principle of shock absorber

TYPES OF SHOCK ABSORBERS

Shock absorbers are classified according to their construction and operation as follows:

1. Classification by operation: single-action type and multiple-action type
2. Classification by construction: mono-tube type and twin-tube type
3. Classification by working medium: hydraulic type and gas-filled type

Of these types, shock absorbers which are used in current models have twin-tube or mono-tube construction and have multiple action. Most recently, many gas-filled shock absorbers of the above types have come into use.

Classification by operation

Single-action shock absorber

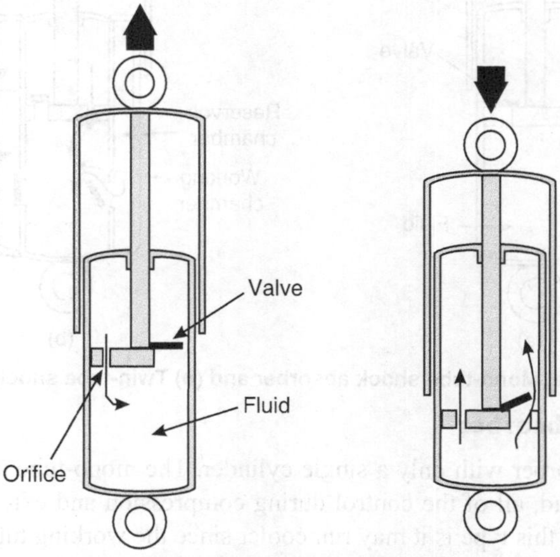

Fig. 13.26 Single-action shock absorber

Damping occurs only when the shock absorber is extended. No damping force is generated when it is compressed.

Multiple-action shock absorber

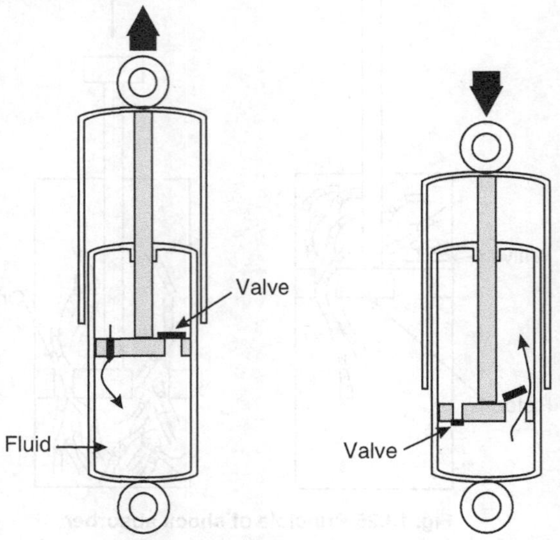

Fig. 13.27 Double-action shock absorber

Damping occurs both when the shock absorber is extended and when it is compressed. Currently, most shock absorbers used on cars are of this type.

Classification by construction

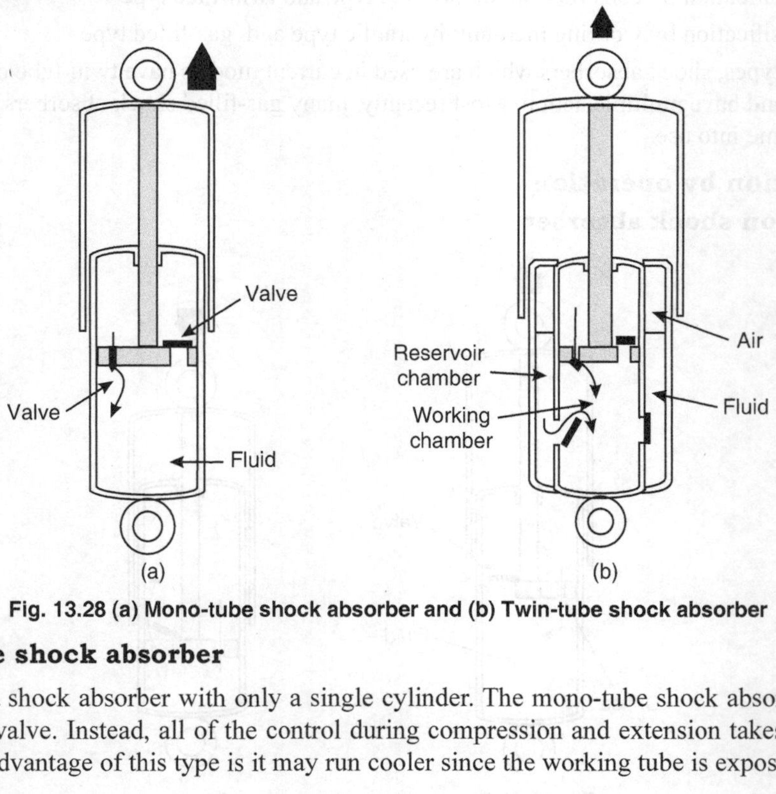

Fig. 13.28 (a) Mono-tube shock absorber and (b) Twin-tube shock absorber

Mono-tube shock absorber

This is a shock absorber with only a single cylinder. The mono-tube shock absorber does not have a base valve. Instead, all of the control during compression and extension takes place at the piston. The advantage of this type is it may run cooler since the working tube is exposed to the air.

Twin-tube shock absorber

The cylinder is divided by working chamber and a reservoir chamber. There is a cylinder in which the piston moves up and down. At the base of the piston rod, a piston valve is installed which generates damping force when the shock absorber is extended (during rebounding). At the bottom of the cylinder there is a base valve which generates damping force when the shock absorber is compressed (during bounding). The inside of the cylinder is filled with absorber fluid, but only 2/3 of the reservoir chamber is filled with fluid, the rest being filled with air at atmospheric pressure. The reservoir serves as a storage tank for the fluid entering and leaving the cylinder.

Classification by working medium

Hydraulic shock absorber

This is an ordinary shock absorber which uses only shock absorber fluid as a working medium.

Gas-filled shock absorber

Gas shock absorbers represent an advance over traditional shocks. At high vehicle speeds, the suspension will be cycling at a tremendous rate, thereby forcing the piston within the shock absorber to move at a tremendous rate as well. When this happens, the oil within a regular shock absorber gets air bubbles forced into it can cause foam of oil and air to form. The oil will flow through the orifices of the piston at unpredictable rates and decreases the performance of any standard shock absorber. The addition of nitrogen under pressure limits this phenomenon and increases efficiency.

The principle gas used is nitrogen (an inert gas), which is kept under either low pressure (3–6 bar) or high pressure (20–30 bar). This keeps the oil from aerating because nitrogen does not mix with the shock oil and forces the oil molecules to stay packed together much more closely, thereby preventing the oil from getting any air bubbles within. This prevents the generation of abnormal noise due to cavitation (air pockets) and aeration (mixing of air with shock absorber fluid) that can occur in shock absorbers using only fluid. Minimization of cavitation and aeration also makes it possible to obtain a more stable damping force, thus improving riding comfort and handling stability.

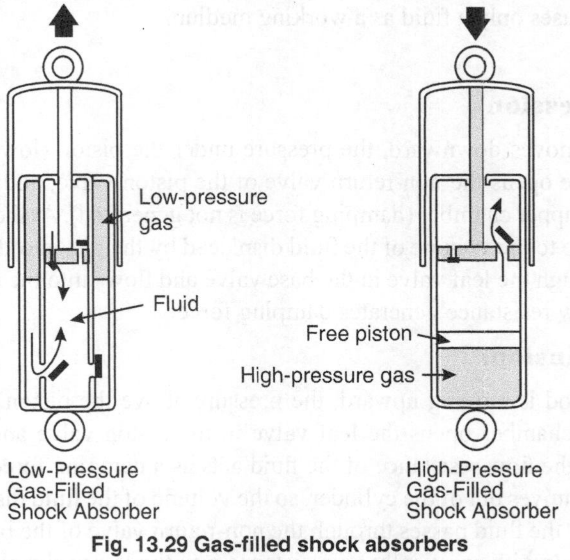

Fig. 13.29 Gas-filled shock absorbers

TELESCOPIC SHOCK ABSORBER

Dampers are usually of the telescopic type. The telescopic damper consists of a steel cylinder that contains a piston attached to a connecting rod. The piston divides the cylinder into two chambers, the upper and lower. The space between the cylinder and the outer casing is the hydraulic fluid reservoir.

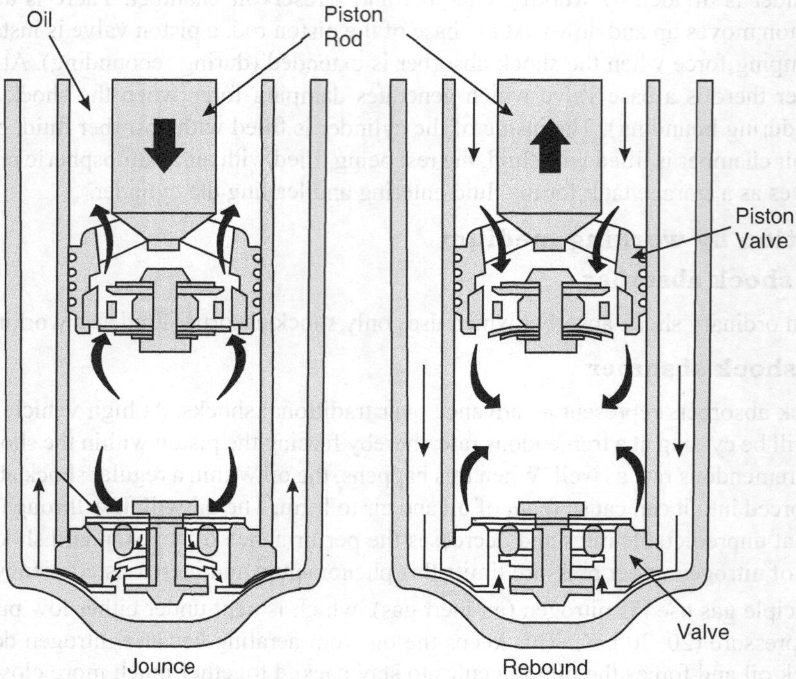

Fig. 13.30 Operation of twin-tube telescopic shock absorber

The cylinder is attached to the unsprung suspension parts (the roadwheel and suspension arm or axle), while the piston and connecting rod are secured to the vehicle chassis or body.

The Fig. 13.30 shows a telescopic type twin tube hydraulic shock absorber. This is an ordinary shock absorber which uses only a fluid as a working medium.

Operation

Bounding (Compression)

When the piston moves downward, the pressure under the piston (lower chambers) becomes high. The fluid pressure opens the non-return valve of the piston valve, and with practically no resistance flows into the upper chamber (damping force is not generated). At the same time, an amount of fluid equal in volume to the volume of the fluid displaced by the piston rod as it is pushed into the cylinder, is forced through the leaf valve in the base valve and flows into the reservoir chamber. It is at this time that the flow resistance generates damping force.

Rebounding (Expansion)

When the piston rod is moving upward, the pressure above the piston becomes high and the fluid inside the upper chamber opens the leaf valve in the piston valve and flows into the lower chamber. At this time, the flow resistance of the fluid acts as a damping force. Since the rod moves upward, a portion of it moves out of the cylinder, so the volume of the fluid displaced by it decreases. To compensate for this, the fluid passes through the non-return valve of the base valve from the reservoir chamber and flows with practically no resistance into the lower chamber.

Although telescopic dampers are compact and require no maintenance, they must be replaced if found to be leaking or defective.

SUSPENSION TYPES AND CHARACTERISTICS

Many different suspension systems are in use. Most of them provide an acceptable degree of roadability and riding comfort. Suspensions can be divided into two types, based on the differences in their construction:

- Rigid axle (or) solid axle suspension in which the right and left wheels are connected by a single axle.
- Independent suspension in which the left and right wheels move independently of each other.

RIGID AXLE SUSPENSION

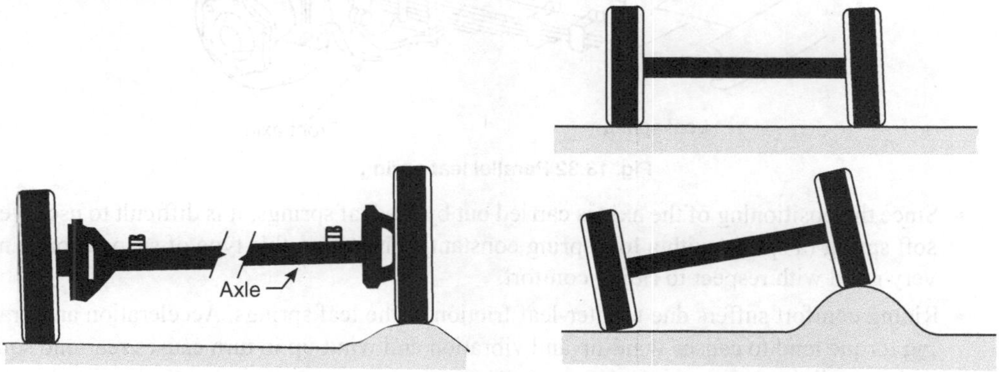

Fig. 13.31 Rigid axle suspension

In rigid axle suspension, a wheel is mounted at each end of a solid axle or axle housing. This type of suspension has the advantages of strength and low cost, but it provides less efficiency and comfort than independent suspension.

Advantages

- The number parts composing the suspension are less and the construction is simple. Therefore, maintenance is simple.
- It is durable enough for heavy-duty use.
- When turning there is little tilting of the body.
- There is little change in the alignment due to the up-and-down movements of the wheels. Therefore, there is less tyre wear.

Disadvantages

- Since the unsprung weight is great, riding comfort is poor.
- Since the movements of the left and right wheels mutually influence one another, vibration and oscillation occur easily.

TYPES OF RIGID AXLE SUSPENSION

Parallel leaf spring type

This type of suspension is used for the front suspension and the rear suspensions in commercial vehicles.

Characteristics

- Since the leaf spring also acts as a linkage for positioning the axle (holding in place), separate linkages are generally unnecessary. Therefore the construction of the suspension is simple but comparatively strong.

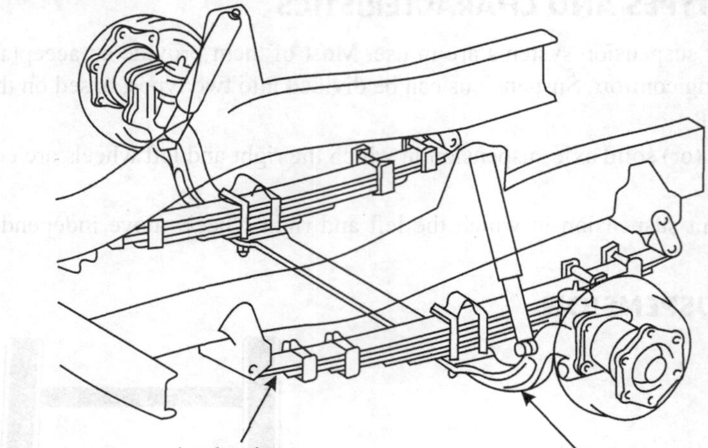

Fig. 13.32 Parallel leaf spring

- Since the positioning of the axle is carried out by the leaf springs, it is difficult to use a very soft spring (a spring with a low spring constant). Therefore, this type of suspension is not very good with respect to riding comfort.
- Riding comfort suffers due to inter-leaf friction in the leaf springs. Acceleration and braking torque tend to causes wind-up and vibration and wind-up in turn causes rear-end squat and nose-diving.

Leading arm and trailing arm types with lateral rods

This type of suspension is used for the front and rear suspension of the SUVs.

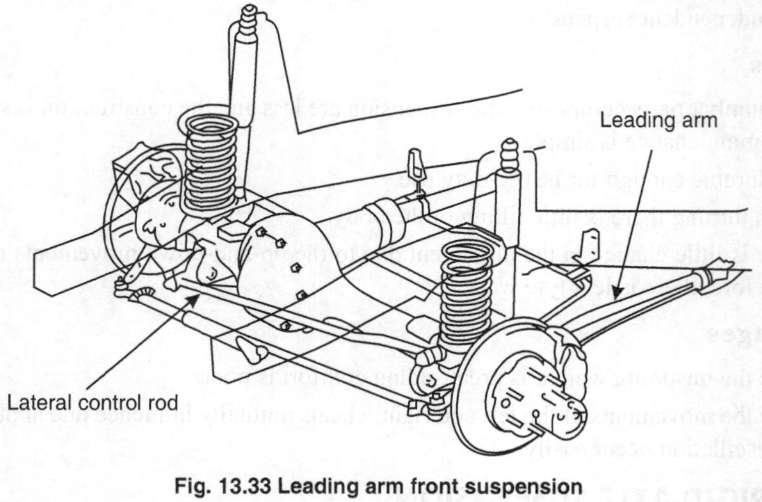

Fig. 13.33 Leading arm front suspension

Characteristics

In this type, the positioning of the axle, which is accomplished by the leaf springs in the parallel leaf spring type, is instead accomplished by leading arms or trailing arms and a lateral control rod. It is superior to leaf springs in the following points.

- Since the spring constant can be made smaller, riding comfort is good.
- Since the trailing arm's rigidity is high, it is difficult for wind-up to occur.

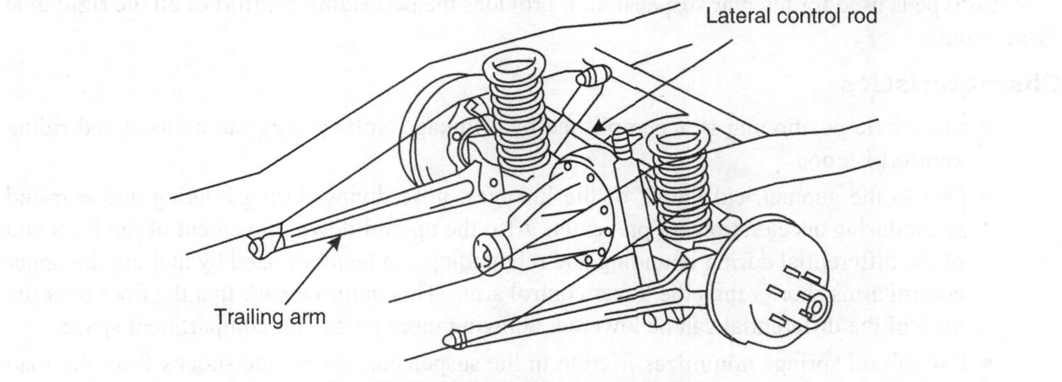

Fig. 13.34 Trailing arm rear suspension

Trailing arm with twist-beam type

This type is mainly used in the rear suspension of compact front-engine front-wheel drive (FF) vehicles and employs a structure consisting of a suspension arm and stabilizer bar welded to a twistable axle beam.

When the wheels bound and rebound in opposite directions, the twisting movement of the ends of the suspension arms is translated into a twisting of the rear axle beam, built-in stabilizer and rear suspension arms. The twisting of the rear axle beam and stabilizer generates a reactive force which opposes the twisting of the suspension arms, aiding the coil springs in providing roll rigidity to minimize body rolling, thus yielding greater steering stability, thereby maintaining vehicle stability.

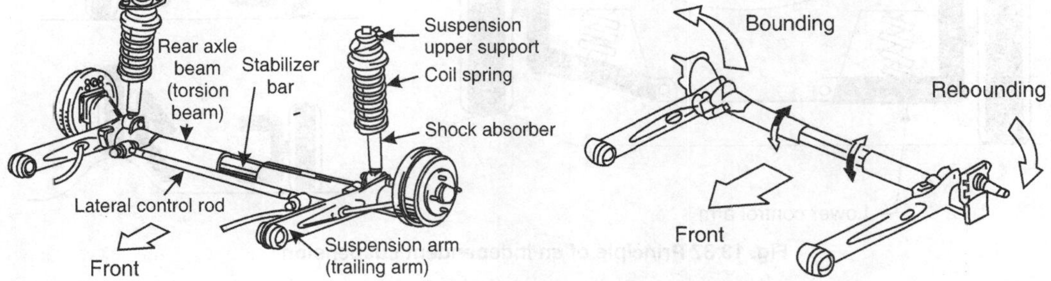

Fig. 13.35 Trailing arm with twist-beam suspension

Due to its simple structure and compact size, unsprung weight can be reduced for a better ride. In addition, it also enables the securing of a luggage space.

Four-link type

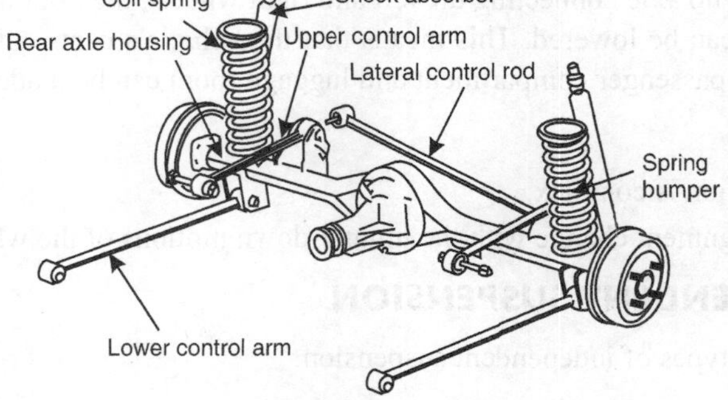

Fig. 13.36 Four-link type suspension

This type is used for the rear suspension. It provides the best riding comfort of all the rigid-axle suspensions.

Characteristics

- Since axle positioning is accomplished by a linkage, soft springs can be used and riding comfort is good.
- Due to the geometrical layout of the linkages, nose diving during braking and rear-end squat during acceleration are prevented. Also the up-and-down movement of the front end of the differential during bounding and rebounding can be minimized by making the upper control arms shorter than the lower control arms. This in turn means that the floor over the nose of the differential can be lowered, allowing more passenger compartment space.
- Use of coil springs minimizes friction in the suspension, so minute shocks from the road surface can be absorbed and riding comfort can be improved.
- Generally, when this suspension system is used in the rear, the linkage is located forward of the axle, and as a result, the capacity of the trunk can be larger on passenger cars.

INDEPENDENT SUSPENSION

Independent suspension systems provide a separate mounting for each wheel. There is no connection between the left and right wheels. Therefore, the linear motion of one wheel is not transmitted to the other, and there is no tilting of an axle, that in turn, might tilt the entire car.

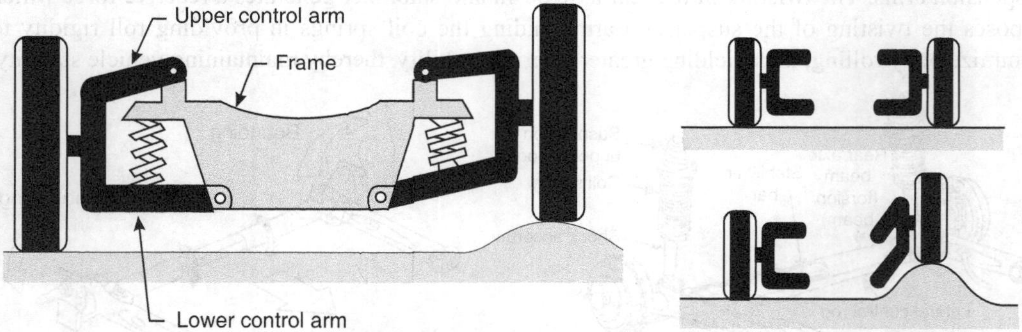

Fig. 13.37 Principle of an independent suspension

Advantages

- The unsprung weight can be kept low and the road-holding characteristics of the wheels are good, so riding comfort and handling stability are good.
- In independent suspensions, the springs only support the body. They do not help to position the wheels (this is being done by the linkages). This means that softer springs can be used.
- Since there is no axle connecting the left and right wheels, the floor and the engine mounting position can be lowered. This means that the vehicle's centre of gravity will be lowered, and the passenger compartment and luggage room can be made larger.

Disadvantages

- The construction is complex.
- Tread and alignment change with the up-and-down motions of the wheels.

TYPES OF INDEPENDENT SUSPENSION

There are various types of independent suspension.

Macpherson strut type

This is the most widely used independent suspension system for the front suspension of small and medium sized cars. This type is also used as the rear suspension of front-engine front wheel drive cars.

In this type only lower wishbones are used. A strut containing shock absorber and the spring carries also the stub axle on which the wheel is mounted. The wishbone is hinged to the cross member and positions the wheel as well as resists acceleration, braking and side forces.

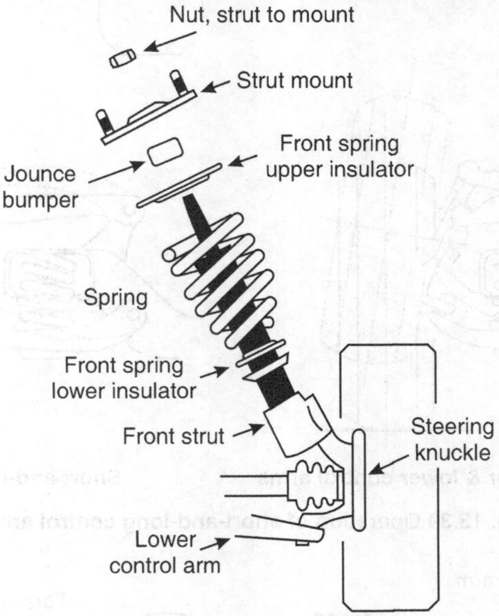

Fig. 13.38 Macpherson strut type

Characteristics

- The construction of the suspension is relatively simple.
- Since there is a small number of parts, it is light, so unsprung weight can be reduced.
- Since the space taken up by the suspension is small, the usable space in the engine compartment can be increased.
- Since the distance between suspension support points is great, there is little disturbance of the front wheel alignment due to installation error or part manufacturing error. Therefore, except for toe-in, alignment adjustments are ordinarily unnecessary.

Double-wish bone (or) Short-and-Long Arm (SLA) type

This type is used widely for the front suspension of small trucks and for the front and rear suspensions of passenger cars. This type consists of upper and lower wishbone arms pivoted to the frame members. The vehicle weight is transmitted from the body and cross-member to the coil spring through which it goes to the lower wishbone member.

The wishbone arms are like the chicken wishbone or letter V in shape, because of which the system is so called. Because of this V-shape, the wishbones not only position the wheels and transmit the vehicle load to the springs, but these also resist acceleration, braking and cornering (side) forces. The upper arms are shorter in length than the lower ones. This helps to keep tyre remains in a more constant position, thus minimizing tyre wear. The wishbone type is the most popular independent suspension system.

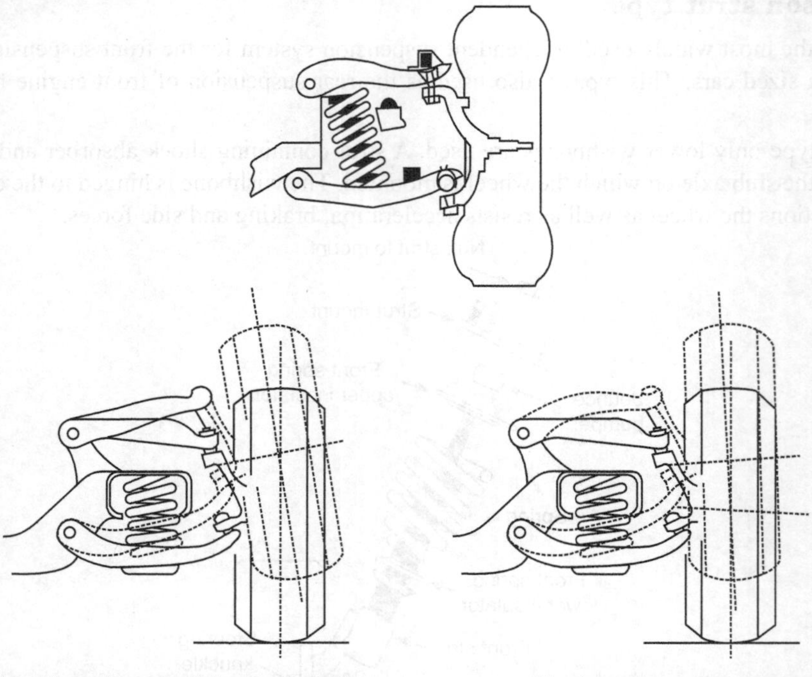

Fig. 13.39 Operation of short-and-long control arms

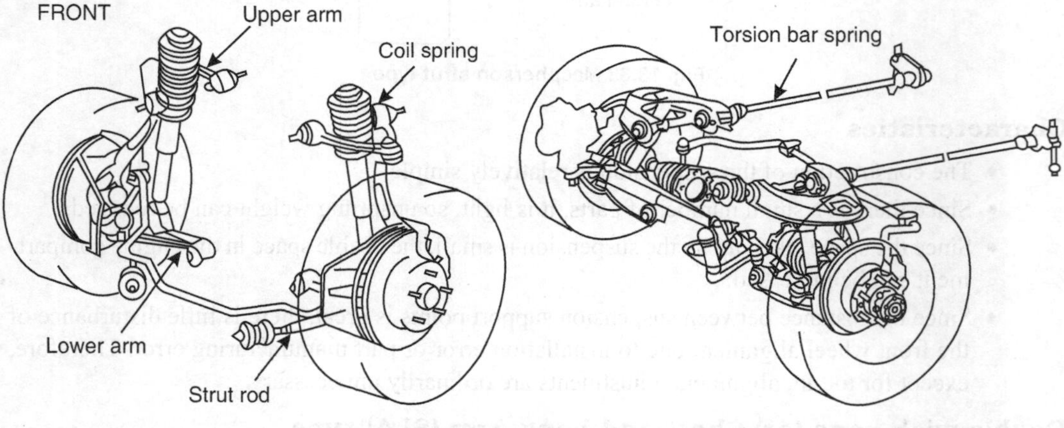

Fig. 13.40 Double wishbone type suspension

Characteristics

In this type, the upper control arm is shorter than the lower control arm. During wheel jounce and rebound travel, the upper control arm moves in a shorter arc than the lower arm. This action moves the top of the tyre in and out slightly, but the bottom of the tyre remains in a more constant position.

Semi-trailing arm type

This type is used for the rear suspension in a few models.

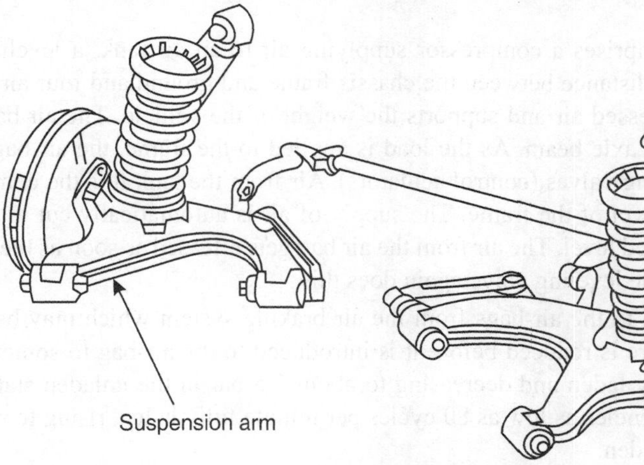

Fig. 13.41 Semi-trailing arm suspension

Characteristics

With this suspension, the amount by which the toe angle and camber change (due to the up-and-down motion of the wheels) can be controlled by varying the length of each arm and setting the arm installation angle and angle of axis sway at the design stage, in order to determine the handling characteristics of the car.

AIR SUSPENSION

Air suspension is a type of vehicle suspension powered by an engine driven or electric air pump or compressor. This pump pressurizes the air, using compressed air as a spring. Air suspension replaces conventional steel springs. If the engine is left off for an extended period, the car will settle to the ground. The purpose of air suspension is to provide a smooth ride quality and in some cases self-leveling.

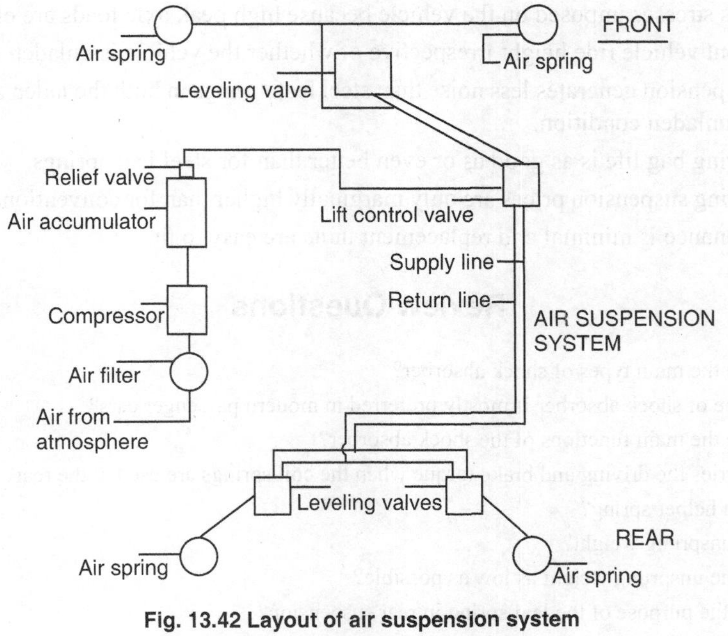

Fig. 13.42 Layout of air suspension system

Operation

The air suspension comprises a compressor supplying air to an air tank, a leveling valve to maintain a pressure a fixed distance between the chassis frame and ground and four air bags. Each air bag is filled with compressed air and supports the weight of the vehicle. The air bag is placed between the chassis and the axle beam. As the load is applied to the frame, the air bags get compressed, actuating the leveling valves (control actuators). Air from the tank fills the compressed air bags and hence raises the level of the frame. The supply of air is automatically cut as soon as the frame reaches a predetermined level. The air from the air bag gets released as soon as the load on the chassis frames decreases. The leveling valve again does this.

Air pressure is supplied to the air-bags from the air braking system which may be as high as 8 bar, but the supply pressure is reduced before it is introduced to the air-bag to something like 5 bar when the vehicle is fully laden and decreasing to about 2.5 bar in the unladen state. Air bags can operate at bounce frequencies as low as 80 cycles per minute fully laden, rising to roughly 100 cycles per minute when unladen.

Advantages

Besides providing vibration isolation, air springs offer many other user-friendly advantages over the traditional leaf and coil springs. Air spring suspensions have become popular with heavy goods vehicles, coaches and buses in recent years, due to the following reasons:

- Maintain a constant frequency of vibration whether the vehicle is laden or unladen.
- Helps to reduce the load while the vehicle in motion i.e. the dynamic loading as the spring rate variation between laden and unladen weight is much less.
- Gives smooth and comfort ride of the vehicle.
- Stiffness of the system increases with the increase of deflection.
- Suspension bounce frequency between unladen and laden operating conditions is much narrower and is much nearer to the ideal frequency for human comfort than conventional steel springs can achieve.
- Protects fragile loads.
- Lowers stresses imposed on the vehicle because high peak axle loads are eliminated.
- Constant vehicle ride height irrespective of whether the vehicle is unladen or fully laden.
- Air suspension generates less noise than steel leaf springs in both the laden and particularly in the unladen condition.
- Air spring bag life is as good as or even better than for steel leaf springs.
- Air spring suspension prices are only marginally higher than for conventional steel springs.
- Maintenance is minimal and replacement units are easy to fit.

Review Questions

1. What are the main types of shock absorber?
2. What type of shock absorber is mostly preferred in modern passenger cars?
3. What are the main functions of the shock absorber?
4. What carries the driving and brake torque when the coil springs are used at the rear?
5. What is a helper spring?
6. What is unsprung weight?
7. Why is the unsprung weight as low as possible?
8. What is the purpose of the leaf spring in rear suspension?

9. What type of spring is used with solid beam axle?
10. Why are leaf springs made of a series of steel strips?
11. What is known as semi-elliptic springs?
12. How are leaf springs lubricated?
13. How is the laminated leaf spring self damping?
14. What is pitching in the suspension system?
15. What do you understand by bouncing in the suspension system?
16. What is meant by independent suspension?
17. Which are the different types of independent suspension system?
18. Why is an independent suspension normally applied to the front wheels and not to the rear wheels?
19. What is known as roll axis in suspension?
20. What are the advantages of rubber suspension?
21. What is known as torsion bar?
22. What is a panhard rod or track bar?
23. What are the advantages of air suspension?
24. Differentiate independent suspension from solid axle suspension.
25. What is the effect of moisture on the leaf spring?.

14 CHAPTER

BRAKE SYSTEM

Once the automobile starts running, its momentum will keep it running even if the engine is stopped or its transmission of power to the driving wheels cut off with the clutch, but this will prevent fulfilling the original purpose of the automobile. Therefore, brakes have been provided to serve the important function of stopping or slowing down the automobile when required to do so. Brakes are also indispensable for safe driving of the vehicle. It is desired that the brakes actuate positively, be highly reliable and have durability. They should also be easy to inspect and adjust.

PURPOSE

Brakes are designed to:

- Decelerate (slow down) the vehicle
- Stop the vehicle, and
- Allow the vehicle to be parked on a slope

They are therefore extremely essential equipment on an automobile to ensure safety driving.

PRINCIPLE

A moving vehicle cannot stop immediately when the engine is disconnected from the power train, due to inertia (the tendency of a moving object to continue moving). This inertia must be reduced in order to bring the vehicle to a halt.

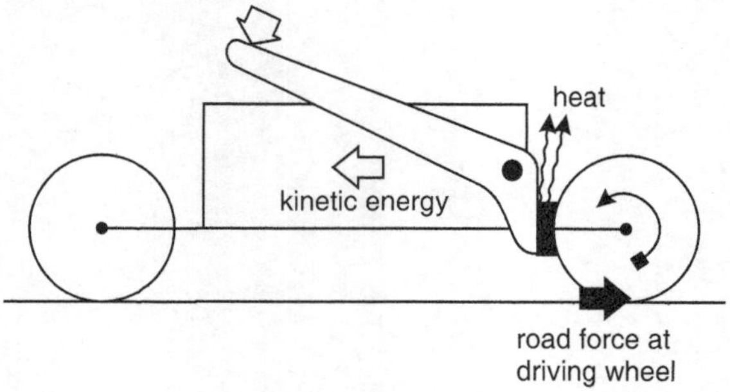

Fig. 14.1 Principle of braking

The engine converts heat (thermal energy) into kinetic energy (energy of motion) to move the vehicle. In contrast, the brakes change this kinetic energy back into heat energy to stop the vehicle. Generally, brakes work by causing a fixed object to be pressed against a rotating object. The braking effect is obtained from the friction that is generated between the two objects. The heat formed at this time is dissipated to the atmosphere.

BRAKING FORCE

Brake pedal operation is based on the principle of the lever and converting a small pedal force into large force acting on the master cylinder.

Based on Pascal's law, the hydraulic force generated in the master cylinder is transmitted via pipe line to individual wheel cylinders. It acts on brake linings and disc pads to generate a braking force.

Principle of lever

The principle of the lever is applied by the brake pedal as follows:

Operating force

$$F_1 \times A = F_2 \times B$$

$$\therefore \quad F_2 = F_1 \times \frac{A}{B}$$

Where, F_1 : Pedal force

F_2 : Push rod output force

A_1: Distance from center to brake pedal to fulcrum

B : Distance from push rod to fulcrum

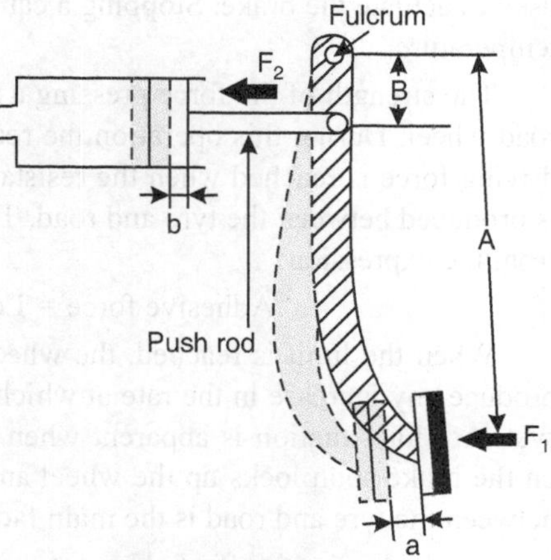

Fig. 14.2 Principle of the lever

Amount of movement:

$$\frac{b}{a} = \frac{B}{A}$$

$$a = b \times \frac{A}{B} \quad \text{(or)} \quad b = a \times \frac{B}{A}$$

a : Amount of movement of pedal edge

b: Amount of movement of push rod

Pascal's law

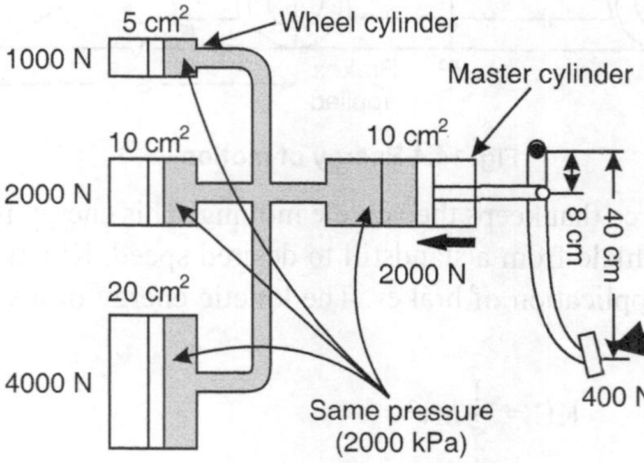

Fig. 14.3 Pascal's law

According to Pascal's law, externally applied pressure upon a confined fluid is transmitted uniformly is all directions. Applying this principle to a hydraulic circuit in a brake system, the pressure generated in the master cylinder is transmitted equally to all wheel cylinders.

The braking force varies, as shown in Fig. 14.3, depending on the diameter of the wheel cylinder. If a vehicle design requires a larger braking force at the front wheels, for example, the designer will specify larger cylinders for the front.

CO-EFFICIENT OF FRICTION AND TYRE ADHESION

Frictional force opposes the motion of the vehicle. Consequently it consumes power and produces heat. Frictional force occurs between the sliding tyre and the road surface when wheel rotation is locked by brakes. The ability of a vehicle to stop depends on the coefficient of friction between the contacting surfaces. Maximum usable coefficient of friction occurs between the tyre and road surface. The amount of energy that can be absorbed by the brakes depends upon the coefficient of friction of the brake materials, brake diameter, brake surface area, shoe geometry, and the pressure used to actuate the brake. Stopping a car suddenly means very high friction, resulting in high brake temperature.

The strength of the force pressing a shoe against a drum governs the resistance to rotation of a road wheel. During this operation the road surface has to drive the wheel around. The limit of this driving force is reached when the resistance of the brake equals the maximum frictional force that is produced between the tyre and road. The latter is called the adhesive force and can be calculated from the expression:

$$\text{Adhesive force} = \text{Load on wheel} \times \text{Co-efficient of friction}$$

When the limit is reached, the wheel starts to skid, so extra force on the brake shoe will not produce any increase in the rate at which the vehicle slows down, no matter how good the braking system. This situation is apparent when a vehicle is braked on a slippery surface. Slight pressure on the brake soon locks up the wheel and very poor braking results. This shows that the adhesion between the tyre and road is the main factor that controls the minimum stopping distance.

Road adhesion is affected by:

- type of road surface.
- condition of surface, e.g. wet, dry, icy, greasy, etc.
- design of tyre tread, composition of tread material and depth of road.

STOPPING DISTANCE

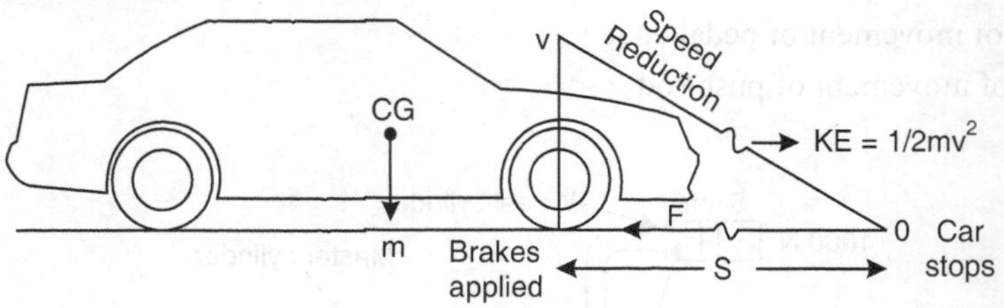

Fig. 14.4 Energy of motion

Kinetic energy is the force that keeps the vehicle moving. This energy is provided by the engine in order to accelerate the vehicle from a standstill to desired speed. Kinetic energy is dissipated as heat by the brakes during application of brakes. The kinetic energy of a vehicle during braking is given by,

$$KE = \frac{1}{2}mv^2$$

Where,
KE = Kinetic energy, J
m = Mass, kg
v = Velocity, m/s

When a vehicle is moving at a given velocity then,

$$\text{Kinetic energy} = \text{work stored}$$
$$= \text{retarding force} \times \text{stopping distance}$$

$$\therefore \quad \text{Stopping distance (S)} = \frac{\text{kinetic energy}}{\text{retarding force}} = \frac{\frac{1}{2}mv^2}{F}$$

Stopping distance is extremely important for emergency braking. The stopping distance is based on the deceleration rate. Also, it is affected by the tyre deflection, air resistance, braking efforts and the inertia of the driveline.

The above expression enables the following conclusions to be formed:

- the stopping distance is governed by the ratio of the retarding force to the vehicle mass as shown in Fig. 14.5.
- the stopping distance varies as the square of the velocity, e.g. the distance required to stop a vehicle travelling at 90 km/h is nine times as great as that required for a speed of 30 km/h (Fig. 14.6)

Fig. 14.5 Stopping distance of vehicle B is similar to that of vehicle A because retarding force is proportional to the mass

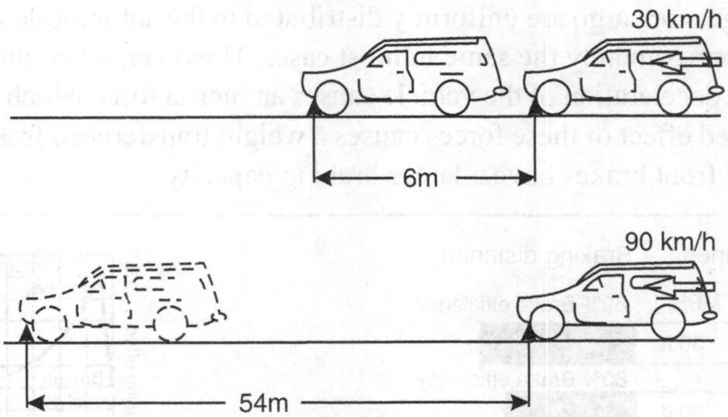

Fig. 14.6 Stopping distance varies as the square of the velocity

The stopping distance remains same with the same tyre and road conditions, when the wheels are locked and skidding, regardless of the weight, number of wheels or vehicle load. Maximum braking force occurs when the wheels are braked just before the locking point or point of impending skid. Non-skid brake systems are designed to operate at or below this point. Any changes in load on a wheel changes the point of impending skid.

BRAKE PERFORMANCE

Brake performance is measured in terms of braking distance, that is, the distance travelled by the automobile from the time the driver depresses the brake pedal to the time the automobile comes to a full stop. The brake performance will naturally be reduced as the speed gets higher or when the load becomes heavier. Road surface conditions will also have a large effect. If the brake linings are worn, soaked with grease or oil or failing to make proper contact with the drum, then the loss in frictional force due to any of these causes will also have a bad effect on the brake performance.

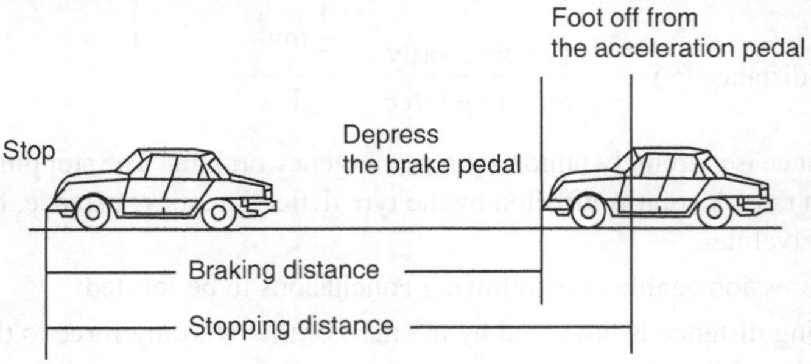

Fig. 14.7 Brake performance

Aside from above, tyre wear or presence of air in the brake lines would also cause reduced brake performance.

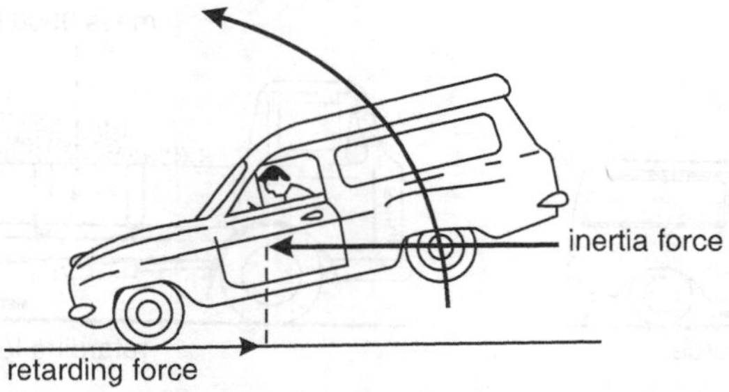

Fig. 14.8 Couple produced by the two forces gives an overturning action

When the passengers or cargo are uniformly distributed in the automobile, the loads on the front and rear wheels are approximately the same in most cases. However, when the vehicle is braked as shown in Fig.14.8, the deceleration of the vehicle causes an inertia force which is equal to the retarding force. The combined effect of these forces causes a weight transference from the rear to the front and for this reason the front brakes have a larger braking capacity.

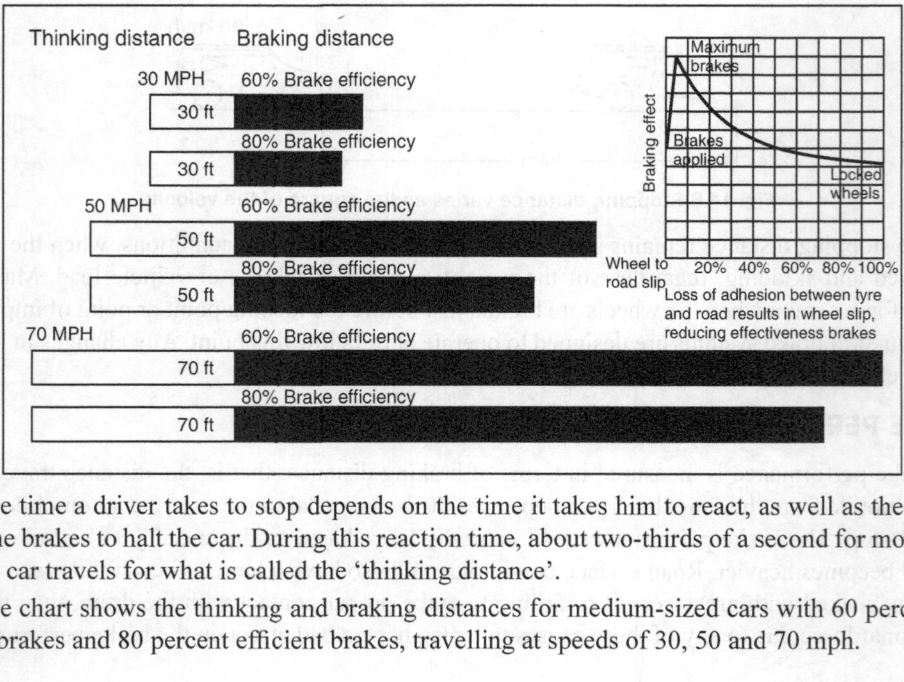

The time a driver takes to stop depends on the time it takes him to react, as well as the time it takes the brakes to halt the car. During this reaction time, about two-thirds of a second for most drivers, the car travels for what is called the 'thinking distance'.

The chart shows the thinking and braking distances for medium-sized cars with 60 percent efficient brakes and 80 percent efficient brakes, travelling at speeds of 30, 50 and 70 mph.

The efficiency of properly adjusted brakes, in good condition, should be at least 80 percent, but in order to obtain the equivalent stopping distances the tyre must provide an adequate grip on the road. If the surface is slippery the stopping distances that can actually be obtained are much greater than those shown on the chart. Locking the wheels does not shorten the braking distance.

It is often difficult to judge the slipperiness of a road surface from its appearance. The only safe rule is to use the brakes cautiously under wet or icy conditions.

BRAKING EFFICIENCY

Gravitational acceleration "g" can be used as the standard for brake efficiency. If a vehicle on a level road was decelerated by the brakes at the rate of 9.81 m/s^2, the braking efficiency is said to be 100 percent.

100 percent brake efficiency = deceleration at the rate of "g"

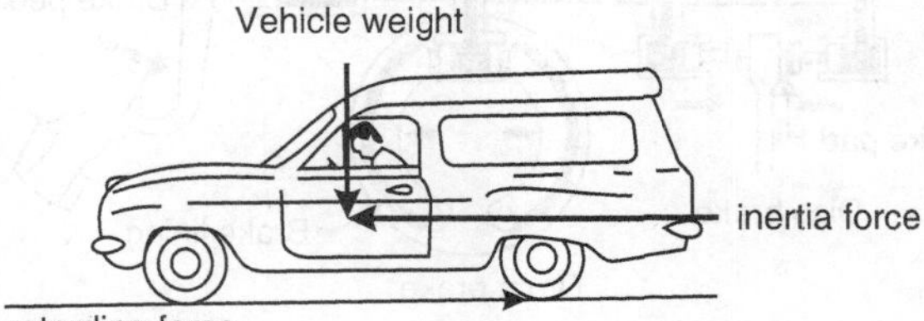

Fig. 14.9 100 percent brake efficiency

To produce an efficiency of 100 percent, the brakes must give, at the road surface, a retarding force equal to the total weight of the vehicle as shown in Fig. 14.9. This would require a coefficient of friction between the tyre and road of 1.0. Since this friction value is far above the average, an efficiency higher than 90 percent is seldom achieved.

100 percent brake efficiency = brakes apply a retarding force equal to the total weight of the vehicle including its load

Statutory regulations specify the minimum efficiency for each type of vehicle, e.g. a four-wheeled car: foot brake 50 percent, and hand brake 25 percent.

WEIGHT TRANSFER DURING BRAKING

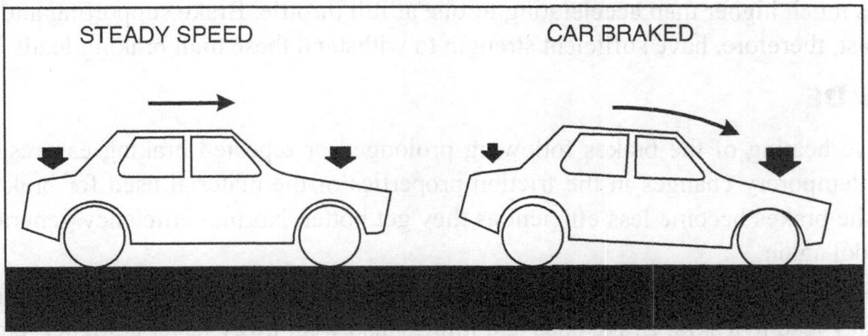

A car travelling at a steady speed has its weight distributed fairly evenly

When the car is braked, weight is transferred forwards, pushing down on the front wheels

Fig. 14.10 Weight transfer during braking

During braking, the weight of the vehicle components transfers forward. On a rear-wheel drive car, about 70 percent of weight ends up on the front. On a front-wheel drive car, as much as 90 percent of the car weight ends up on the front during heavy braking. Due to weight transfer, the ratio of braking effect at the front and at the rear wheels should be minimum of 60% at front and 40% at rear.

This 60/40 apportionment is chosen for safety reasons because it ensures that under maximum braking the front wheels do not lock up before the rear. The vehicle's momentum and weight combine to cause the rear wheels to lift and the front wheels to be forced down. This is why front brake systems are more efficient and larger than rear brake system. The 60/40 ratio can be achieved by using more effective brakes at the front as follows:

- disc brakes at the front and low capacity drum brakes at the rear.
- twin-leading shoe type drum brakes at the front and leading-and-trailing shoe type drum brakes at the rear.
- larger area wheel cylinders at the front.
- larger diameter drums or discs at the front.

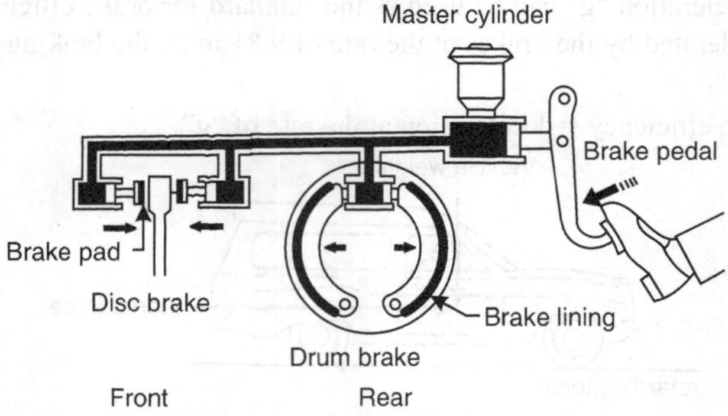

Fig. 14.11 Common arrangement of brakes

As disc brakes are more efficient than drum brakes, disc brakes are mostly used at the front and drum brakes are used at the rear as show in Fig. 14.11. This is the most common arrangement in present day cars.

BRAKING TORQUE

The braking torque is the twisting action caused by the drum or disc on the shoes or caliper anchors during the application of brakes. The amount of torque is determined by the effective axle height and stopping force between the tyre and road surface.

Brake torque on the front wheels is absorbed by the knuckle and suspension control arm. In rear, it is absorbed by the axle housing and the leaf spring or control arm. Braking torque during an emergency stop is much higher than accelerating torque at full throttle. Brake supporting and anchoring members must, therefore, have sufficient strength to withstand these high braking loads.

BRAKE-FADE

Excessive heating of the brakes following prolonged or repeated braking can result in fade. Heat causes temporary changes in the friction properties of the material used for brake pads and linings and the brakes become less efficient as they get hotter. Normal efficiency generally returns when they cool again.

If one brake goes on harder than the others, it may fade much sooner and cause uneven braking, which may lead to a skid. Brake pads and linings also wear away faster at higher temperatures.

ENGINE BRAKING

Engine braking is a method of braking a vehicle without using the foot brake. This method uses the rotational resistance of the engine to help reduce the vehicle's speed.

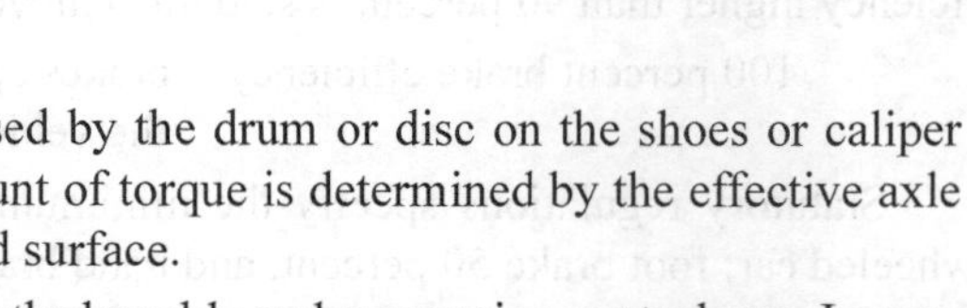

Fig. 14.12 Engine braking

For example, on a steep downhill slope, when the accelerator pedal is released with the transmission engaged, the drive wheels continue to turn, forcing the engine (i.e. crankshaft) to turn, even though no fuel is being supplied to the cylinders. However, the crankshaft resists turning due to the resistance of the air being compressed in the cylinders, friction between moving parts, etc. The drive wheels therefore turn more slowly, causing the vehicles to slow down.

Furthermore, the lower the gear, the faster the crankshaft turns at the same vehicle speed. And since the crankshaft's resistance to rotation is higher at higher engine speeds (when no fuel is being supplied), the engine's braking force increases with the lower gear.

TYPES OF BRAKES

Brakes that are used on motor vehicles can be grouped into several types depending on their purpose.

1. The service brakes, operated by a foot pedal, which slow or stop the vehicle.
2. The parking brakes, operated by a foot pedal or hand lever, which hold the vehicle stationary when applied.
3. Auxiliary brakes are used in combination with the ordinary service brakes by diesel trucks and other heavy-duty vehicles.

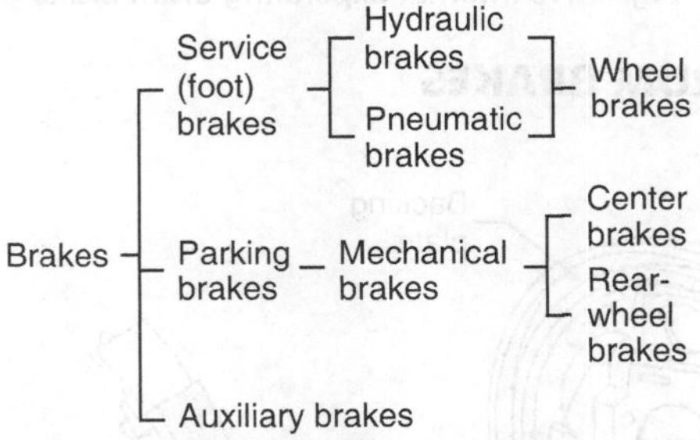

SERVICE BRAKES (or FOOT BRAKES or FOUNDATION BRAKES)

Different types of service brake system are used in different vehicles, depending on the application:

- Mechanical brakes
- Hydraulic brakes
- Air brakes

Most automotive service brakes are hydraulic brakes. Dual-circuit hydraulic brake systems are used in passenger cars and small commercial vehicles up to 7.5t. Combined disc/drum brakes or just disc brakes are usually used.

The service or foundation brakes on many medium and heavy-duty trucks and buses are operated by air pressure (pneumatic). These are air brakes.

All these braking systems depend on friction between moving parts and stationary parts for their stopping force.

There are two main types of service brake: drum brake and disc brake.

DRUM BRAKE

So if disc brakes are so great, how come we still have cars with drum brakes? The reason is cost. While all vehicles produced for many years have disc brakes on the front, drum brakes are cheaper to produce for the rear wheels. The main reason is the parking brake system. On drum brakes, adding a parking brake is the simple addition of a lever, while on disc brakes, need a complete mechanism, in some cases, a complete mechanical drum brake assembly inside the disc brake rotor.

In a drum brake, braking power is obtained by causing non-rotating shoes to be pushed (by a cam in mechanical brakes or hydraulic pressure in hydraulic brakes or compressed air in air brakes) against the inner surface of a drum that rotates together with the wheel. When the pressure is released, return springs pull the shoes back to their rest position.

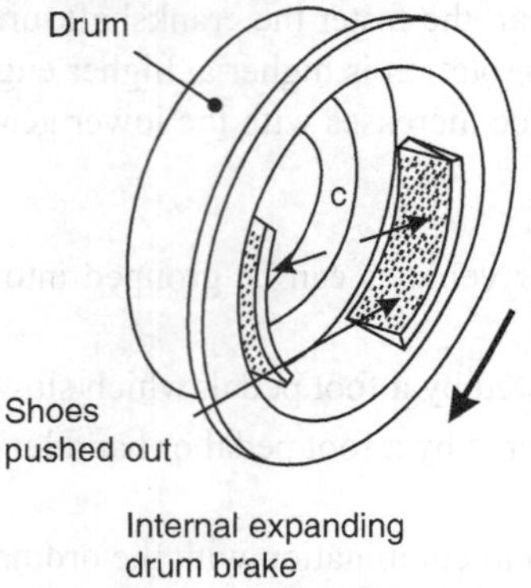

Fig. 14.13 Internal expanding drum brake

COMPONENTS OF DRUM BRAKES

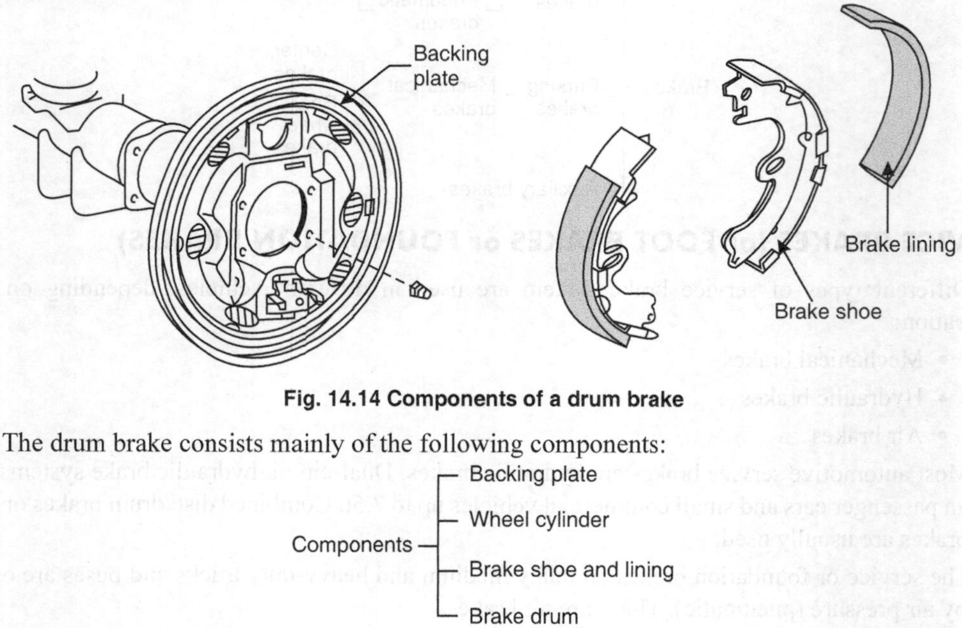

Fig. 14.14 Components of a drum brake

The drum brake consists mainly of the following components:

Components
- Backing plate
- Wheel cylinder
- Brake shoe and lining
- Brake drum

Backing plate

The backing plate is a pressed steel plate bolted to the rear axle housing or rear axle carrier. Since the brake shoes are fitted to the backing plate, all of the braking force acts on the backing plate.

Wheel cylinder

The wheel cylinder is used to expand the brake shoes against the brake drum. One or two wheel cylinders are used for each wheel. Some systems have two pistons (operated by hydraulic pressure) to operate two shoes, one at each side of the wheel cylinder, while other systems have only one piston to operate only one shoe.

Brake shoe and brake lining

The brake shoe is semi-circular in shape. Brake shoes are usually made of steel plates. The brake lining is attached to the shoe by rivets (on large vehicles) or by adhesives (on small vehicles). The material used for lining must have the following qualities:

- Good frictional properties
- Wear resistance
- Heat resistance

Linings were once largely made of asbestos, but the health risks associated with this substance have brought about its replacement with synthetic materials.

Brake drum

The brake drum is generally made of gray cast iron. It is positioned very close to the brake shoe without actually touching it and rotates with the wheel. As the lining is pushed against the inner surface of the drum when the brake is applied, friction heat can reach as high as 200°C to 300°C.

SELF-ENERGIZING ACTION

In the drum type brake, braking power is obtained by causing non-rotating shoes to be pushed against the inner surface of a drum that rotates together with the wheel. There are two types of brake shoe: the leading (primary) shoe and the trailing (secondary) shoe. The shoe facing the front of the vehicle is called the leading shoe and the shoe facing the rear of the vehicle is called the trailing shoe.

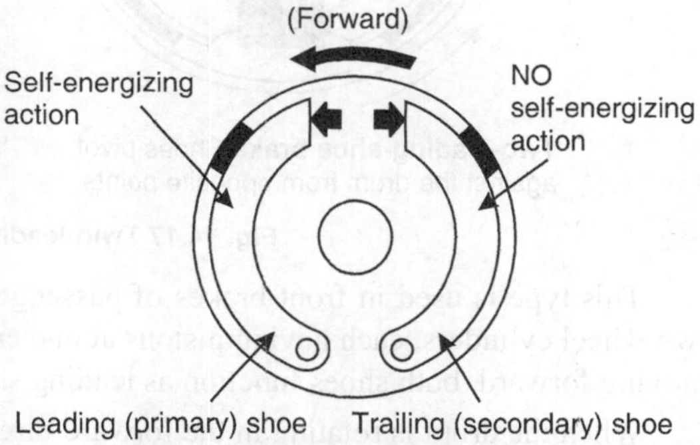

Fig. 14.15 Self-energizing action

The action of the drum, in which it tries to force the leading shoe to rotate with it, is called self-energizing or self-servo action. Self-energizing action creates a greater braking force results from a relatively small pedal effort. Although leading shoes provide more braking power, there is a disadvantage to this in that they wear faster than trailing shoe.

TYPES OF DRUM BRAKES

Leading-and-trailing shoe type

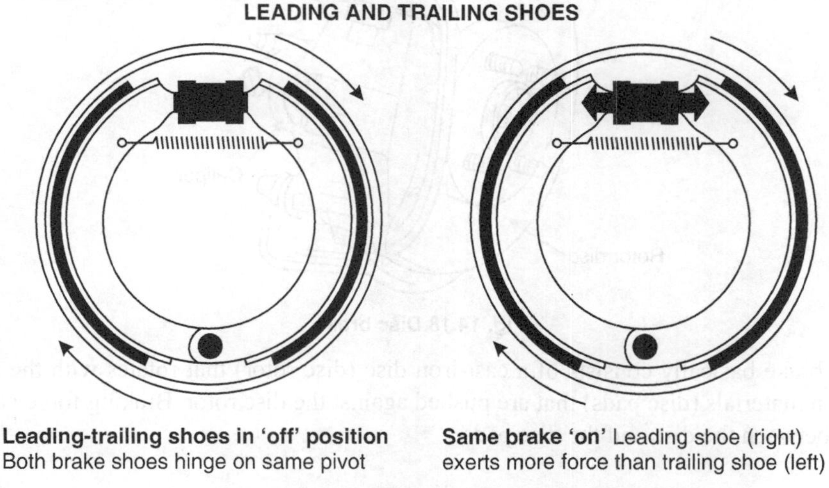

Fig. 14.16 Leading-and-trailing shoe drum brake

In this design, both shoes pivot about the same point and a single expander unit is employed to force the other ends of the shoes in an outward direction with the shoes being applied in opposite directions.

The leading shoe wears faster than the trailing shoe because of the self-energizing action. This type is used in the rear brakes of passenger cars and small commercial vehicles.

Twin-leading shoe type

TWIN LEADING SHOES

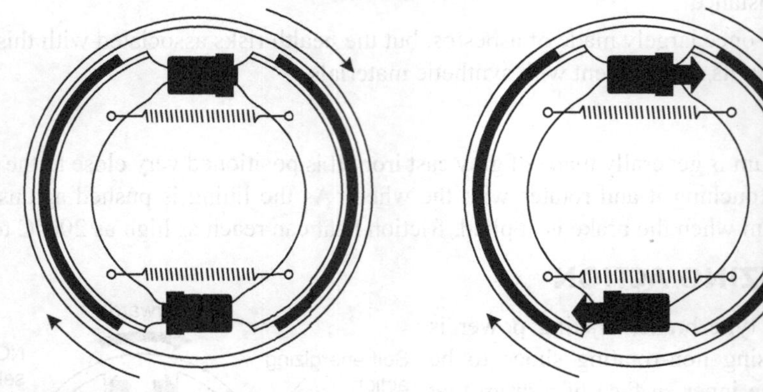

Two-leading-shoe brake Shoes pivot against the drum from opposite points

Same brake 'on' Both shoes are leading. so they exert equal force

Fig. 14.17 Twin-leading shoe drum brake

This type is used in front brakes of passenger cars and commercial vehicles. This design has two wheel cylinders, each having pistons at one end. When the brake is applied when the vehicle is moving forward, both shoes function as leading shoes.

When the drum is rotating in the forward direction, this type exerts a high braking force. However, a disadvantage of this type is that when the drum rotates in the opposite direction (reversing the car), both shoes work as trailing shoes exerting only a small braking force.

DISC BRAKE

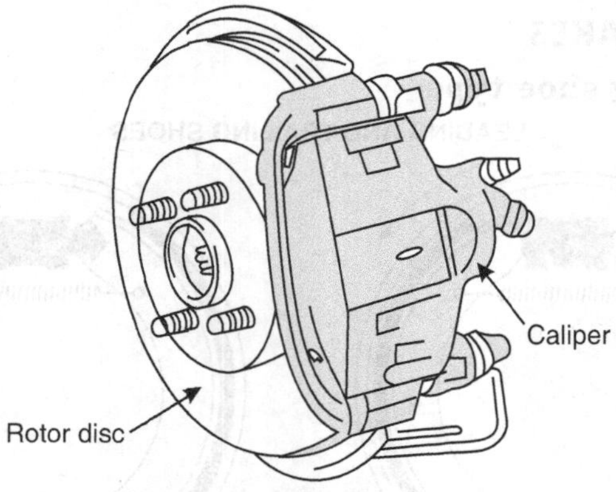

Fig. 14.18 Disc brake

A disc brake basically consists of a cast-iron disc (disc rotor) that rotates with the wheel and fixed friction materials (disc pads) that are pushed against the disc rotor. Braking force is generated by friction between the disc and the disc pads.

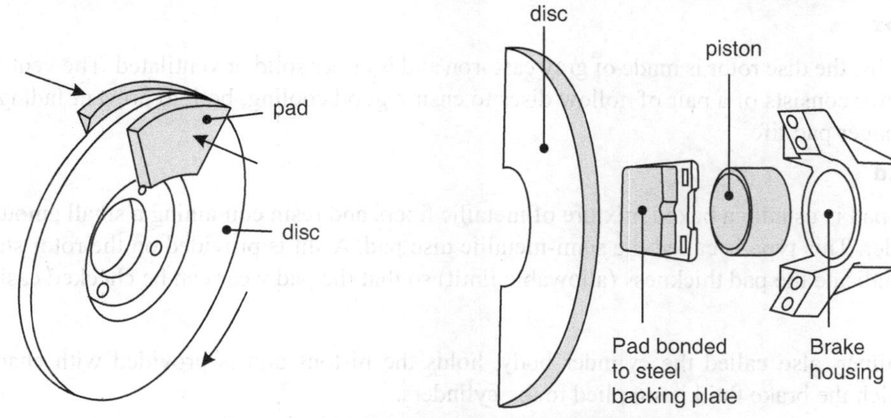

Fig. 14.19 Components of a disc brake

Advantages & disadvantages over drum brakes

The disc brake has the following disadvantages over drum brakes:

- Not as effective at slow speed.
- Needs more pressure to work effectively.
- Size of the disc pad is limited.
- Pads wear faster than drum brake shoe lining.

However, the disc brake has many advantages:

- Has the same stopping power in forward or reverse.
- Has progressive action. The greater the effort applied to the pedal the more effective the brake will be.
- Self-adjusting.
- High braking efficiency.
- High stability.
- Because the friction surface is constantly exposed to the air, good heat radiation is ensured. This minimizes fading.
- Good water recovery. Water that splashes onto the discs can be removed by centrifugal force.
- Simpler design facilitates easy maintenance and pad replacement.

COMPONENTS OF DISC BRAKES

A disc brake basically consists of a cast-iron disc (disc rotor), brake pads and caliper.

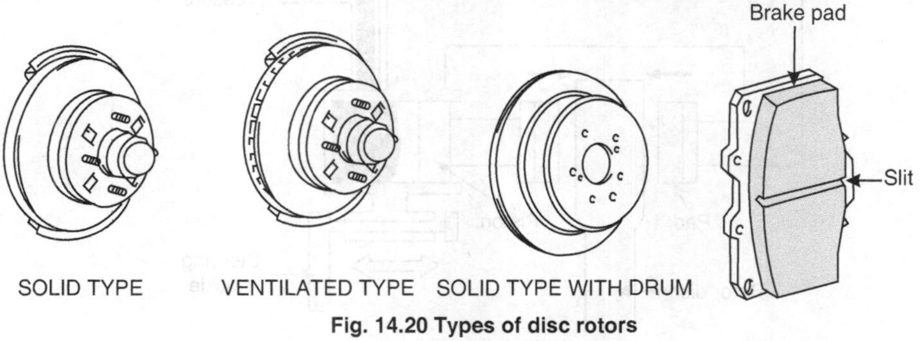

Fig. 14.20 Types of disc rotors

Disc rotor

Generally, the disc rotor is made of gray cast iron and is either solid or ventilated. The ventilated type disc rotor consists of a pair of hollow discs to ensure good cooling, both to prevent fading and to ensure longer pad life.

Brake pad

A disc pad is usually a baked mixture of metallic fibers and resin containing a small amount of metal powder. This type is called the semi-metallic disc pad. A slit is provided on the rotor side of the pad to indicate the pad thickness (allowable limit) so that the pad wear can be checked easily.

Caliper

The caliper, also called the cylinder body, holds the pistons and is provided with channels through which the brake fluid is supplied to the cylinders.

Calipers are grouped into the following types by the way in which they are installed: Fixed caliper type and floating caliper type.

Fixed caliper type

The caliper is fixed to the axle or strut. As illustrated in Fig.14.21, the fixed caliper is provided with a pair of pistons. Braking force is obtained when the pads are pushed hydraulically by the piston against both ends of the disc rotor.

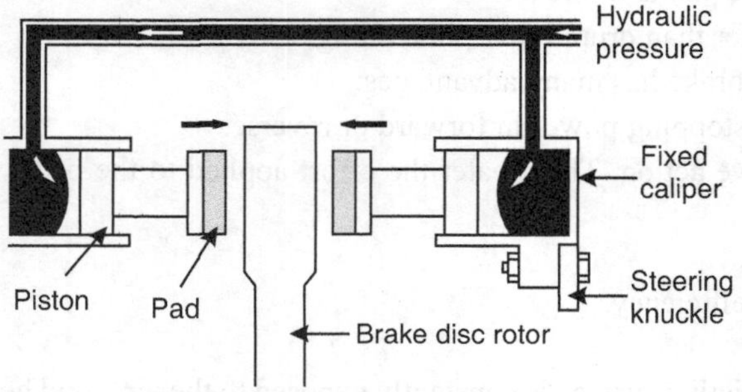

Fig. 14.21 Fixed caliper type

The fixed caliper is the most basic design and ensures accurate operation. However, it requires a large number of components. For this reason, the fixed caliper type disc brakes are used only for some high performance models today.

Floating caliper type

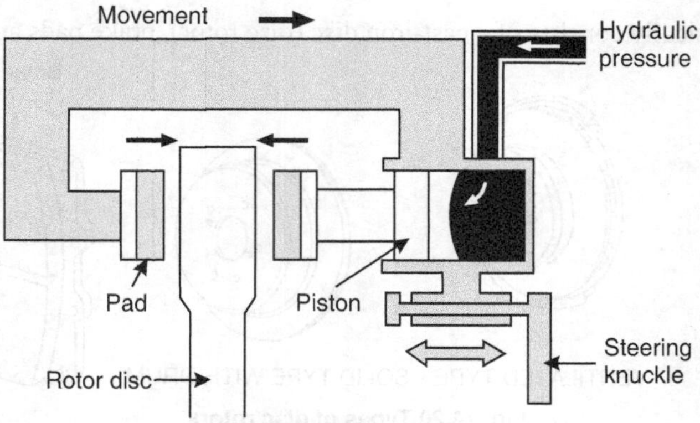

Fig. 14.22 Floating caliper type

As illustrated in Fig. 14.22, the piston is located in one side of the caliper only. Hydraulic pressure from the master cylinder pushes the piston (force A) and thus presses the pads against the disc rotor. At the same time equal hydraulic pressure (reaction force B) acts on the bottom of the cylinder. This causes the caliper to move to the right and presses the pad located opposite the piston against the disc rotor to exert braking force.

MECHANICAL BRAKING SYSTEM

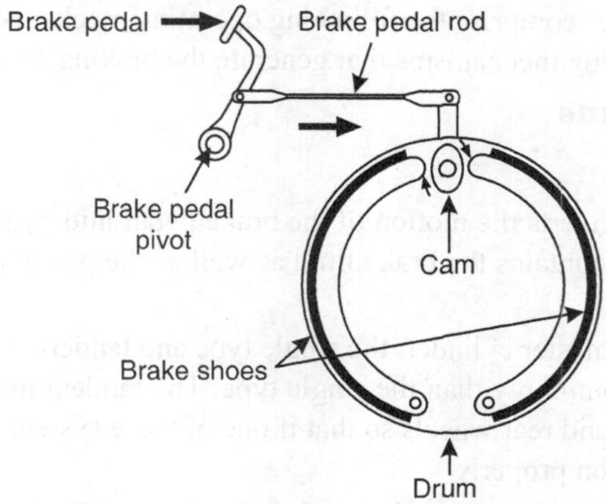

Fig. 14.23 Mechanical braking system

Brakes systems operated purely mechanically are usually limited today to the parking brakes on vehicles fitted with a hydraulic brake system or the service brakes of lightweight and medium-weight motorcycles and single-axle trailers.

The efficiency of a mechanical brake system is low (in the region of 50%). In cold, wet weather or frost, the actuating linkage may freeze and impair operation of the brakes. The brake cables are wires passing over rollers or moving within a metal outer sheath. To reduce friction and prevent icing up, the outer cables are packed with grease. Screw adjusters are provided for accurate brake adjustment.

Brake equalization between the left and right wheels on an axle can be ensured by incorporating a balance beam in the linkage or by means of a pulley.

Lengthy brake rods must be guided halfway along to avoid vibration or buckling. The linkage can be arranged to generate additional force by incorporating levers at the appropriate points.

The rod or linkage is connected to pivots on the brake back plates. In contrast to wire cables, no equalization is possible nor can wear be compensated for by means of screw adjusters.

HYDRAULIC BRAKE SYSTEM

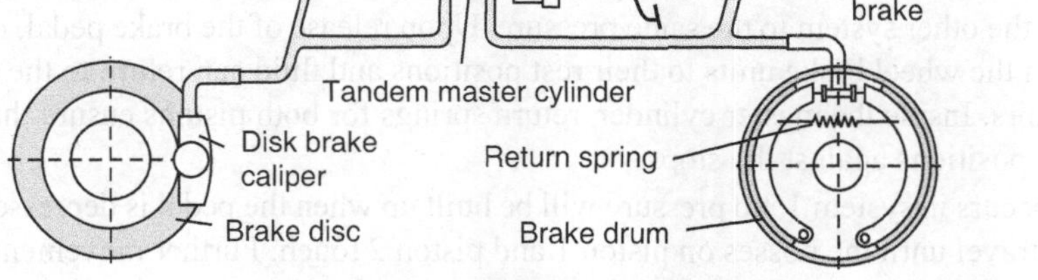

Fig. 14.24 Hydraulic braking system

Fluid is not compressible. Any effort applied at one place will be transmitted without loss of pressure or movement anywhere in the system. So the hydraulic brakes can respond much faster than other types and are simpler in design. Hydraulic brakes also have superior design flexibility. Due to these advantages, hydraulic brakes are most commonly used with passenger cars and light-duty trucks today.

Hydraulic service brakes comprise the following operating mechanisms that transmit the brake applying force and the braking mechanisms that generate the braking force.

Operating mechanisms

Master cylinder

The master cylinder converts the motion of the brake pedal into hydraulic pressure. It consists of the reservoir tank which contains the brake fluid as well as the piston and cylinder which generates the hydraulic pressure.

There are two types of master cylinder: the single type and tandem type. The tandem type master cylinder is used more commonly than the single type. The tandem master cylinder has separate hydraulic systems for front and rear wheels so that if one of these systems becomes inoperative, the other system can still function properly.

The tandem master cylinder is basically two single master cylinders mounted end-to-end and operated by the same pushrod. The cylinder contains two pistons, dividing it into two chambers. The first piston is operated by the brake pedal and a push rod. The second piston is normally operated by the fluid pressure created by the first.

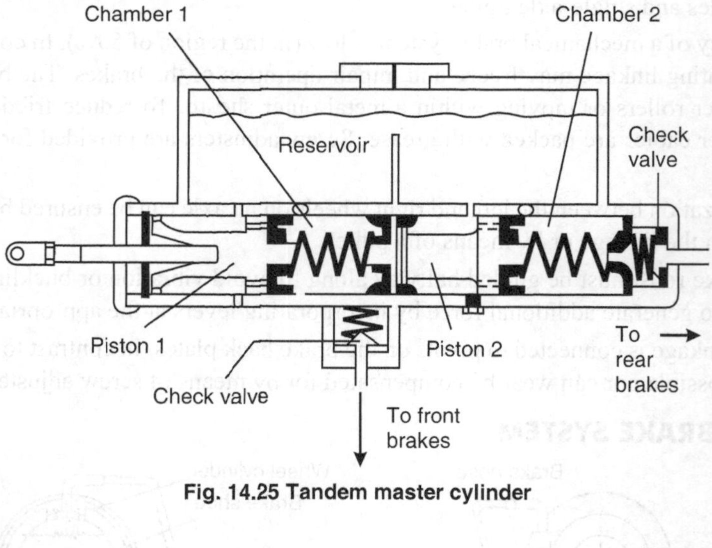

Fig. 14.25 Tandem master cylinder

Operation

Two reservoirs or one divided, supply fluid through ports to each half of the master cylinder. Separate reserves of brake fluid keep one system operating if the other drains away.

When the brake pedal is depressed, the fluid in chamber 1 becomes pressurized and moves fluid into the first system. At the same time, this pressure also moves piston 2 and pressurizes the fluid in chamber 2 and the other system to the same pressure. Upon release of the brake pedal, return springs and seals return the wheel brake units to their rest positions and fluid can return to the master cylinder and reservoirs. Inside the master cylinder, return springs for both pistons ensure that they return to their correct positions against the stops.

If failure occurs in system 1, no pressure will be built up when the pedal is depressed. There will be extra pedal travel until the bosses on piston 1 and piston 2 touch. Further movement of the brake pedal will pressurize system 2 in the normal way.

Failure of system 2 also results in extra pedal travel until piston 2 reaches the limit of its travel. From then on chamber 1 is pressurized by piston 1 in the usual way.

Wheel cylinder (Slave cylinder)

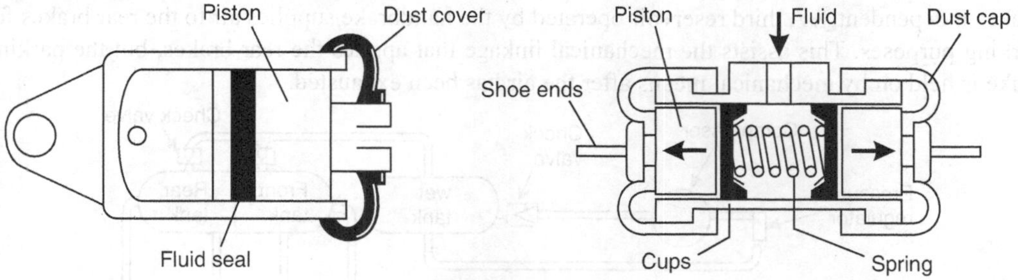

Fig. 14.26 Wheel cylinder

These are sometimes called expanders or actuators. It is the purpose of the wheel cylinder pistons to force the brake shoes into contact with the brake drum. There are detail differences, but all of them work on the same principle.

The wheel cylinder consists of a cylindrical casting made from cast iron or aluminium alloy. It is rigidly attached to the back plate, but is sometimes free to slide slightly to centralize its position.

There are two basic types: single acting and double acting. Internally both have a machined bore, but in a single-acting cylinder one end is blind and contains only one piston. A double-acting cylinder is open at both ends and contains two pistons separated by a spring. The pistons are free to move inside the cylinder.

Rubber cups or seals are fitted to each piston to prevent fluid from leaking out of the system. Correct fitting is essential to avoid brake failure.

AIR (PNEUMATIC) BRAKE SYSTEM

Most heavy commercial vehicles now use air operated brakes. In this system compressed air (around 7 bar) is used to actuate the brake mechanism. Air pressure from the compressor is transmitted through pipes equally in all directions, in exactly the same way as fluid pressure in a hydraulic system. The actuation of each brake is similar to the simple cam brake through diaphragm in the brake chamber.

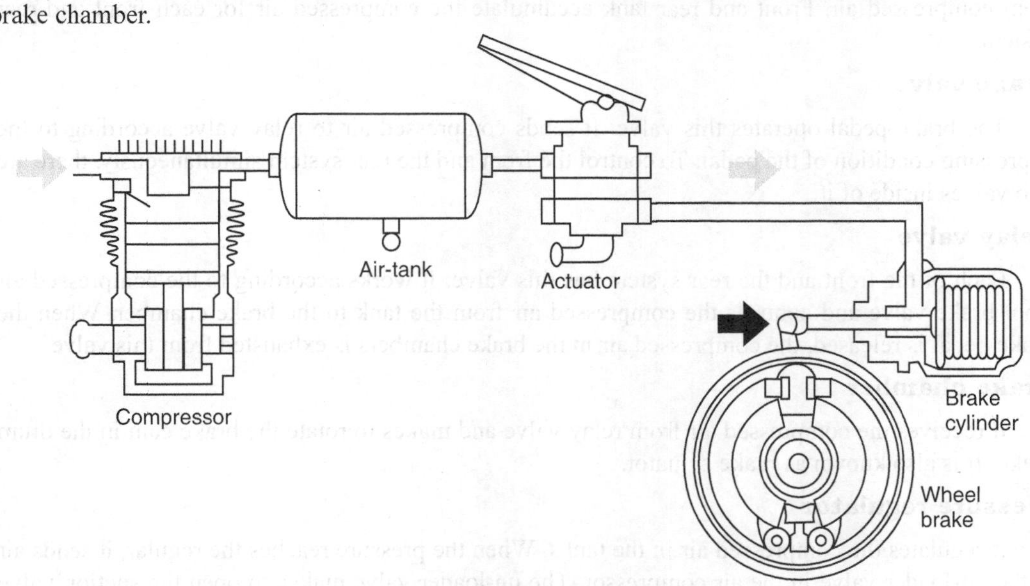

Fig. 14.27 Air braking system

Split system

This is used mainly on rigid vehicles. The main system is divided into two separate circuits. A dual foot valve is used to supply and control air from two separate reservoirs to the front and rear brakes independently. A third reservoir operated by the handbrake supplies air to the rear brakes for parking purposes. This assists the mechanical linkage that applies the rear brakes, but the parking brake is held on by mechanical means after the air has been exhausted.

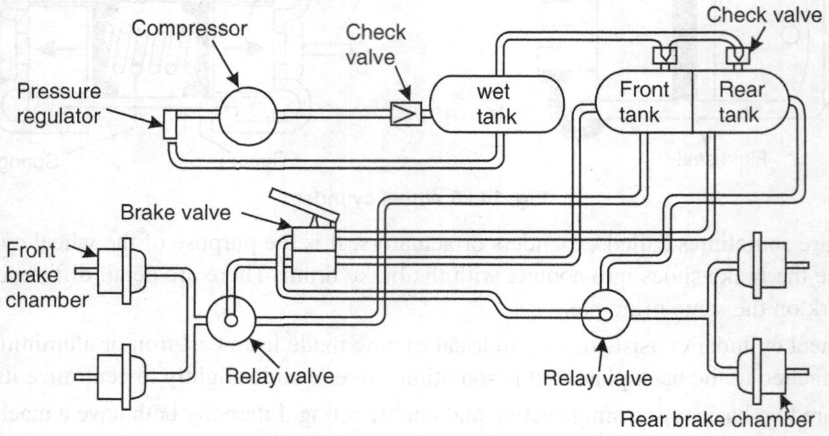

Fig. 14.28 Air braking system (split system)

The whole structure is like the Fig. 14.28. Front and rear systems work separately. In the case of there is leakage in one system, the other system works for safety.

Components

Air compressor

The compressor is a piston type driven by the engine or in some cases, the gearbox. It supplies air under pressure (7 bar) to a reservoir tank for storage.

Air tank

There are 3 kinds of tanks, wet tank, front tank and rear tank. Wet tank is to remove moisture from compressed air. Front and rear tank accumulate the compressed air for each front and rear system.

Brake valve

The brake pedal operates this valve. It sends compressed air to relay valve according to the depressing condition of the pedal. To control the front and the rear system simultaneously, there are two valves inside of it.

Relay valve

Each of the front and the rear system has this valve. It works according to the compressed air from brake valve and controls the compressed air from the tank to the brake chamber. When the brake pedal is released, the compressed air in the brake chambers is exhausted from this valve.

Brake chamber

It receives the compressed air from relay valve and makes to rotate the brake cam in the drum brake. It is also known as brake actuator.

Pressure regulator

It regulates the compressed air in the tanks. When the pressure reaches the regular, it sends air to the un-loader valve in the air compressor. The un-loader valve makes to open the suction valve to stop the compression.

Operation

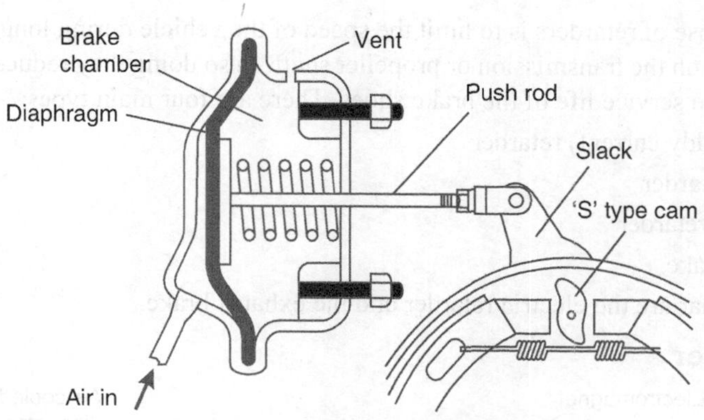

Fig. 14.29 Single-diaphragm chamber

The brake valve, which is operated by the driver's foot pedal, allows the compressed air to travel from the reservoir to the diaphragm in the brake chamber at each wheel. The valve is designed to permit controlled application of the brakes. The brake chambers are fitted with a movable diaphragm, which operates a rod connected to the brake shoe operating mechanism. The admission of air pressure to the diaphragm in the brake chamber moves the diaphragm and linkage to apply the brake. A quick-release valve is used to speed up the release of air pressure to the atmosphere once the brakes have been released. A relay valve speeds up the application and release of the rear brakes.

SERVO BRAKE

One problem that vehicle manufacturers have is that drivers are of different strength. It is impossible to make an effective braking system that can be operated with ease by everybody. As a driver can exert only a limited amount of force on the brake pedal, a means of power assistance is required that will enhance that effort. This is usually supplied by the servo. A servo mechanism fitted to the braking system reduces the physical effort the driver has to use on the brake pedal.

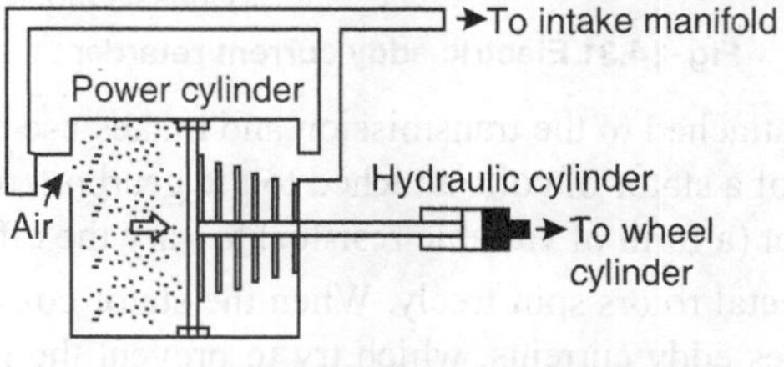

Fig. 14.30 Principle of brake booster

The servo cylinder contains a diaphragm. When air is exhausted from one end of the cylinder and atmospheric pressure is admitted to the other end, the difference in the pressures on the two sides of the diaphragm can be used to help the driver to apply the brakes. The amount of servo assistance increases with the physical force used on the pedal.

All servo units are powered by the engine. The more common type of servo uses the partial vacuum in the inlet manifold. Others have a separate vacuum pump.

In one simple arrangement, the engine exhausts air from both sides of a diaphragm which is held in a state of balance until the brake pedal is used. This admits atmospheric pressure on one side, while a partial vacuum remains at the other side. As a result, the diaphragm moves, applying force to a slave piston, which then adds to the pressure applied by the driver.

If the servo fails for any reason, the driver can still apply the brakes, but the pedal effort required is greatly increased.

RETARDER

The main purpose of retarders is to limit the speed of the vehicle during long descents by proving a braking action on the transmission or propeller shaft. In so doing they reduce the risks of brake fade and increase the service life of the brake shoes. There are four main types:

1. Electric (eddy current) retarder
2. Friction retarder
3. Hydraulic retarder
4. Exhaust brake

The most popular are the electric retarder and the exhaust brake.

Electric retarder

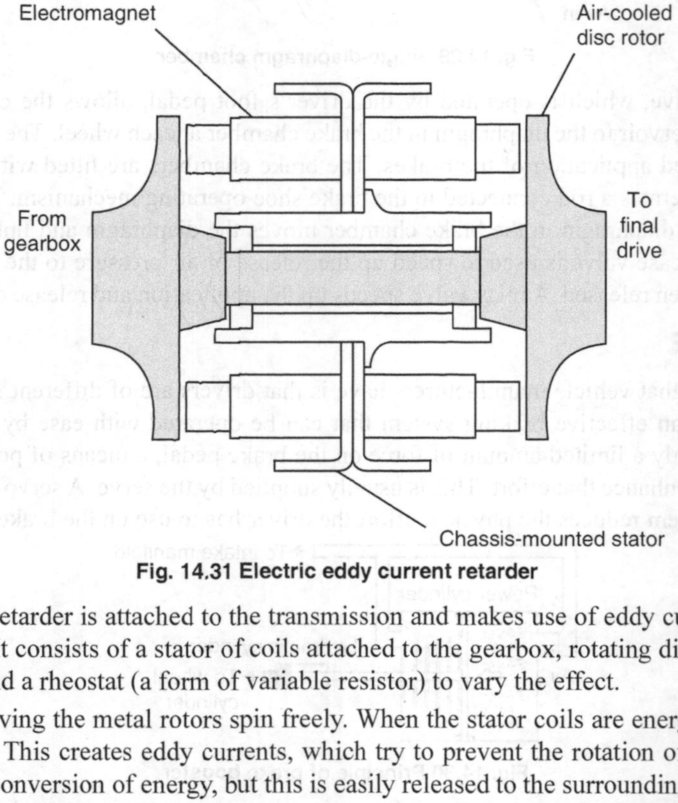

Fig. 14.31 Electric eddy current retarder

The electric retarder is attached to the transmission and makes use of eddy currents created by a magnetic field. It consists of a stator of coils attached to the gearbox, rotating disc rotors attached to the driveline and a rheostat (a form of variable resistor) to vary the effect.

In normal driving the metal rotors spin freely. When the stator coils are energized, a magnetic field is produced. This creates eddy currents, which try to prevent the rotation of the rotors. They heat up from the conversion of energy, but this is easily released to the surrounding air. The braking effect depends on the current flow to the stator and this is varied by the rheostat control.

Hydraulic retarder

Some hydraulic retarders used with automatic transmissions are mounted between the torque converter and the range gear housing assembly. The hydraulic retarder acts as a braking device. A rotor in the hydraulic retarder rotates within a stationary, vaned stator housing. The rotor is an integral part of the torque converter output shaft. Since the rotor is the only moving part in the hydraulic retarder and the rotor does not contact the vaned housing, there is very little wear on these components. There are no adjustments required on the hydraulic retarder. A foot pedal switch or a hand-operated valve is used to activate the hydraulic retarder. The amount of hydraulic braking is directly proportional to the movement of the hand-operated valve or foot pedal switch.

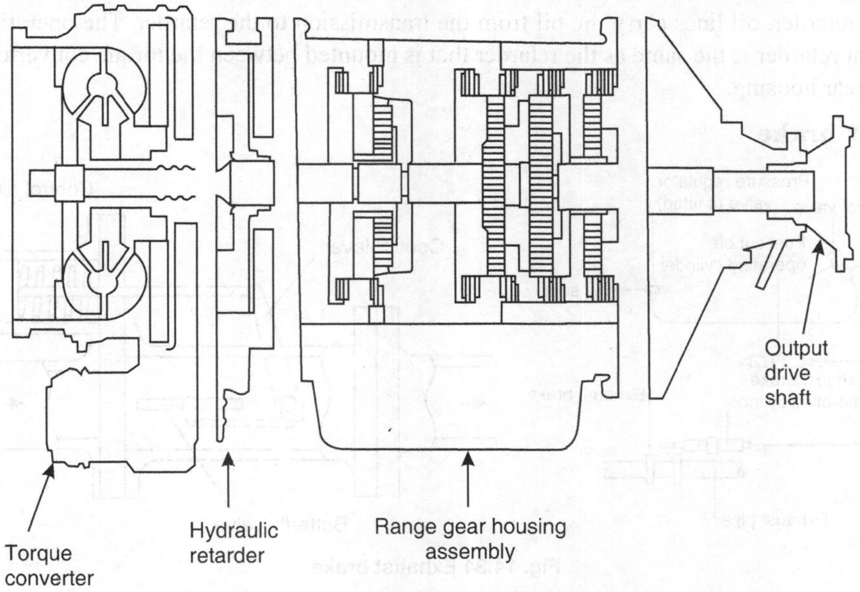

Fig. 14.32 Mounting of a hydraulic retarder

Operation

When the hand-operated valve or foot pedal is in the "OFF" position, there is no oil in the retarder housing. Therefore, the rotor turns freely, and the retarder has no effect.

Depressing the foot pedal or moving the hand-operated lever moves a control valve that allows transmission oil to flow from the transmission pump into the hydraulic retarder housing. This oil in the hydraulic retarder housing is under pressure. Since the rotor is turning with the torque converter output shaft, the rotor vanes are forced through the pressurized oil. This action of forcing the rotor vanes through the pressurized oil works against the rotor rotation. Under this condition the rotation of the rotor is slowed, and this provides braking power to the driving wheels.

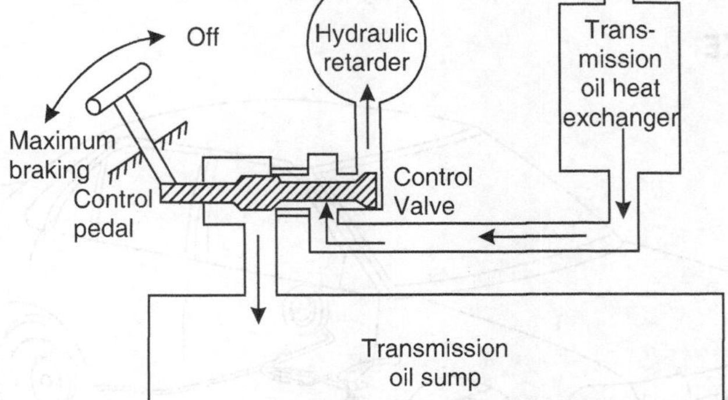

Fig. 14.33 Oil flow through a hydraulic retarder

The rotor pumping action moves oil from the hydraulic retarder to the transmission heat exchanger to cool the oil. Heat is dissipated from the transmission heat exchanger into the engine cooling system.

A mid-mount hydraulic retarder is used in some applications. In this type of hydraulic retarder, the retarder is mounted on the transmission output shaft external to the transmission. In a mid-mount hydraulic retarder, oil lines carry the oil from the transmission to the retarder. The operation of the mid-mount retarder is the same as the retarder that is mounted between the torque converter and the range of gear housing.

Exhaust brake

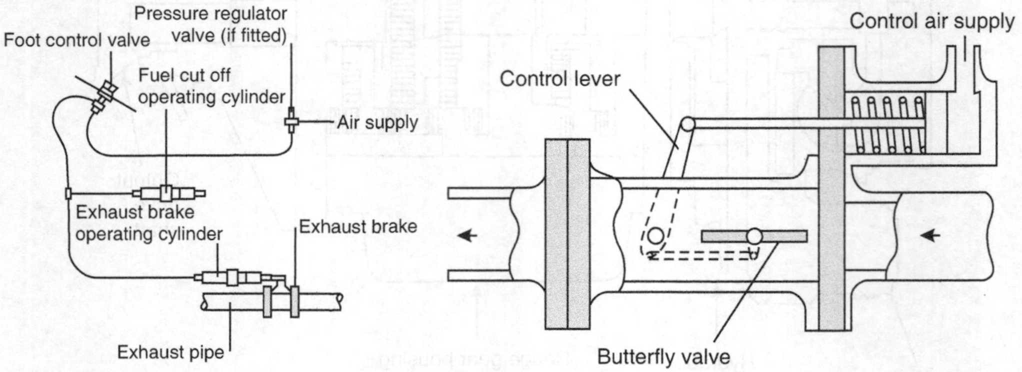

Fig. 14.34 Exhaust brake

Exhaust brakes were first introduced in about 1910. The function of an exhaust brake is to increase engine's natural braking effect. This is achieved by blocking off the exhaust system and turning the engine into a low-pressure single-stage compressor.

There are many ways of bringing the system into operation but basically a butterfly valve or sliding vane valve, electrically or air-operated, closes the exhaust pipe between the engine manifold and silencer. When this valve is closed the fuel supply to the combustion chambers is also cut off.

Pressure builds up as air is pushed into the closed-off manifold. When the air has built up sufficient pressure, it is strong enough to overcome the exhaust valve springs and force its way back into the cylinder. Good seals are necessary on the exhaust system flanges because the pressure can build up to around 3.5 bar. Maximum working pressure is the pressure required to overcome the exhaust valve springs sufficiently to allow this flow back of air. The piston is therefore working against this air pressure on every compression and exhaust stroke. When at working pressure sufficient new air is drawn in through the inlet valve to replenish any air lost through leakage.

PARKING BRAKE

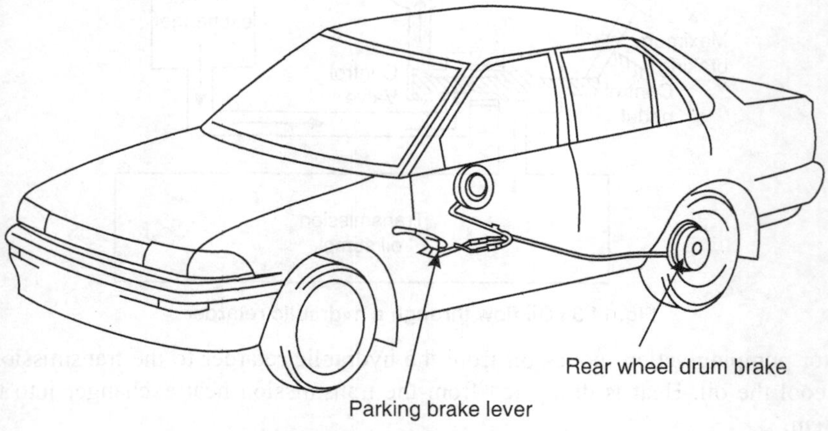

Fig. 14.35 Rear wheel drum type parking brake

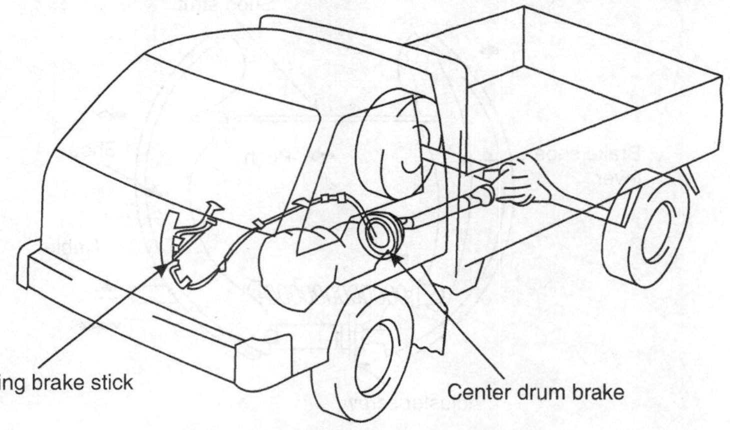

Fig. 14.36 Center drum type parking brake

Parking brakes are mainly used for parking the vehicle. Passenger cars and small commercial vehicles have rear wheel type parking brakes that share the brake drums of the service brakes (foot brakes), or exclusive parking brakes that are connected to the rear wheels. Large commercial vehicles use the center brake type parking brakes that are fitted between the propeller shaft and the transmission.

Operating mechanisms

A parking brake system consists of a parking lever, cable or rod type operating mechanism and the brake drums or disc rotor and shoe that generate the braking force. Pulling the parking brake lever operates the brakes via a cable connected to the lever.

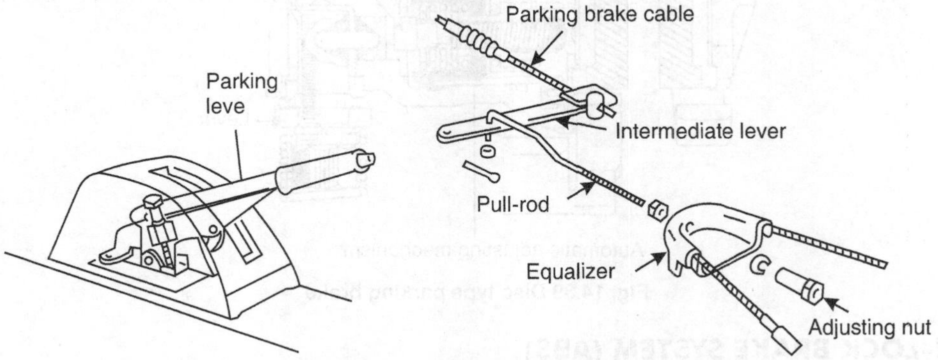

Fig. 14.37 Operating mechanisms of parking brakes

The lever is provided with ratchets to maintain the lever at the position to which it was set.

Intermediate lever, rod and cable

The parking brake cable transmits the lever movement to the brake drum sub-assembly. The intermediate lever is provided to increase the operating force.

Parking brake in vehicles having drum brakes

In this type of parking brake, the brake shoe is expanded by the brake shoe lever and the shoe strut. The parking brake cable is fitted to brake shoe lever, and the operating force of the parking brake lever is transmitted via the parking brake cable to the brake shoe lever.

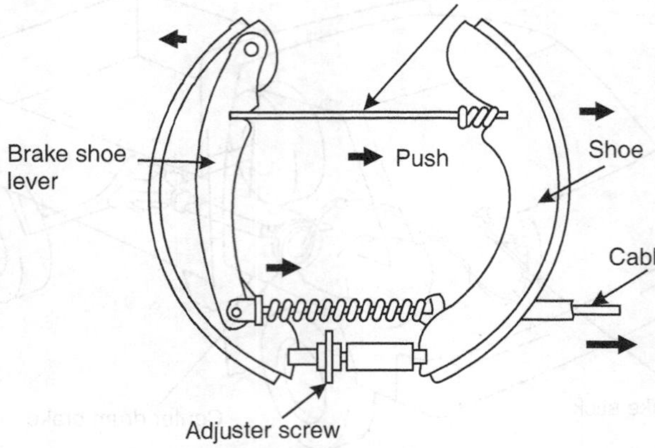

Fig. 14.39 Drum type parking brake

Parking brake in vehicles having disc brakes

In this type of parking brakes, the parking brake mechanism is built into the caliper of the disc brake. As shown in Fig. 14.39, the movement of the lever causes the crank pin to rotate which in turn causes the spindle to move the piston. The pad pressed against the disc rotor as a result.

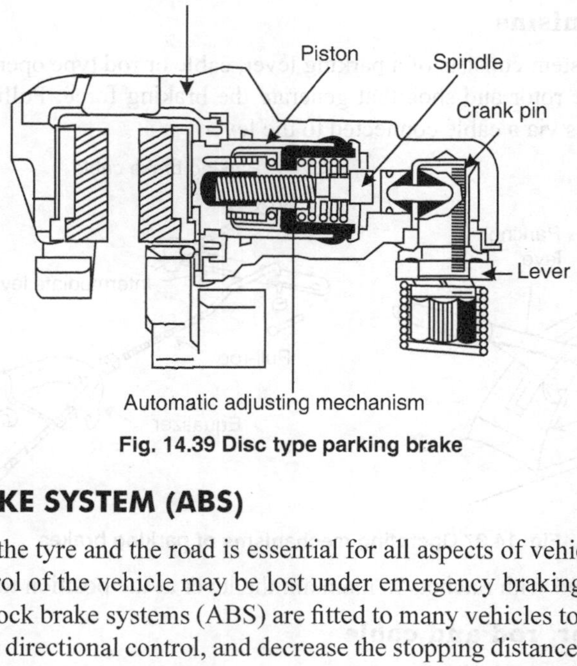

Fig. 14.39 Disc type parking brake

ANTI-LOCK BRAKE SYSTEM (ABS)

Friction between the tyre and the road is essential for all aspects of vehicle control. The brakes may lock up and control of the vehicle may be lost under emergency braking or when the road surface is slippery. Anti-lock brake systems (ABS) are fitted to many vehicles to overcome this danger. Such devices maintain directional control, and decrease the stopping distance in slippery conditions.

Ordinary brakes work to slow or stop a vehicle by utilizing two types of resistance. These are the resistance between the brake pads and discs (or brake shoes and drums) and the resistance between tyres and the road surface. Braking can be controlled in a stable manner if the following relationship between the resistance between the road and tyres exists:

$$\text{Brake system resistance} < \text{Resistance between tyres and road}$$

However, if this relationship is reversed, the tyres will lock up and the vehicle will begin skidding:

Brake system > Resistance between
resistance tyres and road

As a result, if the front wheels lock up, it will become impossible to steer the car. If the rear wheels lock up, the differences in the coefficients of friction (μ) between the left and right sides on the road surface will cause a tail spin to occur.

The ABS controls the hydraulic pressure acting on the wheel cylinders to prevent the wheels from locking up when the brakes are applied on a slippery surface or during panic braking. It also maintains directional stability during braking so that the vehicle can be steered.

Components and operation

The heart of the ABS system is an electronic control unit (ECU) which is provided with inputs from sensors and gives outputs to the controls. The sensors are located at each wheel and send pulse generated signals to the ECU. They indicate whether each wheel is revolving and how fast it is turning. The ECU then controls the output of a hydraulic pump assembly. Based on the input signals from the wheel sensors, the ABS system's ECU knows the speed of each wheel. When the brakes are applied, the wheels and the vehicle start to slow down. The ECU monitors the reducing pulses from each of the wheel sensors. If a wheel seems about to lock up, the ECU reduces the pressure at that wheel until the tyre grips again.

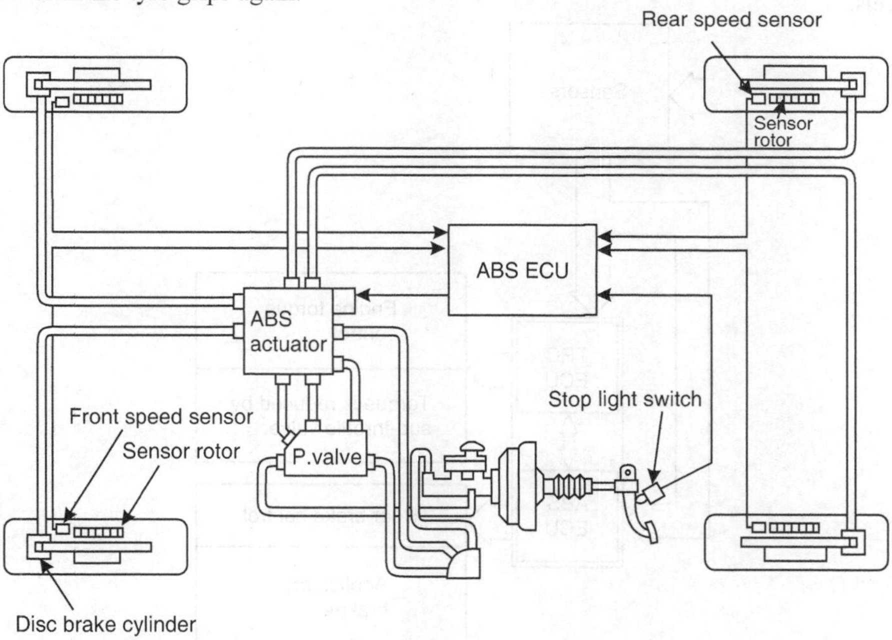

Fig. 14.41 ABS braking system

TRACTION CONTROL SYSTEM (TCS or TRC) or VEHICLE STABILITY ASSIST (VSA) SYSTEM

On roads with a low coefficient of friction (μ), such as snowy, icy or wet roads, the drive wheels spin if the vehicle is started or accelerated quickly, resulting in loss of torque and possibly causing vehicle skidding.

The maximum torque that can be transmitted to the wheels is determined by the coefficient of friction generated between the road and the tyres. If the attempt is made to transmit torque exceeding that level to the wheels, it will become easy for the wheels to spin.

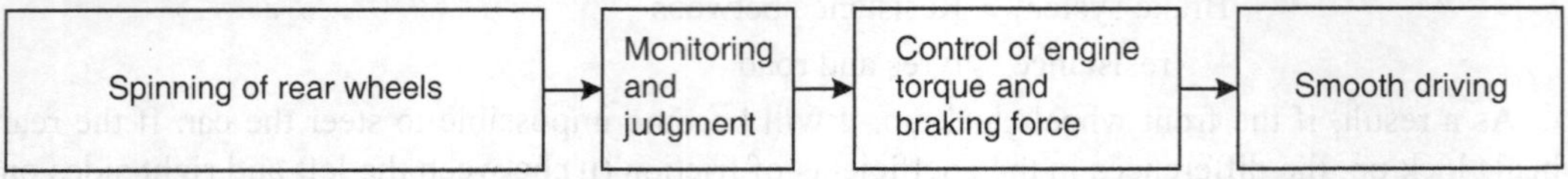

Maintaining the torque at a level appropriate to the coefficient of friction at such times is sometimes difficult for the driver. In most cases, when attempting to start the vehicle quickly, the driver presses the accelerator pedal too hard and the wheels spin, causing a loss of traction and of torque.

The traction control system lowers the engine's torque, regardless of the driver's intentions, when the wheels start to spin, while at the same time controlling the brake system, thereby reducing the torque transmitted to the road surface to appropriate levels. In this way, stable and rapid starting and acceleration can be achieved.

In modern vehicles, traction-control systems utilize the same wheel-speed sensors employed by the antilock braking system. These sensors measure differences in rotational speed to determine if the wheels that are receiving power have lost traction. When the traction-control system determines that one wheel is spinning more quickly than the others, it automatically "pumps" the brake to that wheel to reduce its speed and lessen wheel slip. In most cases, individual wheel braking is enough to control wheel slip. However, some traction-control systems also reduce engine power to the slipping wheels.

Fig. 14.42 Traction control system

Traction control does not have the ability to increase traction. It just attempts to prevent a vehicle's wheels from spinning. For drivers who routinely drive in snowy and icy conditions, traction control, antilock brakes, and snow tires are must-have safety features.

Traction control is basically an anti-lock braking system in reverse. Anti-lock brakes prevent the wheels from locking up when the car is decelerating. Traction control keeps the wheels from locking up or skidding when the car is accelerating.

BRAKE FLUIDS

Brake fluid is a chemically inert hydraulic fluid used to transmit force and motion. It also lubricates the pistons in the master cylinder, wheel cylinders and calipers. Most brake systems use a glycol (glycerin-alcohol) fluid with additives to meet the requirements. Some vegetable and mineral based fluids are also recommended.

A wide variety of materials is used within a standard braking system. Several types of metal, rubber and plastics come into contact with the brake fluid. Brake fluid must be compatible with all materials in the brake system and maintain stability under varying conditions, both in temperature and pressures. Because of these conditions, brake fluid must possess the following six characteristics:

1. Viscosity-must be free-flowing at all temperatures.
2. High boiling point-must remain liquid at high operating temperatures without vapourization.
3. Non-corrosive- must not attack metal, plastic or rubber parts.
4. Water tolerance-must be able to absorb and retain moisture that collects in the system. This characteristic is called hygroscopic. Water causes pitting in the brake system.
5. Lubricating ability-must lubricate pistons and cups to reduce wear and internal friction.
6. Low freezing point-must meet a certain freezing point as established by safety standards.

BRAKE BLEEDING

Most brakes should be bled every two or three years to keep your brake system at optimum performance. Small amounts of air can become trapped in the brake line, creating a spongy feeling when you step on the pedal. If large amounts of air enter the brake line, your vehicle can suffer a complete braking failure. Air can enter into your brake system during certain types of servicing or if there is a leak. The main steps in the operation are:

- Ensure that the reservoir is full.
- Attach one end of rubber tube to bleeder valve and immerse other end in fluid contained in jar.
- Open bleeder valve and slowly pump pedal until there are no more bubbles appear. Close bleeder valve as pedal is being depressed.
- Repeat at all wheel cylinders.
- Top up reservoir.

Review Questions

1. What is the purpose of braking system?
2. Why are vehicles fitted with disc brakes at the front and drum brakes at the rear?
3. What are the main advantages of a disc brake?
4. List three factors that can affect a vehicle's braking efficiency.
5. Why is the braking effect at the front and rear wheels not identical in magnitude?
6. What is the difference between leading and trailing shoes in a drum brake?
7. How can the self-servo effect of a drum brake be made use of for more effective braking?
8. What properties must the brake fluid possess?
9. How is the hydraulic brake system bled?
10. What are the advantages and disadvantages of a disc brake?
11. What are the advantages of an air brake?
12. What effect results from brake lining wear?
13. What is meant by a retarder, and what advantage does it offer?
14. Explain the basic operation of a hydraulic retarder.
15. Explain the basic operation of an electric retarder.

16. What is referred to as co-efficient of friction in brakes shoes?
17. List five factors that contribute to brake effectiveness.
18. Name the types of brakes.
19. Why is an internally expanding brake preferred in automobile?
20. How does a mechanical brake work?
21. What are the advantages of mechanical brakes?
22. What features should an efficient braking system possess?
23. What is meant by brake binding? What are the indications?
24. Why do we not use brakes with more than 80% efficiency in automobiles?
25. What is fading of brakes? What causes it?
26. What is brake compensation?
27. Why does high pedal produce better braking action than low pedal?
28. Define reaction time as referred to brake application?
29. List four factors that tend to increase brake temperature?
30. What is self-energization?
31. How does disc brake function? What is the major advantage of a disc brake?
32. What is the function of a brake shoe?
33. Why are hydraulic brakes popularly used in vehicles?
34. What are the main constituents of brake fluid? What are the qualities of good brake fluid?
35. The brake pedal becomes soft and spongy, why?
36. What is bleeding of brake?
37. What is the function of the brake lining?
38. What are the different types of brake lining?
39. Give two main types of brake lining materials.
40. Out of the leading and trailing shoes which wears out faster? Why?
41. What is meant by power brake?
42. What is meant by servo brake?
43. What is meant by a brake being 100% efficient, why is this not achieved in practice?
44. What is an anti-lock system in brakes?
45. Why do front brake shoes have a larger lining area than rear brake shoes?
46. What is the advantage of a dual or split braking system?
47. Explain the transfer of weight during the application of brakes. Discuss how it affects wheel skidding.
48. ---------------- is the device, which helps the braking system while the vehicle is on slope.
49. What is the principle of hydraulic brakes?
50. What are the disadvantages of hydraulic brakes?
51. Why does the hydraulic brake not work when air enters into it?

15
CHAPTER

WHEEL AND TYRE

Vehicles ride on pneumatic tyres filled with pressurized air. Tyres are the only vehicle components that come into direct contact with the road surface. However, that tyres cannot be used independently on a vehicle. The wheel and tyre correspond to the human foot and shoe. They must be mounted on wheels in order to be used. They roll along the road while supporting vehicle weight. The tyre serves to absorb the road shocks and prevent them from entering into body.

WHEEL

Vehicle wheels have developed from wooden spoked wheels via cast wheels to the sheet metal disc wheel of today. This is the most commonly used wheel in automobiles at the present time. The wheel must be able to resist and transmit all forces which act between the road and the vehicle.

REQUIREMENTS

It is not enough for a wheel to be round. The following essential demands are made on automotive wheel :

1. Must be strong enough to withstand the vertical and lateral loads, driving and braking forces and various other forces imposed upon it.
2. Must be as light as possible.
3. Must be well-balanced so that it will rotate smoothly at high speeds.
4. Must be cheap to produce, easy to clean and simple to remove and refit.
5. Good dissipation of frictional heat.
6. Adequate space for accommodating the brake system.
7. Long service life.

CONSTRUCTION

Most wheels have similar constructional features. The middle of the wheel rim is recessed and is called the well base. This well enables the removal and refitting of a tyre. The outer edge of the wheel rim is called the rim flange and this is normally tapered. The taper ensures that, as the tyre is inflated, the tyre bead is forced into the taper, creating an air-tight seal. The rim shown in Fig. 15.1 is also humped, to prevent the tyre from readily dislodging if it is deflated.

The wheel (disc) is secured to the threaded studs (hub bolts) on the axle hub by the wheel nuts. The wheel-nut bosses and the ends of the wheel nuts are tapered so that the wheel will automatically center itself on the axle hub during assembly.

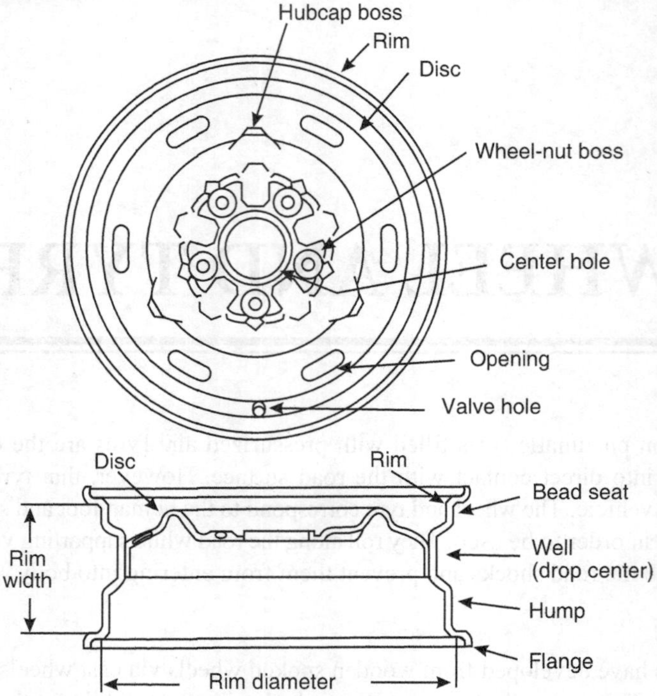

Fig. 15.1 Construction of a wheel

TYPES OF WHEELS

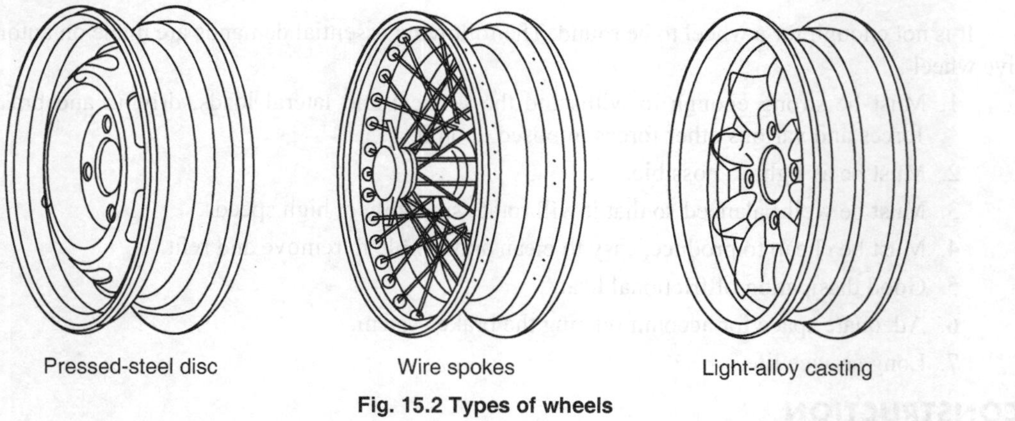

Fig. 15.2 Types of wheels

The type of wheel used depends on a number of factors, such as cost, design considerations and the use for which the vehicle is intended. Three types of wheel are commonly used on today's vehicles: pressed-steel discs, wire-spoke wheel and light alloy castings. The last two are more expensive to produce.

DISC WHEEL

Disc wheels are classified according to the method of their manufacture and the materials from which they are made. Two types are in common use at present: pressed steel and cast light alloy.

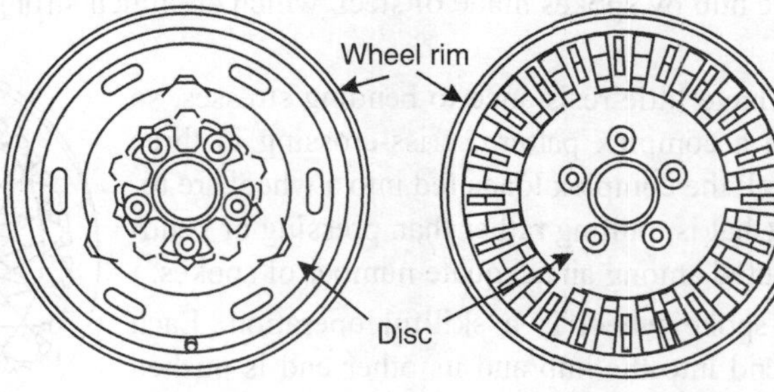

Fig. 15.3 Disc wheels

Pressed-steel disc wheel

Most automobiles today are fitted with pressed-steel disc wheels. They are light, strong, stiff and resistant to accidental damage. They are also easy to produce in large numbers at low cost.

The disc wheel made of a single steel plate pressed into suitable shape (stamped). Rims are welded on the outer circumference of the wheel to allow installing the tyre. This type of construction is well suited for mass production.

The wheel is attached to the hub or axle shaft with four or six bolts. Small weights (balance weights) are sometimes installed on the outer circumference to balance the wheel. Bolts used to attach the wheel are called hub bolts and the cover over these bolts is called wheel cap.

It was once a disadvantage of this design that the disc had to be liberally perforated to allow for the passage of cooling air to the brakes and piercing holes in the disc could weaken it. By using a slightly more expensive technique, modern designers can turn the disadvantage into an advantage. The holes are swaged *i.e.* their edges are turned smoothly inwards and this may actually increase the strength of the wheel. Swaging of this kind is now a standard technique on production cars.

Cast light-alloy wheel

During recent years, the lightness of the wire wheel and the ease of cleaning of the pressed steel wheel have been combined in a wheel made of light alloy. Although much more costly, the appeal of attractive styles of aluminium and magnesium alloy wheels has made this type popular for use on the high performance type car. A light alloy wheel is cast to shape and then machined to give the final finish. At present the number of production cars fitted with these wheels as standard is relatively small, but it is increasing.

Because of their light weight compared with steel, aluminium and magnesium alloys permit the use of thicker sections, which promise stiffness and distribute stresses over a wide area.

The wider rim possible with light-alloy wheels is the main reason for their use on some sports cars. They allow wider tyres to be fitted, so improving road-holding, especially on corners.

Light alloys are also good conductors of heat and therefore disperse the heat generated by brakes and tyres more quickly than steel does. Some precautions are necessary with light-alloy wheels. They react badly to salt spray and must be checked regularly for signs of corrosion.

There is also a danger of electrolytic corrosion, which may occur when steel comes into contact with a light alloy. To prevent this, the holes through which retaining or locating studs pass should be greased and if balance weights are used, avoid those which are held in place by steel clips or screws.

WIRE-SPOKE WHEELS

The earliest type of wheel still in production is the wire-spoke variety, a light but very strong wheel now used mostly for motorbikes and sports and racing cars. All loads on the wheel are transmitted from the rim to the hub by spokes made of steel, which are much stronger in tension than in compression.

Spokes individually have little resistance to bending stresses, so they have to be laced in a complex pattern, criss-crossing in three planes. This ensures that all the complex loads fed into a wheel are resolved into tensile loads (that is, pulling rather than pressing or bending loads), evenly distributed among an adequate number of spokes.

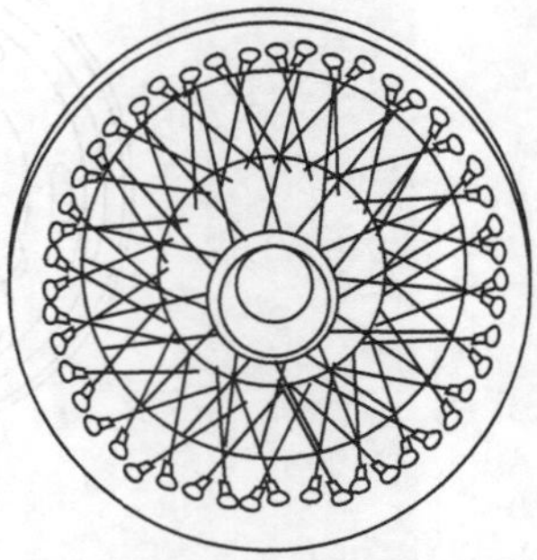

Fig. 15.4 Wire-spoked wheel

Assembling a wire-spoke wheel is a skillful operation. Each spoke is hooked at one end into the hub and its other end is pushed through a hole in the wheel rim, where a tapered nut (the nipple) is screwed down to pull the spoke tight. If any spokes are too loose or too tight, the relatively flimsy rim will distort.

Advantages

- Strong and light.
- Centre lock mounting. Single large nut screwed on to the hub to retain the wheel. It is therefore very easy to change the wheel when required, because only a single nut has to be removed.
- Ensures good circulation of air to the brake system.

Disadvantages

- Wire wheels are expensive because of their complicated construction.
- Difficult to clean.
- The pierced rim of a wire wheel makes it impossible to fit tubeless tyres, as they need air-tight rims.

Coping with stresses from different directions

The car wheel is subjected to extreme loads and stresses even in normal road use. It has to withstand the car's weight and forces of acceleration, braking and cornering and it often has to cope with several of these stresses at once. Cornering, for instance, can be combined with acceleration or braking, which subjects the wheel to different stresses at the same time.

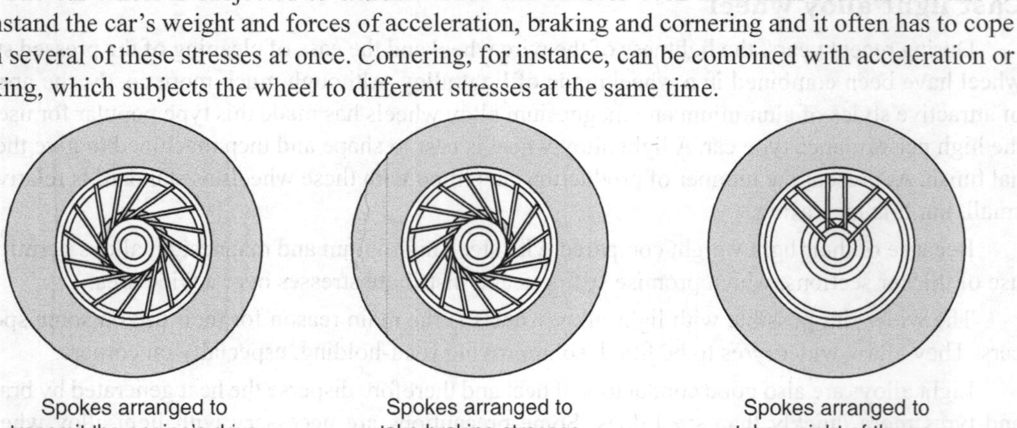

Fig. 15.5 Stresses from different directions

For steering control the wheels must be of rigid construction. There is no difficulty in obtaining the necessary stiffness with a cast light-alloy wheel, because the short spoke portion can be cast in the form of substantial radial ribs. With a pressed-steel wheel, the spoke portion is usually of near-conical shape for extra lateral (side-to-side) stiffness.

In the traditional wire wheel, where the spokes are the only connection between the hub and the rim, this essential side-to-side stiffness is achieved by using a relatively wide hub with two or three sets of spokes arranged at different angles. The spokes are arranged in pairs, inclined so that, with the hub, they form a series of rigid triangles for resisting side-to-side forces when the car is cornering.

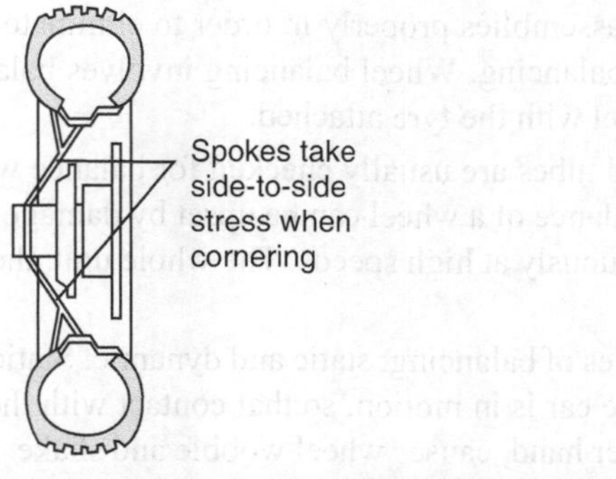

Fig. 15.6 Section showing traingular arrangement of spokes

Backward and forward weight transfer, when the car is braking or accelerating, is absorbed by the steel spokes acting alternatively in tension. Properly designed disc or alloy wheels cope readily with these forces.

WHEEL DIMENSIONS

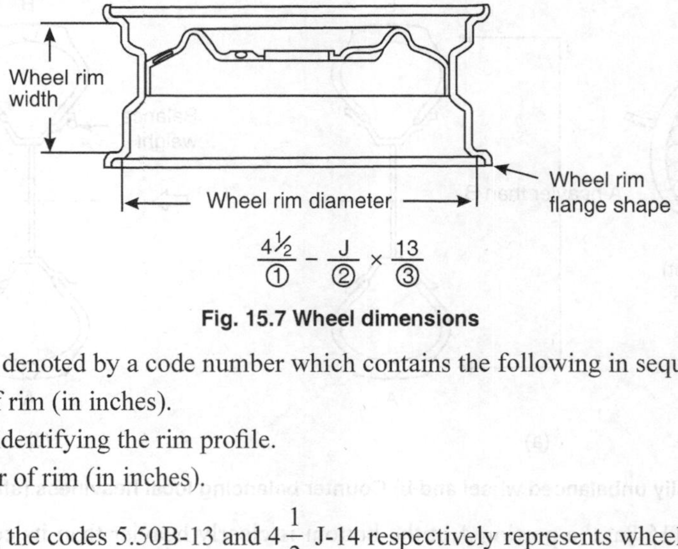

Fig. 15.7 Wheel dimensions

The wheel is denoted by a code number which contains the following in sequence.

1. Width of rim (in inches).
2. A letter identifying the rim profile.
3. Diameter of rim (in inches).

For example, the codes 5.50B-13 and $4\frac{1}{2}$J-14 respectively represents wheels described in the table 15.1 below:

Table 15.1: Wheel dimensions

Width (W)	Rim Type	Diameter (D)
5.50″	B	13″
$4\frac{1}{2}$	J	14″

WHEEL BALANCING

Due to improvements in engine performance, handling and braking performance it is becoming possible for automobiles to operate at higher and higher speeds every year. At high speeds, an unbalanced wheel assembly (wheel plus tyre) can create vibrations which are transmitted to the body through suspension components, causing annoyance to the driver and passengers. A wheel that is not properly balanced may affect steering control even at moderate speeds. Therefore, it is necessary to balance the wheel assemblies properly in order to eliminate such vibrations and this operation is what is called wheel balancing. Wheel balancing involves balancing the weight of the entire wheel assembly *i.e.* the wheel with the tyre attached.

Wheels, tyres and tubes are usually checked for balance within certain limits before they leave the factory. But the balance of a wheel can be upset by damage and that of a tyre by wear, especially on a car driven continuously at high speeds. The whole unit, therefore, should be checked every few thousand kilometers.

There are two types of balancing: static and dynamic. Static imbalance causes the wheel to jump up and down when the car is in motion, so that contact with the road surface deteriorates. Dynamic imbalance, on the other hand, causes wheel wobble and shake. This overloads various steering gear components such as track rod joints, and the steering gearbox.

Static balancing

Static balancing can be done, as its name implies, with the wheel almost stationary. Small lead weights are clipped to the wheel rim to counter balance any local heaviness of rim and tyre at the opposite point on the wheel.

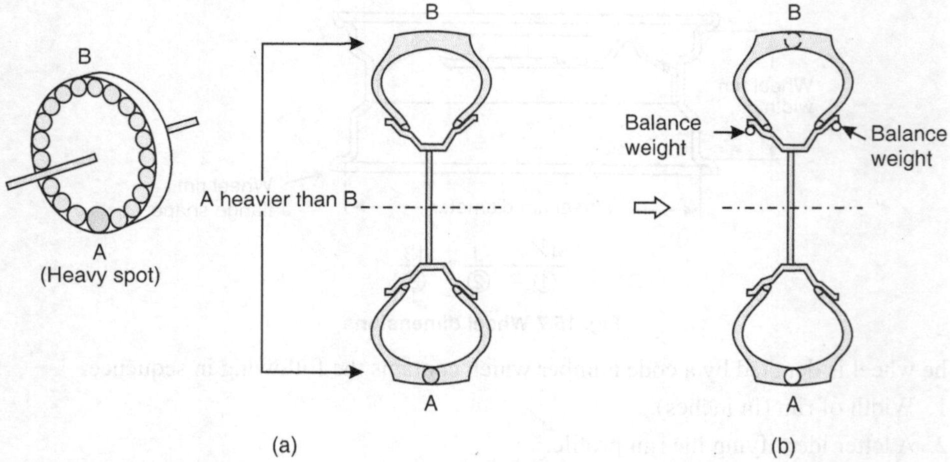

Fig. 15.8 (a) Statically unbalanced wheel and b) Counter balancing local heaviness (statically balanced)

From the Fig. 15.8a, the portion A at the bottom is clearly heavier than its counterpart on the opposite side of the wheel B. If the weight is not uniformly distributed around the axis as shown, the wheel is said to be statically unbalanced.

Attaching a weight W_2 equal to A's extra weight W_1 to B, which is 180° opposite A and the same distance from the center, will eliminate the vibration problem, because W_2 will counter balance W_1. Since it is impossible to attach weight to the tyre tread itself, two counter balance weights (Fig. 15.8b) of equal size are attached to the inside and outside of the disc wheel rim, opposite part A.

Dynamic balancing

Whereas static balance refers to the balance of weight in the radial direction under static conditions, dynamic balance refers to the balance of weight in the axial direction as the wheel turns. By definition, dynamic unbalance is not visible while the wheel assembly is at rest.

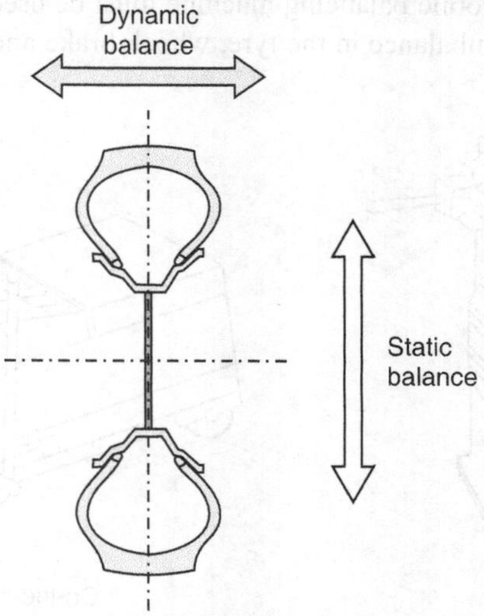

Fig. 15.9 Static and dynamic balance

A wheel that is in static balance can still need dynamic balancing. Dynamic balancing of a wheel is done when it is rotating. The effect of a wheel being dynamically out of balance is as if it had a concentration of weight at one point on the edge of its rim so that, as the wheel spins, it wobbles rapidly from side to side. The wider the rim the greater the chances of this imbalance being troublesome.

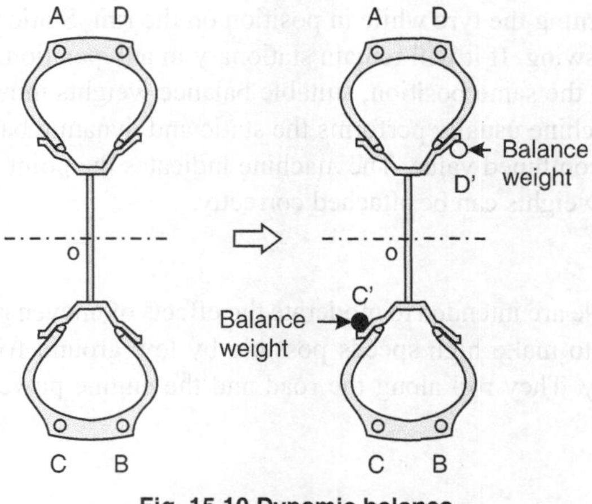

Fig. 15.10 Dynamic balance

Improper dynamic balance is corrected by attaching two weights to the wheel assembly, one with the same weight as A at position C and another with the same weight as B at position D. Attaching these weights will cancel the moments around the center G_0, thus eliminating the vibrations. On an actual automobile, balance weights of the proper size are attached on the wheel rim, at points C' and D'.

WHEEL-BALANCING MACHINES

Each wheel has to be statically and dynamically balanced. Both static and dynamic balance can be checked and eliminated on wheel balancing machines which most large garages have.

These machines are normally set up permanently at a suitable point in the workshop and used to balance complete wheels and tyres which have been removed from the vehicle. If wheel balancing on the vehicle is called for, a mobile balancing machine must be used. It is capable of determining total imbalance, that is to say imbalance in the tyre, wheel, brake and wheel hub as a complete assembly.

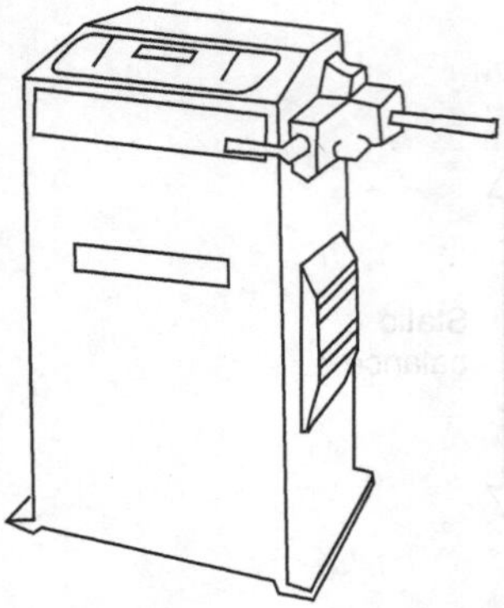

Off-the-car type

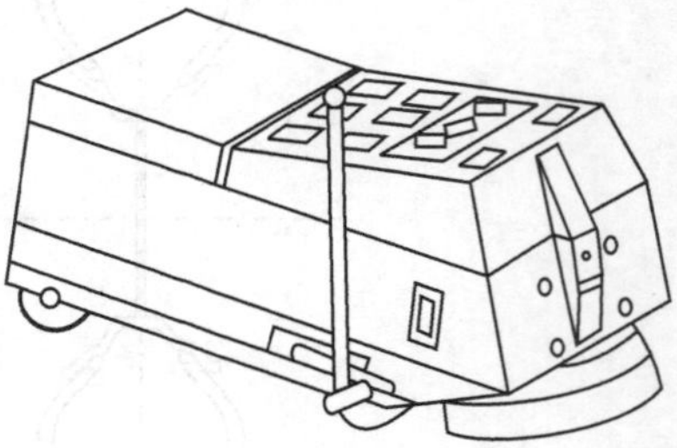

On-the-car type

Fig. 15.11 Wheel-balancing machines

On modern balancing machines, imbalance down to grams can be determined accurately. Before wheels removed from a vehicle for balancing, stones and dirt must be removed from the tyre tread or else the results will be falsified. The old balance weights, if any, must be removed and the tyre checked to ensure that it does not run out of true. Vertical run out not exceeding 0.8 mm can usually be tolerated without affecting tyre and wheel balance. If more severe vertical run out is detected, it can be eliminated by turning the tyre while in position on the rim. Static imbalance is established by allowing the wheel to swing. If it will remain stationary in any position, it is in static balance. If it always swings round to the same position, suitable balance weights must be attached to the rim. The mobile balancing machine usually performs the static and dynamic balancing work in a single operation and displays a combined value. The machine indicates the point of imbalance as well, so that the required balance weights can be attached correctly.

TYRE

The tyres of the vehicle are intended to moderate the effects of uneven road surfaces, to improve the driving qualities and to make high speeds possible by low ground friction. Today pneumatic types are used exclusively. They roll along the road and the engine power is transmitted through them.

TYRE FUNCTIONS

The tyres perform the following basic functions:

- Support the overall weight of the vehicle.
- Directly contact the road surface and transmit the vehicle's driving and braking forces to the road, thus controlling starting, acceleration, deceleration, stopping, and turning.
- Reduce shocks caused by irregularities in the road surface.

TYRE CHARACTERISTICS

Tyres have four characteristics that are important in understanding their design. These include:

Tyre traction

Traction is defined as a tyre's ability to grip the road and to move or stop the vehicle.

Ride and handling

Tyres are measured by their ride and handling ability. This is an indication of the degree of comfort a tyre delivers to vehicle passengers. It is also a measure of the responsiveness to the driver's steering actions.

Rolling resistance

Rolling resistance is a term used to describe the weights of force required to overcome the resistance of a tyre to rotation. As rolling resistance of a tyre decreases, fuel mileage typically increase.

Noise

All tyres make a certain amount of noise. Tyres can be made 'quiet' by scrambling or changing the size, length, and shape of the tread elements. Scrambling prevents the sound frequency buildup that would develop if all of the patterns of the tread were spaced evenly.

TYRE CONSTRUCTION

The following illustrates (Fig. 15.12) the basic construction of a tyre.

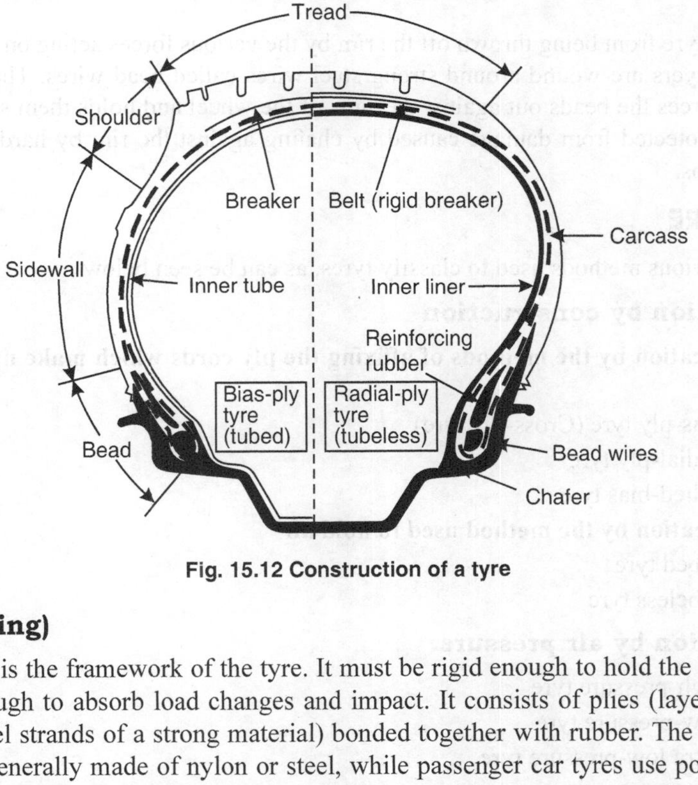

Fig. 15.12 Construction of a tyre

Carcass (casing)

The carcass is the framework of the tyre. It must be rigid enough to hold the high pressure air and flexible enough to absorb load changes and impact. It consists of plies (layers) of tyre cords (sheets of parallel strands of a strong material) bonded together with rubber. The cords in bus and truck tyres are generally made of nylon or steel, while passenger car tyres use polyester or nylon. Tyres are generally classified, according to the direction of the cords, into radial-ply and bias-ply types.

Tread

The tread is an external rubber layer protecting the carcass from wear and external damage caused by the road surface. It is the part that directly contacts the road and transmits the vehicles driving and braking forces to the road. The tread pattern consists of grooves moulded into the tread surface, and is designed to help the tyre more effectively transmit these forces to the road.

Side wall

The side walls are rubber layer that cover the sides of the tyre and protect the carcass from external damage. The largest, most flexible tyre constituents, they continuously flex under the loads applied during travel. They bear the manufacturer's name, tyre size, and other information.

Breaker

The breaker is a fabric layer between the carcass and the tread and helps to reduce the shocks passed from the road to carcass. Breakers are commonly used in bias ply tyres. Tyres for buses, trucks and light-duty trucks use nylon breakers, while those for passenger cars use polyester.

Belt (rigid breaker)

Belts are used in radial-ply tyres. Running like a hoop along the tyre circumference between the carcass and the tread rubber, they hold the carcass securely in place. Tyres for passenger cars use rigid breakers constructed of steel, rayon or polyester cords, while those for buses and trucks are fabricated of steel cords.

Bead

To keep the tyre from being thrown off the rim by the various forces acting on it, the free edges or sides of the layers are wound around strong steel wires called bead wires. The pressurized air inside the tyre forces the beads out against the rims of the wheel and holds them securely in place. The beads are protected from damage caused by chafing against the rim by hard strips of rubber called chafer strips.

TYPES OF TYRE

There are various methods used to classify tyres, as can be seen below.

(*a*) Classification by construction

- **Classification by the methods of affixing the ply cords which make up the carcass of the tyre**
  - o Bias-ply tyre (Cross-ply tyre)
  - o Radial-ply tyre
  - o Belted-bias tyre
- **Classification by the method used to hold air**
  - o Tubed tyre
  - o Tubeless tyre

(*b*) Classification by air pressure

- o High-pressure tyre
- o Low-pressure tyre
- o Extra low-pressure tyre

(*c*) Classification by use

- **Classification by the type of vehicle on which the tyre is meant to be used**
  - o Passenger car tyres
  - o Light truck tyres
  - o Trucks and bus tyres
- **Classification by the road surface on which the tyre is meant to be used**
  - o Snow tyre
  - o Spiked tyre

- o All-weather tyre
- o Sand tyre
- **Others**
  - o Compact spare tyre
  - o Low-profile tyre

Here we will describe the functions and features of tyres with emphasis on the classification of the tyres by the construction and air pressure.

BIAS-PLY AND RADIAL-PLY TYRES

Tyres are classified, according to the construction of the carcass, into bias-ply and radial-ply tyres.

Bias-ply tyre

The bias-ply tyre carcass is made up of alternating layers of ply cords bonded together, and lying at an angle of 30° – 40° relative to the tyre's circumferential centerline. This arrangement supports loads applied both along the tyre circumference and across the diameter.

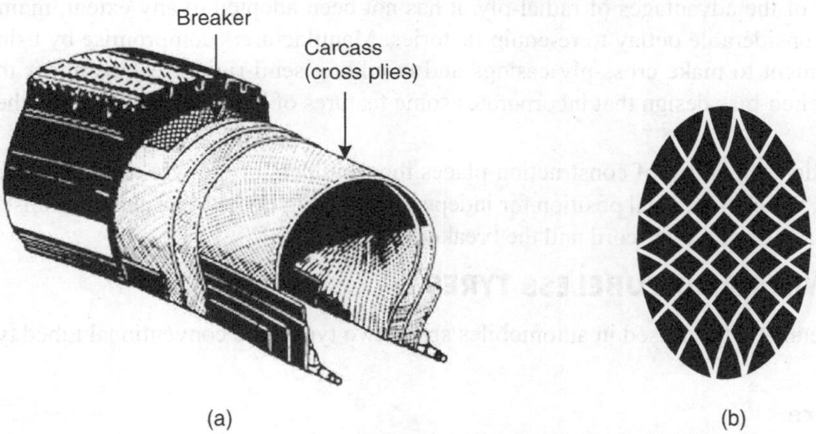

Fig. 15.13 (a) Sectional bias-ply tyre and (b) Bias-ply tyre squirm

However, when the tyre is subjected to a vertical load from the road surface, the ply cords tend to 'squirm' or deform as shown in the illustration 15.13b above.

Bias-ply tyre tread tends to 'squirm' as it meets the road, while radial-ply tyre tread tends to remain apart. Bias-ply tyres give a softer ride, but are inferior to the radial-ply tyres in terms of cornering performance and wear resistance.

Radial-ply tyre

The radial-ply tyre carcass consists of layers of cords bonded together with rubber perpendicular to the tyre circumference. This construction gives the tyre great flexibility in the radial direction. Nevertheless, such a carcass alone cannot withstand the full load applied along the tyre circumference. The radial-ply tyre, therefore, is provided with belts (sometimes called rigid breaker) made of strong textile cords or steel wires bonded together with rubber which bind the carcass in a manner similar to the hoops binding a barrel. This arrangement also increases the tread rigidity.

Radial-ply tyres have a high belt rigidity, which means their cornering performance and high speed performance are good and rolling resistance is low. Tyre wear resistance is high also, but they are inferior to bias-ply tyres in terms of riding comfort when the car goes over small bumps at a low speed.

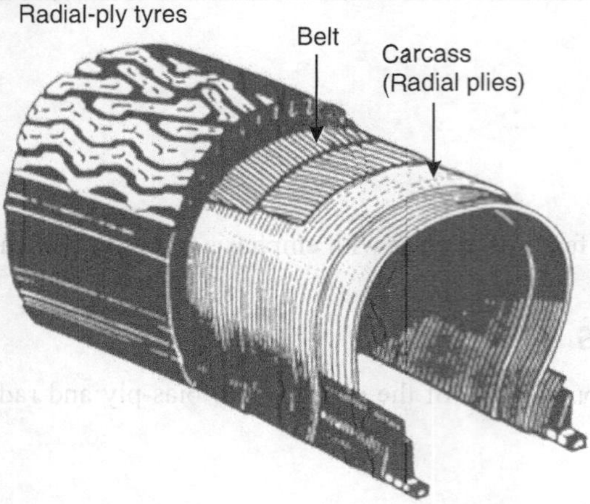

Fig. 15.14 Sectional radial-ply tyre

Belted-bias tyre

In spite of the advantages of radial-ply, it has not been adopted to any extent, mainly because it involves considerable outlay to re-equip factories. Manufacturers compromise by using their existing equipment to make cross-ply casings and moulding semi-rigid breakers under the tread, to produce a belted-bias design that incorporates some features of both the cross-ply and the radial-ply tyres.

In addition, this form of construction places the shoulders of the tyre right at the edges of the breaker belt, which is an ideal position for independent flexing of the tread and the walls. The casing is usually made of polyester cord and the breaker of glass fibre.

TUBED TYRES AND TUBELESS TYRES

The pneumatic tyres used in automobiles are of two types: the conventional tubed type and the tubeless type.

Tubed tyre

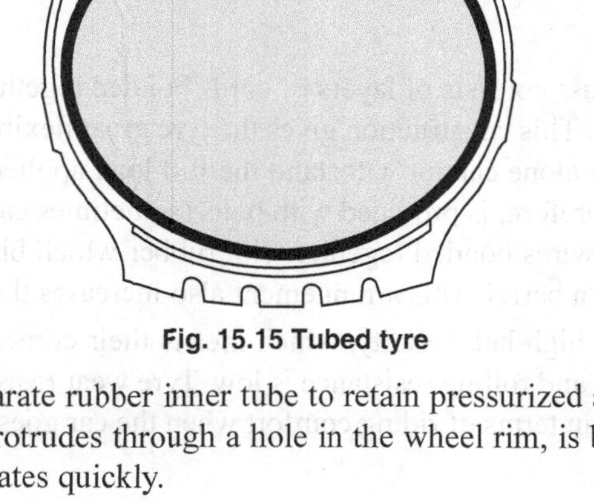

Fig. 15.15 Tubed tyre

A tubed tyre has a separate rubber inner tube to retain pressurized air inside the tyre. The tyre valve or air valve, which protrudes through a hole in the wheel rim, is bonded to the inner tube. If punctured, a tubed tyre deflates quickly.

Tubeless tyre

The tubeless tyre, as the name indicates, has no inner tube. The pressurized air is held in by an inner liner, a specially formulated thick rubber lining with high sealing effectiveness. Since the tubeless tyre does away with the inner tube, the air valve is secured directly to the wheel rim.

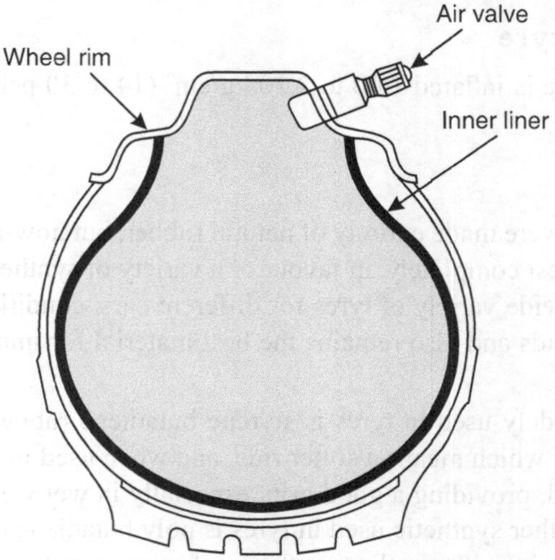

Fig. 15.16 Tubeless tyre

Differences between tubed and tubeless tyres

Tubed and tubeless tyres are made in similar ways. The difference between them is that the tubed tyre has a separate rubber inner tube to hold the air, whereas the tubeless tyre holds the air itself. The tubeless tyre has a number of advantages over the tubed:

- It is easier to fit, since no tube has to be inserted.
- Lower weight, since there is no tube.
- Greater driving safety, since a sudden tyre burst can be almost completely ruled out. When punctured it deflates slowly, because the soft lining has a self-sealing effect. Slow loss of pressure can be soon noticed by the driver.
- Reduced heat build-up, since there is no friction between outer cover and inner tube. Furthermore, the air inside the tyre keeps cooler because it is in direct contact with the wheel rim.
- A temporary puncture repair can be made without removing the wheel, by stopping the hole with a special rubber plug.

Tubed tyres are still necessary for wire wheels, because of the difficulty of making an air seal at the spoke ends.

HIGH-PRESSURE AND LOW-PRESSURE TYRES

The amount of air in the tyre can be designated by the air pressure. Depending on the air pressures, tyres can be classified into high-pressure tyre, low-pressure tyre (balloon tyre) and extra low-pressure tyre.

High-pressure tyre

High pressure tyres have a thick casing and can withstand heavy loads and inflated 4.22 to 6.32 kg/cm^2 (60 to 90 psi).

Low-pressure tyre

The cross-sectional area of low-pressure tyre is about two times larger than that of high-pressure tyre. Ground contact area is also larger. Since air volume is greater and pressure is lower, the cushioning effect is better. These tyres are generally inflated 2.10 to 2.53 kg/cm^2 (30 to 36 psi).

Extra low-pressure tyre

Extra low-pressure tyre is inflated 1.00 to 2.10 kg/cm^2 (14 to 30 psi) and used chiefly on passenger cars.

TYRE MATERIALS

For many years, tyres were made entirely of natural rubber, but now-a-days most tyre manufacturers have given it up almost completely, in favour of a variety of synthetic rubbers. These, used in various blends, produce a wide variety of tyres for different cars, conditions and purposes. Natural rubber is used in some blends and also remains the best material for impregnating and coating the carcass fabrics.

The synthetic most widely used in tyres is styrene butadiene rubber (SBR). It has much less bounce than natural rubber, which means a softer ride, and when used in tyre treads SBR maintains closer contact with the road, providing a good grip, especially in wet weather. It also has excellent resistance to abrasion. Another synthetic used in tyres is poly butadiene (PB). This is hard-wearing and less sensitive to temperature than other synthetics, but too much of it in a blend makes tyres scream in the dry and slip in the wet. PB is usually mixed in small quantities with SBR, with natural rubber or with both.

Other synthetics are used in small quantities. But whatever the blend, it must have other additives, including oil, carbon black and sulphur. Oil improves road holding at the expense of rapid tyre wear. Carbon black adds abrasion resistance, and sulphur acts as a vulcanizing agent.

The number of plies and the relative angle between the cord and the tyre bead governs the tyre characteristics. In the past cotton was the main cord material, but modern tyres use manmade fibres such as rayon and nylon. These materials are much stronger and offer greater resistance to the heat built up by the flexing of the tyre. Heavy vehicles and some cars require an even stronger material, so steel cords are needed in these cases.

The bead consists of a number of hoops of steel wire which are responsible for retaining the tyre on the rim.

TYRE SPECIFICATION CODING SYSTEM

The tyre sidewall usually bears the codes representing the tyre width, the inside diameter (rim diameter) and the ply rating. A high-speed tyre usually bears an additional code such as H, S, etc., a radial ply tyre, an R. Some coding systems include the aspect ratio.

Ply rating

This indicates the number of plies that are used in the construction of the tyre. The more plies that are used, the stronger the tyre will be. Due to improvements in tyre construction, the actual number of plies used has steadily reduced. For example, a tyre marked '6 ply/4 ply' has the same load carrying capacity as a 6 ply tyre, but is constructed with only 4 plies. Because there is no common standard for the definition of ply rating, a more reliable indicator of a tyre's strength is the load index.

Aspect ratio

This term describes the relationship between a tyre's cross-sectional width and its sectional height. This is usually expressed as a percentage.

Early pneumatic tyres had aspect ratios of 100 percent, which meant that the width of the tyre was approximately the same as its sectional height. Now that vehicles have become faster, many are fitted with tyres that have a low aspect ratio. This means that the tyre's sectional height is smaller than its cross-sectional width. A tyre which is 5 inches wide and 4 inches from tread to rim has an aspect ratio of 80 percent. Some of the advantages of using tyres with a low aspect ratio include the following:

- More of the tyre is in contact with the road surface, which improves the vehicle's road-holding and steering characteristics.
- Because of the tyre's smaller sectional height, the vehicle's centre of gravity is lower.

They do have the disadvantage of a more harsh ride as the sectional height is reduced.

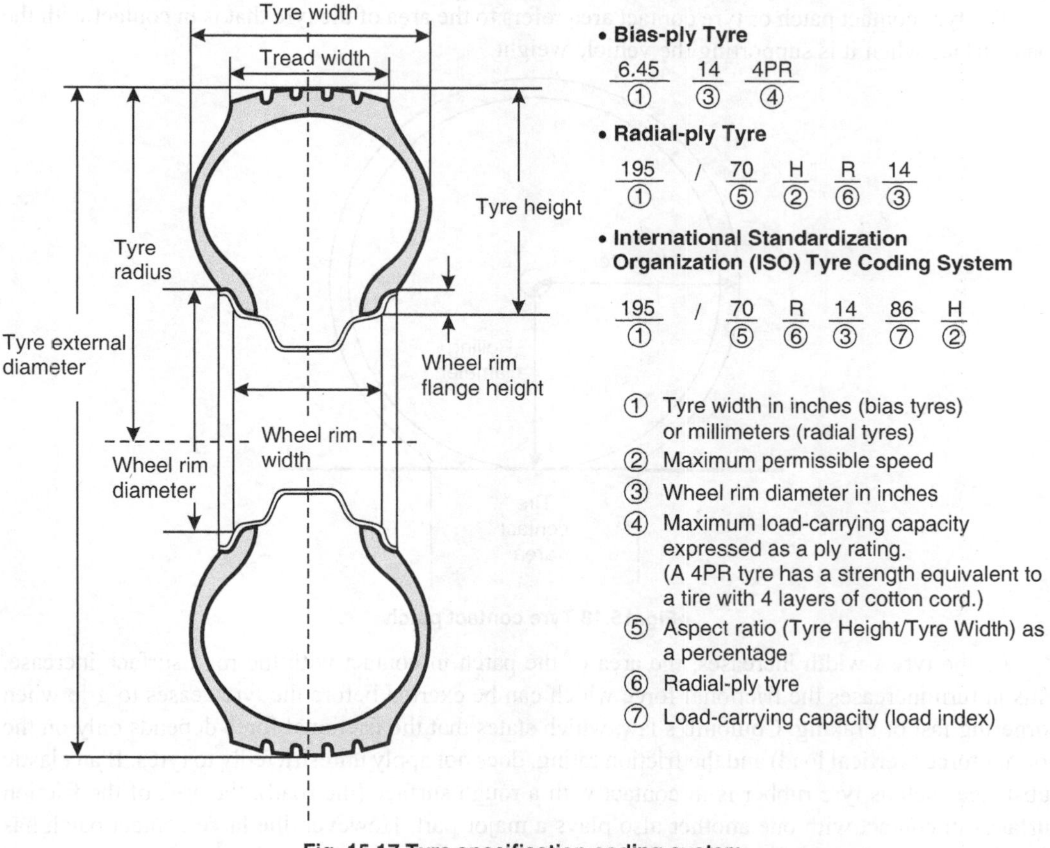

Fig. 15.17 Tyre specification coding system

Speed rating

Tyre manufacturers now stamp each tyre with a speed code letter. This indicates the speed at which the tyre can safely be driven.

Table 15.2 shows a sample selection of speed rating codes. The letter H is out of alphabetical order because originally there were only three speed rating letters: S-slow, H-high speed and V-very high speed.

Table 15.2 Tyre speed rating codes

Code	S	T	U	H	V	W	Z
Speed (km/h)	180	190	200	210	240	270	270 or more

Load index

This is a number that indicates the carrying capacity of a tyre. A sample load index chart is shown in table 15.3. For example, a tyre with a load index code is 102 is capable of safely carrying a weight of 850 kg under normal road conditions.

Table 15.3 Tyre load index

Code	78	82	86	90	94	98	102
Load (kg)	425	475	530	600	670	750	850

TYRE CONTACT PATCH

The tyre contact patch or tyre contact area refers to the area of the tyre that is in contact with the road surface when it is supporting the vehicle weight.

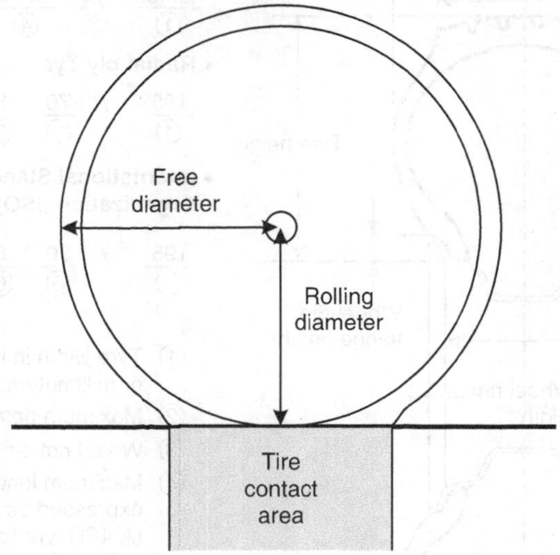

Fig. 15.18 Tyre contact patch

As the tyre's width increases, the area of the patch in contact with the road surface increase. This in turn increases the frictional force which can be exerted before the tyre ceases to grip when cornering fast or braking. Coulomb's law, which states that the frictional force depends only on the normal force (vertical load) and the friction rating, does not apply unrestrictedly to tyres. If an elastic substance such as tyre rubber is in contact with a rough surface (the road), the area of the friction surfaces in contact with one another also plays a major part. However, the large contact patch has disadvantages such as high steering effort at parking speeds and poor traction in winter on account of the low specific ground contact pressure.

HYDROPLANING (AQUAPLANING)

On a dry road the best grip is afforded by a fairly smooth tyre, as this provides the greatest possible contact patch, that part of the tyre is direct touch with the road at any moment. But on a wet road a smooth tyre has hardly any grip and the least trace of water acts as a lubricant. If there is a lot of water on the road, it will form a wedge in front of and underneath a smooth tyre, causing a form of skidding known as hydroplaning or aquaplaning. The tyre, lifted off the road and riding on the water, stops turning and steering control is lost.

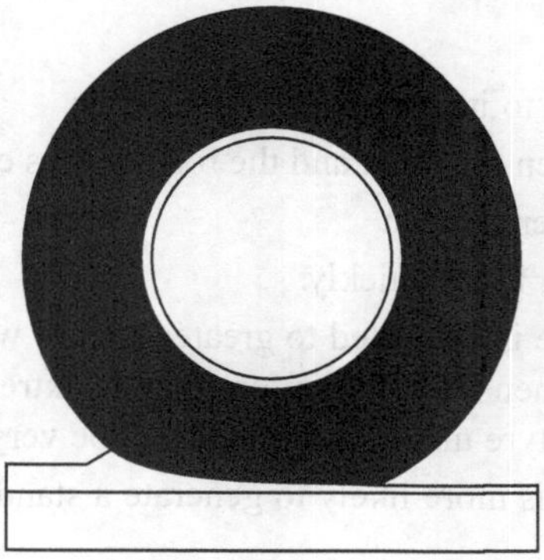

Fig. 15.19 Hydroplanning

TYRE INFLATION PRESSURE

This is governed by the load carried by a given tyre, although manufacturers vary the pressure to modify the steering characteristics. Large-section tyres use a lower pressure for a given load, and so greater comfort is achieved, but the resistance to rolling is increased. The pressure recommended by the manufacturer is applicable to a cold tyre, i.e., it is the pressure before the tyre is used and takes into account the average pressure rise which is caused by the temperature increase during use. Recommended pressure is normally suitable for sustained speeds up to 130 km/h, but a higher pressure is advised if speeds or loads are increased.

If the inflation pressure rises due to heat, do not release the excess air from the tyre. The pressure will return to normal once the tyre has cooled down. If air is released when the tyre is hot, the pressure will drop below normal after the tyre cools off.

The inflation pressure of tyres plays a vital role in terms of total vehicle performance and safety. Although tyres are made up of more or less airtight materials, they still allow minute quantities of air to gradually leak away over time.

Therefore, the tyre inflation pressure must be checked regularly and adjusted as necessary whenever it differs from the specified pressure.

Fig. 15.20 Tyre inflation pressure: correct, over-inflated and under-inflated

Overinflation

An inflation pressure above the specified level can lead to the following problems:

- The narrower tread width reduces driving stability and braking performance.
- Driving comfort suffers.
- The middle part of the tread wears more quickly.
- The tyre's ply cord layers are extremely tense and prone to damage due to external impacts.

Underinflation

Insufficient inflation can lead to its own special problems:

- Increased friction between the tread and the road wastes energy and consumes more fuel.
- Front tyres become harder to steer.
- The tread shoulders wear more quickly.
- When in motion, the tyre is subjected to greater flexure which sharply increases the tyre's internal temperature. When the inflation pressure is extremely low and the vehicle is running at high speeds, the tyre may burst, which can be very dangerous.
- At high speeds, the tyre is more likely to generate a standing wave and experience hydroplaning.

TYRE LIFE

Tyre life, which depends to a very large extent on operating conditions, can be as high as 50,000 km on a passenger car, or 100,000 km on a commercial vehicle. The loads to which the vehicle is subjected must not be exceeded, and the correct tyre pressures must be maintained. Excessive speeds, violent starting and stopping and fast cornering naturally reduce tyre life quite severely. Excessive wear is also caused by incorrect wheel alignment, worn or incorrect shock absorbers, incorrect tyre fitting and poorly balanced wheels and tyres.

RETREAD

Remoulds and retreads can be used up to 112 kmph on 10 inch diameter wheels and upto 120 kmph on wheels over 10 inch diameter. But they are not suitable for prolonged high-speed driving, such as on a motorway.

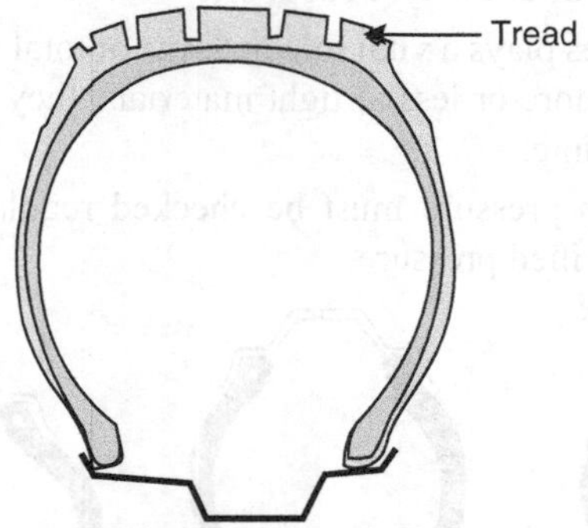

Fig. 15.21 A new tread on an old carcass

On a remould, the rubber is completely renewed from bead to bead, but the tyre will still remain only as good as its carcass. On a retread, however, only the tread of the tyre is renewed.

TYRE DAMAGE AND DEFECTS

In Fig. 15.22, several types of tyre damage are shown. Tyre damage may develop due to non-compliance with the specifications given by the manufacturer, for example incorrect inflation pressure or exceeding of the maximum permissible speed limit. Damage to a tyre side wall is shown in Fig. 15.22a. It develops due to overloading. This can be caused by overloading of the vehicle and exceeding the load-carrying capacity of the tyre.

The tyre damage in Fig. 15.22b is due to excessive inflation pressure. The total weight of the vehicle and its load are supported by the tyres. For this reason, each tyre is given a specified inflation pressure, according to its size and intended load-carrying capacity, which must not be exceeded. If the inflation pressure is exceeded, the tread becomes damaged and the service life and mileage capacity are reduced.

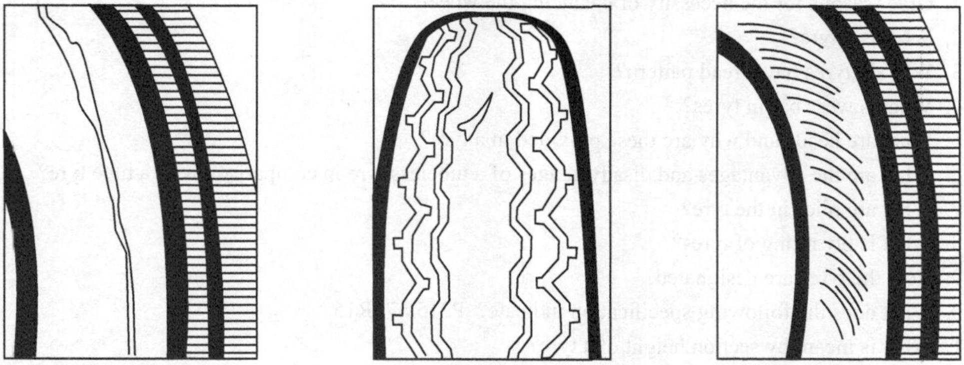

(a) due to overloading (b) due to excessive inflation pressure (c) due to insufficient inflation pressure

Fig. 15.22 Tyre damage

In Fig. 15.22c the casing plies of the side walls have been damaged by insufficient inflation pressure. Due to the load, the tyre is compressed at the point where it comes into contact with the ground, and it starts to spring. If the inflation pressure is constantly too low, springing can lead to the destruction of the carcass.

To increase the service life of the tyre it is necessary to check the inflation pressure regularly. If the vehicle is driven at a very high cruising speed, the tread becomes overheated. The rubber gets warm and peels away from the carcass. If a vehicle passes too quickly over sharp obstacles, punctures may occur, rendering the tyres unserviceable. If the wheel camber, toe-in and brakes are adjusted incorrectly, the tyres will rub and will wear quickly. Defective shock absorbers can be recognized by irregular wear of the tyre tread.

Review Questions

1. What are the factors on which the number of wheels in an automobile depends?
2. What type of rims are generally used in common motor vehicles?
3. Why are mag wheel so called?
4. Why is it important to paint the rims periodically?
5. To which wheels should new tyres be fitted? Why?
6. What is the cause for more wear on one side than the other, in the front wheels?
7. What is wheel tramp?
8. Why should not brake drums be too close to the rim?
9. What are the parts which make up a road wheel?
10. What advantages do light alloy wheels possess?
11. How is wheel balanced?
12. In which circumstances must wheel rims with a hump be used?
13. Describe the design of a wheel.
14. Describe a taperd bead seat rim.
15. Describe the fitting of a tyre to a well-base rim.
16. Explain the function of the wheels and the tyres.
17. What main demands are made on the wheels?
18. List the most common types of wheels.
19. What do you understand by a wide base rim? Give some examples.
20. What do you understand by a well-base rim?

21. Give reasons for the necessity of balancing the wheels.
22. What is a tyre?
23. Why do tyres have tread pattern?
24. What is wear bar in tyres?
25. What are beads and why are these provided in a tyre?
26. What are the advantages and disadvantages of a tubeless tyre in comparison with a tube tyre?
27. What are plies in the tyre?
28. What is ply rating of tyres?
29. How the tyres are designated?
30. What does the following specification indicate? P215 / 75R15.
31. What is meant by section height of a tyre?
32. What is an aspect ratio of a tyre?
33. What is the effect of cuts in the tyres?
34. What is the air pressure recommended for a tyre?
35. What is meant by under inflation?
36. What determines the correct pressure for a particular tyre?
37. How often should the tyre pressure be checked?
38. What will happen by running a tyre below the correct pressure?
39. Is it necessary to run tyres at lower pressures in hot weather?
40. State the effect of oil and grease on tyres.
41. What is the reason for high braking efficiency of radial ply tyres on wet roads?
42. How does a belted bias tyre differ from a bias ply tyre?
43. What is meant by hydroplanning?
44. How should tyres be treated when the vehicle is laid up?
45. Usually, scooter tyres are of ------------- ply.
46. Usually, heavy truck tyres are of ------------- ply.
47. How many types of tyres are there on the basis of pressure?
48. What items make up the complete tyre?
49. What is meant by the effective dynamic tyre radius?
50. What are the advantages of a tyre with a 70% aspect ratio?
51. How are radial-ply tyres constructed?
52. What must be borne in mind when fitting tubeless tyres?
53. What types of tyres do you know?
54. What types of tyre damage do you know? Give the reasons for them.
55. Name the factors which affect the service life of tyres.
56. What effect does the condition of the tyre have on the road safety and petrol consumption of a vehicle?

16

CHAPTER

EMISSION AND CONTROL

AIR POLLUTION

Air pollution may be defined as the presence of undesirable substances in the air either by natural means or due to the activities of men. The natural undesirable substances are dust, spores, pollen, bacteria, sea salt, hydrogen sulphide, ammonia, ozone, etc. In small concentrations, few of these types may have a beneficial effect but the high concentrations are definitely not desirable. The man-made pollutants are smoke, carbon monoxide (CO), sulphur dioxide (SO_2), oxides of nitrogen (NO_X), various hydrogens (HC), fumes of acids, etc.

Burning of fossil and bio-fuels, industrial processes and running of vehicles in the transport sector-all contribute heavily to air pollution. Air pollution is very crucial from public point of view, because every individual person breathes approximately 22,000 times a day, inhaling about 16 kg of air daily. Polluted air also affects vegetation, promotes corrosion, blocks out sunlight and causes deterioration of rubber, paints, etc.

> **Note:** The average percentage composition (by volume) of pollution-free dry air is
>
> $N_2 - 78.09$; $O_2 - 20.94$; $Ar - 0.9$ and $CO_2 - 0.0318$
>
> Hydrogen, methane, carbon monoxide, etc are present in very small amounts.

ENVIRONMENTAL EFFECTS

Acid rain

Acid rain represents one of the major consequences of air pollution. Enormous emissions of SO_X and NO_X from big industrial areas pollute the atmosphere greatly. In these areas, the falling rain reacts with these oxide pollutants to produce a mixture of sulphuric acid, nitric acid and water. This is known as acid rain.

Acid rain causes extensive damage to buildings and sculptural materials made up of marble. These materials become pitted and mechanically weak due to the attack of acidic components. The Tajmahal in India will face a similar threat if proper measures are not taken.

Acid rain also causes extensive damage to terrestrial ecosystems such as water, fish, vegetation, mankind, etc. Acidification of soils by means of acid rain leads to reduced forest productivity. The productivity of fish is also declined due to acidification of water. The heavy metals released by acid rain may also cause potential threat to human health. Acidification of drinking water reservoirs and concurrent increase in heavy metal concentrations may exceed public health limits and may cause dangerous effects.

The only practical approach to counter the problem of acid rain is to reduce SO_X and NO_X emissions. These emissions can be reduced (a) by using low sulphur and low nitrogen fuels and (b) by generating power by alternate energy sources.

Photochemical smog

It is the product of a combination of automobile exhausts and a damp climate. It is characterized by brown hazy fumes which irritate the eyes, reduce visibility and damage plants and rubber goods.

When NO is emitted into atmosphere, it is slowly oxidized by oxygen to NO_2. The NO_2 is dissociated by UV radiations from the sun to give NO and O atoms.

$$NO_2 \rightarrow NO + O$$

Free oxygen atoms are extremely reactive and combine with molecular O_2 to give ozone.

$$O + O_2 \rightarrow O_3$$

Because ozone is a powerful oxidizing agent, it reacts destructively with many materials including rubber, paint and vegetation. It also reacts with hydrocarbons that are released into the atmosphere from automobile exhausts. These reactions produce a variety of organic molecules such as organic peroxides and peroxoacetylnitrates which are strong eye irritants.

Photochemical smog was observed in some parts of Los Angles and Denver in USA and sometimes it is referred to as Los Angles smog. The notorious London smog of 1952, which lasted for 5 days caused 4000 deaths. Latest destructive smog was reported from Indonesia in 1998 which caused much damage to man and property.

Ozone hole

Ozone is an important chemical present in the atmosphere (above 30 km). The ozone layer present in the atmosphere acts as a protective shield for the life on earth. It absorbs UV radiations from the sun, thereby protecting life on earth from skin cancer.

Ozone is destroyed by man-made chlorofluorocarbons. The CFC molecules decompose to release chlorine in the ozone layer and each atom of chlorine thus liberated attacks several ozone molecules.

$$Cl + O_3 \rightarrow ClO + O_2$$

Due to this continuous attack, thinning of ozone layer takes place which leads to the formation of ozone hole.

Greenhouse effect

The greenhouse effect may be defined as the progressive warming up of earth's surface due to the blanketing effect of man-made CO_2 in the atmosphere.

In fact, the greenhouse gases are responsible for keeping our planet warm and thus sustaining life on earth. The earth is heated by sunlight and some of the heat that is absorbed by the earth is radiated back into space. However, some of the gases in the lower atmosphere, acting like glass in a greenhouse, allow solar radiations, but do not allow the earth to re-radiate the heat into space. In other words, these gases in the atmosphere are transparent to the sunlight coming in but they strongly absorb the infrared radiations which the earth sends back as heat. A part of the heat so trapped in these atmospheric gases is re-emitted to the earth's surface. The net result is the heating of the earth's surface by this phenomenon called greenhouse effect. The gases that are responsible for this greenhouse effect are CO_2, water vapour, CH_4, etc. If the concentration of greenhouse gases is larger, they may trap too much of heat, which may threaten the very existence of life on earth.

It is estimated that the atmospheric CO_2 content is increased by 25 percent during the last two centuries. This is the reason for the slight increase in the global temperature (0.5°C). The concentration of greenhouse gases is increasing constantly due to deforestation, industrialization, increased burning of fossil fuels, etc. The CO_2 content in the atmosphere may be doubled within next 50-100 years. If this happens, the global temperature may increase by 4-5°C.

HEALTH EMPACTS

The following substances found in a motor vehicle's exhaust represent a health risk:

Pollutant	Major Sources in Atmosphere	Major Harmful Actions
CO	• Automobiles 93% • Power generation, etc. 7%	Hinders the exchange of oxygen in the blood and causes carbon monoxide poisoning. Atmospheric CO at concentrations of 30 to 40 PPM paralyzes the autonomic nervous system; at 500 PPM or higher concentrations, it causes shortness of breath and headaches when body movements are attempted. At very high concentrations, it can cause death.
HC	• Automobiles 57% • Petroleum refining, use of solvents, etc. 43%	• Irritates the linings of the respiratory organs. • Irritates eyes and nose. Cancer risk. Odour.
NO_X	• Automobiles 39% • Factories, power generation, petroleum refining, etc. 61%	• Irritates the eyes, nose, and throat; if the irritation is severe, it causes coughing, headaches and lung damage. • Atmospheric NO_2: gives off an irritating odour at 3-5 PPM. Irritates the eyes and nose at 10-30 PPM. Causes coughing, headaches and dizziness at 30-50 PPM.
SO_2	• Automobiles (diesel) 1% • Factories, power generation, heating systems, etc. 99%	Irritates respiratory system membranes and causes inflammation of the windpipe.
Pb	• Added to petrol to raise octane rating	Toxic to humans, causing blood poisoning and nervous disorders.

PPM: abbreviation for parts per million. Used as a unit to indicate concentration or content.

AUTOMOBILE EMISSIONS

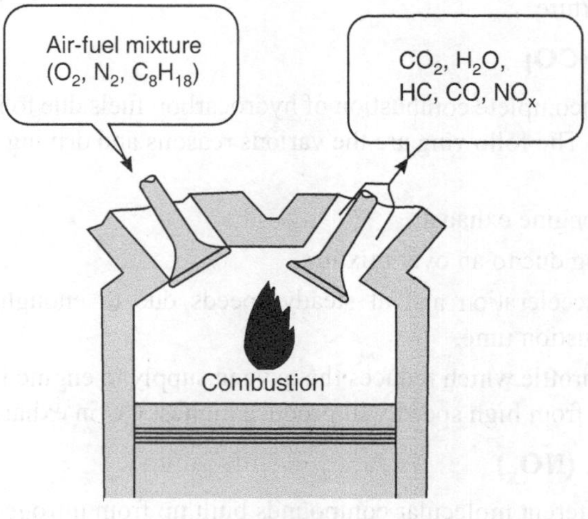

Fig. 16.1 Combustion

Exhaust emissions from the automobiles are just the by-products of combustion of a fuel. The major portion of the exhaust gas is composed of the three components: nitrogen (N_2), carbon dioxide (CO_2) and water vapour (H_2O). These are non-toxic. However, emission of carbon dioxide are being subjected to increasing scrutiny due to their contribution to the greenhouse effect.

Unfortunately 100% combustion is not possible and so there is a small amount of products of incomplete combustion. These are carbon monoxide (CO, hydrocarbons (HC) and oxides of nitrogen (NO_X). These are all gaseous components. Additionally, an engine produces some solid emissions of lead, sulphur, smoke and other particulates, as well as some sulphur oxides These emissions are unpleasant to breathe and are in many cases harmful or even dangerous t human beings, animals or plants. It is reported that the transport sector contributed most of the population load (27 percent NO_X, 74 percent carbon monoxide, 11 percent volatile organic compound and 100 percent lead) in urban areas.

The vehicular pollution is caused because of the following factors:

- Many vehicles are in poor condition, creating more particulates and burning fuel inefficiently.
- Lower quality fuel is used, leading to the emissions of far greater quantities of pollutants.
- Motor vehicles are concentrated in a few large cities.
- There is a lack of public transport and travel demand management.

Hydrocarbon (HC)

HC is raw unburnt gasoline emitted as gas from the automobile. It comes from the following sources:

- Gasoline is evaporated from the fuel tank and escaped into the atmosphere as hydrocarbon gas (HC).
- Carburetor emits hydrocarbon gas (HC), which has evaporated mainly from the float bowl.
- Blowby gas refers to the burnt and unburnt gases that pass between the piston and the cylinder wall during the compression and ignition cycles and escape into the atmosphere via the crankcase.
- Raw gas escaped by overlapping of intake and exhaust valve timing.
- Raw gas remaining near the cylinder walls (quenching) after burning and exhausted during the exhaust cycle.
- Raw gas created by incomplete combustion due to insufficient combustion time or an over rich air-fuel mixture.

Carbon monoxide (CO)

CO is produced by incomplete combustion of hydrocarbon fuels due to insufficient air (oxygen) and time for combustion. The following are the various reasons and driving conditions under which the CO is produced.

- Occurs only in engine exhaust
- High when idling due to an over mixture.
- Lowest when acceleration and at steady speeds due to enough oxygen available and sufficient combustion time.
- Closing of the throttle which reduces the oxygen supply to engine is the main cause of CO. So deceleration from high speed will produce highest CO in exhaust gases.

Oxides of nitrogen (NO_x)

There are several different molecular compounds built up from nitrogen (N_2) and oxygen (O_2), such as NO, NO_2, N_2O, N_2O_3, etc. These are all called 'Oxides of nitrogen' and are expressed for convenience sake as 'NO_X'. The reasons for NO_X formation are high temperature and oxygen availability.

NO_X is produced by nitrogen and oxygen in the air of the air-fuel mixture which combine if the temperature inside the combustion chamber rises above about 1800°C (3300°F). It happens that NOx is formed during complete combustion rather than during incomplete combustion as in the cases of CO and HC, because it is only then that the temperature is high enough to support the chemical reaction in which NO is formed.

If the temperature does not rise above 1800°C, then N_2 and O_2 will be exhausted as is from the exhaust system without combining to form NO.

Lead compounds (pb)

Lead is present in the exhaust when tetra methyl lead /or tetra ethyl lead is used as a cheap additive to improve the octane rating of a fuel, i.e. to improve the fuel's resistance to combustion knock. Lead compounds are toxic to humans, causing blood poisoning and nervous disorders. If leaded gasoline is used, the surface of the catalyst and O_2 sensor will become coated with lead and lose its effectiveness. For this reason, vehicles equipped with a catalytic converter must always use unleaded gasoline.

Smoke

Smoke consists of finely divided particles produced by incomplete combustion. It consists predominantly of carbon particles and other combustible materials. Generally the size of the particles is less than 1μ. The size of the oil smoke particles from 1.0 to 0.03μ.

Black smoke from diesel engines is due to the soot component of diesel particulate matter. Under most operating conditions, nearly all of this soot is oxidized in the cylinder, so the exhaust plume from a properly adjusted diesel engine is normally invisible-with a total opacity (absorbance plus reflectance) of 2 percent or less.

Visible smoke is generally due to injecting too much fuel for the amount of air available in the cylinder, or to poor mixing between fuel and air. These conditions can be prevented by proper design.

Under some conditions, diesel engines may also emit white, blue or grey smoke. These are due to the pressure of condensed hydrocarbon droplets in the exhaust. Unlike soot, these droplets scatter light, thus giving the smoke a bluish or whitish cast. Blue or grey smoke is generally due to vapourized lubricating oil and indicates an oil into the cylinder or exhaust system. White smoke is common when engines are first started in cold weather and usually goes away when the engine warms up.

Sulphur dioxide (SO_2)

Most crude petroleum products (particularly diesel) contain less than 1% sulphur. Sulphur dioxide from automotive vehicles is small compared with the sulphur dioxide released by the burning of coal. However, sulphur dioxide combined with fog was primary ingredients responsible for the famous 1952 London Smog and the deaths at Donora, Pennsylvania in 1948. The combination of moisture and sulphur dioxide produces sulphuric acid particularly when high temperatures are present. It should be noted that much of the sulphur dioxide combines with other materials in the atmosphere to form sulphates and consequently settles out as particulate matter.

Particulates (or) Particulate matter (PM)

Diesel particulate matter consists mostly of three compounds: soot formed during combustion, heavy hydrocarbons condensed or absorbed on the soot and sulphates. In order diesel engines soot was typically 40 to 80 percent of the total particulate mass, but soot emissions from modern emission-controlled engines are much lower. Most of the remaining particulate mass consists of heavy hydrocarbons absorbed or condensed on the soot. This is referred to as the *soluble organic fraction (SOF)* of the particulate matter. The SOF is derived from compounds formed during combustion.

Primary soot particles are small spheres of graphitic carbon approximately 0.01 mm in diameter. These are formed by the reaction of gaseous hydrocarbons such as acetylene under conditions of moderately high temperature and oxygen deficiency. The primary particles then agglomerate to form chains and clusters of linked particles, giving the soot its characteristic fluffy appearance.

Most of the soot formed during combustion is subsequently burned during the later portions of the expansion stroke. Typically, less than 10 percent of the soot formed in the cylinder survives to be emitted into the atmosphere. In modern emission-controlled diesel engines, less than one percent may be emitted.

EURO AND INDIAN EMISSION STANDARDS

The first Indian emission regulations were idle emission limits which became effective in 1989. These idle emission regulations were soon replaced by mass emission limits for both gasoline (1991) and diesel (1992) vehicles, which were gradually tightened during the 1990's. Since the year 2000, India started adopting European emission and fuel regulations for four-wheeled light-duty and for heavy-duty vehicles. Indian own emission regulations still apply to two- and three-wheeled vehicles.

The emission standards adopted for different class of vehicles in India and equivalent Euro emission standards are detailed below.

Table 16.2: Emission standards for two and three wheelers

BS-III

	Effective Date	Category	CO g/km	HC + NO_x g/km	PM g/km
Gasoline	1.10.2010	2W	1.00	1.00	-
Diesel		3W	1.25	1.25	-
		3W	0.50	0.50	0.05

Table 16.2: Emission standards for passenger cars and light commercial vehicles

	Effective Date	Category	Class	RM (kg)	CO (g/km)	HC (g/km)	NO_x (g/km)	HC + NO_x (g/km)	PM (g/km)	Evap. Emission (g/test)
Gasoline	**BS-III** 1 April 05 - NCR* 10 Cities† 1 Oct 10 + Nationwide	M (GVW 2500 or up to 6 seater)			2.30	0.20	0.15	----	----	
		N1 & M (GVW > 2500 or above 6 seater)	I	RM ≤ 1305	2.30	0.20	0.15	----	----	2.00
			II	1305 < RM ≤ 1760	4.17	0.25	0.18	----	----	
			III	1760 < RM	5.22	0.29	0.21	----	----	
	BS-IV 1 April 10 + NCR*, 12 Cities††	M (GVM 2500 or upto 6 seater)			1.00	0.10	0.08	----	----	
		N1&M (GVW>2500 or above 6 seater)	I	RM ≤ 1305	1.00	0.10	0.08	----	----	2.00
			II	1305 < RM ≤ 1760	1.81	0.13	0.10	----	----	
			III	1760 < RM	2.27	0.16	0.11	----	----	

* National Capital Region (Delhi)

† Mumbai, Kolkata, Chennai, Bangalore, Hyderabad including Secunderabad, Ahmedabad, Pune, Surat, Kanpur and Agra

†† Mumbai, Kolkata, Chennai, Bangalore, Hyderabad including Secunderabad, Ahmedabad, Pune, Surat, Kanpur, Agra, Solapur and Lucknow.

	Effective Date	Catogory	Class	RM (kg)	CO (g/km)	HC (g/km)	NO_X (g/km)	HC + NO_X (g/km)	PM (g/km)
Diesel	**BS-III** 1 April 05 - NCR*, 10 Cities† 1 Oct 10 + Nationwide	M (GVW ≤ 2500 or up to 6 seater)			0.64	----	0.50	0.56	0.05
		N1 & M (GVW > 2500 or above 6 seater)	I	RM ≤ 1305	0.64	----	0.50	0.56	0.05
			II	1305 < RM ≤ 1760	0.80	----	0.65	0.72	0.07
			III	1760 < RM	0.95	----	0.78	0.86	0.10
	BS-IV 1 April 10 + NCR*, 12 Cities††	M (GVW 2500 or above 6 seater)			0.50	----	0.25	0.30	0.025
		N1&M (GVW>2500 or above 6 seater)	I	RM ≤ 1305	0.50	----	0.25	0.30	0.025
			II	1305 < RM ≤ 1760	0.63	----	0.33	0.39	0.04
			III	1760 < RM	0.74	----	0.39	0.46	0.06

* National Capital Region (Delhi)

† Mumbai, Kolkata, Chennai, Bangalore, Hyderabad including Secunderabad, Ahmedabad, Pune, Surat, Kanpur and Agra

†† Mumbai, Kolkata, Chennai, Bangalore, Hyderabad including Secunderabad, Ahmedabad, Pune, Surat, Kanpur, Agra, Solapur and Lucknow.

Table 16.4: Emission standards for heavy duty commercial engines
Heavy Duty Vehicles (GUW>350 Kg)

	Effective date	Category	Test cycle	CO (g/kWh)	THC (g/kWh)	NO_X (g/kWh)	NMHC (g/kWh)	CH4 (g/kWh)	PM (g/kWh)[a]	ELR smoke (m^{-1})[a]	Free accl. smoke (m^{-1})[a]
Diesel, CNG or LPG Engines	1.04.05 BS-III	Diesel, CNG or LPG vehicles with GVW > 3500	Engine Steady state cycle (ESC)	2.10	0.66	5.00	NA	NA	0.10/ 0.13[b]	0.80	2.45
		Diesel, CNG or LPG vehicles with GVW > 3500 with advanced exhaust after treatment system	Engine Transient Cycle (ETC)	5.45	0.78	5.00	NA	NA	0.16/ 0.21[b]	0.80	2.45
	1.04.10 BS-IV	Only Diesel vehicles with GVW > 3500	Engine Steady state cycle (ESC)	1.50	0.46	3.50	NA	NA	0.02	0.50	2.45
		Diesel, CNG or LPG vehicles with GVW > 3500	Engine Transient Cycle (ETC)	4.00	-	3.50	0.55[a]	1.10[d]	0.03	NA	NA

a- Only for Diesel Engines,

b- For engines having swept vol. < 0.75 liter per cylinder & rated power speed > 3000 rpm,

c- A manufacturer may choose to measure the mass of THC instead of NMHC,

d- Only fo CNG vehicles.

Table 16.5: Comparison between Bharat Stage and EURO norms

Standard	Reference	Date	Region
India 2000	Euro I	2000	Nationwide
Bharat Stage II	Euro II	2001	NCR*, Mumbai, Kolkata, Chennai
		2003.04	NCR*, 11 Citiest†
		2005.04	Nationwide
Bharat Stage III	Euro III	2005.04	NCR*, 11 Cities
		2010.04	Nationwide
Bharat Stage IV	Euro IV	2010.04	NCR*, 11 Cities

* National Capital Region (Delhi).

† Mumbai, Kolkata, Bangalore, Hyderabad, Secunderabad, Ahmedabad, Pune, Surat, Kanpur and Agra.

EXHAUST EMISSIONS CONTROL MEASURES

To reduce the level of pollutant substances in the exhaust, the advanced technologies or control techniques such as fuel injection, catalytic converter, thermal after burning, exhaust gas recirculation, evaporative emission control have been developed and adopted:

However, exhaust emission problems are not easy to solve. For example, as the CO content is reduced, the proportion of equally toxic oxides of nitrogen tends to rise.

The air pollution due to internal combustion engines can be reduced in the following ways.

1. Modification of internal combustion engines to reduce the amount of pollutants formed during fuel combustion.
2. Development of substitute fuels for petroleum based fuels which will yield low concentration of pollutants during combustion.
3. Addition of emission control devices to remove or to decompose pollutants into harmless gases.

Each car now has the following major systems for controlling pollutants.

Positive crankcase ventilation (PCV)

This is a system that sends fresh air through the crankcase to sweep out blowby and fuel vapours. The air then enters the engine where the pollutants from the crankcase have another chance to burn.

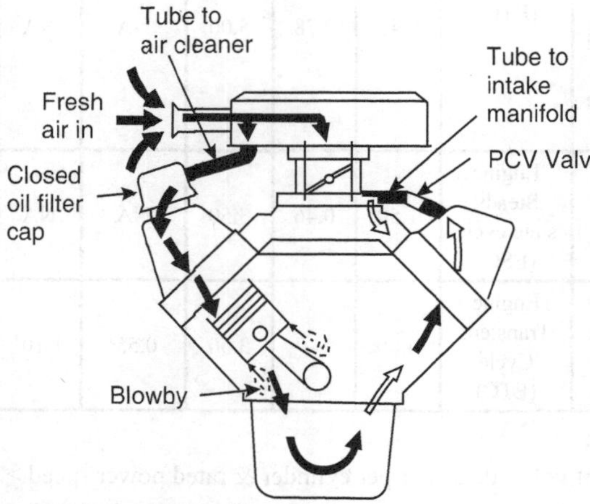

Fig. 16.2 Positive crankcase ventilation

During normal engine operation, some combustion gases leak past the piston rings (blowby) and tend to pressurize the crankcase. In addition, traces of water appear, and some unburned fuel may reach the crankcase. Without ventilation, all these would have a deteriorating effect on the engine oil and also on mechanical parts. Earlier ventilation systems merely vented the crankcase to the atmosphere, but this contributed to air pollution. Closed-crankcase ventilation systems were therefore developed. This type of system is referred to as closed crankcase ventilation or positive crankcase ventilation (PCV). Clean air is drawn in through the filter in the air cleaner, where it mixes with the blowby gases in the crankcase. The gases are then drawn from the crankcase through a flow control valve (PCV valve) into the intake manifold and then to the combustion chambers, where they are burned.

Evaporative emission control

This is a system that captures any fuel vapours coming from the fuel tank and float bowl. It prevents the vapours from escaping into the atmosphere.

Charcoal canister (some models only)

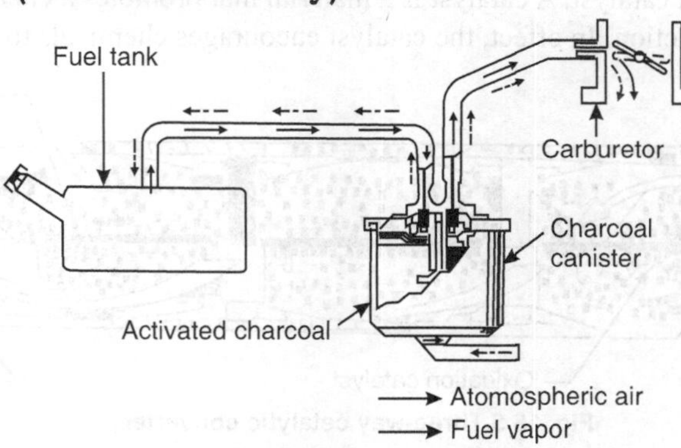

Flow of fuel vapour and air

Fig. 16.3 Charcoal canister

Harmful hydrocarbon (HC) gas is generated in the fuel tank, and must not be discharged into the atmosphere. In some engines, such fuel vapour is stored temporarily in a container when the engine is off and is sent to the combustion chamber to be burned when the engine is turned on again.

The charcoal canister is one such fuel vapour container. It is filled with activated charcoal and the fuel vapour is directed into it along with air. The HC gas is separated from the vapour by the charcoal. When the engine is turned on, the gas is sent through the intake manifold to the combustion chamber where it is burned and becomes a harmless exhaust gas.

Exhaust emission control

This includes a variety of systems such as catalytic converters, air-injection system, exhaust gas recirculation etc. These work together to reduce the pollutants in the exhaust gas emitted from the tailpipe.

Air-Injection (AI) and Air-Suction (AS) systems

In this method, fresh air is supplied to the exhaust manifold by an air injection pump or reed valve. So that it provides additional oxygen to burn HC and CO coming out of the cylinders.

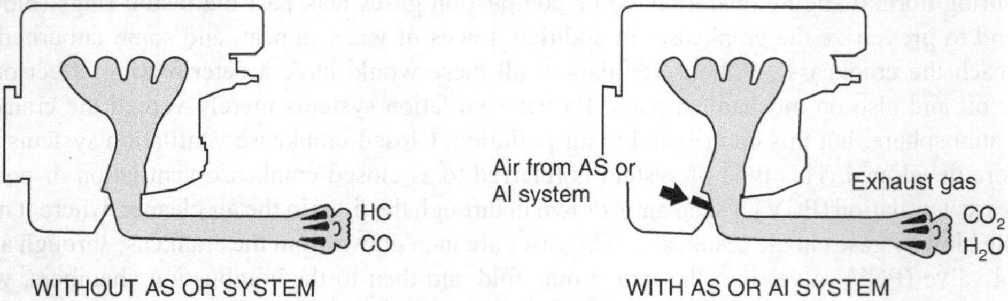

Fig. 16.4 Air-injection/Air-suction system

Catalytic converter

Catalytic converters provide another way to treat the exhaust gas. These devices located in the exhaust system, convert harmful gases into harmless gases. Inside the catalytic converter, the exhaust gases passover a catalyst. A catalyst is a material that promotes a chemical reaction without being affected by the reaction. In effect, the catalyst encourages chemicals to react with each other.

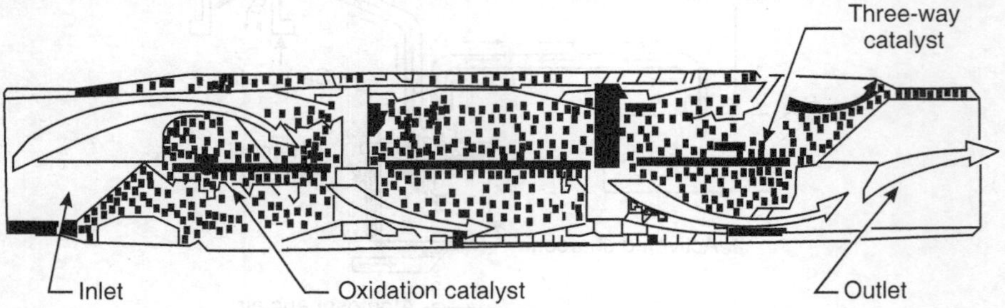

Fig. 16.5 Three-way cetalytic converter

Converter systems with both oxidation and reduction catalysts are called 2 stage or 3-way catalytic converter systems. The three way catalytic converter is the most ideal type of catalytic converter since it can convert not only CO and HC, but also NO_X into non-polluting substances.

Some of the newest converters have even started to use gold mixed with the more traditional catalysts. Gold is cheaper than the other materials and could increase oxidation, the chemical reaction that reduces pollutants, by up to 40 percent.

The oxidizing converter handles HC and CO, using platinum or palladium as the catalysts. The air helps the oxidizing catalyst convert the HC and CO into carbon dioxide and water. The reducing converter handles NO_X using metal rhodium. It splits oxygen from the nitrogen. The NO_X becomes harmless nitrogen (N_2) and Oxygen (O_2).

Converter design

There are two kinds of converter design: pellet type and monolithic. In either kind, the oxidation and reduction catalysts are on ceramic substrates in a steel housing or shell.

In pellet type converters, the catalyst metals are deposited on ceramic pellets, which are placed in beds in the converter housing. In a monolithic converter, the catalysts are deposited on a large ceramic honeycomb block or biscuit, which is installed in the converter shell. Exhaust flows through the pores of the ceramic monolithic, which provides a large surface area for the catalytic reaction. Most cars today use a honeycomb structure.

Oxidation and reduction converter systems work best when the engine air-fuel ratio is regulated at 14.7:1 (stoichiometric ratio). The stoichiometric ratio provides the most complete combustion of gasoline and air and the fewest harmful by products. Fig. 16.6 shows that HC and CO emissions are high at air-fuel ratios richer than 14.7:1. NO_X emissions increase rapidly with ratios leaner than 14.7:1. Therefore, a 3-way catalytic converter system has an exhaust oxygen sensor to measure oxygen in the exhaust. The voltage signal from this sensor goes to engine control computer. The computer then controls the air-fuel mixture for the needed 14.7:1 ratio. All 3-way converter systems are used with an air-fuel metering feedback system or electronic engine controls.

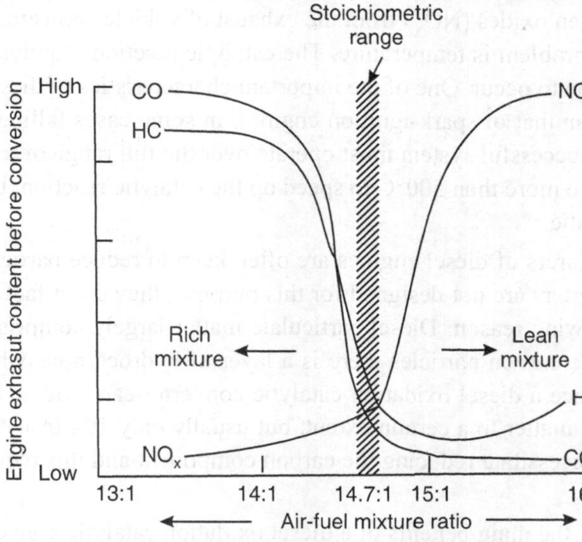

Fig. 16.6 Pollutants vs Air-fuel mixture ratio

Efficient working conditions

All exhaust catalysts work best when hot. In fact, they do not work at all when cold. A catalytic converter must heat up to 204ºC to 260ºC (400ºF to 500ºF) to start working. Engineers call this the light-off temperature, at which the catalyst is 50% effective. A fully hot converter reaches temperatures of 480ºC to 870ºC (900ºF to 1600ºF) for complete efficiency.

Exhaust Gas Recirculation (EGR)

Oxides of nitrogen (NO_X) can be controlled by diluting air-fuel mixture entering the engine with an inert or non-combustible substance. During the combustion the inert substance will absorb a portion of the chemical energy released, thereby reducing the combustion temperature and consequently NO_X emission level.

In the exhaust gas recirculation (EGR) method, a portion of the exhaust gas is recirculated to the cylinder intake charge. This reduces the peak combustion temperature, since the inert gas serves as a heat sink. This also reduces the quantity of oxygen available for combustion.

About 15% recycle will reduce NO_X emission by about 80%. The maximum percentage which can be recirculated is limited by rough engine operation and loss of power.

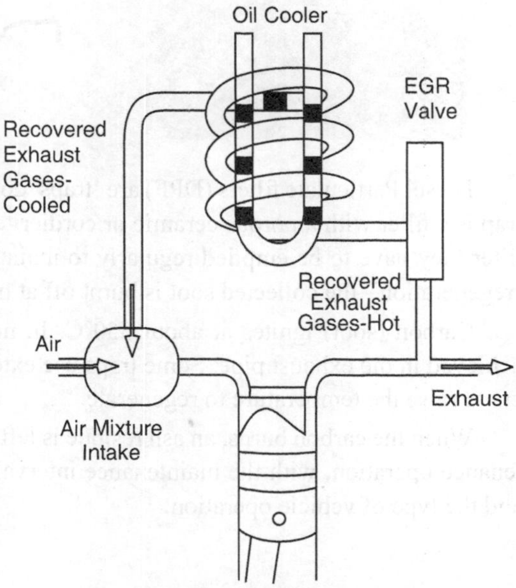

Fig. 16.7 EGR

Diesel Oxidation Catalyst (DOC)

Diesel engines always run 'lean'. One outcome of this is that the catalytic converter can only operate in a 'two-way' mode which means that it can oxidize carbon monoxide and hydrocarbons but will not be able to reduce NO_X. For this reason, a catalytic converter used on a diesel engine is often known as a 'diesel oxidation catalytic converter'. No catalytic system has yet been commercialized that can eliminate nitrogen oxides (NO_X) from the exhaust of vehicles powered by diesel and other lean-burn engines. The problem is temperature. The catalytic reaction requires certain temperature criteria for NO_X reduction to occur. One of the important characteristics of diesel engines is that the exhaust gas is cooler than that of spark-ignition engines, in some cases falling to a temperature of barely 100°C at idle. A successful system must operate over the full range of temperatures found in vehicle exhaust: 150°C to more than 500°C to speed up the catalytic reaction, the low temperatures being the most problematic.

Users and manufacturers of diesel engines are often keen to reduce particulate emissions, and although catalytic converters are not designed for this purpose, they do in fact have a small beneficial impact for the following reason. Diesel particulate matter largely comprises carbon (soot) but around the outside of the carbon particles there is a layer of hydrocarbons which add to the mass of particulate matter. Since a diesel oxidation catalytic converter can oxidize hydrocarbons, it can reduce diesel particulate matter to a certain extent, but usually only 10-20%. Achieving greater reductions than this will necessitate reducing the carbon component and this requires the fitment of a filter (particulate trap).

As described above, the main benefits of a diesel oxidation catalytic converter are its ability to oxidize toxic carbon monoxide and hydrocarbons into non-toxic carbon dioxide and water.

Particulate trap (or Particulate filter)

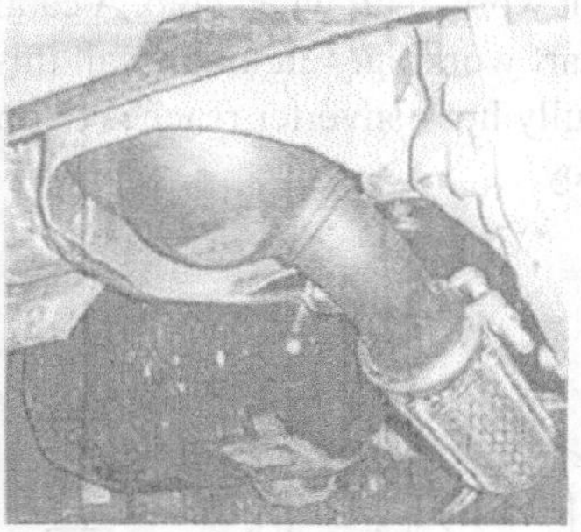

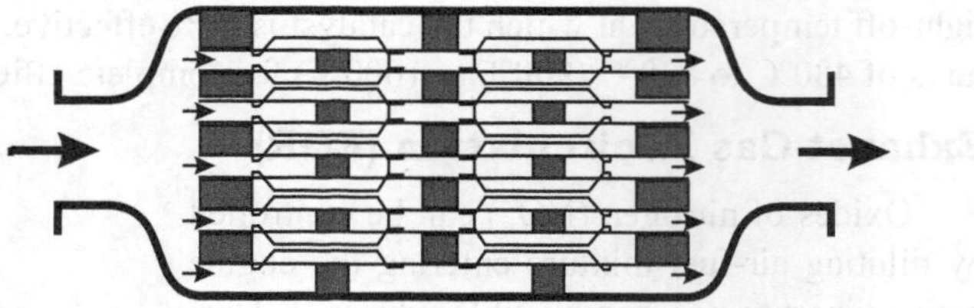

Diesel Particulate filters (DPF) are 'traps' do just that, they catch bits of soot in the exhaust. The trap is a filter with a porous ceramic or cordierite substrate or fine mesh metallic filter. As with any filter they have to be emptied regularly to maintain performance. For a DPF this process is called 'regeneration'–the collected soot is burnt off at high temperature to leave only a tiny ash residue.

Carbon (soot) ignites at about 550°C. In normal operation this temperature would rarely be achieved in the exhaust pipe. Some traps use external means such as fuel burners or electrical heaters to raise the temperature to regenerate.

When the carbon burns, an ash residue is left which needs to be removed. This is a simple maintenance operation, with the maintenance interval varying depending on which type of trap is used and the type of vehicle operation.

Review Questions

1. What are the sources of air pollution?
2. List out the factors affecting pollution formation?
3. Discuss about pollutants that are produced by automobiles in Delhi?
4. What methods are adopted to control diesel emissions?
5. What is EGR? Why it is provided?
6. What is known as Smog in an automobile?
7. What are the methods to clean the exhaust gas?
8. What is a charcoal canister?
9. What may cause white smoky exhaust?
10. What may cause black smoky exhaust at slow speed?
11. What is meant by positive crankcase ventilation?
12. Enumerate the sources of hydrocarbon (HC) emission from Automobiles. Write its effects on human health and natural environment.
13. What are the possible sources of emissions from automobiles?
14. What are the causes of formation of CO in engine exhaust?
15. What are the causes of formation of NOx in engine exhaust?
16. What do the catalytic converters do in the exhaust system?
17. What do you understand by blowby? What are its effects?
18. Write a note or Euro and Bharat emission standards.

17
CHAPTER

ALTERNATE FUELS

Environmental awareness, stimulated fuel diversification and the high price of conventional fuels have led to the creation of incentives to promote and further evaluate alternative fuel sources for conventional internal combustion engines.

NATURAL GAS

Natural gas comes from the decay of ancient organisms, but it naturally takes a gaseous form instead of a liquid form. It is often dissolved in crude oil at the high pressures existing in a reservoir. There are also reservoirs of natural gas, known as non-associated gas, that contain only gas and no oil. Most natural gas comes from three types of wells: natural gas-and-condensate wells, oil wells, and coal bed methane wells. Natural gas is composed primarily of methane, the smallest and simplest hydrocarbon.

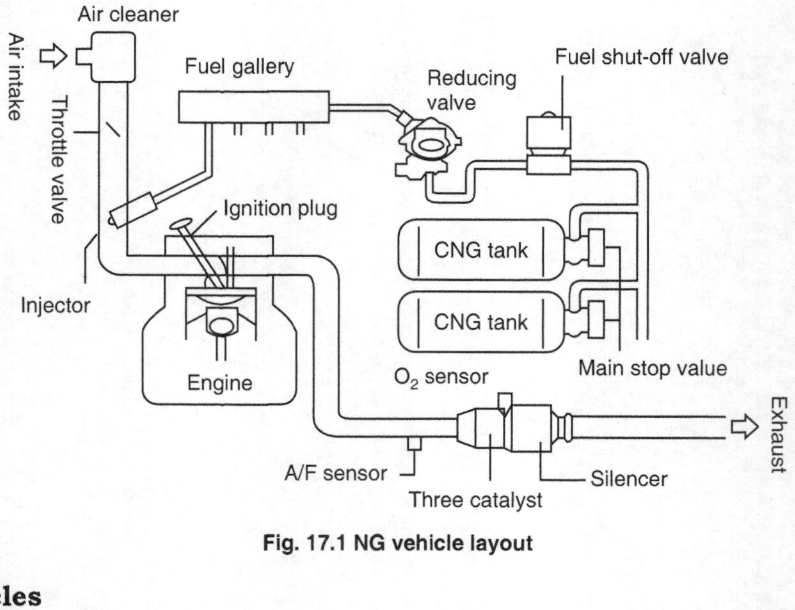

Fig. 17.1 NG vehicle layout

NG Vehicles

Methane mixes readily with air and has a high octane rating which makes it a very good spark-ignition engine fuel. It has a high ignition temperature that makes it unsuited for use in compression-ignition engines, though it can be made to work in such engines for heavy-duty vehicles. Diverse engine technologies running on natural gas include: a) stoichiometric combustion, b) lean burn; c) single point injection; and d) multi point injection. Natural gas is stored on-board as either compressed natural gas (CNG) or liquefied natural gas (LNG). When used as a transportation vehicle fuel, natural gas must be either compressed (CNG) or liquefied (LNG) to decrease its storage volume. CNG is the most common option for cars. The gas is stored in pressurized 200-270 bar cylinders made of steel or composites, which are located within the boot space. Being pressurized, it is heavier than conventional fuel tanks and increases the car total weight by around 60 kg.

Engine modifications required

Gasoline conversions to CNG, accepting the limitations that go with the low compression ratio inherited from the original fuel, have provided the basis for large conversion programs around the world. In the case of diesel engine conversions, some rework of the engine is needed to match the compression ratio to that of natural gas. This work usually involves machining the pistons to lower the compression ratio. The addition of an ignition and fuel control system are the other main modifications. This results in an engine with long life and very low particulate emissions. With the use of the advanced fuel control equipment that is now available, both converted gasoline and diesel engines can meet today's emissions regulations easily.

Advantages

- Produced at relatively low cost and is cleaner burning than gasoline or diesel fuel.
- They reduce environmentally harmful emissions. Natural-gas vehicles can achieve up to a 93 percent reduction in carbon monoxide emissions, 33 percent reduction in emissions of various oxides of nitrogen and a 50 percent reduction in reactive hydrocarbons when compared to gasoline vehicles.
- Natural gas costs are lower than gasoline. On average, natural gas costs one-third less than gasoline at the pump.
- Natural gas is convenient and abundant.
- Natural gas vehicles (NGVs) have lower maintenance costs. Because natural gas burns so cleanly, it results in less wear and tear on the engine and extends the time between tune-ups and oil changes.
- Octane number is around 110, which makes it a very good SI engine fuel. Because of this high octane number the flame speed is higher and engines can operate with a high compression ratio.
- No smoke

Disadvantages

- Low energy density resulting in low engine performance.
- Low engine volumetric efficiency because it is a gaseous fuel.
- Need for large pressurized fuel storage tank. There is some safety concern with a pressurized fuel tank.
- Inconsistent fuel properties
- Refueling is a slow process

Performance characteristics

Vehicle engines using natural gas can increase their power and efficiency by increasing the compression ratio. Compared to typical gasoline, natural gas has a high octane rating that will support higher compression ratios. Since natural gas enters the engine entirely as a gas, while gasoline typically enters the engine as part liquid and part gas, for the same displacement, the gasoline engine will be able to draw more air and fuel and produce higher power. Natural gas engines can overcome this inherent disadvantage by increasing compression ratio, cylinder displacement or increasing volumetric efficiency.

The energy efficiency of engines running on natural gas is almost equal to that of gasoline engines in new cars, where dedicated injectors are used for the alternative fuel but are lower compared with modern diesel engines. Gasoline vehicles converted to run on natural gas suffer because of the engine low compression ratio, resulting in a cropping (10-15%) of delivered power while running on natural gas. In recent bi-fuel gasoline-NG vehicles, the efficiency loss is reduced to 5-10%. CNG dedicated engines use a higher compression ratio due to the fuel's higher octane number of 120–130.

Emission characteristics

Natural gas is composed primarily of methane which dominates its emissions characteristics. Methane barely participates in the atmospheric reactions that produce ozone, though it does contribute to global warming when released into the atmosphere. Because of its high hydrogen-to-carbon ratio (the highest at 4 to 1), the combustion of methane produces about 10% less carbon dioxide than combustion of the energy-equivalent amount of gasoline or diesel fuel.

Compared to petrol, cars running on natural gas offer a CO emissions reduction of 90% to 97%, 25% reduced CO_2, 35% to 60% reduced NOx emissions, and 50% to 75% reduced non-methane hydrocarbon emissions. In addition to this, there are fewer toxic and carcinogenic pollutants, little or no particulate matter and no evaporative emissions.

LIQUEFIED PETROLEUM GAS (LPG)

LPG is a generic term for fuels that include butane, propane and small amounts of other hydrocarbons. The common characteristic among these fuels is that they are easily liquefied by the application of modest pressures (less than 300 psi).

Propane and butane are obtained from oil and gas wells. Propane is a type of liquefied petroleum gas (LPG) made from crude oil. When pressure is applied to a container of propane, the gas becomes a liquid. When the pressure is released, the liquid propane turns into a gas.

For automobile engines, two types of LPG are used. One is propane and the other is butane. Sometimes, a mixture of propane and butane is used as liquid petroleum gas in automobile engines.

Modifications required (Conversion)

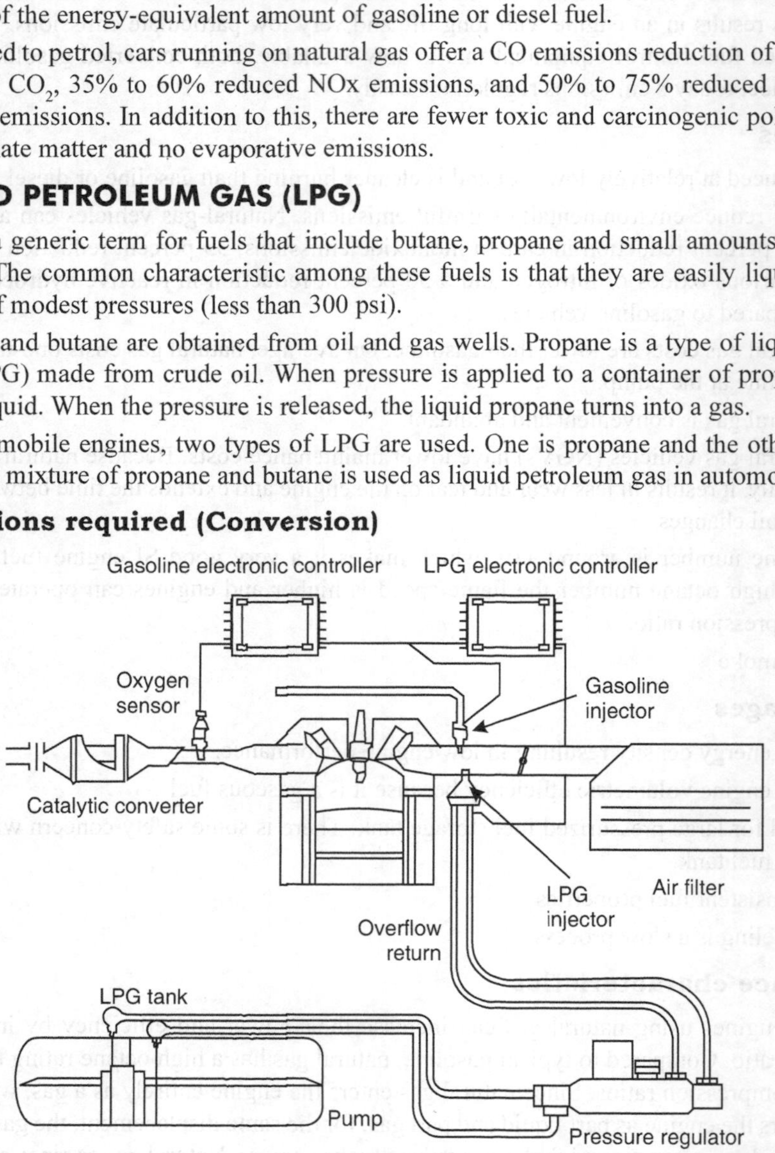

Fig. 17.2 General layout of LPG equipment, devices and units installed in petrol vehicles

LPG vehicles work much like gasoline-powered vehicles with spark-ignited engines. LPG is stored as a liquid in a separate steel or composite vessel at the pressure of 10 bar. LPG supply to the engine is controlled by a regulator or vaporizer, which converts the LPG to a vapour. The vapour is fed to a mixer located near the intake manifold, where it is metered and mixed with filtered air before being drawn into the combustion chamber where it is burned to produce power, just like gasoline. LPG injection engines, developed over the past 15 years, do not vaporize the LPG. Instead, the LPG is injected into the combustion chamber in liquid form. These systems have proven to be reliable in terms of power, engine durability, and cold starting.

Advantages

- Has an octane rating of well over 100. This allows the engine compression ratio to be raised for greater power and efficiency.
- Propane burns cleanly. Less engine wear occurs. Therefore, less maintenance is required.
- No fuel pump and little emission control equipment is used.
- LPG mixes with air at all temperatures.
- Has high anti-knock characteristics.
- LPG costs are lower than gasoline. On average, costs 50% less than gasoline.
- Engine may have a 50% longer life.
- No smoke

Disadvantages

A special fuel system is needed to handle the pressurized liquid and gas. The system includes special fuel tanks to hold reserve supplies of propane under pressure.

Performance characteristics

For vaporized propane fuel systems, propane enters the engine as a gas instead of part liquid and part gas as gasoline does. By entering the engine fully vapourized, some air that could otherwise be used for combustion is displaced. Therefore, theoretically, propane vehicles should have lower power and slower acceleration than their gasoline counterparts, especially in bifuel configuration. In practice, however, these differences do not always show up though power and acceleration are typically reduced. Acceleration in terms of 0-50 mph time can be up to 10% slower. Propane should theoretically have a cold-start advantage over gasoline since it vapourizes so quickly, even at low temperatures.

Emission characteristics

Like natural gas, propane vehicles do not have any evaporative or running loss emissions associated with fuel. Unburned hydrocarbons from propane are easier to oxidize in oxidation catalysts than methane, which results in low unburned hydrocarbon emissions. Being a gas, propane mixes very well with the air before entering the engine, resulting in low carbon monoxide emissions. When using a three-way catalyst, oxides of nitrogen emissions can also be reduced to very low levels if the air-fuel ratio is kept at the stoichiometric value.

BIODIESEL

The esterified versions of vegetable oils have been given the generic label of "biodiesel". Initially it was believed that vegetable oils could be used directly with minimal processing and preparation. However, extensive engine testing proved that while diesel engines operated satisfactorily on raw vegetable oils, combustion residues and deposits would quickly cause problems with fuel injectors, piston rings and oil stability. By reacting the oils with methanol or ethanol, esters (biodiesel) are formed which have much improved characteristics as fuels.

The most popular types of crops from which biodiesel can be extracted include soybeans, sunflowers, jetropha, peanuts, rapeseed, etc.

Biodiesel is made from renewable feedstocks through simple refining processes such as transesterification with low molecular weight alcohols, dilution with low viscosity miscible solvents, micro emulsification, and pyrolysis. These techniques decrease the viscosity of fuels containing vegetable oil. It can be concluded that out of the four methods, transesterification method is simple and cost effective.

Engine modifications required

Engines are designed, manufactured, and warranted for a fuel that has certain specific properties. Therefore, it is important to take endorsements from engine manufacturers for the use of biodiesel and their blends. For some of the caterpillar and other manufactures engines, a blend of 5% biodiesel with diesel fuel (B5) is approved. More than 5% biodiesel in diesel fuel in not covered under engine warranty.

Several marine engine manufacturers of Japan, the U.S. and Europe endorse the use of 100% biodiesel (B100) as fuel in diesel engines. Some manufacturers warranty the newer engines and insist on a change of hoses, seals, and rubber parts in their older engines, while other engine manufacturers give warranties on a case-by-case basis.

Advantages

1. Runs in any conventional, unmodified diesel engine.
2. Can be used alone or mixed in any amount with petroleum diesel fuel.
3. More lubricating than diesel fuel, so it increases the life of engines.
4. Biodegradable and non-toxic.
5. Has a high flash point, or ignition temperature, of about 300°F compared to petroleum diesel fuel, which has a flash point of 125°F. This means it's safer to transport.
6. Auto ignition, fuel consumption, power output, and engine torque are relatively unaffected by biodiesel. So basically, the engine just runs like normal (except for the smell).
7. Biodiesel is an oxygenated fuel, thus implying that their oxygen content plays a role in making fatty compounds suitable as diesel fuel by "cleaner" burning.
8. Esters have lower viscosities than the parent oils. Accordingly, they improve the injection process and ensure better atomization of the fuel in the combustion chamber.
9. Cetane number of esters is greater than those of both vegetable oil and No. 2 diesel fuel.
10. Reduced exhaust emissions such as sulfur dioxide, hydrocarbons, particulates, carbon monoxide and carbon dioxide by 100, 56, 55, 43 and 78 percent respectively.
11. 90% reduction in cancer risks, according to Ames Mutagenicity Tests.
12. Provides a domestic, renewable energy supply.

Disadvantages

1. Slight increase in NO_X emissions (up to 10% depending upon blend).
2. Slight decrease in fuel economy on energy basis (about 10% for pure biodiesel).
3. Thickens more than diesel fuel in cold weather, may need to use blends in sub freezing conditions.

Performance characteristics

Straight biodiesel has a cetane rating significantly higher than typical No.2 diesel fuel, slightly lower heating value, slightly higher viscosity and contains approximately 10 mass percent oxygen. The lower heating value will cause a small loss in maximum power if the engine fuel system is not recalibrated.

On a mass basis, neat biodiesel (100% biodiesel-B100) has approximately 13% less energy than typical diesel fuel. This loss in energy is caused by the oxygen content of biodiesel of approximately 10%. Biodiesel's higher specific gravity of approximately 0.88 compared to approximately 0.82 for diesel fuel regains some of the loss in energy on a mass basis for an overall impact of approximately 7% loss in energy per unit volume. Thus, an engine adjusted for diesel fuel should experience a loss of power of approximately 7% when using neat biodiesel (blends with diesel fuel should experience power losses proportionate to the blend level).

Emission characteristics

In a diesel engine, 100% biodiesel (soy methyl ester) showed a significant reduction in hydrocarbon emissions, no significant change in carbon monoxide emissions, a slight reduction in oxides of nitrogen emissions and reduced particulate emissions.

ALCOHOL

Ethanol (ethyl alcohol) can be made from ethylene or from fermentation of grains and sugar. Much of it made from corn, sugar beets, sugar cane and even cellulose (wood and paper).

Ethanol is a single compound and much lighter than the typical hydrocarbons that make up gasoline. The specific gravity of ethanol is higher than gasoline. A litre of ethanol weighs 20-80 g more per litre than typical gasoline. Ethanol's viscosity is higher than gasoline but is still less than diesel fuel. No problems are known for handling of ethanol in cold weather due to high viscosity.

Ethanol boosted engine

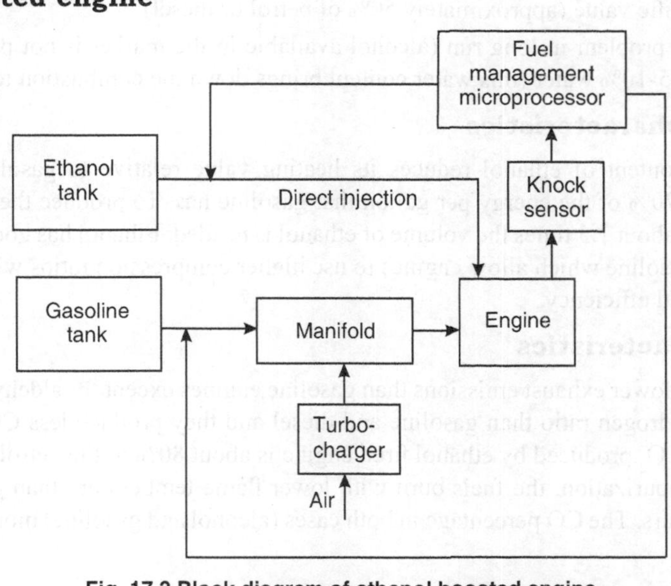

Fig. 17.3 Block diagram of ethanol boosted engine

Ethanol boosting starts with a small turbocharged engine with separate gasoline and ethanol fuel injectors for each cylinder. The gasoline system mixes fuel and air in the motor's intake manifold using port injection. The second system injects small amounts of ethanol directly into the combustion chamber to control premature detonation, or knock, that results from the high temperature and pressure of a turbocharged engine. The ethanol prevents knock by cooling the air/fuel mixture until the engine is ready for combustion.

Engine modifications required

The use of ethanol blends in conventional gasoline vehicles is restricted to low mixtures, as ethanol is corrosive and can degrade some of the materials in the engine and fuel system. Also the engine has to be adjusted for a higher compression ratio as compared to a pure gasoline engine, in order to take advantage of ethanol's higher octane rating and higher oxygen content, thus allowing an improvement in fuel efficiency and a reduction of tailpipe emissions. Stock pistons with flat or dished tops can be replaced with domed pistons, which reduce the size of the combustion chamber and thus increase the compression ratio.

The adaptation of the engine management systems to the ethanol is found to be specific to the vehicle manufacturers control strategy.

Advantages

- Used as fuel in dual fuel engine
- Low NO_X (combustion temperature is low)
- Oxygenated fuel – complete combustion
- No major engine modifications required
- Less HC & CO
- Higher compression ratio is possible – higher efficiency

Disadvantages

- Aldehyde emissions
- Cold starting problem
- Less availability
- Low calorific value (approximately 50% of petrol or diesel)
- Corrosion problem in long run (alcohol available in the market is not pure, i.e., 90-95% alcohol + 5-10% water (this water content brings down the combustion temperature).

Performance characteristics

The oxygen content of ethanol reduces its heating value relative to gasoline. Ethanol has between 64% and 70% of the energy per gallon that gasoline has. To produce the same amount of power as gasoline, about 1.5 times the volume of ethanol is needed. Ethanol has good octane properties compared to gasoline which allow engines to use higher compression ratios with the benefits of improved power and efficiency.

Emission characteristics

Alcohols have lower exhaust emissions than gasoline engines except for aldehydes. Ethanol has lower carbon to hydrogen ratio than gasoline and diesel and they produce less CO_2. For the same power output, the CO_2 produced by ethanol fired engine is about 80% of the petrol engine. Because of high heat of vapourization, the fuels burn with lower flame temperature than gasoline and less NO_X formation occurs. The CO percentage in both cases (alcohol and gasoline) more or less remains same.

5. GOSOHOL

Gasohol is gasoline (petrol) to which a small amount of alcohol has been added. Usually the alcohol is about 10 percent of the fuel. The alcohol can be made from corn or other agricultural products. Advocates of gasohol say that it reduces our dependence on foreign sources of oil.

Gasohol can be used in engines without any changes in the fuel system. However, when fuel with a larger percentage of alcohol is used, the carburetor or fuel injection system must be recalibrated.

Note: 30 % of India total foreign exchange earnings is utilized on oil imports.

6. HYDROGEN

Hydrogen has many characteristics that makes it the ultimate alternative fuel to fossil energy fuels. Hydrogen can be combusted directly in internal-combustion engines or it can be used in fuel cells to produce electricity with high efficiency.

Hydrogen is now produced primarily from the steam reformation of natural gas, though it can be produced from almost any source containing hydrogen in its composition. Hydrogen can also be produced from the electrolysis of water.

Engine modifications required

One of the primary problems that have been encountered in the development of operational hydrogen engines is premature ignition due to hot spots in the combustion chamber, such as spark splug electrodes, exhaust valve or carbon deposits. Most modern fuel metering systems deliver the fuel and air separately to the combustion chamber. Thus, hydrogen can be added to the air mixture at a point where the conditions for preignition are less favourable. Techniques that thermally dilute the charge, such as water injection or residual exhaust gas recirculation (EGR), are also often added to hydrogen engines to help control problems of preignition. Some research works suggested that the most effective method of solving the problems of preignition and knock would be to redesign the combustion chamber and coolant systems to accommodate hydrogen's unique combustion properties.

Direct injection hydrogen engines need high-pressure leak free hydrogen injector to improve hydrogen-air mixing rate and thereby thermal efficiency.

Hydrogen cannot be used directly in a diesel engine since hydrogen's auto ignition is too high. Thus, diesel engines must be outfitted with spark plugs or use a small amount of diesel fuel to ignite the gas.

Advantages

- Clean fuel – carbon is not present – less pollution (almost zero emission)
- Calorific value is better than petrol (on mass basis) – 2 to 4 times
- Light weight
- Fuel availability. There are a number of different ways of making hydrogen, including electrolysis of water.
- Fuel leakage to environment is not a pollutant.

Disadvantages

- Process is costlier
- Production, storing and handling are difficult
- High NO_X emissions because of high flame temperature

Performance characteristics

Only experimental hydrogen vehicles have been built to date and it is not possible to derive meaningful conclusions about vehicle performance characteristics from them. Based on the internal combustion engine work conducted to date, hydrogen engines should be able to produce the same amount of power that petroleum fuel engines do with superior efficiency since the lean limit of hydrogen is much lower than petroleum or other alternative fuels. A major concern about hydrogen vehicles will be operating range. A highly efficient drive train combined with a vehicle design that has low aerodynamic drag and rolling resistance may be necessary to achieve practical operating range.

Emission characteristics

When hydrogen is oxidized in fuel cells, the only emission is water vapour. When hydrogen is combusted in internal combustion engines, water vapour is again the major emission, though some oxides of nitrogen may be formed if combustion temperatures are high enough. Therefore, the use of hydrogen as a transportation vehicle fuel would result in few or no emissions that would contribute to ozone formation.

Like CNG or propane vehicles, hydrogen vehicles should not produce evaporative emissions since the fuel system would be closed. Even if hydrogen is released (eg. Fuel spills or vehicle maintenance) it rises quickly (being lighter than air) and does not cause any reactions in the atmosphere.

7. ELECTRIC VEHICLE (EV)

The conventional internal combustion electric vehicle (ICEV) employs a combustion engine for propulsion. Its energy source is liquid petrol or diesel. In contrast, the electric vehicle (EV) employs an electric motor and the corresponding energy sources are batteries, fuel cells, capacitors and/or flywheels.

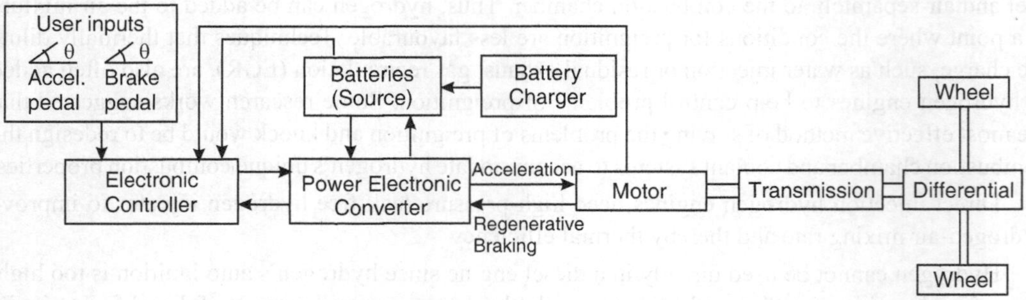

Fig. 17.4 Block diagram of an electric vehicle

An electric vehicle consists of a battery that provides energy, an electric motor that drives the wheels, and a controller that regulates the energy flow to the motor.

Previously, the EV was mainly converted from the ICEV, simply replacing the combustion engine by the electric motor while retaining all the other components. This converted EV has been fading out because of the drawback of heavy weight, loss of flexibility and degradation of performance. At present, the modern EV is purposely built. This purpose built EV is based on original body and frame designs to satisfy the structural requirements unique to EVs and to make use of the greater flexibility of electric propulsion.

Fig. 17.4 shows the general configuration of the EV, consisting of three major subsystems-electric propulsion, energy source and auxiliary. The electric propulsion subsystem comprises the electronic controller, power converter, electric motor, mechanical transmission and driving wheels. There are no gearbox and clutch in these vehicles.

Automobile manufacturers have identified three types of rechargeable battery as suitable for electric car use. Those types are lead-acid batteries, nickel metal hydride (NiMH) batteries, and lithium-ion (Li-ion) batteries and the space occupied by these heavy batteries is large. Operational problems include the limited range of the vehicle and its comparatively low maximum speed.

Advantages

1. The running cost is 40 paise per kilometer
2. Zero emission vehicle
3. While running, it does not produce noise and vibrations
4. As there are no gears and clutch in these vehicles, they are extremely reliable, safe and easy to drive and manoeuvre in the congested cities
5. Easier to service and maintenance
6. They are ideal for stop-start conditions.

Disadvantages

1. The vehicle range is limited on one charge. The vehicle can run 80 km on a single charge
2. The top speed is limited
3. It is heavy and bulky

Note: Reva electric car company of Bangalore had already launched the electric vehicle in India.

HYBRID ELECTRIC VEHICLES (HEV)

A hybrid is a vehicle that has two or more power sources to propel it. An example that is often seen is a moped. The petrol engine is one power source and the rider provides the second power source by 'pedal power'. Other vehicles that are classed as hybrid include some trains (diesel and electric) and submarines (nuclear and electric).

Although very quite in operation and producing almost zero emissions, the disadvantages of the electric vehicle is often the heavy weight of batteries required to propel it, and also the very short distance which can be covered before it is necessary to recharge the batteries.

Petrol engine cars are both lightweight and can cover extensive distances before they need to refill the fuel tank. Refilling the fuel tank is very rapid compared with the time taken to recharge batteries. The disadvantages of the petrol engine are high emissions and high fuel consumption when compared to electric power.

A hybrid car combines the low emissions and fuel consumption of an electric vehicle and provides a lightweight vehicle that can travel a long distance. The hybrid vehicle effectively makes use of one or both of the power sources to propel the vehicle. Depending on how the hybrid system is designed, the petrol engine simply function as a means of driving a generator. The generator then charges the batteries that power the electric motors, which provide power to the vehicle transmission. Alternative designs allow the petrol engine and/or the electric motors to be selected to provide power to the vehicle transmission system.

Research has shown that the average driver of a vehicle uses the maximum power of an engine less than 1% of the overall driving time. Therefore, the size of the petrol engine used in the current range of hybrid cars provides sufficient power to be acceptable to most drivers.

A typical hybrid car contains the following components.

Petrol engine: The engine is similar to those fitted to conventional vehicles e.g. four cylinders, four-stroke normally aspirated, etc. However, the capacity of the engine used is usually relatively small. These engines are lightweight and very fuel efficient. They typically produce approximately 70 brake horsepower which is supplemented with a electric motor rated typically at approximately 50 horse power.

Electric motor: The electric motor is used to propel the car, however with the use of electronic technology, the motor can also function as a generator to recharge the batteries.

Transmission: The transmission can be either manual or automatic.

Fuel tank: The fuel tank is used to store petrol for the petrol engine.

Batteries: The batteries provide the energy source for the electric motor, either recharged by an external power source or recharged by the generator or electric motor when it is functioning as a generator.

HEV Configurations

The two power sources are combined in one of two forms, either in parallel or in series.

The parallel hybrid connects the petrol engine and the electric motor to the gearbox, so both power sources can apply their energy to the gearbox independently or simultaneously.The series hybrid utilizes the power of the petrol engine and electric motor in a different manner, the power of the petrol engine is applied to a generator, which is then used to either charge the batteries or to directly power an electric motor. The electric motor then applies power to the gearbox. Note that on series applications, the petrol engine is never used to directly supply power to the gearbox. The power sources are connected in series, hence the name series hybrid.

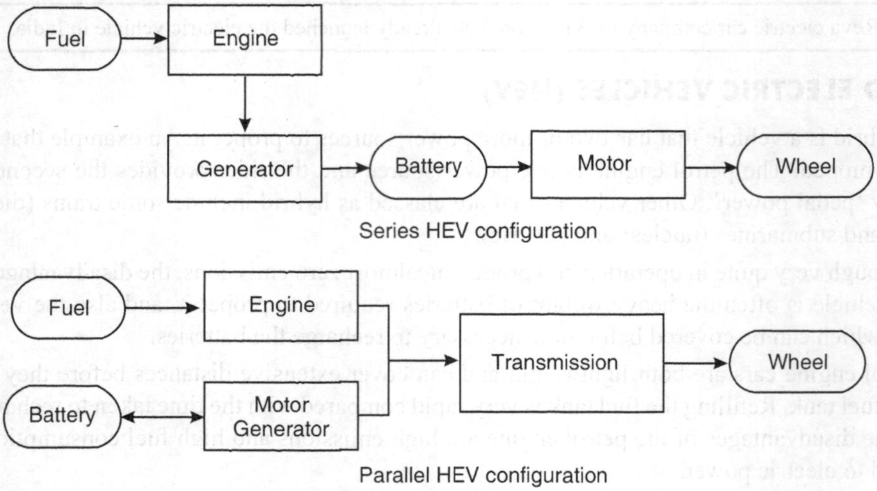

Fig. 17.5 HEV configurations

The hybrid car offers high efficiency yet it also has high performance. It utilizes the power of the electric motor to supplement the energy provided by the petrol engine during situations such as accelerating from a standstill or driving up hills.

The hybrid car can reduce the waste of energy and the production of emissions in many driving situations, e.g. the petrol engine is switched off while the car is stationary. The car generally operates on battery power alone, but when additional power is required for accelerating or if the batteries require charging, the petrol engine starts and supplements the battery power. Battery power alone can accelerate the car to around 42 kilometers per hour. Additionally, a separate starter motor is no longer required to start the petrol engine because the hybrid car uses the electric motor to start the engine when the vehicle is moving.

The initial cost of a hybrid car is normally higher than that of a conventional petrol engine car, however the emission levels and fuel consumption are lower than petrol engine vehicles. Due to the high efficiency and low emissions, some governments and local authorities encourage the use of hybrid cars with special tax reductions and waiving of levies and tolls.

Advantages

1. Low exhaust emission levels
2. Operating range of the hybrid vehicle is comparable with that of conventional vehicles

Disadvantages

1. Bulky and heavy
2. Require very complicated control systems
3. Cost is very high

FUEL CELL

A fuel cell is an electrochemical energy conversion device. A fuel cell converts the chemicals hydrogen and oxygen into water and in the process it produces electricity (DC voltage) with water and heat as its by-product. In principle, a fuel cell operates like a battery. Unlike battery, a fuel cell does not run down or require recharging. It will produce electricity as long as fuel is supplied.

There are different types of fuel cells, each using a different chemistry. Fuel cells are usually classified by the type of electrolyte they use.

- Alkaline fuel cell
- Phosphoric fuel cell
- Solid oxide fuel cell
- Molten carbonate fuel cell

Construction

A fuel cell consists of two electrodes sandwiched around an electrolyte. Oxygen passes over one electrode and hydrogen over the other, generating electricity, water and heat.

The pressurized hydrogen gas (H_2) entering the fuel cell on the anode side, which is negative post of the fuel cell. It conducts the electrons that are free from the hydrogen molecules so that they can be used in an external circuit. It has channels etched into it that disperse the hydrogen gas equally over the surface of the catalyst.

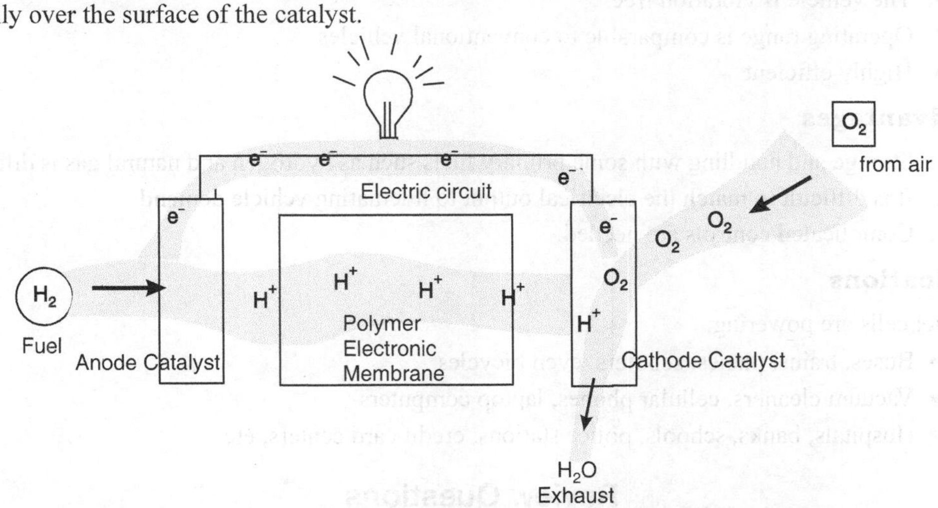

Oxygen (or air) enters through the cathode, which is the positive post of fuel cell. The cathode also has channels etched into it that distribute the oxygen to the surface of the catalyst. It also conducts the electrons back from the external circuit to the catalyst where they can combine with the hydrogen ions and oxygen to form water.

The electrolyte is the proton exchange membrane. This specially treated material only conducts positively charged ions. The membrane blocks electrons.

The catalyst is a special material that facilitates the reaction of oxygen and hydrogen. It is usually made of platinum powder very thinly coated onto carbon paper or cloth. The catalyst is rough and porous so that the maximum surface area of the platinum can be exposed to the hydrogen or oxygen. The platinum-coated side of the catalyst faces the Polymer Electrolyte Membrane [PEM].

Working principle

The pressurized hydrogen gas (H_2) entering the fuel cell on the anode side. This gas is forced through the catalyst by the pressure. When a hydrogen molecule comes in contact with the platinum on the catalyst, it splits into two H^+ ions and two electrons (e^-). The electrons are conducted through the anode, where they make their way through the external circuit (doing useful work such as turning a motor) and return to the cathode side of the fuel cell.

Chemistry of a fuel cell

Anode side : $2H_2 \Rightarrow 4H^+ + 4e^-$

Cathode side : $O_2 + 4H^+ + 4e^- \Rightarrow 2H_2O$

Net reaction : $2H_2 + O_2 \Rightarrow 2H_2O$

Meanwhile, on the cathode side of the fuel cell, oxygen gas (O_2) is being forced through the catalyst, where it forms two oxygen atoms. Each of these atoms has a strong negative charge. This negative charge attracts the two H^+ ions through the membrane, where they combine with an oxygen atom and two of the electrons from the external circuit to form water.

This reaction in a single fuel cell produces only about 0.7 Volts. To get this voltage up to a reasonable level, many separate fuel cells must be combined to form a fuel-cell stack.

Advantages

1. There are no emissions from the vehicle
2. The noise levels are very low
3. The vehicle is vibration free
4. Operating range is comparable to conventional vehicles
5. Highly efficient

Disadvantages

1. Storage and handling with some primary fuels such as hydrogen and natural gas is difficult
2. It is difficult to match the electrical output to fluctuating vehicle demand
3. Complicated controls are needed

Applications

Fuel cells are powering:

- Buses, trains, planes, scooters, even bicycles
- Vacuum cleaners, cellular phones, laptop computers
- Hospitals, banks, schools, police stations, credit card centers, etc.

Review Questions

1. What is the need for alternate fuels?
2. List out the merits of alcohol as fuel?
3. List out the demerits of alcohol as fuel?
4. Compare the properties of alcohols and gasoline as engine fuels.
5. Discuss the suitability of vegetable oils as fuel for diesel engines.
6. What is biodiesel? Why it is used?
7. Compare CNG and LPG with Diesel as fuel.
8. List out the merits of LPG as fuel?
9. List out the demerits of CNG (or LNG) as fuel?
10. Discuss the basic idea of an electric vehicles? What are its components?
11. What parameters of a battery are important for automotive applications?
12. What is meant by hybrid car?
13. Indicate the different types of hybrid vehicles.
14. List out the merits of hydrogen as fuel?
15. List out the demerits of hydrogen as fuel?
16. What is gasohol?
17. What is fuel cell?

18
CHAPTER

SAFETY

An important design feature of any modern vehicle is its ability to protect the occupants from serious physical harm resulting from a collision. In recent years the regulations governing vehicle construction have been updated, making safety a primary consideration. All vehicles are now required to pass certain technical safety standards.

Automobile safety is the study and practice of vehicle design, construction, and equipment to minimize the occurrence and consequences of automobile accidents. As a result of improvements in highway and automobile design, the incidence of injuries and fatalities per mile driven has decreased significantly, but road traffic injuries still represent about 25% of worldwide injury-related deaths (the leading cause) with an estimated 1.2 million deaths each year by World Health Organization (WHO).

Major factors in accidents include driving under the influence of alcohol or other drugs; inattentive driving; crash compatibility between vehicles; driving while fatigued or unconscious; encounters with road hazards such as snow, potholes, and crossing animals; or reckless driving. While human error still plays a big part in causing road accidents, technologies such as anti-lock braking systems, structure-borne sound airbags and innovative ideas, such as airbags on the outside, do promise a safer ride. However, the next big milestone being looked up to is where the highways, automobiles, GPS and ever sophisticated gadgetry would "conspire" to keep a vehicle's occupants safe.

The terms "active" and "passive" are used in the context of automobile safety. At the most basic level, the terms apply to the vehicle occupant's involvement in the function of the safety device or system. Active safety devices and systems are those which the vehicle occupant must act to make functional, as for example by fastening a seat belt. Passive safety devices and systems are those, such as air bags, which operate without any input or action from the vehicle occupant.

The following important active and passive safety systems are employed in the modern vehicles.

Seat Belt: Seatbelts limit the forward motion of an occupant, stretch to slow down the occupant's deceleration in a crash, and prevent occupants being ejected from the vehicle.

Airbag: Airbags inflate to cushion the impact of a vehicle occupant with various parts of the vehicle's interior.

Laminated windshield: Laminated windshields remain in one piece when impacted, preventing penetration of unbelted occupants' heads and maintaining a minimal but adequate transparency for control of the car immediately following a collision. Tempered glass side and rear windows break into granules with minimally sharp edges, rather than splintering into jagged fragments as ordinary glass does.

Crumble zone: Crumple zones absorb and dissipate the energy of a collision, displacing and diverting it away from the passenger compartment and reducing the impact force on the vehicle occupants.

Collapsible steering column: Collapsible steering columns reduce the risk and severity of driver impalement on the column in a frontal crash.

Traction control system: Traction control systems which restore traction if driven wheels begin to spin.

Tyre pressure monitoring systems or deflation detection system: Tyre pressure monitoring system refers to the use of a pressure sensor directly mounted on the wheels or tyres of a vehicle. The pressure inside the tyre is measured using a pressure transducer with the pressure information being subsequently sent to the vehicle to warn the driver of under or over inflation of a tyre.

Electronic stability control: Electronic stability control, which intervenes to avert an impending loss of control.

Adaptive cruise control: Adaptive cruise control which maintains a safe distance from the vehicle in front.

Anti-lock braking system: An ABS (anti-lock braking system) is a system that helps a driver to avoid skids during panic stops. In a car with a normal braking system, all four wheels will lock and cause the car to skid if the driver jams on the brakes in a panic situation. An anti-lock braking system lets a computer monitor the wheels. If one of them locks, the computer can pulse the brake on that wheel so that the wheel keeps spinning. Because the wheels continue to spin, the driver can continue to control the car with the steering wheel.

Emergency brake assist system: Emergency Brake Assist (EBA) is a safety system in vehicles designed to ensure maximum braking power is used in an emergency stop situation.

Rearview camera: Driving on congested city streets might be a little easier if you had some help from a rearview camera system. Rear-view camera display monitor on sun visor rear-view mirrors allows drivers to view a large portion of the area behind their vehicles. However, trunks and rear decks often limit the view of the road as much as ten to 15 feet behind the vehicle. Rear-view cameras, also known as "reversing cameras" or "backup cameras," resolve this problem. These cameras enable drivers to see objects and people directly behind their vehicles.

SEAT BELT

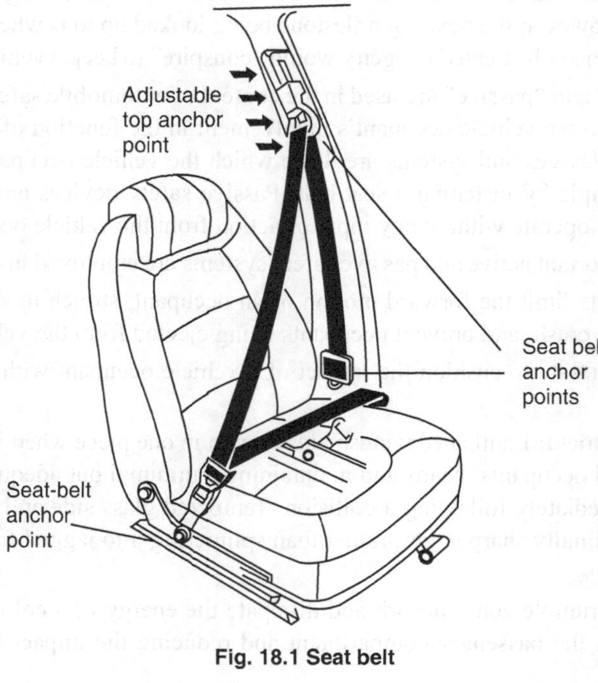

Fig. 18.1 Seat belt

The purpose of a seat-belt is to prevent the wearer from being thrown forwards and possibly being injured during a frontal impact. It is essential to have an automatic device to restrain the body, because in a collision the time to act is too short-one tenth of a second-and the forces are too great to resist. In a really severe crash a human baby effectively weighs the same as a baby elephant.

A seat-belt is made of a woven fabric usually mounted on a spring-loaded inertia mechanism. Under normal driving conditions the seat-belt can be easily pulled off the spool against spring tension. When the vehicle decelerates rapidly as a result of hard braking or impact, a sensor ball is thrown forwards and by means of the actuator plate prevents the spool from unwinding. The seat-belt is now locked in position. When the vehicle comes to rest the ball falls back and the seat-belt is released. It is important that the seat-belts and anchorages are checked frequently and are maintained in good condition.

To make seat-belts more effective by taking out the free play and stretch of the fabric, most are now fitted with an automatic tensioner or pre-tensioner. In an impact, special sensors activate a mechanism to pull the belt tight. This mechanism, usually housed in the seat-belt reel housing, is commonly operated by a small explosive charge.

AIRBAG

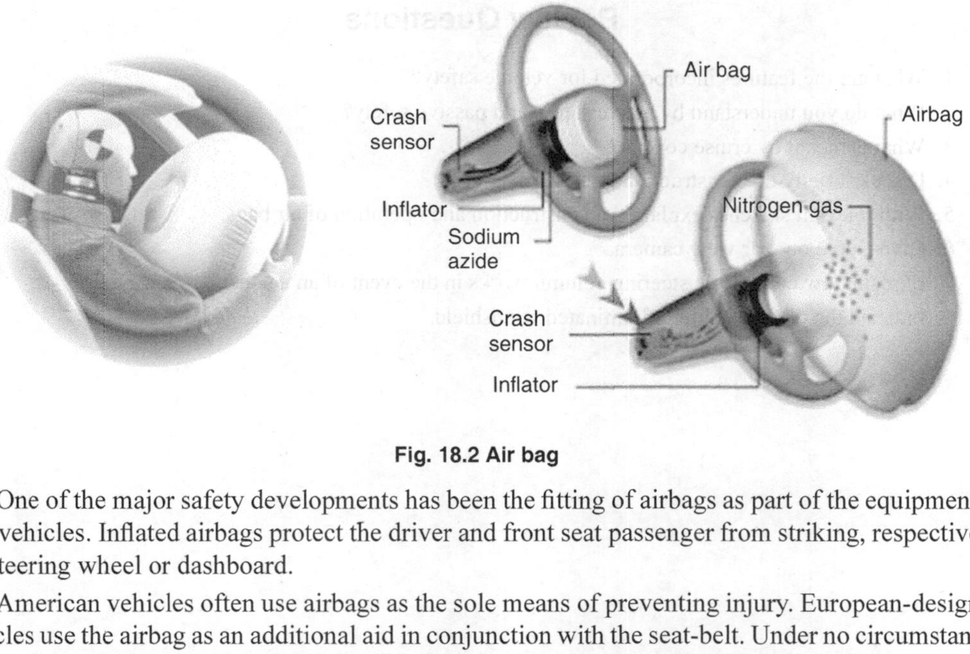

Fig. 18.2 Air bag

One of the major safety developments has been the fitting of airbags as part of the equipment of new vehicles. Inflated airbags protect the driver and front seat passenger from striking, respectively, the steering wheel or dashboard.

American vehicles often use airbags as the sole means of preventing injury. European-designed vehicles use the airbag as an additional aid in conjunction with the seat-belt. Under no circumstances European-designed vehicle with airbags be driven without using the seat-belts if full protection is to be retained.

Side airbags, where fitted, give extra protection against side impact.

In a frontal impact the airbag inflates and then empties in one tenth of a second. In that time the occupant moves forwards into the inflated bag under the influence of inertia and then as the vehicle comes to rest, relaxes back into the seat again.

Airbag operation

In an impact above 25 km/h, crash sensors send a signal to the electronic control unit (ECU), which triggers the igniter unit. Pellets that create a gas when burnt are then ignited and the airbag inflates. As the body of the occupant sinks into the airbag, the gas is forced out of vent holes.

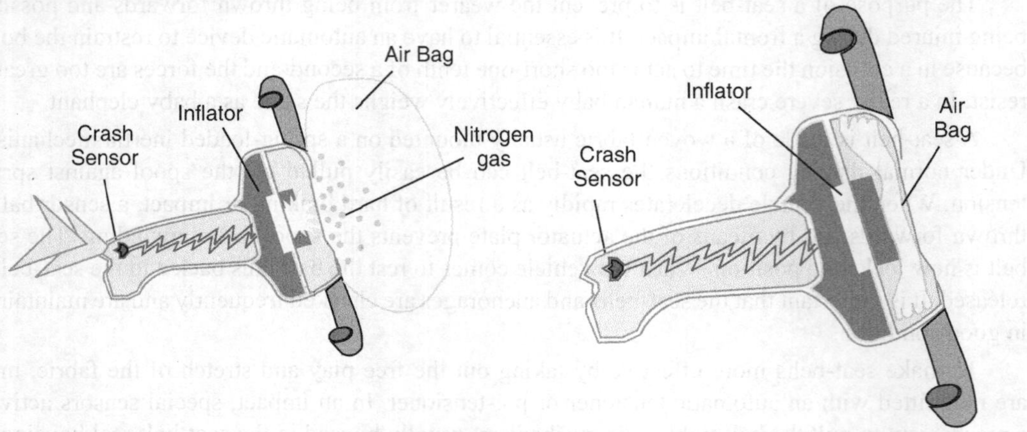

Fig. 18.3 Airbag Inflation System

The nitrogen gas that inflates the airbag is part of the air that we breathe and is quite harmless.

Review Questions

1. What are the features incorporated for vehicle safety?
2. What do you understand by active safety and passive safety?
3. What is meant by cruise control?
4. Discuss briefly the construction of seat belts.
5. With relevant sketches explain the construction and operation of air bags.
6. Give a note on rear view camera.
7. Explain how collapsible steering column works in the event of an accident.
8. Indicate the design feature of laminated windshield.

INDEX

A

B

C

D

E